Teaching Reading

J. Estill Alexander, General Editor

J. Estill Alexander
Arnold R. Davis
Betty S. Heathington
Phyllis E. Huff
Lester N. Knight
Brenda Kolker
Thomas N. Turner
Sammye J. Wynn
All of The University of Tennessee, Knoxville

Leonard G. Breen
Mississippi State University, Mississippi State

Mona M. Donnelly
Nancy B. Tanner
The University of Tennessee, Knoxville, Emeriti

Teaching Reading

Second Edition

Little, Brown and Company
Boston   Toronto

Library of Congress Cataloging in Publication Data

Main entry under title:

Teaching reading.

    1. Reading (Elementary) — Teacher training — Addresses, essays, lectures. I. Alexander, J. Estill.
LB1573.T385 1983   372.4'1   82-22841
ISBN 0-316-03127-5

Library of Congress Catalog Card Number: 82-22841

ISBN 0-316-03127-5

9 8 7 6 5 4 3 2 1

HAL

Published simultaneously in Canada
by Little, Brown & Company (Canada) Limited

Printed in the United States of America

Cover and interior design by Dianne Schaefer/Designworks
Cover photograph © Susan Lapides 1981

Portions of this text were originally published under the title *Rise: Reading*, copyright © 1977, 1976, 1975 by J. Estill Alexander, Leonard G. Breen, Arnold R. Davis, Mona Donnelly, Betty S. Heathington, Phyllis Huff, Lester N. Knight, Brenda Kolker, Nancy B. Tanner, Thomas N. Turner, and Sammye J. Wynn.

Acknowledgments: Page 2, Lynn McLaren/Photo Researchers Inc.; pages 24, 96, 118, 324, 416, Charles Temple/Hobart and William Smith Colleges; pages 48, 198, 246, 280, 450, Bohdan Hrynewych/Southern Light; page 68, Anne Goodrich; page 142, Rene Burri/Magnum Photos, Inc.; pages 166, 220, Ralph H. Granger; page 302, Susan Ylvisaker/Jeroboam, Inc.; pages 356, 390, Bob Bouchal; page 470, Suzanne Szasz; page 494, Culver Pictures.

Preface

This text is intended for teachers and prospective teachers enrolled in an elementary reading methods course. Our principal goal in creating this book — from class-testing preliminary materials in the mid-1970s to most recently revising all chapters for this edition — has been to help students of reading methods acquire the knowledge, skills, and strategies that are an integral part of effective teaching.

In this second edition we have retained, refined, and updated those features and chapters that instructors who used our first edition found most useful. Special chapters on the history of reading instruction, basal readers, the language experience approach, and organizational patterns have been retained. New material has been added to chapters on comprehension, vocabulary development, affective dimensions, additional approaches, and aspects of word recognition. For example, attention has been given to schema theory, to newer information on developing vocabulary and comprehension, and to assessment factors. A totally new chapter focusing on teaching the culturally and linguistically different has been added.

Based on positive reactions from users of the earlier edition, this second edition employs the organization of its predecessor. In Part One, "Foundations," we consider the nature of the reading act and examine the readiness skills and abilities learners need to process print. Part Two, "Recognizing Words," will help teachers with five word recognition techniques — sight vocabulary, phonics, context clues, structural analysis, and dictionary aids to pronunciation — that are useful to learners trying to decode printed symbols. Comprehension, the ultimate purpose of reading instruction, is covered in Part Three, "Getting Meaning." Included are vocabulary development, basic comprehension skills, higher levels of comprehension (inferential, critical, and creative), questioning techniques, study skills, and content area reading. We discuss how teachers most commonly provide instructional frameworks for developing word recognition skills and comprehension abilities in Part Four, "Approaches, Materials, and Programs." Part Five, "Program Planning," covers six crucial areas that we feel are sometimes overlooked by teachers: affective dimensions, working with culturally and linguistically different children, evaluation of reading performance, classroom organization, parental involvement in programs, and the history of reading instruction. Introductions to each part give an overview of the material that follows.

Teaching Reading is eminently flexible because there are a number of alternate sequences in which users can read its chapters. For example, some instructors may wish to begin with Chapter 20, "A Historical Perspective," while others may wish to use this chapter as a summary for Part Four, "Approaches, Programs, and Materials." Some instructors may wish to use Part Four prior to Parts Two and Three so that specific skill development can be addressed after students have studied more general approaches, programs, and materials. The chapters in Part Five on program planning may be presented in a variety of orders to meet the needs of instructors or students.

To help students master the content of this book, we have included and strengthened useful features of the first edition. "Questions to Guide Reading" precede each major heading. The questions focus on three levels of comprehension — literal, inferential, and evaluative — the same levels we hope teachers will use as they plan and conduct comprehensive lessons. You will find answers to the literal questions in the text. You should have a basis for answering the inferential questions as you think about the reading. The evaluative questions are designed to promote further thought about the topic under consideration. Answers to inferential and evaluative questions will not be found in the text. Some questions, of course, do not have definitive answers. You may wish to read further and discuss possible answers to these questions.

"Questions for Further Reading and Thinking" are provided at the end of each chapter. We hope that these questions will guide the interested student to pursue the teaching of reading in greater depth. Also included at the end of each chapter (except Chapter 20) are "Activities and Projects" to enhance learning and give some practical experience with ideas, strategies, and concerns. We think that they will help develop more effective teachers of reading. Most chapters include materials for elementary school students, and you will find a comprehensive bibliography at the end of the text.

Certain viewpoints that we share as a team appear throughout the text. Among these threads of common philosophy are the following:

1. It is important to balance research and theory with practical suggestions. Teachers need to know what to do, but they also should know why they do it.
2. We do not accept the arbitrary dichotomy that students learn to read in the primary grades and read to learn in the intermediate grades.

3. The reading act involves processes that may change from one learner to another and from one developmental level to another.
4. The development of certain prerequisite skills is important prior to processing print. However, readiness is needed for specific reading tasks at all ages and at all levels of instruction.
5. Basic skills are important, but attention must be given as well to the affective domain.
6. Comprehension should be emphasized from the beginning of the school experience and in all instructional settings in which print media are used.
7. Higher level comprehension skills — critical and creative reading — as well as basic comprehension skills should be stressed.
8. Effective use of questioning strategies aids comprehension.
9. Children who differ in ability and who are culturally and linguistically different need special attention.
10. No one approach to reading instruction is best for all learners.
11. The teacher is more important than any technique, approach, or organizational pattern used.
12. Parents are an effective, but frequently overlooked, source for improving the reading program.

A great many people helped us develop this and the previous edition. Listing them all is impossible, but we do want to acknowledge here several individuals and groups. The inservice teachers from whom we have learned and the pre-service teachers who evaluated the text and made suggestions were particularly helpful. The text could not have been developed without the support of Dr. Jerry J. Bellon, Head of the Department of Curriculum and Instruction at the University of Tennessee, Knoxville, and of Dr. John Ray, Director of the Service Center of the Department of Curriculum and Instruction. The contributions of Dr. Paul N. Terwilliger of our staff in the planning stages of the text are appreciated.

We are especially grateful to Mary Jane Hays who typed and proofed much of the manuscript in this and in the first edition. Our thanks also go to Fay Benjamin, who helped with the typing of the second edition; and to Sandy Zecchini, who helped check the accuracy of references.

For work on the first edition that has carried over in part to the second edition, we thank Patsy M. Davis and Ann Keller, who worked on several aspects of the manuscript, and Melinda Eastham, who checked most of the first edition references for accuracy.

We wish to thank Mylan Jaixen and Cynthia Mayer of Little, Brown and Company for their encouragement and support in developing this second edition. The comments and support expressed by users of the first edition in our users survey were most appreciated. Reviewers of this edition provided deeply appreciated and helpful comments: Susan Daniels, University of Akron; Joan Gipe, University of New Orleans; Sam Miller, University of Oregon; Nancy Padak, Northern Illinois University; and Dorothy Troike, State University of New York–College at Cortland.

Finally, we thank our families, who were understanding as work progressed on the text, and each other for the many constructive suggestions made.

Contents

Chapter 5   Context Clues, Structural Analysis, and Dictionary Aids
to Pronunciation / Leonard G. Breen   96

Chapter 10 Study Skills / Arnold R. Davis   220

Chapter 11   Reading in Content Areas / J. Estill Alexander and
              Mona Donnelly   246

Chapter 16 Reading for the Linguistically and Culturally Different /
Lester N. Knight 390

Part One

FOUNDATIONS

The purpose of this text is to help teachers and prospective teachers develop the knowledges, skills, and teaching strategies that will help elementary school students become efficient users of print media. Part One will focus on two crucial foundation areas: processing print and reading readiness.

Chapter 1 discusses insights into the nature of reading, showing that the reading act involves processes that may vary from one learner to another and from one developmental level to another. Although research has not yet yielded a definitive description of a reading process (or processes), there is information available to help a teacher understand how learners process print. We the authors believe that the development of certain prerequisite skills is important prior to processing print. The development of these skills is discussed in Chapter 2. In that chapter and elsewhere throughout this book, we shall demonstrate that readiness is needed for specific reading tasks at all ages and at all levels of instruction.

Brenda Kolker

1

Processing Print

Children do not generally choose whether they will learn to read. It is assumed that they will learn in order to function in and be able to contribute to society. Learning to read, for the purposes of this book, is defined as learning to perceive the potential meaning in written messages and to relate this potential meaning to cognitive structures (what is already known) in order to comprehend it (Ausubel 1968, p. 68). Children at different levels of reading achievement do not appear to act on, or process, written materials in the same ways. A beginning reader, for example, differs from a more mature reader in concept development, knowledge of the world, skills used to obtain information, and strategies used to retain and recall information. Differences in the content to be read may also affect the processes a reader uses. These processes appear to be affected by many background factors that interact and influence what happens from the time a reader sees a stimulus in print through the time he responds in some fashion. These interactions are long term and developmental, continuing through adulthood.

This chapter is intended as an overview of three important interacting factors — affect, cognition, and language — as they relate to learning to read. Simply stated, affective behavior refers to feelings, cognitive behavior to thought, and linguistic behavior to the child's language. Certain assumptions underlie the descriptions presented: (1) the way the child feels about himself and his environment influences his reading achievement; (2) in order for the reader to understand what he reads, he must understand the concepts in the material he is reading; and (3) reading is a communication process between the writer and the reader, utilizing written language. In subsequent chapters, we will show how these assumptions affect reading instruction.

Biologically, reading is a totally human act; but whether humans are "prewired" to act automatically or whether they respond to environmental factors is not the predominant issue for teachers. Rather, the issue is: "How can I teach reading so that children can learn effectively and efficiently?" This question implies that teachers know some of the interactions that function when children read.

Affect

QUESTIONS TO GUIDE READING

Literal
What are five affective factors that influence reading achievement?
How do attitude, motivation, attention, comprehension, and acceptance work together in the reading process?

Inferential
What are five nonverbal cues to suggest positive feelings?
What behaviors are exhibited by students who are not independent in thought and action?

Before a person thinks about an idea or reacts to objects in the environment, the stimuli he saw, heard, or touched pass through the pleasure-pain area of the brain, where their impact is colored by how the person feels (Robeck and Wilson 1974, p. 77). The stimuli are then thought about or acted on. Although it may take only a fraction of a second for a stimulus to pass the affective portion of the brain, how a person cognitively or physically acts is affected.

Imagine walking down the street with a friend and seeing a woman walking toward you whom you do not particularly like. You might find yourself saying "Oh-Oh" and ducking into a store, or giving a curt nod in quickly passing, or trying to look at something in your environment so she will think you haven't seen her. Now imagine seeing someone approaching that you like very much. How do you feel? What would you do? Compare these two sets of reactions. Your feelings undoubtedly dictated your mental and physical reactions.

Children also react with feelings to people and environmental stimuli, including reading and reading-like tasks. If a student has feelings of "I can't do it" or "I hate this" when presented with a reading task, he will probably not try to do the task well. On the other hand, if a student has feelings of "this is easy" or "I like this," he will probably do well on the reading task presented.

WHAT ARE THE AFFECTIVE FACTORS?

Several affective factors that are related to reading achievement have been delineated by research. Athey (1976) has identified the following factors: self-concept, autonomy, environmental mastery, perception of reality, and anxiety.

A positive *self-concept* can be thought of as self-confidence, liking oneself, and a feeling of appreciation by others. In some instances, students have failed in-school tasks repeatedly and have come to believe they cannot succeed. Their report cards have D's, Unsatisfactory Progress (UP), or similar marks. Other children call them dumb and perhaps do not want to work in a learning group with them. Sometimes the teachers also show, by nonverbal cues such as frowns or lifted eyebrows, dissatisfaction with the child's progress. Children understand such nonverbal cues easily. Because of other children's or the teacher's behaviors, a child may feel that he is not liked or competent. As a result, the student may give up and become a disruptive force in the classroom. In such situations, reading achievement may stay at a low level because the child cannot or will not concentrate on the task at hand.

Research appears to support the position that a relationship exists between a positive self-concept and reading achievement. The self-concept of good readers has repeatedly been found to be higher than the self-concept of poor readers (Athey 1966; Brazemore and Gwalthney 1973). (See Chapter 15 for a fuller treatment of self-concept).

Autonomy is another affective factor related to reading achievement. Autonomy refers to independence in thought and action. Children with this independence tend to possess (1) the ability to complete tasks they understand without disturbing the teacher every minute with a question, (2) the ability to follow a series of task directions one after the other instead of completing one task and getting sidetracked, and (3) the ability to plan for themselves rather than waiting to be told what to do. Research suggests that good readers are more independent than poor readers (Carillo 1957).

Environmental mastery is a third factor related to reading achievement. When a child has mastered his environment he is satisfied that he can affect what happens to him; he has some control over his own fate, and he can see that what he does matters. A boy who bullies other children and wonders why the teacher scolds him (or a girl who doesn't study and fails a test but blames the teacher) is generally not responding appropriately to environmental stimuli. The child who has a limited environmental mastery will probably read less well than a child who has appropriately mastered his environment (Abrams 1969; Zimit, Rose, and Camp 1973).

Another affective factor in reading achievement is *perception of reality*. A child perceives reality when he sees himself accurately as an individual and as a person relating to his setting. The fourth grader who tells her teacher she has selected and can read a fourth-grade-level library book is not facing reality if she actually reads only on a second grade level. Studies have shown that poor readers appear to be less realistic than good readers in estimates of themselves as readers (Bouise 1955).

The final factor Athey identified was *anxiety* (1976). Anxiety affects learners in different ways. Many students are anxious when confronted with a test situation, and some perform less well on the test than would be anticipated. Other students perform better when they are anxious. Students experience comparable reactions to anxiety when approaching reading tasks: anxiety may inhibit prose processing or it may enhance it. The role of anxiety in learning to read remains inconclusive because students' reactions vary so much and because different levels of anxiety produce different responses even in one student.

Affect has generally been neglected in models of the reading process(es) because of the lack of explicit definition of the role that it plays. Recently, however, Mathewson (1976) has described the function of affect in learning to read by focusing on five basic components — attitude, motivation, attention, comprehension, and acceptance. In his model he proposed attitude — a favorable feeling — as the central component.

Both attitude and motivation are prerequisites to actual reading. If a child has a positive attitude toward books, and is motivated (will act), he will want to pick up material to read. But attitudes and motivation can be selective: a child might like motorcycles and read avidly any magazine or book on this topic but will not read anything else. Regardless of scope, however, a motivated child with a positive attitude does direct his attention toward the reading material. He reads and begins to comprehend it. He fits ideas from what he has read into his own thought system by comparing it to what he believes. The total process thus involves attitude, motivation, attention, comprehension, and acceptance; the process continually repeats itself each time the student reads.

If attitude, the first prerequisite for reading, is not positive, then it is likely that the others will not occur at all or will occur haphazardly. The role of the teacher, then, is to foster positive attitudes so that children will want to read. (For a fuller treatment of attitude and interests as motivators, see Chapter 15.)

Cognition

QUESTIONS TO GUIDE READING

Literal
What does the cognitive function deal with?
What is a concept?
What are Piaget's four periods of intellectual development?
According to Samuels, how do students learn words?
How does building specific reading skills relate to conceptual development?

Inferential

How do Piaget's developmental theory and schema theory differ?

What stages might a child go through in building a concept of "elk" or "fruit"?

What are several different schemes that might be developed for sled riding?

Evaluative

In planning a reading program, what importance should a teacher give to cognitive factors?

What prerequisite ways of thinking are needed by a student to master a first grade reading lesson in a basal reader?

The cognitive function concerns the nature of the mental processes involved in learning to read. In this section we will consider studies of children on a long-range, longitudinal basis as well as experimental studies of children at one point in time. Both ways of studying children yield insight into how students think and learn. This review is not intended to be all-inclusive; rather, it contains important viewpoints selected to provide a framework in which to consider how the cognitive function affects reading. You should find this information to be very useful as you further develop your understanding of cognition through reading from other sources.

Basic to cognition is a child's ability to form concepts. Concepts are classes of stimuli that have common characteristics. Concept formation, which represents a person's attempts to classify experiences, is fundamental to thinking and hence to reading. For example, a family has a dog, and the child has learned the word "doggie" as a label for her four-legged pet. When the family drives to a farm and the child sees a calf in the barnyard, she calls the calf a big "doggie." The child is probably responding to the size and shape of the calf and dog. She has formed a concept of "doggie" as a creature having four legs, ears, and a tail; but she has not yet included various more discriminating attributes — for example, that one barks and the other moos. On the other hand, if the child never sees a calf at this stage, she misses the experience of discriminating between calf and dog. Discrimination experiences are vital to concept development, for people develop and change their concepts as a result of interaction with their environment. If a child has not had a variety of direct or vicarious experiences with his environment, his concept development will be limited. Limited conceptual development will affect reading in that, although students may "call" ("say") words correctly, they will not understand what the words actually mean. Clearly, comprehension is integral to reading.

Schema Theory

Another term in use recently to explain the basic cognitive functions is schemata (plural for schema) (Rumelhart 1980; Rumelhart and Ortony 1977). Schemata are functions in the brain that interpret, organize, and retrieve information; in other words, they are mental frameworks. In our brain we hold actions, concepts, situations, and their interrelationships in our memory. Schemata organize these experiences as well as enable us to retrieve information when we need it.

In schema theory, the role of past experiences in learning to read and continued understanding of concepts in learning from prose is of prime importance. You have probably heard of or seen people who skim five or six newspapers per day and seem to understand all of the news. These people probably have prior information on all of the topics and are looking for new ideas or developments. They already have the basic concepts and experience, thus allowing them to skim. The way(s) we organize prior information in our memory so that we can retrieve the information while reacting to and interacting with print is explained by schema theory. In other words, schema theory is one explanation of how we comprehend written material.

Initially, a learner must have concepts about his environment and place these concepts into nonrandom categories. Nonrandom categories are called schema. For example, children might categorize cats as shown in Figure 1.1.

The categories may be incomplete. Through accommodation and assimilation new information is added, and categories are refined and changed. For example, a child visits a zoo and observes a leopard. He and his parents talk about the leopard. The child has added a new subclassification under wild cats. When a student does not have the concepts there are voids in schemata. Beginning readers and/or mature readers might thus not comprehend assigned materials. For example, do you understand the sentence "The inspector magnafluxed those welds"?[1] (Hint: You are at a construction site.)

As with concept development, schemata function in organizing our experiences so that we may have access to thoughts and concepts while we read, thereby enabling us to interact with print in a meaningful way.

A Point of View about Thinking

The specific view of thinking we will take up in this section is that of Jean Piaget. He has not applied his view on cognition primarily to reading, but other researchers have done so because it is assumed that reading cannot occur without thinking. Recall that in Ausubel's definition of reading,

1. From Charles Sailor, *The Second Son* (New York: Avon Books, 1979), p. 9.

Figure 1.1. Schema for cats.

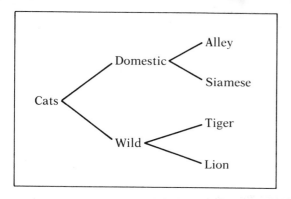

stated at the beginning of this chapter, the reader relates the message's potential meaning to what is already known in order to comprehend the message. We must understand thinking processes if we are to gain insights into why a child reacts as he does when presented with a reading task.

Piaget (1970) has presented a useful developmental view of intellectual development. He has delineated periods through which children progress, with certain levels of thinking or actions accompanying each period or stage. These are the sensorimotor, preoperational, concrete operations, and formal operations periods. In Piaget's framework, operations are actions that can be carried out mentally, and not necessarily physically.

The duration of the sensorimotor period is from birth to approximately 2 years. The child progresses from uncoordinated body movements to walking, from passive responding to searching actively for objects, and from reflex to intentional behavior. Although this period does not relate directly to reading, it does form the basis for future cognitive development. The second period, preoperational, lasts from about 2 years to 7. A child begins to represent his ideas through drawings and symbolic play, he continues to form and refine concepts, and he begins to think with prelogical reasoning. In the concrete operations period, from age 7 to 11, the child can carry out operations mentally, including those dealing with reversibility and conservation (for example, he knows one quantity of water is the same amount in different size containers); also, he can understand relationships among concrete groups. During the formal operations period, ages 11 to 15, the student begins to utilize abstract thinking as an adult does.

The periods Piaget described are not defined in terms of the child's age per se, but rather in terms of the operations the child can perform. The age ranges give only a rough approximation of the periods. Intellectual development in Piaget's research does not refer to an IQ score but to the ways children act on their environment. In order to know an object, a person must act on it mentally or physically. Mental or physical activities that people perform on objects are called schemes. When a pushing scheme is established, a child can push a variety of objects with his body or various implements.

Intelligence, for Piaget, is the result of increasing ability to coordinate actions. For example, consider the rural child who has grown up on a farm and has developed schemes for manipulating the tools used for plowing, planting, and harvesting. Compare him with another child who has lived in an urban area all his life and has developed schemes for dealing with subway riding and taxis. These two children have experienced different aspects of their environment and they coordinate actions differently. If both these children were in the same first grade and used the same reading text, their experiences with actions or schemes could facilitate or hinder their ability to understand the concepts presented.

Children progress within and through the various periods by acts of assimilation, accommodation, and equilibrium. Assimilation, according to Piaget, enables the child to act on something new by using that which is already familiar. For example, a child under eight months old usually does not notice a new picture hung where there was none before. However, after eight to twelve months, the child will actively search for missing objects and will notice new objects.

New schemes develop out of old schemes through the process of accommodation. Accommodation is the change of a scheme by the elements it assimilates. In the example of the calf and dog, imagine the child when the calf moos instead of barks. The child assimilates the fact that the two types of four-legged animals make different sounds. The scheme of "doggie" is changed and a new scheme is developed — that of other four-legged creatures "not doggie." This process of "attributes" continues to develop until the child reaches an equilibrium state that is a balance between assimilation and accommodation.

Consider further the example of the dog and the calf. The child goes home from the farm and sees a Chihuahua. She waits until the dog yaps and now has achieved equilibrium. She knows that it falls in the doggie class. The child is also beginning to distinguish size concepts as well as to distinguish indoor pets from outdoor animals. Accommodation, assimilation, and equilibrium continue through adulthood. If the same child encountered a Basenji, which is a dog that does not bark, she would begin the processes over. Again, if the student has limited experiences, his concept development will be limited. Also, not all students will be in the same stages of acting on objects at a given grade level.

Formal reading instruction generally begins sometime during the later part of the preoperational period or the beginning of the concrete operations period. Some children might be in one stage while others are in the other. In addition, children might have developed different concepts because of their different experiences.

There are differences between the thinking of a child in the preoperational period and that of a child in the concrete operations period. These differences are crucial because a reading task will evoke dissimilar responses from children in the different stages. An example of the different types of thinking involved in each stage is the reaction of a child to three differently shaped bottles, each containing the same amount of water. A child in the preoperational period knows that each bottle contains water but cannot realize that the amounts of water are the same, even when this fact is demonstrated for him. He can respond only to the one variable that is visible or concrete — the water — and not to the water plus volume. A child in the concrete operations period, on the other hand, understands that the shape of the bottles influences the apparent quantity of water. He is able to think about the two factors, shape and quantity, at once and abstracts them. In other words, in the preoperational period the child has difficulty combining classes to form a larger class, while in the concrete operations period he does not. Imagine a first grade student who has been instructed to group pictures into the categories of vegetables, fruits, and meats. This type of task is a typical reading readiness task. In general, children in either period will be able to complete the task successfully because it is a relatively straightforward task with only one dimension. However, if the grouping task were to categorize pictures of transportation vehicles into those with four wheels or two wheels (one dimension), and those which are motorized or nonmotorized (the other dimension), the student in the preoperational period would have difficulty because the task is two-dimensional.

An example of a lesson from a first grade text illustrates the preceding concept. The lesson deals with how /ed/ shows past action (MacGinitie 1976). The teacher's manual asks the teacher to "tell the children that /ed/ stands for /t/ when it is added to a word that ends with any voiceless consonant letter except ⟨t⟩." Many children have difficulty with this concept because of the multidimensional thinking involved. In addition to learning and understanding the rule, the children also have to know the concepts of /ed/, /t/, a voiceless consonant, and a voiced consonant.

One inference for teachers from these examples is that the teacher must analyze the task she is going to ask the student to perform before the student performs it. Seven- and eight-year-olds beginning school are usually in the preoperational or concrete operations period. If the task the student is required to complete is too difficult for his thinking, he will not be able to perform it to the satisfaction of the teacher. Because he cannot perform does not mean that he is slow or dull, but only that his logical thinking processes are not developed enough for him to complete a particular task successfully.

Another inference is that the concepts of the reader will influence how much meaning he derives from the text. If a child is expected to read about alligators in the Florida Everglades but has no concept of either alligators or the Florida Everglades, his comprehension of the text will be low. In other words, he will call words only.

It appears that not only does the level of cognition affect reading, but that the learning of basic skills potentially affects cognition. Powell (1976a; 1976b) synthesized reading research findings and, using Piaget's mental operations concept, constructed a framework for understanding the effects of learning basic skills on cognition. Learning to read assumes that students learn skills, principles, and concepts. The question posed by Powell was "What concepts are built by learning isolated reading skills?" We know that beginning readers learn to associate sounds with the written symbol (see Chapter 5) and that they learn to associate spoken words with their written counterpart, the skill (see Chapter 4). The concept that these types of learnings represent is the associative concept; the beginning reader discovers that one item is consistently associated with another item. That is, he learns to associate the written "and" with the oral "and." He incorporates the concept into the logical thinking process of associativity. In chart form, the learning process would look like this:

Skill	Concept	Logical thinking process
Letter names	Associative	Associativity
Basic sight vocabulary	Associative	Associativity

This means that while a child is learning a skill, such as sight vocabulary, that skill is helping the child to form a concept because he is mobilizing his thinking processes. Hence logical thinking processes are enhanced through the mechanisms of assimilation, accommodation, and equilibrium. Most of the reading readiness and basic reading skills can be thought of in relationship to logical thinking processes. The skill learned is not as important as the concept that learning the skill helps to build.

TYPES OF SPECIFIC READING BEHAVIORS

Piaget deals with mental operations and abilities — that is, with types of thinking. Another way to study the cognitive processes in reading is to give the child a reading task and manipulate what the child sees or does.

One specific type of behavior that can be manipulated is learning to recognize sight words. The earliest stages of learning to read can be thought of as a five-stage process (Samuels 1976). First, a stimulus must be presented. Second, the student discriminates the cue (word, letter) from others. Third, she learns to recognize the cue again, thus using visual memory. Fourth, she must have at her command the appropriate response for the cue. And last, when she has hooked up the cue and response, she has learned the letter or word.

Keeping this five-stage process in mind, imagine a first grader whose teacher has decided to teach the words *paper*, *came*, and *come*. In the first step he presents the words on the chalkboard (stimulus presentation). For the second step the student must be able to indicate that the three words are different, thus discriminating each from the other. The student might have difficulty discriminating *come* and *came,* so she will have to cue in to the second letter of each word because the words begin alike, end alike, and are of the same length. After the teacher has worked on the discrimination task, he erases the words from the chalkboard. Later in the day he again writes the words on the board. The successful student says, "I saw those this morning"; she has visually recognized the prior list and has passed stage three. Next, the response has to be available in the student's vocabulary to call the word correctly. (If the student is learning English as a second language, the response might not be in her vocabulary.) When the word *paper* and the response /paper/ are hooked up together, the student has learned the word. According to Powell, then, the student is beginning to develop the Piagetian concept of associativity.

Research has been conducted by many professionals on how children perceive and learn words. It appears that a beginning reader must distinguish among and between letters. Each letter has a distinctive feature (Gibson and Levin 1975, pp. 15–20) that distinguishes it from another letter. For example, are the letters straight or curved, or horizontal or vertical?

Another question asked was "Which part of the word or graphic cue do beginning readers use most often?" It has been found that the beginning part of the word is used most, followed by the ending, with the medial letters next (Marchbanks and Levin 1965). One implication from this finding is that if beginning readers are expected to learn the words *cat* and *cut* in isolation in the same day, the words have a high probability of being confused because the graphic difference is in the medial position.

An additional question was whether children learn to read words more quickly when a picture is presented with the word or when the word is presented alone (Samuels 1967). Beginning readers were asked to learn words they did not know in a timed test with or without a picture. It was found that children learned words more quickly when there was no picture. This finding has an implication for teaching: when teaching children to read words, the teacher should present only the word to be learned with no picture, because childrern will tend to focus on the picture instead of on the word.

Another specific process that applies to students' learning is the concept of imagery, which influences memory (Paivio 1965; 1969). Imagery is the nonverbal picture that a word evokes in a person's mind. With a concrete noun, such as *arrow,* a picture (arrow) is seen in the mind more readily than with an abstract noun, such as *attitude.* First graders thus will learn a concrete noun more readily as a sight vocabulary word, because they have an image of the referent for which the word stands (Terwilliger and Kolker 1981). Not only does imagery influence the recall of words, but it influences the recall of text material. When a child is told prior to his reading task to form pictures (or images) as he reads, he will remember the content of the assignment better and for a longer period of time (Kulhavy and Swenson 1975).

Language

QUESTIONS TO GUIDE READING

Literal
What is phonology?
What is syntax?
What is the role of dialect in reading achievement?
What role does attention play in learning to read?
What are the main subclassifications in language development?
What are four major cues used during reading?

Inferential
What might be the differences in level of language development between a three-year-old and a six-year-old?
Which of the linguistic and affective factors might vary from one subculture to another?

Evaluative
What stages in language acquisition and cognition are most similar?

In this section we will discuss how language affects reading under the headings of language acquisition, language as a social process, and psycholinguistics. Language acquisition refers to the process by which the child develops a system for communicating, whereas language as a social process involves the social setting or the environment in which language develops. Psycholinguistics is the study of language and thought, the fusion of psychology and linguistic units (Osgood and Sebeok 1965, p. 61). The psycholinguist considers a linguistic unit, such as a word, to see if that unit is the one people actually use to take information to the brain (decode) and then react to in speech or gesture or writing (encode).

Reading is language dependent because students use the concepts they have formed and used in their oral language as they begin to react to print. Oral language is a mediator for perceiving written messages in the initial stages of processing the written word. For example, when children begin to learn to read, they have difficulty reading silently because they have heard spoken language all their lives. Hence, they translate the written message to oral language so that they can comprehend.

Reading, however, is different from listening or speaking (DeStefano 1981). Reading print makes extra demands on the reader because he has to rely on printed linguistic forms only. That is, there are no facial expressions to "read" as in listening; there are also no voice inflections and no gestures. The reader has to rely only on printed words, and written language is often more complex than spoken language.

LANGUAGE ACQUISITION

Language learning is a developmental process. It begins with cooing as an infant, proceeds to first words, and then advances to simple sentences. The groundwork for language production and reception has generally been laid by the time the child reaches school age. There are three major components of language developed by students from birth through adulthood. These are phonology (the sound system), semantics (meaning), and syntax (grammatical rules). The following discussion will highlight aspects of the three components.

The child babbles during the first year of life, making sounds possible in all languages. These sounds narrow to the sounds he hears in his immediate environment. Ultimately, the American child will make sounds of the English language and the German child will make German sounds, because they are what the child hears and they are reinforced by his family. McCarthy (1954) analyzed and summarized existing data on the changes of prespeech vocalization. Several of the changes she found are: (1) the frequency of vowel sounds is greater than that of consonant sounds in the first three months; (2) there is a steady increase in vowel sounds until 2 years of age, and then there is a rapid spurt in vowel frequency as speech emerges; (3) consonant frequency does not equal vowel frequency until 2½ years; (4) by 2½ years, the child uses practically all the vowel sounds but only two thirds of the consonant sounds; (5) sex differences emerge around 26–27 months, with girls being more vocal; and (6) final consonants are negligible in the first half-year, and then are mastered at an accelerating rate.

Another summary on the acquisition of phonemes (the smallest units of speech sound without meaning) was done by Templin (1957). She tested children and reported the age at which 75 percent of those tested could produce the phonological elements correctly. For example, only at age 6 could 75 percent of the students pronounce /th/, /v/, and /skw/ in the initial position and /th/, /v/ and /ek/ in the final position. The development of a phonological system is a continuous process. In a kindergarten or first grade class, there will be variation among students on the development of sound production, which is normal. If students cannot produce a sound, they will probably have difficulty discriminating it auditorially because of the positive relationship between sound production and auditory discrimination (Templin 1957).

During the time the child is acquiring the sound system of language he is also acquiring meaning (semantics). By 18 months, there are approximately 200–300 words in his vocabulary (McNeill 1966). Semantic development has probably elicited the most diverse research and theory of the language functions, and several theories of meaning are in existence. One point of view is that meaning is conditioned. That is, meaning is defined as a relationship between a stimulus and a response (Nobel 1952). The more associations one has with a word, the greater will be the increase in meanings. Consider all the meanings of the word "run." A child may have encountered the word in several contextual settings: "I will run away" and "Mother has a run in her hose." An adult will have encountered the word in more and varied contexts ("Still waters run deep." "He's running for mayor." "Ever since I dropped it, it runs slow.") The adult will have had more stimulus-response connections and therefore have more meanings in his repertoire.

Another point of view is that words become meaningful when they: (1) recall images for the object named, and (2) are incorporated into the thinking of the person. The acquisition of new meaning is the incorporation or subsumption of the new word under more general ideas already held by the learner (Ausubel 1965, p. 6).

Yet another point of view is that the syntactic and the semantic features of language learning are related. Meaning occurs in the context of other words; therefore, meaning and grammar cannot be separated (Fodor 1980). Assigning meaning to sentences requires rules, and the way sentences are put together influences meaning. This point of view is that semantics is not a conditioned response but a combination of rules and their systematic interrelations.

The syntactic rules the child develops along with sound and meaning enable him to combine words into sentences. Among the syntactic rules are placement and use of (1) connecting words; (2) designative words; (3) inflections indicating tense, number, gender, and case; and (4) word order. These rules serve as communication devices to bring meaning to ideas (Ausubel 1968, p. 67). In learning syntax the child tries out rules, which are not mere imitations of adult speech.

Brown and Bellugi (1964) have described three processes in the child's acquisition of syntax. In the first stage, the child imitates an adult but reduces the utterance. That is, the adult may say "Look at that big brown dog," and the child will say "Look dog." The word forms retained during this stage are usually nouns and verbs, and the word order is kept the same. In the second stage, the child says something and the adult expands it. The child might say "Daddy go," and the adult expands it to "Yes, Daddy is going to work." The word order is again retained. The third process is induction of latent structure, which is determining where structural components such as noun phrases and descriptive adjectives are placed. For example, the child would induce that an adjective precedes a noun when the noun is being described: "A black dog" instead of "A dog black."

By the age of 3, the child uses plurals (Ervin and Miller 1963). They appear to be learned first as separate vocabulary items, but later a rule develops. A child might say "Some mans are coming," or "Lots of childs was there." The plurals of man and child are made to fit the rule the child has developed. Still later, the irregular forms of plurals are used appropriately.

At 4 or 5 years of age, all parts of speech are used by the child (Ervin and Miller 1963), and sentences increase in length and complexity as a child matures (Cazden 1968; McNeill 1970; Slobin 1966). Syntax continues to develop throughout the elementary school years, including "if" and "so" clauses (Menyuk 1963) and sentence complexity (Strickland 1962).

Strickland (1962) found the average sentence length in first grade was approximately 11 words, and in sixth grade it was approximately 14 words. The range of sentence length for first graders was from 1.92 to 22.56; the range for sixth graders was 4.60 to 26.32 words. Perhaps the most significant finding of this research was that the length of oral sentences varies more within one grade than it does from grade to grade. Longer sentences are usually more complex because they have clauses and phrases. Consider a first grade classroom with twenty-five students. Several students speak with an average of 3 words per sentence, and others speak with an average of 15 words per sentence. The primer-level book in which the children are reading has an average sentence length of 3 words. All the children should easily relate the sentence length to their oral language and understand it. However, if the sentences contained an average of 15 words per sentence, not all the children could relate it to their oral language.

Specific examples of the way the child's understanding of sentences progresses have been documented by Carol Chomsky (1969). Children from 5 to 10 years of age were presented with sentences containing no semantic or contextual clues to influence interpretation of the sentence. In one instance, the children were shown a blindfolded doll and were asked "Is the doll easy to see?" (Chomsky 1969, p. 26). The children could interpret the question in two ways — first, that the doll is doing the seeing, and second, that someone else is seeing the doll. There was mixed interpretation from children between the ages of 5.6 and 9 years, and, generally, success from 9 years of age on. From this example we can infer that, even though a student can call the words correctly while reading, he may not grasp the author's meaning of the sentence because the student does not understand the syntax.

A teacher can help to overcome this inability by making children more objectively aware of the language (DeStefano 1981). Five-year-olds appear to react to a sentence based on a description of reality. That is, when asked whether "John read the book" is a good sentence, children answered no because maybe John does not know how to read. As children mature, they begin to develop linguistic awareness of the structure of the language, thus increasing their ability to relate to prose more abstractly.

A child's procedure for understanding and generating utterances can be seen as a five-step procedure (Menyuk 1963, pp. 154–155).

1. The child acquires some rules to understand and reproduce sentences.
2. Using his rules, he samples and determines the structure of an utterance.
3. Using his rules, he generates an utterance but sometimes does not complete the order of rules needed for a well-formed structure.
4. He stores the rules in memory but has only enough memory to store some of the rules of grammar.
5. The set of grammar rules expands when this memory increases and is reorganized.

This procedure does not preclude the idea of language modeling behavior by the child or of the child's predisposition for language production. It only explains what the *child* does.

Language acquisition, then, is a developmental process. It appears to be controlled by cognitive abilities that increase with age (Slobin 1966). Reconsider Piaget's sensorimotor period (0–2 years). During this time the child imitates in both motor and language acts. It is also the time in which the child imitates and reduces utterances (Brown and Bellugi 1964). Therefore, cognitive abilities and language development are interwoven; as a child matures in both, they affect text processing.

Reading acquisition and oral language differ in several respects: level of anxiety of the learner, of the teacher, and of the parents is higher during reading acquisition; there is more conscious instruction in reading; and the rate of acquisition expected is quicker (Wardhaugh 1971). In addition, when students are learning to read they appear to relate what is written on the page to their oral language. When they are learning to speak, however, they need the first-hand experiences to associate with the words they are learning.

LANGUAGE AS A SOCIAL PROCESS (SOCIOLINGUISTICS)

A speech community is any human population characterized by regular and frequent interaction by means of shared verbal signs. The verbal behavior of the group constitutes a system that can be studied, and it is related to shared social norms. For example, in general, America shares a common language, as does Mexico. However, within a large speech community here are subcommunities whose speech forms a system. In America, a Southerner's pronunciation of words, syntax of sentences, and semantics will be different from a New Yorker's. Some authors refer to these differences as dialect. The student's use of these dialect components is an indicator of the part of the country he lives in, his social position, his background, and his education (Gumperz 1968, p. 383).

The term used to describe language in social contexts is sociolinguistics. Consider the following example (Shuy 1977). A preadolescent boy keeps his mouth shut in class. If he's white, it might be interpreted as shyness. If he is black, it might be interpreted as nonverbalness. Now toss in the concept of masculinity. Mix. What might be possible reasons for a boy keeping his mouth shut in class? Is there peer pressure not to be intelligent? Are boys less articulate than girls? Does the macho image apply to sports but not to school? Sociolinguists study language in this type of context.

Early language stimulation appears to be a key factor in establishing vocabulary and patterns of communication. Noel (1953) found that parents, or the immediate family, are the strongest influence on oral language development. Milner (1951) found that high-scoring achievers in first grade had an enriched verbal environment and more books in the home than low-achieving peers. The high achievers also engaged in conversation with their parents more often.

Students in classrooms have experienced different degrees of verbal interaction with their families and peers. If students do not have the concepts and vocabulary presented in text material, they will be hindered in their understanding of the material. Therefore, a teacher's observation of student oral language will help in two ways: first, if concept development is limited, the teacher will need to provide experiences with the environment and oral language; second, the teacher should put aside materials that do not match the student's concept development and oral vocabulary level and should supply materials that do match.

Dialect is another dimension of the social process of language. Recall the stage of language development when the child imitates the adults surrounding him in establishing a communication system. If the adults speak a dialect, the child will naturally imitate the sounds he hears. In different geographical areas words are pronounced differently. In some areas, for instance, many persons do not orally differentiate between short /i/ and short /e/; they pronounce /pin/ and /pen/ the same. Also, /greasy/ ends like /easy/. Sentence structure, also, is diverse among speakers. Some speakers say: "I be comin'," "Where he at," "He is no here," and "He might could come." Vocabulary differences are also notable, as in "spider" for "skillet" and "sack" for "paper bag." The phonology and sentence structure of diverse speakers and their relationship to reading have been studied. Research findings show that dialect, both phonological and syntactic, does not result in poor reading (Melmed 1971; Mitchell-Kernan 1969). Rather, the way the teacher presents material and his feelings about a dialect speaker have a greater influence on reading achievement (Goodman 1976b).

The major implication of language as a social process is that teacher attitudes and teaching methodology are more important than the language differences themselves. It appears that when teachers' or school systems' values, expectations, or attitudes are dissonant with those of the students, failure to learn is the result (McDermott 1976). Language variation from "standard English" has nothing to do with lack of or abundance of cognitive abilities or creative thinking abilities. Teachers should understand and allow for dialect variation in teaching reading (Horvath 1977).

PSYCHOLINGUISTICS

Psycholinguists study language and thought processing. It has been theorized that efficient reading is the ability to select the fewest, most productive cues necessary to produce right guesses the first time. Reading, according to Goodman (1976b), is a psycholinguistic guessing game. A reader has to anticipate what will happen next.

For example, a noun is expected in the sentence "The ——— was in an accident," and a preposition in the sentence "He poured juice ——— the pitcher." Another dimension of the guessing game is redundancy. Many words or phrases are used with each other so often that a fluent reader knows what to expect before reading the word. (For *example*, the little *red* wagon, park your *car* in the lot). A fluent reader can anticipate what the preceding italicized words will be because they are used so frequently in those same word settings. The ease in identifying a given word depends on the words around it, as well as on prior knowledge or on the frequency of having used the phrase in oral language (or reading it in print before).

There are four major types of cues used in reading (Smith et al. 1970): (1) cue systems within words, (2) cue systems in language or text, (3) cue systems within the reader, and (4) those cues within neither the language nor the reader. For the cue system within words, the reader looks for phonics, shape, parts of words, or words that are in his sight vocabulary. The cue systems within language itself include use of redundancy, of sentence structure, of function words, and of context clues. Cues within the reader are his facility with language, concept development, physical factors, and ability to transfer his knowledge of language to the reading task. External cues are illustrations, help from the teacher, and skill charts.

Reading as a psycholinguistic process is the interaction of the reader (who possesses a unique combination of language and concept development) with the textual material, which has built-in cues. The student has already learned much of his language when formal reading instruction begins and must learn to transfer his knowledge to the cue systems in written prose. The purpose of the transfer is to extract meaning.

Another view fusing language and thought involves attention as the major factor in reading comprehension — the learner's attention both to the task and to the linguistic features (Wanat 1977). Attention to the task assumes that the child is actively listening to what the teacher is saying (rather than concentrating on tying his shoelace, for example). Attention to the linguistic features means that the child is cuing into what is on the printed page. Linguistic features include letters, sound–symbol correspondences, word parts, spelling patterns, syllables, words, phrases, clauses, sentences, and the total text.

The linguistic features into which the child cues depends on the nature of the reading task, how advanced his reading skills are, and the method by which he is being taught to read. Imagine a beginning reader in first grade who is using a text in which there are three words. "Tom is running." The students in this particular classroom are being taught by a sight word and sound–symbol (phonics) method. The students would naturally tend to use these two skills in reading the three words and not other skills because these two are what they have been taught to use. As the same students mature or develop and refine their reading skills, they will use additional skills or even combinations of different skills.

As the students progress in reading skill to the larger linguistic units such as phrases, clauses, sentences, and text, the real skill involved is one of thinking. The skills necessary in these larger sized linguistic units are not specific to reading initially, but rather to listening and oral language first, and then to reading. Thus a student has to understand the meaning of these larger linguistic units as he would use them in speaking or listening, and then has to transfer his knowledge to the reading task. In fact, when the sentences in the passage of the reading material reflect the child's normal speech patterns, then his reading comprehension is higher (Ruddell 1965). This finding implies that before the students can read passages with complete understanding they must be able to use the basic sentence structure of phrases and clauses in their oral language. Meaning is the key idea.

Summary

Certain affective, cognitive, and linguistic factors interact and affect reading achievement. Affect functions as a liking–disliking gauge before cognition. Children, through overt behavior, tell the teacher how they feel about themselves, the teacher, other students, and the reading task itself. Five affective factors that show a relationship to reading are self-concept, autonomy, environmental mastery, perception of reality, and anxiety. The role of the teacher is to build and enhance positive attitudes toward reading so that children will want to read and will continue to want to read.

Thought, the cognitive aspects of reading, functions as a basis for understanding what has been read. A student needs to develop concepts similar to the ones he encounters in print. The brain stores, changes, and retrieves schemata so that one can react to print. According to Piaget, children progress through certain stages of thinking, and the type of thinking utilized enables the child to act on reading tasks in certain ways. Therefore, the teacher should observe children's reactions to tasks they are asked to perform, then adjust the tasks to be compatible with the child's thought process level. Learning the specific reading skills, according to Powell, enhances the child's conceptual ability.

Concepts and the building of new concepts are important to reading processing, as is mental imagery. For example, when students learn nouns, they respond more quickly if they have a mental image or mental picture for the word. Also, in learning sight words, children must progress through the processes of visual discrimination and visual memory, and have the item in their oral vocabulary.

Concepts and thought manifest themselves through oral language. Oral language functions as one basis, in beginning readers, for understanding the meaning of written text. The adage that children learn what they live holds particularly true for oral language development. Children reflect their nationality (American or Russian, for example) in their use of phonemes at an early age. Furthermore, they reflect their background in their use of grammar and vocabulary before they enter school. When a child begins to read he uses his oral language as a mediator. He probably has difficulty reading silently at first because he has never had to do that type of task before; he has always been responding to spoken language. The more compatible the written sentences are with the child's oral language, the higher will be his understanding of the written message. Understanding what has been read will not occur, however, if the student is not attending to the task.

Concepts in Processing Print

1. Learning to read is perceiving potential meaning in written messages and relating this potential meaning to existing cognitive structures to understand it (Ausubel 1968, p. 68).
2. Reading is a complex interaction of linguistic, affective, and cognitive functions.
3. Affective factors related to reading achievement are self-concept, autonomy, environmental mastery, perception of reality, and anxiety (Athey 1976).
4. The function of affect in reading includes the components of attitude, motivation, at-tention, comprehension, and acceptance (Mathewson 1976).
5. Conceptual development of the child is one base for reading achievement; another is language development.
6. The way the child thinks logically will influence his performance on reading tasks.
7. Learning isolated reading skills is not as important as the concepts being built while learning the skills.
8. Language learning (phonology, semantics, syntax) is a developmental process.
9. A child needs to have concepts and vocabu-

lary labels in his oral language in order to understand the written counterpart initially.

10. Children will be in various stages of oral language and concept development when formal reading instruction is expected to begin.
11. Parents, or the immediate family, exert the strongest influence on oral language development.
12. Dialect, per se, does not interfere with a student's reading achievement; rather the attitude of the teacher toward the dialect may interfere.
13. The purpose of building appropriate concepts and background before the child reads textual material is to facilitate the student's understanding of what he reads.
14. Reading may be viewed as a "guessing game" in which the reader should anticipate what will follow.

Questions for Further Reading and Thinking

1. What affective factors, other than those discussed in this chapter, relate to reading achievements?
2. How do authorities differ in the ways they define self-concept? With which definition do you agree?
3. How can a teacher evaluate the development of a given child's affect as it relates to reading?
4. For some children, why are some concepts more difficult to learn than others?
5. What are additional implications of affective, cognitive, and language developmental factors for beginning reading instruction?

Activities and Projects

1. Compare the views on the reading process presented in this chapter with other sources on the same topic such as:
   Spache, George D.; and Spache, Evelyn B. 1977. *Reading in the Elementary School.* 4th ed. Chapter 1. Boston: Allyn and Bacon.
2. Read in greater depth about the role of oral language development and its relationship to and effect on reading achievement. Write a paper on what you find.
3. Read *Discovering American Dialects* (Champaign, Ill.: National Council of Teachers of English, 1967) by Jean Malmstrom and A. Ashley. Observe student dialect in a classroom and compare the student dialect with those presented by Malstrom and Ashley.

Lester N. Knight

2

Readiness for Beginning Reading

The general concept of readiness — being prepared to begin a particular task — is not difficult to grasp: some things should be attempted and mastered before other things can be undertaken. A child's first piano lesson may include learning to identify some notes on the musical staff but not a rendition of a Chopin étude. Everything we do involves mastery of some simpler and related competency or skill, one that enables us to perform a task at the next level.

Learning to read also appears to involve mastery of skills. Although there is no universal acceptance of a particular sequence, there has been a general acceptance of some concept of reading readiness. Perceptions of reading readiness, however, have been divergent, with the result that reading readiness (unlike the general concept of readiness in life) has been in some ways rather poorly understood.

Several things have led to the divergent views regarding readiness. Primary among these is the complexity of reading itself. The answer to "What happens when one reads?" is not simple. Researchers have identified a set of skills, but no universally acceptable model has emerged as yet. It is known that various experiential, cognitive, linguistic, affective, and perceptual skills are at work, but these skills require further research. Related questions regarding reading are: "What is (true) reading instruction?" and "Is reading instruction restricted to teaching useful skills?" In addition, the role of mental maturity and the home or school's possible influence on that maturity has been considered. Perhaps the somewhat complex state of the art is the reason for such differing positions on reading readiness as the following:

We have evidence to prove that a perfectly "normal" child — I.Q. 100 — cannot learn to read until he is about six years, six months old. . . . When the time comes he can master it readily (Heffernan 1960, p. 316).

Reading is begun by very different materials, methods, and general procedures, some of which a pupil can master at the age of five with reasonable ease, others of which would give him difficulty at the mental age of seven (Gates 1937, p. 508).

We begin with the hypothesis that any subject can be taught effectively in some intellectually honest form to any child at any stage of development (Bruner 1960, p. 33).

Reading Readiness

QUESTIONS TO GUIDE READING

Literal
In what ways are one's concept of the reading act related to one's concept of reading readiness?
What particular skills and competencies are related to reading success?

Inferential
How is reading readiness related to beginning formal instruction in reading? to ongoing instruction? to reading at all levels?

Evaluative
In what way does a child's desire to read influence his development of the skills necessary to do so?
With which of the preceding three viewpoints on reading readiness do you most agree? Why?

A POSITION

In spite of the divergent interpretations of reading readiness in general, it is possible to reach a position on reading readiness from which to work as a teacher. First, consider the question "Is this child ready to begin to learn formal word recognition skills?" As we saw in Chapter 1, word recognition is only one aspect of reading. But if this narrow question *is* asked, then what is to be done with the child for whom the answer is no?

There are many other important skills related to reading, so perhaps a better question might be "What aspect of reading is this child ready for?" This question appears to lend itself to the broader interpretation of reading, and more importantly, to possibilities for some precision in assessment and subsequent instruction. It would be an exceptional child whose strengths and weaknesses could not be profiled somewhere along a reading continuum (see Figure 2.1).

The practical answer to the question "What aspect of reading is this child ready for?" is a broad-based interpretation of reading readiness.

Figure 2.1. A reading continuum. These factors are not skills to be learned in sequence but are interrelated factors that relate to success in reading.

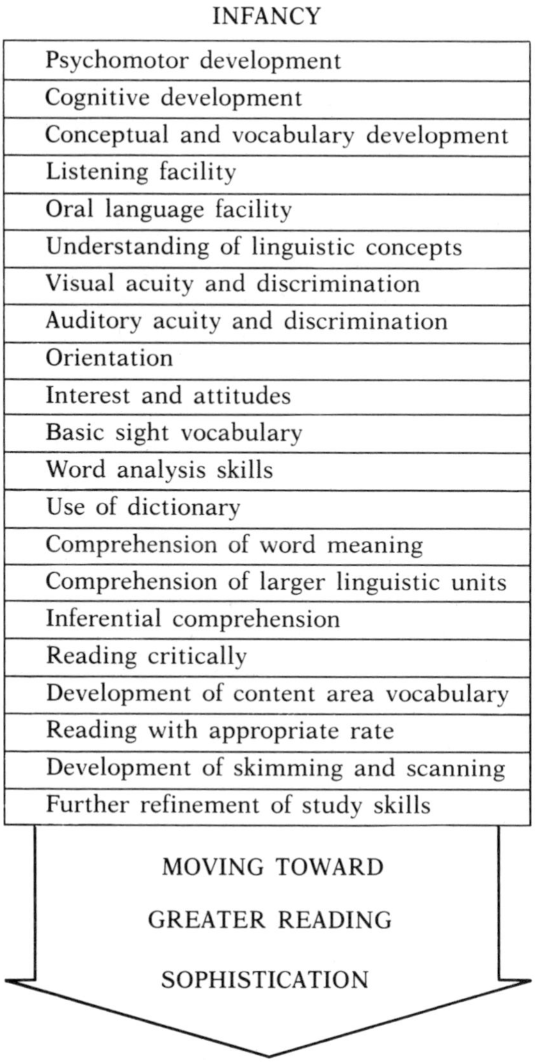

INFANCY

Psychomotor development
Cognitive development
Conceptual and vocabulary development
Listening facility
Oral language facility
Understanding of linguistic concepts
Visual acuity and discrimination
Auditory acuity and discrimination
Orientation
Interest and attitudes
Basic sight vocabulary
Word analysis skills
Use of dictionary
Comprehension of word meaning
Comprehension of larger linguistic units
Inferential comprehension
Reading critically
Development of content area vocabulary
Reading with appropriate rate
Development of skimming and scanning
Further refinement of study skills

MOVING TOWARD

GREATER READING

SOPHISTICATION

Within this interpretation there also rests the possibility for readiness considerations in the traditional ("predecoding" instruction) sense.

Broadly considered, reading readiness is an issue not for any one age or grade level but for all ages and grades. For example, the high school senior will need to develop particular concepts and vocabulary *before* he can read his chemistry text adequately. The same is true for the middle grade youngster as he pursues situation problems in math. Readiness in reading is an ongoing concern and must receive its due attention at every level. The new concepts must be developed directly or vicariously.

PREREQUISITES TO FORMAL READING

We must recognize, however, that there are some reading-related skills, abilities, and understandings for which a minimum of development is prerequisite to the beginning of formalized reading instruction.[1] Included among these are an adequate experiential base that facilitates the development of concepts and associated vocabulary (labels), cognitive development, language development, interest in and attitudes toward reading, visual and auditory discrimination, and orientation skills. (These prerequisites will serve formal reading best when the child also possesses good hearing, vision, emotional health, psychomotor skills, and a definite pattern of handedness).

Experiential base. Fortunately, most children enter kindergarten and first grade having had sufficient experiences to develop a speaking vocabulary of several thousand words. For these children there is usually little problem in relating the concepts they have developed to the first words they learn to recognize in print. Teachers must be alert, however, to those children whose experiences, because of linguistic or cultural reasons, have produced a vocabulary different from that which is encountered in initial reading.

Cognitive development. Children's mental development initially (birth to age 2) enables them to deal with reality and associated meanings only when that reality (e.g., object) is present and can be manipulated. It is only after a period of years (typically fifth or sixth grade) that most children can be expected to deal with their world abstractly. Children between 5 and 7 are in a transition period (from preoperational to operational thought) in which they *begin* to think representationally. This means "knowledge is no longer exclusively tied to external acts" (Furth 1970). Though the child may now pretend that the chair is a car (one object represents another), he or she may not be able to cope with reality representations (such as the written word *boat*) bearing no resemblance to that reality. Since written language as a representative for the objects and activity of the child's world is somewhat abstract, teachers must be aware of children's mental abilities as formal reading is encountered.

Language development. Language is now widely viewed as the basic tool of the reader (Goodman 1976b; Loban 1976; Smith 1971). The degree to

1. Formalized reading instruction is defined here as the systematic teaching of skills used to translate print into a comprehensible message.

which materials that teach reading correlate with the child's ent
language development is important. As printed words, and ult
longer written passages, are encountered, the reader must proce:
through her own language code. Since most children enter schc
considerable, though incomplete, skill in understanding and usi:
native language (Chomsky 1969; Dale 1976), it is essential that the
experiences in reading capitalize and build on their linguistic s
At the same time areas of incomplete development must be rec
and instructional procedures chosen accordingly.[2]

Interest and attitudes. Interest and attitudes are affective fac
must be considered in readiness. Unless children develop and maintain a
desire for reading, much of what is good about learning to read will be
lost. Children who have a fascination with the printed word will often
indicate that interest by asking questions, looking at books, etc. Teachers
should be aware of this interest and respond in positive ways to ensure
that the child moves into reading to the extent that his abilities and
desires dictate.

Visual and auditory discrimination. Both visual and auditory discrimination abilities have been shown to be associated with success in reading
(Church 1974; Robeck and Wilson 1974). The ability to discriminate
among the various sounds used *in the language* and to associate them with
their printed counterparts in the alphabet is what appears to be crucial.
It is not surprising, therefore, that research has repeatedly shown that
isolated training (which often has included such nonlinguistic features as
geometric shapes) in these abilities does not improve achievement in
reading (Church 1974; Hammill et al. 1974; Neuman 1981; Witkin 1973).
Children entering school are better equipped in auditory discrimination
of linguistic differences than they are in visual ones, since much of the
oral component of the language has already been learned (Groff 1975).
However, any phonological features that have not fully developed will
result in auditory discrimination weaknesses in those areas.

Orientation skills. In our culture reading involves the ability to proceed
from left to right and up to down. Unless children come to school with
considerable experience with these processes, they will have to learn
them. Those who are already familiar with them have usually learned
them by being read to or by some other language-reading related experience. Therefore, teachers of children entering school should make sure
that those who have not had such experiences have them.

These skills must be emphasized in readiness programs in light of their

2. Examples of possible incomplete development include delineation of *ask* and *tell* in certain
imperatives (Chomsky 1969) and certain concepts related to math (Hargis and Knight 1975).
In addition, children frequently are confused about key terms used to teach reading, such
as *letter* and *word* (Downing et al. 1975).

relationship to reading and the children in the programs. Reliable and ongoing assessment can assist teachers in determining whether the skills are established. Although it is important for teachers to develop an interpretation of readiness as inclusive as that shown in Figure 2.1, much of the material in the remainder of this chapter deals with assessment and suggested methods of instruction of traditional readiness skills.

Teachers frequently encounter a broad range of readiness within their classes. Some children will require many experiences, particularly language oriented ones, that are related to reading but do not involve formal instruction, whereas others are advanced to the point of success in actual reading. Most of the other skills for which readiness is a concern will be dealt with in other chapters.

Assessing Readiness

QUESTIONS TO GUIDE READING

Literal
What are the various informal ways to assess strengths and weaknesses of readiness skills?

Inferential
How accurate are standardized tests for assessing readiness?
What guidelines should we follow in using standardized tests for assessing readiness?

Evaluative
How important should standardized tests be in assessing readiness?

Procedures for assessing reading readiness skills vary from teacher observation to the use of standardized tests. Experience has shown that experienced teachers often develop a sensitivity and skill that enables them to identify children who are ready to move successfully into formal reading instruction.

INFORMAL ASSESSMENT

Some teachers can tell which children are ready to read simply by working with them and systematically observing their *patterns* of behavior and achievements. Conclusions are made based on what appears to be the pattern rather than on occasional behavior. In so doing most of these teachers appear to rely heavily on informal ways of conducting an ongoing assessment. Examples of such informal assessment procedures follow. Observation is the logical starting point. In some cases written mechanisms such as checklists and anecdotal records may be used along with observation.

Observing experiential base. There are many opportunities in the classroom to note which experiences seem to be relevant to children. Responses to the children's literature shared may give a clue. Observations of free play will indicate how the available objects are related back to previous experience. Oral language activity, such as sharing time, will also give some indication of the experiences and associated concepts each child has.

Observing cognitive development. Note the children's activity in play to determine their ability in representing an absent object with another. This may occur in a "let's pretend" situation when a chair becomes a "car." This expertise may also be noted in art activities and creative dramatics. Activities can also be devised to check the child's abilities in placing objects in categories such as food items. Abilities in memory can be observed in follow-up activities at story time.

Observing language development. As children participate in oral language activities and language experience activities the teacher can expect to notice some children still having difficulty in articulating sounds such as the /th/ in *their* or *that* or the /skw/ in *square*. These problems are age-appropriate and should be self-corrected in time. The presence of many articulation problems or a native dialect different from reading related materials must be considered so that instructional procedures do not place the child in a situation in which he cannot succeed.[3] The teacher must be alert to the child's language competence as well as production. For example, it is evident that some of the terminology used in reading instruction, such as *letter, word,* and *sentence,* are not clearly understood (Downing et al. 1975; Holden and MacGinitie 1972; Reid 1966; Roberts 1981). Also some language constructions are poorly understood by children at this level (Chomsky 1969; Hargis and Knight 1975). Some children will place a "tell" interpretation on the imperative "Ask Mary what time it is." Teachers must take this into consideration in giving directions and in selecting materials for reading. Other children may experience difficulty in comparative construction in mathematics. Therefore, mathematics reading problems that deal with terms such as "smaller" or "taller" may be beyond the child's competence.

3. Both regional and social class differences should be considered, especially when teaching word recognition skills. See Chapter 16 on reading for the linguistically and culturally different.

Observing orientation. Orientation can be observed as a child identifies letter sequence in words, order of words in experience stories, or left-to-right use of the chalkboard.

Observing interest and attitude. A child's interest in reading can be noted by such things as:

1. questions regarding word identification.
2. apparent interest in printed material as evidenced by browsing through magazines and books.
3. desire to read experience charts devised in the classroom.

Use of checklists. The teacher may find it helpful to use some general checklists to record some observations. Listening skills, for example, are closely correlated with the ability to read. The checklist in Table 2.1 can be adapted for use with students at various levels. Checklists might be devised for the other skill areas as well.

An analysis of general speaking qualities can provide an overall assessment of such items as clarity, organization, and articulation. A potentially useful mechanism for this type of assessment is a checklist as in Table 2.2.

Table 2.1. A Checklist of Listening Skills

	Always	Sometimes	Never
1. Can the student tell the difference between kinds of sounds?	☐	☐	☐
2. Does he listen to and follow directions for games?	☐	☐	☐
3. Does he listen to and follow directions at other times?	☐	☐	☐
4. After listening to a story, can he tell what happened first, next, and last?	☐	☐	☐
5. After listening to a passage, can he answer questions about the details?	☐	☐	☐
6. Does he recognize the main idea of a paragraph?	☐	☐	☐
7. Can he describe the mood of a story he listens to?	☐	☐	☐
8. Does he remember what he hears?	☐	☐	☐
9. Does he get the idea the speaker is suggesting something even when he isn't actually?	☐	☐	☐
10. Does he recognize it when the speaker gets off the subject?	☐	☐	☐

Table 2.2. Checklist for Speaking Qualities

Qualities	Child A	Child B	Child C
Ideas are worthy			
Expresses ideas clearly and with variety			
Selects and organizes ideas effectively			
Usage appropriate for situation			
Appropriate voiced articulation			
Appropriate postured body actions			

Source: Reprinted by permission of the publisher, F. E. Peacock Publishers, Inc., Itasca, Ill. From Paul C. Burns, *Diagnostic Teaching of the Language Arts*, 1974, p. 67.
Key: I — needs instruction and teaching
     R — needs review and practice
     S — satisfactory
     E — enrichment/extension are appropriate

Anecdotal records. Anecdotal records can be kept to indicate strengths and weaknesses in an area. This technique can be applied to any of the areas of observation listed earlier in the section on informal assessment. Such records might result in a diary-type list of observations such as the following:

> *Steve Mayo*
> 9/15 — Noted repeated requests for repetition of instruction.
> 9/18 — Did not follow instructions several times today.
> 9/21 — Interest and listening really "perked up" when I shared the story today on space giants.

As the observations are continued perhaps the teacher can pinpoint the cause of Steve's problem and begin to solve it.

Auditory discrimination tests. Teacher-made auditory discrimination tests and games can require children to respond by a predetermined signal (e.g., a raised hand or a clap) to such things as:

1. words that rhyme (*pig, big, rig, jig, pin*): have the children note the one that is different.
2. words that have similar or different beginning sounds or medial sounds.

Visual discrimination tests. Visual discrimination can be tested by having children do such things as:

1. Identify the same letters placed in two columns but in different order.
2. Find the word on the board that is on the flashcard.
3. Mark letters from choices on a page as they are called out by the teacher.

STANDARDIZED TESTS

Over the years a number of authorities on reading have developed reading readiness tests and established norms to predict success probabilities for children in reading.

Many of these published standardized tests include subtests to measure achievement in such skills as visual discrimination of letters and words and auditory discrimination of beginning and ending sound. Others include measures of listening, comprehension, following directions, visual-motor coordination, and ability to understand spoken language. Among the more commonly used readiness tests are the following:

> *Gates-MacGinitie Reading Tests: Readiness Skills*, Grades K–1. Teachers College Press, Columbia University.
> *Harrison-Stroud Reading Readiness Profiles*, Grades K–1. Houghton Mifflin Company.
> *Lee-Clark Readiness Test*, Grades K–1. California Test Bureau.
> *Metropolitan Readiness Tests*, Grade 1. Harcourt Brace Jovanovich.
> *Murphy-Durrell Reading Readiness Analysis*, Grade 1. Harcourt Brace Jovanovich.
> *The Boehm Test of Basic Skills*, 1971 Ed., Forms A & B. Grades K–2. The Psychological Corporation.

When using standardized reading readiness tests, teachers should be concerned about whether the tests are useful as assessment tools. Questions regarding the tests' validity, reliability, population used for reading norms, comprehensibility, and true usefulness as a predictor should be answered. All such questions relate to the degree to which the test results can be believed.

General information concerning such questions can be found in the *Mental Measurements Yearbooks* by Oscar Buros, as well as in many professional texts in reading. In addition some information is provided by the test publishers themselves. It should be remembered, however, that much of this information relates to the general validity and reliability of the test itself; that is, it treats the question of whether the test measures what it says it does and how consistently it does so. Such general validity and reliability are frequently reported positively.

Users of these tests must probe deeper. For instance, the norms established for the tests are often based on a population sample that does not adequately represent varying socioeconomic and minority groups; therefore the norms apply very little to those groups not represented. While the general validity and reliability of a particular readiness test may look good, we should recognize that test authors usually disagree among themselves as to what should be tested to predict success. Rude's (1973) study of five major reading readiness tests indicated a lack of unanimity on what should be tested on every item but one; letter recognition was the only unanimous choice. Some important skills such as attention span, cognitive learning style, and experiential background are omitted from all the standardized tests.

The primary purpose of standardized readiness tests is to permit predicting the probability of success in beginning reading. The research indicates, however, that they are *not* very good predictors. Karlin (1980, p. 171) reports that independent investigators have reported correlations from below 0.30 to as high as 0.75, with most between 0.40 and 0.60. This means that only 40 to 60 times out of 100 are the tests good predictors. It is not too surprising, then, that careful, experienced teacher observation and judgment often yield predictions just as reliable as any readiness test.

In view of the problems involved in the makeup and use of standardized tests, we must deal with the question of their place as assessment tools for reading readiness. The following suggestions are offered:

1. Exercise a high degree of selectivity in choosing tests. Attempt to choose those which appear to have the highest potential for your particular population and need.
2. Use standardized tests as only one indicator of the possible needs of children. Continue to use ongoing informal measures as well.
3. Note in particular the subtests. Some subsections of tests are better than others in the same test or in other tests. However, subtest reliabilities may be lower than those of the total test.
4. Note the specific items of the test and look for patterns of strengths or weaknesses that may be apparent.

Teaching Procedures

QUESTIONS TO GUIDE READING

Literal
How can a child's ability in the following areas be strengthened: listening? speaking? knowledge of the alphabet? auditory discrimination? visual discrimination? left-to-right orientation?

Inferential
What does research indicate about the value of isolated instruction and drill in the various readiness skills?

Evaluative
How would the selection of teaching strategies be affected by such factors as cognitive (thinking) style and physical factors (such as visual and auditory acuity)?

Working out an instructional program in reading readiness has an inherent problem — one that arises because of the divergent views of what constitutes a reading activity as opposed to a readiness activity. We established that in general no separation should be made — that the question to raise is "What aspect of reading is this child ready for?" We feel that a whole continuum of skills relates to the reading act. But we did establish that there is some sequence to these skills and that achievement in some of them seems to be prerequisite to formal reading instruction, the actual instruction in such skills as decoding and comprehension.

The major emphasis of this section on teaching procedures is on developing and improving those skills often associated with "preformal" reading. First, however, we should consider some general guidelines.

GENERAL GUIDELINES

There is no conclusive evidence, as noted earlier, that separate, formal training in those skills normally associated with preformal reading is truly beneficial to reading achievement. Whether the skill be visual discrimination, auditory discrimination, auditory blending, etc., there is "almost no evidence that the increased teaching of these skills will ensure success in learning to read" (Farr 1969, p. 154). This seems to be particularly true with respect to the use of nonverbal stimuli such as pictures and geometric figures in visual discrimination training (Rosen 1966).

Although separate, formal training in so-called readiness skills does not appear to be positively correlated to reading achievement, we should not conclude that there is no value to working on these skills when a weakness exists. On the contrary, special instruction and assistance is sometimes in order. But perhaps such instruction should just occur as a part of the total reading program.

Attempts at separate instructional programs for isolated skills related to the complex process of reading often seem ludicrous. Would one attempt to separate the skills of learning to speak? Imagine some separate and distinct instructional programs to teach pronunciation of voiced versus voiceless sounds (/d/ or /t/ for example), or differentiation of nouns from verbs, or the proper use of intonation. The futility of such an approach to learning to speak is quite obvious. The child in large measure learns to speak (as he learns many other skills) by plunging in and trying it. He doesn't wait for complete mastery of a lot of related skills.

A useful position on the teaching of readiness skills might be summarized with the conclusion Robinson reached (1972, p. 145):

> There is little in the research which indicates that delaying reading instruction is necessarily helpful. On the other hand it may well be that initiating reading instruction, pacing the instruction according to the capability of the youngster, and giving additional training in skills which he is deficient in may prove to be of value.

The suggestions that follow might help a teacher who, having determined by a variety of assessment techniques that a particular weakness in a reading-related skill exists, goes about systematically meeting that need. It is not suggested that the teacher work with a particular skill and that skill only; instead, activities should fit together as coping responses to the question: "What aspect of reading is this child ready for?"

In addition, teachers are advised to determine the general cognitive and emotional status of the child in order to make judgments concerning his or her learning style. The determination of the skills the child lacks is not enough in making prescriptive decisions. The teacher must also try to predict the likely response of the child to instruction in those skills.

Language Arts Skills

The fallacy of considering reading as a skill separate from the other language arts (listening and speaking, in particular) has been emphasized repeatedly. As we saw in Chapter I, reading involves the processing of language. Although reading does involve some skills that are unique to it (see Wardhaugh 1971), it relies mostly on language ability. An integrated program involving development of all the language arts is essential, and probably the most promising such program is the language experience approach.

The use of the language experience approach has some built-in advantages, which are detailed in Chapter 13. Certainly the experiential, conceptual, and linguistic strengths that most children bring to school must be utilized fully. Such an approach is also very useful for the atypical child, such as the linguistically different, because it reflects both the language and culture of the child. Freeman and Wolfgang (1978) have suggested that children who are not ready to move into formal reading should have much experience in representational symbolism for reality such as clay sculpturing. They suggest further that the language experience approach may help to bridge the gap from this type of symbolization to representation by signs such as words.

Listening is the first communication skill a baby develops; it serves as the basis for perception of sound so essential to reading. It is also quite clear that listening vocabulary and comprehension correlate highly with reading vocabulary and comprehension. As a matter of fact, a child's achievement on a test of listening comprehension is sometimes used as a measure of his potential in reading achievement. Lundsteen (1971), among others has emphasized the relationship between listening and reading.

The development of speaking as an essential component in reading readiness has received considerable stress in recent years (Knight 1972). This emphasis has resulted, in part, from the influence of linguists and psycholinguists such as Bloomfield and Barnhart (1961), Fries (1963), Lefevre (1964), and Goodman (1976a). Loban approached the same theme as an educator. His report, *The Language of Elementary Children* (1976), stated that competence in reading depends largely on a child's competence in spoken language and that the oral language with which a child is familiar provides the basis for his learning the visual recognition of the words in that language. The degree to which materials that teach reading correlate with the child's speaking or oral language development is of considerable importance.

How to Improve Listening and Speaking Skills

1. Provide time, materials, and a climate for free play.
2. Provide listening centers that include clearly delineated and stated purposes, directions, materials, procedures, and evaluation keys.
3. Choose stories and poems from children's literature to share with the children.
4. Utilize the various records and tapes available for listening activities.
5. Encourage children to play games involving listening and speaking.
6. Provide specific lessons and training in the various types of listening — such as marginal, appreciative, attentive, and analytical or critical listening (see Smith 1973).
7. Use the language experience approach to help show the relationship between speech and reading and writing (see Chapter 13).
8. Provide opportunities for the student to develop speaking skills in informal settings, such as:
   a. participating in sharing time.
   b. telling stories.
   c. communicating by telephone.
   d. participating in conversation.
   e. developing discussion roles.
   f. planning for daily activities.
   g. producing creative dramatics.
   h. participating in choral readings.
   i. utilizing art and music to capitalize on the opportunities for description, comparison, and classification.
   j. solving problems associated with topics in science and social studies.
   See also suggested materials at the end of this chapter.
9. Read aloud to children and have them respond in such ways as:
   a. providing the ending for unfinished stories.
   b. retelling parts of all of the story, with particular attention to sequence.
   c. drawing conclusions.
   d. supplying words that are omitted.

OTHER SKILLS

A number of other skills, as we have seen, are often associated with readiness for formal reading instruction. There is apparently, for instance, a high correlation between knowledge of the alphabet and success in reading, although just learning the alphabet does not ensure this success. Some letter processing appears to be done not only by the beginning reader but by the mature reader as well. Other factors include visual discrimination, auditory discrimination (closely associated with phonics), left-to-right orientation, and interest in reading.[4]

4. A necessary prerequisite to good visual and auditory discrimination is good sight and hearing, respectively. Teachers should consider the possibility that a child not succeeding

Teaching the alphabet

1. Teach the child to become familiar with the letters in his own name.
2. Capitalize on any other word the child recognizes, such as a cereal name or a soft drink brand, and teach the letters used in the labels.
3. Teach the alphabet song while pointing to the letters on a transparency used in an overhead projector.
4. Utilize the various alphabet books available.

Auditory discrimination

1. Note likenesses in the sounds of words; for example:
   a. Give a word and then list on the board those words children identify as having the same *beginning* sound.
   b. Give a word (e.g., *sat*) and ask children to name other words that *rhyme* with the word.
   c. Read nursery rhymes that children can complete such as:
      "Hickory, dickory, dock
      the Mouse ran up the ——— ."
2. Note differences in the sounds of words; for example:[5]
   a. Give a series of words (e.g., *pal, pet, pull, ball, post*) and have children raise their hands when they hear a word not beginning with the same sound.
   b. Have children tell you which pair of words (*mother, man* or *little, dog*) begins with different sounds.
   c. Pronounce a series of words such as *lot, got, met,* and *rot* and have children indicate when they hear a word with a different medial sound.
   d. Give a word such as *seen* and have children give two or three other words that begin with a different sound.
   e. Do the same as in (d) above, but ask for different *ending* or *medial* sounding words.

Visual discrimination

1. Print labels for co⌐ on index cards. P dren to choose a object.
2. Develop indivi writing the le word, and draw.
3. Ask children to note lin⌐
   a. Have a child draw a circle ⌐ in a chalkboard list that is the sam⌐ word on a card shown to the class.
   b. Print two columns of words and ask the child to draw lines from words in the left column to same words in the right column.
   c. Have children find one word in several magazines and cut it out for his "word scrapbook."
   d. Suggest that a child group word flashcards according to words that begin the same or end the same.
4. Ask children to note differences:
   a. Present letters that are grossly different and have a child identify the different one, such as NNNB.
   b. Do the same thing with letters that are somewhat similar, such as CCOC.
   c. Do the same thing with letters that are very similar, such as bbdbb.
   d. Ask the child to discriminate between words that are very different, such as *man* and *mother*. Later, ask the child to discriminate between such similar words as *over* and *oven*.

Orientation

1. Teach left to right through such songs as "Looby Loo."
2. Sweep your hand from left to right when reading back to the children any material they have dictated in language experience work.

---

in these skills might not have the necessary prerequisites. Also note that visual discrimination of letters and words is of more value to reading achievement than general discrimination of nonlinguistic forms.

5. In each case care should be taken to choose examples consistent with the child's dialect.

child where to begin on charts when
ting something as he looks on.
rrange pictures to tell a story in left-to-
right progression.

Interest in and attitude about reading

1. Read to the children often and secure a reaction to the stories through discussion or
other language-related activities.

2. Provide as much attractive printed material
as possible for the child to browse through
and pursue his interests.

3. Encourage children to share orally the picture books they have particularly liked.

4. Make class and individual booklets from
stories resulting from the language-experience approach; display them prominently.

Reading in the Kindergarten

QUESTIONS TO GUIDE READING

Literal
Why has there been a shift in emphasis relative to reading in the
kindergarten?
What are some general characteristics of the kindergarten child that
relate to reading readiness?
What kind of reading program does the author advocate for
kindergarten?
What is the major change that has occurred in the teaching of reading
in the kindergarten?

Inferential
What reasons could be given for opposing reading instruction for all
children in kindergarten?

Evaluative
Is the current emphasis on reading in the kindergarten beneficial to the
development of a good total reading program?
Are some of the listed characteristics of the kindergarten child more
important than others in program planning?

Reading instruction in the kindergarten at one time was limited almost
exclusively to activities related to the development of so-called prereading
(readiness) skills as outlined previously in this chapter. However, whether
for valid or invalid reasons, the situation has often been reversed so that
a good many kindergartens now teach reading in the formal sense. In a
growing number of kindergarten classes children are being taught with
highly structured reading programs in spite of a number of unanswered
questions (Lesiak 1978).

The reasons for this shift in emphasis do not appear to be coming from any clear-cut research base proving that it is the best strategy for all children. Some research has suggested some achievement advantage (Shapiro and Willford 1969; Sutton 1969) for those beginning reading in the kindergarten; but it has not been without flaw and the findings cannot be interpreted to support early reading instruction for all. Perhaps the shift in emphasis has come instead from less direct influences. For example, the increased evidence that intellectual development is extremely significant during the early childhood years has led to increased concern for intellectual pursuits. There has also been a lot of attention given to the so-called disadvantaged in various compensatory programs in order to make up for their intellectual and language "gaps." The inclusion of formal reading instruction at an earlier age has seemed to be a natural end result from these and other influences. In addition, in a joint statement of concerns about pre–first grade reading, a group of professional organizations have indicated that the push for early reading may be coming at least in part from economic and political pressures rather than from our knowledge of young children and how they learn.[6]

Thus there is no sound reason for advocating *wholesale* reading instruction in any formal sense at the kindergarten level. But we cannot dismiss the issue so simply: the reason is that all children are different and some of them are in fact ready to move into reading instruction. Others come to school already reading (Durkin 1966). The basic implication is that reading in kindergarten must be individualized just as at every other level. We must meet the child where he is; again, we ask, "What aspect of reading is this child ready for!"

Because of the younger age of the kindergarten child as compared to other grades it is essential that educators be aware of some characteristics that are more generally descriptive of children at this age than other ages. Some of the characteristics that are related are the following:

1. Although many children by age 5 are no longer far-sighted and do have 20/20 vision, the teacher must take care to note those who have not reached such visual maturity.
2. Children at this level are extremely active and may be turned off by extensive use of "sit down and be still" reading activities.
3. Most "fives" are preoperational and work generally at a concrete level. This means that many phonic programs dealing essentially at abstract levels of cognition are inappropriate. It also suggests that the teacher must be careful in establishing comprehension expectations and guidance. She may find, too, that some children have trouble learning generalizations and rules.

6. American Association of Elementary/Kindergarten/Nursery Educators, Association for Childhood Education International, Association for Supervision and Curriculum Development, International Reading Association, National Association for the Education of Young Children, National Association of Elementary School Principals, and National Council of Teachers of English.

4. Some evidence (Meltzer and Herse 1969) exists indicating that even some first grade children have difficulty with the concept of word boundaries. Such children may encounter initial difficulty in reading because letter identification appears to be related to success in reading (Pick 1972).

5. A good oral language base representative of the material being read is essential. Although kindergarteners in general have an excellent beginning in language, they still have some developing to do. For example: Some of the words used by the children, although seemingly used accurately, are frequently labels for ill-defined concepts. Find alternate ways to test the students' understanding. A few children will still be working out some articulatory deviations and will probably have corresponding difficulty with sound–letter matching. It is clear that syntactical development occurs throughout the elementary years (Chomsky 1969) and that the period of kindergarten through grade one is a period of rapid syntactical development (O'Donnell et al. 1967, p. 33). Keep this in mind as you listen to the children and implement reading instruction.

6. Some children will show a strong interest in the printed word and will by their questions and enthusiasm indicate that they are at least ready to begin a limited sight vocabulary. A few of these children will indicate that they can move ahead to further reading instruction.

7. Occasionally a child will come to kindergarten already reading.

The preceding list of kindergarten-age characteristics suggests something of the continuum teachers of kindergarten might find in any one classroom with respect to potential for reading. As indicated earlier the implication is to individualize.

GUIDELINES FOR KINDERGARTEN READING

Recognize that the basic goal in all reading instruction is for every child to learn to read as easily and successfully as possible and to develop a yen to read. Any kind of general "let's hurry up and learn to read" policy is totally antithetical to this goal, for the goal is both cognitive *and affective.*

Be supportive of the kindergarten reader. Provide appropriate materials to read and praise and encouragement for his accomplishment. Realize that much of the readiness curriculum is inappropriate and should be skipped. Attempt to ensure that the postkindergarten curriculum is adjusted accordingly. At the same time recognize that there are still many levels of social, cognitive, and language development to be reached.

Allow a child to move ahead when she indicates a readiness to read by her interest or advanced total development. Remember there are children at both extremes of the continuum. But take care to choose materials and methods that are appropriate for each child.

Utilize a language oriented program. For the majority of kindergarten children the most appropriate reading curriculum will be reading-related activities that are not formal reading instruction per se; the curriculum should be geared toward the language and cognitive development of the child, with reading experiences as an integrated part of that emphasis. Such a language oriented program probably holds the best promise for meeting the basic reading goal of enthusiastic, smoothly achieved competence. Also, as pointed out earlier, K–1 is a period of crucial language growth. It is interesting to note that Durkin (1977), when describing the experiences of children who read early, suggests that a language arts approach is an apt description of the instructional program that took place in the homes and that deliberate attempts to teach reading were uncommon. Examples of the many language oriented activities appropriate for use (after careful assessment of each student) are the following:

1. Utilize play and movement experiences to develop many concepts and the related language.
2. Select art and music activities that provide opportunities for perceptual, language, and motor development.
3. Provide plenty of manipulative materials: encourage children to be creative with them and elicit verbal interchange about the experiences children have.
4. Plan to have available such materials in print as comics, newspapers, game directions, charts, and books. The teacher must be prepared to respond to questions.
5. Utilize children's literature by reading to the children. This practice has been shown to have a positive influence on vocabulary development (Cohen 1966).
6. Strongly encourage as much application of language in as many situations as possible. For instance, after listening to a selection from literature it may be particularly beneficial to follow the experience up with choral readings, story telling, creative dramatics, or group discussions (Cullinan et al. 1974).

Avoid mass instruction. There is never any good reason for mass instruction, using any one material to teach reading; this is particularly true of phonics workbooks.

Utilize all the possibilities inherent in the language experience approach. This basically informal method can often indicate to the teacher which students might be ready to move on in reading and which are not.

Help parents play a key role in developing the child's readiness for reading. The importance of this role has been clearly demonstrated in the studies by Durkin (1966) of children who learn to read early. Parents are not teachers of reading but can do much to serve in a supportive role and to provide an environment that stimulates growth in language and interest in reading. Teachers are frequently asked by parents what they can do to help their children succeed in reading. There are a number of things they can do. Chapter 19 contains many specific suggestions.

Summary

Learning to read, like most skills, involves some constellation of skills. This fact makes a consideration of reading readiness imperative. The complex nature of the reading process, along with the tentative models dealing with all the skills and their interrelationships, have led to a diversified view of readiness.

The position on readiness we have advanced here is an attempt to accommodate the present "state of the art." Reading readiness is a pervasive concern for all ages and grade levels, which means that there *always* needs to be attention to the question "What aspect of reading is this child ready for?"

There are several skills traditionally associated with preformalized reading instruction. The major attention in terms of assessment and suggestions for instruction is therefore geared to those skills.

Most ways of assessing the child's level of interest in reading, his listening and speaking development, auditory and visual discrimination skills, and left-to-right orientation place major emphasis on the use of informal measures. In addition, this chapter lists the most used standardized reading readiness tests, along with guidelines for their use.

Instruction in the areas of weakness must be based on careful assessment. Since there is no conclusive evidence that isolated training in any of these reading skills truly benefits reading achievement, we suggest that work in weak areas be only part of the total program. Furthermore, complete mastery of any of the preformal reading skills is not prerequisite to formal reading instruction.

Kindergarten teachers are in many instances being pressured to teach formal reading. These pressures are not always based on sound research, and the teacher must take great care to individualize the program so as to provide the reading or reading-related activities needed by each child. The range of need in any one kindergarten may be wide indeed.

Parental roles in reading are viewed as more supportive than instructive. Parents, although not teachers of reading, can do a number of specific things to stimulate growth in language and interest in reading.

Questions for Further Reading and Thinking

1. Assume you are a kindergarten teacher. How would you go about determining your students' places on the reading continuum? As an intermediate grade teacher, how would you make this determination?
2. What evidence supports the contention that "Experienced first grade teachers can predict the reading potential of their students better than standardized readiness tests"?
3. Consider that you have made the following diagnoses in grade one. What will be your instructional procedure? (Assume other skills are developed.)

   Case A: Sam is from a culturally different background and has a different oral language background from the middle-class youngster.

   Case B: Jill's hearing is normal, but she has virtually no ability to discriminate the contrasting phonemes.

   Case C: Mary's sight is normal, but she is very poor in visually perceiving differences in letters and words.

   Case D: Ed is a poor listener, has little interest in reading, and has no left-to-right orientation.
4. Specify what you might say to a parent who asks: "What can I do to help my child in reading?"
5. What readiness assessment procedures could you apply for students in the intermediate grades?
6. To what extent are elementary schools currently concerned with reading readiness at *all* levels?
7. Is there any evidence to make you believe that formal reading instruction should or should not begin even earlier than kindergarten?

Activities and Projects

1. Develop a collection of files of informal assessment techniques such as:
   a. checklists in listening and speaking.
   b. checklists for visual and auditory discrimination.
   c. summative checklists giving a general profile.
   d. individual profile sheets.
   e. anecdotal record sheets.
2. Develop a notebook of reputable standardized tests along with data on each test.
3. Begin to collect lists of recordings that could become part of a listening program.
4. Select samples of children's literature that students could use to develop the various language skills.
5. Find appropriate games and organize them according to the various readiness skills.
6. Develop learning centers that deal with the various readiness skills.
7. Devise a system of record keeping as a quick and easy reference of the current status of each child.
8. Develop a set of strategies for dealing with children who have hearing or visual losses.
9. Determine ways to deal with children whose socioemotional adjustment inhibits their progress in reading related activities.

Readiness Materials

For the teacher

Anderson, Paul S. 1963. *Storytelling with the flannel board.* Minneapolis, Minn.: T. S. Denison.

Bailey, Carolyn S.; and Lewis, Clara M. 1965. *Favorite stories for the children's hour.* New York: Platt.

Corcoran, Gertrude. 1976. *Language experience for nursery and kindergarten years.* Itasca, Ill.: F. E. Peacock.

Gambell, Trevor J. 1976. *Developing children's language through the elementary school media centre.* ED 137 792. New York State Department of Education.

Henry, Mable Wright. 1967. *Creative experiences in oral language.* Urbana, Ill.: National Council of Teachers of English.

Huck, Charlotte S. 1976. *Children's literature in the elementary school.* 3rd ed. New York: Holt, Rinehart and Winston.

Listening and speaking, K–3: a packet for teachers. 1975. New York State Department of Education.

McIntyre, Barbara. 1974. *Creative drama in the elementary school.* Itasca, Ill.: F. E. Peacock.

Moffett, James. 1973. *A student center of language arts curriculum, grades K–6: a handbook for teachers.* Boston: Houghton Mifflin.

Possein, Wilma M. 1969. *They all need to talk.* New York: Appleton-Century-Crofts.

Russell, David; and Russell, Elizabeth. 1959. *Listening aids through the grades.* New York: Teachers College Press.

Spache, George D.; and Spache, Evelyn B. 1973. *Reading in the elementary school.* 3rd ed. Boston: Allyn and Bacon. (See pp. 119–123 and 128–129 for suggested materials to develop perceptual skills.)

Tooze, Ruth. 1959. *Storytelling.* New York: Prentice-Hall.

For use with the elementary school student

Alpha time. Jackson, Miss.: Central School Supply.

A pocket guide of movement and activities for the elementary school by Marjorie Latchaw. Englewood Cliffs, N.J.: Prentice-Hall.

Creating with materials for work and play. Washington, D.C.: Association for Childhood Education International.

Developing prereading skills by Rachel G. Brake. New York: Holt, Rinehart and Winston.

Directionality program. Glendale, Calif.: Bowmar Records.

Kindergarten fun by Cole and Appleyard. Cincinnati, Ohio: McCormick-Mathers.

Kindergarten readiness. New York: Harper and Row.

Learning readiness system by Scott, Ratekin, Kramer, Nelson, and Dunbar. New York: Harper and Row.

Letters in words by Helen A. Murphy and Donald D. Durrell. Wellesley, Mass.: Curriculum Associates.

Listening-doing-learning tapes (Levels K–1) by Don Parker, Shelby Parker, and William Fryback. Chicago: Science Research Associates.

Listening time (Albums 1–3) by Louise Bender Scott. Glendale, Calif.: Bowmar Records, Inc.

Peabody early experience kit (Levels P–3) by Lloyd M. Dunn. Circle Pines, Minn.: American Guidance Service.

Peabody language kits (Levels P, I, II, III) by Lloyd M. Dunn et al. Circle Pines, Minn.: American Guidance Service.

Readiness for learning clinic by McLeod. Philadelphia: J. B. Lippincott.

Part Two

RECOGNIZING WORDS

We believe that fluent reading is based on the acquisition of certain crucial skills. Basic among these is the ability to recognize words — either instantly or through techniques that facilitate or mediate recognition. In Part Two, we will consider five important techniques for recognizing words: sight vocabulary, phonics, context clues, structural analysis clues, and dictionary aids to pronunciation. We feel that each technique has value in a word recognition program and should be made available for efficient use by students. Some techniques are more appropriate for one level of instruction than another and some are more efficient in certain contexts than others. When teachers understand the use of each, they can select the technique or combination of techniques most efficient for use in a given situation.

Sammye J. Wynn

3
Developing a Sight Vocabulary

A sight word has been defined as a word that is immediately recognized as a whole and that does not require the use of word analysis skills (Harris and Hodges 1981, p. 295). Any definition of vocabulary must, however, include understanding of the meaning of instantly recognized words. Acquisition of an initial sight vocabulary is one of the first steps a child takes in a successful reading program. It provides a foundation on which to teach word attack and other vital reading skills. Mastery of this step in no way signals the demise of sight vocabulary development. It is an ongoing process with the ultimate goal of instantaneous recognition and understanding of words most frequently occurring in all written materials.

In commenting on the importance of learning sight words, Heilman, Blair, and Rupley (1981, p. 155) make these statements:

1. If a child knows a number of words as sight words (instant recognition) she can be taught to see and hear similarities between these words and the new words she meets. A sight vocabulary is an invaluable tool in helping her identify other words.
2. When words are recognized instantly, analysis is not necessary. The reader can put known words together in phrases, thus focusing on reading for meaning.
3. There are numerous high frequency words that should be learned as units simply because they are met over and over in any reading situation and contribute significantly to using syntax as a means of getting meaning from what is read.

Since the acquisition of a storehouse of sight words is essential to all future reading and contributes to all facets of reading (including word analysis, comprehension, fluency in oral reading, and the creation of a permanent interest in reading), sight vocabulary development should be an important objective of teachers at all levels of instruction. This chapter is designed to answer many questions raised by students and teachers in the area of sight vocabulary development. Ideas, activities, procedures, and exercises presented here have been tested in classrooms with a high degree of success and have been enthusiastically received by the children who tried them.

Selection of Sight Words

QUESTIONS TO GUIDE READING

Literal
What are two sight word lists?
What are the distinguishing features of each of the sight word lists discussed?
On what basis are sight words selected?

Evaluative
Why might sight word "lists" differ?

The major thrust of sight vocabulary development is mastery of those several hundred words appearing over and over in printed materials. Included in this group are words with which children are familiar in the spoken form and words that are irregular in terms of letter-sound association. Although there is no single sight vocabulary, there are many prepared lists to serve as guides. Though challenged by some, the Dolch Basic Sight Vocabulary of 220 service words is still the most frequently used checklist, according to Bush and Huebner (1979). They state that these words "make up over half of all the running words children read in their elementary textbooks" (p. 71).

Fry's revised list of Instant Words (1980) should not be overlooked in selection of sight words to be taught because of the "high frequency of occurrence in all material written in the English language." As further stated by Fry, half of all material in English is composed of just the first hundred Instant Words and their common variants. The 300 New Instant Words and their common variants are reported to comprise 65 percent of "all words in any textbook, newspaper or writing sample in English." Fry's list appears at the end of this chapter.

Although no specific list can be agreed on, there seems to be a consensus among authorities in the field that sight words should be selected on the basis of their high utility value, their irregularity in terms of letter-sound association, their frequency in classroom materials, and their common occurrence in the speaking vocabularies of children.

Major Approaches to Sight Vocabulary Development

QUESTIONS TO GUIDE READING

Literal
What are some techniques for developing sight vocabulary?

Inferential
How is a sight vocabulary acquired?

Evaluative
How does a teacher choose from among the many procedures available for developing sight vocabulary?

There are many roads leading to sight vocabulary development; among them are direct teaching of individual words, the language experience approach to reading, use of basal programs, wide reading in easy material, creative writing, and the teaching of words through games, exercises, and activities. It is important to remember that the teacher does not have to undertake this teaching unassisted. Parents can provide valuable assistance and often want to be involved. (See Chapter 19 for specific ways parents may assist in the education of their children.)

Findings from research help to provide insights to teachers as they work with children in developing a sight vocabulary. Recall from Chapter 1 that children appear to go through a five-stage process in word learning — from the stimuli being presented to the hookup stage of cue and response (Samuels 1976). Recall also that children perceive the distinctive features within a word (Gibson and Levin 1975, pp. 15–20); and most often utilize the beginning part of the word as a cue (Marchbanks and Levin 1965). In learning a word in isolation, it appears that a picture/word combination is not as efficient as a word presented alone (Samuels 1967). Recall also that high imagery words are learned more easily than low imagery words; low imagery words need more repetition and exposure. In addition, children need to know how to use a word before the word is considered for inclusion in sight vocabulary study.

Repetition has been considered significant in the learning of sight words since the early McGuffey Readers. The amount of repetition will depend on factors in the learner such as language background, interest, knowledge, and ability, and on the type of word to be learned (concrete versus abstract). There are not many definitive positions taken on the amount of repetition in the literature. In an early study, used here *only to illustrate* the fact that the amount of repetition will need to vary, Gates (1930, p. 35) noted that the number of repetitions needed may depend on level of intelligence. This variation was as follows:

IQ	Number of repetitions
120–129	20
110–119	30
90–109	35
80–89	40
70–79	45
60–69	55

Remember that the factors in the learner mentioned above (other than intelligence) also affect the number of repetitions needed. Teachers will find that the number of repetitions needed will vary from child to child.

FIVE STEPS FOR TEACHING SIGHT WORDS DIRECTLY

Smith and Johnson (1980, p. 69) suggest these five steps for the direct teaching of a sight word. Reinforcement will, of course, need to follow direct teaching.

1. Seeing — The word is printed on the chalkboard, is on a flashcard, or is used as a label on a picture caption. The word should also be used by the teacher in a sentence.

2. Discussing — After the word has been read orally by the teacher and repeated by the children, a short discussion is held so that the word can be related, if possible, to the lives and experiences of the group. If, for example, the word is pet, children will be asked about their own pets or one they would like to have. Since many words are not labels for actions or objects, the next step is important.

3. Using — Pupils are asked to use the word in a sentence, or to think of a synonym for the word. This is done orally.

4. Defining — Providing a definition for a word is often harder than using the word in a sentence. But after the class has used it in several sentences, it is not too difficult (for many children) to arrive at a tentative answer to the question, "What does the word mean?" or "What does this word do in the sentence?"

5. Copying — Many elementary teachers have their children keep a personal dictionary of new words. Fernald (1943), in advocating a kinesthetic approach to reading, believed that writing a word reinforces its learning. Common sense would seem to bear this out. The words should be written alone and in sentences.[1]

1. Smith/Johnson. *Teaching Children to Read,* © 1980. Addison-Wesley, Reading, MA, p. 69. Reprinted with permission.

Developing a Sight Vocabulary

LANGUAGE EXPERIENCE APPROACH

In the language experience approach, which is more fully discussed in Chapter 13, the child learns a sight vocabulary largely through participation in a variety of experiences that develop group and individual experience stories, employ the child's language, and use the word bank. The word bank, which may be a 3- by 5-inch file box with index cards, serves as a repository for the child's known words. As he identifies words in group or individual stories, he adds to the word bank cards on which the teacher has written his new words for him.

As various activities and experiences occur and more experience stories develop, the children learn many words because the vocabulary is not controlled. Later, the class builds a group word bank.

The following are some categories that may be established in the word banks:

1. Color words
2. Words we use for things
3. Words we use for people
4. Words we use for animals
5. Days of the week
6. Weather words
7. Question words
8. Words that tell when
9. Words that tell where
10. Words that tell how many
11. Words that tell what we can do
12. Words that tell what kind (descriptive words)
13. Words we use a lot (a catch-all category for high-frequency words that fit no specific grouping)

The use of the word bank is not limited to the language experience approach. It may be effectively used for sight words learned in any situation, especially after the child grasps the similarity between the parents' bank, which is a repository for money, and his word bank, which holds his language possessions. Additionally, the word bank provides a tangible record of the child's progress in acquiring sight words and serves as a source of words for practice when children play games with cards from the word bank.

Many teachers use the language experience approach to develop a basic stock of sight words even when the basal program is used; this technique gives a child the delightful experience of being able to read the preprimer when it is first introduced. This initial successful encounter with reading is a joyous one for the child and a rewarding one for the teacher.

USE OF BASAL READERS

Although the vocabulary is somewhat controlled, most basal programs do an excellent job of teaching sight words and provide many opportunities for repetition and reinforcement. The teacher can introduce words in a meaningful context by using a parallel chart story (a short, teacher-composed story using words of the story in a different context) or by recalling a class experience that can be described with the new words. The teacher repeats the words in a carefully planned sequence; sometimes she uses them in game situations, thereby furnishing further contact. She reviews the words with the children each day in basal and parallel stories as she adds new words.

WIDE READING

One of the most effective means of building an extensive sight vocabulary is through wide reading in easy materials — an approach that lets the child meet the same words again and again.

It often happens, however, that the child with the limited sight vocabulary is not the avid reader: it therefore becomes the responsibility of the teacher to devise ways to bring children and books together and promote greater interest in reading.

Many avenues lead to promotion of wide reading, including these:

1. Display appealing books attractively in the library center and other places in the room.
2. Discover and capitalize on the child's special interest.
3. Read part of an intriguing book to the class.
4. Read fascinating short stories to children on a regular basis; also read part of a very interesting story and stop at a dramatic point.
5. Have other children recommend to the class books that they have read with pleasure.
6. Help children identify with and develop friendships with storybook characters.
7. Provide free time for reading and make it a very special occasion.

Organizing a book club (and devising a recording system that shows the number and variety of books read) is another example of how interest in reading may be created. The class will have numerous suggestions as names for the club. After they agree on one, help them make a display that categorizes the books into such areas as adventure, science, social studies, humor, fairy tales, animals, poetry, and others. As each pupil completes a book, he makes a colorful bookmark from construction paper and places it in the appropriate category (see "The Read Away Book Club" in Figure 3.1). He shares his experience with the book if he wishes, but

Figure 3.1.

there is no required book report. There must be a large collection of books covering a variety of interests with a wide range of difficulty.

These are just a few of the ways that enthusiasm for reading may be created. There are, of course, many other ways to bring children and books together to promote sight vocabulary development.

CREATIVE WRITING

Second only to wide reading in its effectiveness in extending the sight vocabulary, is creative writing, which can be used with excellent results at all grade levels. Just as the child often encounters the major service words in reading (words identified as being especially serviceable or useful because of their frequent appearance in written material), he uses them again and again in writing, learning them so thoroughly that recognition is immediate.

An invitingly arranged writing center should be focal point of the classroom with "story starters" and other suggestions available for those students in need of stimulation in this area. A very good way to get the reluctant writer primed is through a "Let's Write a Story" folder from which pupils can select a picture and write a story, or select an idea and develop a story. This folder also contains "word helpers" under headings such as:

1. words that tell what we can do
2. words that tell what we did
3. words that tell what kind
4. words that tell about occupations (for the "I want to be . . ." stories)

As the junior authors write stories, they draw on the story folder, their word banks, word books, word train, and dictionaries for words as needed. Additionally, the students experience more contact with high-frequency words as they exchange stories for the purpose of proofreading or for pleasure. Creative writing adds immeasurably to the pupils' stockpile of immediately recognized words by providing many opportunities for practice with words in varied contexts.

SIGHT VOCABULARY GAMES, EXERCISES, AND ACTIVITIES

In addition to the approaches to sight vocabulary development already discussed in this chapter, there are many games, exercises, and activities that are highly successful for this purpose. Examples of a few of these techniques are described in the following pages.

Stepping stones. A child is delighted to walk his way to an improved sight vocabulary with stepping stones. Circular shapes (footprints or any shape) are cut from brightly colored construction paper to make stepping stones. (See Figure 3.2.) Then high-frequency words are printed on them. Children take turns identifying words as they step on them. After stepping on each word, the pupil uses it in a sentence. This exercise can also be used to introduce and review words from the reading lesson.

Word ladders. The word ladder adds an element of delight to sight vocabulary development as cartoon figures challenge the child to climb the ladder. (See Figure 3.3) The pupil climbs the ladder by selecting words from the pocket at the bottom of the ladder and placing one on each step. Words placed on the ladder may be selected from the reading lesson, from experience charts, and from the Daily Bulletin (see p. 61); or they may be high-frequency words on which practice is needed.

Sentences may be written on sentence strips and used in the same manner on a sentence ladder as words are used on the word ladder.

Labeling and action words. The traditional procedure of labeling objects in the classroom and constructing matching cards (to facilitate learning

Figure 3.2.

through paired association) is still a very effective tool in developing a sight vocabulary. In conjunction with the labeled objects, action words (such as climb, jump) are illustrated on clue cards to be used with matching cards as above. In addition to the matching activity, children's names are used with action words and labels to facilitate development of a large stock of instantly recognized words. The children are delighted to see their names in print and are highly motivated to read the sentences, which results in an increased sight vocabulary. Sentences such as the following may be printed on sentence strips, chart paper, and the chalkboard:

John can jump up.
Jimmy can jump up on the table.
See Rose jump up on the table.

Word train. The word train is an ageless device for sight vocabulary development and still enjoys popularity with young children. You can construct the train of oak tag, posterboard, or construction paper and call it the "Wordland Express" or a similar name. (See Figure 3.4.) Label the cars of the train with words being taught (or with words on which practice is needed). Of course, you change the labels as new words are introduced. Often children want to learn words of special interest to them and request the teacher's help. In responding to this personal interest, the teacher can label each car with a child's name and put his words on the car along with his name. As he learns to recognize these words at sight, the child removes them to his word bank.

Picture dictionary bulletin board. A picture dictionary bulletin board, placed within easy reach of the children, is an excellent tool for helping them recognize a variety of words. (See Figure 3.5.) The picture dictionary is developed parallel to ongoing activities in the classroom, changing as activities shift. When the class is studying a unit on the family, the dic-

Figure 3.3.

tionary illustrates family members; when they are studying the weather, the dictionary shows weather words. Thanksgiving, Christmas, Easter, Children's Book Week, and other holidays and special events generate their own vocabularies for inclusion in the picture dictionary. Trips to places of interest develop their own vocabularies too: when the children visit the public library, they can add words such as library, librarian, book, spine, and author. Each time the children rearrange the picture dictionary, the teacher makes a set of matching label cards so that chil-

Figure 3.4.

Figure 3.5.

dren may pair these cards with those on the bulletin board. Children can learn an amazing number of words in this manner. They can also develop their own individual picture dictionaries by cutting pictures from magazines or drawing their own illustrations; this provides a handy reference if a child forgets a word.

Figure 3.6.

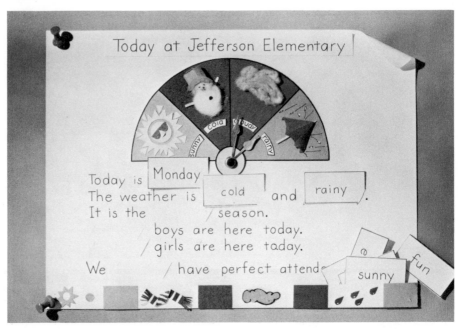

Weather and attendance charts. Days of the week, weather words, seasons, and a number of other words can be learned when children use a device similar to the weather and attendance chart you see in Figure 3.6. In the pocket are placed days of the week, including Saturday and Sunday, plus weather words, seasons, numerals, and "do" and "do not" for recording attendance. Pupils take turns charting the weather and attendance, using the hands of the weather chart and inserting words from the pocket in the appropriate slots. This activity tends to generate much enthusiasm. Duty charts and written instructions may also be used in this way to develop sight vocabulary.

Accordion charts. An accordion chart can be constructed from squares of posterboard and construction paper. Its illustrations and labels teach color words, number words, foods, clothing, and other names for things. (See Figure 3.7.) Many high-frequency words can also be taught this way by illustrating phrases and sentences. For example, the color chart illustrates the major colors with color words printed beneath the pictures. Print an identical set of color words on separate cards for matching. As students work in teams or with partners matching the color words, these words become part of the sight vocabulary. The same procedure can be followed for teaching other words.

Figure 3.7.

Sorting and classifying. To add diversity to practice in recognizing words instantly, try sorting and classifying tasks. A kangaroo's pouch makes an excellent receptacle for words and adds a dimension of delight to sight vocabulary development. For this activity, make kangaroos from colorful construction paper — one large one and several small ones. Paste envelopes underneath the kangaroo's pouch to hold words. The pouch of the large kangaroo holds the words to be classified. As words are classified, they are placed in the pouches of the small kangaroos, whose bodies wear the category label; for example, color words, action words, careers, words that tell how many, words that tell what kind, and names of things.

The Daily Bulletin. The Daily Bulletin is a chart that records highlights of daily happenings with personal mention of individual children. It may include information about holidays and special events such as United Nations Day and Children's Book Week, weather reports, and general background information in the areas of social studies and science. Initially the Bulletin is read by the teacher, who calls attention to words that occur again and again and to words that have the same beginnings. By the second or third day children are recognizing a few words and are eagerly pointing to them. After the second week, the Bulletin is read only after children have had an opportunity to identify all words known to them. The number of known words increases dramatically with this activity.

A milestone is reached when, after three or four weeks, a child is able to read an entire section of the Bulletin independently. This, of course, provides a feeling of great accomplishment. Words of three syllables or

Figure 3.8.

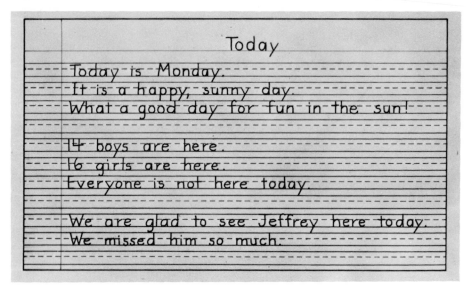

more are referred to as "giants" and children who recognize these words are "giant killers," which adds an element of delight. Many sight words are acquired via the Bulletin, and daily reading of this chart provides a good opportunity for practice. As a child takes the Bulletin home each day, he can share it with his family, at which time he gets further practice. Words learned in this way are added to the word bank in the appropriate category.

We show a sample Bulletin in Figure 3.8 to give you an idea of how effective its simple format can be.

These are some of the games, activities, and exercises that lead to growth in sight vocabulary. There are many, many more that you will devise as you work with boys and girls.

SYSTEMS APPROACH

Words can be added to the sight vocabulary through a systematic procedure for teaching words. The pupil and teacher together should set a goal for learning a specific number of words, altering the number only if the progress rate makes that a good idea.

Steps in the Systems Approach

1. Introduce words to be taught in context.
2. Discuss individual words and present them in varied contexts.
3. Write words on a chalkboard and flash cards.
4. Point out letter-sound association and call attention to familiar parts of words.
5. Flash words for the pupils to identify.
6. Have students write words while looking at them and again without a copy.
7. Let students read sentences containing the new words in an entirely different context.
8. Provide additional practice through word games.

Summary

Acquisition of a sight vocabulary is basic to the development of word attack skills, comprehension, proficiency in oral reading, and all other reading skills. The teacher must utilize many approaches to help children continually add to their stock of sight words: language experience activities; use of the basal program; wide reading in easy materials; creative writing; and teaching words through games, exercises, and activities. Instant recognition of words is not enough; the child must also understand the meaning.

There is no single sight vocabulary. Words should be selected on the basis of a high frequency of occurrence in printed materials; they should include words that are irregular in terms of grapheme–phoneme correspondence and words that are in the speaking vocabularies of children.

The foundation for sight vocabulary development is laid during the early years the child spends at home with his parents. It is, therefore, crucial that the teacher consider the pupil's background of experiences when planning ways to teach sight words.

Since so much practice is needed in sight vocabulary development, the teacher must devise numerous ways to keep the constant encounter with words interesting and meaningful. Activities, procedures, and exercises suggested in this chapter are mere beginnings, points of departure; many other effective ideas will be generated as teachers work with boys and girls.

Questions for Further Reading and Thinking

1. How may children from economically deprived homes be helped to acquire an enriched experiential background for understanding words in their spoken form?

2. What is the relationship between sight vocabulary and meaning vocabulary?

3. What supplementary activities can you suggest for children experiencing difficulty in

acquisition of a sight vocabulary? Suggest at least four activities.

4. What are the bases for deciding whether a given technique for developing sight vocabulary is effective or ineffective?

Activities and Projects

1. Develop a learning center designed to teach sight words through paired association. Make provision for practice in reading words in meaningful contexts.
2. Develop three activities for using the word bank to teach sight words.
3. There are four children in your teaching situation who appear to lack the ability to discriminate visually between words. Plan two activities to help them develop skill in noting likenesses and differences in words. Identify grade level.
4. Plan a language experience activity to teach sight words.
5. After reading the section on approaches to sight vocabulary, make the following teaching aids:
   a. picture dictionary bulletin board
   b. accordion chart of action words
   c. stepping stones

Sight Vocabulary Materials

ABC Game. Buffalo, N.Y.: Kenworthy Educational Services.

Basic Sight Vocabulary Cards. Champaign, Ill.: Garrard.

Basic Word Concepts and Vocabulary Development Charts. Chicago: ETA Division of A. Daigger.

Build-It (Grades 3–8). Washington, D.C.: Remedial Educational Press.

Dolch Games by E. W. Dolch. Includes *Basic Sight Word Cards, Group Word Teaching Game, Phrase Cards, Picture Word Cards, Popper Words, Who Gets It.* Champaign, Ill.: Garrard.

Educational Password Game. Springfield, Mass.: Milton Bradley.

Flash X, A Hand Tachistoscope for Rapid Word Recognition. Huntington, N.Y.: Educational Development Laboratories.

Match. Champaign, Ill.: Garrard.

Pictocabulary Series. Rockville Centre, N.Y.: Barnell Loft.

Picture Words for Beginners. Springfield, Mass.: Milton Bradley.

Rolling Reader. Glenview, Ill.: Scott, Foresman.

Spello Word Game. Oak Lawn, Ill.: Ideal.

Fry Instant Words

The Instant Words — First Hundred

First 25 Group 1a	Second 25 Group 1b	Third 25 Group 1c	Fourth 25 Group 1d
the	or	will	number
of	one	up	no
and	had	other	way
a	by	about	could
to	word	out	people
in	but	many	my
is	not	then	than
you	what	them	first
that	all	these	water
it	were	so	been
he	we	some	call
was	when	her	who
for	your	would	oil
on	can	make	now
are	said	like	find
as	there	him	long
with	use	into	down
his	an	time	day
they	each	has	did
I	which	look	get
at	she	two	come
be	do	more	made
this	how	write	may
have	their	go	part
from	if	see	over

Common suffixes: s, ing, ed

The Instant Words — Second Hundred

First 25 Group 2a	Second 25 Group 2b	Third 25 Group 2c	Fourth 25 Group 2d
new	great	put	kind
sound	where	end	hand
take	help	does	picture
only	through	another	again
little	much	well	change
work	before	large	off
know	line	must	play
place	right	big	spell
year	too	even	air
live	mean	such	away
me	old	because	animal
back	any	turn	house
give	same	here	point
most	tell	why	page
very	boy	ask	letter
after	follow	went	mother
thing	came	men	answer
our	want	read	found
just	show	lead	study
name	also	land	still
good	around	different	learn
sentence	form	home	should
man	three	us	America
think	small	move	world
say	set	try	high

Common suffixes: s, ing, ed, er, ly, est

The Instant Words — Third Hundred

First 25 Group 3a	Second 25 Group 3b	Third 25 Group 3c	Fourth 25 Group 3d
every	left	until	idea
near	don't	children	enough
add	few	side	eat
food	while	feet	face
between	along	car	watch
own	might	mile	far
below	close	night	Indian
country	something	walk	real
plant	seem	white	almost
last	next	sea	let
school	hard	began	above
father	open	grow	girl
keep	example	took	sometimes
tree	begin	river	mountain
never	life	four	cut
start	always	carry	young
city	those	state	talk
earth	both	once	soon
eye	paper	book	list
light	together	hear	song
thought	got	stop	leave
head	group	without	family
under	often	second	body
story	run	late	music
saw	important	miss	color

Reprinted with permission of Edward B. Fry and the International Reading Association. From *The Reading Teacher* (December 1980), pp. 284–289.

Nancy B. Tanner

4

Phonics

Phonics can be defined as the use of letter-sound relationships to pronounce an unknown printed word. The reader looks at the word, gives the sounds represented by the parts, and then blends them into a whole word. If the unknown word is one he uses in speech or one he understands when he hears it, even an approximate sounding combined with the context will usually lead him to recognize the word and understand the meaning. In this way, phonics becomes a very vital means to developing a much larger reading vocabulary and increasing a child's reading independence. On repetition, new words eventually become part of the sight vocabulary and no longer require sounding out or decoding; this is the end goal of all word recognition training. The child must be encouraged to move from phonic analysis, which is the slowest and least economical method, to more efficient methods.

The fewer the number of phonics clues needed to identify the word, the quicker the recognition. The beginning reader needs phonics skills, but as he becomes more proficient he will not have to use phonics except as a last resort. The more advanced reader will combine sight recognition of words and phrases with anticipation from the meaning and the syntax of the sentence. He will make an intelligent attempt at the unknown word from the context, and if he needs more clues he may try context plus the sound represented by the initial letter. If he still cannot recognize the word, he will try the first syllable or, if necessary, divide the word into its root and affixes. Only as a last resort, for a word that does not yield to these methods, will he give the sounds represented by the phonic units and then blend them into a word. In addition, if he does not understand the meaning of the word, he will use the dictionary.

This does not mean that phonics skills are not important. Jeffrey and Samuels (1969) found that knowledge of letter-sound correspondence has a positive effect in reading new words. One conclusion from the First Grade Studies sponsored by the USOE (Bond and Dykstra 1967) showed that a basal reading program strengthened with supplemental phonics material produces greater achievement in reading than does a program using the basal materials alone. Furthermore the most recently published basal series are continuing to present considerable phonics instruction. For the reader who is developing reading skill, phonic analysis must be recognized as a vital tool.

Since teachers cannot teach what they do not know, they must first learn the content of phonics before learning how to communicate phonics to children. This chapter will therefore focus on both content and instructional methods. First we shall take up the content of phonics, which is limited here to the minimum skills necessary for phonic analysis. Teachers must become thoroughly familiar with the skills necessary for decoding before going on to the rest of the chapter, which will discuss the major tasks, the principles, and the methods of instruction (these are the authors' preferred methods, which incorporate a number of contributions made by linguists to the area of reading instruction).

Content of Phonics

QUESTIONS TO GUIDE READING

Literal
After reading the definitions, can you define each of the terms and give examples?
Why should the speech sounds of consonants not be pronounced in isolation?
When would you expect the phonemes /c/ and /g/ to have soft sounds?
How do you pronounce the short sounds of vowel phonemes, the long sounds, the sounds of vowels controlled by /r/, the diphthongs? What are some words illustrating each of these sounds?
In decoding a word, when would you first try the short sound represented by the vowel letter and when the long sound? (Give words as examples.)
What are three visual clues that help in dividing an unknown word into syllables? (Illustrate with words.)

Evaluative
Why is it important for teachers of reading to have a knowledge of phonics terminology?
Why is a knowledge of phonics content relevant for teachers of reading?

The following phonics content is given in a very simple, elementary way and is followed by a self-test. Teachers cannot have just a vague idea about sounds, but rather must understand the subject matter thoroughly. A limited amount of phonics is needed, but this minimum amount must be understood very well if teachers are to be able to communicate it to their pupils. Teachers should first learn the definitions of phonics terms, referring back to that section whenever necessary. They would also find it helpful to pronounce the example words aloud and try to discover the phonics generalizations for themselves before reading the author's statements.

Definitions of Phonics Terms

Phonetics: The whole science of raw speech sounds, how these sounds are produced vocally, how sound changes develop, and how speech sounds relate to the whole language process.

Phonics: Using speech sounds represented by letters and groups of letters as an aid to word recognition in reading. This is only a small part of the total field of phonetics.

Grapheme: A graphic representation of a basic sound unit. The grapheme may be one letter or several letters. For example, the sound heard at the beginning of the word *mud* is represented by the grapheme ⟨m⟩. The sound heard at the beginning of the word *chair* is represented by the grapheme ⟨ch⟩.

Phoneme: The smallest class of distinctive and significant speech sounds. For example, the word *mud* is made up of three phonemes, /m/, /u/, /d/ represented by the written symbols ⟨m⟩, ⟨u⟩, ⟨d⟩. In the words *bit* and *pit*, the spoken words are identical except for one phoneme. The speech sounds of /b/ and /p/ are phonemes, distinguishing one spoken word from another.

A consistent phoneme-grapheme relationship: A speech sound heard is always represented by the same printed symbol. English has many irregular spellings and therefore is not a language with a consistent phoneme-grapheme relationship; rather, it is an alphabetical language of 26 letters representing approximately 45 different sounds for any given speaker.

Morpheme: The smallest meaningful unit of language. For example, *tie* is a morpheme and *un* is a morpheme; therefore *untie* is made up of two morphemes. Morphemes include word bases, prefixes and suffixes, and inflectional endings.

Initial sound: The beginning sound of a word or syllable.

Medial sound: The sound found in the middle of a word or syllable.

Ending sound: The final sound in a word or syllable.

Syllable: A unit of pronunciation that contains one vowel sound and to which consonant sounds may or may not be attached.

Closed syllable: A syllable that ends with a consonant sound (based on final sound, not final letter). Examples: /un/ in *untie* is a closed syllable. /Bough/ is not a closed syllable because it does not end with a consonant sound.

Open syllable: A syllable that ends with a vowel sound (based on final sound, not final letter). Examples: /ho/ in *hotel* is an open syllable. /Sigh/ is an open syllable because it ends with a vowel sound.

Phonogram: A group of consonants and vowels representing a speech sound that remains constant in many words. A sound family, such as /all/, /ay/, /ight/, /tion/, /er/.

Blending: The process of joining together the sounds represented by letters or syllables.

CONSONANTS

Consonant phonemes are all the sounds represented by the letters of the alphabet except ⟨a⟩, ⟨e⟩, ⟨i⟩, ⟨o⟩, ⟨u⟩. ⟨W⟩ is sometimes a vowel. ⟨Y⟩ is a consonant only at the beginning of a syllable. Consonants are relatively stable, but only ⟨m⟩ and ⟨v⟩ represent constant sounds in all words. ⟨B⟩, ⟨k⟩, ⟨l⟩ also represent only one sound each, but in some words they are silent. The sounds represented by the remaining consonants are fairly stable but are sometimes affected by other letters in the word.

Method of pronunciation. In general, consonant phonemes should not be pronounced in isolation because they become distorted unless used with a vowel. For example, the sound represented by ⟨b⟩ pronounced alone is apt to become *buh*. The sound represented by ⟨d⟩ tends to be *duh*. Thus if the word *bed* were blended letter by letter, the resulting *buh-e-duh* would be distorted beyond recognition. Therefore the sound represented by ⟨b⟩ must be combined with the sound represented by the ⟨e⟩ that follows it.

There are some consonant phonemes called continuant consonants that can be sounded alone without distortion. If for purposes of illustration the teacher is tempted to give consonant sounds in isolation, the ones to use must be /s/, /f/, /m/, /n/, /l/, /v/, /z/, where the sound can be maintained as long as the breath lasts. Words with these continuant consonants in the initial positions can be decoded without distortion by sounding the consonant and then blending it with the next sound, as in /m/ — /at/, or /s/ — /at/.

Note: The other consonants must *always* be combined with the vowels that follow them: /bi/ — /g/, /ca/ — /t/.

Consonant letters that sometimes represent no sounds include ⟨k⟩, ⟨w⟩, ⟨g⟩, ⟨l⟩, ⟨b⟩. Examples: *knee, write, sign, talk, lamb*.

/C/ and /g/ phonemes. The consonants ⟨c⟩ and ⟨g⟩ each represent two different sounds, called hard and soft sounds. The hard sound is made in the back of the throat.

Hard /c/: *cat*	Hard /g/: *game*
cot	*go*
cut	*gun*

The soft sound represented by ⟨c⟩ is like /s/; the soft sound represented by ⟨g⟩ is like /j/.

Soft /c/: *cell*	Soft /g/: *gem*
city	*ginger*
cycle	*gym*

A quick analysis of the preceding material shows that the soft sounds occur before the vowels ⟨e⟩, ⟨i⟩, ⟨y⟩. The grapheme ⟨c⟩ follows this pattern with great consistency, since in spelling there are the three letters (⟨c⟩,

⟨k⟩, and ⟨s⟩) representing the two sounds. The grapheme ⟨g⟩ is not as consistent. The most common words that are exceptions are *get, give, girl,* and *begin.*

Consonant blends. Consonant blends, or clusters, are two or three consonants together. Although actually each consonant phoneme is sounded, they are pronounced almost simultaneously so that one blend results. For example, in the word *play,* the lips form the phoneme /p/ as the tongue and roof of the mouth form the phoneme /l/, and the sounds blend together. Examples of common blends are: combinations in which the second letter is /l/, as in /bl/, /cl/, /fl/, /pl/; combinations in which the second letter is /r/, as in /br/, /cr/, /pr/, /tr/; and combinations in which the first letter is /s/, as in /sm/, /st/, /scr/, /spr/.

Consonant digraphs. Consonant digraphs are two consonants together that represent one sound, not a blend of the two. Pronounce the following words: *chair, think, shut, who, phone,* lau*gh,* si*ng.* In syllabication these consonant digraphs are never divided but always remain together. The common digraphs are /ch/, /th/, /sh/, /ph/, /gh/, /ng/, and /nk/, and sometimes /wh/.

VOWELS

The vowel letters are ⟨a⟩, ⟨e⟩, ⟨i⟩, ⟨o⟩, ⟨u⟩, and sometimes ⟨y⟩ and ⟨w⟩. ⟨Y⟩ functions as a vowel when it is not at the beginning of a syllable, and ⟨w⟩ functions as a vowel when it follows a vowel in a syllable.

Each vowel letter represents many different sounds depending on its position in the word and the other letters with it. For the purpose of using phonics as an aid to word recognition, teaching of the vowels may be limited to the following:

Short vowel sounds. Teachers must become very familiar with the short sounds represented by vowel letters. Pronounce the following and hear the sound represented by each vowel:

an, can, canter
Ed, red, redden
it, sit, sitting
odd, nod, nodding
up, pup, puppy

There are speech variations in different parts of the country and in different social and educational classes. Since the short vowel sounds are particularly subject to variation, the teacher should accept those commonly used by the children. As you can see from the preceding list, the short vowel sound is often given to a single vowel that is followed by a consonant sound in a syllable. (Using ⟨v⟩ to stand for a vowel letter and

(c) to stand for a consonant letter, the spelling pattern would be represented by ⟨vc⟩ or ⟨cvc⟩.)

To help children associate the sounds with the short vowels, you should first make an auditory-visual association, and then reinforce it (how to do this will be explained in the section under methods). In addition many teachers find it helpful to choose a word beginning with the short vowel sound to use as a clue for the children. Some teachers choose familiar objects to display, labeled with the appropriate vowels.

For short /a/: an *apple*
/e/: a toy *engine*, or *hen*
/i/: a wooden *Indian*
/o/: a beanbag *octopus*
/u/: a doll's *umbrella*

Warning: The word *egg* is not a good choice to use as a clue to the sound represented by short /e/ because its pronunciation varies with different dialects. If there is a similar problem with *engine*, try using *hen*.

Warning: It is important that teachers themselves have instant recognition of the sounds represented by the vowels, enabling them to make appropriate selections of words to illustrate the sound they are teaching. For example, in choosing words to help children inductively discover the short /a/ sound, it would be correct to choose *cat* and *man* but incorrect to use *wasp*, which does not have the short /a/ sound. Since teachers cannot rely just on spelling patterns, they must know the sounds themselves. Another example: although *cup, but, rub*, all illustrate the short /u/ sound, the words *put* and *push* do not. Teachers who do not know the sounds represented by the vowels fall into the trap of including words that do not follow the generalization being taught; this only serves to confuse the learner. Such errors are sometimes found in workbooks, too. Teachers should also be aware that they can distort sounds if they are not careful of their own pronunciation of words.

In decoding a word, the short vowel sound would be the first sound to try if there is a single vowel in a closed syllable, which is a syllable that ends with a consonant *sound* (vc or cvc). However, there are many exceptions. In separate research and using different lists of words, Clymer (1963, pp. 252–258), Emans (1967, pp. 419–425), and Bailey (1967, pp. 413–418) all studied this type of syllable. They used one-syllable words and found the generalization of a "single vowel followed by a consonant is short" was useful in only 62 percent of the words (Clymer), or 73 percent (Emans), or 71 percent (Bailey). The exceptions to be aware of are as follows:

Vowel followed by /r/, as in *car, for, sir, her, fur.*
/i/ followed by /gh/ or /nd/, as in *sight, blind.*
/i/ and /o/ followed by /ld/, as in *child, cold.*

As long as the teacher is aware of the exceptions and teaches the children to be flexible, it is still helpful to know that the short sound would be the first sound to try in decoding a syllable that has a single vowel followed by a consonant. Burmeister (1968, pp. 349–356) listed this as an especially helpful generalization.

Long vowel sounds. A vowel with a speech sound similar to its name is called a long vowel. The following generalizations are not infallible but suggest when to first try the long sound of the vowel in decoding a word.

1. Examples: *be, go, fly.* A single vowel at the end of a one-syllable word is usually long (cv). Clymer found this generalization useful in 74 percent of primary words, and Burmeister classified it as especially useful.

   Warning: The teacher must be aware of exceptions in choosing illustrations. For example, although following the same spelling pattern, neither of the words *do* or *pa* represents the long sound of the vowels.
2. Examples: *ho-tel, lo-co-mo-tive.* Similarly, open syllables in words such as these often have the long sound represented by the vowel. However, multisyllabic words are not as consistent in this as one-syllable words. For example, *na-tion* conforms to the generalization but not *na-tion-al.* Burmeister considered this to have only limited usefulness.
3. Examples: *cake, hope, like.* In words with the spelling pattern vowel-consonant-final ⟨e⟩ (vce), Clymer found in 63 percent of the words he studied that the first vowel represents the long sound and the final ⟨e⟩ is silent. Greif (1980, pp. 290–292) found only 53 percent. Burmeister (1971, pp. 439–441) found 73.7 percent but suggested that the following generalization would be more useful for teaching children: "When a word ends in a single vowel-single consonant-e, the ⟨e⟩ is silent, and the vowel usually represents its own long or short sound — try the long sound first."

   Warning: Again, the unwary teacher relying solely on spelling pattern may make the mistake of including such irregular words as *done* and *love.*
4. Examples: *say, paid, meat, beet, coat, suit.* When there are two adjacent vowels in a syllable, the first usually represents the long sound and the second is silent (vv) — or almost silent, as in *lion* and *giant.* (This does not apply to vowel diphthongs or vowel digraph exceptions, which represent special sounds given in the next sections.) This generalization is useful in the following, where Clymer (1963) found it to apply most of the time:

   oa (97 percent of the time)
   ee (98 percent)
   ay (78 percent)
   ai, ea, and *ui* (66 percent)

Vowel digraph exceptions. These adjacent vowels represent a sound unlike either vowel.

1. Examples: *saw, sauce, paw, pause.* ⟨Au⟩ and ⟨aw⟩ usually represent the sound heard in these words. The grapheme ⟨au⟩ is found in the initial and medial positions in the word, and the spelling ⟨aw⟩ on the endings of words but occasionally in the other positions too.
2. Examples: *book, foot,* and *food, moon.* These two sounds are represented by ⟨oo⟩.
3. Examples: *new, few.* This is the usual sound represented by ⟨ew⟩.

Vowel diphthongs. Examples: *joy, join,* and *how, house.* Diphthongs are two adjacent vowels representing a special sound made with a change of mouth position in the middle of the sound, as if gliding from one sound to another. One diphthong sound is represented by ⟨oi⟩ and ⟨oy⟩ and the other by ⟨ou⟩ and ⟨ow⟩. Both ⟨y⟩ and ⟨w⟩ function as vowels in these diphthongs. The ⟨oi⟩ and ⟨ou⟩ spellings are used in the initial and medial positions, and the ⟨oy⟩ and ⟨ow⟩ on the endings of words but occasionally in the other positions too.

Warning: ⟨Ou⟩ is not consistent in the sound it stands for, representing different sounds in such words as *cough, rough, though, through;* but where it does have any regularity, it is pronounced as in *out.* ⟨Ow⟩ represents the diphthong sound as in *now* in 61 percent of primary words Clymer studied; the remainder of the time it represents the long /o/ sound as in *slow,* following the adjacent vowel pattern outlined under the section on long vowels.

Vowels controlled by /r/. Examples: *car, for, her, sir, fur.* Vowels followed by the consonant /r/ are usually changed in the sound they represent and are neither long nor short. Note in the examples that ⟨ar⟩ represents a distinctive sound, as in *car, farm, part.* The sound represented by ⟨or⟩ is distinctive as in *torn,* and *short,* but when it is used as a suffix it often is similar to /er/, as in *sailor, tailor.* The sounds represented by ⟨er⟩, ⟨ir⟩, and ⟨ur⟩ are indistinguishable from one another, as in *herd, hurt, fir, fur.*

Summary of spelling patterns. The abbreviated information in Table 4.1 may be helpful, but only after you have mastered the whole section on vowels. These are only guidelines for which vowel sound to try first.

SYLLABICATION

The ability to divide an unknown word into syllables is vital to phonics because the syllable is the unit of pronunciation. The sound that a letter represents often depends on its position in the syllable. For example, if you examine the vowel sounds in *rip* and *ripen,* or in *cab* and *cable,* the

Table 4.1. Spelling Patterns

	Vowel pattern in the syllable	Example
Short vowels	vc or cvc	an, can
Long vowels	cv	be
	vce	ate
	vv	paid
/R/-controlled	vr	art, her
Exceptions (vowels are neither long nor short):		
Digraph exceptions (au, aw, oo, ew)	vv	saw, book, food, new
Diphthongs (oi, oy, ou, ow)	vv	boy, out

importance of the syllable becomes apparent. Fortunately there are visual clues that help in syllabication when trying to decode an unknown printed word. Too often children are only given directions such as: "Pronounce the word and decide where the syllables occur." Such directions do not help at all in dividing unknown words the child cannot pronounce, but there are principles based on visual clues that do help.

1. Examples: *mar-ket, lad-der, num-ber.* When there are two consonants between two vowels (vccv pattern), the division usually occurs between the consonants. Clymer gives the utility of this principle as 72 percent, Emans as 80 percent, and Bailey as 78 percent. Then pronounce according to the vowel pattern in each syllable.

   Warning: consonant digraphs are not divided.

   sing-er   not *sin-ger*
   au-thor   not *aut-hor*
   a-shamed not *as-hamed*

2. Examples: *pi-lot, ho-tel, be-gin.* When one consonant is between two vowels (vcv pattern), try dividing so that the second syllable begins with the consonant. This is a helpful visual method, resulting in an open syllable (cv), and the long sound would be represented by the vowel letter. However, the percentage of utility is not high (Clymer found 44 percent, Emans 47 percent, and Bailey 50 percent), and the resulting blend may not yield a familiar word. In that case, try the consonant with the preceding syllable, as in *sal-ad, pan-el*, resulting in a closed syllable (cvc), and therefore the short sound represented by the vowel letter.

3. Examples: *bri-dle, ta-ble.* In words ending in one consonant plus *le*, the consonant joins the *le* to form a syllable. Clymer found this useful in 97 percent of the cases, Emans in 78 percent, and Bailey in 93 percent. The first syllable is an open syllable.

4. Examples: *sad-dle, can-dle.* If there are two consonants plus *le* on the end of a word, divide between the consonants; the second consonant plus *le* still forms the final syllable. The first syllable in this case is a closed syllable.

5. Examples: *re-write, in-correct.* Prefixes and suffixes are separate syllables:

im-press   not *imp-ress*
tough-er   not *tou-gher*
re-print   not *rep-rint*

Summary of syllabication patterns. Table 4.2 will give some visual clues for dividing unknown words in independent reading.

Table 4.2. Syllabication Patterns

	Vowel-consonant pattern	Division	Example
Divide between consonants	vccv	vc-cv	mar-ket
	vccle	vc-cle	sad-dle
Divide before the consonant	vcv	v-cv	ho-tel
	vcle	v-cle	ta-ble
Divide after the consonant in some words	vcv	vc-v	sal-ad

SELF-TEST ON PHONICS

How much do you know about phonics now? Are you confused? Test yourself on the following questions. If you cannot pass the test, you are not yet ready to study methods of teaching phonics in the classroom.

The answers are given at the end of this section. Since there are potentially fifty correct answers, credit yourself with two points for each one you get right. There may be more than one correct answer per line.

1. This question tests your knowledge of terminology. Underline those examples that illustrate the term you are asked to identify.
   a. Closed syllable
      1. bough   2. luck   3. low   4. be   5. sigh
   b. Single grapheme
      1. pr   2. t   3. oi   4. sh   5. cl
   c. Two-syllable words
      1. locate   2. hotel   3. rote   4. able   5. deny

        d. Diphtong
            1. ch   2. ou   3. ea   4. aw   5. an
        e. Long vowel sound in medial position
            1. eaten   2. elope   3. be   4. ache   5. flyer
2. This question tests your knowledge of sounds represented by vowel
    letters. Pronounce each word to yourself, and then underline each word
    that contains the correct *sound* asked for.
        a. Short /o/ sound
            1. cold   2. to   3. rob   4. torn   5. howl
        b. Long /e/ sound
            1. men   2. seat   3. send   4. bread   5. meter
        c. R-controlled sound
            1. care   2. burden   3. fear   4. chart   5. fire
        d. Short /u/ sound
            1. push   2. fuel   3. pull   4. rust   5. amuse
        e. Diphthong sound
            1. coon   2. show   3. oyster   4. though   5. coincide
        f. Short /e/ sound
            1. weigh   2. need   3. herd   4. tent   5. peace
        g. Soft /g/ sound
            1. gate   2. hedge   3. give   4. gym   5. gut
        h. Short /i/ sound
            1. bridge   2. pie   3. shirt   4. bind   5. wine
        i. Long /o/ sound
            1. do   2. mole   3. motor   4. gone   5. soap
        j. Short /a/ sound
            1. able   2. date   3. match   4. pa   5. haul
        k. Consonant digraph
            1. break   2. ring   3. shell   4. throw   5. slide
        l. Long /i/ sound
            1. piece   2. mile   3. thin   4. die   5. whip
3. This question tests your ability to apply generalizations helpful in vis-
    ual identification. Underline each nonsense word containing the sound
    asked for.
        a. Begins with long vowel sound
            1. ican   2. inpud   3. oaner   4. arf   5. oge
        b. Begins with short vowel sound
            1. aib   2. epto   3. urby   4. ifent   5. obteck
        c. Begins with soft /c/ or /g/
            1. cenno   2. gop   3. cibe   4. cag   5. gylo
        d. Begins with a diphthong sound
            1. uity   2. oib   3. aine   4. oudy   5. oobe
        e. Begins with the medial sound in *Bert*
            1. arpe   2. urfe   3. irde   4. org   5. ersy
        f. The first syllable ends with a long vowel sound
            1. dolen   2. gorso   3. faupy   4. efip   5. bollen

4. Underline the nonsense word that illustrates the correct division into syllables.

   a. mogle: 1. mog-le   2. mo-gle
   b. boflet: 1. bo-flet   2. bof-let
   c. duthil: 1. du-thil   2. dut-hil
   d. siffle: 1. siff-le   2. sif-fle
   e. faugher: 1. faugh-er   2. faug-her

(Answers to this self-test can be found inverted at the bottom of this page.)

The Phonics Program

QUESTIONS TO GUIDE READING

Literal
What are some major tasks to be taught in a phonics program?
What is a suggested sequence for teaching phonics?
Why are consonants usually taught first?

Inferential
How can a teacher help a child who is confused by diverse dialectical pronunciations?

Beginning reading instruction depends very much on the child's previous experience with language. The chapter on readiness has already stressed the need for auditory discrimination of speech sounds and for visual discrimination among written symbols. Later chapters emphasize the need for sizable speaking and listening vocabularies (words used in speech and words understood when heard). Another prerequisite is that children be able to pronounce words correctly so that they will not be confused when trying to associate the written symbol with the spoken word. Children with a speech defect who cannot pronounce words clearly may have difficulty in making the correct associations. For example, a child with a tongue thrust may pronounce the phoneme /s/ like /sh/, and *see* like *she*,

Question 4 Answers: a — 2; b — 2; c — 1; d — 2; e — 1.
3, 5; f — 1, 4.
Question 3 Answers: a — 1, 3, 5; b — 2, 5; c — 1, 3, 5; d — 2, 4; e — 2,
— 2, 4; h — 1; i — 1; j — 3, 5; k — 2, 3, 4; l — 2, 4.
Question 2 Answers: a — 3; b — 2, 5; c — 2, 4; d — 4; e — 3; f — 4; g
Question 1 Answers: a — 2; b — 2, 4; c — 1, 2, 4, 5; d — 2; e — 2, 5.

causing possible confusion. There may be even more of a problem for children for whom English is a second language and for those with different dialects. Dialect, as we have seen, is the speech used by people in a particular part of the country or in a particular social and educational class. Even so-called "Standard English" is actually but one dialect of English; a grapheme may represent one phoneme in one dialect and another phoneme in a different dialect. The five short vowels are particularly apt to vary in different dialects, as are the final consonant clusters. The teacher's responsibilities are to know and understand the dialect of the children and to accept their pronunciation. She will not try to change their speech patterns. A dialect difference is acceptable and not to be considered a reading error.

Important Concepts in a Phonics Program

1. Understanding that written symbols represent speech sounds.
2. Understanding that the sounds represented by these written symbols can be used in conjunction with other word recognition skills to decode the pronunciation of a word.
3. Knowledge of sounds represented by consonant letters — initial consonants, final and medial consonants, consonant blends or clusters, consonant digraphs.
4. Knowledge of sounds represented by vowel letters and their uses — short sounds, long sounds, vowel digraphs, vowel diphthongs, r-controlled vowels.
5. Knowledge of common phonograms.
6. Skills of syllabication from visual clues.
7. Ability to use substitution and blending skill.
8. Flexibility in word attack; acceptance of the fact that generalizations are helpful in knowing which sounds to attempt first, but alternate approaches must be tried when necessary.

SEQUENCE OF TEACHING PHONICS

The following is a suggested sequence for teaching phonics skills. Of course the skills overlap as they are taught, and they are continually reinforced as needed through the primary grades.

1. Consonants are usually taught first for a number of reasons: They are more consistent than the vowels; most English words begin with consonants; in many instances use of context plus just the initial consonant suggests the unknown word that makes sense in the sentence; the sound represented by a vowel letter is often determined by the consonant following it; and lastly, when the children know the consonants, they are ready to use phonics substitution, which will be explained in a later section. The simpler consonants are begun during the preprimer stage and completed by the end of the primer level, but the harder consonants are introduced during the first reader and completed by the end of the

second. The harder consonants are ⟨z⟩, ⟨r⟩, ⟨j⟩, soft ⟨g⟩ and ⟨c⟩, ⟨q⟩, ⟨v⟩, ⟨l⟩, ⟨x⟩, and ⟨s⟩ pronounced as /z/.

2. The short sounds represented by the vowel letters are begun at the preprimer level and completed by the end of the first grade. They are very necessary because the consonant speech sounds are distorted if pronounced without a vowel speech sound.

3. The long sounds represented by the vowel letters are introduced at the primer level after the short vowel phonemes are established.

4. Consonant blends and consonant digraphs are begun at the first reader level and completed by the end of the third.

5. Vowels controlled by /r/ are begun in the first reader and completed by the second.

6. Vowel digraphs are begun in the first reader and completed by the third.

7. Vowel diphthongs are begun in the first reader and completed by the third.

8. Common phonograms are begun at the primer stage and completed by the third (such as /all/, /ight/, /and/, /ay/, /ing/, /tion/).

9. Syllabication is generally introduced in third grade (Barbe 1965).

Not all commercial materials follow this sequence. Teachers with helpful manuals would want to follow the sequence suggested for their own material.

Principles of Instruction

QUESTIONS TO GUIDE READING

Literal
What are the advantages of the inductive approach?
What do we mean by saying that phonics is taught in conjunction with other learnings?

Inferential
How does phonic substitution differ from finding little words in big words?

There are several important principles of phonics instruction teachers should consider.

1. *A teacher-guided inductive approach to learning phonics* uses familiar words to help children discover for themselves various phonic generalizations. A *deductive* method starts with the rules that the children must

then apply to words. There are proponents of both inductive and deductive methods (Bleismer and Yarborough 1965; Chall 1967; Cleland and Miller 1965; Durrell 1968; Gurren and Hughes 1965). The inductive method has both the advantage of using self-discovery, which is good for motivation, and the advantage of starting with the familiar, which is a sound principle of learning. So the approach in this chapter will be the teacher-guided inductive method — of starting with the familiar and the specific and leading to the general. "Teacher-guided" refers to the fact that the teacher selects what is to be learned and decides when to clarify and restate the learnings. The teacher may also decide in the interest of economy of time that once a pattern or principle has been established inductively, it may be helpful to step in to teach similar principles deductively. But in general the inductive method should be used as much as possible.

An example of the inductive method would be this: the teacher selects some words already in the children's sight vocabulary; he makes his choices to illustrate one auditory-visual association, such as the phoneme-grapheme relationship for /f/. He lists on the chalkboard sight words beginning with /f/, like these:

fat
fun
five
fish

The children discover for themselves the sound represented by the initial consonant letter in those words. Inductive instruction leads children to independence in word attack, since they learn they can discover some relationships for themselves. The teacher reinforces the inductive learnings and moves the children on to new discoveries. A pure inductive method would not be economical in time, but a teacher-guided method of children's self-discovery leads to interest, application, and self-confidence.

2. *Phonics skills are not taught in isolation.* Since the only reason for knowing phonics is to increase independence in word attack on unknown words, sounds are dealt with in words. The words should be used in sentences because the structure of the sentence helps to convey meaning.

3. *Children learn to use other clues* to word recognition simultaneously with phonic clues: word form, picture clues, context clues, or structural analysis (dividing into the meaning or pronunciation units). Thus word recognition is an integral part of the reading process (see Chapter 5).

4. *Informal phonics instruction in the first grade begins at the preprimer level,* teaching sounds represented by consonant letters that appear in words that have become part of the children's sight vocabulary. If experience charts have been written, these will provide the words to be used.

5. *Reading, writing, and spelling go together* and reinforce one another. For example, children learn the name of a written letter and the sound it represents; at the same time they learn to write it.

6. *Phonemes are first taught in the initial position* and then in the final position if applicable. Last, children learn to hear them in the medial position.

7. *Teachers should not introduce exceptions until the principle being taught is firmly established,* so as to prevent confusion.

8. *Phonics substitution* is one of the most helpful methods leading to independence in word attack. Substitution can be used when an unknown word is very similar to a known word, with perhaps just one difference. If the unknown word is *can*, the child recognizes that it is similar to a known word, *man*, but starts with the phoneme beginning the word *cat*. He can then substitute the initial phoneme and come up with *can*. For a more advanced student, the same method is helpful. If he knows the words *concert* and *perform*, he can substitute and arrive at the pronunciation of *conform*.

9. *It is not helpful to teach children to look for the "little words in big words."* The danger is evident if you consider the "little word" *at*, and try to read it in the "big words" *date, nation, athlete*; or read *as* in *aside, ashame*; or *so* in *sock, sonnet*. *The syllable is the important unit of pronunciation, not the "little word,"* which may straddle two syllables. What is helpful is the sound of the phonogram in the syllable. For example, the sound of the phonogram /at/ can be used to aid pronunciation of the syllable, as in *bat, at-tend, fat-ten*. A phonogram is a useful clue, particularly in the primary grades where some 1,500 words have ending phonograms with a consistent sound (Wylie and Durrell 1970, pp. 787–791), such as *man, can; sick, pick; cake, make*. But hunting for "little words" causes more confusion than it helps.

10. *Children must be helped to apply phonic skills in their independent reading,* and this transfer cannot be left to chance. Opportunity must be systematically provided.

Instructional Methods

QUESTIONS TO GUIDE READING

Literal
What are the steps necessary for good instruction of a phonics skill?
What steps should a reader follow in applying phonics skills to attack an unknown word? (Try using these steps to decode the following: *sonance, dermo, ukase.*)
What is the synthetic approach to teaching phonics? What do its proponents emphasize? What criticisms have been made of this approach?

What is the analytic approach? By what rationale do its proponents support this approach?

Evaluative
When would a teacher elect to use a synthetic rather than an analytic approach to phonics instruction?

Available research does not prove any method of teaching phonics to be the most successful one. There is as yet no proof as to the exact sequence, timing, or method that is superior. To present a number of conflicting approaches to teaching phonics would do little but confuse the prospective teacher; it seems preferable first to examine in some depth one method that adheres to sound psychological principles of learning. This is not to lay claim that this method is the only one, but rather that it works well and is commonly used very successfully. A comparison with another approach appears at the end of this section.

PROCEDURE

The optimal procedure in teaching phonics will vary according to the particular skills you are teaching and the amount of reinforcement you need to give; but in general it will follow these steps:

1. Auditory-visual association and teacher clarification. The children make an auditory-visual association leading to self-discovery of the desired learnings.
   The teacher then clarifies, restates, and fills in any necessary details.
2. Reinforcement and application. The teacher reinforces the learnings, first by similar examples, second by using contrast, and third by identifying examples from a mixed group.

Then the teacher provides opportunities for practice and review until the auditory-visual association becomes automatic. Exercises should be easy enough to ensure success, and it is important that the teacher correct any errors immediately to reinforce positive learnings.

Finally and most important, the children (and teacher) apply the learnings in reading and writing. There is not necessarily any carryover from practice sheets to actual application in reading stories, and so the teacher must provide for transfer. These steps are used in the following sample lesson.

Teaching Consonant Speech Sounds: Sample Lesson

To learn sounds represented by consonant letters, the child should first know a few words by sight. A knowledge of thirty to fifty words or more is very helpful. If the children know several words beginning with the same consonant, they are ready to associate the name and sound with the written symbol. To illustrate with the letter ⟨s⟩, use words from the children's sight vocabulary and print them in a column on the chalkboard.

Warning: In teaching the auditory-visual association, choose words that have the /s/ sound being taught, and do not introduce words as *sugar* and *sure*. Do not use words beginning with blends or digraphs.

Auditory-visual association and teacher clarification.

saw
said
see
Sam

Help the children discover the visual similarity in the words:

"Do you see anything that is the same in all these words?"
"Yes, they all begin alike. We call this letter ⟨s⟩."
"The big ⟨S⟩ is called a capital ⟨S⟩ (or uppercase ⟨S⟩)."

Help the children make the auditory-visual association:

"Let's read these words and listen to the sound they begin with."
"Now, what other words can you think of that begin with the same sound?"
"Yes, *sit, sun, silly* begin with the same sound. Let's write them here with the others."

Some child may suggest a word such as *city*. Accept it with an explanation such as this: "*City* does begin with the same sound, doesn't it. Let's write it over here. What do you see that is different? Yes, it begins with a different letter. Sometimes words with this letter also begin with the same sound as words beginning with the letter ⟨s⟩."

Reinforcement and application.
The teacher will reinforce the name, written symbol, and sound represented by the letter ⟨s⟩ through various exercises and seat work, such as these examples:

1. Have children dictate sentences using the words just listed. Write them on chart paper for posting and review.
2. Prepare a page of pictures of familiar objects such as *sand, sock, sun, chair, table*. The child says the name to himself and then writes ⟨s⟩ under the pictures that begin with the /s/ sound.
3. If several consonant speech sounds have already been learned, contrast

the sounds. Prepare a page with columns of three words, each beginning with a different consonant, such as *sat, fat, bat.* The teacher reads one word, and the child marks the word beginning with the speech sound heard.

4. Similarly, the child can sort mounted pictures into boxes labeled with the consonant letter corresponding to the initial speech sound of the object pictured.
5. Make a deck of cards from pictures of objects beginning with the simpler consonant letters, two different pictures for each consonant. The object is to match the two pictures beginning with the same speech sound. Play as in Old Maid or Go Fish.
6. In Consonant Bingo the teacher reads a word, and the children cover the consonant on the card that represents the initial speech sound of the word.
7. Substitution of initial letters: if the children know the word *run,* they can substitute the /s/ sound and combine it with the /un/ sound heard in *run.* Write *run* on the chalkboard, erase the ⟨r⟩ and substitute ⟨s⟩. Put the words in sentences, underlining the words.

> See the dog *run.*
> It is hot in the *sun.*

8. After the speech sound of the consonant in the initial position is well established, introduce the sound in the final and medial positions, and prepare exercises similar to the examples above for practice.
9. Apply to independent reading: put unknown words containing the letter ⟨s⟩ in sentences on the chalkboard. Demonstrate to the children that they can now use what they have learned to help figure out unknown words. For independent reading, distribute teacher-prepared stories that have new words containing the letter ⟨s⟩.

This sample lesson can be adapted to teaching various phonics skills. The following sections point out additional suggestions that apply to specific phonics tasks.

Teaching Consonant Blends (Clusters)

Select consonant blends to teach in the order in which they are occurring in the reading material. Lead the children to discover that the speech sounds represented by the consonant letters are combined into a blended sound.

Since it would take considerable time to teach two dozen blends one by one, we can be more efficient by teaching the children to pronounce each phoneme in the consonant blend and then blend them; thus they learn a tool to use in meeting future blends. Although in decoding words it is important to follow the left-to-right direction, in teaching the blending of consonants it may be necessary to alter that rule; first, read the word with one consonant only and then precede the word with the other consonant. For example:

pin — spin   *rain — train*
pill — spill   *rail — trail*
pot — spot   *rap — trap*

For children who have trouble blending phonemes, put the word in context. For example:

rain — train   The little engine pulled the __?__ .

After the children have learned several blends in this fashion, they should be able to apply this principle to other blends as they meet them.

TEACHING CONSONANT DIGRAPHS

Because consonant digraphs represent a speech sound that is not a blend of the two letters, it is necessary to teach each digraph separately. Teach them first in the initial position, and later in the final and medial positions. Take ⟨sh⟩ as an example.

Auditory-visual association and teacher clarification.

shell   *ship*
shave   *short*

Because this digraph does begin with the consonant ⟨s⟩ previously taught, possibly causing confusion, the teacher should contrast the sound represented by the single consonant and the sound represented by the consonant digraph, pointing out the visual difference.

shell — sell   *ship — sip*
shave — save   *short — sort*

Reinforcement and application. The teacher will reinforce the speech sound represented by the consonant digraph ⟨sh⟩ by putting words beginning with the digraph into sentences, and by preparing various exercises and seat work similar to what has already been suggested. For example:

sell — shell   Bill saw a __?__ on the sand.

After the speech sound is learned in the initial position, present it in the final and medial positions. Finally, provide opportunities to apply the newly acquired knowledge in independent reading.

The same procedure is used with ⟨ch⟩, ⟨wh⟩, ⟨th⟩. These are the most common digraphs. Later, as they appear in the reading vocabulary, ⟨ph⟩, ⟨gh⟩, ⟨ng⟩ will be added, and the other sounds represented by ⟨ch⟩, ⟨th⟩.

Teach only the one sound represented by a given digraph until it is established.

TEACHING THE SHORT VOWEL SPEECH SOUNDS

A few sight words listed on the chalkboard can illustrate the short vowel sound; the words should have the vowel in the initial position. After the children discover the vowel speech sound, the teacher can point out the vowel pattern (vc and cvc). Take ⟨a⟩ as an example.

Auditory-visual association and teacher clarification.

at   and
an   add

After using the vowel in the initial position, list words using the consonant-vowel-consonant pattern and have the children listen for the sound represented by the vowel in the medial position.

hat   man
pat   pan
sat   tan

Columns of rhyming words can be used, as above; later the words may be mixed, to focus on the medial vowel speech sound. Point out the vowel pattern.

cat   man   bag   bath

Reinforcement and application. The following are in addition to the suggestions in the sample lesson.

1. When the short /a/ sound has been established, it is helpful to choose a word with the initial short /a/ sound to use as a clue word with which to associate the sound. For short /a/, the word *apple* is often used. (See page 74 for clue words for the other short vowel speech sounds.)
2. For further reinforcement, contrast words to see if the children can hear the correct vowel in the words you pronounce. Have them indicate when they hear the short /a/ in a word.

   mad — mud
   hid — had
   rag — rug

3. After several short vowel speech sounds have been learned, prepare sentences with one word omitted and follow the sentence with a choice of two words differing only in the vowel. The child chooses the correct word to write in the blank to make sense in the sentence.

It is a very _____ day. (hut/hot)
Bill _____ the ball. (hit/hat)
Jane writes with a _____. (pen/pan)

Reminder: It is important that each phonics skill be applied to reading and writing so that the children become independent in applying the skill.

TEACHING THE LONG VOWEL SPEECH SOUNDS: THE VOWEL-CONSONANT-FINAL ⟨E⟩ PATTERN

Since the speech sounds of long vowels are similar to their names, the sounds are generally quickly understood. The beginning reader's main problem is to know when first to try the long sound represented by the vowel letter in decoding a word. Spelling patterns are helpful clues.

Auditory-visual association and teacher clarification.

ate
age

"Let's read these words. What sound do you hear at the beginning of the words? Yes, we hear a sound that is like the name of the letter ⟨a⟩. We call that the long sound of ⟨a⟩."

cake
make
lake

"What do you see is the same in all these words? Yes, they all end in ⟨e⟩."

hate
plane
made

"Let's read them again and see if you can hear any sound for the ⟨e⟩? No, it is silent."

Reinforcement and application.

1. To establish the pattern (vce), contrast the long vowel spelling pattern with the short vowel in the cvc pattern.

    at — ate
    hat — hate
    mad — made
    plan — plane

"Here are some words with the short /a/ sound. I am going to change each word by adding ⟨e⟩ on the end. What happens to the /a/?"
Use the other vowels in a similar way.

hid — hide   bit — bite
hop — hope   rob — robe
cut — cute   cub — cube
pet — Pete

2. Prepare seatwork with pictures of objects. Write the name below the picture, leaving a blank for an ⟨e⟩ to be added. The child adds the ⟨e⟩ to those names that have a long vowel sound represented.

Pictures: *plane*   *cat*   *cake*   *hat*
Names: *plan__*   *cat__*   *cak__*   *hat__*

3. Put words with the vce pattern in sentences, because the structure of the sentence helps convey meaning. Prepare exercises similar to ones already described.
4. Words occurring in the reading material will be pointed out to reinforce the vowel-consonant-final ⟨e⟩ pattern whenever one occurs that represents the long first vowel. Do not pick out the exceptions until the children question them. Words such as *some, done* can be explained as exceptions and taught as sight words. In words such as *give*, point out that although the long vowel sound is tried first, if that does not result in a word, then try the short vowel sound.
5. Provide opportunities for using this new phonics skill in independent reading.

TEACHING THE LONG VOWEL SPEECH SOUNDS:
THE ADJACENT VOWEL PATTERN AND THE OPEN SYLLABLE

The spelling pattern with adjacent vowels (vv) is taught by the same procedure, first listing words with the long vowel phoneme in the initial position, then adding rhyming words, and finally showing a mixed group with the vowel in the medial position.

eat
meat
seat

bead
mean
real

Continue with other vowel digraphs: ⟨ee⟩, ⟨oa⟩, ⟨ai⟩. Then present columns of words with the cvc pattern contrasted with words with the vv pattern.

man — maid
ran — rain
bed — bead

And so on, through the usual steps, until the generalization is well established. Do not use exceptions when first introducing the principle.

Use these same methods, where applicable, in teaching the long vowel sounds on the end of a syllable: *be, so, ho-*tel.

Teaching /r/-controlled Vowels and Diphthongs and Phonograms

The same procedure — auditory-visual association and teacher clarification, reinforcement and application — is used in teaching the /r/-controlled vowels, the vowel digraph exceptions, the diphthongs, and the phonograms.

Syllabication

For the principles of syllabication based on visual clues, refer back to the content section on pages 76–78. Teach the syllabic patterns by the same inductive method used in teaching the spelling patterns for long vowel speech sounds. Accent and more on syllabication will be discussed in Chapter 5.

Steps in Sounding Out an Unknown Word

The following procedure shows how the phonics skills presented in this chapter assist in word recognition. These are the questions the children would ask themselves when attacking a new word in their independent reading.

1. What is the sound represented by the initial letters? Used with the context clues, will the initial sound of the word be sufficient clue to the unknown word?
2. If not, is the word similar to a known word so that phonic substitution may be used (man — ban)?
3. If not, how many vowels are in the word (or syllable) and where are they?
   a. If there is only one vowel in a closed syllable (cvc), try the short sound represented by the vowel letter (*ban*).
   b. If a single vowel is followed by ⟨r⟩, try the /r/-controlled sound (*bar*).
   c. If a single vowel is at the end of the word or syllable (cv), try the long sound represented by the vowel letter (*be, be-*gin).
   d. If the word contains the vce pattern, first try the long sound represented by the first vowel letter (*bake*). Then try the short sound (*give*).
   e. If the word contains the vv pattern, try the long sound represented by the first vowel letter (*beat*).
   f. If there is a vowel diphthong, try the diphthong sound (*bout*).
4. Blend the whole word. Does it sound familiar? Does it make sense in the sentence?
5. If not, try blending it again with the other vowel sound.

6. Is it now familiar? Does it make sense? If not, ask for help, or go to the dictionary (if the student has developed the necessary dictionary skills).

COMPARISON OF THE SYNTHETIC APPROACH WITH THE ANALYTIC APPROACH

Most of the preceding description of instructional methods has used the analytic approach, which starts with the whole and analyzes its parts. The analytic approach presents a whole word first and then analyzes the word into the speech sounds represented by its graphemes.

However, there are a number of materials designed for the synthetic approach. The synthetic approach is basically a decoding process that teaches graphemes, phonemes, and phonograms — often in isolation. Then the reader combines the speech sounds into words. This method starts with the small parts and synthesizes them into the whole. Most synthetic materials start with words arranged according to repetitive spelling patterns. Much of the teaching is done deductively, and it relies heavily on rote memorization, with little attention to reading for meaning.

The controversy over analytic versus synthetic approach has been going on for decades. Proponents of the synthetic approach emphasize the imperative need to be able to work out the pronunciation of unknown words (Hay and Wingo 1967). But the critics of the synthetic approach say that it produces slow reading and word calling because too much attention is focused on the mechanics of decoding and too little on the meaning of the passage. The proponents of the analytic approach feel there is no true reading without understanding and thinking; and since there is no meaning in a phoneme, the emphasis should be on whole words and on a method that develops immediate sight recognition of words and phrases.

Many formal phonics systems and linguistic readers utilize the synthetic approach. Most basals use the analytic approach. Chall (1967) attempted to resolve the debate on approaches in her intensive review of the research on phonics systems compared to other methods; she came out on the side of the synthetic, but her analysis has itself been questioned.

In this chapter the analytic approach has been emphasized, but some suggestions from the synthetic have been adopted, such as the use of clue words for the short vowel sounds. The best features of both approaches can be utilized, but what the teacher must keep in mind is that there needs to be a comprehensive program adaptable to individual differences and flexible enough for the particular class being taught.

Summary

Phonics is the art of using a knowledge of letter-sound relationships as an aid to word recognition in reading. Phonic analysis is used not in isolation but in conjunction with other word recognition clues, and there must be flexibility in approach. New words should be assimilated into the sight vocabulary as rapidly as possible because overreliance on phonics leads to slow, laborious reading. As the reader develops his sight vocabulary and becomes more proficient, he will need to use phonic analysis less often.

Phonics is a very essential tool for the beginning reader if he is to gain independence in reading, and it needs to be well taught. But teachers can teach well only what they themselves know thoroughly. Since the English language has many irregularities, teachers must be so well grounded in phonics that they recognize irregularities and do not confuse the children.

The methods of instruction suggested in this chapter have been influenced by a number of the insights of linguists. For example, we saw that phonemes, particularly consonants, should not be isolated from the words in which they occur because they are realized differently in different spelling patterns. Furthermore the student should see the words used in sentences because the structure of the sentence helps to convey meaning. Other linguistic contributions to reading instruction that are included are the use of rhyming elements and the contrasting of pairs of words that differ in only one phoneme. The influence of linguistic terminology is apparent, and the suggested use of the inductive method agrees with the linguistic philosophy.

We favor the analytic approach and believe that a teacher-guided inductive method should lead to motivation, understanding, and application. Such instruction utilizes auditory-visual association, teacher clarification, reinforcement, and application to reading and writing. Throughout the teaching of phonics, the focus must always be on the goal, which is to help the child become an independent reader.

Questions for Further Reading and Thinking

1. Examine a formal phonics program that uses the synthetic method, such as *Reading with Phonics* (J. B. Lippincott Co.); *Phonetic Keys to Reading* (The Economy Co.); or the *Open Court Basic Readers* (Open Court Publishing Co.). Do you prefer this approach to the one outlined in the chapter? Defend your position.

2. Examine one of the systems designed to provide a consistent phoneme-grapheme relationship in spelling English words, such as i/t/a, Unifon, or Laubach's Alphabet. Would

you wish to use this method in teaching beginning reading? Defend your position.
3. What are the strengths and weaknesses of selected commercial materials designed to improve phonics skills?

Activities and Projects

1. Make a skills box for reinforcing phonics skills in the primary grades.
2. Make a chart showing the relationship of the 45 phonemes to the graphemes.
3. Prepare a set of at least five games for developing phonic skills. Identify the purpose and suggested grade level for each.
4. Plan a learning center for reinforcing a phonics skill. Include well-defined objectives, self-directions for the child, immediate feedback to the child, provision for different ability levels, and manipulative materials more motivational than just seat work.
5. Prepare a tape to be used in a learning center for reinforcing a phonics skill.
6. Prepare a lesson plan for presenting a new phonics skill to a particular age group, preparing the objectives, the methods, and the actual teaching materials.

Instructional Materials for Elementary Students

Basic Primary Phonics (filmstrips). Chicago: Society for Visual Education.

Discovering Phonics We Use. Chicago: Rand McNally and Company.

The Ginn Word Enrichment Program by Theodore Clymer et al. Boston: Ginn and Company.

Merrill Phonics Skilltexts and Skilltapes by Josephine B. Wolfe. Columbus, Ohio: Charles E. Merrill.

New Phonics Skilltexts. Columbus, Ohio: Charles E. Merrill.

The New Phonics We Use Learning Kits. Chicago: Rand McNally and Company.

Open Court Basic Readers by Arthur S. Trace, ed. La Salle, Ill.: Open Court Publishing Company.

Phonetic Analysis by Virginia Middlemas et al. New York: Center for Programmed Instruction.

Phonetic Keys to Reading and *Keys to Independence in Reading* by Theodore M. Harris et al. Oklahoma City: The Economy Company.

Phonics and Word Power. Columbus, Ohio: American Education Publications.

Phonics Plus by Charles T. Mangrum II and Peter B. Messmore. Englewood Cliffs, N.J.: Prentice-Hall.

Phonics Practice (filmstrips). Chicago: Science Research Associates.

Reading with Phonics by E. C. Wingo and Mary C. Hletko. Philadelphia: J. B. Lippincott Company.

Speech-to-Print Phonics: A Phonics Foundation for Reading by Donald A. Durrell and Helen A. Murphy. New York: Harcourt Brace Jovanovich.

SRA Reading Laboratory I-Word Games (grades 1–6). Chicago: Science Research Associates.

SRA Skills Series. Chicago: Science Research Associates.

Steck Teaching Aids. Austin, Texas: The Steck Company.

Take and *Vowel Lotto* by E. W. Dolch. Champaign, Ill.: Garrard Publishing Company.

Word Analysis Charts by William Kottmeyer and Kay Ware. St. Louis: Webster Publishing Company.

Word Rummy. Detroit: Educational Cards.

Leonard G. Breen

5

Context Clues, Structural Analysis, and Dictionary Aids to Pronunciation

For most nonprofessionals writing on the subject of reading and for some teachers and producers of reading materials, phonics and sight words make up the program of word recognition teaching. In reality, sight words and phonics are just two of several basic word recognition techniques. Many reading specialists commonly talk about five word recognition skills and list along with sight words and phonics the teaching of context clues, structural analysis, and dictionary aids to pronunciation. Because nothing works all the time, children need this full range of word attack tools to give them flexibility in word recognition. Likewise, teachers must be prepared to instruct and to encourage flexibility in the use of all word recognition strategies. If overall reading development is to occur, each of these skills must be integrated into the reading program.

Context Clues

QUESTIONS TO GUIDE READING

Literal
What is contextual analysis?
What is the difference between syntactic and semantic context clues?

Evaluative
What is the value of any context clue for intelligent guessing on unknown words?
Should a teacher help children decide when to use contextual rather than phonic or other clues?
Why is a picture or illustration a type of context clue?

The utilization of context clues as a word recognition skill is nothing more than the use of surrounding information to identify a word that is probably known aurally but not visually. As with sight words, the use of context clues is often criticized by advocates of the phonics approach to decoding as one that involves guessing. The writers, however, feel that intelligent guessing is often a desirable procedure and consider skill in making use of context clues significant at all stages of reading development.

Goodman (1965a) found that first grade readers were able to read 62 percent of the words they had missed on a list when these same words occurred in the context of a story. Second graders correctly read 75 percent missed in isolation, and third graders got 82 percent of the words they had missed in isolation. In a similar study Freeman (1973) found that context, plus a limited number of graphic clues, aids in decoding most of the unknown printed words in a child's listening or speaking vocabularies. Carol Chomsky (1974) writes that readers in her study were often surprised to discover that words they thought were unfamiliar when presented in isolation were actually known when viewed within their contexts.

Readers using context clues rely on three kinds of information for making decisions about unknown words: semantic, syntactic, and picture clues. Semantic clues involve making use of the meaning of words in phrases, sentences, or combinations of surrounding sentences. Using semantic clues requires use of prior knowledge and experience as well as the reader's speaking and listening vocabularies to predict unknown words. In using syntactic clues the reader utilizes his intuitive knowledge of language and its patterns to look at the position and function or grammatical fit of an unknown word in order to make logical predictions as to its pronunciation. Pictures, drawings, graphs, and other forms of illustration serve as graphic extensions of the printed word and can aid the reader in pronunciation, comprehension, and interpretation.

Before discussing these types of context clues more fully we should point out that it is very difficult to separate them. Readers utilizing context clues rarely develop a reliance on only one type of signal but instead rely on the natural redundancy of language to supply them with a combination of semantic, syntactic, and pictorial clues. These are then used in conjunction with knowledge of graphophonic skills to assist with reading.

SEMANTIC CLUES

The utilization of semantic clues as a word recognition skill deals with helping children read for meaning. (See Chapter 6 for further discussion of context clues as they relate to meaning.) A behavior many readers display when encountering an unknown word is to stop and wait expectantly for the teacher to supply it. Teachers who supply the reader with the needed word are inadvertently teaching dependence on themselves as instructors rather than dependence on context for meaning or pronunciation. Training children to utilize contextual clues might best be started by encouraging them to read the entire sentence before attempting to derive the pronunciation or meaning of an unknown word. For example:

Student (reading orally): Betty went to the store and — (*stops at the word* bought *and looks at the teacher for help*).

Teacher: Yes, read the rest of the sentence and see if you can think of a word that makes sense here.

Student: Betty went to the store and (*slight pause*) her mother a present. Oh yes, bought! Betty went to the store and bought her mother a present.

In the event that the reader miscalls the word intended, teachers might still encourage the child to use context to work out the correct pronunciation.

Student (reading orally): Betty went to the store to buy her mother a present.

Because the essential meaning of this sentence won't change, the teacher should probably ignore it at the time it occurs but return to it afterward to work out the new word with the child.

Teacher: Let's look back at this sentence: "Betty went to the store . . ." Do you remember what you read? You said *to buy.* That's good because it makes sense, but what else would make sense here if we use the word *and,* which is in the story? "Betty went to the store and . . ."

If the child suggests *bought* the teacher might respond as follows.

Teacher: Bought? All right, let's put that in the sentence to see if it sounds right. Could this possibly be the correct word? How can we tell?

The teacher might find that it is necessary to supply even more clues to the child by drawing his attention to beginning and ending sounds or by pointing out that the word rhymes with fought (graphophonic skills).

The important thing to recognize is that in both examples the teacher focused on meanings in context rather than on the decoding of an isolated word. The teacher required the reader to use context to predict which word or words might come next, and then to check the accuracy of the prediction by listening to the word's meaningfulness and by checking its graphophonic similarity. In utilizing this process of predicting, guessing, and verifying, the teacher encourages the child to approach decoding as a meaning-getting process rather than as a process of simply combining letters and sounds (see also Chapter 1).

Several ways in which writers provide semantic context clues to help readers deal with the possibility of unknown words or concepts are suggested by the classification of context clues delineated by McCullough (1945, pp. 1–5):

1. *Definition.* The descriptive context defines the unknown word. For example, "A *square* is a closed figure with four straight equal sides."
2. *Experience.* Children use past experiences to complete a thought. For example, "After school Dick hung his clothes in the *closet.*"
3. *Comparison and contrast.* The unknown word is compared to something known. For example, "You don't always have to run. You can sometimes *walk.*"
4. *Synonym.* The context offers a synonym of the unknown word. For example, "The fat giant was large and round and *rotund.*" fat
5. *Familiar expression.* The word is recognized by its use in a familiar language pattern or verbal experience. For example, "As he left he shouted, 'See ya later, *alligator.*'"
6. *Summary.* The unknown word serves to summarize several previous concepts. For example, "Hammers, nails, saws, and ladders are all building tools for a *carpenter.*"
7. *Mood or situation.* The tone or mood of a sentence suggests the nature of the new word. For example, "The old cellar was dim and cool and quiet. After being out in the hot sun all day, I had a feeling of *relief* when I went down."

Additional semantic contextual aids have been identified by Wilbur S. Ames (1966, pp. 57–82). He bases these on reading behaviors exhibited by numbers of adult readers and says that such readers also rely on such aids as:

1. Modifying words, phrases, and clauses. For example, "A tall, *muscular* bystander finally broke up the fight."
2. Words connected in a series. For example, "Hamburgers, hotdogs, and *pizzas* are among the favorite foods of teenagers."
3. Referents or antecedents. In this case readers use a pronoun and accompanying context to refer back to the unknown word. For example, "A broken *fishing* line is useless. It won't help catch fish."

All of these examples of semantic clues rely on a natural behavior of language users. The reader uses words and experiences that he has or knows to trigger an inferred recognition of unknown words.

SYNTACTIC CLUES

English is a positional language. That is, the meaning of phrases and sentences depends on the order of words. Consider, for example, these sentences: *The man just missed the train* and *The train just missed the man.*

Context Clues, Structural Analysis, and Dictionary Aids to Pronunciation

In the first sentence the man simply lost some time, whereas in the second he very nearly lost his life. Occasionally phrases also illustrate the significance of word order for meaning, as can be appreciated by contrasting the word order for *house cat.* A child's knowledge of these positional relationships (syntax) comes from his understanding of and experience with language. Additionally, though less often, it comes from grammatical concepts learned at school. It should be noted that a knowledge of formal grammar is not necessary in order to use syntax as a word recognition tool. Readers do not need to know that "a noun is a name of a person, place, thing, or idea" in order to use the fact that nouns follow articles as a word recognition tool. Combined with semantic clues and a teacher's guiding questions this knowledge of the way language works can be used by readers to make intelligent guesses at the pronunciation of unrecognized words. At the very least syntactic clues can reduce the number of possible pronunciations of unknown words to a reasonable few. The following syntactic generalizations illustrate some of the ways that language works to help readers and can be helpful to teachers in guiding practice in this skill.

Nouns follow articles. Articles such as *the, that, these, some, a,* and *an* serve as signal words to readers that the word that follows is a noun. Their value in predicting probable singular and plural nouns can be seen in the following example sentences. Assume that the child does not know the italicized words in each sentence.

> The record playing on the *phonograph* was old but in good condition.
> Those *camels* all have two humps.

In the first sentence probable pronunciations might include *radio, phonograph,* or possibly *machine.* In the second, readers will use the plural markers *those* and *all* as well as the final /s/ to hypothesize perhaps *camels* or *craters.* In either case logical predictions will be nouns or naming words because each is preceded by an appropriate noun marker or article. Further narrowing toward the correct word can be accomplished by relying on semantic clues, the content of surrounding sentences, and appropriate phonic clues.

Noun-adjective relationship. The relationship of nouns and descriptive modifiers can be capitalized on as a pronunciation aid when either the noun or the modifier is unknown, as in the following sentences:

> The ice made the drink *cold.*
> The spaghetti *sauce* left stains on the table cloth.

Teacher questions can lead readers toward combining their own natural awareness of the use of descriptive words and the use of semantic clues to arrive at the unknown word. "Why," she might ask, "do we add ice to a drink?" "What part of a spaghetti dinner would leave stains on the table cloth?"

Subjects announce verbs. The relationship between nouns and verbs can be used to help predict unknown words. In the sentence, "The snake *slithered* cross the gravel road," children will generally be able to distinguish between the naming part of the sentence (noun phrase) and the action part of the sentence (verb phrase) by virtue of their being able to use language orally. Additionally, by using structural analysis they know that *slithered* is the past-tense action verb that describes some form of moving. At this point the teacher might inquire of the readers, "What words might tell how a snake moves?" Their suggestions plus further looks at appropriate phonic clues will help the children unlock this new word in a meaningful, language-based way.

TEACHING CONTEXTUAL ANALYSIS

Using an array of context clues to assist with reading should be emphasized from the earliest stages in the reading program. Children taught these skills soon begin seeing reading as a natural extension of already known language skills. They approach new words with an attitude of meaning-getting and understanding rather than merely "sound and say." Most useful of all, they learn through example and practice that decoding unknown words is best done through an integration of *all* of the cues available to them through print and language.

There are many exercises and materials teachers can draw on to help readers become skilled in recognizing and using the contextual clues available in sentences. Beginning readers can play oral games to help them understand that language makes sense. A teacher can ask, "Who can finish this sentence?" and then read aloud sentences like the following:

1. We often watch fireworks on the Fourth of _____.
2. The _____ of our flag are red, white, and blue.
3. When the telephone _____, I answer it.

Picture clues, diagrams, and charts are helpful for introducing new words in advance of reading. Before the class begins to read a selection, the teacher may direct their attention to an accompanying picture in the book. Discussion of the picture can make mention of the new word in the text, which can then be pointed out and emphasized.

Simple cloze selections, sentences from which certain words have been deleted, can be written to give readers practice in using context to fill in words omitted from reading passages. The simplest would be short sentences requiring readers to select the most appropriate word for completing each statement.

1. I caught some $\frac{\text{bass}}{\text{soon}}$ in the lake.

Word choices given to the reader could be varied as they become more skilled to include words more and more semantically, syntactically, and graphically similar to the correct choice.

2. I caught some $\frac{\text{bass}}{\text{barn}}$ in the lake.

Older readers might receive longer sentences utilizing a maze procedure (see also page 135). After selecting a passage from a story or textbook, the teacher substitutes three alternative words for each word deleted. The passage then resembles a maze in that pupils must continually decide which path will lead them through the sentence or story.

                       most   lighted
It was dark by the time the meal was prepared, and he roared a lamp
                        train   loudly

           money
and put it on the easily .
          table

As readers become more confident in their ability to use context to make correct word choices, less visual information can be supplied to them. Exercises such as the following require readers to rely upon all of the semantic, syntactic, and graphic cues available:

1. I had a large breakfast of bacon, eggs, and t_____.
2. At school I got ten of my math pr_____ correct.
3. I went to the bakery to buy some c_____.

Emans and Fisher (1967, pp. 243–246) conducted a study of six kinds of instructional activities designed to utilize contextual deletions. Children were asked to read sentences and provide the missing word in each sentence. Their results indicated a hierarchy of difficulty in contextual analysis skills for children in grades three to ten. The teacher can use the hierarchy to plan instructional exercises in order, from easiest to most difficult, to help the student develop contextual ability. Their hierarchy of skills is as follows:

1. (Least difficult.) Consonants given, vowels omitted.
   The c_rp_nt_r built a new sailboat.

2. Four word choices given.

The _____ built a new sailboat.

insect   carpet   machine   carpenter

3. Beginning and ending letters given.

The c_____r built a new sailboat.

4. Length of the word given.

The _____ built a new sailboat.

5. Beginning letter given.

The c_____ built a new sailboat.

6. (Most difficult.) No clues given other than context.

The _____ built a new sailboat.

Structural Analysis

QUESTIONS TO GUIDE READING

Literal

What is meant by the term structural analysis?

What is a morpheme?

What are the major elements to be found in a program of structural analysis skills development?

Inferential

What are the basic principles that should be observed in teaching structural analysis?

Why is it easier for children to understand compound words than combinations of bound and free morphemes?

Another method of analyzing words is through the use of structural analysis. Simply stated, structural analysis is the investigation of unknown words for known meaningful parts — such as root words; compound words; contractions; prefixes and suffixes; plurals; past tense endings; and comparison endings in words like fast, faster, fastest. In phonic analysis the reader deciphers a word by means of sound (represented by letters or combinations of letters in a word); but in structural analysis he recognizes the "meaning units" of a word. According to Robeck and Wilson (1974, p. 38), structural analysis is an important word recognition technique, and readers "who do not master this kind of analysis will continue to sound on a letter-by-letter basis." Those who continue to depend on letter-by-letter analysis are slow readers who frequently feel they have not adequately mastered the reading act; thus motivation as well as efficiency may suffer.

Linguists refer to the units of meaning as morphemes. There are two general types of morphemes in English, as in other languages — free forms and bound forms. Units of language that are meaningful in isolation, such as *cat, house, school,* or *month* are called *free morphemes.* Units of language that have meaning but that cannot stand alone as words are *bound morphemes.* Prefixes, suffixes, plural endings, comparison endings, and some roots are bound morphemes; for example: *un, sub, re, geo, intra, bio, ing, ed, er.* Because structural analysis concerns itself with word derivatives (that is, combinations of prefixes, roots, and suffixes, which are combinations of bound and free morphemes), some authors refer to this reading skill as morphemic analysis.

Exactly which elements and generalizations in structural analysis should be taught in the elementary school is a question having few definitive answers and a limited research basis. Most authorities suggest that teachers keep the following criteria in mind in making this decision: (1) the frequency of occurrence of the structural form; (2) the ease with which the learner can identify the form; (3) the value of the element to the development, speed, and independence in word recognition; and (4) the recommendations of the reading series being used for instruction.

COMPOUND WORDS

Other things being equal, the elements easiest to learn and apply should be taught first. This being so, it is easier for children to understand compounding, especially when two free English morphemes are used. The following types of compound words might easily be used in the early stages of a reading program: *cowboy, into, fireman, milkman,* and *snowman.* First grade children generally have these words in their oral vocabularies. They can also discuss the reasons for combining the small words and can generalize that the pronunciation of the roots is maintained and that the roots have a connected meaning. For example, *snowman* is a man made of snow, and *drawbridge* is a bridge that can be drawn up or aside. (The only exceptions to this rule of connected meaning are structural words such as *however* and *nonetheless.*) These criteria of maintaining original pronunciation and having connected meaning will automatically eliminate the teaching of such words as *manage, orbit, target,* and *together* as compound words.

For children who have been taught to rely on semantic meanings in context, the underlying linguistic structures of compound words can sometimes be confusing. For example, *sunlight* is light from the sun, but a *button hook* is a hook used for buttons, not a hook from buttons. *Wallpaper* is paper for walls but a *frogman* is a man who swims like a frog not a man for frogs.

A second confusion can arise because compound words sometimes appear as two separate words when written instead of as a single word.

Truck driver (someone who drives a truck) is often written as a single word whereas *brick layer* (one who lays brick) is written as two. *Turtle neck* (a neck like a turtle's) is two words and is similar in meaning to the single word *bulldog* (a dog like a bull). Although it is tempting to call the first word in the two-word combinations an adjective modifying a noun, this cannot linguistically be done. A true adjective can appear as a relative clause. A red shirt, therefore, is a shirt that is red. However, it cannot be paraphrased that a turtle neck is a neck that is turtle. Linguistically, words like *turtle neck, elevator operator,* and *brick layer* are best regarded as compound nouns similar to *truckdriver* and *bulldog* (Johnson and Pearson, 1978, pp. 87–89). The following structural breakdown of different types of compounds is suggested for teachers who wish to teach this structural form.[1]

1. B *is of* A. A mudslide *is* a slide *of* mud, and a riverbank *is* the bank *of* a river. Here are others:

tarpaper	housework	piecrust
heartburn	countertop	housewife

2. B *is from* A. Sunburn *is* a burn *from* the sun, and starlight *is* a light *from* a star. Others include:

bookworm	sawdust	goat skin
		horse hair

3. B *is for* A. A washbasin *is* a basin *for* washing and a dining room *is* a room *for* dining. Others:

housedress	fryingpan	dishpan
bookcase	pigpen	

4. B *is like* A. A bulldog *is* a dog that looks *like* a bull and a catfish *is* a fish that looks *like* a cat. Others might include:

crabgrass	rattlesnake	house boat
bull horn	turtle neck	Batman

5. B *is* A. Darkmeat *is* meat that is dark and a pipeline *is* a line that is made of pipe. Others include:

blackberry	manservant	snowman
blueberry	White House	blueprint

6. B *does* A. A jumping bean is a bean that *jumps*, and a pipe fitter is a man that *fits* pipes. Others include:

fireman	towtruck	postman
brick layer	policeman	

1. Adapted from pages 87–89 of *Teaching Reading Vocabulary* by Dale D. Johnson and P. David Pearson. Copyright © 1978 by Holt, Rinehart and Winston. Reprinted by permission of Holt, Rinehart and Winston, CBS College Publishing.

Although teachers are encouraged not to overemphasize this structured-group approach to compounds, it is a very interesting way of thinking about compound words and may prove useful in organizing lessons about them. As always, after children have discussed the meanings of compound words, they should be given the opportunity to use the words in sentences. The words might be used in sentences of the children's own construction, or used in modified cloze activities that require children to select the appropriate compound words to fit in sentences or short paragraphs that the teacher composes.

PREFIXES AND SUFFIXES

As a next step, commonly bound morphemes might be combined with free morphemes. Knowledge of the most common prefixes and suffixes will assist some children in unlocking many new words. Hoisington's research (1968) showed that children who received direct instruction in prefixes, suffixes, and root words scored significantly higher in reading comprehension than those who did not receive such instruction. Common inflectional suffixes to be taught in the beginning grades include:

s	*doors, calls, girl's, hosts*
es	*boxes, hostesses*
ed	*called, cried*
ing	*calling, diving*
er	*softer, drier*
est	*softest, driest*

Harris and Sipay (1980, p. 464) state that many suffixes in English have multiple meanings. Thus, generalizations are particularly difficult. They suggest that the following are the most appropriate for instruction since they are fairly common and have a relatively constant meaning:

er, or, ist, ion (performer of)
tion, sion (art of)
ry, ty, ity (conditions of)
al (pertaining to)
is (pertaining to)
ence, ance (state of)
ble, able, ible (capable of being)
ment (result of, act of)
ful (full of)
man (full of)
ous, eous, ious (like, full of)
ly, y (in the manner of)

Prefixes are usually introduced in the second year reading program in the form of morphemes such as *un* (unkind) and *re* (rebuild). From such combinations children easily learn that, when a prefix is added to a word they know, the meaning of the word is changed or altered by the meaning of the prefix. For example, *unkind* means not kind and *unable* means not able. Stauffer (1942) suggests that the following fifteen prefixes have the highest utility:

ab (from)
ad, ap, at (to)
be (by)
con, com, col (with)
de (from)
dis (apart, not)
en, em (in)
ex (out)
in, im (in, into)
in, im (not)
ob, ot, op (against, away, from)
pre, pro (before, in front of)
re (back)
post (behind)
super (over, above)
trans (across)
sub (under)
un (not)

Instruction in the use of prefixes and suffixes as a pronunciation aid should be designed to help readers (1) correctly pronounce whatever prefix or suffix is being taught; (2) understand how this word part changes the meaning of the root word; and (3) be able to transfer this new learning to other new words being learned. Children who have learned the pronunciation and meaning of the prefix *un* to learn the words *unkind* and *unlikely* should be able to use these learnings to work out the pronunciations and probable meanings for new words encountered such as *unabridged* and *unresponsive*. (Chapter 6 also focuses on instructional procedures for teaching meanings of unknown prefixes, suffixes, and roots).

Dictionary Aids to Pronunciation

QUESTIONS TO GUIDE READING

Literal
What are some skills and understandings a child must possess in order to use a dictionary to identify the pronunciation of a word?

What are a few ways knowledge of the dictionary can help a reader with word pronunciation?

Inferential
How will the development of dictionary skills help a child in reading?

Evaluative
Which dictionary skills should be taught first?
When should a child use the dictionary to determine the pronunciation of words?

Because dictionary analysis is often perceived as a study skill or as part of a total unit in vocabulary development, teachers seldom promote this important skill as an aid to word recognition. Additionally, readers are often reluctant to use dictionaries because of the interruptive nature of looking up an unknown word. Stopping to "look it up" seems to detract more than it adds to the act of reading. Also, to be able to deal with dictionaries effectively, one must have many skills, including understanding the nature, organization, and format of dictionaries.

There are times, however, when reliance on semantic and syntactic clues, word structure clues, and graphophonic clues cannot help the reader with the pronunciation or meaning of an unfamiliar word. The word *terpsichorean* in the sentence "The display of terpsichorean skill was dazzling" serves as a good example. The four-step process that children should be taught to follow just does not work in this case.

1. When you come to a word you do not know, skip it and read to the end of the sentence. Then use context clues to go back and figure it out. (If you have never seen or heard the word as in the sentence above this probably will not work.)
2. If that does not work, try sounding it out. (Because the word is of foreign origin this will get the reader nowhere.)
3. If *that* does not work, see if it has word parts you know. (It does not.)
4. If nothing works, ask someone for help. (Just your luck. You have found a word that nobody else knows either!)

No amount of guessing or word analysis will lead to either its meaning or its pronunciation. The only alternative left for resolving this impasse is the dictionary.

The skills to be learned in using a dictionary are complex and teachers should know what subskills they wish children to practice for word recognition purposes. To locate an unknown word in order to determine its pronunciation children should be able to (1) use alphabetical order and general alphabetical position; (2) use guide words; (3) identify a root word in an uninflected or derived form. Zintz (1975, p. 261) provides a helpful listing of skills that children need in order to use the dictionary effectively for pronunciation purposes. (See also Chapter 10 for a discussion of many of these dictionary skills.)

Necessary Skills for Using the Dictionary

1. Ability to use the pronunciation key at the bottom of the page.
2. Ability to use the full pronunciation key in the front of the dictionary.
3. Ability to use and interpret accent marks, both primary and secondary.
4. Ability to select the proper heteronyms, for example: *rec'ord* or *re·cord'*; *ob'ject* or *ob·ject'*.
5. Ability to identify silent letters in words pronounced.
6. Ability to recognize differences between spellings and pronunciation (lack of phoneme-grapheme relationship).
7. Ability to use phonemic respelling for pronunciation.
8. Ability to discriminate vowel sounds.
9. Ability to use diacritical marks as an aid in pronunciation.
10. Understanding of the way syllables are marked in dictionaries.
11. Ability to identify unstressed syllables in words.
12. Arriving at the pronunciation and recognizing it as correct.

This suggested list of skills places major emphasis on being able to find the pronunciation of a word by means of respellings and use of diacritical marks as interpreted by the pronunciation key at the bottom of the page in a dictionary. The performance of these skills rests on the student's ability to use previously taught phonic and word structure clues. The student must, for example, be able to identify root words and recognize their modification by inflectional endings. She also needs a knowledge of syllabication skills and the understanding of accents and the use of accent marks. Equipped with these skills, she can approach the task of learning to use pronunciation aids in the dictionary, including the use of diacritical marks and respellings, with confidence. To summarize then, using the dictionary for pronouncing a new word requires the reader to (1) be able to use dictionary respellings; (2) be able to identify roots and inflectional endings; (3) be able to identify syllables and use accent marks.

DICTIONARY RESPELLINGS

The following are some activities that might be used in working with dictionary respellings. See the teacher's manual or your dictionary for many more activities.

1. Discuss with children the key words following the symbols a, e, i, o, and u and review the sounds these symbols represent. Point out the

horizontal line (macron) over the vowel to represent its long sound. Make a chart of the key words on your chalkboard:

long ā — as in *made*
long ē — as in *me*
long ī — as in *smile*
long ō — as in *hope*
long ū — as in *mule*

Write the dictionary spellings given below and ask pupils to use their key to pronounce and spell the words that they represent.

chēz (*cheese*) pād (*paid*)
fōn (*phone*) kūt (*cute*)
rīz (*rise*) frāt (*freight*)

This technique can then be used to introduce each of the major diacritical markings used in your school dictionary.

2. Write the pronunciations given below and tell the children that five of them are pronunciations of words that name things to eat. Ask the children to correctly spell each of the edible items. (Example: mēt — *meat*)

a. mēt e. chēz i. hămlĭt
b. skwŏt f. hwāl j. shō
c. sōp g. sāləd
d. skwŏsh h. măkərōni

IDENTIFYING ROOTS AND INFLECTIONAL ENDINGS

Although this type of exercise will more than likely be review for most middle and upper grade youngsters, it is important to train them to identify the root or base word that will be found in the dictionary. Students must understand that the inflected forms of words do not ordinarily appear as first entries in the dictionary.

Exercise: What is the root word for each of the following words? Write it on the blank at the right of each word.

loneliest _____ promiscuously _____ parted _____
operating _____ haughtier _____ intensified _____

Then ask the child to identify the inflectional ending and put it in parentheses after listing the root.

Accent and Syllables

Accent is the stress given to the syllable in a word and has an important bearing on how a word is sounded. Because of this, children should learn what an accent is and how accent marks are interpreted in pronouncing words. Probably the best way to develop this skill is in an incidental way. Notice which readers accent the wrong syllable when pronouncing unfamiliar words. After the reading or discussion of a story, return to the mispronounced words to discuss the correct pronunciation and to develop certain accenting principles. Because of the nature of this skill, it is often best taught as a part of the ongoing program in the development of dictionary skills.

In a multisysllabic word, the syllable that receives the greatest stress is said to receive primary accent. Other syllables receive either secondary stress or weak stress. There are few hard and fast rules in regard to accent, but a few generalizations of high utility were isolated in a study by Winkley (1966, p. 224). They could be useful to certain children who are having difficulty in knowing where to accent a word and should probably be taught in grades four to six.

1. When there is no other clue in a two-syllable word, the accent is usually on the first syllable. Examples: *ba' sic, pro' gram.*
2. In inflected or derived forms of words, the primary accent usually falls on or within the root word. Examples: *box' es, untie'.*
3. If *de, re, be, ex, in,* or *a* is the first syllable in a word, it is usually unaccented. Examples: *debate', explain'.*
4. Two vowel letters together in the last syllable of a word may be a clue to an unaccented final syllable. Examples: *com*plain', con*ceal'.*
5. When there are two like consonants within a word, the syllable before the double consonants is usually accented. Examples: *be*gin' ner, let' ter.*
6. The primary accent usually occurs on the syllable before the suffixes *ion, ity, ic, ical, ian, ial,* or *ious,* and on the second syllable before the suffix *ate.* Examples: *affecta' tion, differen' tiate.*
7. In words of three or more syllables, one of the first two syllables is usually accented. Examples: *ac' ci*dent, de*ter' mine.*

A good way to introduce the concept of identification of syllables might be to have children orally pronounce words familiar to them and to count by clapping out the number of syllables. Their own names can be used to start: *John* (1 clap): *Bob by* (2 claps): *Lo ret ta* (3 claps); etc. They can also listen to see which syllable receives the greatest stress (or accent) when they and others pronounce it. Does it change the sound of their name if they change the place of stress (accent); i.e., Lo ret' ta; Lo' ret ta; or Lo ret ta'?

Some sample activities follow:

1. Add the accent mark after the right syllable in each word below.

but·ton	gar·den	o·mit	de·cide	blos·som
bar·rel	rai·sin	en·joy	a·gain	re·turn
bush·el	sig·nal	e·vent	ex·pect	sec·ond

2. Write each italicized word in syllables. Then mark the syllable that is accented.

   1. Colorado has *rugged mountains* with very high peaks.

   _____

   2. The *pilot* of the airliner circled the airport *again* and again.

   _____

   3. Do you *believe* that your dog can pull that big *wagon*?

   _____

3. (des'·ert) (de·sert')   Which one is a very dry area with little rain?
   (rec'·ord) (re·cord')   Which one do you play at a dance party?
   (re·fuse') (ref'·use)   Which one of these goes out as trash?
   (ob'·ject) (ob·ject')   Which one names the way some boys and girls feel about doing the dishes?

TEACHERS' MANUALS FOR DICTIONARIES

Several school dictionaries used in today's classrooms have well-developed teachers' manuals and teaching resources that facilitate the introduction and reinforcement of important dictionary skills. The *Thorndike-Barnhart Beginning, Junior,* and *Advanced* dictionaries published by Scott, Foresman and Company and the *Dictionary of Basic Words* by Childrens Press are two excellent examples.

Summary

Skill in word recognition is the result of an interactive working of sight words, phonic analysis, context clues, structural analysis, and, when needed, dictionary analysis. When a reader derives pronunciation and meaning of an unknown word from the context in which it occurs, he is making use of context clues. Because reading is primarily a process of communication, many reading authorities consider the use of these semantic and syntactic clues, in conjunction with phonic and structural analysis, to be the best word recognition techniques a reader can employ.

Structural analysis deals with the use of base or root words, prefixes and suffixes, compound words, and contractions. It requires the reader to examine the meaningful parts or units of words.

Dictionary analysis as an aid to pronunciation involves (among other skills) the use of the pronunciation key of a dictionary or glossary and phonemic respellings for the determination of the sounds of a word. Dictionary skills can be quite complicated and require much teacher guidance as well as student practice before they are thoroughly mastered.

Questions for Further Reading and Thinking

1. How may the contributions of psycholinguists change instructional procedures relative to context clues?
2. How might the steps suggested for teaching phonic elements be adapted for teaching aspects of structural analysis?
3. "The dictionary is the last resort for discovering the pronunciation of words." Why is this so?
4. How can children be motivated to use dictionaries and glossaries more effectively?
5. On what basis does a teacher decide how many dictionaries are appropriate for a given classroom?
6. Should structural analysis skills be taught in a systematic developmental sequence or as children have need for given skills?

Activities and Projects

1. Compile several activity cards for an idea file for each of the following skills: use of context clues; syllabication; teaching dictionary usage or accent; structural analysis.
2. Using the form presented in Figure 5.1, study a teachers' manual and summarize the word analysis skills listed in Activity 1.

Figure 5.1.

Your Name	Date	Title of Reading Book	Gr. Level of Text

Type of Skill	Example & Page No.	Example & Page No.

Context Clues, Structural Analysis, and Dictionary Aids to Pronunciation

Word Recognition Materials

For context clues

Context Puzzles. Glenview, Ill.: Scott, Foresman.

Context Vocabulary (Levels 4–6). Sun Valley, Calif.: Teaching Technology Corporation.

Using the Context (Levels A–F of Specific Skills Series) by Richard A. Boning. Baldwin, N.Y.: Barnell Loft.

Using Word Cues (Levels A–C of Supportive Skills Series) by Richard A. Boning. New York: Dexter and Westbrook.

For structural analysis

Activities for Reading Improvement (Levels 7–9) by Norman Schachter and John Whelan. Austin, Tex.: Steck-Vaughn.

Affixo. Washington, D.C.: Remedial Education Press.

Compound Word Game and Compound Words — Preliminary. Niles, Ill.: Developmental Learning Materials.

Diagnostic/Prescriptive Program for Word Analysis by Elizabeth C. Adamson. Indianapolis, Ind.: Bobbs-Merrill Publishing Company.

Reading Compound Words (Levels A–C of Supportive Skills Series) by Richard A. Boning. New York: Dexter and Westbrook.

Reading Skills Series: Working with Prefixes and Working with Suffixes (Grades 4–6). New York: Guidance Associates.

Student Word Set. Washington, D.C.: Wordcrafters Guild.

Syllable Game. Champaign, Ill.: Garrard Publishing Company.

Using Syllabication (Levels A–F and Advanced 1–3) by Richard A. Boning. New York: Dexter and Westbrook.

Webster Word Wheels by William Kottmeyer. New York: McGraw-Hill.

Word Analysis Practice: Intermediate Series by Donald Durrell. New York: Harcourt Brace Jovanovich.

Word Building Slide Rule. Cleveland, Ohio: E-Z Grader Company.

Word Prefixes and Word Suffixes. Buffalo: Kenworthy Publishing Company.

For dictionary aids

Dictionary of Basic Words, Day A. Perry, ed., and M. Hughes Miller, coordinator. Childrens Press.

Giant Golden Dictionary, Stuart A. Courtis and Garnette Watters, eds., six volumes. Golden Press, Inc.

The Holt Basic Dictionary of American English. Holt, Rinehart and Winston, Inc.

The Holt Intermediate Dictionary of American English. Holt, Rinehart and Winston, Inc.

Illustrated Golden Dictionary for Young Readers, Stuart A. Courtis and Garnette Watters, eds., rev. ed. Golden Press, Inc.

Thorndike-Barnhart Beginning Dictionary, Edward L. Thorndike and Clarence L. Barnhart, eds. Scott, Foresman.

Thorndike-Barnhart Junior Dictionary, Edward L. Thorndike and Clarence L. Barnhart, eds. Scott, Foresman.

Webster's A Dictionary for Boys and Girls, a Merriam-Webster book (American Book Company).

Webster's Elementary Dictionary, a Merriam-Webster book (American Book Company).

The Winston Dictionary for Schools, Thomas K. Brown and William D. Lewis, eds. Holt, Rinehart and Winston, Inc.

Word Wonder Dictionary, Doris Whitman and Lewis Parker. Holt, Rinehart and Winston, Inc.

The World Book Dictionary, Clarence Barnhart, ed. 2 volumes. Field Enterprises Educational Corporation.

Part Three

GETTING
MEANING

Among the major goals of reading instruction in elementary schools today is the development in learners of these abilities: *to understand* concepts presented in print; *to think* about the material read; *to use* that which is read for relevant purposes. Reading for meaning should occur from the onset of instruction, and reading instruction should occur at all times during the school day when the print medium is being utilized. Thus a major portion of this text (six chapters) is devoted to the challenge in reading instruction of helping a child learn how to derive meaning from what he reads.

   Part Three begins with a discussion of the development of a knowledge of word meanings, which is crucial to comprehending printed materials. Other chapters take up the development of basic comprehension skills, the development of inferential, critical, and creative reading abilities, and the use of reading to learn specific subject matter through effective processing of content area texts. A highlight of Part Three is a chapter on the use of effective questioning techniques in probing for greater meaning.

J. Estill Alexander

6
Developing a Meaning Vocabulary

The acquisition of word meanings is basic to comprehension. Words are labels for concepts. Recall from Chapter 1 that concepts were defined as classes of stimuli that have common characteristics, and, as stated by Johnson and Pearson (1978, p. 34), are meanings associated with words as they occur in speech or print.

The relationship between a good vocabulary and success in reading has been strongly suggested in research and in theoretical positions of reading authorities. Davis (1968), for example, found that the factor that correlated most highly with comprehension was a knowledge of word meanings. Manzo and Sherk (1971–72, p. 78) have stated that "vocabulary is central to formation, acculturation, articulation, and apparently *all* learning." The size of a learner's vocabulary as he enters school correlates well with success in school (Ames 1964) and is probably the best single index for predicting achievement in reading.

In developing a meaning vocabulary it is important for teachers to understand how concepts are related to the labels that represent them; how such concepts and labels can be assessed; and how to develop or extend a meaning vocabulary. These topics will be discussed in this chapter. The importance of first-hand experiences, of direct instruction, and of incidental learning will be featured.

How Meaning Vocabularies Are Developed

QUESTIONS TO GUIDE READING

Literal
How are concepts organized?

Inferential
What is the best way to develop concepts?

Since words are labels for concepts, it is important that teachers understand something of the organization of concepts. A useful way to describe the organization of concepts is in terms of class relations, example relations, and property relations (Johnson and Pearson, 1978, pp. 32–37). Knowledge of these relationships is useful for teachers in considering ways to develop or enrich vocabulary. In the discussion that follows, concrete nouns are used for illustrative purposes. Concepts relative to concrete objects are easiest to teach since their class, example, and property relationships are easiest for children to learn. Concepts are, of course, built that are more abstract (such as *love*, *happiness*, and *anger*). Additionally, concepts (schemata) may be related to each other and indeed may organize whole experiences. "Going to a basketball game" is an example of such a total experience.

Class relations refers to a group of things (such as dogs) that have recognizable characteristics or properties (see Chapter 1). An *example* refers to particular individuals (Jane's dog Spot) or groups (Chihuahua) within the class. Chihuahuas are members of the larger class *dogs*. Spot is an individual member of the class *dogs* and may or may not be a member of the group *Chihuahua* depending on the kind of dog he is (what properties he has). *Property relations* are attributes or characteristics of the concept. For example, the class *dogs* generally has such attributes or characteristics as four legs, tails, ability to bark, and hair. Property relationships interact with class relationships. That is, if Spot (an example) is a dog, then Spot probably has four legs, hair, and barks.

From experience, relationships among classes, examples, and properties are developed. These relationships are the concepts that individuals have about reality. Such relationships may be rich or they may be incomplete, imprecise, or even inappropriate. It is the teacher's responsibility to help learners develop relationships to facilitate the formation of concepts and to help them attach appropriate labels to these concepts. In developing concepts, there is no adequate substitute for first-hand experiences (discussed in the next section). If such direct experiences are not possible, direct teaching through the provision of vicarious experience and of opportunities for incidential learning becomes necessary.

FIRST-HAND EXPERIENCES

The basis for early vocabulary development is first-hand experiences — visual, tactile, auditory, and psychomotor. Innate capacity sets limits to vocabulary development but does not mean that children with below-average abilities (slower learners) will be unable to develop an adequate meaning vocabulary for many school tasks. A child with slightly below-average ability who has grown up in an environment in which there is good verbal interaction is likely to have a larger meaning vocabulary than a child with slightly above-average ability who has not had stimulating verbal interaction.

The environment in which children live and learn impinges on the teacher's efforts in vocabulary development. For example, children spend many hours of linguistic activity in the home and in play activities with peers. If this environment projects an attitude unfavorable to the use of words other than those of its own linguistic community, the teacher will find it difficult to promote vocabulary growth because a word really becomes internalized only through use.

Some learners may hold concepts for which the labels are unique to their linguistic or cultural setting (Ching 1976, p. 15). For example, until recent years the attribute of machismo would have been one that only the Spanish-speaking school child could have understood. In some situations, labels are common words that carry unique meanings in the minority setting, thus causing confusion. For example, "the Man" had until recently a unique meaning for the Black community.

DIRECT TEACHING

Time does not permit us to learn all concepts and words through first-hand experience, so teachers must include in their programs the direct teaching of many words and concepts. Direct teaching is more fruitful in vocabulary development than incidental learning is (Gray and Holmes 1938). Several strategies for direct teaching have been found effective. These will be discussed in a later section of this chapter. The importance of practice or reinforcement will also be discussed.

INCIDENTAL LEARNING

Incidental learning plays an important role in vocabulary development though it is not as fruitful as first-hand experiences or direct teaching. It is through wide reading in relatively easy material (one form of incidental learning) that students meet words in many contexts with different shades of meaning; thus an opportunity is presented to refine the precision with which they can select and use words. Provision for wide reading in areas of student interest (possibly through Sustained Silent Reading, discussed later) is a vital aspect of a good vocabulary development program. Silent reading, according to Manzo and Sherk (1971–72, p. 84), facilitates greater vocabulary growth than does oral reading in the classroom or being read to by either the teacher or another student.

Assessing Vocabulary

QUESTIONS TO GUIDE READING

Literal
How may a teacher assess conceptual knowledge?
How may a teacher assess specific word knowledge?

Inferential
Why should the ways vocabulary are assessed be similar to those used in the instructional process?

Evaluative
What assessment techniques seem most appropriate for the age/grade level you are teaching or plan to teach?
Which is more appropriate for assessing vocabulary — a criterion-referenced test or a norm-referenced test?

Teachers should know whether students have an adequate store of concepts (and their appropriate labels) in order to handle the materials available for use in the instructional program. It is important to distinguish between concepts and labels since the instructional task for the teacher will differ depending on which is the deficiency. When conceptual background is lacking, the teacher will need to provide the experiences necessary for the development of the concept — the class, example, and property relationships. When the student lacks an appropriate label, or word, the teacher's task is simpler. Teachers then teach the new label, relating it to the concepts or schemata already present in the learner.

ASSESSING CONCEPTUAL KNOWLEDGE

Bader (1980, pp. 99–101) states that conceptual knowledge can be assessed through interviews, observations, and informal tests. She suggests that the criterion in each type is a comparison of a given student with other students at his age/placement level. An additional criterion would be the concepts needed for reading the printed material planned for use in the instructional program.

In constructing an informal concept test, the teacher would assemble a series of statements based on the instructional materials involving concepts that would be necessary for adequate understanding of those materials. With individual children then, through discussion of these statements, the teacher could determine whether that student's level of conceptual development was adequate for handling the material. For example, a statement might be: "The farmer stored his combine in the barn." The teacher could ask "What does this statement mean to you?" The assessment may be made in a group setting when students are at an age/grade/ability level that enables them to write responses. Then the teacher may prepare a series of statements on a ditto sheet, with students responding underneath given statements.

ASSESSING LABELS (WORDS)

Informal tests of students' knowledge of the labels (specific words) needed for understanding a particular text can be assessed in several ways. The teacher first identifies, from instructional materials planned for use, those words necessary for comprehension or successful learning, and then develops a technique for ascertaining whether students know the meanings needed.

For best results, the assessment format for tests should be similar to that used in regular classroom instruction; that is, do you usually check word knowledge by asking the students to use words in sentences, to define them in isolation, or to fill in blanks? In addition to constructing tests according to one of the ways mentioned above the teacher may construct a synonym test (see page 130) or a maze test (see page 133). An Informal Reading Inventory (IRI) taken from materials in current use also samples vocabulary. The number of words sampled is generally small however (see Chapter 17).

In evaluating responses, remember that young children tend to give more concrete definitions, whereas older children tend to give synonyms or to classify words in a given category. Responses should be interpreted relative to the context of the test. Although a child may recognize a word in the context of the test or be able to select the appropriate response in a multiple-choice format, he may have difficulty in other contexts or formats.

General word knowledge can be assessed through norm-referenced or criterion-referenced tests. There are strengths and limitations to the use of these tests. Norm-referenced tests may be used to measure overall vocabulary development as compared to a norm group. The words sampled on such tests, however, are limited in number and may not realistically assess the child's usable vocabulary. In addition such tests may not assess specific words needed in the curriculum. Criterion-referenced tests are designed to assess mastery of general vocabulary needed at a given level. They too may not assess specific words needed for success in a given program. See Chapter 17 for a discussion of norm- and criterion-referenced tests.

Planned Instructional Procedures

QUESTIONS TO GUIDE READING

Literal
What are five teacher behaviors that provide a good model for children?
What are three ways first-hand experiences can be used to develop vocabulary?
What are three points in each vocabulary lesson at which discussion of word meanings is important?
What are ten ways of direct word study?
What are three ways that word study can be individualized?
What steps may a child follow in unlocking word meanings?

Inferential
What does a teacher's attitude toward word study have to do with children's attitudes?
What factors affect the expansion of listening and speaking vocabularies?
How does a semantic feature analysis help students develop or refine concepts?

Evaluative
Why is direct teaching of word meanings crucial?
Why is the SSR plan generally effective?

Planned experiences are generally necessary for adequate vocabulary growth. In this section we shall consider ways that meaning vocabularies may be developed.

THE TEACHER AS A MODEL

The importance of a good teacher model cannot be underestimated in vocabulary building. The teacher's attitude toward and interest in words is frequently "caught" rather than "taught." How can the teacher provide a good model? By exhibiting the following behaviors:

1. Genuinely enjoy words and word study yourself. Set an example by using a word new to students to explain a concept, or use a new word to explain something familiar to students.
2. Read to children and let the students see you reading and working crossword puzzles.
3. Use bulletin board displays to emphasize new or interesting words. These may be puns, plays on words in advertising, or words from cartoons and comic strips, for example.
4. Use dictionaries and reference books to look up words the children need for classroom activities, but don't yet know.
5. Provide a time when all class members can read without interruption.

Developing Listening and Speaking Vocabularies

The building of a listening and speaking vocabulary prior to, or in conjunction with, learning to read is crucial because these vocabularies provide a base on which to build a reading vocabulary. How does a teacher develop adequate listening and speaking vocabularies? In general, those vocabularies expand in a school environment in which there is much opportunity for experiences with language. Durkin (1978, pp. 379–385) suggests the following specific ways:

1. Teacher use of important words in conversation and discussion.
2. Experiences in which children express themselves through discussion, conversation, role playing, and dramatics.
3. Many opportunities for media to provide vicarious experiences.
4. Reading aloud to children.

Providing Experiences

First-hand experiences are best for developing concepts and words associated with them. The more experiences a child has relative to a concept, the greater his depth of understanding and the more precise his use of words. First-hand experiences that develop vocabulary may be provided both in school and out of school.

Examples of appropriate experiences include planned out-of-school trips that provide first-hand experiences chosen to promote vocabulary development; opportunities in school for manipulating toys, simple tools, and equipment in the early school years; role playing in social studies classes; and in-school demonstrations and laboratory work in later school years in areas such as math and science.

Both in-school and out-of-school experiences should be planned if they are to be maximally effective. Such experience should include the following three opportunities for discussion in which children actually use the words being studied:

1. Discussion prior to the experience, using key vocabulary items to be developed or refined through the experience.
2. Discussion during the experience, in which children have an opportunity to use the new words as they observe, listen, and learn.
3. Discussion after the experience to solidify learnings.

It is impossible to develop vocabulary through the use of first-hand experiences only; to save time, many concepts must be developed vicariously. Media such as books, films, slides, tapes, records, pictures, and TV are all important sources of vicarious experiences. The teacher should provide opportunities for discussion of key words before, during, and immediately after the planned vicarious experience.

After both real and vicarious experiences, there should be opportunities for later use of the words learned, because words are seldom really learned from one instructional session. Ways to provide for opportunities for later use include discussion, reports, and creative dramatics.

WIDE READING

One of the most effective ways to develop a meaning vocabulary is to read widely in varied, suitable, and interesting materials. Through wide reading the student meets words in varying contexts and develops new associations with words, thereby forming for himself more precise definitions than he would be likely to learn through drill exercises. An awareness of differing connotations and shades of meaning can also emerge from wide reading.

Although wide reading is an effective way to develop a meaning vocabulary, it does not solve all the difficulties of acquiring new words or provide the only route to vocabulary growth. Students in greatest need of vocabulary development often do not read widely. These students may lack adequate concepts, reading skills, mental abilities, or good attitudes toward reading. It is important that these children receive direct instruction and that the problems interfering with wide reading be corrected as soon as possible.

Many students will not read widely without proper encouragement, adequate opportunity, and the provision of appropriate materials. It is difficult, if not impossible, to get all students to read widely. An effective way to encourage wide reading, however, is to provide an environment in which wide reading is a valued activity and in which students are rewarded for the experience. The following suggestions may be helpful:

1. A wide selection of books should be available — on both the interest levels and independent reading levels of the children.
2. Opportunities should be provided for children to share or discuss books. It is more effective to do this on a voluntary basis because routine book reports tend to lead to boredom and negative attitudes.
3. A time should be set aside that gives each child an opportunity to read to himself.

A useful plan for ensuring that all students have an opportunity to read — designated as Uninterrupted Sustained Silent Reading (USSR) — was suggested in the 1960s by Lyman C. Hunt, Jr. This plan, now known as Sustained Silent Reading (SSR), is used in many schools throughout the United States.

The SSR plan provides a regularly scheduled time during which all persons in the classroom (including the teacher) or in the whole school (including the principal and custodian) read. Robert A. McCracken (1971, pp. 521–522) has suggested some rules for initiating SSR. He feels that these rules should be followed rigidly until the habit of reading during SSR periods is established.

McCracken's Rules for Initiating SSR

1. Each student must read silently.
2. The teacher reads, and permits no interruption of his reading.
3. Each student selects a single book (or magazine or newspaper).
4. A timer is used, to prevent clockwatching.
5. There are absolutely no reports or records of any kind.

6. Begin with whole classes or large groups of students heterogeneously grouped.

Source: Robert A. McCracken, "Initiating Sustained Silent Reading," *Journal of Reading* 14 (May 1971): 521–522. Reprinted with permission of Robert A. McCracken and The International Reading Association.

McCracken's rules need to be modified for beginning readers since they may lack the skills needed for independent reading. Teachers may need to work with small groups of six or seven providing guidance and assistance with word recognition, answers to children's questions, and general help when requested (Hong 1981).

A variety of activities is important for motivation in SSR as in all other areas of reading instruction. Gambrell (1978) suggests that interest and motivation may be kept high in the following ways:

1. developing a "Book Sharing Bulletin Board" so that students can "advertise" the books they particularly like.
2. creating a comfortable "Reading Corner" with pillows and rugs, and artwork based on the books read.
3. giving choices relative to place for SSR, such as the classroom or library (or perhaps outside under a tree)
4. inviting parents and others to share in the period occasionally.
5. talking with students about what you (the teacher) have read.

DIRECT METHODS OF INSTRUCTION

Realistically, it is most beneficial to teach directly those words which are crucial to the successful comprehension of assigned materials. These words might include:

1. core vocabulary words in basal readers.
2. special words essential for understanding content area materials.
3. words in assigned reading materials that cannot be unlocked through context.

"Crucial words" will vary from one child to another. Thus, in addition to group instruction, individualized word study is frequently appropriate. Teaching large groups of words from master lists to all pupils is generally a waste of both teacher time and pupil effort: for almost every child there would be some words from master lists that are inappropriate, already known, or not needed. The child learns best those words he needs to know and wants to learn.

Explanation and discussion. One method of direct instruction is explanation and discussion. Typically, the teacher chooses the words to be explained and discussed from suggestions in teachers' manuals for basal readers and content area texts. In addition, she should include words from assigned materials that her students may not know.

One appropriate way to introduce the new words is to write them on the chalkboard in sentences. The sentences should provide a contextual setting that is familiar to students and that provides clues to a meaning or meanings that will be needed for understanding the material to be read. The students should then discuss the words so that any meanings not fully understood can be clarified (Gipe 1980).

The teacher should realize when using this method that learning may be *superficial*. The child may learn a single meaning that may not fit other contexts. It is often helpful, therefore, to explore other common meanings of the words being studied as the discussion proceeds.

Semantic feature analysis for synonyms and antonyms. Concepts were discussed earlier in terms of class, example, and property relationships. A semantic feature analysis based on these relationships is effective as a way of developing vocabulary. Such an analysis is particularly helpful in developing synonyms and antonyms. In such analyses it is important for children to understand that an "identical synonym" is not possible. Each word is unique, and a word that is called a synonym is a word that is "something like" the other word.

A semantic feature procedure suggested to Johnson and Pearson (1978, pp. 39–41) is as follows:[1]

1. Begin with a list of known words that have some features in common. For example: type of conveyances such as bicycle, motorcycle, car, and skateboard.
2. Have students suggest features that at least one of the words possesses. For example: two wheels, four wheels, etc.
3. Prepare a matrix on paper or the chalkboard, listing the features across the top of the matrix.
4. Have students fill in the matrix with pluses or minuses as appropriate beside each word under each feature as appropriate (see Table 6.1).
5. Through discussion ask children to suggest more words that share the same features; then ask them to suggest additional features that are shared by two or more of the words.
6. Inductively, help students discover that no two words are identical on all features. Even if such a situation does occur at this stage, the addition of more features (class, property, or example) will likely result in a feature difference.

It is probably best to begin synonym study with categories of concrete words — such as plants, food, pets, or clothing — that are within the experience of the students. More abstract categories such as feelings, shapes, or entertainment can be added later (Johnson and Pearson 1978, p. 40).

Table 6.1. Semantic Feature Analysis for Means of Transportation

	2 Wheel	4 Wheel	Motor	Passengers	Enclosed	Handlebars	Rubber tires
Bicycle	+	−	−	+	−	+	+
Motorcycle	+	−	+	+	−	+	+
Car	−	+	+	+	+	−	+
Skateboard	−	+	−	−	−	−	−

1. Adapted from pages 39–41 of *Teaching Reading Vocabulary* by Dale D. Johnson and P. David Pearson. Copyright © 1978 by Holt, Rinehart and Winston. Reprinted by permission of Holt, Rinehart and Winston, CBS College Publishing.

After students become familiar with the procedure, it is appropriate to have children develop lists of words that have meanings or features opposite those of the words being studied — thus beginning a study of antonyms. Pearson and Johnson (1978, pp. 55–58) state that there are probably true antonyms; that is, words that are opposite in meaning. There are many kinds of "opposition." Teachers need to be aware of these when constructing exercises that deal with opposition. Three types are probably true opposites: contradiction (alive, dead), contrary (white, black), and reversal (stop, go). A fourth category that Pearson and Johnson label as "counterparts" includes relative pairs in which one term implies another, such as parent-child; words that are alike except in one aspect, such as brother-sister; and reciprocal (one attacks, one defends). A fifth category is contrasted terms (words that do not clash as do contradictory or contrary terms). Examples are: night-day and begin-end. All categories should be included in instructional programs. At beginning levels, teachers may not communicate these specific categories to students. At upper levels with the better students, exercises may be developed with specific antonym types (Pearson and Johnson, 1978, pp. 55–58).

There are many types of appropriate reinforcement exercises a teacher can prepare once the learner knows what synonyms and antonyms are. The following three suggestions may be helpful in devising such exercises.

1. List words in columns and ask children to match words having the same or similar meanings. For example:

1. finish	4	a.	sure
2. creek	1	b.	conclude
3. supply	3	c.	furnish
4. certain	2	d.	stream

Similar exercises may be constructed for reinforcement work with antonyms.

1. sad	2	a.	hot
2. cold	3	b.	big
3. little	4	c.	hard
4. soft	1	d.	happy

2. A variation of the first exercise involves supplying a set of possible synonyms or antonyms for a given word. The child then selects the word most appropriate. It is desirable that the child be able to defend his choice through discussion of the meanings of the correct and the incorrect responses. For example:

Choose a synonym: Pretty (beautiful, ugly, happy)
Choose an antonym: Long (short, big, hard)

3. Children may learn to state ideas in different ways through the use of synonyms. The teacher may select some common, overworked words and then use discussion to develop other ways of stating the same ideas. For example, there are a variety of ways to deal with the concept of *said*.

John *said* that he was going home.
John *stated* that he was going home.

After the children learn some synonyms, they should be encouraged to find instances of them in their reading materials.

Classification. One of the most effective ways to extend vocabulary growth is to help children categorize and differentiate words. Such categorization involves feature analysis (discussed above) since it deals with class relationships. By helping children categorize and classify, one aids them in developing schemata for future use in extending and refining word meanings. It also helps them learn where the new concept "fits" in relationship to what they already know. Children can begin early in the primary grades classifying concrete words that share one feature. As the child progresses more features and/or abstract categories may be added. Children of lower ability will progress more slowly, of course.

Pearson and Johnson (1978, pp. 62–63) state that classification activities are among the most helpful a teacher can develop to improve vocabulary and that such activities can be used at any developmental level. They suggest the following:[2]

1. Begin as early as kindergarten asking children to categorize pictures that belong to a single class, such as food or pets.
2. Then reverse the procedure and ask children to name the category when pictures that are related are shown in a display.
3. Ask children to put pictures into two categories.
4. Repeat steps 1, 2, and 3 with words when children have learned to read words. Use only clear, common categories (foods, pets, etc.) until about third grade.
5. Then begin categorizing by attributes (things that have hair, things that fly, for example).
6. Then add categories that are not mutually exclusive (that is, words that can fit into more than one category under consideration, such as *meat* and *food*).

Analogies. When children understand something of synonyms and antonyms, instruction in analogies becomes appropriate. Such instruction

2. From pages 62–63 of *Teaching Reading Comprehension* by P. David Pearson and Dale D. Johnson. Copyright © 1978 by Holt, Rinehart and Winston. Reprinted by permission of Holt, Rinehart and Winston, CBS College Publishing.

helps students think about words and relationships because problem solving is involved. The activities also help learners cope with aptitude tests. An analogy is an abbreviated form of a sentence (Ignoffo 1980). For example, *lead : pencil :: ink : pen* can be read as "A pencil uses lead to write and a pen uses ink." This is an example of a part-to-whole analogy. Other types that may be used with elementary students are (Ignoffo 1980, p. 521):

refrigerator : cold :: oven : hot   (object and function)
car : metal :: book : paper   (object and its composition)
mechanic : pliers :: sculptor : chisel   (craftsman and tool)
stream : river :: sea : ocean   (size or degree)
ice cream : olive :: sweet : sour   (opposite in sensation)
water : cup :: picture : frame   (object function)
quart : gallon :: quarter : dollar   (proportions of measure)
dog : fish :: lungs : gills   (characteristics)

Teachers can introduce types of analogies through discussion of the relationships involved. In beginning lessons, it is best to focus on only one type of relationship. Analogies should be written in sentence form and then rewritten in analogy format. Students can practice developing analogies by writing their own in sentence form and then rewriting them in analogy format.

An appropriate activity to introduce early in showing relationships is the establishment of lists of word pairs that are analogous in some way and may be sorted in one to two categories. For example:

Animals	Food eaten
cat	tuna
dog	hamburger
bird	seeds
squirrel	nuts
horse	grass

Later, more complex relationships and a broader range of categories may be used.

Context clues. Context clues as an aid to word recognition were discussed in Chapter 5. The use of context clues is also an effective technique in unlocking meanings of unknown words. Hafner (1965) found that children attained higher levels of reading comprehension when they received planned instruction in using context to build meaning than when they had received no such instruction.

When the context *will help* clarify the meaning of a word, the teacher may encourage the child to read to the end of the sentence or passage and then attempt to determine the meaning. But children should not be asked to "read on" when there are no clues available; to do so encourages guessing of word meanings. When there are no clues available, it is more appropriate for the teacher to supply the meaning or to suggest that the child use the dictionary (if the child possesses appropriate dictionary skills.) Many times, especially in content area texts, context alone will not help determine meaning.

Constance M. McCullough (1958) has identified types of context clues that may be effective in unlocking meaning. These types, discussed in Chapter 5, are: definition, experience, comparison and contrast, synonym, familiar expression, summary, and mood or situation. When one of these clues is appropriate for unlocking an unknown word, the teacher should explain the type of clue and encourage the child to use that clue to determine the meaning.

Children who have difficulty using a given type of clue need additional help with that clue type. The teacher may construct exercises (sentences or short paragraphs) that utilize the clue with which the child is having difficulty. These exercises are more effective when the child discusses with the teacher the word meaning he has derived from the context. In this way, the teacher can help the child understand better how the clue type functions.

Another type of exercise (utilizing cloze procedure) involves deleting words and replacing them with blank spaces or lines. Refer back to page 102 for a hierarchy of instructional activities involving the use of contextual deletions. A third technique, known as maze procedure, may also be useful. Although Guthrie and others (1974, pp. 161–168) presented the maze procedure as an assessment tool, we feel it is helpful in teaching the use of context clues. In this procedure, series of sentences from a given text are modified by having alternatives supplied for given words in the sentence. For example:

> begin
> John played ball   after school.
> roads

The alternatives supplied should include the word originally used by the author, a semantically incorrect word that is the same part of speech, and an incorrect word that is a different part of speech. In constructing maze exercises, it is important to insert the correct word randomly among the three possibilities and to select distractors at approximately the same level of difficulty as the omitted word.

Exercises designed on the maze format provide the teacher with an opportunity to work with both semantic and syntactic clues.[3] Discussions

3. The teacher may find additional specific help in *Using the Context, Levels A–F* of the Specific Skills Series (see the materials cited at the end of Chapter 7).

of reasons for correct choices should be a part of the instructional procedure. (See Chapter 5 for more examples.)

Two cautions seem appropriate when considering asking children to use context to unlock meanings. First, a single contact with a word in context will help the child with that meaning only. Second, this approach may encourage word guessing. Guessing is particularly undesirable in content areas because the highly technical meanings of many content words could be misunderstood. It is often helpful to explore other common meanings of the words under study as the explanation and discussion goes along.

Prefixes, suffixes, and roots. Knowledge of the most common prefixes, suffixes, and roots will assist children in unlocking many new words. For lists of commonly taught prefixes and suffixes, see Chapter 5. In addition, James I. Brown (1966) has identified the fourteen roots that account for 10,000 words in a typical desk dictionary and for 100,000 words in an unabridged dictionary. A knowledge of these roots is especially helpful for gifted intermediate students. The roots are given in Table 6.2.

The meaning of prefixes, suffixes, and roots may be taught deductively or inductively. Generally, the inductive approach appears to be superior. A sample inductive lesson for prefixes follows.[4] Similar lessons may be prepared for suffixes or roots.

Table 6.2. The Fourteen Words that Make All the Difference

Root	Its other spelling	Its meaning
tain	ten, tin	to have or hold
mitt	miss, mis, mit	to send
cept	cap, capt, ceiv, ceit, cip	to take or seize
fer	lat, lay	to bear or carry
sist	sta	to stand, endure or persist
graph	—	to write
log	ology	speech or science
spect	spec, spi, spy	to look
plic	play, plex, ply	to fold, bend, twist or interweave
tend	tens, tent	to stretch
duct	duc, duit, duk	to lead, make, shape or fashion
pos	pound, pon, post	to put or place
fic	fac, fact, fash, feat	to make or do
scribe	scrip, scriv	to write

Source: James I. Brown, "Reading Improvement Through Vocabulary Development, the CPD Formula," in *New Frontiers in College-Adult Reading,* ed. George Schick and Merrill May (Milwaukee: The National Reading Conference, 1966), pages 197–202. Reprinted by permission. Copyright © 1966, American Educational Research Association, Washington, D.C.

4. Based on unpublished materials prepared by Dr. Wallace Z. Ramsey of the University of Missouri at Saint Louis. Reprinted with his permission.

Step 1: Decide what prefix you want to teach.
　　　　Example: Prefix "un" meaning "not"
Step 2: List on the chalkboard some words for which students know the meaning and to which the prefix may be added.
　　　　Example: *wanted*
　　　　　　　　able
　　　　　　　　armed (verb)
Step 3: Discuss the meaning of each word. Let the students supply the meanings by making up sentences using each of the words or by directly defining the words.
Step 4: Add the prefix to each of the words in the list in Step 2.
　　　　unwanted　unable　unarmed
Step 5: Discuss the new meaning of the words. Follow the procedure in Step 3.
Step 6: Ask the students to define the prefix.
Step 7: Ask the students to supply other words in which the prefix is used.

Because of instructional time constraints, it may not be possible to teach all prefixes, suffixes, and roots inductively. In general, it seems preferable to begin instruction in this area using the inductive approach in order that students understand how these items function in English. After children have this understanding, other items may be taught deductively. In the deductive approach, the teacher supplies the meaning of the item, then students find examples to illustrate the meaning.

Reinforcement activities may often be needed to fix learning. Two examples of exercises designed for this purpose follow:

1. Ask children to substitute a phrase for a word containing a prefix or a suffix. For example, "The man was *un*able to climb the tree" may be restated as "The man was *not* able to climb the tree." The activity may also be reversed, with the child being asked to change a phrase into a single word utilizing a prefix or a suffix. For example, "I *read* the story *again* to my little sister because she liked it so much" may be restated as "I *reread* the story to my little sister because she liked it so much."

2. Children can "build" words from roots by adding prefixes and suffixes. For example, the teacher puts a prefix or a suffix on the chalkboard. The children may then suggest root words to which the prefix or suffix can be added to build a new word. The child who supplies a root word should be able to demonstrate that he is able to use both words correctly in some contextual situation. Examples are:

Prefix *dis-*	Suffix　*-ness*
agree	sweet
grace	blunt
place	sick
like	glad
arm	weak

Dictionary use. The development of the skills necessary for pronouncing words in dictionaries was treated in Chapter 5. The focus here is on the use of the dictionary as it relates to the development of a meaning vocabulary. Chapter 10 provides added information on the use of the dictionary as a study skills aid.

It is essential that students learn that the choice of a definition depends on the context of the material from which the word is taken. Too often a student who looks up a word meaning will look for the first or shortest definition. Exercises that encourage this practice, such as having children look up long lists of words, should be avoided.

It is helpful to work with small groups of children in developing the ability to select an appropriate meaning. Such group instruction facilitates discussion and comparisons of responses. Each student can select for an unknown word a meaning he feels best fits the context. The students can compare their selections, then select the most suitable definition through discussion. In this way, it is possible for a student to learn why he made a correct or incorrect response.

Homonyms. Homonyms are words that are pronounced the same but which have spellings and meanings that are different. Some examples are *mail* and *male*, *to* and *two*, and *made* and *maid*.

Since homonyms sound the same, it is essential that children see the difference in the written words. Thus, instruction should include provision for the child to see the word pairs in written meaning contexts. For example:

The dog is a *male.*
I received a letter in the *mail* today.

Discussion of the words in other sentence contexts should follow the initial example.

Study of multiple meanings. Many of the most frequently used words in English have multiple, and often quite diverse, meanings. One effective way to make children cognizant of a word's multiple meanings is to discuss other common meanings of words as they occur in reading assignments.

In addition, special exercises that give the child an opportunity to demonstrate his knowledge of multiple meanings may be useful. One type of exercise involves selecting a common word that has several different meanings (for example, *rise, drop, quick, sharp*). Use this word in sentences in which the context provides a clue to the meaning. Ask the children to define each word. You may also ask them to verify their definition by checking the dictionary (assuming dictionary skills are known, of course). Some examples follow:

1. It will break if you *drop* it.
2. Gum *drops* and jelly beans may hurt your teeth.
3. When the sun sets, the temperature *drops* rapidly.
4. Use eye *drops* and don't wear your glasses.

Study of word histories. An effective way to interest many students in words is to study the ways word meanings have evolved or changed. Word history study is appropriate for all ability levels, but is especially appropriate and challenging for the gifted.

In the teaching of word meaning changes, three stages seem appropriate. First, the teacher may begin with the origin of surnames (Warren 1960). Students may have fun tracing the meaning of the surnames of friends and classmates. For example, some surnames represent objects, such as *Ball* and *Bell*; others are derived from characteristics, such as *Fair* and *Good*; others represent occupations, such as *Smith* and *Taylor,* and still others relate to animals, such as *Beaver, Bull,* and *Bird.*

Dechant (1970, p. 396) suggests that the second stage of instruction could involve the study of the foreign origin of words — such as *camouflage, sombrero, pagoda,* and *pizza.* During the third stage, the teacher may deal with the ways words change in meaning through time (Alexander and Burns 1974). The following types of meaning change are appropriate for intermediate grade children: elevation and degeneration, widening and narrowing, hyperbole and litotes, euphemism, and shifts in association. Understanding how word meanings come to be is often the stimulus needed to trigger an interesting word study project.[5] The study of slang words serves as a good beginning.

Word history activities seem less like an assignment if they are placed on individual activity cards and located in interest or learning centers. Activity cards are very appropriate for use with word histories (as with many other activities in this chapter). Figure 6.1 is an example of an activity card for such a center which illustrates elevation and degeneration.

Figurative language. Children need to be able to understand the figurative use of language they meet in reading materials. Our language is rich with such items. Suggestions for teaching figures of speech are found in Chapter 8.

INDIVIDUALIZING WORD STUDY PROJECTS

Individualized word study projects are effective ways to promote vocabulary growth for many students. Individualized word study may take many forms. Three suggestions follow.

5. For a list of sources for obtaining word histories see "Words and Their Changing Ways" by J. Estill Alexander and Paul C. Burns, *Elementary English,* (April 1974), pp. 477–481.

Figure 6.1. Activity card.

Elevation and Degeneration

Which words have "better" meanings today than in earlier times? Which have "poorer" meanings?

nice	*villain*
silly	*lady*
parson	*marshall*

Meaning banks. Words with specialized meanings are often associated with hobbies and special content area units. An individual student may have an interest in a special area and may be interested in words associated with that area. He may collect words that interest him and form a "meaning bank." The meaning bank is a set of 3″ × 5″ or 4″ × 6″ cards with one word written on each card. On the back of each card a definition (definitions) applicable to the interest area is written. The cards are filed alphabetically in a file box, or bank. The owner of the bank may become the resource person to supply words and word meaning to other members of the class when they need a word or word meaning related to the area.

Notebooks and pupil-made dictionaries. As an individual project, notebooks and pupil-made dictionaries are effective when the student is interested in the activity. But if this traditional activity is required of all students, it tends to be busywork and is of little value in promoting vocabulary growth.

Crossword puzzles. One interesting way to stimulate vocabulary growth at the upper elementary levels is to have students prepare crossword puzzles for other students to solve. These puzzles may deal with a specific topic or they may be general in nature. Both the puzzle builder and the puzzle worker profit.

PROVIDING PRACTICE

Since children tend to forget much of what they have been taught, opportunities to practice using or meeting the words introduced must be provided. Practice should follow soon after the initial introduction and again later as often as needed to fix learnings. The following suggestions may be helpful:

1. Provide practice in situations that are meaningful in the school day or in the child's life. One way to do this is to provide many opportunities to use the words in discussion in class.
2. Provide opportunities for the student to meet the words learned through wide reading in easy materials that contain the words studied.
3. Use practice exercises that are carefully and clearly constructed. Such exercises provide the opportunity to distribute practice over time. Page 130 contains samples of such activities for synonyms and antonyms. Crossword puzzles are also examples of effective practice experiences.
4. Construct or secure games that children enjoy playing. Games provide excellent opportunities for practice and are generally motivating to children. Examples include modification card games such as Bingo, Concentration, and Old Maid.

A SYSTEMS APPROACH FOR UNLOCKING WORD MEANINGS

It is important that a learner use the meaning-getting aids available to him in the most efficient manner possible. In unlocking unknown word meanings, a student may find the following steps helpful:

Step 1: Read on to the end of the sentence or paragraph. Is a context clue available to provide the needed meaning?
Step 2: If context does not supply the meaning, try breaking the word down into its smallest meaning units. Does a knowledge of prefixes, roots, or suffixes provide the meaning?
Step 3: If context or a knowledge of word parts does not supply the meaning, consult a dictionary (if needed dictionary skills are known) or ask the teacher or another student.

Summary

A knowledge of word meanings is dependent on the schemata present in the cognitive structures and is essential for effective communication. Teachers should not assume that students will develop an adequate meaning vocabulary from maturation and incidental learning. It is necessary to provide direct instruction, especially for the slow learner and for a child from an environment that is linguistically different from that which facilitates easy learning in school.

Children learn vocabulary through three primary processes: first-hand experiences, direct teaching, and incidental learning. First-hand experiences and wide reading are basic sources of concept development and word knowledge and should receive strong and continuous emphasis.

Since not all learning can occur from first-hand experiences and wide reading, all instructional programs should include direct teaching strategies. Individual word study activities should also be provided to capitalize on individual interests and to make learning more meaningful.

Questions for Further Reading and Thinking

1. What special problems do linguistically and culturally different learners have with the development of meaning vocabulary?
2. What can a teacher do for a child who has difficulty in mastering vocabulary independently?
3. What should a teacher do in a fourth grade class to develop the meaning vocabularies of a group of students whose word knowledge is considerably below that necessary for success at grade level?
4. What vocabulary development activities do you feel would be most appropriate for the slower learner? Why?

Activities and Projects

1. Prepare a card file of at least thirty vocabulary development ideas. Include on each card source, type of activity, and the age and grade levels for which each idea is appropriate.
2. Prepare an interest center that focuses on word histories. Prepare at least ten task cards. (See Chapter 18 for help with interest centers.)
3. Construct five activity sheets to teach each of the following direct methods of vocabulary development (state age or grade level):
   a. Multiple meanings of words
   b. Synonyms
   c. Analogies
4. Construct three crossword puzzles on a special content area topic. Prepare one appropriate for grade two, one for grade four, and one for grade six.
5. In your field experience program, observe five ways teachers promote vocabulary growth effectively. Write a brief statement describing each.
6. Construct five teacher-made games that will help teach or reinforce vocabulary development.
7. Prepare a notebook of interesting word histories that may be used in the development of activities on word origins.
8. Prepare and illustrate five bulletin board ideas designed to promote vocabulary growth.
9. Choose two different content area texts. Plan a lesson for a study unit in each that

would help strengthen word knowledge prior to the student's reading the material.

10. Choose an age or grade level and describe the characteristics of the children in a classroom (IQ, interests, linguistic environment, cultural setting, language development, etc.). Suggest vocabulary development activities that would be appropriate for this group.

11. Illustrate how you would develop a lesson using semantic feature analysis.

12. Read Chapters 4 and 5 in *Teaching Reading Comprehension* by P. David Pearson and Dale D. Johnson (New York: Holt, Rinehart and Winston, 1978). How has your reading refined your understanding of conceptualization?

Vocabulary Development Materials

For the teacher

Ching, Doris C. 1976. *Reading and the bilingual child*. Newark, Del.: International Reading Association.

Dale, Edgar; and O'Rourke, Joseph. 1971. *Techniques of teaching vocabulary*. Palo Alto, Calif.: Field Educational Publishers.

Deighton, Lee C. 1959. *Vocabulary development in the classroom*. New York: Teachers College Press.

Johnson, Dale D.; and Pearson, P. David. 1978. *Teaching reading vocabulary*. New York: Holt, Rinehart and Winston.

O'Brien, Carmen A. 1973. *Teaching the language-different child to read*. Columbus, Ohio: Charles E. Merrill.

Platts, Mary C. 1970. *Anchor: A handbook of vocabulary discovery techniques for the classroom teacher*. Stevensville, Mich.: Educational Service.

Russell, David H.; and Karp, E. E. 1981. *Reading aids through the grades*. 4th ed. New York: Teachers College Press.

Thonis, Eleanor Wall. 1976. *Literacy for America's Spanish-speaking children*. Newark, Del.: International Reading Association.

For the elementary school student

Building Word Power, Levels C–F by Sandra M. Brown. (Modern Curriculum Press Skillbooster Series). Cleveland, Ohio: Modern Curriculum Press.

First Book of Words (good for lower primary grades) by Samuel Epstein and Beryl Epstein. New York: Franklin Watts.

Growth in Word Power (word games and exercises for upper elementary grades) by Natalie Moreda. Pleasantville, N.Y.: Reader's Digest.

Homonyms, Synonyms and Antonyms (programmed material for grades 4 and 5). Tempe, Ariz.: Learning, Inc.

In Other Words (a junior thesaurus) by Andrew Schiller and William A. Jenkins. Glenview, Ill.: Scott Foresman.

Multiple Skills Series (Levels 5–6) by Richard A. Boning. Baldwin, N.Y.: Barnell Loft.

Picturesque Word Origins (interesting word origins). Springfield, Mass.: G. and C. Merriam.

Probe (game for intermediate grades). Salem, Mass.: Parker Brothers.

Supportive Skills Series (*Mastering Multiple Meanings*, levels 1 and 2; *Reading Homographs*, levels 1–9; *Reading Homonyms*, levels 1–9; *Reading Heteronyms*, levels 3–9; *Interpreting Idioms*, levels 1–9) by Richard A. Boning. New York: Dexter and Westbrook.

Tumble Words (vocabulary building game for any elementary grade). New York: Kohner Brothers.

Using the Context (exercises on using the context in grades 1–6), The Specific Skills Series. New York: Barnell Loft.

Vocabulary Development (six programmed books for grades 3–8), The Macmillan Reading Spectrum of Books by Lee C. Deighton. New York: Macmillan.

Vocabulary Improvement Practice (intermediate grades) by Donald Durrell. New York: Harcourt Brace Jovanovich.

Thomas N. Turner

7
Comprehension: Reading for Meaning

Reading comprehension involves getting meaning from the printed page. To be fully comprehended, experiences and perceptions gained from reading are received or recalled with clear, broad understanding. The individual may be said to comprehend something within a passage read when he can:

1. recognize that which is experienced or perceived for what it actually is (obtain literal meaning).
2. associate meanings both denotative and connotative from his own experiences to that set of impressions.
3. recognize how the experience or his perception of it fits into contextual situations and into surroundings.
4. be aware of the relationships between the experience or perception and others having similarities and differences.

Comprehension of anything that is read can be highly individual. Each individual has a different set of experiences that affects his comprehension. Value systems, beliefs, and attitudes differ widely. Therefore comprehension of ideas, perceptions, and experiences will vary as much. The same experience may be shared by several people and understood differently by each one. Their comprehension of the experience will vary in degree and nature.

Since comprehension is an unobservable mental process, at least three questions about it are important to the reading teacher: (1) How does comprehension relate to the cognitive act of processing print that is called reading? (2) What is the nature of reading comprehension? (3) What teaching approaches and techniques will bring about optimal progress in reading comprehension?

Ability to decode or translate the printed symbols is necessary for comprehension. But decoding alone is not a sufficient condition for comprehension to occur. LaBerge and Samuels (1974) have stated that only a fixed amount of attention is available to a reader at a given time. Their observations indicated that until decoding becomes automatic, comprehension suffers. Once decoding is easy and unconscious, the individual can give closer attention to understanding. Comprehension success is difficult to identify. It might be said, though, that absolute comprehension of any given passage is unlikely (in the sense that every shade of possible meaning is fitted together). However, a degree of accuracy and completeness of comprehension is desirable and necessary for real reading to occur. Without minimal success in this regard, the individual is not reading.

This chapter and the following one will deal with maximizing growth in comprehension both while decoding is a major focus of a child's reading development and as decoding becomes more automated. In this chapter we will introduce the idea that the same passage may be read with different levels of comprehension. Though levels of comprehension are not distinctly separable, we will focus on overall comprehension, especially to what is termed literal comprehension. Chapter 8 will give more specific attention to higher level comprehension skills including inference, critical reading, and creative reading.

To understand reading comprehension one should begin by analyzing what comprehension involves and how it relates to the entire reading process. Smith (1975a, p. 185) contended that fluent reading entails two fundamental skills: (1) prediction of meaning and the "sampling" of surface structure sufficiently to make predictions certain; and (2) making the most efficient use of visual information, which is all the cues to meaning available in the printed text. Smith's position was that a child learns to read by reading materials in which he has an opportunity to test hypotheses. As a child becomes better able to predict or hypothesize what a sentence or paragraph will say, he becomes a better reader.

This suggests that development of reading comprehension is a complex process. The ability to comprehend is closely interrelated with all reading skills and interfaces with the entire language development of the child. When teacher and children work on developing reading, writing, listening, and speaking vocabularies, they are attempting to improve comprehension.

Comprehension: Definitions and Influencing Factors

QUESTIONS TO GUIDE READING

Literal
What are some ways of describing levels of reading comprehension?
What are some of the factors that may influence reading comprehension?

Before a teacher can work toward improving a child's comprehension, he must have a thorough understanding of what is involved in this complex intellectual operation. This section attempts to extend the definitional concept of comprehension for reading teachers and to examine the factors associated with its development.

DEFINITIONS

Reading with comprehension is variously defined by both practice and theory. In many reading achievement tests and in some basal reading materials, success in tasks defined as comprehension requires mere memory of factual detail from any reading selection, along with knowledge of word meanings. Other definitions of comprehension range from narrow descriptions, which tend to limit the view of comprehension to word meaning and word identification, to extremely broad definitions. The latter sometimes become global. They imply that comprehension involves anything and everything related to the act of reading. Some of these more complex definitions include long listings of skills described as interpretive.

It seems futile to attempt to deal with comprehension as though it were a finite ability in which success was simply distinguished. Readers comprehend differently. A useful definition of comprehension seems to be one in which success in gaining meaning is examined in light of the achievement of the reader's purposes. If the reader discovers the meaning needed to achieve purposes set for him, or by him, he has successfully comprehended. If the reader's purpose is to find a particular piece of information or solve a problem through reading, then adequate comprehension is achieved when that purpose is accomplished. When the reader's purpose is very broad, there are varying degrees or levels of comprehension with which he may correctly read a passage. The term "levels" does not imply greater difficulty. It does mean that the reader reacts differently to what he reads. If he is merely getting the facts or the literal meaning, he is assuming a passive role. That is, he is trying to receive what the author has to say. Some literal comprehension is necessary for reading; otherwise the reader will merely be calling words nonsensically. Higher levels of comprehension involve reading beyond or between the lines. If the reader brings more knowledge and experience to the act of reading to draw inferences and apply reading to life situations, he is reading actively. For literal comprehension the reader needs only to understand exactly what is stated to receive the author's literal message. For higher levels of comprehension, the reader is involved in an interchange of ideas with the author. He is reading for a specific purpose of his own and goes beyond the surface meaning and message.

A child is likely to reach higher levels of comprehension with easier materials. Therefore, if a child or group makes little response to a reading activity, the teacher has at least two alternatives: move to activities at an easier (more literal) level of understanding or abandon that reading selection in favor of one that is easier. In implementing the second decision the teacher may continue activities requiring higher levels of comprehension. The choice of the teacher should be a conscious decision based on whether the goal of a particular reading activity is to raise the level of comprehension or to deal with more difficult materials.

A single definition of comprehension acceptable to all concerned with the reading process is clearly impossible. However, Robinson (1966) developed a definition that adequately describes the parameters of comprehension. She has depicted comprehension as a "clear grasp of what is read" at the levels of literal meanings, implied meanings, and possible applications beyond the author's meanings. This definition may actually encompass more than mere comprehension; it might more fairly be used to describe what is termed "critical and creative reading." In any case, it does provide a framework of meaning that this author finds to be useful.

Factors Influencing Comprehension

The total program of reading instruction; the child's own personality, motivation, and habits; and his out-of-school environment all influence his development of reading comprehension. Adverse effects may come from overemphasis on word recognition, overemphasis on oral reading, and insufficient experiential background for a reading selection. All but one of these factors involve concentrating the reader's attention on matters other than "meaning" in the reading process. Lack of sufficient guidance may also be a major factor in low reading comprehension of particular reading assignments.

Reading rate also may have some influence on comprehension. Good reading comprehension requires a flexible reading rate. There is no verification from research that readers with a fast reading rate comprehend less well than readers with slower rates. Fast reading simply saves time, and the proficient reader will use the rate demanded by the occasion. An appropriate comprehension and reading rate goal, according to Tinker and McCullough (1975, pp. 251–252), is to "comprehend as quickly as possible."

The purpose for which a reader reads has a great deal of influence on comprehension. Smith (1967) listed various appropriate and motivating purposes for reading: (1) enjoyment, (2) intellectual demands, (3) utilitarian purposes, (4) socioeconomic demands, (5) vocational or avocational interests, (6) personal social needs, (7) problem solving, and (8) spiritual or religious needs or personal stimulation.

Several approaches to reading instruction involve the reader in setting his own purpose or stress having the teacher declare a purpose before the children begin the reading assignment. There is some evidence that questions devised to set a purpose for reading may limit, or at least set restrictions on, comprehension. This seems only to emphasize the important role such purposes play.

Yet another factor within the reading instruction program is the length and difficulty of material. Determining the proper length and difficulty of a reading selection for good comprehension is related to such variables as the age, reading ability, experiential background, and general intellectual abilities of the child. Materials themselves have wide ranges of difficulty with regard to language organization and writing styles, as well as concept diversity (the number, newness, and degree of abstraction of concepts).

The abilities and experiential background, including the cultural language patterns, of the reader are crucial to reading comprehension. Reading materials that contain language patterns close to the child's oral patterns are better comprehended.

The abilities to recognize "inductive" sequences of ideas leading to a conclusion; to apply deductively a principle to new situations; and to recognize cause-effect, comparison, contrast, and other idea relationships relate to the level of the intellectual powers of the learner.

Memory plays an important role in reading comprehension. The reader must recall what he reads as well as his own experiences and other relevant readings; altogether, these factors result in comprehension, expanding the meaning the reader is able to take from what he reads. Smith (1975b) has shown the importance of prediction for reading comprehension. He described prediction as ability to make guesses about what is to be read. These guesses are largely based on prior knowledge and memory of experiences. Such memories are enhanced by the original impact of the experience or knowledge, the recency of its occurrence, and the number of times it has occurred (repetition of experience). Other experiential relationships will be discussed further in the section on schema theory. Chapter 16 will deal with specific implications and problems related to how the culturally and linguistically different learner comprehends.

Specific Comprehension Skills

QUESTIONS TO GUIDE READING

Literal
What were the eight comprehension skills Davis identified?
Which of these skills did Spearritt's study support?
What abilities, according to Dunn, are needed for successful performance on comprehension tasks?

Inferential
How are comprehension skills taught?

Evaluative
Why should teachers use a variety of techniques in developing comprehension skills?
Of what use is division of comprehension into subskills?

Among the best-known research related to the differentiation of the various comprehension skills is the work of Frederick B. Davis.[1] Davis (1968, p. 517) identified eight comprehension skills through a factor analysis procedure (factor analysis is a statistical procedure that attempts to identify the unique component elements of a competency):

1. recalling word meanings.
2. drawing inferences about the meaning of a word from context.
3. finding answers to questions answered explicitly or merely in paraphrase of the content.
4. weaving together ideas in the content.
5. drawing inferences from the content.
6. recognizing a writer's purpose, attitude, tone, and mood.
7. identifying a writer's technique.
8. following the structure of a passage.

Davis determined that the mental abilities used in the eight skills were to some degree independent of one another. He advocated direct and supervised instruction and practice for each of the eight skills. Bruton's (1977) critical analysis of comprehension research confirmed the importance of a knowledge of word meanings and the importance of the ability to infer from context.

Thorndike (1973), analyzing Davis's data, concluded that only word knowledge was distinguishable and that all others could be described as

1. A summary of his nearly forty years of research (as well as some related work by other researchers) appeared in 1968 in the *Reading Research Quarterly.*

reasoning. Spearritt's research (1972), however, supported the independence of four of the skills of comprehension: recalling word meanings; drawing inferences from the content; recognizing a writer's purpose, attitude, tone, and mood; and following the structure of a passage. Vocabulary acquisition was the most distinguishable comprehension skill in all the studies and is recognized as the most essential skill for reading comprehension.

More recently Drum, Calfee, and Cook (1981) identified the abilities needed for successful performance on comprehension tests. Since such tests should reflect teaching objectives and instructional content these qualities are worth noting. They include:

1. accurate and fluent word recognition.
2. knowledge of specific word meanings.
3. knowledge of syntactic/semantic clause and sentence relationships.
4. recognition of superordinate/subordinate idea structure of passages.
5. identification of the specific information requested in questions.
6. evaluation of the alternative choices in order to select the one that best fits
   a. the syntactic/semantic requirements of the questions.
   b. the idea structure of the passage.

The significance of all of the skills research for teaching may be not so much that skills are learned separately but that separating skills provides a way of focusing instruction. It seems that the more distinctly identifiable skills are those which relate to obtaining literal meaning. Higher level comprehension skills are difficult to measure and depend on previous development of literal comprehension.

COMMONLY TAUGHT SKILLS

Reading comprehension has traditionally been taught from a skills perspective. Long lists of comprehension skills have been developed by a number of writers and researchers. Recently, however, a great deal of criticism has been leveled at skills-based teaching of comprehension. According to Pearson and Johnson (1978), lists of skills have served only to confuse the teaching of reading comprehension. The major agreement for a skills program is that separate attention is convenient for planning and organizing teaching. It assumes that at least some attention will be given in the classroom to comprehension development. In one way or another nearly all basal reading programs, as well as other comprehension materials, identify and teach what their editors believe to be key comprehension skills. Skills have also been the heart of classroom practice in teaching comprehension for many years. In fact, Durkin (1978–1979) found that most of the reading period was spent in discussing comprehension questions that seemed to cluster around a group of subskills of comprehension. She observed that teachers meeting reading groups tended to ask such questions to see how well children have remembered, understood, and comprehended silent reading.

Attempts to name and classify all comprehension skills are known as comprehension skills taxonomies. The best known of these is Barrett's Taxonomy (1974). Table 7.1 shows such a taxonomy, developed by this author after considering Barrett's. Among the most commonly taught comprehension skills are finding the main idea, remembering detail, recognizing sequence, following directions, summarizing and organizing information, generalizing, and predicting outcomes. Most of these may be found under the heading of literal comprehension of the taxonomy in Table 7.1. In this section we give attention to each of these skill areas and suggest activity ideas for each. The most fundamental and important skill related to comprehension is the development of word meaning and vocabulary. However, Chapter 6 covered that subject, and it will not be given further treatment here. Three of the comprehension skills discussed here (main idea, details, and following directions) are given additional attention in Chapter 10. It is of some note that the focus of most activities in specific comprehension skill development at elementary levels is on literal comprehension. Content area subjects require a high level of development of many of the comprehension skills, especially those involving reading work/study skills (see Chapter 10).

Finding main ideas. Techniques for teaching children to find the main idea are numerous. These most often involve summarization or searching for key words and topic sentences. Initial teaching-learning experiences should involve many examples and explanations by the teacher, not only with reading but also with listening and observational experiences. Teachers should ask questions wherever the opportunity occurs, calling children's attention to the essential meaning of the lesson. Terms like, "the main point," "the theme," "the moral" should be used often and illustrated. Teachers need to take the time to have children vote or discuss which sentence or word says the most, which sentence or word is most important, etc. Students might be given help by having them leave out different sentences in a paragraph to see which ones are missed most.

The sample activities suggested below illustrate practicing searching for main ideas at several reading levels:

1. Divide children into groups of five or six. Have each group read the same short selections. Give each group a different title, or main idea, for each selection. Then have the groups debate, each trying to establish its own "right" main idea.
2. Cut the topic sentence out of a paragraph. Let the children write the topic sentence.

Table 7.1. A Taxonomy of Skills in Comprehension

I. Literal Comprehension
1.0 *Recognition/Identification* of:
  1.1 Main ideas
  1.2 Supporting ideas
  1.3 Details
  1.4 Vocabulary meanings
  1.5 Cause and effect relationships
  1.6 Similarities and comparability of language, plot, and structure
  1.7 Figurative language
  1.8 Direct statements of opinions
  1.9 Character traits, sequence, setting, and mood
2.0 *Recall* of:
  2.1 Main ideas
  2.2 Sequence
  2.3 Details of plot and information
  2.4 Character traits, setting, and mood
  2.5 Vocabulary meaning
  2.6 Cause and effect relationships
3.0 *Analysis and Reorganization* by:
  3.1 Summarizing
  3.2 Synthesizing, reducing, and capsulizing ideas
  3.3 Transfer and restatement
  3.4 Outlining
  3.5 Classifying
  3.6 Response to questions that analyze organization or organize differentially

II. Inferential Comprehension
4.0 *Interpretive*
  4.1 Interpreting themes, overall purposes, or moral lessons not directly stated
  4.2 Interpreting character
  4.3 Interpreting meaning of plot and mood
  4.4 Interpreting figurative language
  4.5 Identifying multiple meanings and symbolism
5.0 *General Inferential*
  5.1 Visualizing unstated supporting details
  5.2 Inferring character traits
  5.3 Identifying character types

5.4 Describing sequence not specifically stated
5.5 Inferring events and information not specifically described
5.6 Identifying missing elements
5.7 Inferring details
5.8 Inferring cause and effect relationships
5.9 Inferring reality base and moral philosophy
6.0 *Predictive*
  6.1 Predicting character development
  6.2 Predicting sequence outcomes and results
  6.3 Predicting language use and vocabulary patterns
  6.4 Predicting philosophy, moral interpretation, and presence or absence of a lesson
  6.5 Predicting style

III. Evaluational Comprehension
7.0 *Judgmental*
  7.1 Philosophical judgments indicating basic agreement or disagreement with author
  7.2 Reality judgments of degree of possibility or impossibility (realism or fantasy)
  7.3 Judgments of evidence, reasonableness, experience to substantiate (fact versus opinion)
  7.4 Relational judgments of appropriateness (determination of relevance or fit of reading selection to a problem or issue)
  7.5 Judgments of completeness (adequacy)
  7.6 Judgments of worth and weight (validity, strength, and importance)
  7.7 Judgments of agreement or acceptability
8.0 *Appreciative*
  8.1 Emotional reactions to content or subjects
  8.2 Extension of emotional and attitudinal aspects of concepts

8.3 Emotional response to story line movements (plot)

8.4 "Draw" and sensory feel of setting

8.5 Identification with and feeling of knowing and understanding characters

8.6 Response to descriptive power of author

8.7 Internalization of emotion and mood

8.8 Appeal of author's use of language patterns

8.9 Response to specific selection of words

9.0 *Critical*

9.1 Questioning of opinions, information, format, and presentation

9.2 Development of definite ideas of dissatisfaction or satisfaction

9.3 Identification of specific flaws either of the whole or of parts

9.4 Taking exception to particular ideas

9.5 Questioning authenticity and authority

9.6 Comparison of style, language, and substance of different writers and reading sections

9.7 Formulation of contrary opinions to those of the author

3. Give children a series of captions and pictures. Have them correctly match picture with caption.

4. Have children give a one-sentence phrase "title" for a particular passage.

5. Have children write new titles for stories or articles.

6. Have children write titles for book chapters that are only numbered.

Remembering details. Reading for details can be developed through some of the questioning procedures discussed in Chapter 9. Some of the study skill techniques developed in Chapter 10 also involve these skills. Descriptions are good places to begin showing children the importance of detail. One child might draw an object with details from a printed description given in order of importance by other children. Some additional activities teachers might use in developing this skill are the following:

1. Make a series of "category" cards (animals, houses, people, character traits, for example). For a given story, flash the cards and have children name all the examples of a given category within the story.

2. Have a fact listing "contest" after a story to determine how many facts about the story the children can give orally.

3. List story character's name (or a place in the story) on the chalkboard. Have children take turns adding a detail of information about the person or place until no child can suggest any more information.

4. Show a picture to the children. Remove the picture from view. Then have the children try to list all the objects in the picture.

5. Have children read a paragraph and then see how many nouns they can remember without looking back at the paragraph.

6. Role play a dramatic event in a story. Afterward have three children leave the room. Ask them, one at a time, to return and describe the dramatization. Discuss the differences in the details of the three accounts.

Recognizing sequence. Ability to recognize a sequence of events is essential to understanding plot and story "direction." The language experience approach discussed in Chapter 13 can be used as one way of teaching children to recognize sequence. Story reconstruction in outline or sentence series can be a good oral teaching technique. Other ideas include the following:

1. Have children practice grouping objects and pictures — in alphabetical order, by size, by age, and by complexity of information contained.
2. Cut apart a small book or booklet and remove the page numbers. Have children arrange the pages in correct order.
3. Prepare summaries of stories read by the children. Cut the sentences apart. Then mix up the order of the sentences. Have children reorder them correctly.
4. Have children list the day's events, then put them in the order in which they happened.
5. Have children sequence newspaper comic strips that have been cut apart.

Following directions. Following directions is a skill of great importance in a print-oriented technological society. As children progress, the directions we give them can have more and more intermediate steps. Ideas for developing this comprehension skill are easy to delineate. Many may be put into game format. For example:

1. Have children make up directions for doing something that they themselves do regularly or for school activities they know well.
2. Let children tell how to play a particular game. Put their directions on a chart or on the chalkboard, then play the game. If a situation involving an omitted direction occurs, the game is over.
3. Compose sets of directions for doing something, leaving out one important step. Have the children attempt to discover (as in a riddle) what step is missing.
4. Have children go through books and other materials. Ask them to identify "direction words." Make a list of the most common words found in their search.

Summarizing and organizing information. Summarizing and organizing information is important to most reading tasks. It is most crucial in content area study. Children can participate both formally and informally in activities such as the following five in learning to summarize and organize ideas.

1. Have children "pull" from a story all the events that one of the less important characters witnessed in order to see the situation from that character's perspective.
2. Identify one event within a story, then have children tell what happened before or what happened after that event.
3. Have children "dry" a story — go through a copy and cross out all but the most essential plot line statements.
4. Have children make one-minute "Who? What? Where? When? Why? How?" book reports.
5. Have children prepare a list of important events in a story. Then organize these events in several different ways, such as: (1) in the order in which they occurred; (2) in order of their importance; (3) as they affected a central character; (4) as they related to the final outcome of the story; (5) as they related to one another.

Generalizing. Generalizing from information is a difficult skill to learn. The ability to generalize usually relates to higher level comprehension (see Chapter 8). Activities for generalizing are sometimes difficult to structure and plan. A few suggestions follow:

1. Have children think of a proverb or motto that could have saved the hero or heroine of a story from difficulty.
2. Have children who have read one story by a given author attempt to anticipate what another story by that author may be like.
3. Have children make lists of traits or characteristics of familiar concept words, such as United States President, horse, TV programs, or trees. Then have them test their traits against an example of the concept.
4. Give children a list of six articles found in a particular home or village of a real or imaginary culture. Then let the children try to define the traits of that home or culture.

Predicting outcomes. Practice in predicting outcomes can be very enjoyable for children. One of the most common techniques is to stop children before they finish reading a story and have them suggest how the story could end. Another is to discuss events that could follow those in the stories; e.g., what happened to Cinderella's step-sisters? what would have happened if Cinderella's feet became sore and swollen?

A few activities for helping children make predictions are described here:

1. Have children predict content from headlines or headings.
2. Have children tell a story just from seeing the book cover or a picture.

3. Cover a sentence or a word within a sentence. Have children guess what the missing part says.
4. Have children guess what the study questions on a chapter will be.
5. Let children write the ending they predict for a story after reading only the first page of the story.
6. Omit the adjectives in a story. Let the children try to guess from pictures or context what the adjectives were.

TEACHING COMPREHENSION SKILLS

Durkin (1981) analyzed five basal program and observational instructional settings. She found that although questions, assignments, and "mentioners" (minimal information given) were used frequently in both the materials and the teaching activities, there was little direct teaching. She concluded that there was a need for direct increased comprehension instruction. There was little or no instruction in the form of direct teaching or other instructional activity related to specific comprehension difficulties. She identified eight categories of instruction that seem to merit comment.

1. *Graphic Signals* (punctuation, indentation, underlining). *Teaching needed:* Point out to children how these signals alter meaning. Direct focused instruction can deal with graphic signals as a whole or specific types. When the teacher follows up the reading of a text, she should include calling children's attention to the graphic signals to help them remember.
2. *Signal Words. Teaching needed:* One word may change the entire meaning of a passage. (e.g., time signals like *before, after, during,* etc.). By grouping related signal words together and by showing lots of examples of how they influence meaning, teachers can help children comprehend more accurately and especially help them see relationships such as sequence and size.
3. *Possessives. Teaching needed:* Pronouns, 's, and possessive phrases are often confusing to children because of their similarity to other forms. More than a practice sheet or two is needed to make their recognition and comprehension automatic.
4. *Language Functions. Teaching needed:* Children need help in recognizing the different purposes that words and phrases serve in context. Teachers should point out how different language functions change meaning.
5. *Anaphora* (especially pronoun referents). *Teaching needed:* Awareness of the need to clarify who or what is being referred to by a pronoun or a general noun is essential to comprehension. Instruction in the form of analysis of examples can help children develop a sensitivity and ability to correctly interpret referents.

6. *Less than a sentence. Teaching needed:* Sentence fragments are often standing alone in reading materials. Conversation, for example, may include utterances that are not whole sentences. It is also important for children to be given help in interpreting phrases and clauses within sentences. For example, they should be able to recognize dependent and independent relationships. Prior to and following reading, teachers can pick out difficult or tricky key sentence parts for discussion.

7. *Sentence. Teaching needed:* Children should be helped to understand what a sentence needs to do and the relative importance of sentences in conveying meaning. Examples and nonexamples of types of sentence structures can be discussed and analyzed in guided learning activities.

8. *More than a sentence. Teaching needed:* Paragraph functions and types of paragraphs should be described and pointed out. Children then need practice in identifying and in writing different types of paragraphs. The ideas of style, theme, sequence, and unity in reading selection can be discussed with children.

Durkin observed that the connection between what was taught and how to read was either minimized or entirely overlooked. Transfer was more or less assumed, which seems inconsistent with research.

Schema Theory

QUESTIONS TO GUIDE READING

Literal
What is schema theory?
What are the characteristics of schemata?

Inferential
How are schemata selected?
How is metacognition of importance to comprehension?

Evaluative
In what ways will schema theory influence classroom practice and materials for the development of reading comprehension?
What are the implications of schema theory for the beginning teacher?

SCHEMA

Probably the most important research and theory regarding reading comprehension in recent years has had to do with the relationship between prior knowledge and reading comprehension. In its simplest form the beginning idea of this theory and research is that the more you know about the topic of any reading material the better you will be able to understand that reading material (see Chapter 1). Schema theory represents an attempt to explain and describe the way that experiences and concepts gained from them are stored in memory. Rumelhart (1980) described schema theory as essentially a theory about what the human mind does with knowledge. A schema is the way knowledge is organized or structured by the mind. Schemata (plural of schema) are internal, informal explanations about the nature of the events, objects, or situations each individual faces. Rumelhart (1981) characterized schemata as active (changing) processes representing knowledge. They occur at all levels of abstraction and are used as recognition devices.

The question, then, is, how does this prior knowledge work in the reading-thinking process? One image that might help is that of a reading selection as a free-floating form. The schemata are the ties between the reader and that form that keep it from drifting off. Some threads are stronger and thicker and some are the thinnest silken threads. Each thread has to be connected before it does any good.

Let us suppose a child is trying to read a selection about Native Americans. If he had no relatable experiences he would find it very difficult to understand and react to the selection. But nearly every child will have developed an assortment of experiences with which he can quickly associate some of the material. The knowledge he has about different tribes and cultures — from the other books he has read or heard, from pictures he has seen, and from any visits to or discoveries about Native Americans — helps with this association. All these knowledges and perhaps many more will present memories that will serve as associations for the new material. So too may his knowledge about tribal or clan cultures of other groups, his experiences with the geographic area where the particular selection takes place, and a number of words he has learned. The individual's use of the category system of his memory will help him make sense of new experiences and changes in his view of the environment. Such alterations are involved in reading.

What are some implications of schema theory for the teaching of reading? The major thrust of the theory and related research seems to suggest that strong emphasis should be given to building background knowledge. Overall prereading preparation as well as comprehension follow-through activities need to be more purposefully selected to develop cognitive structures (Jenkins and Pany, 1981). Vocabulary development remains a key target of planning with experience-based vocabulary teaching occurring prior to reading. Yet another implication of schema theory is that comprehension can be helped if the teacher pays special attention to building bridges between the reading material and student experience.

Lack of comprehension of a given passage may be accounted for in at least three ways according to Pearson and Camperell (1981). To each of their three reasons a logical teaching follow-through seems indicated and has been noted: (1) The reader does not have appropriate schemata. This means the teacher should develop experience when she discovers the lack. (2) The clues provided by the author are not sufficient to suggest the appropriate schemata. Teachers need to suggest relationships by stimulating the child with questions and by taking comparisons to known experiences of children. (3) The reader finds a consistent interpretation that is not intended by the author. Obviously, the teacher needs first to discover that this has occurred. The reteaching task may be the most difficult. Teachers should try to bring reading material classes closer to the children's prior experience base by:

1. use of comparisons and analogies connecting reading material to the experiences of children in preparation for and follow-through of reading tasks.
2. frequent careful questions calling for comparisons of reading encounters to previous reading experiences, television experiences, and personal lives of pupils.
3. ongoing assessment of the ways in which children are able to relate to materials.

Motivation, which by definition stresses personal relationships to reading material and need for reading, cannot be ignored. Mathewson (1976) found that comprehension for a liked story was higher than for a disliked story but that with sufficient extrinsic motivation comprehension of both a disliked and a liked story was high.

METACOGNITION

One of the most promising related areas of research deals with metacognition. Metacognition is the deliberate conscious control of one's own cognitive actions (Brown 1980, p. 453). The idea is that there are various degrees of control and awareness of consciousness one has over one's own thinking. Many people neither cause themselves to think in special ways nor realize they can. Metacognition skills, then, have to do with the ability to control one's own thinking and to be aware of one's own cognitive processes. Research seems to indicate that this level of awareness affects comprehension. The greater an individual's awareness of his thinking processes and his sense of control of these processes, the better he is able to understand the thing he is thinking about. This suggests that teachers should give special attention to reading study skill techniques such as those described in Chapter 10. It also suggests that there should be a stronger development of prereading activities with children so that they have a more urgent sense of direction, sequence, and purpose. Teachers can spend time with questions and purpose setting before assigning independent reading. They can help children tell themselves what to think and how to think by discussing reading materials more before they are read and helping children organize their own thoughts to maximize what they are to get out of the reading material.

In a slightly different but related area, metacomprehension may be seen as an aspect of metacognition. Baker and Stein (1981, p. 42) have cited growing evidence that young children have poor "metacomprehension skills." That is, they do not know when they do not understand. Part of the teacher's role then is to help students become more sensitive to their own thought processes and to think more clearly, specifically to identify their own difficulty. Simple questions such as "Why do you think so?" or "How did you come up with that answer?" may suffice. Additional techniques are described in Chapter 9. Practice in outlining talks and reports may also help. It is often very good just to sit down with children and summarize in an organized way with them the ideas they stated or encountered. The point of such interpreting should be in focusing thought.

The classroom preparation and follow-through needed for optimal comprehension will eventually involve the reader in a series of steps such as the following:

1. Developing purpose and reason for reading.
2. Focusing attention on themes, main ideas, and special issues, problems, and concerns.
3. Developing a sense of relationship between the reading material and the reader's own experience.
4. Maintaining concentration throughout the reading act.
5. Attaching meaning to different terms and passages.
6. Remembering and restructuring the thrust of the reading material.
7. Extending structural knowledge, including significant details.
8. Clarifying meaning.

The independent reader goes through step 1 when he asks himself, "Why am I reading this?" or identifies an author, a type of story, or a kind of writing he particularly enjoys. Focusing attention and developing relationships may be achieved by motivation, exposition, and inquiry teaching preparation. Maintaining concentration, attaching meaning, remembering and restructuring, and clarifying meaning require careful teacher follow-through. Teachers need to be aware of the child's ability to achieve these steps independently and of the amount of help the child needs.

Comprehension of Longer Printed Messages

QUESTIONS TO GUIDE READING

Literal
What is one technique for developing a sense of subject and predicate?
What are some different ways paragraphs are organized?
What are three structured approaches or plans designed to increase comprehension of longer selections?

Inferential
What are some organizational considerations a teacher should know to help children understand longer reading selections?
What factors in the English language make learning its structure a useful tool for readers?

Evaluative
Would it be possible to read with comprehension without having some knowledge of the structure of sentences? Why or why not?
What are the implications of this section for the widely used technique of discussing a story after children have read it?

As the length of the author's message increases, the skills and tools the reader needs are likely to change. Some of these changes are subtle, involving only a different degree of ability. Complexity and amount of information to process increases as compensation to the reader. Longer messages create within themselves additional clues to meaning that can aid the comprehension process. Increase in length also makes it more difficult for the reader to apply experience or to identify appropriate schemata. Schemata become more complex, overlapping, and embedded within one another in longer printed passages.

SENTENCE STRUCTURE

Lefevre (1964, pp. 8–11) has described the basic sentence order of English as rigid and arbitrary. These characteristics constitute a convenience to learning because they make our language structure predictable and useful to understand. A knowledge of basic sentence order plays an important part in a child's ability to anticipate, predict, and therefore understand when reading. Another facet of sentence sense is the words themselves, and the role they play. For example, suppose that a child is asked to complete the following sentence: The boy ran down the _____. First, he knows (without knowing the terminology) that the sentence must be completed with a noun or nominal. Second, because of his past experience with oral language, the child already knows that only certain vocabulary items could reasonably be anticipated.

Teachers need to develop activities to enhance children's understanding of sentence order; that is, to help them learn what kinds of words are likely to fit into each part of a sentence. It is helpful to practice with open-ended sentences and with the completion of phrases. (She was taller than _____. He ran toward _____. I like _____. My favorite _____. The king raised _____.) Worksheets, wall charts, and bulletin boards are among the possible vehicles for such exercises. Oral exercises are also useful; for example ask children to read stories, then complete sentences from the stories differently from the way the author chose.

Understanding sentences is not difficult for children in beginning reading because the sentences are simple at this stage. However, difficulty increases as sentences grow longer and more complex. Karlin (1975) suggested that having children write paired sentences is an effective way of developing a sense of subject and predicate. For example, show them this pair:

Cinderella lived happily.
Cinderella and the Prince lived happily ever after.

After seeing a series of examples such as the preceding, the children are given a single sentence and asked to write a paired sentence for it.

PARAGRAPH MEANING

There are numerous "standard" techniques for developing understanding of paragraph meaning. These include: writing titles for paragraphs, writing summary sentences, drawing pictures to depict the events of a paragraph, identifying which paragraph among several describes an illustration, and identifying topic sentences.

Many authors advocate teaching children to recognize the logical structure of paragraphs. They are convinced that such a skill aids children in finding an appropriate reading speed and leads to a better reading rate as well as better comprehension, especially in being able to skim and scan well.

Karlin (1975, p. 227) has emphasized teaching children to recognize patterns of organization in paragraphs — such as time order, enumeration, topic, comparison or contrast, or cause and effect. Karlin further noted that children should learn to recognize that some paragraphs serve special functions — such as summarizing ideas, or giving examples, or as transitions between sets of ideas.

Another type of paragraph structure has been suggested by Robinson (1978). Each structure suggests the kind of information that the paragraph contains and often gives clues about how the information will be sequenced. Understanding the structure and function of the paragraph is important to literal comprehension. Robinson viewed these paragraph structures as important to comprehension in the school setting since most of the reading in school is of expository or explaining material. The following basic structures are described by Robinson as most common in expository materials.[2]

1. *Explanatory* paragraphs tell about something factual as opposed to describing a scene or unfolding a plot. The reader usually needs to understand the words and attend to the information to arouse incomplete or hazy concepts. It is also likely that explanation extends beyond single paragraphs and the reader needs skill in grasping paragraphs.

2. *Definitional* paragraphs (which may also be explanatory) focus on clarifying the meaning of one or more words, phrases, or clusters. Again, a cluster of paragraphs may be used to define. Understanding such paragraphs is aided through approaching them by first asking *What is defined?* followed by *What does it mean?* Readers need to learn to use graphics and pictorial aids to definition.

3. *Introductory* paragraphs are usually broad in nature and set purposes for reading. The reader should look for words that will serve as clues to focusing attention in later paragraphs.

4. *Summarizing and concluding* paragraphs may be used as reviewing aids before reading and as comprehension checks after reading. They occur either at the beginning or at the end of a chapter, section, or book and serve to repeat major concepts, restate major ideas, redefine terms, and make transitions. Writers almost always let the reader know by cue phrases and sentences when a summarizing paragraph will occur. Such paragraphs may require several readings.

5. *Transitional* paragraphs tersely summarize one idea or set of ideas or introduce another, and point out relationships. They are used for smoothness and to add unity of structure.

6. *Narrative* paragraphs tell a story. Such stories sometimes are used to illustrate major points in expository writing. Students need to be alerted to the double purpose of such paragraphs. Such paragraphs often provide an attitude mindset for further reading. They move the action of a story or exposition and usually contain a sequence.

7. *Descriptive* paragraphs "paint a picture," suggest mood, and provide detailed information. They are usually unified around a single topic. The topic features are related to one another. Sequence is often in descending or ascending order of the significance of the traits.

8. *Persuasive* paragraphs are most frequently found in advertising and editorial material. They are attempts to convince a reader, sometimes through emotional means. They usually either tie off a series of arguments or thoroughly explain one.

2. Based on pages 137–155 of H. Alan Robinson's *Teaching Reading and Study Strategies: The Content Areas.* Boston: Allyn and Bacon, 1978. Used with permission.

Teachers may help students become aware of the relationships of structure of paragraphs to meaning by pointing out examples as well as by direct teaching of types of paragraphs. A number of structural features may help the reader identify exactly what sort of paragraph he is reading. Among these features are:

1. The location of the paragraph within the reading material.
2. Internal structure clues especially from the first and last sentence.
3. Clue words and phrases.
4. The nature and focus of the content totally (the topic, the purposes, the nature of the target audience, etc.).
5. The type of writing (for example, fictional stories contain different types of paragraphs than do descriptive articles).

UNDERSTANDING STILL LONGER SELECTIONS

Learning to understand entire pages, stories, chapters, and books requires special attention in reading instruction. Levels of comprehension — literal, interpretive, and evaluative — are of ultimate concern here. Many of the strategies for developing comprehension of longer passages involve the approaches to questioning that Chapter 9 explores.

Teachers need to help children learn to utilize the reading aids that most reading selections have within them. They may want to have children develop (through discussion) habits of using chapter titles, headings, and subheadings to predict the content of sections of books and stories.

Summary

Reading comprehension, though difficult to define, centers on the ability to derive meaning from what is read. Without comprehension, a child does not really read. Researchers disagree as to whether comprehension is a single general skill or a competency composed of several differentiated skills. The research of Davis (1968) has indicated that there are a number of distinct comprehension skills. Recalling and identifying word meanings is the special comprehension skill most uniformly agreed on. However, drawing inferences; recognizing author tone, mood, attitude, and purpose; and following passage structure are some of the other skills research has suggested to be important.

A number of factors are believed to influence reading comprehension. Although it is true that readers with a fast rate do not comprehend less well than readers with a slower rate, the ability to adjust rate is important. Reading instruction can actually retard growth in reading comprehension if it draws the pupil's attention exclusively to such factors as word recognition or oral reading or if it gives insufficient guidance. Setting purposes for reading that are meaningful and motivating to the pupil facilitates comprehension.

Among the most significant developments in comprehension research and theory in recent years have been schema theory, which stresses the importance of previous experience to reading comprehension, and metacognition, which stresses understanding how one thinks about a reading selection. If the reader fits a passage into a structural framework in his mind, he is more likely to comprehend a reading passage better.

Approaches to developing comprehension are numerous and differ according to the length of the passage. Children need to become aware of the basic structural patterns of phrases, sentences, and paragraphs. This knowledge will help them anticipate and understand the order of elements in their reading.

Questions for Further Reading and Thinking

1. In what ways does a child's experiential background influence comprehension?
2. What response could be made either to support or to argue against the contention that typing the comprehension skills is misleading since all reading skills relate to comprehension?
3. Why are some comprehension skills seemingly more vital than others to total reading comprehension?
4. Why is there no evidence that readers with slower reading rates comprehend better than fast readers?
5. How can a teacher be assured of comprehension when children read silently?
6. Do all children need to comprehend a reading selection in the same way in order to enjoy it?
7. Will a higher level of comprehension enhance a reader's enjoyment of a particular selection?

Activities and Projects

1. Develop several activities in which children can evaluate their own comprehension.
2. Select a short story and show how it might be comprehended at each of several levels.
3. Make a list of twenty kinds of activities that reinforce reading comprehension.
4. Develop a lesson plan to teach one specific comprehension skill at a given grade level. Provide activities that allow for different stages in comprehension.
5. Develop and make the materials for a reading comprehension skill game (for a small group of children).
6. Look at the various comprehension skills and levels of comprehension in relation to Piaget's stages of cognitive development. Describe the inferences of your comparison.
7. Study a basal reading series. How are the "basic" comprehension skills taught?

Comprehension Materials for Elementary School Children

Comprehension Skills Laboratory. Santa Monica, Calif.: BFA Educational Media.

Gates-Peardon Reading Exercises (for grades 2–6) by Authur I. Gates and Celeste Comegys Peardon. New York: Teachers College, Columbia University.

Increasing Comprehension (for grades 3–6). Modern Curriculum Press Skillbooster Series. Cleveland, Ohio.: Modern Curriculum Press.

Love, Marla. *20 Reading Comprehension Games.* Belmont, Calif.: Fearon Pilman Publishers. 1977.

New Reader's Digest Reading Skill Builders (for grades 1–9). Pleasantville, N.Y.: Reader's Digest.

New Reading Skilltext Series (for grades 1–6). Columbus, Ohio: Charles E. Merrill.

Reading Comprehension (for grades 3–8) by Adrian B. Sanford and others. New York: The Macmillan Company. (Revised Macmillan Reading Spectrum.)

Reading Comprehension Series (grades 3–6). New York: Scholastic.

Reading for Concepts (for grades 2–6) by William Liddle. New York: McGraw-Hill Book Company, Webster Division.

Reading for Meaning (for grades 4–12). Philadelphia: J. B. Lippincott.

Scholastic Comprehension Practice Books (one for each of grades 3–6). New York: Scholastic.

Specific Skill Series (one for each grade, Grades 1–6) by Richard A. Boning. Baldwin, N.Y.: Barnell Loft. Specific titles include *Detecting the Sequence, Drawing Conclusions, Getting the Main Idea, Locating the Answer, Getting the Facts, Using the Context, Following Directions.*

SRA Reading Laboratories (for all levels). Chicago: Science Research Associates.

Strategies for Reading by H. Alan Robinson and others (workbooks: *Sentences; Paragraphs; Language Selections*). Boston: Allyn and Bacon.

Working with Facts and Details (levels C–F) Modern Curriculum Press Skillbooster Series by Sandra M. Brown and Mollie L. Cohen. Cleveland, Ohio: Modern Curriculum Press.

Thomas N. Turner

8

Higher Levels of Comprehension: Inference, Critical Reading, and Creative Reading

Chapter 7 introduced the comprehension processes as a whole. Helping the child obtain a clear understanding of what is directly stated in reading material is the most direct aim of the activities and skills described in that chapter. However, total comprehension often requires that the reader go well beyond the simplest and most obvious meaning of the message. The type of thinking required to obtain more than literal meaning is referred to as higher level comprehension. Much of what was said in Chapter 7 about the comprehension process also applies to higher levels of comprehension. However, since the necessary guidance, activities, and instruction to develop such comprehension is often neglected at the elementary school level, special focus is needed in these areas. This chapter is intended to add depth of understanding about higher levels of comprehension. Higher levels of comprehension are not always more difficult. They simply involve thinking that is greater in abstraction and further removed from the literal meaning of the reading material. Reading at such levels of comprehension puts greater demands on the reader to supply images, ideas, and reactions and to make inferences.

The first of these more abstract types of comprehension to be dealt with here is reading for inference, sometimes described as reading between the lines or finding the hidden meanings (those not directly stated but implied). Inferential comprehension as discussed here involves use of context, awareness of language usage patterns, choosing among alternative meanings of words and expressions, and understanding relationships implied by language to discover an author's message and the meaning that author intends to convey.

Inferences are a routine part of the comprehension process. Ability to recognize what an author implies is both normal and necessary for comprehension. When the reader comprehends inferential meaning he deals with ambiguities in text, correctly identifies referents (anaphora), and catches context signals. Inferential comprehension also describes the reader's understanding and ability to recognize connotative meaning of words and figurative language. Obviously, understanding even a simple, brief communication requires a reader or listener to make many inferences.

The second and third sections of this chapter will deal first with critical and then with creative reading. Critical reading and creative reading have been defined and described in many ways. Psychologists, linguists, and reading specialists are not always in agreement about the two terms. Some definitions build in unnecessary confusion by treating critical and creative reading as though they were the same thing. Such definitions do not seem to give the reading teacher any help in developing critical and creative reading abilities. This chapter is built on definitions of critical and creative reading that treat them as separate, thought-related sets of abilities and ways of thinking about reading.

Critical reading is reading with an awareness of similarities and differences between what the reader has already seen and what he is seeing in the work he is reading critically. Critical reading compares experience to the new material on elements such as style, expression, information and ideas, opinions, or values of an author. Creative reading, on the other hand, is reading with awareness of the stimuli of imaginative thought present in reading materials. Such stimuli may be in the form of problems sensed or of new ideas or ways of expression.

Thus, critical reading involves analytic thinking for the purpose of evaluation of what is read. In contrast, creative reading involves selective and productive thinking for the purposes of divergence from that which is read. Creative and critical reading are similar in that both involve higher, more difficult levels of thinking and comprehension, interaction of the reader with the substance of reading material, and a search for personal use and meaning in reading.

The three levels of comprehension presented in this chapter seem to have a strong relationship to metacognition (discussed in Chapter 7). That is, as the individual reader comprehends at higher levels he may become more sensitive and aware of his thought processes. A kind of growth cycle seems to follow with increased awareness tending to develop increased ability to comprehend.

Although it is convenient conceptually to deal with these three aspects of reading comprehension separately, it does not follow that they occur in isolation in the reading-thinking process. Comprehension is a dynamic integrated and unified process. One level does not have to end for another to begin since there is an interdependence of all the thought processes involved in reading comprehension. Higher level comprehension tasks are memory dependent (Wertsch 1972) and dependent on literal comprehension. Literal comprehension is, then, necessary but not sufficient for such comprehension to occur. Inference, critical reading, and creative reading involve greater amounts of information and often deal with greater complexities of relationships (see Chapter 7). Therefore, greater difficulty is often involved in the thinking processes.

Inference: Finding More Meaning

QUESTIONS TO GUIDE READING

Literal
What does a reader do when he makes an inference?
What are some types of difficulties involved in determining causal relationships?
What are figures of speech and why are they difficult for children?

Inferential
How do inferences help a reader comprehend more effectively?
What are the differences among the stages of ability to deal with figurative language?

Evaluative
Should inferential comprehension be taught directly?
How does a teacher determine when readers should be introduced to inferences?

Inferential comprehension involves understanding an author's intent and getting his intended message. According to Trabasso (1981, pp. 56–57), a reader who makes an inference either fills in missing information or finds semantic and/or logical relationships among elements in a narrative. The reader is involved in an active process of choosing meanings from among alternatives and deriving meaning from the surface structure of a text. That is, he examines all the information the author provides. However, the meaning the reader derives is not necessarily limited to that information. The reader himself supplies meaning by the information and background he possesses.

Each sentence of a piece of reading material consists of at least one conceptualization. The reader creates a connective chain that adds underlying meaning and structure to what is read.

Inferences are complex and have a variety of functions related to comprehension. Included among those identified by Trabasso (1981) were:

1. Inferences help solve ambiguous individual words and phrases. (This ambiguity is sometimes intended, as in puns, double-entendre, and use of nuance.)
2. Inferences help interpret pronouns and other references (anaphora).
3. Inferences relate content to context, helping to generalize.
4. Inferences establish a larger framework for interpretation.

There are many types of cognitive operations that could be described as inferences. Frederiksen (1977), for example, identified twenty-six types of inferences. However, this section can focus only on the most common ways in which teachers can develop inferencing ability in children. The aspects of comprehending text that demand inferencing skill and will be treated here are: ambiguity, anaphora (pronoun reference), context signals, causality, and figurative language.

AMBIGUITY

Many words and sentences confuse the reader because two or more meanings may be attached. Often these are intentional, as when people use puns or double-entendre or when hints or innuendoes are dropped in conversation. However, more often ambiguity is unintentional and can be avoided by looking at the passage logic. Some teaching activities that might be useful in helping children deal with ambiguities follow:

1. Have children keep a file box of sentences with multiple meanings. Then have them invent contexts that will pinpoint one of the meanings.
2. Occasionally look up a multiple-meaning word in a story. (Chapter 6 offers a related suggestion.)
3. Have a "pun of the day" contest.
4. Collect a scrapbook of cartoons that show words with double meaning.
5. Collect homographs (words that are spelled alike but are pronounced differently and have different definitions) and homophones (words that sound alike but are spelled differently).
6. Develop lists of near-synonym words that mean *nearly* the same thing. Have children talk about the differences. As noted in Chapter 6 all synonyms are "near" synonyms with slight differences in meaning.

ANAPHORA

Anaphoric expressions include pronouns, and "proverbs" (Webber 1980). They maximize the meaning that can be derived from a single word by substituting that for other single words and groups of words. The word "it," for example, can be used to evoke from the reader a very complicated group of ideas. Complex and often difficult thinking is involved in understanding anaphora.

The following are a few of the activities that the teacher may want to develop to help children grow in ability to deal with anaphora.

1. Have children orally read passages substituting the correct name for each pronoun.
2. Draw children's attention to sentences in which there are pronouns that confuse in a humorous way (use the chalkboard to display). For

example, "I'll hold the nail and when I nod my head hit it with the hammer."

3. Make handouts in which paragraphs and longer passages are printed leaving blanks where pronouns would usually be.
4. Have students identify descriptive substitutes other than pronouns or rementioning nouns. For example, children might look for synonyms for "boy" such as child, male, young man, lad, etc., and put these in the place of pronouns.
5. Prepare pages in which *only* pronouns are used. Have children create "sense" by replacing *enough* of the pronouns with nouns of their own.

CONTEXT SIGNALS

Context signals are hints given by authors to the relationships among words and phrases. The most common context signals to meaning are connectives. Robinson (1978) described the following connectives:[1]

> *Go signals* are words that inform the reader that he is going to encounter another equivalent or similar idea. The word *and* is the most common example. Some "go signals" are "sequence signals" giving order to content. (For example: *and, also, then too*, etc.).
> *Caution signals* tell the reader to pay special attention to the next point, suggesting that it will be a conclusion or summary. (For example: *therefore, so, hence,* and phrases such as *in conclusion, as a result*.)
> *Turn signals* warn readers that they are about to read a different view, an opposing idea, or a change of direction. (For example: *although, despite, otherwise*.)
> *Relationship signals* are connectives that point to time, space, degree or amount, cause and effect, or conditional associations and comparisons between or among elements in a passage. (For example: *while, when, soon, there, here, many, less, fewer, if, unless*.)

Teachers need to help children become aware of signals and to help them use them for optimal meaning. When children read orally teachers might have them point to connectives and tell what they indicate about the next section. Handouts with missing or improper connectives substituted might also heighten awareness. In follow-up sessions teachers should be alert to confusion and lack of clarity due to failure to note or understand connectives. When this occurs they need to take the students to the spot where the connective signals are provided.

1. Based on a discussion on pages 70–71 of *Teaching Reading and Study Strategies: The Content Areas*, 2nd ed., by H. Alan Robinson. Boston: Allyn and Bacon, 1978. Used with permission.

CAUSALITY

Causal relationships are often very confusing to young readers. Pearson and Johnson (1978) suggested a series of difficulties related to causal relationships. These all require that the reader make inferences.

1. Many causal relations are not signaled by special terms and words (*because, since, wherefore, since,* etc.) that give explicit clues.
2. Many causal relations are disguised as time relations. (For example: *when, then* statements.)
3. There are multiple causes for many events.
4. There is a difficult distinction between physical cause and other relationships. (For example, those which enable an event to occur, and those which explain an event.)
5. In *if-then* causal statements it is not known whether the *if* statement has occurred.
6. Predicting outcomes (forward inferencing) and drawing conclusions involve stored conditional relationships. (We believe that something will happen because in similar prior experiences we saw the results.)

In order to improve children's ability to understand causal relationships, the teacher might do activities such as the following:

1. Have readers practice in discussion finding the tip-off words or phrases to causal relationships in sentences.
2. Give children questions involving choices after reading a passage in which causal relationships are implied.
3. Cut sentences in a story apart and have children correctly order them.
4. Have children make a dictionary of cue words that indicate causal relationships, telling what each indicates.
5. Use comic strips, with children being given choices for second, third, and fourth frames. Students are given the first frame and asked to identify the proper result. If frame 1 is the cause, what frame should follow?
6. Jokes and riddles are excellent examples of causality. They also illustrate many types of inference. Have students invent last lines for jokes and riddles.

FIGURATIVE LANGUAGE

Understanding figurative language is often difficult for children. Figures of speech are uses of language that build and extend sensory images. They do so by attaching one thing or action or idea to another with which it is not normally associated. In order to help children develop their ability to understand figurative language effectively in reading, the teacher needs to have an awareness of figures of speech himself.

Most children have used figurative language. It is prominent in dialects and in standard English and makes up the greater part of most slang expressions as well. Children begin to imitate these slang expressions at a very young age. Thus, by the time they encounter figurative language in reading, most children are already using it often in their speaking vocabulary. But it gives them great difficulty in written form. This trouble is due, in part, to specific unfamiliarity with the expressions used — for the message of figurative language goes beyond literal meanings. To understand it, one must be able to recognize contrast, comparison, and exaggeration.

The major purpose of figurative language is to add to the sensory images and affective meanings we can derive from reading, speaking, or listening. Such language also adds to the beauty and appeal of the language and is a distinctive element of writing "style." Almost all writers of literature employ many figures of speech. All forms of writing depend on such language patterns to expand meaning for the reader. The ability or inability to recognize and imagine figurative language may influence the reader's understanding of the author's idea. To fail to catch the meaning of a figure of speech may cause the reader to miss or confuse the author's message altogether. At the very least it will diminish the amount and intensity of personal meaning he derives from reading.

Figurative meaning is not given by the writer. It is supplied by the reader's experience. Arriving at figurative meaning is a creative reading and thinking process. The more imaginatively the reader interacts with the language, the richer the meaning becomes. Teachers should attempt to build a sensitivity to the presence of figurative language. Children need to be able to detect *when* words are being used figuratively. Figurative expressions used in reading selections create comprehension difficulty only in situations in which the reader is unaware that figurative speech is being used and in situations in which the referents are unfamiliar.

There seems to be a number of discernible stages in a reader's growth in ability to deal with figurative language. Though each stage is in constant development and is interdependent with all the others, it might be useful to look at one conceptualization of the various focuses of the process. Turner (1976*a*) has proposed the following.[2]

Experience stages of oral language. Awareness of the use of figures of speech in the language of ordinary oral communication (normal conversation patterns).

Recognition of the frequent and continual figurative language in the reader's own speech patterns.

---

2. Adapted from "Figurative Language: Deceitful Mirage or Sparkling Oasis" by Thomas N. Turner, *Language Arts* 53 (October 1976), pp. 158–161, with the permission of the National Council of Teachers of English.

Ability to verbalize, describe, and explain the expanded meanings created by figurative expressions, especially in terms of sensory images and feelings.

Consciousness of the role that figures of speech play in creating distinctiveness in dialects and slang.

Reading and writing stages. Awareness of the presence of figures of speech in reading materials and ability to see meaning in these when they are pointed out.

Ability to distinguish between words (and groups of words) in reading of materials that the author uses with figurative meanings rather than literal meanings.

Ability to recognize specific types of figurative language and to create new examples.

Realization of and ability to describe and imitate those effects that figurative language has on such qualities as mood, style, viewpoint, and the language beauty of a reading selection.

There are many classroom approaches that facilitate growth in dealing with figurative language. The one thing that really should not be expected of children is incidental and accidental growth. If untaught, figurative

Common Figures of Speech in Elementary School Materials

Simile: A comparison of two things or actions (or a person and a thing, etc.) that usually uses the words *like* or *as*. (Example: "Big John was as strong as an ox.")

Metaphor: An analogy or a simple comparison without the words *like* or *as*. (Example: "Big John was an ox.")

Allegory: A prolonged metaphor — a story that is in total a comparison. (Example: *Pilgrim's Progress* or "The Grasshopper and the Ant.")

Personification: Attributing to an inanimate object or an abstract idea or a lower animal form the characteristics of a human being. (Example: "The dog smiled in an evil sort of way." "The tree was lonely.")

Onomatopoeia: Using words with sounds that suggest their meaning. (Example: "The locomotive engine *hissed* and its wheels *screeched* against the tracks.")

Antithesis: A contrasting of ideas, showing opposites next to one another. (Example: "He was tall. The other man was short.")

Epigram: A short and succinct, usually humorous and satirical, statement. Used in car-

toons, often by newspaper columnists, and as a daily "chuckle" in a newspaper. (Example: "If he were to beat his head against a stone wall, only the wall would feel pain.")

Hyperbole: An exaggeration used for the special effect or impression it will create. (Example: "I could eat a million hamburgers.")

Euphemism: The substitution of a milder expression that will not be offensive for one that is stronger and may seem harsh or offensive. (Example: *pass away* is a euphemism for "die"; *perspire* is often used for "sweat.")

Synecdoche: The use of a part of something as though it were the whole thing. (Example: "All *hands* on deck!")

Irony: An expression or outcome of plot in which the results are deserved but their meaning is contrary to what is expected. (Example: The ogre in "Puss in Boots" chooses to show his power by turning himself into a mouse, which is the natural prey of Puss.)

174   **Higher Levels of Comprehension**

language encountered in reading will most likely remain unnoticed or misunderstood.

A number of ideas are listed below to help children become more aware of figurative language in reading (Turner 1976a).

1. Play the "What do people call you?" game. Pet names and nicknames are a very special kind of metaphoric language. During the discussion, the teacher may list a number of them on the chalkboard or on a chart. Offensive names that hurt children should be discussed, too, but care should be taken to avoid embarrassment. Discussion concerning why their particular names are used can help children become more aware of language meaning.
2. Collect examples of descriptions that are rich in figurative expression. Then have children draw the object or person described using literal meanings.
3. Have children create similes and metaphors to describe events that give feelings. For example: a clear sunny day; a happy optimistic person; the excitement someone feels when he receives especially good news; the feelings of a team that has just won an important game (or lost one); a terrible accident; a noisy, confused crowd.
4. Discuss the figurative and literal meanings of expressive sayings and proverbs. For example: "You're as pretty as a picture"; "Time is money"; "Fit as a fiddle"; "Don't beat a dead horse"; "Don't change horses in the middle of the stream"; "Where there is smoke, there is fire."
5. Read short poems that have a good deal of figurative language in them. Underline the figures of speech and have children think of other ways of expressing these ideas. They might take a short verse and rewrite it in language that tries to convey the same meaning literally. Or they might try to find alternative figures (e.g., metaphors for similes).
6. Have children imagine and perhaps describe something they have never seen before. Then they can try to help others understand it by using comparison as a figure of speech. Possible sources: a new invention; a new kind of vehicle; a creature from outer space; an organism that cannot be seen with a microscope; a character in a book that has no pictures.

It is especially important that children recognize the purposes of figurative language. Figurative expressions are used principally to aid in description. Through comparison, contrast, and exaggeration authors are able to increase the number of, and make more real and alive, the sensory images and feelings of the reader. Figures of speech sometimes evolve into habitual, common ways of saying things. Everyone uses them. Their meanings become blurred and they become cliches and begin to lose their power of sensory imagery. Good reading materials are continually supplying children with figures of speech that create fresh and new sensory images. When children become involved in understanding and "seeing" these images, they are reading creatively.

The Critical Reading Process

QUESTIONS TO GUIDE READING

Literal
Why does a reader need to develop the skill of dealing with a writer's viewpoints?
What are some reasons for developing skills for dealing with propaganda and advertising materials?
What five purposes are authors usually trying to achieve?
What are some criteria for distinguishing fact from opinion?
With what qualities are values concerned?

Inferential
What critical reading skills relate to opinion formation and decision making?
What are the differences between inductive and deductive approaches to teaching children to read materials containing propaganda?
What difficulties does an individual encounter in relating his own values to those encountered in reading?

Evaluative
Is one set of skills required for analysis and evaluation of literary materials and another set for dealing with informative and persuasive materials? Are there really any differences between the two types?
How are informational and persuasive skills related?
Should teachers encourage children to be critical of fantasy in literature?
Should particular values be taught as "right"?
Why does a reader tend to interpret values encountered in reading as supportive of his own central value system?

The development of critical readers is an irrefutable purpose of the reading program. This goal applies to every subject in the school curriculum, and critical reading skills are acknowledged as bread-and-butter tools needed by the individual in modern society.

In the sections that follow, we suggest a few ways of developing some of the critical reading skills. Many of these teaching techniques depend on discussion, which is essential because critical reading is a type of interactive reading. The reader is interacting with what he believes the author to be saying, and interaction is dialogue. Discussion helps to extend and develop the dialogue capabilities of students, to improve their questioning skill by sharing questions, and to improve their ability to compare evaluation responses they and others give.

DEALING WITH AUTHOR VIEWPOINT

An important area of critical reading skill is that of dealing with author opinions, viewpoints, and biases. Every reader needs to develop this area of skill in order to reconcile the views of the author with his own thinking.

There seems to be a negative, or at least reactive, feeling about author viewpoint in much of the literature of critical reading. Some writers go so far as to hint that authors are evil in having any view or opinion at all. To exemplify the evil, they point to the hidden and hypnotic power of reading materials to sway and stir the reader. Somehow, critical reading skill is supposed to steel the reader with a suspicious, skeptical attitude that will not be swayed.

Certainly, writers are trying to tell readers something, to communicate ideas. That is why they write. They feel they have a message that has not been communicated in just this way before. Generally, authors are attempting to achieve one or a combination of these purposes: (1) to entertain, (2) to inform, (3) to teach a skill or technique, (4) to persuade, or (5) to express an idea, opinion, or philosophy. Just as importantly, people read because they want to hear and know what the author is trying to say. They may share concerns and interests. If the writer did not believe in his message he would have had no reason to write. If the reader had no interest in getting the message, he would have no reason to read.

The first purpose of critical reading instruction related to author viewpoint is to teach children to recognize author opinion. A second purpose is to help the child to reconcile those opinions with the way he himself views the topic. A number of techniques have been used, including these:

1. Get children to ask questions about reading selections, such as the following: "Why did the writer write this story?" "What do you think was the purpose?" "How did the writer make you feel in the story?" "Did the writer bring you to feel as though you were a character in the story or that you wanted to be one?"
2. Have children skim a series of short poems or song lyrics. Ask them to describe the mood or feeling the author of each is trying to create and try to decide his reasons for wanting this mood.
3. Have children convert the messages of short opinion articles into cartoons or comic strips. (You should review with them any previous discussions of political cartoons and the ideas of comic visuals.)
4. Give all children colored slips of paper. Read several short selections to them. Have them hold up the color the reading makes them feel. Discuss color variety and how reader mood relates to author purposes.

5. Have students read biographical sketches of authors to identify factors that give their books the authority of being from experience.
6. Have students group books and stories and show ways in which the authors' biases differ.

DISTINGUISHING FANTASY FROM REALITY

Many children have difficulty in determining when, where, and how fantasy and reality diverge. Children are more likely to accept magic, myth, and unexplained mystery as real than adults. Their experiences are insufficient to enable them to make accurate judgments. After all, they are exposed daily to many strange, new, difficult-to-believe ideas that are presented as fact. Greater accuracy in making the distinctions between what one ought to believe to be an accurate picture of the real world and what is merely imaginary is needed in reading. A number of critical reading approaches exist that can help the child develop this skill. The more obvious and often taken route is to shatter fantasies by showing how unrealistic and ridiculous they are. In a way, this seems to be unnecessarily destructive.

In a recent study, Harms (1975) found that 5-year-olds are beginning to understand some of the concepts of fantasy. By the age of 9, her subjects were able to internalize fantasy, to comprehend concepts of causality in fantasy and reality, and to see some shifts from fantasy to reality.

A number of suggestions for dealing with fantasy and reality in reading are described in the following list:

1. Have children talk about the reality of such statements as these:
   "Each snowflake is different (unique)."
   "There is a person who looks just like you somewhere in the world."
   "Animals can talk."
   "Toys come alive on Christmas."
   "Frogs cause warts."
2. Have children examine the comic page of the newspaper. Discuss how the pictures are like real things and people and how they are different. Talk about how conversation and characters are real and how they are unreal.
3. Have children compare with real-life situations some specific television programs about the police, emergency workers, and the medical profession.
4. Brainstorm a list of "impossible" things we would like to do or have. Talk about why the things are "impossible." Do the same for a list of "possible" things.
5. Make a list of characters from favorite stories or television. Discuss the things these characters do. Classify the characters into categories of "very much like real people" and "very unlike real people."

DISTINGUISHING FACT FROM OPINION

Children need to become aware of the existence of both fact and opinion in reading material. Most of what we read is, to some degree, based on opinion, but it is often stated as though it were totally fact. (This paragraph is an example.) Fact might be defined as what is true. Opinion is what we believe to be true but cannot verify.

Distinctions between fact and opinion are not always clear-cut. Indecision usually arises from conflict in consciously or unconsciously weighing a statement simultaneously by a number of criteria. Some are necessary attributes of fact; some just look good but prove nothing. These criteria include the following:

1. The statement comes from a believable authority.
2. The statement is substantiated by other evidence or other authorities.
3. The statement is reconcilable with what we know from personal experience.
4. The statement seems logical and reasonable.
5. It is stated in terms that are value-free or that do not require value judgments.
6. The statement is generally accepted to be true or accepted by those we trust.
7. The statement is open to few or no exceptions.
8. The statement has been repeated often with little or no contradiction to this point.
9. The statement is made with authority.
10. The statement *can be* checked.

We do not weigh these criteria equally in making our decision. At varying times one or two of the criteria may totally (or nearly totally) influence our decision. To help children develop their abilities to make decisions about fact and opinion, you might apply some of the following suggestions:

1. Have children generate or discuss a set of statements of fact and opinion around a single topic. For example, some children assembled these statements on apples, then evaluated them for factual context.
   a. "Apples grow on trees."
   b. "Green apples will make you sick if you eat them."
   c. "The redder an apple is, the better it tastes."
   d. "The biggest apples are sweetest."
   e. "Apples are most crisp in the autumn."
   f. "There are several varieties of apples."
   g. "Apples taste better than oranges."
2. Simulate a courtroom trial in which witnesses have different stories. Nursery rhymes and fairy tales are fun to use for the cases. For example:

"Who really stole the Queen's tarts?" "Was Tom, the piper's son, guilty of pignapping?" "Was the wolf in 'The Three Little Pigs' guilty of malicious destruction of property?"

3. Put a story on an acetate transparency. With two colors of felt-tip markers underline statements of fact in one color and statements of opinion in another. With questionable statements take a vote after discussion.

4. Place a statement of controversy on the chalkboard, such as any of those in the following list. As the children debate it, give the arguments for the statement on one side and those against it on the other.
   a. "The bathtub is the most dangerous place in the home."
   b. "People who wear seatbelts in their cars are more likely to survive an accident."
   c. "Eagles may become extinct."
   d. "There are more police stories on television than any other form of show."
   e. "The world is overpopulated."

5. Have children list as many ways as they can of "proving" particular statements of fact. Begin with easily proven ideas (i.e., Washington was the first president of the U.S.A.) and move to more difficult ones. Set up a chart of items. This can be run as a contest or game, with the goal as obtaining the most ways of establishing proof.

6. Develop with the children a list of resource people. Then make a list of questions or problems. Have the children identify who the best two or three authorities would be for assistance in solving each problem. Problems should range from easy to difficult.

Sample list of resource people

Home economist	Mechanic
Plumber	Hobby shop owner
Mechanical engineer	Lawyer
Ex-Burglar	Insurance agent
City mayor	Forest ranger

Sample problems
How to bake a cake.
How to open a locked safe.
How to put an electric wire in a house.
How to write a will.

Note: Discuss other background experiences of these people that might make them better authorities.

DETERMINING RELEVANCY

The critical reading skills of drawing relationships and seeing associations are needed for all research and problem solving. The same data can be structured in different ways to reach different conclusions and solutions. These are "selecting" skills. It is appropriate to master them at the same time or even before developing skimming abilities. A few ideas for activities are listed below:

1. Write class outlines of stories after children become familiar with the technical aspects of outlining. Work on headings that depart from the author's sequence (e.g., characters, settings). See what children can do with extraneous information.
2. Give children a question such as the following, and have them choose the relevant facts from among several pieces of (mostly irrelevant) information: What is the capital city of Ohio?
   a. The largest city in Ohio is Cleveland.
   b. Many presidents come from Ohio.
   c. The Ohio River runs past Cincinnati, Ohio.
   d. The governor and the state legislature are in Columbus, Ohio.
3. Mix up lines from different songs or panels from different cartoons along with some unrelated lines and cartoon frames. Have the children correctly sort them.

ASSESSING PROPAGANDA

Propaganda and advertising materials are often used to teach critical reading. To many teachers, these materials seem to be the most appropriate types to use, for reasons such as the following:

1. Propaganda and advertising materials are abundant, current, and free.
2. Children are usually already very familiar with such materials and recognize most of them immediately.
3. Propaganda and advertising have but one single purpose — to sell something to somebody.
4. The simplicity of purpose makes it easier to identify and isolate the techniques being used.
5. Once isolated, the techniques and devices used in propaganda and advertising can be easily categorized.
6. In a society in which children are constantly confronted by mass media, it seems important to teach them how to deal with the advertising and propaganda being directed toward them.
7. In a democratic society in which citizens are supposed to help make many decisions, it seems important that they recognize forces attempting to influence those decisions.

Teaching children to read, view, and listen critically to propaganda may begin with either inductive or deductive approaches. In inductive approaches the teacher begins by focusing children's attention on many examples of propaganda and advertising. She can do this in many ways. The teacher may collect or have children collect examples of advertising from magazines and newspapers. Recorded samples of radio and television sales approaches are also useful. Once the examples are collected, they can be utilized in a number of ways. One is simply to have the children discuss and work at categorizing the advertisements. Common guide questions could be: "Which ones seem to go together?" and "What are some different ways of categorizing?" The first result will probably be a grouping of like products. When this occurs, the teacher needs to guide the children to look for other ways of grouping and arranging. Good discussion leadership will guide and enable students to discuss the common elements employed by advertisers in selling different products and ideas. Eventually, children can learn to form generalized concepts that will help them to categorize other attempts to influence their thinking.

Another inductive approach is to have children role-play and artistically recreate political and commercial advertisements they have seen or heard on television and radio or in magazines and newspapers. Perhaps they can create fictional products with fictional names and try to imitate the approaches read or heard. This application leads to analyses in detail of propaganda that children see every day. It also leads to a more critical attitude. The applicational level of this technique stimulates imaginative as well as critical thinking. It is one approach to critical reading in which creative thinking is important to the learning process.

Deductive approaches to teaching critical reading using propaganda normally begin with the listing and defining of propaganda techniques. The teacher may then give several examples of each technique from current and familiar sources. Afterward, it is the children's task to come up with additional examples. A follow-up or alternative assignment could require children to identify which techniques are being used in an additional group of examples. The children could try pantomiming or role playing to test their assessments. Or the teacher may simply ask, "What techniques do 'Pepsi' and 'McDonald's' use?" Lists of propaganda techniques are abundant. The following paragraphs describe some typical techniques:

Loaded words: Words that stir up strong emotions in people are used. The reader or listener will not be able to be objective about the words. Good propagandists use loaded terms to draw people to their point of view. Examples: Society for Freedom and Democracy in American Life, The Eternal Rest (name of a cemetery).

Name calling: This involves smearing (or building) someone's reputation without rational arguments related to issues. (Mud slinging is one description often given to this device.)

a. *Glad names:* The reader's interest is kept away from the issues. Examples: "handsome," "smiling."

b. *Bad names:* Judgments are made and conveyed without facts. Examples: "He's a communist." "He's a rampaging liberal." (Note: Bad names are often used in conjunction with loaded words.)

Card stacking: All the facts favoring the propagandist's point of view are presented. All the contrary or qualifying arguments are omitted. Example: "This dogfood has more of the protein your dog needs than any other, and dogs love the taste." They omit mentioning that most of the protein consists of hair, nail clippings, and other types that the dog's body cannot use and that dogs get sick after they eat it.

Straw man: A case for the opponent's point of view is built, but in a carefully selected way so that it can later be destroyed or broken down. Example: "My opponent has taken a firm stand on human rights. He is a family man, a church goer, an active worker in charities." (Prepare now to hear about the opponent's actions, which disprove all these assertions — for example, that he owes $250 in parking fines, belongs to a club with prejudicial membership requirements, and beats his horse.)

Slogans: Simple, catchy, and easily remembered sentences or phrases are associated with the product or person. They are repeated until people begin to believe them. Examples: "You deserve a break today"; "I like Ike"; "A choice not an echo"; "Have it your way."

Unproved assertions: Statistics and factual-sounding information may have no evidence or at least cannot stand up to close examination. But the assertions are repeated so often that people begin to believe them. Examples: "The best you can buy"; "a man for our time."

Testimonial: A well-known person endorses a product or another person. The celebrity may or may not have any expertise related to the selection, but his individual reputation is attached. Examples: A football player advertising hamburger cookers, a well-known singer endorsing a particular automobile, famous comedians talking about discovering a great new soft drink taste.

Bandwagon: This approach invites the reader to do what "everyone" is doing, to go along with the crowd. Example: "Join the Dodge Rebellion."

Snob appeal: This technique invites the reader to follow an "elite" bandwagon. The reader will act as the propagandist wants *if* he is that special kind of person. Examples: "For the person who wants something more"; "Not for the average man"; "For the discriminating customer."

Individualizing approach: This technique invites the reader to be different. Nonconformity is for the sake of nonconformity. Examples: "Be your own man"; "What's good enough for other folks is not good enough for me."

Plain folks: An attempt is made to associate the product or person with the common man, *usually country* (often with country folks or the working man or woman). Examples: "For that downhome, country flavor"; "He is a man of the people." Note: Most often visual and sound effects add to these images.

We may also examine advertisements by asking the following questions: "What forms do the advertisements take?" "What is the target audience?" "How often is the format changed and why?" and "How is the advertising timed?" All these and many more questions need to be asked. One of the essential understandings that should be part of every approach to propaganda is the notion that the propagandist is simply trying to convince the reader or media audience of a point of view. It is an attempt to sell something to somebody, to make them feel they need something. One important question that the critical reader asks is, "Are the propagandists really sold on the product or person themselves?"

CRITICAL READING AND DECISIONS ABOUT VALUES

An ultimate purpose of critical reading is the development of abilities to select, reject, and adapt information and ideas found in reading. The reader evaluates both the form of presentation and the substance of the ideas and information. Further, he may evaluate the whole reading selection or only the smallest detail. So, critical reading instruction must be involved with the student's competency in interrelating the values inherently put forth by reading materials with his own personal values. It may also relate to his awareness of his own values and how well he is able to put these aside while examining the opinions of others. Reading materials reflect many values concerns. Values are relatively prevailing, qualitative opinions. They generally relate to a number of identifiable overlapping categories (Turner 1977):[3]

1. *Goodness* (moral values, social values, religious values)
2. *Power* (political values, physical values)
3. *Beauty* (aesthetic values)
4. *Satisfaction* (personal values, psychological values)
5. *Truth* (philosophical values, scientific values)
6. *Order* (organizational values)
7. *Worth* (human values, economic values, historical values)

Most people have a large number of values related to each of these classifications. These are sometimes vague ideas, not at all clearly defined. The total set is always changing and shifting, but the central value core remains fairly constant for most individuals. We are more likely to notice ideas that agree with our central values than to see those that disagree. If possible, we interpret ideas encountered in reading as being supportive of our central values. Where there is unavoidable conflict, we have to reconcile that conflict, which we do by shutting it out (ignoring or failing to see it), or by finding reason to reject the intruding value (rationalizing),

3. Adapted from "Critical Reading as a Values Clarification Process" by Thomas N. Turner, *Language Arts* 54 (November–December 1977), pp. 909–917. Reprinted with the permission of the National Council of Teachers of English.

or by accepting it and changing our own value system (adaptation). Quality, relevance, importance, strength, and interest or concern are all judgments that influence the process.

There are many techniques and activities a teacher can use to strengthen a child's awareness and skill in making values decisions. A few ideas are listed below.

Activities to Strengthen Skills in Making Values Decisions

1. Discuss a number of old fairytales, taking the side of the villain. Example: "Jack in the Beanstalk was a thief and murderer."
2. Have children identify things that story characters *should* have done but did not do (either because they did something else or because they did nothing at all).
3. Brainstorm a list of "Hero" traits. Then look at heroes and heroines of specific stories to see which of these traits most of them exhibited.
4. Give children a list of problem situations or occupations. Then have them talk about what different story characters would have done in these instances. Examples of situations:

a. On a sinking ship with three people and no lifeboats . . .
b. As the "underdog" in an election campaign for president . . .
c. Trying to find a lost child . . .
d. Getting people out of a building that is about to fall down . . .
5. Have children switch characters among stories (you can incorporate television characters too). Discuss with them how some new character would have acted differently in a story from the way the original one acted.
6. Have children make a list of books or stories they think everyone should read.

BEGINNING CRITICAL READING

Primary children can be taught to read critically. McCullough (1957) found no special difficulty attributable to grade level with such higher comprehension or critical reading skills as seeing relationships, drawing conclusions, and passing judgments. Wolf and her associates (1967) also concluded that children in any of the grades one to six can learn to read critically.

Two questions may be asked of any primary grade child to initiate instruction in critical reading. The first general question is the same as the initiating question for the most advanced student of literature: "Do you like what you have read?" A series of follow-up questions naturally flows from this: What do/don't you like? Why do/don't you like it? What do you like about the characters? Are you pleased by the events that happen in the story?" Whenever children arrive at controversy, diversity, indecision, or doubt, a critical reading discussion can follow. The eventual goal is to have children initiate, ask, and grapple with these kinds of questions themselves. Similar questions may be directed toward expository materials.

A second general question should be: "What does this mean?" Answering this may involve the child in written tests — selecting the most appropriate from among several possible meanings of words and sentences. It may involve paraphrasing and putting ideas into one's own words. But the idea of "meaning" includes more than literal translation in reading. It implies power or significance as well as relevance and utility. The larger question is "What does this mean to *you*?"

While such questions probe for likes and dislikes (which are opinions), they more essentially are leading the child to ask about the impact of the reading selection upon his senses, his thinking, and his emotions. Such impact (or the lack of it) is importantly related to what the selection means to him and how it affects the way he views the world.

Aspects of Teaching Creative Reading

QUESTIONS TO GUIDE READING

Literal
What are some features of a classroom environment that help children become creative readers?
What can a teacher do to create a stimulus-rich environment?
What are some features of assignments that encourage creative reading?

Inferential
What is a stimulus-rich environment?
What is there about fantasy that makes it a "natural resource" in creative reading?
What makes creative reading a risk-taking behavior?

Evaluative
How can a teacher know if the atmosphere of his classroom is conducive to creative reading?
Why is the assignment of creative tasks so important to the development of creative reading?

Different teaching personalities and types of environments may bring growth in creative reading. The child, the classroom situation, and the teacher are all too complex for there to be a single "right" way. A number of qualities, however, seem to characterize the teacher whose students grow best. There are at least three aspects of a teacher's role that can promote creative reading: providing a conducive environment, creating stimulating reading tasks, and making the student who reads creatively feel that he has done something worthwhile.

SETTING THE CLASSROOM ENVIRONMENT

The creative environment is one in which apparent contradictions exist. This environment needs to make children feel psychologically safe and at the same time it must create a tension toward excitement. The child has safety without boredom and adventure without fear. A second feature is that the child has leisure time to dream and to create and yet does not feel pressured to do the creating or to complete the creation.

Perhaps the most important feature of the environment needed for creative reading is that it makes the child feel a need to create. The term *creative set* is often used to describe this feeling the child must have. Creative set can be defined as an attitude of anticipation that what is read will prove useful and will be applicable to doing something or creating something. Both teachers and students need to have this creative set in the classroom.

Stimulus-rich environments are essential for creative reading. Torrance (1970) pointed out the importance of providing children with materials that develop the imagination and, especially, with those that enrich imagery. Not the quantity, quality, or variety of the materials essential for stimulating creativity can ever be overdeveloped in a school setting. The display, focus, and highlighting of the best imaginative qualities are all crucial teacher responsibilities. The teacher can select and keep available books and stories of high imagination. He can cut up old storybooks, eliminating endings and beginnings to stimulate creative writing. Both teacher and students can examine newspapers and magazines for pictures to illustrate stories. The teacher can keep children's written work and artwork from year to year. He can make bulletin boards and invent creative reading games. Learning or interest centers can be full of tasks that require creative reading. The teacher is really limited only by his own imagination in making the learning area into a treasure house of creative stimuli.

One aspect of a stimulus-rich environment is the provision for experiences to expand reading. Visual representations of stories (such as pictures, movies, and artwork by children) provide sensory experiences with the things and people found in reading materials. Field trips, artifacts, and other activities involving sensory perception also contribute to the building of such experiences. The world of the school should be filled with sights and sounds, smells and tastes. It should be an ever-changing, choice-filled (yet patterned) kaleidoscope of experience.

Providing Creative Reading Tasks

Creative tasks are crucial to creative behavior. Turner and Alexander (1975) have given a number of suggestions to teachers about the nature of assignments that encourage creative reading, including:

1. Give students challenging choices among tasks.
2. Vary the way in which a child is asked to put his reading to creative use. If he must always respond in writing to a set of questions, the tasks soon become noncreative. Use all the means of expression available, including oral and written language, musical experiences, artistic expressions, and body movement.
3. Encourage children to vary and deviate from the tasks set.
4. Keep tasks flexible so that individual movement of "mood and inspiration" may be utilized.
5. Maintain a high degree of imagination in the task and task descriptions. Be creative and exciting. Change the patterns of tasks often.
6. Provide as rich a sensory background to the reading task as possible, adding dimensions of sound when appropriate.

An array of strategies and techniques is needed to develop creative reading skills in children. No one type of approach is sufficient by itself. Torrance (1970, pp. 13–14) has said that "creativity is encouraged in the classroom whenever teachers and pupils respond to one another's creativity needs." This is a complex and difficult job to accomplish because every individual has a constantly changing set of immediate needs.

A natural resource for creative reading tasks seems to be stories of high fantasy and imagination. Fairytales, tall tales, wonder tales, talking animal stories, myths, and legends all provide, by their very imaginative qualities, models for creative thinking. Gendler (1975) described a technique in which he approached myths by looking at modern names (days of the week, for example), then explored the natural phenomena they describe. After reading the myths, the children carefully examined the word that the myth attempted to explain. Creative analysis was needed to see how the inventors of the myths could have used the particular myth to explain or account for aspects of their environment. Tall tales and stories of superheroes also provide excellent models. Alternative endings for the stories or additional episodes can be written or talked out repeatedly. (A tape recorder is useful.)

All the written fantasy forms can be reexpressed well in symbolic and impressionistic art. They may provide entry into a study of this type of art and into the development of models, sculpture, paintings, and drawings by the children in symbolic and impressionistic styles based on stories read. Some of the science fiction and wonder tales have rich and lively illustrations that may serve as models. Stimuli for creative reading should not be totally and exclusively drawn from the world of fantasy.

This is limiting in itself; and it necessarily excludes some children from being able to create in a satisfactory way. Gould (1972, p. 26) has concluded from her research that some children are reality-bound and unable for psychological reasons to engage in fantasy. Although these children are limited in their range of creations, they can still be creative readers. The ability to create and the ability to fantasize are distinguishable traits; they are not the same thing. Children incapable of fantasy are simply restricted in their creations to imagining and creating the "possible" in their perceptions of the real world. To expect such children to react to fantasy stimuli is unrealistic.

Smith (1969) suggested that tasks that involve having children think about questions can be used to stimulate creative reading. Questions for recall or comprehension differ from creative questions. Witty (1974) charted the differences in convergent and divergent questions as follows:

Convergent questions	*Divergent questions*
1. Ask only for information that is in the story.	1. Ask for information not in the story.
2. Do not ask for reader's personal ideas.	2. Ask for the reader's personal ideas.
3. Ask for correct answers that can be determined by analyzing the story.	3. Evoke open-ended, inferred responses.
4. Focus on the author's meaning.	4. Focus on what the reader can add.

Children should be encouraged to record their ideas, but they need a purpose for recording. One purpose could be to keep a notebook or folder to fill with writing, which they could share from time to time. Class and school publications provide another purpose. Specific occasions also offer opportunities to make creative reading purposeful. For example, children may be encouraged to make and send greeting cards (Christmas, birthday, get-well, and sympathy).

Creative tasks should involve choices. Children should be allowed to decide among several means of creative responses to reading. These choices should not always be limited to a poem, a written story, or any other narrowly defined form.

Following are a number of ideas for assignments and pupil tasks that encourage creative reading. The sample sources used are games, newspapers, and poetry:

Gaming activities and game making for creative readers. Remake a board game such as "Uncle Wiggley," "Candy Land," or "Monopoly." The game can be one in which the objective is either to move pieces around or to move toward a goal. Rename the stops and hazards along the way using the events, places, and characters in a story or series of stories. Play the game.

Make a checkerboard ditto or transparency. Label each square with name of a character in a story or a place in a story. (Several different stories can be used.) To move into a square with a checker a player must be able to describe what happened or who the character was.

Change question-asking games like 20 Questions, television's "Jeopardy," or "Hollywood Squares" into creative reading games by having children make up both questions and answers. (For example, the occupants of each square in the "Hollywood Squares" game could be a book character who answers in character.)

Reading the newspaper creatively (adapted from Turner 1973). *World leader — Dear Ann Landers.* Give the children a chance to write an advice column for leading political figures in the news. Using current news and knowledge, they can pretend they are both the leaders and the columnist, or they can set up an exchange to answer each other's letters. The gossip columnists can be paralleled in the same way.

Photo-essay. Newspapers and magazines provide exciting resources for this creative technique. With short captions, or no captions at all, a story can be told or an idea put across using a series of newsphotos and diagrams. The creativity is in the selection and sequence. Subjects can vary from world peace to community helpers, to a new engine design, to sports, to society. This is especially useful for the early school years and for children who have trouble with written communication or verbal communication in general.

Comic page news. Comics and cartoons are among the newspapers' first and biggest attractions to children. Their use can begin in the earliest primary grades and extend through the highest levels of schooling. They can be used in a number of ways that promote creative writing while developing a child's understanding of and interest in the news. Comics and cartoons provide in themselves a running commentary on our society and its values and symbols. The teacher, or each child, needs to select one or more comic strips or cartoon series to clip and save over a period of time to provide and build up an inventory. Then the children can use them in any of the following ways:

1. Cut off captions on cartoons and exchange them. Then have children match cartoons to news stories or write their own captions.
2. Write a comic "philosophy": Over a period of time a comic or cartoon expresses a total view of life. See if children can pick this out and describe it, using the cartoons as illustrations. The intermix of the children's own developing views makes "right" or "wrong" inappropriate. If the teacher can convince the children that they will not be judged on interpretation, they can enjoy this task. It may be a little frustrating for children at first, but after they get started, it can be a lot of fun.
3. Create a new cartoon form. Some suggested possibilities might be car-

toons using newspaper weather maps, textbook circle graphs or picture graphs, or clothing. The children create their own humorous comments about our life and times.

Classified news. Again, this is a rich and unused source for creativity. Children can write their own advertisements using their humor and descriptive abilities: For example: (1) selling something, real or imaginary; (2) describing a job to fit their qualifications or ambitions; (3) announcing an event that is going to happen or that they want to happen.

Using headlines. Children learn some creative reading skills and have fun at the same time when using headlines they have clipped or invented.

1. Newspaper articles can be clipped and mounted on cardboard. Afterwards the headlines can be separated from the articles. Groups of children then play matching games trying to put the proper article and title combinations together. This can be done as a relay race game among several groups of children, or it can be used as a creative activity, with children finding appropriate or ironic headline and article combinations.
2. Collect a large variety of newspaper headlines; cut out and mount if possible. Children can use these to write a complete story using headlines only. The story need not be in complete sentences since headlines are not always complete sentences.
3. Have the children put stories from their reading books into the language and style of newspaper headlines.

Using poetry. Have children invent motions to accompany the oral reading of a poem. Or have children visually represent short poems on posters.

Involve children in writing additional verses to favorite songs. Have children find recordings or songs to sing that match the mood of a poem.

Have children do book "reports" in some poetic form. Or let children try to imitate a particular poet's style.

Let children make copies of poems in which the style and lettering fit the mood of the poem.

RESPONDING TO THE CREATIVE READER

The determination of how to receive creativity is not easily researchable. Golub (1971) has pointed out that the teacher necessarily takes sometimes conflicting roles of literary analyst and psychologist. These roles require a thorough knowledge of the creator and his background as well as an understanding of what the creative reader is trying to communicate.

There is general agreement that two important factors in encouraging creative reading are: (1) an atmosphere of acceptance of each creative work or idea as something of value and (2) the recognition and reward of creative effort. The two are interrelated factors. Rewards and acceptance may both be provided in countless ways. The teacher must realize that it is not any single action she takes but the complex concerts of all actions that must be directed at encouraging and rewarding if creativity is to flourish. No behavior is too small or too insignificant to have impact on a child's view of how he or his ideas have been received. Consciously and unconsciously, verbally and nonverbally, overtly and covertly the teacher and the class are constantly giving the child feedback about himself and his ideas. Creative drive can be damaged as much by acts omitted as by acts committed. Failure to notice a child's work or idea can hurt as much as showing negative reactions. A facial expression interpreted as disinterested, preoccupied, or hostile is as demoralizing as a verbal brush-off or destructive verbal criticism. Stopping class activities to "look" can be damaging at one time or to one child and rewarding and helpful in a different situation.

Creative thinking in reading, as in any curricular area, is a risk-taking behavior. A person creatively reacting to reading is engaging in behaviors that are not "safe" ones. A safe action is one in which the individual can judge how people will receive what is said or done. The exact reaction is not known, but the general type of reaction is. People avoid actions that will bring hurt or injury; in fact, the subconscious often blocks out unsafe answers, and they never surface. School situations that demand a response usually have a right-answer range that is "safe." That is, the students know how the teacher and peers will receive the kinds of answers given. The especially timid often find that no answer is safer from criticism or ridicule than a wrong answer.

Part of the creative response environment is an openness to "serendipity" or chance happenings and ideas. Teachers are sometimes too busy for such unexpected creativity. One of the most difficult arts for teachers to master is to take time to recognize and encourage things that children do outside of the tasks assigned in school. It seems that teachers even take it as a sign that they are not giving enough work if a child brings something that took some time to do. Yet it is that kind of act that teachers need to encourage. Probably the best sign of the accomplishment of creative set in children is when they do something not assigned. The independently creative reader is the best evidence that creative reading has been "taught."

Beginning Creative Reading

Creative reading should be a part of the earliest reading experiences. It will enable the child to make reading "real" and "alive" if he begins to reshape and rethink what he has read. Only when reading becomes more than words, sounds, and letters does the reading process take on meaning.

Language experience approaches to reading instruction provide real

Figure 8.1. The cycle from experience to reading.

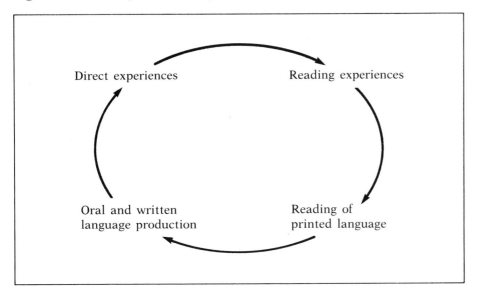

opportunities to relate creative thinking to reading (see Chapter 13). These approaches recognize the importance of experience and personal language reading. They allow children to see the continual exchange in the cyclical process of experience to language productions to reading (see Figure 8.1).

Reading is itself an experience. A language experience story can be created by a group of children who retell a story they have all read (or who create a new story). This telling gives children an opportunity to verbalize what they understand of plot, character, and setting.

Early creative reading experiences need not take a great deal of time. A few illustrative ideas follow:

1. Writing a sentence identifying each of the characters.
2. Making tools or objects described in stories.
3. Dressing dolls or paper dolls as story characters.
4. Making up a song about a story character to be sung to a well-known tune.
5. Making puppets or masks and role-playing some stories. (Puppets can be such as a sock puppet, a paper bag puppet, a mask puppet, a stick and nylon stocking puppet, or a metal hanger puppet; all are within the capabilities of primary age children.)
6. Orally reading short stories and poems and making up motions to go with them.
7. Making posters to "advertise" or "sell" stories to other children.
8. Rereading a single line or sentence of a story or poem several times to show different ways of expressing it.

Any number of sets of principles have been formulated to help the teachers organize the early creative reading experiences of children. The following guidelines seem to incorporate many of the best features of these (Turner 1976*b*):

1. Creative reading problems initially should be mostly concrete.
2. First creative tasks should relate productive thinking to literal meaning of stories.
3. In the beginning creative problems and tasks should be of the types that can be completed in a short period of time (say, five minutes).
4. Creative tasks for young children should be finite, that is, they should give a sense of accomplishment and completion.
5. Questions and reading-related assignments seeking creative response can and should begin with first experiences in reading.

HOW EXCEPTIONAL CHILDREN EXPERIENCE CRITICAL AND CREATIVE READING

All children can learn to read creatively and critically. However, critical and creative reading skills are built on literal comprehension. That is, some level of literal comprehension of a reading passage is almost always necessary to enable the reader to think creatively and critically about the passage. The implications are important for working with children with learning difficulties. The critical and creative reading skills of these children need development, but the materials used should be of lower difficulty than those used with more able children. Generally, these materials should be well within their independent reading level. If the materials are too difficult for children to read independently, teachers should develop literal comprehension through discussion. A high degree of teacher guidance may be required.

Gifted children generally read more than their average peers and perform more critical and creative tasks with relative ease. The range of independent-level materials they can comprehend literally is far greater than the comparable ranges of their normative classmates. Catalytic ideas and encouragement of freedom of thought and expression represent their chief needs.

Summary

Inferential reading, critical reading, and creative reading are interactive types of reading. That is, the reader is engaged in a dialogue of thought with the author. The differences between critical and creative reading are to be found in the manner and purposes of the dialogue. Reading for inference involves selective application of prior experience and knowledge. Critical reading is reactive and comparative. The reader is constantly testing what is read in the balance of experience and judgment. It is analytical in that the reader seeks to identify what delights, what satisfies, what is missing, what horrifies, what bores, and what engrosses. Creative reading is provocative and, again, selective. It involves the reader in finding that within the reading which can be made his own and which can be adapted for use. The reader is constantly seeking to see things not as they are but as they could become.

Inferential reading, critical reading, and creative reading are all skill related. Each requires competency in several skills basic to the reading process. These reading skills are prerequisite to higher levels of comprehension and are involved in their development. Since these higher levels involve the reader in going beyond the literal content of what is read, inference, critical reading, and creative reading demand highly developed comprehension skills. Problem-solving and questioning skills are necessary for the nurture of all these levels. The reading skills required to read inferentially, critically, and creatively are developmental. Therefore, inferential, critical, and creative reading can and should begin with the earliest reading experience.

Questions for Further Reading and Thinking

1. What are some ways in which teachers can better anticipate misleading inferences or insufficient inferences?
2. How are inferencing problems detected?
3. How does imagery relate to inferencing skills?
4. How could each of the following be used to develop creative reading?
   a. adventure fantasy
   b. tall tales
   c. folk tales and fairy-tales
   d. talking animal stories
   e. biographical fiction
   f. humorous stories
   g. lyric poetry
5. Which of the following would you want children to read most critically? Most creatively? Explain your reasons.
   a. the Bible
   b. the local newspaper
   c. the dictionary
   d. a novel
   e. a historical account
   f. a legal contract
   g. the telephone book
6. How could you recognize the point at which a child understands what he is reading well enough to think creatively or critically about it?
7. What influences do parents and peers have on critical and creative reading abilities?
8. What could be some creative reading "products" of such familiar pieces of literature as the following:
   a. "The Emperor's New Clothes"
   b. "The Blind Men and the Elephant" (old Indian story)
   c. *Where the Wild Things Are* by Sendak
   d. *Little House on the Prairie* by Wilder

e. The Rhymes of Mother Goose
f. "The 23rd Psalm"
g. "The Selfish Giant" by Oscar Wilde
h. "Peanuts" (comic strip)
i. "Rocky Mountain High" (song)
j. "Rumpelstiltskin"
9. How would you describe critical reading? Take the definition from the literature that best fits your own concept and expand it.
10. Do techniques and strategies for teaching critical reading vary with the type of material read? Why or why not?
11. Is creative reading only for gifted children? Explain your reasoning.
12. What are some of the specific behaviors of teachers you have seen that promote creative thinking about reading?
13. What is the pattern or sequence of skill development that can be expected of children in critical reading?

Activities and Projects

1. Develop an annotated bibliography of stories, articles, and books for children that are especially good for stimulating inferential, creative, or critical reading. Justify each by explaining your reasons for selection.
2. Develop a set of probing questions for readers for each of the materials in the bibliography of activity 1 to help them read more critically or creatively or to obtain more accurate or varied inference.
3. Go through one or more reading games and activities books. Identify those games and activities you feel would be useful in developing inferencing skills, or creative or critical reading. Explain your reasoning.
4. Analyze a set of poems for inferential meanings.

5. Make a materials notebook of poems, short stories, and readings that can be read creatively or critically. Point out the techniques to be used with each (creative motion, dramatization, interpretive oral reading, specific questions, for example).
6. Collect a group of open-ended stories in which children have to decide how the stories should end, on the basis of one of the following:
   a. moral judgments   d. legal judgments
   b. aesthetic judgments e. realism judg-
   c. ethical judgments   ments
7. Collect a set of stories with double or multiple meanings.

Activities and Materials Sources

For teachers

Altick, Richard D. 1956. *Preface to critical reading.* New York: Henry Holt.

Christensen, Fred. 1971. *Springboards to creative writing.* Monterey Park, Calif.: Creative Teaching Press.

Ehrlich, Harriet W., ed. 1971. *Creative dramatics handbook.* Philadelphia: Office of Early Childhood Programs, The School District of Philadelphia.

Hopkins, Lee Bennett. 1972. *Pass the poetry, please!* New York: Citation Press.

Kirg, Joyce; and Katzmar, Carol. 1976. *Imagine that.* Pacific Palisades, Calif.: Goodyear.

Modely, Robert; and Gibb, Sylvia. 1971. *The writing center.* Toronto: Holt, Rinehart and Winston of Canada.

Murray, Donald M.; and Albert, Burton, Jr. *Write to communicate.* (4 kits; Base levels 3, 4, 5, and 6) Pleasantville, N.Y.: Reader's Digest Services, Educational Division.

Write on! Read on! Right on! 1975. Newburgh, N.Y.: Newburgh City School District. (1st, 2nd, and 3rd year writings of students using ITA reading materials).

For children

Becoming somebody: Creative activities for preschool children by Dr. Charles E. Schaefer. Buffalo, N.Y.: Disseminators of Knowledge.

Creative reading enrichment duplicating masters (K–3). Grand Rapids, Mich.: Instructional Fair.

Creative reading program (Readiness–3). New York: Harper and Row.

Find your own way — experiences in language by Dr. Terry Borton. New York: Harcourt Brace Jovanovich.

Logic cards and *reaction cards.* Niles, Ill.: Developmental Learning Materials.

Reading, thinking, and reasoning by Don Barnes et al. (grades 1–8, skills emphasis on analyses, synthesis, and evaluation). Austin, Tex.: Steck Vaughn.

Thomas N. Turner

9
Questioning Techniques: Probing for Greater Meaning

Any statement that requires a response may be called a question. Teachers and children use questions as a continual part of the communication process. Teachers often find that questions may be the only way that they can discover how well children understand what they read. Reading itself is a cognitive process and is not unobservable. Questions can probe for children's effectiveness as readers. Did they get the author's message? Were main ideas and details understood? What inferences were made? In reading groups, in individual conferences, and in both written and oral forms, questions help teachers to estimate students' success.

The role of questions in the teaching of reading is broader than that of an evaluation tool, however. Questions provide ways of guiding, directing, and focusing the mental activities involved in reading. They provide both the teacher and the reader with keys to better reading.

The ability to ask questions and to teach children to ask themselves questions — thus exploring their own curiosities purposefully — is essential; it contributes not only to the total development of the reader but also to the child's success in all areas of the school curriculum and in life itself. Questions can be a focusing and refining device for expanding vocabulary and for developing all levels of comprehension, including critical and creative reading. Questioning by both teachers and pupils should help to pinpoint direction of inquiry and to identify problems. It is essential as a way of delving into difficulties in content area fields.

Analyzing Your Teaching Questions

QUESTIONS TO GUIDE READING

Literal
What are Sanders's categories of questions?

Questions provide much of the teacher-learner dialogue. They also can be purposeful and significant for the reader in communicating with an author. Questions readers ask themselves about the nature and purpose of an author provide important gateways to understanding the structure and organization of what is read and the concepts involved (Anderson et al. 1977). Recent research and writing in comprehension has stressed metacognition (see Chapter 7), which may be described as the reader's awareness of his own cognitive processes — such as memory, attention, comprehension, and communication (Baker and Stein 1981). Questions may be used to heighten this awareness.

Classifying questions in various ways may be useful in helping both teachers and children to become more aware of the importance of purposeful, effective questions. Such awareness can lead to greater proficiency in the skills involved in both asking and answering questions. Classification of questions may also increase ability to use questions as communication tools.

Questions related to reading may be sorted or classified in any number of ways. The simplest is to look at the wording of a statement itself. What makes the statement a question? Is a question word used? The "wh" words, forms of the verb "to be," and helping verbs such as *have, do, would,* and *should* are most common. Each question word indicates a particular kind of answer. For example, *who* questions commonly look for a name of a person or group; *where* questions ask for a place, and so on. By giving children examples showing the important directive power of each question word they can be helped to anticipate the nature of required answers better.

Yet another way of looking at categories of questions is to examine the qualities that make various types of questions ineffective or confusing. One such system was that of Napell (1978), who classified many classroom questions that are likely to confuse thinking and suppress responses.

1. The "Dead-End" (a type of yes-no) questions are often addressed to entire groups with the intent of making sure the student understands. (Example: Does everyone see what the author's main point is?)
2. The "Chameleon" (a run-on question) involves a simultaneously imposed series of questions that appear to be unrelated and different from one another to the person(s) to whom they are addressed. (Example:

Why did Snow White go to live with the Dwarves? Didn't she love her father? Did she have something to fear? How did she manage to escape? Was she helped? . . .)

3. The "Programmed Answer" question directs respondents away from expressing their own thoughts and prestructures, or dictates the answer. (Example: Do you feel that Jack was justified in disobeying his mother? Does a sudden unforeseen opportunity present itself? Was the cow really worth anything at all?)

4. The "Put-Down" question is one that is stated so as to prevent further questions. (Example: I have just explained the reasons for the theft in the story and I am sure you found this easy to follow in the book. Any more questions?)

5. The "Fuzzy" question uses unclear and inaccurate language, obscuring what is really wanted in the answer. (Example: Do you "sort of" understand the moral of the story?)

Still another way of classifying questions is to look at the purpose of the questioner. Questions serve many communication purposes. Some are rhetorical, seeking no really important response. Some rhetorical questions are only rituals, but even rhetorical questions must be seen in their context as providing important information to the listener. Pragmatic linguists, who study the communication purposes of language, would suggest that several other social functions could be served by questions. "Would you like to . . . ?" questions and "Are you going to . . . ?" questions, for example, can be commands instead of true questions. (The General who says to the soldier "Well, are you ever going to salute?" is in effect ordering the soldier to salute immediately.)

Questions might also be helpful in seeking information; asking opinions; enlisting reinforcement or support; trying to get a response showing acceptance, forgiveness, love, etc.; showing issues or concerns; causing awareness, demanding attention; analyzing critically; etc. Being able to identify what kind of response the questioner is looking for is very helpful to the individual answering the question.

Sanders's system of classifying questions is another that can be very useful to teachers who want to learn to ask more effective questions. Sanders (1966, p. 3) defined a "question" as any intellectual exercise calling for a response. His approach to analyzing questions was based on ideas taken from the *Taxonomy of Educational Objectives: Cognitive Domain* (Bloom 1956). The "taxonomy" attempted to identify and define distinct categories of mental processes. In terms of these categories, all educational objectives, if stated specifically enough, can theoretically be classified according to the mental processes required to accomplish them. With some slight adaptation and retitling of the categories, Sanders used the categories defined in Bloom's *Taxonomy* to analyze and classify questions. His categories were:

1. *Memory:* The student recalls or recognizes information.
2. *Translation:* The student changes information into a different symbolic form or language.
3. *Interpretation:* The student discovers relationships among facts, generalizations, definitions, values, and skills.
4. *Application:* The student solves a lifelike problem that requires the identification of the issue and the selection and use of appropriate generalizations and skills.
5. *Analysis:* The student solves a problem in the light of conscious knowledge of the parts and forms of thinking.
6. *Synthesis:* The student solves a problem that requires original, creative thinking.
7. *Evaluation:* The student makes a judgment of good or bad, right or wrong, according to standards he designates.

To illustrate Sanders's classification of questioning, we give examples of each category. The examples are based on the story of Cinderella and are probably appropriate to a fourth- or fifth-grade reading level.

Memory: "By what time did Cinderella's fairy godmother tell her to be sure to be home?" (The student is asked to recall a specific fact read.)

Translation: "Put in your own words the warning that Cinderella's fairy godmother gave her." (The student is asked to find a different way of expressing the idea read.)

Interpretation: "What is a fairy godmother?" (The student has to examine the actions taken by the fairy godmother in the story for both their magical qualities and their special focus on Cinderella.)

Application: "Sometimes we have chances as Cinderella did to do some very special and exciting things. What are some of these, and what brought these good times of ours to an end?"

Analysis: "What special qualities did Cinderella have that made the prince want to find her?" (The student has to pick out the character traits as well as the special beauty Cinderella had.)

Synthesis: "How would the story have ended if Cinderella had not lost her slipper?"

Evaluation: "If you were Cinderella, how would you treat your stepsisters after you married the prince?" (This question requires speculative evaluation, which combines synthesis with evaluation. The student is asked to decide on a "right and good" course, a course of action based on his values.) "Do you think there were ever real fairy godmothers? Why or why not?" (This question involves analytical evaluation in terms of real-imaginary worlds.)

Some research indicates that effective questions involving lower-level thinking are most crucial to developing thinking, even for higher-level thinking (Gatheral 1979). But, Ryan (1973) concluded from his research that higher-level questions are more efficient than lower-level questions in moving students toward both high- and low-level understanding.

Teacher Questioning Skills to Deal with the Unexpected or Unfamiliar

QUESTIONS TO GUIDE READING

Literal
How can a teacher prepare to help or evaluate children who are reading material unfamiliar to the teacher himself?
What are some general questions that apply to any reading material?

Inferential
What are the skills involved in effective questioning techniques?
What is meant by the term "restructuring" when applied to questions?

Evaluative
What are the "dangers" in a teacher's being either too good or not good enough in thinking on his feet?
What are the dangers of inadequate preparation?

Reading teachers often must be ready to guide children in stories and books with which the teacher himself is not familiar. In most individualized reading programs this happens frequently. Even with a story the teacher has read and is prepared to teach, a child may bring up ideas and aspects the teacher has missed or forgotten.

With question asking, as with any other teaching behavior, a teacher probably cannot be overprepared. It is likely that most teachers do not plan enough for the question asking. Questions asked orally, either individually or in group discussions, are often all too spontaneous. Preparation of questions should involve:

1. careful examination of the reading materials.
2. consideration of objectives involved (reading objectives, social growth objectives, knowledge mastering objectives, etc.).
3. purposeful decision making about the nature, purpose, and direction of the questioning strategy itself.
4. knowledge and understanding of the needs, levels of abilities, and likely reactions to different techniques of particular children.
5. consideration of the total instructional context.

The teacher should remember that no question ever occurs in isolation. Each inquiry has a context of reading experiences, attention to the discussion, and personal interrelationship. Even a seemingly simple question such as "What time of day is it in the story?" develops a complex context. This context includes the conflicting and reinforcing ideas given in the story, which the child relates.

Regardless of how well prepared a teacher is, the questions for every reading situation cannot always be anticipated. The complex events and details of a long school day make such planning too time consuming. Moreover, no one can predict what children will say and how they will respond to questions.

The reading teacher's ability to think on his feet to meet the complex uncertainty of each minute in the classroom is one of the qualities that make teaching challenging and enjoyable. Spontaneity, sensitivity, and responsiveness to the children and their needs are valuable teaching skills. In discussion, the teacher who uses questions most effectively is one who is able to restructure his approach quickly. A delicate sense of timing is required. The ability to judge when more information or rewording is needed from the questioner is also important. A teacher develops this sense with experience. However, the teacher can be sensitive to the possibilities when a poor answer or no answer is given. It may be a problem with the statement of the question instead of a fault of the student. Although one can react too quickly and too often, that may be better than never changing the question.

A teacher asks a child, "What is one means of transportation?" The child may know the answer quickly and easily. The line of questioning may then be to get the student to name other forms of transportation or to explain why transportation is so important. For another child, the teacher may need to apply the question personally: "How did you get to school?" The teacher may ask a child with limited verbal abilities to act out a means of traveling.

GENERIC QUESTIONS

A reading teacher can generally prepare for at least some of the uncertainties of not being familiar with a story or book that a child is reading by thinking through a set of questions he can apply to a variety of stories or books. Question words such as *who, what, how, when, where, which, why,* and evaluation words such as *would, should, could* make it relatively easy to invent and remember such questions. The teacher can also probe for descriptions of the child's concepts of the plot, characters in the book, setting, and mood. Such probes typically begin with such expressions as "Tell me about" or "What did you think of." Questions that can be used with many stories and books are sometimes called generic questions. Such questions should not be thought of as substitutes for specific preparation; instead they serve as a supplement.

When a teacher uses these approaches exclusively, without reading himself, the stories used in reading instruction will lose effectiveness. Developmental instruction in conceptual, vocabulary, and word attack skills will not take place. Children will soon lose motivation and respect.

Following is a starter list of some of the generic questions a teacher may find useful with stories. Although these questions may appear to be only evaluative, they also have instructional value. Follow-up questions based on student responses to generic questions can be most helpful as teaching devices.

1. What can you tell me about the characters in this story?
2. Who is your favorite character?
3. What is the most exciting part of the story?
4. Could/would you have done what the person did in the story?
5. Why do you think the author wanted to write the story?
6. Does the story teach a lesson? What is it? (or, Why don't you think so?)
7. Where/when does the story take place?
8. How does the writer try to get you interested in the story?
9. Is this like any other story you have read? (movies or TV shows you've seen?)
10. Have you ever felt like the people in the story? (Have you ever wanted the same kinds of things?, etc.)

General Questions for Use with Content Areas

Generic questions may also be used with content areas. Starter lists are given below for science, social studies, and mathematics. Obviously there is much overlapping among these areas, and questions appropriate for one content area may also be appropriate for another.

Sample questions for science

1. What is the problem?
2. Can you restate the problem in other words?
3. Where could there be a mistake here?
4. What are the attributes (traits, features, characteristics) of this?
5. How are these two things alike (or different)?
6. How long did it take?

Sample questions for social studies

1. What was significant?
2. What happened and in what order did events occur?
3. When/where did it happen?
4. Who was involved?
5. What were the results (consequences) and causes?
6. How are we influenced by this event?

Sample questions for mathematics

1. What needs to be done? (What process should be followed?)
2. Which mathematical information is needed to solve this?
3. Does the order matter?
4. Is there more than one way of doing this?
5. Why does it work this way? (or Why does it not?)
6. What does the answer tell us?

Using Questions to Prepare Children for Reading

QUESTIONS TO GUIDE READING

Literal
What are some purposes for which teachers use questions?
In what ways should the abilities of children be considered when using guide questions?

Inferential
How do questions help the reader get started in reading a passage?

Evaluative
What makes a question interesting or motivating?
When should questions be used to "slow down" a child who reads too quickly?
What societal factors tend to minimize the distance between values found in reading and the child's own values?

Teachers use questions before reading to achieve a number of purposes: (1) to motivate and arouse interest; (2) to give the children reasons for reading; (3) to assess and develop background concepts and information; (4) to provide comprehension tasks by which the child may guide and evaluate his own understanding during independent reading time; (5) to serve as a basis for deciding whether or not children should read the selection; (6) to help determine the most appropriate reading rate.

MOTIVATIONAL AND INTEREST-AROUSING QUESTIONS

Motivational and interest-arousing questions may call attention to pictures, titles, subheadings, settings, characters, and plots. The pictures in a story could be used to pique curiosity by asking such questions as:

1. What do you think this story will be about?
2. Have you ever seen anything like this before?
3. How does this picture make you feel?
4. What do you see that is unusual in the picture?

Whether pictures, titles, or other devices are used, if questions can initiate in children a habitual spirit of wanting to read to find answers, reading will become self-motivating. When trying to get children to develop their own questions prior to reading, one should practice a few cautions. The teacher should allow and encourage children to share their curiosities and questions. Contrived and useless questions in which children have no real interest should be avoided.

PROVIDING REASONS FOR READING

Questions may also be used to set the purpose for reading and move the child toward determining his own purposes. People read to relax, to find out, to be inspired, to experience adventure vicariously, for intrigue, for romance, and for excitement — in fact, for every reason imaginable. Approaching a reading task, a child needs to have identifiable and direct reasons for reading. Questions can clarify and focus attention on the specific purposes that are appropriate to the reading situation. The different purposes are going to influence the rate of reading, the style of reading, the number of times an assignment is read, and many more subtle yet important aspects of the act of reading. Reading to tell sequence ("What happened in the story?") or to react ("How could you reenact the story?") should require careful reading and rereading. Reading to answer a question seeking a detail (such as the color of an animal in the story) can be accomplished by skimming. Other differences in reading rate and style result logically from other objectives — questions that probe for a favorite part or paragraph, for a paragraph or section that can be read expressively orally, for a description of the setting, or for a character.

Sometimes questions can be used as a means of directing children's reading to something they might otherwise miss or to which they might pay insufficient attention. Questions may be used in this way, for example, when several stories of one type are read. The teacher may use questions to get children to compare setting, main character development, plot, author's style, vocabulary, or other features among stories. Within a single story a teacher may want to use focusing questions to call attention to the importance of details in developing the total impression the story makes.

To provide the best reasons for reading, the teacher needs to first decide what about the story is similar to or familiar in the children's lives. As a basis for this the teacher needs to know the children's records, other places where they have lived, and the experiences of close relatives. The creative and autobiographical writing of the children provides one key; but discussions, school records, opinionaires — in fact, the sum total of the teacher's knowledge of the children — is called for in every way. With a sound knowledge of the children, the teacher can design a line of questioning that draws out those experiences that can help the children to relate to or to identify with the elements in the story.

AIDS TO COMPREHENSION

In the upper grades, written responses to questions are often used as seat work. Such questions lengthen the reading task. Obviously, they may become dull and frustrating busywork. However, such questions can provide children with a guide to independent reading and a measure by which they may evaluate when a reading task has been done well and thoroughly understood. Such questions may sometimes aid in controlling the child who impulsively — even compulsively — thinks he has read a story by racing over the words without ever registering them in his consciousness. Questions remind the child of the purpose for reading. However, this is not true if written questions are not followed by oral discussion.

When written questions are carefully formulated, they add to the child's well-being: he knows in advance what is expected. Followup in the form of grading, group discussion, or conference is crucial to the success of written questions in promoting comprehension.

The abilities of each child should be considered when asking guide questions. The length of the required answer, the level of the question, the degree of abstraction, and the number of questions to be answered are all factors that need careful consideration. Children of high ability need to be challenged with questions that are not insulting. Slower children need to be questioned with great caution. They need the satisfaction of success and need to avoid the frustration of failure. They also need the opportunity to learn how to decide not to read particular stories or books. Questions can help alert them to logical, important reasons for rejecting the reading. Will they be bored by it? Will they think it is silly or juvenile? Will they find the material too difficult? too highly technical? too detailed or lacking in detail?

Questions That Follow Up Reading

QUESTIONS TO GUIDE READING

Literal
What are four questioning strategies?

Inferential
What purposes do specific questioning strategies serve?

Evaluative
How would different types of question clusters be used to serve different needs?
Can children's own language difference be utilized effectively to improve their reading comprehension?

Questions asked after children have completed reading a portion of a story serve to improve comprehension, help them review and reinforce concepts and ideas, and aid them in remembering significant thoughts and facts dealt with in the story. Such questions may be an integral part of an overall teaching strategy such as the DR-TA activity discussed in Chapter 11.

Both Rothkopf (1966) and Frase (1967) have concluded from their research that postreading questions play an important part in comprehension and learning. The length of the passage read and the amount of time that lapses between reading and answering questions appear to be significant factors to consider in using questions after reading. Shorter passages immediately followed by questions seem to be most effective. These findings indicate that the practice of teachers meeting with individuals or reading groups to discuss an entire story may be questionable. Shorter, more frequent questioning and discussion periods may be more valuable.

The reading teacher should take care not to move too quickly beyond literal postreading questions. They deal with the easiest level of meaning to understand, requiring less abstract and complex thinking than do questions focused on what the reader can infer from a particular reading passage. Critical reading questions demand a still higher level of thinking. The transition from questions that explore the literal meaning of a passage to those requiring inferential and critical thinking should be a gradual one. Sequencing of such questions should be carefully thought out. According to Taba (1965), moving too rapidly to questions requiring such higher levels of thinking may cause comprehension to deteriorate.

Alexander and Filler (1973) summarized questioning strategies by which reading comprehension may be at least facilitated if not increased after reading. These strategies stress how a series of questions is put together. Following are some organizational patterns.

1. *A question cluster* is a set of two or more questions that require related thinking from the reader. An example of a question cluster from science follows: "Which is larger, a star or a planet?" "Is the earth a star or a planet?" "Is the sun a star or a planet?" "Which is larger, the earth or the sun?" The answer to the first question often determines in part how the second and all following questions must be answered.

Guszak (1969) identified several types of question clusters. *Purpose-setting follow-up clusters* pose purpose questions prior to reading, and follow up after reading by exploring how the readers met that purpose. The prereading questions would typically begin "Read to decide . . . ," "Read to find out . . . ," "Read to explain . . . ," and so forth. After the child reads, questions follow up the purpose. Follow-up questions explore the resulting decision, findings, and explanation. Using "Cinderella" again, the cluster could go something like this: (before reading) "Read to find out how the prince found Cinderella"; (after reading) "What did Cinderella leave behind?", "How did the prince use the shoe to find her?"

Verification clusters represent a second type. Typically, this cluster asks the reader to establish the truth of his answer to a prereading question by finding and reading the appropriate portion of the reading selection. For "Cinderella" the cluster might go this way: "Why didn't the prince recognize Cinderella? Find the sentence that tells why she was difficult to recognize."

Judgmental clusters also focus on followup. A reader's literal answer to one question contains a fact that is then evaluated. Typical of judgmental clusters are questions that require the reader to judge a factual answer to a first question on the basis of morality, strength, goodness, appropriateness, wisdom, beauty, or carefulness. In "Jack and the Beanstalk," for example, a factual question examining Jack's "trade" or his stealing would be followed by questions like "Was Jack a clever fellow?" "What do you think of Jack's honesty?" "Is it right to steal even from 'bad' giants?"

Justificational clusters demand that the reader reason out and defend his answer to a judgmental question. For example, a justificational cluster might begin with this question: "What did Jack do when he saw the beanstalk?" Follow-up judgmental questions might be: "Was this the right (or the wisest) thing to do?" or "Would you have done this?" A justificational cluster is most often concerned with having the reader give the reasons for a decision or judgment. The series of questions on "Jack and the Beanstalk" would become a justification cluster if the teacher followed with "Why do you think that Jack did the wise (or good, or best) thing?"

2. *Cognitive-level questioning* is based on the work of Hilda Taba (1965). This strategy attempts to relate questions to the stages that a reader goes through in developing and being able to deal with concepts. Three question stages are identified: (1) Concept Formation, or "what," questions in which the reader is aided in such operations as differentiating, grouping,

and categorizing perceptions; (2) Interpretation, or "why," questions requiring the reader to generalize, relate previously gained concepts, and make inferences; and (3) Application, or "what does it mean," questions, which require the reader to explain and predict. To illustrate these levels of questions we will use the story of "The Bremen Town Musicians":

Level 1. (Concept Formation): "What did all the animals have in common? How did the animals get the robbers out of the house?"
Level 2. (Interpretation): "Why did each of the animals leave home? Why did the animals want to get the robbers to leave the house?"
Level 3. (Application): "What has happened to people and animals you know who are unable to work any longer? Are they happy about it?"

Taba advocated beginning with concept formation questions in discussing a reading passage and moving to the more advanced levels only when the slowest children are ready. A related practical teaching consideration may be the size of groups of children the teacher is to work with. Questions that ensure mastery of concept formation are essential before interpretation or application questions are attempted. The implication is that until a reading teacher really has very carefully determined the ability of a class, he needs to prepare alternative sequences of questions.

3. *Inquiry strategies* of questioning attempt to develop a systematic process approach children can apply to solving a problem or making a decision. Once the children learn the process, the teacher becomes a guide and source of data, and the children are in control of the strategy. Inquiry requires questions similar to the steps in the classic scientific method. Suchman (1966) has named the types of questions that accomplish these steps as verification, experimentation, necessity, and synthesis. As with the scientific method, each type of question relates to a central problem or inquiry question. *Verification* is the gathering of facts. For example, in the story of "The Brave Little Tailor": "What made the little tailor think he was brave?" "How did he convince the giants that he was brave and invincible?" "How did he convince the king?" "How do we know that everyone in the story could read?" *Experimentation* questions are used to manipulate the information gained. In the tailor's tale: "Was bravery alone the reason for his success?" "Was the tailor a good judge of his own abilities?" "How did factual information lead to a misunderstanding?" *Necessity* questions test the relevance of information to the central problem. Questions appropriate to the story of "The Brave Little Tailor" might include the following: "Did the fact that the little tailor outwitted stronger enemies instead of outfighting them mean that he wasn't brave?" "Was the tailor's belt, which announced that he had killed 'seven at one blow', important to what happened later in the story?" *Synthesis* questions evaluate the validity of tentative conclusions to the main problem. Such questions for the story of the little tailor might include: "How do we know

that the little tailor really was brave?" "Why is being clever important when someone is being brave?"

4. *Reciprocal questioning* involves an exchange of questions between teacher and child. According to Manzo (1979) this approach is most useful for the first few paragraphs of a story. Remedial readers may benefit from extended use of the technique, however, especially since it is aimed at developing reader purpose. Reciprocal questioning (Manzo calls it Re-Quest questioning) involves silent reading of a very short passage, even as short as one sentence. Following the silent reading, the student asks his teacher a question about the materials. Then the teacher and the student alternate asking questions to which the other responds. Of course, the student is encouraged to imitate the teacher's questioning technique. All questions are answered. The student must either answer or explain why he cannot answer the teacher's questions. The objective is to develop various skills (depending on the content of what is read) in asking questions that seek different kinds of answers. Manzo suggests that a tally be kept of questions demanding the different kinds of answers: (1) Immediate reference (What happened in what we read?). For example, "How did the tailor help the giant carry the tree?" (2) Common knowledge (What does the author assume *everyone* knows about what was read?). For example, "What is a tailor? a giant?" (3) Related information (What other information would help the understanding of the passage?). For example, "What was life like at the time the tailor's story took place?" (4) Open-ended discussion (What different opinions exist about what was read?). For example, "Should the tailor have been so quick to leave home?" (5) Further reference (What else can we read or observe that will increase understanding, enjoyment?). For example, "What other stories deal with courage and cleverness? How would you find them?" (6) Translation (What does it all mean?). For example, "What moral does the story of 'The Brave Little Tailor' show?" "Do cleverness and courage always win over strength and power?"

Turner (1981) has suggested that question-asking games may be effective in developing good question-asking habits and skills in children. Children sometimes feel uncomfortable asking questions. Teachers nonverbally and verbally, intentionally and unintentionally convey the impression that questions from children are out of order, unwanted, or inappropriate. Games may instill for the first time the notion that it is all right to ask questions about what is read. As puddles are for stepping in and holes are for digging, so questions are to be asked. Realization of this is in itself a novelty for many children. Twenty questions is a typical childhood game that illustrates this. Turner developed and adapted a series of games in which children are required to frame and ask (rather than merely answer) questions related to material being studied.

Many TV programs have involved panels asking questions. These provide excellent models for question-asking games. Turner also pointed to the importance of teaching children the function of particular question words and what the question word tells about the nature of the answer. For example, the word *who* in a question indicates that the answer will include a person or several persons; *where* indicates a place description or name; *why* suggests a reason or set of reasons or causes; and *when* requests a time. By knowing more about the direction and nature of the answer to a question asked him, a child should respond with more confidence and accuracy.

Building the Questioning Environment

QUESTIONS TO GUIDE READING

Literal
What are some features of a good questioning environment?
What are some forms of positive motivation a teacher can use in reaction to solid effort and good responses to questions?

Inferential
What are some of the major difficulties involved in developing a sound response environment for questions?

Evaluative
Why are personal security and safety so important in the questioning environment?
How can a teacher distinguish a genuine effort of the learner to answer a question well?
Should a teacher deal in similar ways with all children who refuse to attempt to answer questions?

The environment in which reading questions are asked is as important as the kind of questions asked. Jackson (1968) reports that in negative reports from school children two themes are predominant: frightening or embarrassing experiences, and boredom from meaningless tasks. Children (and teachers as well) have conflicting types of needs that should be met in a wisely balanced manner by the questioning approaches used in teaching reading. One need is for security and safety. Soar (1966) found that teaching with a high proportion of acceptance and encouragement of student ideas and a low proportion of direction and criticism of student ideas produced higher reading achievement. The way questions are worded, where the teacher stands or sits, every movement and use of eye contact, the manner in which children are chosen to answer questions, how the teacher or other children react to answers — all these and other factors as well influence the child's sense of security. An atmosphere in which children feel severely frustrated, frightened, threatened, or tricked is not conducive to good discussion or learning. Intimidating children by an inquisition style of questioning may make a few teachers feel somehow superior, but it will not help children learn. Instead, what may occur in children is some form of withdrawal — not volunteering, being silent, daydreaming, or saying "I don't know"; or rebellion — in the form of attempts at sarcastic angry humor, argument, active refusal to answer, or even physical violence; or sublimation — escaping by substituting success in some other form for success in answering questions.

Attention to planning details may also help the child feel more secure. For example, if the complexity (vocabulary usage or concept level) of the question itself is beyond the child's ability to comprehend, it can never be answered. Frustration occurs immediately. Careful wording of questions and anticipation of any other difficulties before children are asked to answer will help a great deal to avoid frustration. Among the many other details teachers should consider are the degree of quietness or isolation children need to answer written questions, the distractive influence that arises when the teacher is working with a child or group, and the multisensory tools students may need to help them understand questions.

Children need to have a feeling of security as well as a knowledge that their responses to questions will be received in a way that will not endanger them. People with strong physical fears — such as fear of heights or of fire — will panic or freeze up when they confront the object of their fears. They do not intentionally come in contact with or take risks with this object. In the same way, the child who fears what will happen when he answers a question tries to avoid ever having to answer. Continued frustration by often answering incorrectly is enough to cause a child's withdrawal. The shy child will even avoid risking failure or exposure from the very beginning by never answering. By being silent he is never vulnerable.

Yet another variable of importance in the secure environment is "wait-time" or "think-time." These terms refer to the period of time allowed between the question asking and the response. When the teacher pressures for instant responses and makes silence uncomfortable, think-time is reduced. The child's inner tension is increased. The quality and accuracy of the responses to questions requiring all levels of thinking suffer. Recent research seems to indicate that increasing the permissible wait-time by even a second improves the responses. The chances for more frequently accurate and qualitative response also improve.

What happens to one child's response to a question in the reading class will have a ripple-like effect on the entire class. The receptiveness of the teacher and the other children is equally important. Every honest effort should be treated as valuable. An atmosphere of acceptance is essential. The way a teacher and class react to answers to questions is sometimes referred to as the classroom climate or the response environment. Most

Questioning Techniques: Probing for Greater Meaning

research indicates that an ego-reinforcing, warm response environment is more nurturing to learning.

This is not to say that each response should be treated in the same way. Answers should be evaluated and dealt with honestly, for every answer is *not* equally valid or significant. Degrees of effort and quality should receive appropriate recognition. There is, however, no place for biting personal sarcasm and personalized criticism in an effective questioning strategy. A teacher who belittles a child for an incorrect answer or for not answering at all is probably only serving his own ego needs. A few children and adults will react with just the right kind of fear or rebellion by taking the criticism as a challenge and preparing better answers the next time to avoid being attacked. More often, though, the response will be to build a shell of withdrawal.

A more effective environment seems to consist of solid and regular reinforcement of top effort and good responses and questions. Answering a question well should be treated as important and valuable. Positive motivation or reinforcement can take several forms: (1) verbal rewards (expressions like "That's good," "Right," or "Good thinking"); (2) displaying good written responses; (3) urging class reinforcement (such as applause from the group or asking individual children to identify "good" things in answers by other children); (4) giving children audiences outside the immediate group; (5) physical acknowledgement by the teacher (smiles, eye contact, moving closer, saluting, or patting on the back); (6) calling attention to good written responses by showing written comments on the response to the class or showing off "gold star" types of approval; and (7) cumulative incremental kinds of rewards so that the child can see his correct or good work accumulate (bulletin boards with each child's growth represented, question files of questions answered correctly, or tokens given as a reward to be used at some terminal date, for example).

Developing the Child's Own Questioning Skill

QUESTIONS TO GUIDE READING

Literal
What does a teacher do for a child by answering that child's questions?

Inferential
What must occur if children are to develop good questioning ability?

Evaluative
Why should children be encouraged to ask questions?
How can children's questioning skill be developed?

Questions that children ask can be irritating, disruptive, and unanswerable. Seemingly pointless inquiries can confuse and sidetrack the direction of a well-planned and organized teaching activity. Some children's questions do not have an answer and others the teacher cannot or does not want to answer. Some children ask questions to get attention or recognition and they have no desire to hear or understand an answer. Others ask questions they could answer themselves if they gave a little thought to it. Some children's questions are about things that seem irrelevant or unimportant to teachers. It is little wonder that the teacher sometimes feels a very natural desire simply to squelch the questioners. "Habit retorts" develop all too easily: "We'll talk about that later," "Ask me again after class," or the near-sadistic, "That's an interesting question; why don't you do a report on it?"

The important but difficult thing to remember is that the objective should not be to silence the questions. If you turn off the questions, you may lose one of the greatest motivations to learning — curiosity — as well. A teacher may teach children that it is not good to ask questions or be curious. Far better, of course, is to teach children to ask better questions, to ask questions in a better way, and to ask them at more appropriate times. A few approaches that can develop children's questioning skill have been previously described in this chapter. Among these are inquiry and reciprocal questioning and question-game strategies.

Experience and practice at both writing questions and asking questions in discussion are essential to the development of the skill. Children need to master the basic mechanics of questioning itself. This requires practice over a long span of time. One simple exercise that does this is turning sentences into questions. ("George Washington was the first president of the United States" becomes "Who was the first president of the United States?")

Teachers often wonder if they should answer children's questions. There are many reasons for doing so. One is that it is often the easiest thing to do. It is efficient in that it saves time and energy. When the teacher supplies an answer, the child is reinforced. When his question is answered the child feels that: (1) his question (and therefore he) was considered important enough to respond to; (2) the teacher has shown a form of concern and love by answering; (3) the teacher to whom he looked for an answer has demonstrated that the trust and respect were justified; (4) he can go on to other things that may have depended on the answer. Giving the answer sometimes is even reinforcing to the teachers who feel success at knowing the answer and knowing that this uplifts them in the eyes of the children. Answering questions can also "save" the direction of the lesson by minimizing the interruption.

When the teacher does answer he should attempt to be simple, direct, and concise. He may need patience to deal with a series of questions, each dependent on the last. Answers should be directed at the questioner; but, if it comes in a group discussion, the entire group should be pulled in if possible. A reasonable (but not ridiculous) effort should be made to bring the question into the mainstream of ideas of the discussion.

Types of questions the teacher chooses to answer and the times that each individual child is responded to will vary a great deal depending on many variables such as class size, teacher personality and style, ability of the children, and schedule pressures. Some children will ask questions as long as answers come and perhaps even when they do not. These children need to be taught to respect others more, to wait their turn, and to limit their inquiries to the most essential. It may be necessary to give children a limited number of questions they can or should ask. This will signify the importance attached to good questions. It may also be a means of teaching the overanxious questioners to be more selective.

Speculative, fanciful, and impossible questions sometimes irritate teachers (What if . . . all the plants were candy? the ocean was fresh water? the moon was a rubber ball?) Such questions should not be discouraged nor their assumptions pushed aside as foolish. A better approach is to take the question seriously. This is the "stuff" out of which imagination is built into reality. Try to answer and give the children opportunities to try as well.

Questions that seem to be distractions or tangents from the reading lesson should not always be treated as mere irritants. Such questions may sometimes provide better, more important directions for the lesson. They may create a kind of teachable moment, by offering an atmosphere where teaching can be most effective because children are interested.

Summary

Questioning serves a number of functions in the teaching of reading. Teachers use questions to introduce a reading task by stimulating interest and curiosity, setting up problems that will require reading, and pointing out important ideas to look for in reading. Questions are also a way of evaluating how well students understand and remember what they have read and of helping reinforce and organize important ideas gained from reading.

The questions that teachers ask require considerable forethought about their purposes and effectiveness in achieving these purposes. One way of analyzing reading questions is by use of a categorization system such as that of Sanders. Such systems allow the teacher to see the variety of types of questions used.

Questions cannot always be preplanned. However, the best preparation for teaching reading includes thoughtful consideration of questions to be asked in discussions and lessons. The development of generic questioning skills is in itself a type of preparation for unanticipated questioning.

Skillful questioning helps develop reading understanding and abilities before, during, and following the reading act. Good questions asked before a child reads provide purposes for reading, help spur motivation and interest in reading, and aid comprehension.

Questions to follow the reading task are especially important. Careful thought needs to be given to the choice of questioning strategies. Alternative strategies include clustering of questions, questioning based on the cognitive level of the reader, inquiry, and reciprocal questioning.

Though purposeful well-planned questions and question strategies are important, the classroom environment also influences the effectiveness of questions. Teachers need to provide a climate in which a child always feels that his best effort will be acceptable and receive praise.

The questioning skill of children must be developed if teacher questions are to have carryover into independent reading. Teachers have difficulty allowing children to ask questions mostly because of the role-conflict problems such questions create. Strategies to develop the questioning skills of children should be a regular part of the reading instructional program. Teacher responses to fanciful questions should be encouraging and appreciative.

Questions for Further Reading and Thinking

1. What are some of the consequences of poorly planned questions in a reading discussion?
2. Why are children reluctant to ask questions in upper elementary grades?
3. What are some of the problems involved in such questioning strategies as questioning clusters and inquiry?
4. What are some of your own particular shortcomings and strengths in asking questions and dealing with the way they are answered?

Activities and Projects

1. Make up a question for each of Sanders's categories based on a reading of some folk- or fairytale.
2. Classify several questions in a basal reader teacher's guide using the Sanders scale.
3. List five generic questions not included in the list on page 205. Try them on three different stories to see if they work.
4. Plan two or three activities in which children's question-asking skills are developed.
5. Write down three to five questions you still have about questioning. Try to develop your own answers by using the references listed at the end of this book or some children's reading materials, or discussion with teachers and other education students.
6. Make up a game involving children in asking or answering questions.
7. Select a story from a basal reader and

write questions to fit each of the categories of Shaftel and of Sanders.

8. Make a lesson plan for the introduction and follow-up discussion of a story with a reading group. List all questions you would ask.

9. Conduct discussions with several children. Use generic types of questions. See how well you can adapt generic questions to each story.

10. Make yourself a personal checklist of "do's" and "don'ts" of questioning. Tape-record or videotape yourself teaching a reading lesson and see how well you have done according to your checklist.

Arnold R. Davis

10

Study Skills

Reading is not an end in itself; it is a means to the achievement of many ends. Reading is central to most school subjects and important in nearly all of them. Since reading is an essential tool, all teachers who make use of printed materials as teaching aids have the responsibility for increasing the student's ability to use that tool.

The term "study skills" is a latecomer to the educational world; consequently, research relating to study skills is relatively recent and not as thorough as in some other areas of reading. But it is known that study skills are important, as evidenced by the work of Howell (1950, 1953). His studies were concerned with work/study skills in grades four through fourteen. The conclusions from the research in grades four through seven were that the use of a central library as a program focus for teaching work/study skills is important and that techniques of work/study skills must be incorporated into lesson plans every day. He concluded that intensive work in study skills should begin in grade four. This should not be interpreted to mean that study skill instruction does not begin earlier. You will surely note as you proceed through this chapter that work on study skills should begin with the earliest school experience.

The term "study skills" can refer, generally, to any technique students use in learning school assignments. Or the term can refer specifically to the application of reading skills to specific study tasks — organizing and scheduling one's time for study, taking notes, preparing reports, or preparing for examinations. In any case, study skills are needed when a learner begins to make use of content materials. Teachers cannot safely assume their students have acquired all the necessary study skills. Study skills cannot be left to chance; they must be taught step by step. The teacher must plan and conduct lessons on how to locate material and use general reference books. Lessons must also be planned and presented on how to select important ideas and translate them into one's own words without sounding bookish. How to organize materials into outlines and summaries should also be taught.

If we subscribe to the idea that reading, study skills, and the entire curriculum are interwoven, and if we believe that study skills should be taught, then we must decide how this can best be accomplished. Study skills can be taught directly in reading, language arts, or English classes; or they can be taught through planned instruction in each content area. Ellis (1965, p. 16) suggests that a skill taught in a given situation has the best chance for successful application if it is used in another situation almost identical to the one in which it was taught. Therefore, it seems preferable for study skills to be taught and practiced when they are needed in a particular area of study. The actual materials in the subject area should be used for both teaching and practice; in this way, the student sees immediately that the skills really are useful.

The rate at which children learn various study skills will vary with individual pupils. The gifted child may be introduced earlier to selected study skills and will be able to master these skills at a faster rate than an average or below-average student. However, as the research seems to indicate, most students can profit from reading methods that teach study skills.

Study Skill Areas

QUESTIONS TO GUIDE READING

Literal
What are the major study skill areas?
What are the location skills?
What skills are needed to use a dictionary effectively?
Why are skills in reading charts, maps, and graphs important?

Inferential
Why is it necessary for students to become proficient in using the Dewey Decimal or Library of Congress classification systems?
Why is selecting appropriate information an important skill?

Evaluative
How do students use note-taking and outlining skills in organizing information?
How would you evaluate a student's proficiency in following directions?

Even though different authors define the study skills differently and pinpoint different specific skills, basically the skills can be grouped into these main headings: locating information that includes using library resources; selecting information; organizing information; following directions; and reading and interpreting graphs, maps, and charts.

Important Skills to Help Students Locate Information

Alphabetizing
1. Knowing letter names
2. Knowing alphabetical order
3. Alphabetizing lists using first letters
4. Alphabetizing lists using second letters
5. Using guide words in dictionaries, glossaries, and indexes
6. Using articles *a, an,* and *the* in locating words or titles

Using book parts to locate information, such as:
1. Title, author, title page, publisher, location of publisher
2. Copyright page and date of publication
3. Preface, introduction, foreword
4. Table of contents
5. List of illustrations, maps, charts
6. Chapter headings, subtitles
7. Footnotes and references at the ends of chapters
8. Glossary
9. Index — selection and use of key words and cross references
10. Appendix
11. Bibliography
12. Summaries at the ends of chapters

Using reference materials
1. Using a dictionary
   a. Using a thumb index
   b. Using guide words
   c. Using pronunciation key
   d. Interpreting phonetic spelling and diacritical marks to determine appropriate pronunciation
   e. Checking spellings
   f. Noting syllabic divisions of words
2. Using encyclopedias
   a. Using information on spine to locate volume
   b. Using initial letters and guide words
   c. Using index in last volume

Locating and using other references, such as:
1. Almanac
2. Atlas
3. Newspapers and periodicals
4. Yearbooks
5. City and telephone directories
6. Government publications

Locating Information

The basic skills needed to locate information are the use of the alphabet, the ability to use book parts, the use of basic works of information, and the ability to use the library. The teaching of location skills begins in the primary grades with finding page numbers and learning the sequence of letters in the alphabet.

One of the objectives of classroom teachers is to provide continuous guidance in using the textbook and other references. When these skills are carefully and systematically developed from kindergarten through grade six, the student develops the ability for effective independent study.

The ever-expanding body of knowledge makes it practically impossible to teach students all the existing information on any one subject. As new theories and facts are discovered, expanded, or discarded, it becomes imperative that students have skills and abilities to locate and use reference materials independently.

Teachers must not take for granted that students possess necessary location skills: they need to be shown how to use the materials. Teachers should plan in-class activities in which the materials can be used with teacher guidance. The activities need to be meaningful so students will be eager to develop and practice the skills as part of a project that stimulates them.

For example, students can be given the opportunity to gather information from reference books needed for work on a unit in science or social studies. Providing students with the opportunity to make a bibliography of materials available in the school library on a given topic can be another meaningful activity.

Other types of activities can also be used to help students learn the skills needed for locating and using information. The following practice exercises illustrate other teaching strategies for helping students get acquainted with location skills.

For dictionaries. Arrange these letters in alphabetical order.

    t, o, s, p, l __ __ __ __ __
    h, f, i, e, g __ __ __ __ __
    z, t, m, q, d __ __ __ __ __

Figure 10.1 shows a boxful of words. Take them out of the box and write them in alphabetical order.

1.   7.
2.   8.
3.   9.
4.   10.
5.   11.
6.   12.

Figure 10.1.

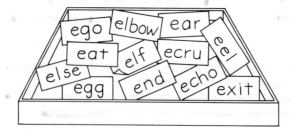

Guide words are at the top of a dictionary page. They show the first and last entry words on that page. Below are guide words and a list of entry words that belong between the guide words. Write the entry words in correct alphabetical order.

Sailboat

1.

2.

3.

Salami

4.

5.

6.

salad, saint, salamander, sake, sailor, Saint Patrick's Day

Here are two guide words: *thwack, ticket.* Look at the list of entry words below. Cross out any that do not belong on this page with these guide words.

them	tinsel	thyself
tick	tie	tic
thyme	they	tibia
tickle	tack	tidy

Find these words in the dictionary. Write the entry word that precedes and the entry word that follows each of these.

_____	beagle	_____
_____	award	_____
_____	safe	_____
_____	vacation	_____
_____	toucan	_____

Commercially produced books for practicing skills can also be used to help meet individual needs as children are learning to locate and use information. Figure 10.2 presents an example of an activity for helping children learn to find information in a book.

For reference books. Match each reference book with the type of information it contains. Place the number of the reference book in front of the description.

1. Dictionary
2. Atlas

3. Encyclopedia
4. Almanac
5. Who's Who in America

_____ maps and points of interest

_____ updated information on many sports, cities, current events, etc.

_____ word definitions

_____ biographies of famous people

_____ facts on many subjects

For encyclopedias. Which volume in Figure 10.3 would you choose to answer these questions?

_____ 1. What part of the boat is called starboard?

_____ 2. What is the purpose of a mirror on a microscope?

_____ 3. When was Napoleon Bonaparte defeated at Waterloo?

Figure 10.2.

Finding Information in a Book

Almost every nonfiction book has two parts that help you to find specific information.

The **table of contents** is at the beginning of the book. It lists the title of every chapter and the page on which each chapter begins.

The **index** is at the end of the book. It lists the topics that are discussed in the book. These topics are listed alphabetically, and are followed by the numbers of the pages on which they are found.

Finding Information in the Table of Contents. Examine the table of contents of your math book. See if there is a chapter for each topic listed below. If there is, write the number of the chapter and the page number on which it begins. If there is not a chapter on the topic, write **No.**

	CHAPTER NUMBER	BEGINNING ON PAGE NUMBER
1. addition	_____	_____
2. subtraction	_____	_____
3. multiplication	_____	_____
4. division	_____	_____
5. fractions	_____	_____
6. percentage	_____	_____
7. metrics	_____	_____
8. geometry	_____	_____

Finding Information in the Index. Look up the following topics in the index of your math book. Write the pages on which each topic can be found.

1. whole numbers _____

2. kilometers _____

3. common denominator _____

4. decimal point _____

5. area _____

6. integers _____

From *Skills Practice Book, Building English Skills*, Silver Level (Evanston, Ill.: McDougal, Littell & Co., 1981), p. 75. Reprinted with permission.

Figure 10.3.

1	2	3	4	5	6	7	8	9	10	11	12	13	14	15	16	17	18	19	20	21
A	B	C– Ch	Ci– Cz	D	E	F	G	H	I	J– K	L	M	N– O	P	Q– R	S– Sn	So– Sz	T	U– V	WX YZ

_____ 4. Who was president of the United States during the bicentennial celebrations of that country?

For an index. In preparing exercise cards on the use of the index, keep in mind that the student must master these points: alphabetical arrangement, main topics, subtopics, punctuation, listing of maps, and abbreviations (such as "illus," and "ff"). Samples of exercises follow.

Give page numbers in your science book on which information on these topics can be found: nuclear energy, solar energy, radium, radio astronomy, uranium, volcanoes, and Celsius scale.

Copy the phrases below onto your paper. If you were looking for information about these topics, for what word would you look first? second? Put one line under the word that would be your first key word and two lines under the second key word (the word you would look for if you did not find enough information under the first key word).

1. Message-carrying nerve cells are neurons.
2. History of highway transportation.
3. Einstein's theory of relativity.
4. Planestesimals are little planets; a theory of the solar system.
5. Bathythermograph: an instrument in oceanography.

Figure 10.4 presents another example of an exercise for helping children learn to use an index.

Newspaper index. Use your newspaper (the sample index in Table 10.1) to locate information and answer these questions.

1. Bill is going to a movie tonight. He should look in section _____ on page _____ to see what time it begins.
2. Joe wants to know who won the baseball game yesterday. He should look on page _____ in section _____.
3. Ann wants to read the latest stock prices. She can find these in section _____, page _____.

Figure 10.4.

Index

Part of an index is shown here. Suppose you are using it to help you find information to answer each question below the index. On the line under each question write the number or numbers of the pages on which you might find the needed information.

dolphin—about 10 feet long (3 meters)

Atlantic Ocean, animals in, 6–9, 15; fish in, 10, 12–14; location of, 5, 116 *m*; plants in, 2–4, 11; temperatures in, 167, 169
Babies. See **Calves**
Blue whales, length of, 33; number of, 38; oil from, 36; weight of, 40
Calves, care of, 24, 26–29; teeth of, 45
Dolphins, color of, 56; flippers of, 55; food eaten by, 47–51; games played by, 43, 57, 59; sounds made by, 44; where found, 73–76, 79. See *also* Porpoises
Jaws. See **Mouth**

Killer whales, hunting habits of, 85–91; length of, 93; teaching tricks to, 103, 110
Monsters, stories about, 153–161
Mouth, of dolphins, 52; of sharks, 83; of whales, 100, 102
Porpoises, harbor, 210
Scrimshaw, history of, 175, 187–190; tools used for, 195, 198 *p*
Sharks, body of, 143, 149 *d*; kinds of, 148, 151–153; senses of, 146; uses of, 157–160
Slings, for rescue work, 170; for transportation of whales, 97–99

KEY: *d*—diagram   *m*—map   *p*—picture

1. Can sharks be used for food?

   157–160

2. Why do killer whales hunt in groups?

   85–91

3. Where would you find a map of the Atlantic Ocean?

   116

4. What are some games that dolphins are known to play?

   43, 57, 59

5. When do teeth begin to grow in a whale's jaw?

   100, 102

6. How much does a blue whale weigh?

   40

7. Do babies get a lot of care?

   24, 26–29

8. When are slings used for carrying whales?

   97-99

9. Where would you find a picture of some tools used for scrimshaw?

   198

10. What kinds of plants live in the Atlantic Ocean?

    2-4, 11

Table 10.1. Sample Newspaper Index

Section B	Section D	Section G
Editorials 2	Baseball 4	Art 1–2
Financial 5–8	Basketball 1–3	Books 3
Obituaries 4	Golf 5–7	Crossword 3
	Swimming 8	Lawn & garden 4–6
		Movies 7
		TV 8–9

USING LIBRARY RESOURCES

Although many classrooms contain book collections or supplementary resources, most reference and resource materials are located in the school library. Students need to be taught the skills that will help them to use the library effectively and to make proper use of the available materials. As with many other aspects of reading, all students should not be learning these skills at the same time. For example, the gifted child may be introduced to these skills at an earlier age than an average child. Learning how to use the facilities of the school library will help free the gifted child to learn and acquire information somewhat independently.

Basic skills needed for using library resources are:

1. Learning to use Dewey Decimal or Library of Congress classification systems.
2. Finding topic, author, or title in card catalog.
3. Using indexes such as *Reader's Guide to Periodical Literature*.

Many school libraries use an adaptation of the Dewey Decimal system or the Library of Congress classification system. Students should not be asked to memorize a classification system but should be taught how to use the system used in their library. Knowing how to use the library facilities enables students to work efficiently and independently.

Library Classification Systems

The Dewey Decimal System

000–099	General works, including bibliography and general periodicals
100–199	Philosophy, psychology, ethics
200–299	Religion, Bible, mythology
300–399	Sociology, economics, education, political science
400–499	Philology, dictionaries, grammars
500–599	Natural science, including mathematics, chemistry, physics
600–699	Applied science, including useful arts, medicine, agriculture, manufacturing
700–799	Fine arts, music, recreation
800–899	Literature
900–999	History, biography, travel

Library of Congress Classification

A	General works	M	Music
B	Philosophy and religion	N	Fine Arts
C	History: auxiliary sciences	P	Philology and literature
D	History: general and Old World	Q	Science
E–F	History: America	R	Medicine
G	Geography, anthropology, folklore	S	Agriculture
H	Social sciences	T	Technology
J	Political sciences	U	Military science
K	Law	V	Naval science
L	Education	Z	Bibliography & library science

The card catalog is an index to the entire collection of learning materials housed in any library. There will be cards for subject, author, and title — for books, filmstrips, films, records, tapes, pictures, and vertical and picture files.

All cards are filed alphabetically in the card catalog by the first line. Figure 10.5 shows an example of information available on an author card.

Nonfiction books can be located with the help of the card catalog and a workable knowledge of the Dewey Decimal system or the Library of Congress classification system. Biographies will probably have a B added to the call number and be listed in alphabetical order according to the person's name about whom the book is written. Fiction books will have an F in the call number and will be listed in alphabetical order by the author's last name. Story collections will probably have an SC added to the call number.

Newspapers (070) and periodicals (050) can be located with their Dewey Decimal number. But these numbers do not help students locate specific articles in them. Students will need to use indexes for the location of specific items of information, such as the *Reader's Guide to Periodical Literature* and the *Abridged Reader's Guide to Periodical Literature*. Each magazine article is entered under both the author's name and the subject, and sometimes under the title.

The *New York Times Index* and the *Christian Science Monitor Index* are examples of indexes that help students locate information in newspapers. These indexes have subject indexes with brief summaries of the articles

Figure 10.5. Information on an author card.

```
Call Number        Author, surname first
                   Title ...................................................
                   ............... Publisher, date.
                   Paging, illustrations
                   Notes ...................................................
                   contents..........................................
                   tracings
```

and dates of events; this information may be used to find articles in local newspapers for which no index is available.

In addition to directed instruction and practice in a school library, workbook activities such as the one in Figure 10.6 can be used to provide reinforcement as children are learning the basic skills needed for using library resources.

SELECTING INFORMATION

Selecting needed information is a basic reading skill. All writing has some kind of organization. Students need to be aware of order and patterns when they read. These patterns may be: topic development, time order, comparison-contrast, or cause-effect. If students can follow the author's patterns, they can learn to look for key words in sentences and key sentences in paragraphs. They can select main thoughts and supporting details.

Since selection skills are basic to many other study skills, they need to be given more than passing notice. The teacher should plan instruction carefully and systematically to provide numerous practice experiences. Teachers should be encouraged to use actual content material (such as social studies or science) in teaching students to become aware of writing patterns and to select the author's main ideas. Research findings have indicated, for example, that science achievement can be increased by:

1. Working with reading and study skills using the course material.
2. Introducing vocabulary symbols and abbreviation.
3. Working on comprehension skills, including the ability to note detail, ability to follow directions, and ability to relate relevant items (Fay 1954).

Practice sessions in the following selection skills would increase comprehension in content areas:

1. Finding key words in sentences and key sentences in a paragraph.
2. Selecting main thoughts and supporting details.
3. Reading for topic development, classification, sequence, comparison-contrast, or cause-effect.

ORGANIZING INFORMATION

The teaching of organizing skills should begin in the primary years when students learn to tell a story in the proper sequence or to designate the most important events that happened. Students learn organizing skills

Figure 10.6.

Using the Card Catalog

The **card catalog** contains alphabetically filed cards on each book in the library. Each card has a call number in the upper-left hand corner of the card.

There are usually three cards for the same book in the card catalog: the *author card*, the *title card*, and the *subject card*. Each has the same information but is found in alphabetical order in·the card catalog. The library system does not capitalize important words in a title.

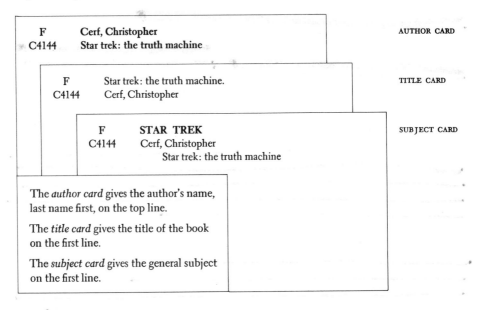

| F | Cerf, Christopher | AUTHOR CARD |
| C4144 | Star trek: the truth machine | |

| F | Star trek: the truth machine. | TITLE CARD |
| C4144 | Cerf, Christopher | |

F	STAR TREK	SUBJECT CARD
C4144	Cerf, Christopher	
	Star trek: the truth machine	

The *author card* gives the author's name, last name first, on the top line.

The *title card* gives the title of the book on the first line.

The *subject card* gives the general subject on the first line.

Finding Card Catalog Information.   Circle the letter of the correct catalog card to use in the following situations.

1. You need a book on butterfly collecting. You will use

   (a) the author card   (b) the title card   (c) the subject card

2. You want to read a book by Mark Twain. You will use

   (a) the author card   (b) the title card   (c) the subject card

3. You are looking for the book, *The Lord of the Rings.* You will use

   (a) the author card   (b) the title card   (c) the subject card

From *Skills Practice Book* (Teacher's Edition), *Building English Skills*, Gold Level (Evanston, Ill.: McDougal, Littell & Co., 1981), p. 69. Reprinted with permission.

when they sort and classify objects into categories. These are readiness activities for the more complex aspects of organizing information.

Location and selection skills are being used when students select main ideas and topic sentences. The teaching of organizational skills should progress developmentally through the intermediate grades, step by step, as the students learn to: write summaries; outline material they have read; develop original outlines from which they can write reports; make notes and collate materials from several sources. Students begin to see an outline as a framework or skeleton with which a writer works (A. R. Davis 1973).

When students make original outlines, they use all the study skills previously taught: location skills, to find available information on a given topic; and selection skills, to choose the important ideas and supporting details. Students must be able to determine the author's pattern to determine sequential order.

Time spent in teaching students the following skills in organizing information will increase comprehension and result in better understanding of content material:

1. Taking notes.
   a. Selecting major and minor points.
   b. Deciding which information will be useful.
   c. Rephrasing author's statement in own words.
2. Constructing an outline.
   a. Outlining what is read.
      (1) Selecting main headings.
      (2) Selecting supporting ideas.
      (3) Putting ideas into outline form.
   b. Preparing original outlines for independent research.
3. Summarizing materials.
   a. Summarizing paragraphs.
   b. Summarizing short selections.
   c. Learning to use summary paragraphs at ends of chapters.

Activities to Teach Students How to Organize Information

Teaching about main ideas

1. Write short paragraphs on cards. Have students read them and write an original title for each paragraph.
2. Have students underline the main idea after reading selections from newspapers.
3. Show a short section from a film. Have children write the main idea and supporting details.
4. Prepare a list of sentences that contain the idea expressed in a paragraph. Have the students select the sentence that best expresses the main thought of each paragraph.
5. Have students write one or two sentences as summaries of a movie, a selection from a book, a news program, a newspaper article, or a group discussion.

Teaching how to relate details to main ideas

1. Select a paragraph that describes details in chronological order. Have pupils list the series of events in order.
2. List the events of a story on the chalkboard. Have students rearrange these incidents in the order in which they probably occurred in the story.
3. Find short selections describing causes and events. Have students list the events and the factors that caused the events.
4. Have students complete outlines as in the following activity.

Americans
  I. Homes
    A.
    B.
    C.

  II. Clothing
    A.
    B.
    C.
  III. Food
    A.
    B.
    C.
  IV. Transportation
    A.
    B.
    C.

Use these words to complete the outline:

potatoes	bicycles	ice cream
apartments	condominiums	hiking boots
airplanes	blue jeans	swimsuits
bread	automobiles	houses

Some activities to use in teaching students to organize information by selecting main ideas and supporting detail appear above (see also Chapter 7).

FOLLOWING DIRECTIONS

Reading to follow directions is a basic skill students will need in all subjects. Directions must be followed in using tools in industrial arts, in baking a cake in home economics, in conducting a science experiment, in working problems in mathematics or in playing a game. Instruction in this skill should begin in the primary grades. It begins with one-step directions given orally and proceeds to multistep directions students read for themselves. Students learn through practice that some directions only give general instructions while others are precise and must be followed exactly and in the correct order. When the teacher checks end products, he will discover which students need additional help in following directions. Students can be helped with practice sessions of teacher-made directions on the student's reading level. Another good practice is to have the student read the directions and tell in her own words what she is going to do. Simple directions in workbooks can be used during the early stages of learning to follow directions.

Exercises such as the ones in the following paragraphs could be useful in helping children learn to follow directions exactly. It is important that children learn there are times when no mistakes can be made — for example, a very small error in adjusting a machine might be the difference between safety and danger.

The first directions may be given orally:

1. Kevin, open the fourth window from the right and close the record cabinet door.
2. Write the date on the chalkboard, Gayle. Under it write the day of the week.
3. Mary, bring me the first library book on the third shelf of the blue bookcase.

When working with written directions, the first ones should be simple, with only one or two exercises in each set. For example:

1. Draw as many lines on the chalkboard as you have fingers.
2. Find a picture of an airplane in the dictionary. Write the number of the page on your paper.
3. Find the word *silhouette* in the dictionary. On what page is it found? How many syllables does the word have? Draw a silhouette.

READING CHARTS, MAPS, AND GRAPHS

Maps, charts, graphs, and tables are used extensively in some content areas, such as science and social studies. The interpretation of such material may be essential to understanding the text, so students should be taught to read tables, graphs, maps, and charts as they appear in the textbooks. In learning to read maps and globes, students need to understand special symbols. Lines, dots, colors, and shadings with their accompanying keys and legends should be converted to what they symbolize — direction, location, topography, and distance. The information presented in graphic form should also be related to that presented in the text.

Students need to become proficient in the following skills:

1. Using and interpreting maps and globes: locating information; using map scales; and interpreting symbols.
2. Using and interpreting graphs, tables, diagrams: interpreting graphs (bar, circle, line); interpreting tables; and interpreting diagrams.
3. Reading and using charts.

Two examples of activities for helping children learn to read charts, maps, and graphs follow:

Provide students with charts, maps, and graphs from different content areas. Ask them to find the answers to questions by using the information portrayed in the charts and graphs. For example, base your questions on a map or chart in a social studies book. The children are to answer questions similar to the following:

Figure 10.7. A sample activity card.

---

1. Choose a statistical topic about which you can gather data from a group of friends or classmates.
2. Gather and organize the data in a table and prepare two different graphs of it.
3. Write a set of questions concerning your table and graph.

---

1. What is the name of the longest river shown on the map?
2. About how high is the tallest mountain on the map?
3. How many miles is Atlanta from here?

Ask students to collect data and organize it in a table or graph so that it can be interpreted easily. Many teachers prefer first-hand data over that taken from encyclopedias, almanacs, or textbooks because they have greater meaning to children. The classroom provides a good source of first-hand data. Some examples of data that can be collected in the classroom are: kinds of books or magazines read by the students, opinion polls, and weekly growth of a plant.

Instructions for the development of charts or graphs may be written on activity cards. An example of an activity card is shown in Figure 10.7.

Map skills can be promoted from selectively using commercially developed activities as in Figure 10.8.

Flexibility of Reading Rate

QUESTIONS TO GUIDE READING

Literal
What factors affect reading rate?

Inferential
Why do educators say reading rate is multilevel?
How does having a clear-cut purpose for reading affect rate and comprehension?

Evaluative
Should teachers in the elementary school work for speed in reading?

Advertisements in the mass media concerning speed reading courses have made a lot of people conscious of reading rates. Too often people believe

Figure 10.8.

Maps

A map key shows the symbols used on a map and explains
what each one means. For example, on this map four-lane
highways are shown with a red line. Two-lane highways are
shown in black. Look at each of the other symbols. Find a place
on the map where each one is used.

Find the direction arrows on the map. Use the arrows and the
key to help you answer each question below the map. Put an X
in each correct box.

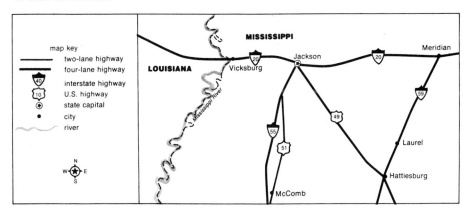

1. Is McComb north or south of Jackson?
   □ north   ☒ south

2. What is the name of the capital of
   Mississippi?
   ☒ Jackson   □ Laurel

3. Is Jackson east or west of Vicksburg?
   ☒ east   □ west

4. Would you take a U.S. highway or an
   interstate highway to travel from
   Jackson to Hattiesburg?
   ☒ U.S.   □ interstate

5. What river does this map show?
   Mississippi River _____

6. What interstate highway would you
   take to travel from Vicksburg to
   Meridian?
   □ Interstate 55   ☒ Interstate 20

7. If you were driving from Hattiesburg to
   Meridian, which direction would you
   travel?
   ☒ north and east   □ north and west

8. How many lanes does Interstate 59
   have?
   □ two   ☒ four

9. How many lanes does U.S. Highway 51
   have?
   ☒ two   □ four

Practice Maps   45

Page 45 from *Sea Treasures* (Workbook Teacher's Edition). Copyright © 1981 by Scott,
Foresman and Company. Reprinted by permission.

that a reader should have only one reading rate, preferably rapid. Actually, the good reader will use many different rates in accordance with the purpose for reading the material.

Some factors that affect reading rate are as follows (Heilman et al. 1981, pp. 302–303):

A. In the reader
1. The reader's experiential/conceptual background in relation to the general subject matter.
2. The reader's motivation.
3. The physiological state of reader (fatigue, for example).
4. The reader's level of reading skills (that is, word recognition and comprehension skills).
5. The reader's familiarity with the printed language, such as sentence structure and word usages.
B. In the printed material
1. The readability of the material as determined by difficulty level of vocabulary and sentence length (factors used in computing readability levels).
2. The readability of material as influenced by style of writing, sentence structure, and difficulty of concepts (factors not indicated in readability formulas).
3. Mechanical factors such as size of print, length of printed line, and type of paper used.
4. The availability of graphic aids such as illustrations, figures, and graphs, and the use of cross references and footnotes to explain more difficult materials.
C. In the reading environment
1. The help teachers give students in establishing a suitable purpose for each reading assignment.
2. The length of the reading period.
3. The physical environment (such as heat, light, and noise level).

Activities for Working with Reading Rate

1. Have students skim a newspaper to find a report on a sports activity.
2. Explain to the students the relations between type and difficulty of material and the appropriate speed at which the material should be read.
3. Ask students to scan a telephone directory to find the name of a specific person.
4. Have students reread a selection in order to answer a specific question.
5. Have students list all the items that support a main idea.
6. Question students on the details of a problem in mathematics.
7. Give students a series of timed reading selections followed by comprehension ques-

tions. You may wish to keep records of the reading rate in words per minute and of comprehension scores. By keeping a careful check on the speed-comprehension balance, you can encourage students with a low rate but high comprehension to read faster. Students who have poor comprehension will have to maintain their present rate and be encouraged to concentrate on their comprehension. Keep the drills short and extend them over a period of weeks. Elementary school children can learn to make significant rate gains. Examples of materials produced commercially that are appropriate for working with rate are included at the end of the chapter.

Different types of material require different rates for reading. The good reader must learn to adjust his reading rate to the material and to his purpose for reading the material. Rate of comprehension must be considered along with rate of reading. Reading without comprehension is not actually reading.

Teachers need to help students improve their speed, but more importantly they need to help students adjust their rate to the purpose and type of material. Actually, there is no best rate teachers and students should strive to attain. The rate should be flexible. Students need to learn to "shift gears" depending on whether they are reading a magazine story, a mathematics problem, science experiment, or history selection. The teacher should plan specific activities to develop the needed flexibility in reading rate.

Harris (1968) reflected on the 1928 study by Yoakam, which distinguished four main rates of reading: skimming for survey or item location; rapid reading in easy material; normal reading; and slow, careful reading in difficult material. Harris's research indicated that most readers are rigid rather than flexible.

Reading rates may be fast for easy, familiar materials we read for general ideas. The rate may be much slower for unfamiliar material or material we read for critical evaluation or depth of meaning. Considerable practice in rapid reading of easy materials helps increase the reading rate.

Although a major focus of the elementary school reading program should be on word recognition and comprehension, training for faster rate and flexibility should also be given attention. When increasing rate is combined with instruction in study skills, the student begins to get the idea of flexibility. A major goal of the elementary school reading program must be to produce readers who know when to read at a rapid rate and when to read slowly and carefully.

Systematic Study Plans

QUESTIONS TO GUIDE READING

Literal
What is one specific study plan?
What are the 3 Rs in Robinson's plan?

Inferential
How can SQ3R be adapted in given content areas?

Evaluative
Should you use SQ3R as you study this text?

Reading authorities have developed a number of systematic study strategies. In most cases they direct the student to follow a series of steps in order to approach study-type reading tasks in an organized manner. One systematic study plan that has been widely used as a teacher-directed activity and as a student-directed activity is the SQ3R (Survey, Question, Read, Recite, Review) reading and study formula developed by Robinson (1961, pp. 29–33; 1962, p. 31).[1]

S = Survey	Read the title of the chapter, the introductory statement, and the main headings. Survey illustrations and read the summary at the end of the chapter. Try to construct a chapter outline in your mind.
Q = Question	Look at the main headings. Ask yourself what they mean. Formulate questions from your survey.
R_1 = Read	Read to find answers to your questions.
R_2 = Recite	Recite answers to your questions. Do the author's answers satisfy you? Do you have new ideas that could help answer the questions?
R_3 = Review	Review the entire chapter or selection in a survey fashion. Reconstruct your outline in your mind. Recall the author's important ideas. Think of ways to use the new ideas you learned.

The SQ3R study strategy has been widely accepted because it is designed to serve not only as a technique for increasing immediate understanding but also as an aid in prolonging retention. The SQ3R study strategy is supported by results from research studies.

1. From Francis P. Robinson, "Study Skills for Superior Students in the Secondary Schools," *The Reading Teacher* 14 (September 1961), pp. 29–33. Paraphrased by permission.

For example, a study designed to determine whether the teaching of SQ3R would increase reading and social studies achievements in grade seven was conducted by Donald (1968). The results showed no significant gain on normed instruments, but a significant gain on teacher-made tests. Teacher observations indicated SQ3R methods resulted in the students' feeling more secure in their ability to do well and in better attack skills for new material.

In educational literature, there are many variations of the SQ3R technique. Spache (1963, p. 94) suggests the PQRST technique for science.

Preview:	Rapidly skim the selection.
Question:	Raise questions for study purposes.
Read:	With questions in mind, read selection.
Summarize:	Organize and summarize information gained.
Test:	Check your summary with the selection.

For problem reading in mathematics, Fay (1965, p. 93) recommends the use of the SQRQCQ technique.

Survey:	Read the problem rapidly to determine its nature.
Question:	Decide what is being asked, what the problem is.
Read:	Read for details and interrelationships.
Question:	Decide what processes should be used.
Compute:	Carry out the computation.
Question:	Ask if the answer seems correct, check the computations against the problem facts and the basic arithmetic facts.

Forgan and Mangrum (1981, pp. 202–217) recommend a five-step instructional procedure for teaching any one of the three study techniques. The five steps in the instructional procedure involve:

1. Selecting appropriate materials (or problems in mathematics).
2. Applying the technique to the materials or problem.
3. Scheduling instruction for a suitable period of time so that the information can be thoroughly taught.
4. Providing appropriate instruction.
5. Including practice sessions following instruction for the purpose of extending their understanding and helping children to become automatic in their application of the newly acquired study technique.

Tierney, Readance, and Dishner (1980, pp. 82–85) describe a technique that is most appropriate for the teacher of history. The study strategy is referred to as the Herringbone technique and provides children with a structured framework for taking notes from a textbook chapter, for observing relationships, and for studying and remembering information.

The Herringbone technique suggests that the important information can be obtained by asking six very basic comprehension questions: Who? What? When? Where? How? and Why? By providing a form to record information, the teacher provides the structure for notetaking and for later study of the recorded information. The Herringbone strategy is intended for use with children in the middle grades and above and is most beneficial to children who are experiencing difficulty with organizing material. A Herringbone format appears in Figure 10.9. The children are taught to seek answers to these questions and record their answers on the Herringbone format as they read the content material.

There are various other study techniques available for helping children better understand and remember information. Some of these strategies are very specific and some are more general. Many of the strategies direct the children to follow a series of steps in approaching content area reading in an organized manner. Some techniques appear to be most effective when used alternatively with other techniques. The teacher should be aware of the similarities and differences among the techniques that are suitable for guiding and improving content area reading. The teacher should select the strategy that seems most appropriate for her children based on an understanding of their needs and abilities. Attempting to teach all strategies to the children could confuse them and defeat the purpose of teaching a tool to guide children in content area reading (Douzat and Douzat 1981, pp. 173–181).

Figure 10.9. The Herringbone technique.

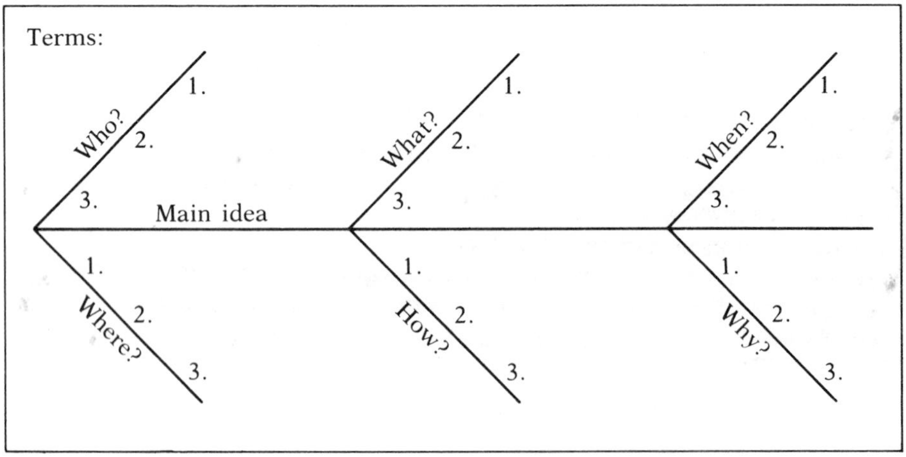

Adapted from Figure 2.3 on page 83 in *Reading Strategies and Practices: A Guide for Improving Instruction* by Robert J. Tierney, John E. Readance, and Ernest K. Dishner. © 1980 by Allyn and Bacon, Inc. Used with permission.

Summary

Developing proficiency in the study skills is a difficult and slow process. Training in the skills should begin in the primary grades and continue through all the school years. The skills should be taught and retaught; each school year the teacher should review, revise, and refine the skills.

Skills do not develop by themselves. Children learn through carefully planned lessons and a followup of consistent guidance. This requires careful planning and systematic teaching. Some classroom teachers are convinced of, and committed to, the value of teaching study skills; but this commitment needs to be extended to all teachers in all grade levels and content areas. The day-by-day contact with students enables each classroom teacher to determine which skills need additional emphasis. Instruction should begin where the learners are and progress from that point.

Study skills are best taught and practiced when the student can apply them. Teaching the skill at the time it is needed does not detract from content coverage; in fact, it should increase understandings. Study skills should be taught in conjunction with a particular subject area, not in isolation. This motivates the student to learn the skill because he can see its usefulness. Classroom teachers should develop skill-building activities that will be appropriate in aiding each student to attain an acceptable level of mastery or proficiency. The teacher can divide the tasks into subtasks as needed, to tailor sessions to each individual child's needs. The teacher should make sure the issue isn't confused by the presentation of too many skills at one time.

The old adage "practice makes perfect" can be applied to study skills. The practice requires teacher guidance and attention. While each teacher is encouraged to become a skills teacher, it does not mean he works alone; teachers should share strategies, experiences, techniques, materials, and talents. The librarian, the reading specialist, the principal, the curriculum supervisor, and other classroom teachers are all sources of ideas for the teacher who is helping his students develop study skill competencies.

In this chapter the study skills emphasized were those which help the student to: locate information; use library resources; select information; organize information; follow directions; and read and interpret graphs, maps, and charts.

Questions for Further Reading and Thinking

1. What constitutes readiness for using dictionaries and encyclopedias?
2. Do you believe that the American schools do a thorough job of developing study skills proficiencies? Why or why not?
3. Advocates of speed reading courses insist that comprehension increases with rate. Do you agree? Can you defend your answer?
4. If you had the opportunity to select encyclopedias for the school in which you were teaching, which set(s) would you choose for the primary grades? Intermediate grades? Defend your selections.
5. In many schools, children have five different teachers for five different subjects during the school day. Who should teach them study skills? Why?
6. What would be a suitable teaching sequence for helping children learn to locate information?
7. Why is the ability to write an effective summary such an important communication and study skill?
8. What are some different types of practice that can be used to increase rate of reading?
9. In what ways are the various study skills prerequisite for each other? What aspects of each skill are necessary to facilitate progress in another skill?
10. Study a basal reading textbook series. How are the study skills taught?

Activities and Projects

1. Check recent issues of *Teacher, The Instructor, Language Arts, The English Journal, The Reading Teacher,* and *The Social Studies* for teacher-tested strategies for instruction in study skills. List ten activities that provide practice for learning study skills.
2. Compare a chapter in a sixth grade social studies book with one from a science text. Which study skills are needed for each? How are the study skills alike? Different?
3. Develop a set of criteria for judging the value of workbooks in teaching specific study skills.
4. Cut graphs and charts from a daily newspaper. Develop a lesson plan for teaching a class of fifth graders how to read these graphic materials.
5. Develop a set of activity cards designed to help students learn specific study skills.
6. Develop readiness activities to prepare students to read a road map.

Materials for Developing Study Skills

Be a better reader (Books A, B, C) by Nila Banton Smith. Englewood Cliffs, N.J.: Prentice-Hall.
Classification and order (Level B) by Raymond Fournier. Englewood Cliffs, N.J.: Prentice-Hall.
Dictionary activity cards. Monterey Park, Calif.: Creative Teaching Press.

Dictionary skills series (Grades 2–6). New York: Scholastic.

EDL study-skills library (four kits; Levels 3–9). New York: Educational Development Laboratories.

Essential reading: study and research skills by Gerald G. Duffy and Laura Roehler. Evanston, Ill.: McDougal, Littell. 1982.

Library reference skills (Books C–F) by Claire Murray. Los Angeles, Calif.: Bowman/Noble.

Map skills, Books C–F. Los Angeles, Calif.: Bowman/Noble.

Organizing information (Levels C–F) by Alvin Kravitz and Dan Dramer (MCP Skillbooster Series). Cleveland, Ohio: Modern Curriculum Press.

Reading improvement activities by Norman Schachter and John K. Whelan. Austin, Tex.: Steck-Vaughn.

Using maps, charts, and graphs (Levels C–F) by Dale I. Foreman and Sally J. Allen (MCP Skillbooster). Cleveland, Ohio: Modern Curriculum Press.

Using references (Levels C–F) by Sandra M. Brown (MCP Skillbooster Series). Cleveland, Ohio: Modern Curriculum Press.

Sea treasures. Glenview, Ill.: Scott, Foresman.

Skills for school reading (Level B) by Katherine Hunt Swartz and (Level C) by Day Ann McClenathan. Atlanta, Ga.: Harcourt Brace Jovanovich.

Skills practice book (Purple, Yellow, Blue, Orange, Green, Red, Gold, Silver, Aqua, and Brown Levels). Evanston, Ill.: McDougal, Littell.

Sky climbers. Glenview, Ill.: Scott, Foresman. 1981.

Specific skills series by Richard A. Boning. Rockville Center, N.Y.: Barnell Loft, Ltd.

Standard test lessons in reading by McCall and Crabbs. New York: Bureau of Publications, Teachers College, Columbia University.

Study skills for information retrieval series by Donald L. Barnes and Arlene Burgdorf. Boston: Allyn and Bacon.

Supportive reading skills: Understanding questions (Levels 1–9), *Using a table of contents* (Levels 1–9), *Using an index* (Levels 1–9), *Learning to alphabetize* (Levels 1–3), *Using guide words* (Levels 4–9). Baldwin, N.Y.: Dexter and Westbrook.

J. Estill Alexander / Mona Donnelly

11

Reading in Content Areas

Many teachers believe that low achievement in reading skills constitutes a serious handicap in any area of the curriculum. This feeling is verified by the research of Herber and Sanders (1969), which suggests that student achievement can be improved when reading instruction takes place in conjunction with content area instruction. The reading of content texts often poses problems for youngsters who have little difficulty with basals or with trade books in which they are interested. This discrepant performance may occur because they lack the motivation for study reading or because they cannot effectively meet the reading challenges inherent in each content area. The intent of this chapter is to present ways teachers can match children more appropriately with texts; to delineate those reading skills and competencies which need special attention in science, social studies, mathematics, and literature; and to present instructional frameworks that facilitate comprehension in content areas.

Readability and Utilization of Content Area Texts

QUESTIONS TO GUIDE READING

Literal
What purposes does a readability formula serve?
What factors determine readability?
What are some commonly used readability formulas available to teachers?
What are some ways that a teacher can reduce the mismatch between a child's reading ability and the difficulty level of the text?

Inferential
How does cloze procedure differ from readability formulas?
Why is it important for teachers to assess readability informally?

Evaluative

When would a teacher use cloze procedure (as discussed in this chapter)?

When would a teacher use a readability formula?

Should a teacher decide not to use a content area text simply because it is too difficult for some children to read?

Readability refers to the "ease of understanding or comprehension because of style of writing" (Harris and Hodges 1981, p. 262). There are many variables that may contribute to readability. These include variables within the text such as format, typography, content, literary form and style, vocabulary difficulty, sentence complexity, idea or proposition density, and cohesiveness. Variables within the reader such as motivation, abilities, and interests also contribute to readability. Text variables and reader variables interact in determining the readability of a given text with a given child (Harris and Hodges 1981, p. 262).

The textual factors determining readability are usually better controlled at lower elementary levels, and seem so; but less concern is obvious at the intermediate and secondary levels. West (1974, pp. 26–27) emphasized that often the authors of content area texts are experts in their fields who have not had training in teaching the reading skills prerequisite for comprehending the text. It is encouraging to note that the overall readability level of elementary social studies texts is decreasing (Johnson 1977). In his study, Johnson also found that the range of reading levels within texts is getting narrower. This range of readability from one part of a text to another has been a concern of teachers for some time.

READABILITY FORMULAS

West (1974, p. 29) states that most authors of readability formulas have attempted to identify the factors that make materials difficult to read. The main objective in developing readability formulas is "to obtain the highest degree of prediction using the least number of factors." West further points out that researchers also agree that vocabulary and sentence length cause the greatest difficulty, with vocabulary being the most significant determiner of reading comprehension. Because of the many nonmeasurable factors discussed in the definition of readability, we *must* accept the fact that readability scores are *approximations*.

Many readability formulas are available for teachers' use. Teachers prefer formulas that are as simple as possible. Such simple formulas often involve simple word and sentence counts noted above. Klare (1974–75, p. 98) states that such counts can provide satisfactory predictions for most purposes and may be used as *one* index of readability. Knowledge of learners and textual factors should be considered also (see page 248).

Teachers should recognize specific limitations of readability formulas as they consider them for use. According to Hittleman (1978) the short-comings include:

1. A criterion of comprehensibility can't be reliably determined.
2. Word frequency and sentence length do not stand in simple relationship to reading disability.
3. The formulas may be of dubious value when used with pupils or materials dissimilar with those used in computing the formulas originally.
4. They do not consider difficulty caused by factors such as concept load, format of the material, organization of the ideas, or the writing patterns.

Among the best-known formulas are the Dale-Chall (1948), Spache (1953), Gunning's Fog Index (1968), SMOG Grading (McLaughlin 1969), the Raygor Readability Estimate (1977), and the Fry Readability Graph (1977). Because of its brevity, simplicity, and comparable accuracy, the Fry formula can be recommended for use by the elementary classroom teacher. Instructions for using the Fry Graph (see Figure 11.1) are given below. In this figure the average number of sentences per 100 words was 6.3 and the average number of syllables per 100 words was 141. Plotted on the graph, the point (dot) at which the two sets of data meet is in the seventh grade area. Hence the material is at about the seventh grade difficulty level.

Expanded Directions for Working Readability Graph

1. Randomly select three (3) sample passages and count out exactly 100 words each, beginning with the beginning of a sentence. Do count proper nouns, initializations, and numerals.
2. Count the number of sentences in the hundred words, estimating length of the fraction of the last sentence to the nearest one-tenth.
3. Count the total number of syllables in the 100-word passage. If you don't have a hand counter available, an easy way is simply to put a mark above every syllable over one in each word, then when you get to the end of the passage, count the number of marks and add 100. Small calculators can also be used as counters by pushing numeral 1, then push the + sign for each word or syllable when counting.
4. Enter graph [Figure 11.1] with *average* sentence length and *average* number of syllables; plot dot where the two lines intersect. Area where dot is plotted will give you the approximate grade level.
5. If a great deal of variability is found in syllable count or sentence count, putting more samples into the average is desirable.
6. A word is defined as a group of symbols with a space on either side; thus *Joe, IRA, 1945,* and *&* are each one word.

Source: Edward Fry, Rutgers University Reading Center, New Brunswick, N.J. 08904.
Note: This "extended graph" does not outmode or render the earlier (1968) version inoperative or inaccurate; it is an extension.

Figure 11.1. Extended Fry graph for estimating readability.

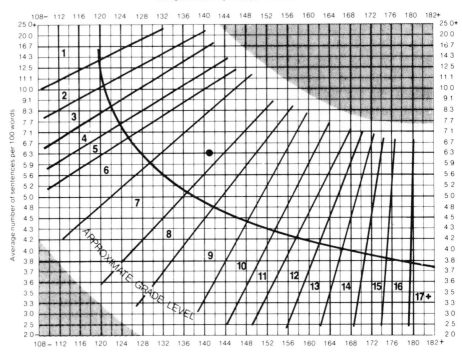

Average number of syllables per 100 words

Source: Edward Fry, Rutgers University Reading Center, New Brunswick, NJ 08904.

7. A syllable is defined as a phonetic syllable. Generally, there are as many syllables as vowel sounds. For example, *stopped* is one syllable and *wanted* is two syllables. When counting syllables for numerals and initializations, count one syllable for each symbol. For example, *1945* is four syllables, *IRA* is three syllables, and *&* is one syllable.

CLOZE PROCEDURE

Bormuth's Cloze Readability Procedure is a newer procedure that involves students, as opposed to a formula that does not take the student into account; its purpose is to predict whether a student can handle satisfactorily a given piece of material in an instructional situation (Bormuth 1969). Directions for constructing, administering, and interpreting a cloze test in content areas have been suggested by Earle (1976, pp. 64–65). We reproduce them in the following seven paragraphs:[1]

1. From Richard A. Earle, *Teaching Reading and Mathematics* (Newark, Del.: The International Reading Association, 1976), pp. 64–65. Reprinted with the permission of Richard A. Earle and The International Reading Association.

1. Select approximately 260 running words from required text material.

2. Print the first sentence in its entirety, unmutilated.

3. Select, at random, one of the next 5 words (i.e., one of the first 5 words in the second sentence). Delete this word and replace it with a blank of standard length. Continue to delete every fifth word until you have 50 blanks. End that sentence. Follow with a complete, unmutilated sentence.

4. Since most students will find the cloze a new experience, it is important to explain the purpose of the test, and to precede its administration by one or two similar very brief and easy exercises, completed with teacher guidance and/or peer collaboration. Administration rarely takes more than 30 minutes.

5. Since the test is not to be graded or returned to the students, the easiest means of scoring is to avoid the search for synonyms. Rather, mark as correct only those words or symbols which are exact replacements according to the original text material. Multiply each correct replacement by two to arrive at percent correct.

6. Research has shown the cloze to be a valid and reliable measure of reading comprehension. As with any test, however, your interpretation of the scores is most important. The research suggests that cloze scores of less than 30 to 35 percent are likely to indicate inadequate comprehension, while scores of greater than 55 to 60 percent are likely to indicate very high comprehension of the text in question.

7. Perhaps the best way to interpret your cloze scores, however, is to organize them in a single frequency distribution, i.e., arrange the scores in order to show that so many kids got 10 percent, so many got 12 percent, so many got 14 percent, and so on. This kind of organization will give a more graphic picture of how well individuals and groups in a particular class comprehended the text.

Cloze procedure passages should be prepared from the materials that the teacher plans to use in her classroom. It is important to note that, at times, texts differ in readability from section to section. Therefore, a representative passage (or passages) of medium difficulty should be chosen.

Cloze procedure may well be preferred over readability formulas in the future. Lundstrum (1976), for example, feels that readability research in the social studies should be more sensitive to the problem of concept loading and states that cloze procedure may provide this greater sensitivity.

Although cloze procedure has the advantage of considering the material to be used and factors within learners, such as conceptual background and interests, there are cautions with this tool also. Among the limitations suggested by Hittleman (1978) are the following:

1. Materials sampled may contain items deleted for which there are no context clues in the text.

2. Deleted items may not be reading related. Responses given may reflect general information rather than that which was read.
3. The deletion of every fifth word may not be suitable for all learners.
4. Cloze results may be greatly influenced by type and number of deletions. Science materials may need more words between each deletion than English or social studies materials if an accurate prediction of readability is to occur.

In addition, cloze may be very frustrating to a child who has not had considerable experience with the procedure in regular classroom work.

TEACHER ANALYSIS

It was noted earlier that both readability formulas and cloze procedure have limitations. In addition to the use of these tools, it is wise for teachers to analyze the text informally themselves. H. Alan Robinson (1978) has utilized the work of Krause (1976) and has developed the following set of criteria for this purpose.[2] Such criteria enable the teacher to look at factors affecting readability that are not assessed by formulas.

1. The density of concepts *isn't* intended to frustrate the student. In other words, each sentence isn't packed with several ideas.
2. The sentence complexity *isn't* usually high. That is, the authors don't tend to always use long compound and complex sentences.
3. The authors *don't* continually choose to use long, difficult words when simpler synonyms would suffice.
4. Captions under graphs, tables and diagrams are clearly written.
5. The text contains both a table of contents and an index.
6. The table of contents shows a logical development of the subject matter.
7. When a text refers to a graph, table, or diagram, that aid is on the same page as the textual reference.
8. Pictures are in color and are contemporary, not dated by dress unless the author's intention is to portray a certain period.
9. Difficult new vocabulary words are highlighted, italicized, or underlined.
10. The main idea or purpose for reading a chapter is stated at the beginning.
11. The authors include a summary at the end of each chapter.
12. Passive tense is used only when essential, since frequent use seems to trouble poor readers.
13. The variety of connectives (consequently, in spite of, thus, however, etc.) is somewhat controlled so they are used sparingly as important signals to the reader.
14. Antecedents and referents are clear, particularly across sentences.

2. From p. 132 of *Teaching Reading and Study Strategies: The Content Areas*, 2nd ed., by H. Alan Robinson. Boston: Allyn and Bacon, 1978. Reprinted with permission.

15. Relative clauses are limited in number in a given sentence, clearly written, and clearly attached to a referent.

MATCHING CONTENT AREA TEXTS AND CHILDREN

A first step in promoting comprehension of content area texts is the matching of children with texts they can read. One effective but time-consuming technique to use is an informal reading inventory (Burron and Claybough 1974) constructed from the content area materials the teacher plans to use. (See Chapter 17 for a discussion of informal reading inventories.) A second technique that is less time consuming is the cloze procedure, which we just discussed in the preceding section. McWilliams and Rakes (1979) have produced a content area inventory based on cloze.

Other techniques are the use of informal observations, study skills inventories, or teacher-made tests (Readance et al. 1981; Thelen 1976; Vacca 1981; Viox 1968).[3] These determine whether students have the study skills necessary to comprehend the text. A study skills inventory utilizes questions requiring the student to use the whole book, a portion of the book, or a particular study skill. Study skills inventories may be constructed to assess internal textual aids (such as table of contents, index, glossaries, pictures, maps), external aids (such as dictionaries, reference guides, and encyclopedias), vocabulary knowledge, explicit and implicit information, and pattern of organization of material (Readance et al. 1981, p. 89).

In addition, a teacher has other options for precluding a mismatch between the difficulty level of a text and the reading capabilities of a child — thus facilitating comprehension. These include:

1. Provision for more than one text on a given topic. The use of trade books on varying readability levels is also encouraged. Supplementary resources such as films, filmstrips, tapes, and records are also helpful (Turner 1976b).
2. The teacher may rewrite the material so that it can be comprehended more easily (Cardinell 1976). All factors determining readability (discussed in the preceding section) should be considered. The teacher should apply a readability formula to the rewritten material. Don't assume that rewriting automatically makes the material more readable. Rewriting is a difficult, time-consuming task. Thus a teacher can realistically rewrite only a small amount of material.

3. For an in-depth treatment of these informal skills tests and inventories see Ruth G. Viox, *Evaluating Reading and Study Skills in the Secondary Classroom* (Newark, Del.: International Reading Association, 1968); Judith Thelen, *Improving Reading in Science* (Newark, Del.: The International Reading Association, 1976); Richard T. Vacca, *Content Area Reading*, Chapter 11 (Boston: Little, Brown, 1981); or John E. Readance and others, *Content Area Reading: An Integrated Approach*, Chapter 5, (Dubuque, Iowa: Kendall/Hunt, 1981).

3. The teacher may give instruction in the general and specific skills needed for success in particular assigned materials.
4. Assignments may be differentiated in terms of both the purposes set for reading and the amount of material to be read.
5. The teacher may construct study guides in which students are provided with questions they are likely to be able to handle (Readance et al. 1981).

Turner (1980) has provided suggestions for working with and around reading problems that may inhibit comprehension of social studies texts. These suggestions are generally applicable to science and literature also. Among his suggestions are:

1. Tape-recording critically important textbook sections.
2. Pairing students to do textbook assignments so that one child may assist another. It is important that these children want to work together.
3. Preparing textbook summaries or outlines of important material.
4. Developing question-asking skills about illustrations so that attention may be focused on important sections of the text.
5. Having the class prepare a cartoon narrative of important parts of the text.

Reading Skills in Content Areas

QUESTIONS TO GUIDE READING

Literal
What specific reading skills are basic for the science area? the social studies area? the mathematics area? the literature area?

Inferential
Why are some reading skills more important than others for content area reading?
In teaching a content area reading skill, why might a teacher need to adapt the way some skills are presented in reading class?

Evaluative
How can a knowledge of paragraph structures, described in Chapter 7, help you become a better content area teacher?
Do content area teachers need to stress vocabulary more?

Reading is the major self-study skill used in all areas of the curriculum. The ability to read materials in all content areas cannot generally be adequately developed and refined through a basal reading program or in language arts activities. Reading abilities *must* be developed and reinforced in the content areas in which they are to be used if a child is to achieve at a level commensurate with his capacity.

Some have argued that content areas have special reading skills and that content teachers need to distinguish between general reading skills that transfer to content situations and ones that do not (Dechant and Smith 1977, p. 315). Others feel that the uniqueness of these "content area" skills may be in the adaptation of these skills rather than an inherent "difference" in the given skill (Herber 1972, pp. 195–197). This latter position forms the basis for the discussion in this section. The skills noted can be introduced either in "reading" class or in a content area class. In any event, the use and application of these skills *must* take place in content area classes for most effective learning.

In each of the four content areas discussed — science, social studies, mathematics, and literature — a list of skills highly important to each area will be given. There is some redundancy in these skills lists; however, this underscores the need and the opportunity to develop or reinforce these skills in each of the areas. Basic procedures for introducing these skills have been presented previously, and word meaning strategies were developed in Chapter 6. Since vocabulary is so important to comprehension, however, additional strategies and modifications are included here. You should notice the need for practice and reinforcement in content area vocabulary development (see Chapter 6 for ideas). Comprehension and questioning strategies were presented in Chapters 7, 8, and 9. Study skills ideas were developed in Chapter 10. Word pronunciation skills were introduced in Part 2. Please return to these chapters to think about what modifications (if any) would be needed in order to apply these strategies to given content area classes. The nature of the modification often depends on the content area. Additional strategies are included in this section.

Recall from Chapter 7 that paragraph structures differ. This difference is basic in working in the content areas. For example, are the paragraph structures primarily explanatory as in a science text or narrative as in literature? Review these paragraph structures as you think about content area instruction.

READING IN SCIENCE

Science is so largely first-hand learning that, ideally, it furnishes the experience and meaningful vocabulary necessary to effective reading. "Young children, so rightly, make full use of their senses in experiencing. They feel, push, lift, pull and shove. They taste, watch and listen." But first-hand experience often falls short of completely meeting a child's needs; reading then becomes a vital supplement (Camden 1954, p. 105).

Specific skills. Forgan and Mangrum (1981, p. 104) list the following skills needed for efficient reading of science materials:[4]

Word Meaning
1. Understand the technical vocabulary of science.
2. Analyze stems, prefixes, and suffixes to determine the meaning of technical words.

Comprehension
3. Read to answer various types of questions.
4. Differentiate facts from opinions.
5. Read and follow directions as required for doing experiments.
6. Read to test, prove or predict outcomes.
7. Organize ideas from reading and understand the relationships between the ideas in order to draw conclusions or make inferences or evaluations.

Study Skills and Strategies
8. Use library skills to locate and research a topic.
9. Interpret such graphic and visual materials as weather maps or diagrams.
10. Use a study technique such as PQRST.

Word Pronunciation
11. Quickly identify symbols, formulas, and abbreviations.
12. Recognize common prefixes, suffixes, and stems as an aid to word pronunciation.
13. Pronounce such multisyllable words.

Foundations: objectivity and vocabulary. The application of specific comprehension skills to science materials depends on two important foundations. The first foundation is an understanding of the objectivity of science. The student needs to understand the scientific procedure — in defining a problem, developing an idea for the solution of the problem, and then trying out the idea to see if it is, in fact, a solution. Biographies of scientists are useful for developing this understanding.

The second foundation is vocabulary. The elementary school child is faced with a vast and rapidly growing technical vocabulary that includes symbolic language and abbreviations. In science, abbreviations often stand for far more than a shortened form of a word. There has been some debate as to the propriety of using technical terms in science materials for children. One of the major characteristics of science writing is clarity and preciseness, which makes the use of technical terms essential.

4. Taken from p. 104 of *Teaching Content Area Reading Skills*, 2nd ed. by Harry W. Forgan and Charles T. Mangrum II. Columbus, Ohio: Charles E. Merrill Publishing Co., 1981. Reprinted with permission.

Teachers can aid students in learning a technical vocabulary in several ways. Some of these practices are described below:

1. Vocabulary cards, on which the student records new words he learns, can be helpful. The student is encouraged to write the definition in his own words, including its use and relationship to other concepts. For slower students a pictorial definition could be beneficial.
2. In reviewing a new reading assignment, the teacher may point out new words, or words that might be troublesome. As the teacher introduces a new word, he can develop a definition through discussion.
3. The teacher may draw attention to the endings of science words and the commonality of those words having the same suffix.
4. The teacher may draw attention to the style of the textbook writer. The author may put definitions in italics or boldface type. Or, he may define a word in technical language and then follow this with a sentence explaining the meaning in simple terms.
5. Visual aids in the forms of films, slides, study prints, maps, graphs, charts, and models serve to clarify a vague understanding of technical jargon. Field trips are especially helpful.
6. Creative writing assignments give students an opportunity to use new words and ideas introduced during specific science activities.

In the teaching of science, teachers need to remember that children may not be accustomed to using words precisely. Science vocabulary must be carefully and specifically defined and used. Teachers need to take extra time to guide children to this realization. One way of doing this is to point out the precise scientific meaning of terms when they are encountered. But more importantly, teachers need to listen to children's vocabulary usage when they are talking about science. Vague expressions such as "You know what I mean" and "This thing . . ." should be probed with teacher questions. Children can be led to think with more specificity if the teacher shows sufficient interest in exact word meanings.

Critical reading of science materials. Students need to develop an attitude of demanding meaning from their reading, for critical appraisal is an essential part of all content reading. Learning to read critically and to appraise findings in a thoughtful and accurate manner requires many years of training and practice. Children need to begin this experience at a very early age.

All of the new science curricula emphasize inquiry, discovery, and process. If a child is going to learn to be a superior problem solver, he must have the opportunity to ask questions, make predictions, and gather and process data. In short, he must be taught to be an inquiring reader. The elementary teacher must guide children in applying reading study skills in all areas of the curriculum and especially in science.

Social studies is essential for developing an understanding of how people live and interact in cultures, societies, and the world. Students learn social studies in many ways; they listen, observe, interact with people, and read people's thoughts in books or other printed materials. Because most social studies content in the elementary and middle grades is learned through written sources, reading becomes the most important learning tool in social studies (Roehler 1974).

Specific skills and competencies. Forgan and Mangrum (1981, pp. 104–105) state that social studies teachers need to be aware of the many reading skills needed for adequate comprehension of social studies texts. These include:[5]

Word Meaning
1. Use such technical vocabulary words as *alliance, autonomy, butte, coniferous, equinox,* and *sovereign.*
2. Recognize the meaning of common prefixes and suffixes, which can be used as aids to word meaning.

Comprehension
3. Answer various types of questions.
4. Find the main idea and supporting details in reading selections.
5. Recognize cause and effect relationships.
6. Read critically to identify propaganda techniques.
7. Read to compare and contrast information and situations.
8. Read to distinguish fact from opinion.

Study Skills and Strategies
9. Be able to use the different parts of a book, such as summaries, chapter introductions, vocabulary lists, glossaries, preface, and footnotes.
10. Use such library resources as *Reader's Guide to Periodical Literature,* the card catalog, and others as may be appropriate.
11. Effectively and efficiently locate information in such reference materials as encyclopedias and almanacs.
12. Read maps (population, rainfall, physical, political, soil, etc.), tables, charts, graphs, and cartoons.
13. Understand time and space relationships.
14. Take notes in outline form from a book or other assigned reading.
15. Use a study strategy such as SQ3R.

5. Taken from pp. 104 and 105 of *Teaching Content Area Reading Skills,* 2nd ed. by Harry W. Forgan and Charles T. Mangrum II. Columbus, Ohio: Charles E. Merrill Publishing Co., 1981. Reprinted with permission.

Word Pronunciation

16. Pronounce such multisyllable words as *ingot* and *typhoon.*
17. Use common prefixes and suffixes to aid in the pronunciation of technical words.

The organization of the material in the social studies is at times more complex than that to which the pupil is accustomed in much of his other reading. Chronological order usually has been the simple determinant of the organization in the basal reader and storybook; in social studies textbooks, it seldom is.

Familiarity with organizational features and patterns can be helpful in the development of analytical and evaluative reading skills. A good social studies student is one who has learned to inquire alertly — always aware that distortion, inconsistency, and unfounded or unsupported reasoning may creep into any author's work. Such a student will be sensitive to and aware of his own biases as well as those of other students and teachers.

Social studies, perhaps more than any other field, can provide an opportunity to help students develop skills in critical reading, and the student's feelings of satisfaction can be personally rewarding to the teacher. It is a turning point in a child's education when he discovers that two authors may have very different ways of looking at the same thing — that they may have different points of view. When he makes this discovery, he has made a giant step toward dynamic, participatory citizenship in a democracy.

Democratic citizenship is based on individual choices. But making choices is not only a freedom — it is a developed ability. A child needs to realize what the alternatives are and what constitutes a sufficient information basis for making decisions among alternatives. Critical reading skills enable him to reach these decisions. (See Chapter 8.)

Vocabulary development. Social studies, like science, conveys its message through a specialized vocabulary. Words typical of and frequently used in social studies materials must be thoroughly understood if the reader is to comprehend the materials. Another aspect of vocabulary knowledge is that the same word may be used in a different manner or with different meanings in the same text. Unless a student understands the meaning of the content words and the function words, he cannot follow the structure of the selection.

In teaching word meanings in social studies, it is useful to know that many of the practices mentioned in teaching science vocabulary are applicable. In addition to those suggestions, Herber (1970, pp. 166–168) recommends the following activities:

1. Exercises that focus on multiple meanings of words. For example, a vocabulary item such as *combine* may have several meanings. These

meanings can be listed, with students selecting and verifying the most appropriate meaning in the contextual setting under consideration.

2. Crossword puzzles utilizing the new words in a given unit. This activity is often highly motivating to intermediate and upper grade students.

3. Exercises that promote recall of word definitions and involve word analysis skills. For example, syllabication can be the basis for some exercises. An example from Herber (1970, p. 168) is: "Give the two-syllable word that describes rich land, good for grain crops. Answer: F _ _ / _ _ _ _ ."

READING IN MATHEMATICS

The reading and study of mathematics is focused essentially on mathematical concepts so that students can develop competence in the mathematical processes. The teacher therefore has a twofold responsibility. He must teach students how to read mathematical materials, and he must teach them concepts and their applications. In order to teach the reading of mathematics, the teacher must know the basic mathematics concepts as well as the skills of reading as they apply to mathematics.

Reading skills in mathematics. To assist students in achieving some independence in the successful reading of mathematics, Forgan and Mangrum (1981, p. 102) recommend the development of the following skills:[6]

Word Meaning
1. Understand such specialized vocabulary terms.
2. Understand common stems, prefixes, and suffixes.

Comprehension
3. Answer various types of questions.
4. Read detailed material slowly to determine the significant and insignificant facts.
5. Follow directions precisely, as in detailed explanations of various processes requiring step-by-step operations.
6. Critically analyze such statistical records.

Study Skills and Strategies
7. Locate and read reference materials on such topics as famous mathematicians or the application of a specific mathematical theory.
8. Interpret materials used to express relationships, such as principles, axioms, formulas, and equations.

6. Taken from p. 100 of *Teaching Content Area Reading Skills*, 2nd ed. by Harry W. Forgan and Charles T. Mangrum II. Columbus, Ohio: Charles E. Merrill Publishing Co., 1981. Reprinted with permission.

9. Read tables.
10. Read various types of graphs, such as bar graphs, line graphs, pictographs, and flowcharts.
11. Read such visual materials as diagrams and geometric forms.
12. Use an index, table of contents, or other aids to locate information.
13. Remember the meanings of symbols and abbreviations.
14. Use an appropriate study strategy, such as SQRQCQ, for reasoning problems requiring reading.

Word Pronunciation
15. Pronounce such multisyllable words.
16. Recognize common prefixes and suffixes.

Reading for main ideas. Main ideas are crucial in mathematics, as in all content areas. Many mathematics texts offer special helps for the student in discovering main ideas. These include chapter headings, subheadings, visual aids that highlight a concept, and chapter summaries (Aukerman 1972, p. 195). Activities suggested in Chapter 7 (page 150) are appropriate for consideration in developing main ideas in mathematics.

Vocabulary development. There are two aspects to the study of mathematical vocabulary. One aspect is the conceptual base of the terms: if a student is to "understand" rather than learn mathematics by rote, he must have the conceptual foundation. The second is that vocabulary load is further increased by mathematical abbreviations and symbols.

The vocabulary that must be mastered in the learning of mathematics falls into four categories (Shepherd 1973, p. 259):

1. Technical terms peculiar to mathematics (*Pythagorean theorem, polyhedron*).
2. General words with mathematical meaning (*prime, exponent, square*).
3. Words describing mathematical processes (*addition, subtraction, column, difference*).
4. General words that have a degree of difficulty (*compare, least, increase, of*).

Because an understanding of the special terminology of mathematics is essential to mastery, study and review on a daily basis are necessary. The following are among the suggestions made by Coulter (1972, pp. 115–117) that may prove helpful in teaching the vocabulary of mathematics.

1. Provide opportunities for studying the basic terms of each new area of study in the mathematics program.
2. Encourage students to spell and pronounce all words correctly. Language accuracy is as important as computational accuracy.
3. Use accurate terminology when a specialized term is needed. Avoid substituting less precise terms.

4. Provide opportunities for using new terms in a variety of ways (reading, writing, speaking, and illustrating) to increase understanding.
5. When testing, check for growth in vocabulary as well as in reasoning and computation. Students should be expected to write definitions, match the term with its arithmetic application, and supply the right term for a described function.

Interpreting symbols and signs. The mathematics teacher must help students build new concepts, and he must also be concerned with the preciseness of the students' understanding of the symbols they use. At times the symbols are words while at other times they are mathematical signs, like %, π, $\sqrt{\ }$. An understanding of symbols and signs should develop sequentially and meaningfully — usually when the concept related to them arises. Whenever a student works an example, he should be questioned about the meaning of the symbols.

Children should learn that formulas and equations are mathematical shorthand expressions for sentences. To facilitate a better understanding of this concept, the teacher should have his students write formulas and equations in sentence form; each sentence must have a subject and predicate. For example, "42 + 18 = 60" may be written as "The sum of forty-two and eighteen is equal to sixty." In such equations, the symbols (+, −, =, ÷, ×) represent verbs. If the formula or equation is given in sentence form, as in word problems, it is helpful to have students translate the sentence into its mathematical equivalent. In this type of activity students may be helped to analyze the written version of the formula or equation if the teacher indicates the basic parts of the sentence and the function of the process and structure words (Shepherd 1978, pp. 284, 288).

Solving word problems. According to research, the development of numerical concepts alone will not guarantee success in mathematics (Corle 1972, p. 80). This is especially true in the solving of "word problems," which is usually cited as the most complex and troublesome part of mathematics. A review of research on problem solving (Glennon and Callahan 1968) identified four factors that underlie success in solving word problems. These are:

1. General reading skills (including vocabulary).
2. Comprehension of statement of the problem, determination of relevant details, and selection of proper procedures for solving the problem.
3. Computational skills.
4. Ability to conceptualize.

Teachers need to be sure that students have adequate skills and abilities before expecting proficiency in solving word problems.

Students need to learn how to "read and study" problems rather than just "how to solve problems." They should be encouraged to try different sets of attack strategies, not just one particular set. Of course, if a student's general reading skills are deficient, he will have difficulty reading math problems as well. The study-attack steps in the following list are taken from Robinson (1978, pp. 253–254).

1. Read the problem thoroughly, asking "What is this all about?"
2. Reread the problem, asking "What am I to find here?"
3. Ask yourself, "What facts are given?"
4. Next, plan your attack.
5. Estimate the answer.
6. Carry out the operations.
7. Check your work.

Interpreting graphic and pictorial representations. Graphs and charts are used with great frequency in mathematics. They often illustrate concisely in a visual manner what is explained verbally. The term *figure* is used to refer to most graphics in textbooks. Some texts distinguish among figures (geometric figures), diagrams (line drawings), graphs, tables, and charts. Aukerman (1972, p. 203) lists the following steps for a student to try in his attempt to understand data and comparisons presented as visuals.

1. Read the title. Know exactly what is being compared with what.
2. Read the labels and figures on the graph. Read the titles on each axis.
3. Study the graph to make comparisons among the different items on it.
4. Interpret the significance of the graph as a whole. Draw conclusions.

Following directions. Following directions is as important in mathematics as it is in science. Students must be able to understand the directions they are to follow. To help this understanding take place Shepherd (1978, p. 298) proposed some steps for the student to try when he first reads a set of directions.

1. Read the directions completely and carefully to get an overview of the total scope.
2. Read just one direction at a time very carefully (if need be, word by word).
3. Think about each direction and be sure that you understand the exact requirement. If not, reread the direction.
4. Carry out the directions.

Only accurate reading will produce the desired mathematical result.

The primary purpose of any literature program is and should be the enjoyment of both prose and poetry. A good literature program will help children become acquainted with the best of many types of literature, including the older classics and those excellent newer works which may become classics (Burns and Broman 1979, p. 460). Children should have experience with a variety of genres — nursery rhymes, picture books, fairytales, poetry, adventure, fantasy, folk tales, biography, drama, and factual books — and should have the opportunity to read freely according to their own special interests.

It is important to remember that many children are particularly interested in literature that deals realistically with their cultural heritage. One reference that assists teachers with selecting literature on a thematic or issues dimension is Rudman's *Children's Literature: An Issues Approach* (1976). Guidelines for evaluating minority literature are provided by Huck in *Children's Literature in the Elementary School*, 3rd edition (1976).

Literary writing tends to be descriptive, narrative, and imaginative. Factual data are rarely employed, as they are in mathematics and science materials. Vocabulary usage, in literature, is usually the appropriate use of general words. There is little technical vocabulary and very little use of diagrams, maps, charts, and tables.

The elementary teacher is confronted with a wide range of differences in the types of reading he must ask of his students in the reading of literature. These differences really become apparent when examined and compared with the range of reading required in social studies, mathematics, or science courses (Hasselriis 1972, p. 32).

In this section on literature, we will give special consideration to poetry, biography, drama, short story, and essay forms. We will also focus some attention on the techniques of reading to students, especially young children.

Skills needed. Forgan and Mangrum (1981, pp. 99–100) have proposed the following skills as necessary for English language arts and literature:[7]

Word Meaning
1. Understand specialized vocabulary.
2. Develop scope and depth of vocabulary by studying word origins, slang, idioms, denotations and connotations of words, multiple meanings, and word relationships such as synonyms, antonyms, and homonyms.

7. Taken from pp. 99–100 of *Teaching Content Area Reading Skills*, 2nd ed. by Harry W. Forgan and Charles T. Mangrum II. Columbus, Ohio: Charles E. Merrill Publishing Co., 1981. Reprinted with permission.

Comprehension

3. Answer various types of questions to identify significant details, central ideas, mood, sensory images, sequence of ideas, and relationships among ideas, and make inferences about characters, settings, and events.

4. Critically evaluate what is read by determining the authors' purpose, distinguishing facts from opinions, identifying propaganda techniques, and identifying characteristics of good writing.

5. Read creatively to respond to the authors' ideas.

Study Skills and Strategies

6. Use the card catalogue, the *Reader's Guide to Periodical Literature*, and other reference materials to locate information.

7. Develop a flexible style and rate of reading appropriate for different types of literature (poetry, drama, fiction, nonfiction, and so forth). Use study strategies as necessary.

8. Organize ideas into an outline, summarize, take notes from a book.

9. Develop skill in using reference materials such as dictionaries, encyclopedias, and a thesaurus.

10. Use a study strategy, such as SQ3R.

Word Pronunciation

11. Pronounce words using context clues, structural analysis, phonics, and the dictionary.

Poetry. For a student to learn to enjoy poetry, it is important for him to appreciate that poetry is our richest spoken language in that imagery and figurative language are prominent and that poems are organized in interesting, special ways. Also important here is the development of good listening skills. Students can achieve them through listening to the reading of simple poetry by the teacher or by a student who reads poetry well. Choral reading is another effective technique.

Since real appreciation for poetry does not develop unless the audience understands a poem, the major reading strategy is to help students understand each poem. However, requiring minute analysis of poetry often turns students away from poems. Once students have learned something about the language patterns used, the nature of the times in which the poem is set, and the types of figurative language employed, they can read to enjoy, appreciate, and understand the poem. The goal of reading poetry in elementary and middle schools is "not a scholarly knowledge of the intricacies of poetry but a deep and lasting appreciation for the ideas of the poem itself . . ." (Bamman et al. 1961, p. 174).

Biography. A biography is an account of one or more individual lives written by someone other than the subject. Even though biographies are nonfiction, they tend to be slanted by the knowledge and perceptions of the writer. It is important that the student know the relationship of the writer to the subject: if he is a member of the subject's family, he may not present the subject's life in an objective manner; on the other hand, if the writer has not done adequate research on the life of the subject, his writings may be grossly inaccurate.

In teaching students to read biographies, the teacher should guide them in focusing on the analyses of human motives and emotions. The reader should come away from the reading experience able to create outlines, summaries, and possibly even pictures of the personality they read about (Robinson 1978, p. 275).

To develop students' interest in biography, a teacher may consider the following suggestions:

1. Encourage students to write their own autobiography, incorporating photography. The autobiography may cover a time span from babyhood to the present.
2. Encourage students to interview each other and write a biography of the person interviewed.
3. Provide students an opportunity to read biographies of famous persons who were involved in specific activities in which the students are interested (such as sports).
4. Read an anecdote from a biography to illustrate concepts in a history class (for example) or to introduce a content area unit of work. Students may also be encouraged to find anecdotes to illustrate a point being discussed in class.
5. Select a biography that lends itself to creative drama. Encourage several students to read the biography. Then provide these students with the opportunity to "act out" aspects of the life of the person in question.

Drama, short story, and essay. No type of literature demands more of the reader than drama. The student who reads drama must be able to visualize the details of the setting, the action, the characters, and numerous implied events; almost the only clues are provided by the dialogue. Students must also be able to account for the gaps in meaning that are unique to drama. Events that have occurred prior to the time the drama is set in must be inferred by the reader from the speeches of the actors. Students should be permitted to read plays on their own and also have the experience of reading various parts of a play orally. A small group may want to read a play together and perform it for the class.

According to Robinson (1978, p. 268) a short story is a compressed view of a segment of fictitious life with some type of plot, and usually an opposition of interests. A short story has no given length or rigid form. Because of the brevity of the short story, many incidents are left unmentioned and the reader must oftentimes use his imagination. Students should be encouraged to make guesses without fear of being wrong. They need to make errors in judgment and then analyze them in order to be able to approach the next story with a sense of security. Magazines are the most common source of short stories other than the anthologies available for classroom use.

An essay usually focuses on a detailed expansion of a single idea or bit of information; it expresses the point of view and personality of the writer. Essays must be impersonal, autobiographical, narrative in nature, or have no set form. To read an essay intelligently, the learner must be able to think logically, to recognize organizational patterns, and to evaluate ideas critically.

Reading to students. One of the best ways of presenting literature to children is for the teacher to read to them. This technique is helpful in developing an appreciation of good literature (Chan 1974). At the same time, it is an excellent way to facilitate concept and vocabulary development (if the content of the selection is acceptable to the listeners). According to Alexander and Filler (1976, pp. 46–47), reading to children may also (for some children) lead to more positive attitudes toward reading. They suggest that if the activity is to be effective, the teacher should keep the following points in mind:

1. The story selected should be one that the teacher likes. Enthusiasm for a story shows and is often contagious.
2. The teacher should know the story well so that he can read it fluently and with appropriate intonation patterns.
3. The story should be of interest to students.
4. In a longer story, it is often desirable to read only the more interesting parts. The more descriptive, less interesting parts may be summarized orally. This conserves time and keeps interest high.
5. At times, it is appropriate to read an interesting episode to students to whet their appetites for more reading. The story should be on a reading level appropriate for the students so that they may finish it if they so desire.

Instructional Frameworks

QUESTIONS TO GUIDE READING

Literal
What are the steps in the DRTA?
What is the role of the teacher in the DRTA framework?
What are the steps in developing a structured overview?

Inferential
What is meant by conceptual density?

Evaluative

How would DRTA differ in a mathematics lesson from the way it functions in a science lesson?

How would you decide which instructional framework or procedure was most appropriate for a given content area? for a given group of students?

When would you consider using ReQuest or Inquiry Strategies with a content area lesson?

It is not enough that a teacher understand the skills involved with reading content area materials; she must also understand how comprehension of that material can be facilitated. One effective way to accomplish this goal is to have a plan, or instructional framework, that provides structure to the teaching-learning process. In support of this concept, Herber (1978, p. 216) asserted: "Teachers can help students experience immediate success and ultimate independence if they provide a structure, or framework, within which students are guided through the process being taught, developing an understanding of both the process and the concepts to which the process is applied."

In this section, the Directed Reading-Thinking Activity and the Structured Overview are presented. A framework presented in Chapter 12, the Directed Reading Activity (DRA), is also appropriate for use with content areas. Teachers often overlook the possibility of using good, established "reading class" methodology as a means of dealing with content area materials. Two other strategies developed in Chapter 9 — In Inquiry Strategy and ReQuest — may also be used effectively.

The DRTA

A framework that can be especially effective in content area reading is the Directed Reading–Thinking Activity (Stauffer 1975, Chapter 2). The DRTA, which is often used in conjunction with basal readers (see Chapter 12), can also aid students in overcoming some of the problems associated with content area materials, such as difficulty in: understanding highly technical and unfamiliar concepts; seeing a need or purpose for reading the material under consideration; dealing with content material at a readability level above the student's ability; and handling content area material independently. DRTAs may be utilized with groups or with individuals.

For group use. The DRTA may be used with a group when a chapter or selection of printed materials in science, social studies, or math is being considered. When using the DRTA in a group setting, a four-step process is advisable (Stauffer 1975, pp. 35–36). Please note the active role of the teacher.

Step 1 — Identifying purposes for reading. Students are encouraged to identify problems, goals, or questions that can be answered by reading the passage under consideration. The problems or questions defined through discussion and interaction of group members and the teacher should be related to the experiential backgrounds of the students. During this introductory part of the DRTA, students often establish hypotheses or guess at possible solutions, answers, or facts they expect to find in the passage. Both group and individual purposes for the piece can be set at this point.

This preparatory stage is also a time when both teacher and students discuss difficult concepts and terms. The concept load of content materials (noted earlier) is an extremely critical problem for many students. The DRTA provides an opportunity to alleviate this difficulty to some extent through a thorough discussion and examination of unfamiliar or technical terms included in the passage. The ability of students to deal adequately with a passage is enhanced when terms and concepts are known and understood before students are asked to deal with the printed material.

Step 2 — Adjusting rate of reading to purposes set. The nature of the material and the purposes set will determine the rate to be sought in reading the material. Purposes may dictate, for example, that the reader survey or skim to get the main idea of the passage, that he scan to find specific information, or that he read carefully and critically in order to reflect or pass judgment. It is the responsibility of the teacher to help establish efficient reading rates.

It seems appropriate at this point to consider the specific reading skills the group will need. For example, maps, charts, or graphs may illustrate the passages, requiring special attention and discussion. (See Chapter 10 for suggestions for teaching these skills.)

Step 3 — Achieving reading purposes. After purposes are established, hypotheses set, concepts explained, and efficient rates determined, the group reads the passage silently. Throughout the reading, students are relating the material to their own purposes and to hypotheses they have generated to see if the purposes are met and the hypotheses supported. During this step, the teacher should be available to assist students who are having problems with clarification of purposes, word recognition skills, or evalution of material in light of purposes set.

Step 4 — Developing comprehension. During this step, the teacher may facilitate comprehension by sharing information as it relates to purposes set. This may involve reporting specific facts, summarizing findings, or orally rereading passages that support or refute hypotheses. In any event, this step should involve discussion — not an oral quiz. Discussion centered on a given concept facilitates comprehension of that concept. After the discussion, the group may need to redefine their purposes and do more reading. In addition, the teacher may also need to teach, reteach, or reinforce skills they will need for further reading.

For individualized use. The DRTA can also be used in an individualized manner with content area material. Stauffer and Harrell (1975) have provided a process to use in dealing with the DRTA on an individual basis. They stress that in using the DRTA with an individual, four conditions need to be considered.

1. The student must identify a problem, goal, or question to be investigated.
2. Resources (library, media center) must be available where the student can seek and obtain information.
3. The teacher must provide the student with the intellectual and physical freedom necessary to obtain information that he can understand and that meets his goals.
4. The student must be able to share his findings with others.

A DRTA lesson in science. As Stauffer (1975, p. 34) notes, a group DRTA desirably should be limited to eight to ten students in order to promote participation and interaction among the members of the group. Such groups should be formed on the bases of interest and reading level when possible. When this occurs, the students' comprehension should be maximized. At times, however, a teacher may wish the entire class to be engaged in work on a given topic. The group DRTA, in conjunction with individual DRTAs, may enable the teacher to realize this goal. In the lesson that follows, notice the contrast to the traditional "read and quiz" procedures.

Imagine that a fifth grade science teacher wishes to present a lesson on cells to a class of thirty pupils.[8] Of the thirty students, ten are reading at a fifth grade level, five are reading at a sixth, and five at a seventh grade level. Five of the remaining students read at a fourth grade level, and the other five read at a third grade level. Although a number of students within the class will have difficulty with the text, through effective teacher guidance in the group setting and through individual work the objectives of the lesson may be accomplished.

The lesson focuses on what cells are like (see Figure 11.2). Utilizing the DRTA framework, the teacher could first ask the students to open their text to the material to be read (page 27) and then to describe what they

8. The writer is grateful to Mark W. Fridge, special teacher of reading in the Knox County, Tennessee, schools for providing the basis for this illustration. For additional illustrations of DRTA lessons see Russell G. Stauffer's *Directing the Reading-Thinking Process* (New York: Harper and Row, 1975).

think they will study under the section entitled "What Are Cells Like?" (without actually reading the material). Some of the students will probably point out that the subtopics of the section are labeled "Characteristics of cells," "Differences in cells," "Parts of cells," "Protoplasm," "Plasma membrane," "Nucleus," "Cytoplasm," "Vacuoles," and "Cell wall." At this point the teacher could ask the students what is meant when they discuss the *characteristics* of something. Discussion should lead to the concept of *characteristics* as referring to such qualities or properties as size, shape, function (what does it do?), composition (what is it made up of?). The teacher may suggest to the students that the reading material offers the answers to these properties of cells.

The teacher could then ask the students to turn to the illustrations of a honeycomb and leaf cells on page 27. Although some of the students may not be able to read the material, all students should participate in discussing the comparison between the honeycomb and leaf cells, and the concept of the cell as a *compartment*.

Discussion may then turn to the illustration on page 28 of different cells, with the students noting the differences in shapes of cells. The teacher may then direct discussion to the need for viewing cells through a microscope since most cells are too small to be seen by the naked eye. The teacher should point out to the students that reading of the text will provide answers to their questions and information about the parts of cells as shown in the illustrations on page 30 of a plant cell and an animal cell.

The next step within the DRTA would be the formation of workable discussion groups. If all of the students could function adequately at the readability level of the text, then the formation of these various groups would be easy. However, in this instance some of the students may encounter difficulty with the passage. Consequently, the teacher could assign the text to those students who could function within this material and acquire supplemental material for the remaining students.

The teacher could suggest the text to those ten students reading at the sixth and seventh grade level, and thus form one discussion group. The second group could be formed by assigning the text to those ten students reading on grade level. In addition, provision must be made for those who cannot handle the text adequately. In this instance, the teacher could use pages 12–17 of *What Is a Cell?* (by King and Otto, Benefic Press). Although the students reading at the fourth grade level may have little appreciable difficulty with the supplemental book, the remaining students could encounter some problems with it. Consequently, those students reading at the third grade level could be paired with the fourth grade readers so an opportunity for peer tutoring could exist within the third discussion group. In this manner the teacher may construct three discussion groups that contain ten students each.

Once the groups have been designated and the appropriate material acquired, the teacher's next task is to discuss with each group the material they will read, helping them establish appropriate purposes or formulate questions to be answered during the reading. It is desirable that the questions for each group sample a variety of comprehension levels (e.g., factual recall and critical thinking) and that each group have its own set of questions. The level of difficulty of the questions, however, should reflect the cognitive level of functioning of the students. Any special skill that will be needed during the reading should be developed by the teacher.

When working with the students who compose the upper reading group, the teacher could point out that the main text topic deals with Living Things and that all living things are made up of cells (the cell as the unit of life). From this point of reference, the teacher and students might formulate questions such as the following:

1. Every living cell is made of protoplasm. What is protoplasm?
2. How do the cell walls of plants and animals differ? Why do they differ?
3. Why would it be important for scientists to study cells?

Figure 11.2. A science lesson: cells.

From *Modern Science*, Level Five, Teacher's Edition (River Forest, Illinois: Laidlaw Brothers, 1974), pp. 27–31. Used by permission of Laidlaw Brothers, A Division of Doubleday & Company, Inc.

1. What Are Cells Like?

Characteristics of cells. All living things are made of cells. Many animals and plants are made up of more than one cell. What is a cell?

You have probably seen a comb of honey before. In the picture notice the many compartments that bees use to store their honey. Each little compartment is complete in itself. Yet each one is a part of the whole comb.

Now look at the section of leaf that is shown. It appears to have compartments similar to those of the honeycomb. But these compartments were not made by bees. This is a picture of a group of things which are alive. What looks like a little compartment is actually a cell. Each cell of the leaf is a living thing in itself. Yet each cell is also one part of the whole leaf. Does this picture give you an idea why a cell is often called a "building block" of life?

Because each cell is a living thing, it must have the characteristics of living things. Therefore, each living cell must carry on these activities— respiration, growth, reproduction, movement, and reaction.

Differences in cells. In the animal kingdom there are many different kinds of animals having varying sizes and shapes. Plants, too, are of different kinds, sizes, and shapes. Name several kinds of animals which are not alike in size and shape. Name a few plants which are not alike in kind, shape, or size.

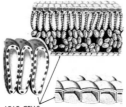

LEAF CELLS

1. The simpler the plant or animal, the more the cells resemble **27** one another. In complex living forms, the cells must vary greatly to assume their specialized life functions.

Once these questions have been formed, the teacher could point out that the students may wish to skim through the earlier pages of the introduction to the unit on Living Things.

Through discussion with the teacher, the members of the second group (on grade level) may formulate questions such as these (which are somewhat less difficult than the first set):

1. What are the functions of vacuoles?
2. What activities of living things does a cell carry on?
3. Why is a cell called a "building block" of life?

The book to be read by the group reading below grade level (*What is a Cell?*) could then be examined briefly. Working with the teacher, this group may create questions such as:

1. What is cytoplasm?
2. What is the purpose of a cell wall? of a cell nucleus?
3. Why are food, oxygen, and water permitted to enter cells?

ACTERIA CELLS

Bacilli

Cocci

OOD CELLS

Red   White

AF CELLS

Epidermis   Palisade

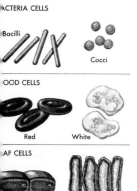

TRY THIS Processes utilized: observing, recording, investigating

Materials Needed: microscope, onion bulb, glass slide, iodine or colored ink

Peel off the dry outer layer of an onion bulb. Cut a piece from this layer about half the size of a dime. Place this small piece of onion on a drop of water on a glass slide. Place a cover slip over it. Examine it under a microscope. Sketch a picture of what you see.

Peel off a moist inner layer of the onion. Cut a small piece from this layer. Mix a drop of iodine or colored ink with a drop of water. Place the mixture on this piece of onion on a glass slide. Cover it. Examine it under a microscope. Sketch a picture of what you see. Describe any differences between the outer and inner layers that you see.

Cells also vary in appearance. Some have the shape of a pancake. Others have the appearance of a rectangular box. There are some cells which are spherical. In the picture find examples of cells having these different shapes. Can you give the name and also describe the shape of each of the examples shown?

Cells can also differ greatly in their size. Consider the size of a pinhead. Some cells are so small that it would take many thousands to cover the top of a pin. There are also some fairly large cells. Some would cover the palm of your hand. Most cells, however, are too small to be seen by the unaided eye.

1. Although the size of the cells above appears to be about equal, actually the leaf cells are many times the size of the blood cells, and the blood cells are much larger than the bacteria cells.

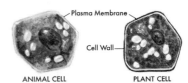

Plasma Membrane

Cell Wall

ANIMAL CELL   PLANT CELL

Parts of cells. Look at the picture of an animal cell as it appears through a microscope. Can you see that the cell has a definite boundary? Trace with your finger the line representing this outside border of the cell. This outer layer is called the *plasma membrane* (plaz'mə mem'brän). This outer layer and most of what is contained by it is living material. This living material is called *protoplasm* (prō'tə plaz' əm).

Suppose you were looking through a microscope at a plant cell. You might see the plant cell shown in the picture. Does it have an outer boundary? Does this outer boundary look like that of the animal cell? The plant cell does have a plasma membrane. As in the animal cell, the membrane and much it contains is protoplasm. But look again at the outer layer of the plant cell. Is it different in any way from the animal cell? Notice that outside of the plasma membrane there is another

layer. This outermost layer of a plant cell is called the *cell wall*.

Because living things are either plants or animals, their cells will have the parts you have seen in these pictures. All cells have an inner part and an outer part. The outer part forms the boundary of the cell.

Protoplasm. Protoplasm is an essential part of every cell. *Every living cell is made of protoplasm.* We have said that all living things are made of cells. Now we can say that all living things are made of protoplasm.

Protoplasm is a colorless, jellylike substance. It is always composed of at least four elements of the universe. You have seen one of these elements, carbon, in the form of charcoal. The air you breathe contains oxygen, another of the elements. The other two elements are also gases of the air. One is called *nitrogen* (ni'trə jən). Nearly ⅘ of the

1. This special feature is made of a non-living woody substance that is completely lacking in animal cells.
2. The four elements needed to make protoplasm are obtained from the food supply of the cell.

During the time that the actual reading occurs, the teacher should circulate among the groups to assist the individual members. This could take the form of helping with word recognition difficulties, or with concept formation.

After the students have finished reading the material and have discussed their questions in small groups, the class could regroup and discuss the material they have read. During this time, each group could present answers to their given questions, and the entire class could discuss these findings or conclusions. As a part of the discussion the teacher could ask the students if they found passages within their material that answered particular questions. The students who found such passages could be asked to read them aloud to the class and tell why they thought the passage answered the questions. Through listening to passages read, poorer readers will gain information. After all of the questions have been answered or discussed, one or more of the students could then briefly review the material they all covered.

Because of the nature of the selection within the text, the teacher may find it necessary to devote some instructional time to the skill of reading charts and diagrams. One useful material would be the S.R.A. skill kit *Graph and Picture Study Skills*. The subsection, "Charts and Diagrams,"

Figure 11.2. (continued)

air is this gas. The other element is called *hydrogen* (hī′drə jən).

Think for Yourself

1 Is the following statement true? "All living things contain the elements carbon, oxygen, nitrogen, and hydrogen." Explain your answer.

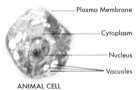

ANIMAL CELL

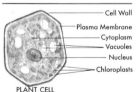

PLANT CELL

Plasma membrane. In the picture you can see drawings of a plant cell and an animal cell. Find the plasma membrane in the picture of the plant cell and the animal cell. Ob-

serve how thin it is. This plasma membrane, being a living part of the cell, is made of protoplasm.

Even though the membrane is extremely thin, it can keep some of the foreign and possibly harmful materials from entering the cell. Sometimes this membrane is seriously damaged. For example, it might come in contact with something very hot. When this happens the plasma membrane, and therefore the cell, is destroyed.

Nucleus. The *nucleus* (nü′kli əs) controls the activities of the cell. 2 How does it compare in size to the size of the entire cell in the picture? The nucleus of a cell may take many different shapes, but it usually is nearly spherical.

In a way the nucleus is like a brain. A nucleus controls the activities of a cell, and a brain controls the activities of a body.

Cytoplasm. All the protoplasm inside a cell, excluding the nucleus, is called *cytoplasm* (sī′tə plaz əm). Spherical *vacuoles* (vak′yü ōlz) are usually found in this cytoplasm. Find the vacuoles in the picture of a cell. How does their appearance differ from that of the nucleus?

Vacuoles. Vacuoles have different functions. Some vacuoles contain 1 food. These act as food storage tanks for the cell. In these vacuoles food is digested. Other vacuoles store and then eliminate waste material and water from the cell.

The parts discussed so far are common to both plant and animal cells.

Cell wall. The outer layer of a plant cell is called the cell wall. Observe the cell walls shown in the picture. These cell walls are made up of *cellulose* (sel′yə lōs). The cellulose is not a living part of the cell, but it is made by the living parts of the plant cells.

Compare cell walls of some newly formed plant cells to those of some older plant cells. Are the cell walls of the newly formed cells thinner than those of the older cells? What happens to the cell walls as these plant cells increase in size?

NEWLY FORMED PLANT CELLS

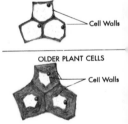

Cell Walls

OLDER PLANT CELLS

Cell Walls

Have you ever wondered why a small sapling is easier to break than a larger one? Size, of course, is one reason. But there is also another important reason. As the cells increase in size, the cell walls become thicker with cellulose. This cellulose is fairly rigid and gives support to the plant. A larger sapling has a greater number of thickened cell walls than a smaller sapling. These thickened cell walls make a larger sapling more difficult to break.

TRY THIS Processes utilized: observing, comparing, associating ideas, measuring
Materials Needed: a small tree branch, vise, spring scale

Cut the branch into lengths about one foot long. Take one stem at a time. Insert one end in the vise. Attach the scale to the other end. Determine how the thickness of a stem affects its breaking point.

30 1. Yes. Protoplasm contains those suggested elements, and protoplasm is found in all living things.
2. Most cells have a nucleus. However, in rare cases, such as the red blood cells, the nucleus is absent.

1. The vacuoles may contain the pigment of the cells, such as 31 the orange coloring of oranges or the purple pigment of purple flowers. In addition, sugars, acids, and special flavors of food may be contained in the vacuoles of the cells.

could prove especially useful. This skill kit could be used by a majority of the students in the class since it begins at the fourth grade reading level. However, some other instructional strategy may need to be developed for those students reading below this level.

STRUCTURED OVERVIEW

The structured overview aids in organizing the learner's cognitive structures in order to facilitate the gaining of meaning from the text.[9] Used as a preparatory activity, it can help guide students toward deductive thinking. The majority of content area textbooks contain such a large number of concepts that mastery of all of them is virtually impossible. Representative concepts could be selected by the teacher and then presented in a structured overview. Earle (1969, p. 166) has suggested a procedure to follow in developing a structured overview. It involves four steps:

1. Select every word you intend to use in this unit which you think is necessary to the students' understanding of what you want them to understand.
2. Take the list of words . . . and arrange them and rearrange them until you have a diagram which shows the relationships which exist among the ideas in the unit, as well as their relationship to the semester's work. . . .
3. On the first day of the unit, write the diagram that you've made on the chalkboard. While you're doing this, explain why you arranged the words as you did and get the students to contribute as much information as they can.
4. Throughout the unit, as it seems appropriate and comfortable, refer to the structured overview. Sketch portions of it on the chalkboard if you wish. The object here is to aid the student in his attempts to organize the information in a meaningful way.

Figure 11.3 depicts a simplified structured overview derived from the science lesson, "What Are Cells Like?" from pages 272 to 274.

As noted above, an overview can be used to emphasize concept development and/or vocabulary development before the actual lesson is presented by the teacher. In addition, it should be stressed that the vocabulary words comprising the structured overview should be reinforced as they are encountered in the text and throughout the planned program of study.

Several follow-up activities may be incorporated to further the effectiveness of the structured overview technique. Students may be required to formulate their own simple overviews of concepts taught. These could then be shared with other class members in order to clarify the concepts.

9. The writer is grateful to Wendy Shearer and Sandra Zecchini, tutors in the University of Tennessee Reading Center, for providing the development of this section. Used with permission.

Figure 11.3. A structured overview.

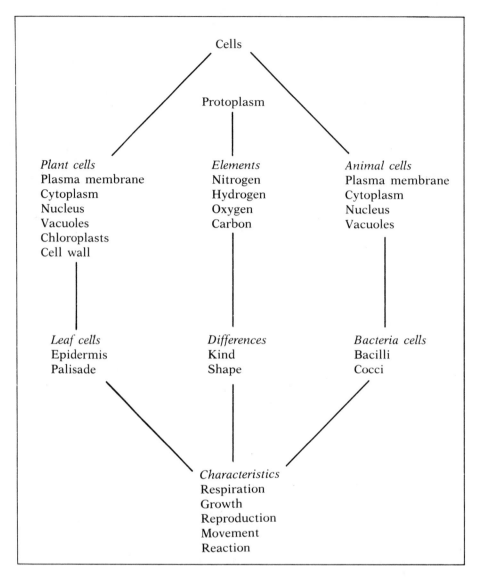

The overview could also be used for test review as well as a skeleton form on which additional information could be noted for future reference or study.

The flexible nature of a structured overview makes it a valuable tool when laying the groundwork for concepts and vocabulary. When incorporated with the students' prior knowledge and experience, this advanced organization aids the reader's understanding of the hierarchial arrangement of both concepts and vocabulary.

Summary

Student achievement can be improved when reading instruction occurs in content area classes. Providing such instruction has been difficult in the past because of the lack of availability of content area texts that were written on a level that students could read. This situation is changing. Authors and publishers are giving more attention to the readability level of the materials they are writing and publishing; and teachers are becoming more aware of the ways they can facilitate comprehension of content area materials.

Reading in content areas requires reading skills appropriate for given areas. It is especially important that teachers give attention to the skills needed in a given type of content, such as specialized vocabulary items. In addition to understanding the skills needed, teachers should be cognizant of plans, structural frameworks such as the DRTA, or structured overview through which instruction may be facilitated.

Students should not "learn to read" in instructional situations that are completely divorced from "reading to learn." When teachers provide more reading instruction through content area classes and when students see the application of reading skills in learning, comprehension in content fields is likely to improve considerably.

Questions for Further Reading and Thinking

1. What are some other readability formulas that a teacher may consider?
2. What are some other ways a teacher can match children with texts?
3. What does the literature say about rewriting materials on lower readability levels?
4. How does the information in the chapter compare with your methods text in social studies? in science? in mathematics?
5. What is the relationship of Piaget's stages of concept development and instruction in content areas?

Activities and Projects

1. Encourage students to read and report on science fiction. Discuss the use of scientific principles and factual knowledge in the development of the story. How did the author depart from the facts to present an interesting story?
2. Make a list of several questions that can be answered only with the use of maps, graphs, tables and other types of illustrations. Discuss the merits of illustrative materials in any textbook.
3. Develop several directed reading lessons

with step-by-step directions for solving word problems in mathematics.

4. Using the Fry Graph for Estimating Readability and another readability formula, determine the approximate grade level of a textbook of your choosing.

5. Select an elementary textbook in each of the following areas: science, social studies, literature, and mathematics. Write to each publisher and request information on the grade levels for which the book is sold. Also find out how the readability levels were determined.

6. Choose a textbook and rewrite a passage to lower its readability level.

7. Choose a typical passage in a content area text and construct a cloze test. Administer the test to a youngster at the age or grade level for which the material was designed. Was the passage on his or her independent, instructional, or frustration level?

8. Study the Readability Checklist developed by Judith Westphal Irwin and Carol A. Davis (*Journal of Reading*, November 1980, pp. 129–130). Apply this checklist in a classroom situation. Report your results to the class.

9. Choose a game from *Science Games* by Arnold R. Davis and Donald C. Miller (Belmont, Calif.: Lear Siegler, Inc./Fearon Publishers, 1974). Try this game with a group of appropriate elementary school students. Describe how this game helped students achieve its stated objective.

Materials for Elementary School Students

Be a better reader (Grades 4–8) by Nila Banton Smith. Englewood Cliffs, N.J.: Prentice-Hall.

Bookmark reading program: Skills readers by Margaret Early et al. New York: Harcourt Brace Jovanovich.

Go: Reading in the content areas by Harold Herber. New York: Scholastic.

Graph and picture skills by Robert A. Naslund and Jack McClellan. Chicago: Science Research Associates.

Map and globe skills by Robert A. Naslund and Charles M. Brown. Chicago: Science Research Associates.

Read better learn more by Theodore Clymer et al. Lexington, Mass.: Ginn and Company.

Reading for concepts by William Liddle. New York: McGraw-Hill.

Scope/reading skills. New York: Scholastic.

Social studies readers by Arthur Flug and Seymour Litman. River Forest, Ill.: Laidlaw Brothers.

Part Four

APPROACHES, MATERIALS, AND PROGRAMS

In the most general sense, *approaches* are philosophies that influence or underlie a program. Language experience (Chapter 13) and individualized reading (discussed in Chapter 14) are examples of approaches as philosophies. A *program* may be described as the way or ways teachers organize materials and techniques or procedures in some logical manner to facilitate the act of processing print. Basal readers (Chapter 12) and management systems (Chapter 14) are good examples of ways materials are organized into programs. Programs may be representative of one approach or a combination of approaches. For example, some basal systems may use a heavy phonic approach to word recognition whereas others may not.

The wide variety of materials on the market today reflects varying philosophies and may be organized in various ways to produce reading programs. Many of the more commonly used materials are discussed in Chapter 14.

We feel that the various approaches and materials are generally best used in certain combinations in programs, with the decision for use based on unique conditions within the instructional situation — such as learners' needs, the teacher's experiences and preferences, and the materials and physical facilities available.

Betty S. Heathington

12

Basal Readers

The vast majority of reading teachers will begin their careers in schools that use basal readers. Basals are by far the most popular reading materials in schools in the United States. There are few school systems that do not use basals as at least part of their reading program. Because of their widespread use, it is imperative that classroom teachers and those preparing to teach be knowledgeable concerning basal reading materials.

Of primary importance is an understanding of: (1) what basal materials are, (2) ways basals are used in the classroom, (3) ways basals are used to meet individual needs, and (4) how to choose and evaluate a basal series. A firm knowledge background in these areas should enable teachers to make appropriate decisions about basal reading materials.

A Definition of Basals

QUESTIONS TO GUIDE READING

Literal
What types of supplemental materials are included in basal reading programs?
What are the steps in a typical lesson plan format of a Directed Reading Activity?
What are the usual steps in the teaching of each reading skill?

Inferential
What is meant by the statement that basals are a systematic and sequential approach to reading instruction?
How can a teacher determine which age or grade level a particular book in a basal series is appropriate for?

If basals are defined as "reading materials that are sequenced in terms of difficulty," then we can trace the use of basals in the United States back to the 1700s. A 1782 publication by Noah Webster called *Grammatical Institute* was made up of three distinct sections: Section I was a beginning reader's book; Section II contained a treatise on grammar; and Section III was designed for advanced readers. The three parts were published separately in 1790. In the 1800s the emphasis on graded schools promoted the use of a different reading book for each grade level. In 1840 the *McGuffey Readers* consisted of one reader for each grade level. From these beginnings, basal readers emerged and gained prominence as central resources for classroom teachers. (See Chapter 20 for more details.)

This basic definition and early historical account merely provide some insight into what is meant by basal materials, but we need further details to account for the many facets of modern series. To expand the definition, we must understand basals as a systematic and sequential program for reading instruction. To provide this understanding, we shall discuss: the leveling and labeling of books, the array of supplementary materials, grouping for instruction, the typical lesson plan format, the development of skills, and vocabulary control in the materials.

The Leveling and Labeling of Books

A basal reading program includes a series of books, each carefully designed to fit into the total "system." The number of books varies from publisher to publisher but an entire series generally spans the period from kindergarten to sixth or eighth grade. In the 1950s and 1960s many basal programs contained the following: a series of softcover books known as readiness books, used in kindergarten or first grade; a series of softcover preprimers and a hardcover book called a primer for first grade; a first reader, designated by a label of 1-2 for midyear of first grade; and two hardcover books for each grade thereafter, one for the beginning of the year and one for midyear. Such labels as 2-1 and 2-2 for second grade and 3-1 and 3-2 for third grade were common designations. For most programs, the upper grade levels had only one book per grade level.

This labeling and numbering for books has changed to some extent during the past few years as the emphasis in school systems moved toward meeting the individual needs of students. Under the old labeling system, teachers and administrators sometimes incorrectly assumed that only books designated for a certain grade level could be used in that grade, disregarding the reading needs of students. For example, the idea was sometimes expressed that only 3-1 and 3-2 books could be used in third grade. A child in third grade reading at a sixth grade level and a third grader reading at a first grade level were both at a disadvantage in such a system. The trend toward meeting the individual needs of students stresses that a child should be placed in a book at her diagnosed reading level.

To aid teachers in a move away from restrictions limiting books to a particular grade level, most publishers in the 1970s adopted a lettering system, such as A through F or A through M, or a numbering system, such as 1 through 15 or 1 through 21. Such labeling was intended to promote the idea of moving children through material as they were ready and not limiting the material to a certain grade in school. However, publishers stressed that each level was built on those which came before it in the series. For example, a child using level 10 should have received instruction equivalent to that given in levels 1 through 9. This recommendation did not imply that every book was to be covered, only that "equivalent instruction" be provided.

In the 1980s, some publishers are again using the 3-1 and 3-2 type of labeling. Teachers must thoroughly familiarize themselves with a specific publisher's system of labeling to ensure that they provide the most appropriate materials for a child.

Current teacher manuals generally include guidelines regarding the probable grade levels for each book in tabular form similar to the one illustrated in Table 12.1.

Some publishers recommend a range of grade levels for a particular book. For example, in Table 12.2, we can see that the level A book is recommended for most children in kindergarten and for some children in first grade; level B is recommended for some children in kindergarten and for most children in first grade, etc.

Table 12.1. Illustration of Book Level–Grade Level Relationship

Book levels	Probable grades	Book levels	Probable grades
1	Kindergarten	12	Grade 5
2, 3, 4, 5, 6	Grade 1	13	Grade 6
7, 8	Grade 2	14	Grade 7
9, 10	Grade 3	15	Grade 8
11	Grade 4		

Table 12.2. Basal Series Levels and Corresponding Grade Levels

| Grade levels | Book levels | | | | | | | | | | | | | |
	A	B	C	D	E	F	G	H	I	J	K	L	M	N
K	×	0												
1	0	×	×	×	×	×	0							
2						0	×	×	×	0				
3								0	×	×	0			
4										0	×	0		
5											0	×	0	
6												0	×	

× = most pupils; 0 = some pupils.

THE ARRAY OF SUPPLEMENTARY MATERIALS

A basal reading series is a major undertaking by a publishing firm. Such a series requires a tremendous investment of time and effort on the part of the company. The publisher must make an outlay of millions of dollars in the production of a basal series.

Current basal series usually have three basic divisions of books in a system: beginning level books, often stressing prereading language development, or readiness materials (see Chapter 2); primary level books, beginning what has been described as formalized reading instruction; and intermediate level books, emphasizing reading in the content areas, along with literature and study skills. In addition to these textbooks for students, an extensive array of supplementary materials for a total system is offered. Such materials as the following are available from most publishers:

Student's text. Softcover books are often used in beginning instruction; hardcover books are introduced during first grade.

Teacher's edition. Often spiral bound, the manual contains reduced pupil pages, comprehensive teaching plans, and teacher resource or reference sections.

Student's workbook. Consumable workbooks are designed to parallel and supplement the lessons in the text by providing independent practice activities.

Teacher's edition of workbook. This reproduction of the pupil's workbook contains answers often marked in a contrasting color to facilitate checking.

Duplicating masters. These sheets provide independent activities to reinforce and enrich the skills program. The teacher's edition of these masters contains a reproduction of the pages with answers marked.

Picture or word cards. These cards are used to introduce, reinforce, and review vocabulary presented in the student text.

Pocket chart. The pocket chart is a holder designed to facilitate the use of picture and word cards.

Placement tests. Such tests — often in the form of informal reading inventories that assess word recognition and comprehension — are used to place pupils at the appropriate instructional level.

Mastery tests. Used to assess a pupil's mastery of the skills developed in a particular unit or level, these tests pinpoint skill areas in which children need additional help.

Other materials available from some publishers are original full-length children's books to correlate with the basal text; filmstrips to accompany the texts; special books for students with learning disabilities; independent supplemental remedial programs; magic slates with special chalk; read-along recordings, which provide aural reinforcement; and many types of games for reinforcement of skills. While a single program will not have all the materials just listed, the wide array of supplementary materials for a single series is sometimes overwhelming. Little wonder that a basal reading series is a multimillion-dollar endeavor!

GROUPING FOR INSTRUCTION

For years, to group students for reading instruction with basal readers, the teacher has typically divided each class into three groups according to ability: above average, average, and below average. The teacher customarily uses test scores or some other evidence of reading ability to make the three divisions. Each group meets with the teacher for a period of time (usually twenty to thirty minutes) for instruction while the other two groups perform seat work tasks. Seat work often involves duplicated reading skills practice, creative art or writing, or reinforcement activities in word recognition. In the primary grades, the teacher generally meets with all three groups every school day. Unfortunately, the three-group organization is often inflexible; a child sometimes remains in the same group throughout the school year or for several years.

Today several basal series, in stressing their adaptability to meeting the individual needs of students, promote continuous progress plans, which allow a child to begin at a certain level and progress through other levels at her own pace. Other grouping practices, in addition to the individualized approach, are also being suggested as alternatives to the three ability groups within a classroom (see Chapter 18). However, the three-group arrangement according to ability is still the most prevalent arrangement in classrooms today.

LESSON PLAN FORMAT

Several basal series provide similar formats for their reading lessons. Although the sequence may vary, generally the contents contain the following phases: (1) preparation for reading the story, (2) guided reading, (3) skills development and practice, and (4) follow-up and/or enrichment activities. The combination of phases is typically referred to as the Directed Reading Activity (DRA).

Preparation for reading the story. This introductory phase is designed to motivate the students to read the story, to create a purpose for reading, to provide background information, and to develop concepts the students may need to understand the story fully. Questions are provided in the teacher's manual to stimulate discussion about some aspect of the story. The teacher strives to create an interest in the story in this initial activity because, presumably, she accepts the underlying assumption that students read only if they are properly motivated.

Before the story is read, the teacher usually introduces a certain number of new words. She may write these new words on a chalkboard or place them on cards and use them in pocket charts. She may present a new word in a sentence, in a phrase, or alone. The reading group discusses the meaning of the new word. Children may be asked to use the words in sentences to establish that they clearly understand the words.

Guided reading. The next step is the developmental phase of the lesson. The teacher's manual contains suggestions for the guided reading and ideas for developing discussion. Picture interpretation, oral reading, silent reading, and comprehension are all involved in this part of the lesson. The student is often directed to examine and discuss a picture at the beginning of the story, then to read a certain portion of the story silently. Generally he does not read the entire story at one time. Directions tell the students to read a certain number of pages, silently, to find the answer to specific questions or for certain purposes; the teacher then discusses the information found in the silent reading and directs additional reading for another set number of pages. This procedure continues until the entire story is read.

At each point, students must wait until all members of the group have read a section before they do further reading. Oral reading is done at certain points in the guided reading. Sometimes the teacher has the students read orally specific parts of the story that answer questions the teacher has asked. For example, the teacher may direct that a student read the part that describes how some character felt about an event in the story. Thus the story is read silently and orally in parts, with the teacher asking questions at various points in the lesson.

Skill development and practice. During this part of the lesson, the teacher gives instruction and activities in such areas as vocabulary development, decoding, comprehension, and study skills. The teacher's manual contains specific suggestions regarding appropriate activities to use. It states objectives and outlines teaching strategies. Usually it suggests several activities, with the recommendation that the teacher is to choose from the activities those that fit the needs of the particular students being given instruction.

Exercises written on chalkboards or charts can help to involve students in the group practice of the skill. For example, let us suppose that the skill under consideration is learning rules for the two sounds of /c/, hard and soft. The teacher might write a list of four words on the chalkbord (mice, lace, cereal, cow) and ask students if the ⟨c⟩ had the same sound in all of them. Discussion would follow. Then the teacher might write a series of words on the chalkboard and ask students if the ⟨c⟩ had a hard or soft sound in each word.

The skill development and practice session may be used effectively for evaluation as well as instruction. Throughout the activity, the teacher will note the various levels of students' proficiencies in the skill and may then assign the appropriate types and amount of reinforcement and practice pages.

Follow-up activities. Students perform follow-up activities independently at their desks or various centers in the room. The assigned workbook pages, involving practice in a certain skill area, are often used as one type of follow-up material. At times, the teacher will recommend additional reading in library books that relate in some way to the story read that day. Art, music, and writing activities are also used to extend ideas and concepts discussed in the group assembly. The teacher's guide outlines specific recommendations for follow-up activities. Usually, more suggestions are given than can be used; therefore, teachers must choose those which best suit the interests of their particular groups of students.

DEVELOPMENT OF SKILLS

A skill chart, such as the one outlined in Chapter 2, may be used to show the skills often covered in a basal reading series. Briefly, the skills listed in Chapter 2 include:

1. Psychomotor Development
2. Cognitive Development
3. Conceptual and Vocabulary Development
4. Listening Facility
5. Oral Language Facility
6. Understanding of Linguistic Concepts
7. Visual Acuity and Discrimination
8. Auditory Acuity and Discrimination
9. Orientation
10. Interest and Attitudes
11. Basic Sight Vocabulary

12. Word Analysis Skills
13. Use of Dictionary
14. Comprehension of Word Meaning
15. Comprehension of Larger Linguistic Units
16. Inferential Comprehension
17. Reading Critically
18. Development of Content Area Vocabulary
19. Reading with Appropriate Rate
20. Development of Skimming and Scanning
21. Further Refinement of Study Skills

Most publishers furnish a scope and sequence chart, which shows the various skills and the level at which they are introduced.

The skills are not presented one time only; rather, those introduced at one level are repeated and reinforced at subsequent levels with increasing depth and sophistication. For each skill there is usually a three-step plan: introduction of the skill, reinforcement of the skill, and review of the skill.

Usually each new skill is thoroughly taught before proceeding to the next. There are many opportunities for reinforcement and review in the workbooks, duplicated material, games, and other supplementary materials. Basal publishers stress that the scope of each skill presented is on a small scale so that children are not overwhelmed with too much to learn at one time.

Many basal programs advocate the use of a diagnostic/prescriptive approach to skill development. This approach includes: diagnosing the skill deficiencies of a particular child through testing; then providing instruction aimed at overcoming the deficiencies; and finally, using mastery testing to determine if the child has achieved a certain degree of proficiency. Many basal programs provide the placement tests and mastery (or end-of-unit) tests as part of their system.

Vocabulary Control

Basal readers have traditionally had strong vocabulary control in the beginning books, i.e., only a limited number of new words are introduced at these early levels with a high rate of repetition of these words in subsequent books in the series. This sequential and limited introduction of words has created a great deal of controversy among reading authorities. On one hand, some experts believe the control is necessary, pointing to the fact that children will make more progress if they are confronted by a small, consistent, repetitious vocabulary rather than a large one. Some authorities have estimated that children must encounter a word approximately thirty times before they recognize it at sight (Harris and Smith 1972, p. 26).

The group on the other side of the controversy feels that vocabulary control leads to uninteresting, artificial reading materials. This group feels the pattern of the "Look! Look!" and "Go! Go!" exclamations found in some basals is an unnatural use of the English language and is more difficult for children to follow. In response to this argument, some publishers stress that their books now follow the natural language patterns of children so that children can take full advantage of their knowledge of spoken English in learning to read. They claim that characters in stories speak in natural, everyday language rather than an artificially controlled vocabulary and sentence structure.

A recent survey of 1970 basal readers reveals that one of the greatest changes that has occurred is in the area of vocabulary control (Rodenborn and Washburn 1974, p. 885). When the researchers compared 1970 and 1960 programs, they found a marked increase in the total number of words included in first grade programs. They also found that new words are not repeated as often in the newer series.

Until research has revealed more definitively which side of the issue is more acceptable — control or natural language — the controversy will probably continue. Basal publishers will continue to modify their approach to that acceptable to the greatest number of those who will use their programs.

The Use of Basals in the Classroom

QUESTIONS TO GUIDE READING

Literal
What are some of the values of basals?
What questions should be asked when a teacher or teaching staff is considering a basal reading series?

Inferential
Why do teachers often misuse basals?

Evaluative
In what priority order would you rank this chapter's recommendations for classroom use?

The value of basal readers has been a topic for discussion for many years. Are basal materials effective in a reading program? Is a basal program superior to other types of reading programs? The most comprehensive research project to provide some answers to this question was the United States Office of Education's First Grade Studies, conducted in the latter part of the 1960s (Bond and Dykstra 1967b). These twenty-seven independent projects conducted across the nation compared the effectiveness of various reading programs — for example, basal, ITA, linguistic, and language experience. The results from the studies did not show that any program was consistently superior to another. The teacher does seem to be an important factor and if a knowledgeable teacher uses basal readers properly, the materials can be effective.

Advocates cite the many benefits basal materials can offer; critics, in turn, level a variety of charges against such a program. Many of the criticisms are aimed at misuses of the basals rather than any inherent fault of the materials. For the classroom teacher to make proper evaluation, he needs a thorough understanding of the various reactions to basal readers. In this section, we will look at these areas: (1) values of basals, (2) criticisms of basals, (3) misuses of basals, (4) alternative lesson plan formats, (5) oral reading and the basal lesson, (6) ways basals may be effectively used in the reading program, and (7) considerations in choosing a basal series.

VALUES OF BASALS

Many positive characteristics have been attributed to basal readers. The primary values associated with basals include the following:

1. The materials save a considerable amount of a teacher's time. If a classroom teacher had to produce or assemble all the materials that are part of a basal series, the time requirement would be exorbitant. A teacher can better spend her time in analyzing children's progress in reading achievement, or assessing attitudes, or personally guiding children in their reading activities. Further, the extensive time spent by reading experts in preparing basal materials may provide a quality that a teacher may be unable to attain owing to time commitments.

2. The structure and guidance of basals are said to be beneficial to the beginning teacher. The exact questions to ask, the workbook pages to be done with each story, and the recommended follow-up activities may provide a structural framework necessary for the novice. However, as the new teacher gains confidence and experience, it seems reasonable and desirable that he will adjust and manipulate the lesson plans to meet the specific needs of students in his class.

3. The workbooks and tests that accompany basal readers can serve as effective diagnostic tools. Presently, with the emphasis on the diagnostic/prescriptive approach to reading, adequate instruments to measure students' skills are always in demand. (See Chapter 17 for more details.) The tests that are part of a basal program are prepared by experts in the field of reading and should contain appropriate items to evaluate skill proficiency.

4. The systematic review used in basals is noted as a positive contri-

bution. The repetition of a word gives students opportunity to deal with the word on more than one occasion, making it a part of their reading repertory. The review of concepts provides enlargement of ideas previously encountered.

5. The extensive array of supplementary material provides variety and breadth to a reading program. Basal publishers continue to add more materials to their offering of supplemental resources.

6. Basals aim at the interests of the students for whom they are designed. Authorities have spent time and effort in preparing inventories of interests of children by grade level and sex. Publishers and writers use such lists as they prepare stories for use in the textbooks.

7. The systematic and sequential presentation of skills helps overcome the possibility that instruction in a certain skill will be overlooked in a reading program. For example, all elementary teachers might ignore instruction in prefixes if each assumed the skill had been taught at another grade level.

8. One of the strongest influences on the use of the basal reader has come from its use in the DRTA (Directed Reading–Thinking Activity), which Stauffer (1975) outlined. As you recall, the procedure involves a group of children dealing with the same material at the same time under a teacher's guidance. Stauffer says the plan is extremely useful when basal readers are the source material in a DRTA. As children examine the same material, they are encouraged to react in terms of their own past experiences, to share ideas, to present evidence to defend ideas, and to respect the thinking of others. (See Chapter 11 for a more complete discussion of the DRTA.)

CRITICISMS OF BASALS

Despite their widespread usage, basals have been the target of criticisms over the years. Some of the most prevalent ones are the following:

1. The language patterns used in the stories are not generally the same as those used by the children who read the book. For example, critics contend that children use more complex sentence structures than are used in basal readers. The concept load in basals is also oversimplified according to these critics. Today's communication, which provides young people with a tremendous background of ideas, calls for a greater concept load than is currently found in most basal readers.

2. Some say basal stories lack literary merit. Critics contend that the quality of the stories is not as good as one finds in various library books. The same criticism is also made regarding the illustrations used in basals. Legenza and Knafle (1978, 1979) developed a Picture Potency Formula, which rates the extent to which a picture is likely to stimulate language. Applying this formula to eight widely used basal series for first and second

graders, they found few high potency pictures. The majority of pictures (60–100 percent) from the first grade series were of low potency and only one series had any high potency pictures. Between 75 and 100 percent of the pictures in the second grade series were of low potency, and no high potency pictures were found.

3. In the past, many critics denounced basal textbooks because of the middle class content. The series of the 1940s and 1950s typically contained stories exclusively about middle-class white families. Very vocal criticisms in the past few years have led to extensive revisions in basal stories: the story characters may now be whites, Blacks, Chinese, Puerto Ricans, or members of other minorities. However, there has been criticism that the recent changes are merely a change in names and not a change in the cultural context in which the characters live. The characters all seem to be the same, with no distinctive manner of acting and talking (McCutcheon et al. 1979).

4. One of the latest attacks has been concerned with the sex bias in the stories. Basals have been accused of advocating stereotyped sex roles through the various character portrayals in the stories. Currently, attention is being concentrated on this bias to show women, girls, men, and boys in the stories in roles other than those traditionally outlined for the two sexes. Although the number of minority characters and females seems to have risen in basal stories, McCutcheon et al. (1979) warn that there may be a tendency to show all people as the same, thereby losing the sexual identity of the characters.

5. Some authorities criticize the way reading comprehension instruction is handled in basal reading series. Durkin (1981) examined five basal reader programs, kindergarten through grade six, to determine the adequacy of suggestions in teachers' guidebooks regarding comprehension instruction. She found that teachers' guidebooks provided more suggestions for assessment and practice than for direct instruction. The coverage in the teachers' guidebooks of procedures to teach children how to comprehend were brief and tended to show little connection between what was being taught and how to read. Therefore, Durkin contends that children never realize the "how" or "why" when applying the comprehension skills to reading they do on their own.

6. The readability levels of the basals are also a concern to some individuals. Eberwein (1979), using the Harris-Jacobson Readability Formula, found the average basal reader had a range of 4.65 levels. The average range was 2.1 levels for preprimers to 7.6 levels for fourth, fifth, and sixth grade textbooks. Bradley and Ames (1978) examined the readability of six basal readers using the Fry Readability Graph. They found substantial variation in the readers studied. Stories from the same book were found to differ considerably both in average readability and range of readability. They also found that stories near the beginning of a basal are *not* generally less difficult than those near the end.

Other criticisms of basals center around misuses of the materials by teachers. Through improper usage of the materials, teachers can negate much of the value that can be derived from a basal program. Misuses that are often cited include the following:

1. Often, the children of a reading group are asked to read silently a certain number of pages; then everyone must wait until each member of the group has completed the section before further reading can be done. Quite often children are impatient and are eager to move on to the rest of the story. If, on the other hand, the group reads orally, one child at a time, each child follows along word by word as another child reads. This practice has also been criticized as a waste of children's time. The critics say it promotes poor habits for the faster child when he is forced to move at the slower reader's rate. In addition, the slower reader is unable to follow the faster reader and often loses his place in the story.

2. The static three-group organization is a practice much criticized. In the fall, three groups are assembled according to reading ability. Ability is judged on scores from previous reading achievement tests, from individual reading inventories, or some other method the classroom teacher feels is satisfactory. Critics say that once this basic three-group pattern has been established, it is very difficult for children to move from one group to another, even though their reading ability increases sufficiently for them to operate in a higher reading ability group. Since many teachers incorrectly believe that every workbook page must be done and every story read, it is hard for a child to "catch up" with the higher ability group after a few months in a certain group.

3. So much time is required for the activities associated with a basal program (workbooks, duplicated materials, silent and oral reading) that there is little time left in the school day for children to read books they have chosen themselves. The reading program is filled with assigned reading activities, making it impossible for most children to have time for free, relaxed reading. Most publishers recommend that teachers be selective in choosing from the activities available. Many teachers, however, feel compelled to assign almost every activity listed. Sometimes, the high-ability reader can finish quickly and use free time in self-selected reading; but the child with lower reading ability rarely has this privilege because of the extensive time he needs to complete all the tasks. Consequently, all the slower child's reading is on an assigned basis and he has little time to learn how to become a discriminating reader able to make appropriate selections of reading materials.

4. Another aspect of the basal reading method which is of concern to many is the stress placed on careful, analyzed reading. During the assembled reading group, each part of the story is carefully analyzed. The teacher asks many questions about each part of the story before going to the next and sees that all words and events are thoroughly discussed.

Critics say this practice creates in children an undue compulsion for analyzing every word or event, resulting in a slower rate. Negative attitudes toward reading may also be formed. The critics emphasize that children should be made aware that all reading does not have to be intense and compulsive but should often be relaxed and flexible.

5. Another practice that has been condemned is that of using only one grade level of basal readers for a class. For example, some teachers use only third grade material for students in third grade. Occasionally, teachers realize that some children are not able to read third grade level material and go back to a lower level for their lowest reading group. However, it is greatly frowned upon in some schools if a teacher uses a reader from the next higher grade. The charge is made that the child will not have a book to read the next year. The labels using letters and numerals to show levels of difficulty have overcome some of this "hands-off" attitude of teachers. The emphasis should be on moving children through the material as they are ready, with the realization that in most classrooms, there is a wide variation in the ability levels of children. This ability span becomes even broader as children move to the higher grades. Most basal publishers now stress that the various levels are to be used by children as they are ready, and not according to grade level.

6. The final misuse of basals involves the lack of record keeping about individual students' skill proficiency. Some teachers assume that after they explain a certain skill and students have done workbook pages related to that skill, the students have a firm grasp of the concept. Some teachers also incorrectly assume that students have mastered skills presented the previous year. When records are not passed from grade level to grade level to specify in which skills the student has proficiency and in which there is a weakness, skill development is hampered. Many publishers provide a record system that, if properly used by all teachers in a school, would provide a complete survey of a child's reading performance.

ALTERNATIVE LESSON PLAN FORMATS

Alternatives to the traditional basal reading lesson have been advocated by some authorities. These options provide variety, an element often needed in the basal reading program.

Pieronek (1979) has suggested a lesson plan format that follows many of the same steps as the DRA. Her model of the "ideal integrated reading lesson plan" has seven steps: (1) concept development, (2) vocabulary recognition, (3) goal setting for comprehension, (4) directed reading and thinking activity, (5) purposeful oral reading, (6) follow-up activities, and (7) enrichment. According to Pieronek (1979), the model can be used independently or as a guide to select parts of lessons from the teacher's guidebook of a basal reading series.

Spiegel (1981), stating that not every story should be approached in the same manner and that not every student needs to follow the same steps, suggests six alternatives to the DRA. Her alternatives include such suggestions as (1) ReQuest Procedure (see Chapter 9), (2) DRTA (see Chapter 11), and (3) semantic webbing.

Freedman and Reynolds (1980) suggest semantic webbing as a procedure for enriching basal reader lessons. Semantic webbing is a procedure for constructing visual displays of categories and relationships. From the story content and their past experiences, students can compile semantic webs that have four elements: (1) a core question, (2) web strands, (3) strand supports, and (4) strand ties. The core questions, usually chosen by the teacher from the story content, begins the webbing. The web strands are composed of possible answers students give to the core question; the strand supports are facts, inferences, and generalizations that students provide; and the strand ties are students' suggestions regarding relationships between the strands.

For example, in the story *Hansel and Gretel*, the teacher may ask, "Who were the main characters in the story?" As seen in Figure 12.1, students may give answers (web strands) of Hansel, Gretel, and the Witch. Facts and inferences about these characters (strand supports) can be organized around the answers (e.g., Hansel made a trail of bread crumbs and made a trail of stones; Gretel tricked the Witch and shoved her into the oven; and the Witch could not see well and liked to eat children). The relation-

Figure 12.1.

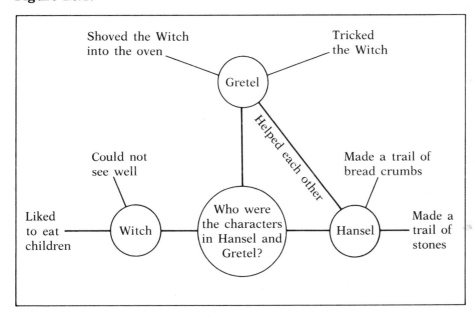

ship between Hansel and Gretel (strand tie) shows that they helped each other get away from the Witch.

Semantic webbing and other variations of the typical basal reader lesson plan format can provide interesting alternatives in the classroom. Such variety should increase motivation in the basal reading lesson.

ORAL READING AND THE BASAL LESSON

Round robin oral reading, in which each child orally reads a passage while others in the group "follow along," has been actively and appropriately denounced. Children are forced to read along at a rate that is either faster or slower than one that is comfortable to them. The idea that a story must be read orally as well as silently may give children an incorrect idea of what reading really is. Often children are bored when asked to read a story again after having just read it silently. However, many feel there are a variety of oral reading activities that can be used effectively in the basal reading lesson.

There are positive functions of oral reading, namely to entertain, to share information, and to provide diagnostic information (see Chapter 17). These functions make oral reading instruction and practice in the classroom worthwhile endeavors. Teachers should provide a variety of oral reading experiences during the basal reading lesson. Activities that may be used include the following:

1. After reading a basal reading story silently, the group closes their books while one member of the group reads aloud the part she found to be the most amusing, the saddest, the most exciting, etc.
2. A student, after practicing reading the story orally until he has achieved fluency, may read the story to a younger brother or sister or a child with less reading ability.
3. Students may read certain phrases or sentences from the story to answer questions or prove a point. Instead of all of the questions being teacher-generated, students should be encouraged to ask questions whose answers can be read by other members in the group.
4. Passages that describe a character's feelings, actions, or demeanor may be read to others in the group. This can be especially effective when it is combined with character evaluation.
5. Poems, which are now included in many basal reading series, are excellent to use for oral reading. Students may read poems to share the beauty or expression of a passage.

Overall, oral reading as part of or an extension of a basal reading lesson can be a satisfying and beneficial activity. Children can gain fluency and find enjoyment in reading to others.

RECOMMENDATIONS FOR CLASSROOM USE

The pros and cons of using basals must be carefully evaluated. You can do a lot of reading on the subject and consult many authorities, but ultimately you, as the classroom teacher, must decide whether basals will be used and what strategies you will follow in using the materials.

We make the following recommendations concerning the use of basal materials:

1. Use basals as part of the reading program, not the whole program. There should be time allowed for self-selected reading in practical, real-life material and in recreational types of resources. When basals become the complete reading program, they may become boring because of the sameness of the format of the entire series.

2. Do not require all children to do all stories and all workbook pages. If a child is proficient in a skill, additional practice may be completely unjustifiable.

3. Oral reading is best handled in other ways than in the reading group. Do not ask students to follow along in their books as a child reads to them. In addition, a child should always have ample time to prepare for an oral reading in front of an audience. Choral reading and other such activities are effective ways to provide oral reading activities in the classroom.

4. A child should be allowed to use the basal reader suitable for her ability, not according to the grade she is in. The child should be allowed to move as quickly or as slowly through the material as is deemed necessary. No set of readers should be used exclusively for one grade in school.

5. The teacher should keep accurate records of each child's progress in skill development. Only those skills which are needed should be practiced. Varied and flexible groupings will allow teachers to have skill practice as needed by certain children.

6. The teacher should never consider that all steps or procedures in a basal lesson must be followed but should use his or her own judgment regarding which activities will be meaningful to students. The guidebook should not be considered as the ultimate authority; a teacher should feel free to use his or her own creative ideas in conducting a lesson.

Choosing a Basal Series

1. Are the stories of interest to the children for whom they are intended?
2. Does the series have a variety of stories?
3. Would the illustrations appeal to children?
4. Are the supplementary materials a positive addition to the basic text? Are the materials too repetitious or do they add variety and reinforcement to the skills presented?
5. Are skills systematically and sequentially presented? Are all skills included in the scope of the program from kindergarten to sixth or eighth grade?

6. Does the series show variety and value in occupational endeavors?
7. Does the book accurately portray sex roles in the stories?
8. Are minorities in our culture portrayed in a positive manner in the stories?
9. Does the series provide for individual differences in reading level?

CONSIDERATION IN CHOOSING A BASAL SERIES

Certain basic considerations should be part of any selection of a basal series. The large financial investment a school system makes when it chooses a series should be preceded by an equally careful analysis of the many series available on the market. The adoption period for most school systems dictates that whatever choice is made must be lived with for several years. Time carefully spent in textbook selection will be a productive investment for a school system. Chapter 14 outlines some of the overall considerations needed in evaluating reading materials. By careful examination of several programs, teachers and administrators will be able to make the best decisions concerning this important instructional aid for classrooms.

Aukerman (1981) has compiled comprehensive data on fifteen major basal reading series. He has examined each of these series by the following components: (1) physical, (2) instructional, (3) literary, (4) graphic arts, (5) directed learning, (6) individualized reading, and (7) management. In addition to the detailed information he provides on each series, Aukerman includes a detailed checklist for teachers to use in determining preferences for one series over another. Reference to such a detailed checklist is encouraged when a decision is being made concerning basal reading series for a classroom or school system.

Meeting Individual Needs

QUESTIONS TO GUIDE READING

Literal
What are some of the strategies of publishers for serving the needs of special children?

Inferential
Do teachers meet all the needs of all pupils? Explain your answer.

Evaluative
Should basals be used with all children? Explain your reasoning.

Teachers recognize that the children in their classrooms have many diversities: different ability levels, family backgrounds, motives, and interests. There are gifted and talented children, slow learners, and linguistically and culturally different students. Meeting the unique needs of such diverse individuals is a challenging task for any teacher.

Basal publishers recommend a variety of strategies to provide the flexibility needed to serve these special children. These are some of the suggestions they make:

1. The use of a nongraded approach promotes the idea that each child should operate at his own instructional level. Teachers do not assume that all children in a certain grade level are reading at the same levels. The nongraded program is meant to encourage teachers to assess the child's abilities to determine the most appropriate level of book for that child.

2. Basals present skills systematically, allowing many opportunities for practice and review and providing different tools such as textbooks, duplicated skill sheets, reading skill workbooks, etc. Some children may move quickly, without using all materials and activities; others require additional involvement, moving slowly, with each step practiced in many settings. It is the teacher's responsibility to evaluate continually to determine when a child needs additional practice in a skill.

3. Many basal series present activities that provide practice in a variety of modes. The student may get to use a visual, auditory, or kinesthetic mode to complete an activity. If learning does not occur using activities involving one mode, the teacher can try another. The teacher must be aware of the learning modes that are most successful with various children and vary the mode as appropriate.

4. In the teacher's manual, most publishers have a special section, usually entitled either "enrichment" or "extension." In this section there are suggestions for the student who can go beyond the basic lesson. It contains extending experiences in reading, writing, research, listening, and language-related activities. The teacher's task is one of carefully planning these activities for children who need them.

5. The way in which publishers are striving to have story content show varied cultures, ethnic groups, and career endeavors makes the books more suitable for the child from a different background. Showing varied groups in a favorable setting promotes the self-esteem of those who have similar backgrounds. Careful acknowledgment and discussion of these groups by the teacher further enhances their worth.

6. The skill assessment materials included with most basal series are helpful in determining those pupils who are having difficulties. Many programs suggest reteaching activities and provide materials to use when testing shows a child has not attained a certain level of skill proficiency.

7. Some programs now have three sets of materials available for each level: (1) basic materials used by all pupils at that level; (2) prebasic

materials used by those children whose abilities are limited by personal, cultural, or classroom experiences; and (3) expansion materials used by those who need a more in-depth level and expansion of critical and creative reading skills. These three sets of materials may be used in a variety of ways: only basic, or basic plus prebasic, or basic plus expansion. The decision must be made by individual teachers.

Summary

An overview of information on basal readers has been the focus of this chapter. We have looked at characteristics of basals and considered a broad definition of what is meant by the term "basal reading materials." We have seen the basal method, along with a description of the steps used in most basal series. We have also weighed some criticisms and values of basal readers and considered some recommended practices for use of the basals. This background information should allow the beginning teacher to make knowledgeable decisions regarding the use of basal materials.

Questions for Further Reading and Thinking

1. In what ways could a reading lesson described in a basal teacher's guide be changed or modified?
2. How could you determine what content and illustrations are preferred by students in your class?
3. What are the arguments for and against using more than one basal series in a single classroom? in a single school?
4. How are basal readers changing today?

Activities and Projects

1. Examine basal readers from three or more publishers. Note the method used to show levels, the sequence of skills, and the steps suggested for a typical lesson. Compare and contrast the various series in a panel discussion.
2. Write to a publishing house for catalogs and descriptive brochures of their basal program.
3. Develop an outline of a reading program that would have a basal reader as one of the parts of the program.
4. Add to the lists given in this chapter regarding pros and cons of basal readers.
5. Ask a local representative of a publishing house to speak about the theory regarding his basals, the background of the authors,

and his recommendations for proper use of the materials.

6. Read "Six Alternatives to the Directed Reading Activity" by Dixie Lee Spiegel in the *Reading Teacher* 34 (May 1981), pp. 914–920. Using a basal reading series you select, develop variations to the selected basal lesson format using ideas suggested by Spiegel.

Publishers of Basal Reading Series

Allyn and Bacon, Inc., Pathfinder, 7 Wells Avenue, Newton, MA 02159.

American Book Co., American Readers, 136 West 50th Street, New York, NY 10020.

Economy Co., Keys to Reading, 1901 N. Walnut Street, Oklahoma City, OK 73125.

Ginn and Company, Rainbow Edition, Reading 720 Series, 191 Spring Street, Lexington, MA 02173.

Harcourt Brace Jovanovich, Inc., Bookmark Reading Program, 757 Third Avenue, New York, NY 10017.

Harper and Row Publishers, Inc., Reading Basic Plus, 10 East 53rd Street, New York, NY 10022.

Holt, Rinehart and Winston, Inc., Holt Basic Reading, 383 Madison Avenue, New York, NY 10017.

Houghton Mifflin Company, The Houghton Mifflin Reading Program, One Beacon Street, Boston, MA 02107.

Laidlaw Brothers Inc., The Laidlaw Reading Program, Thatcher and Madison, River Forest, IL 60305.

J. B. Lippincott Co., Lippincott Basic Reading, East Washington Square, Philadelphia, PA 19105.

Macmillan Publishing Co., Series r — Macmillan Reading, 866 Third Avenue, New York, NY 10022.

Charles E. Merrill Publishing Co., The Merrill Linguistic Reading Program, 1300 Alum Drive, Columbus, OH 43216.

Open Court Publishing Co., The Headway Program, LaSalle, IL 61301.

(Rand McNally and Company) Riverside Publishing Company, Rand McNally Reading Program 1981: Young American Basic Series, 1919 South Highland Avenue, Lombard, IL 60148.

Scott, Foresman, and Co., Scott, Foresman Reading, 1900 East Lake Avenue, Glenview, IL 60025.

Phyllis Huff

13

Language Experience Approach

Most teachers of young children agree that children come to school eager to learn to read. This eagerness can be quickly and effectively put to constructive use in a reading approach commonly called the language experience approach (LEA). The definition of the language experience approach is expressed in the words used to identify the process — experience and language. *Experience* is just what it says: the child is involved in an active happening. *Language* refers to the spoken word, the written word, the listened-to word, and the word read by others.

How can this approach be utilized in reading instruction? Many reading authorities writing about language experience agree that children who can think, talk, and listen can learn to write and to read. They point out that anything a child can talk about, he can write, and anything he can write, he (or others) can read (Allen 1965, p. 7; Ashton-Warner 1963; Bush and Huebner 1979, p. 256; Hale 1981, p. 24; Lee and Allen 1963, p. 5; Veatch et al. 1979, pp. 12–13).

The language experience approach to teaching reading is built on the premise that children will decode printed words more easily if they have been the authors or composers of these words and if these words reflect a part of their everyday, familiar language and describe a personal experience. A more concrete description explains the steps: a child experiences a phenomenon, an event, or a happening; then uses language to share it with others and to record it for his own use at a later time.

The utilization of language experience involves all four of the skills areas of communication: speaking, listening, writing, and reading. This makes it a total communications approach, which is supported by Lee and Allen (1963, pp. 1–2) in their six assumptions about language:

1. There is a close interrelationship between the language skills of speaking, listening, reading, and writing.

2. The background of experiences of the individual learner provides the meaning of the words to that learner.
3. Words, by themselves, have no inherent meanings. The meaning comes as the words relate to the experience of the reader.
4. When the visual symbols are combined with the known sound symbols, then meaning occurs in the mind of the reader.
5. Spoken words are sound symbols that the listener uses to arouse meaning.
6. Reading is the means of developing meaning from patterns that one recognizes. Reading merely arouses meanings based on the experience of the learners. It does not provide them.

The six assumptions declare that in order for reading to have any meaning, the reader must be able to associate mentally some meaning based on experience with the printed word. Merely calling is not reading. Stauffer (1970, p. 2) concurs, defining the language experience approach as "the method founded on the oral-language facility of children." He goes on to say that ". . . by school age most children have had oral language sufficient to provide the foundation for reading instruction." But the foundation is sufficient only if the teacher patterns the reading instruction on the natural spoken language of the child. That is to say, we must use the language of the children as it is spoken by them, instead of imposing the adult-accepted language standard of the commercially printed materials. Children come to school eager to talk, to share their experiences and ideas, and to read. Advocates of the language experience approach believe that this method capitalizes on this natural motivation by having children talk and write about familiar experiences or concepts in a language they fully understand.

The Language Experience Procedure

QUESTIONS TO GUIDE READING

Literal
What are the steps in the language experience procedure?

Inferential
Can you outline the sequence of activities in the language experience lesson described in this section?

Evaluative
Are language experience stories built on common experiences of children more desirable than those built on the unique experiences of a single child?

The basic procedure for teaching beginning reading using the language experience approach will be the subject of this section. Detailed suggestions for usage will make up a later section.

The language experience approach differs from most other beginning reading programs in one respect. It is based on the language and writing of the children. No commercial or teacher-prepared materials are used except as they relate to the stories created by the children. In this program, skill development depends on the knowledge and ability of the teacher to correlate student-developed materials with instructional strategies for word recognition and other basic beginning reading skills. As such, it requires a teacher who has thorough basic knowledge of the developmental reading process and who is able to apply this knowledge creatively to day-by-day language experience activities.

The initial experience for writing a language experience story can involve either a total class or smaller groups. Most teachers favor the smaller groups as the more effective but use the total group as a way to introduce the process. For this reason this experience is described as a total class project.

To see how the language experience approach works, and how it builds on each preceding day's learning, let us consider what happens on the first days of first grade. On the first day, the teacher usually takes the students on a tour of the building and points out the places that will be of interest and importance to them — such as the cafeteria, the restrooms, the principal's office, the nurse's office, and the library. Let us assume that the tour has been completed and the children are back in the classroom discussing what they have seen. After a short discussion, the teacher says to the children, "Let's write a story about the trip you have just taken." The teacher moves to the chalkboard or to a chart paper she has previously set up. The teacher and students decide whether to write the title before or after the completion of the story. (If a teacher insists that the title be written first, it can often prove to be a stumbling block.) The teacher may ask if anyone has a title or if the students wish to wait until the story is finished before deciding. If the decision is to wait before giving the story a title, the teacher leaves space and begins the writing of the students' dictation.

The teacher asks the children questions that will lead into a story sequence. For example: "What did we do today?" "How can we say that in a story?" "What did Mark say?" Each child with a contribution is recognized and what he says is recorded exactly as he dictated it. In recording the story it is important that the child's language be recorded

Figure 13.1. A language experience story.

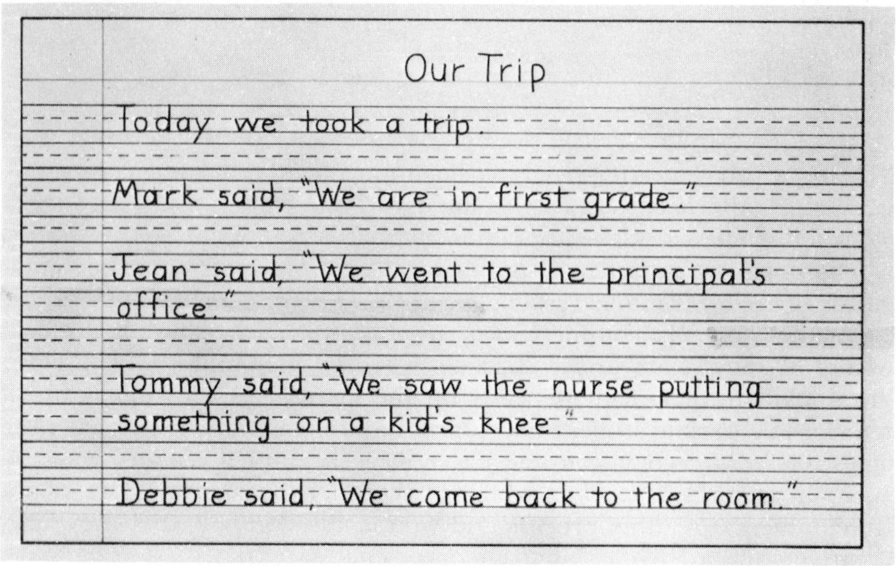

```
                        Our Trip
      Today we took a trip.

      Mark said, "We are in first grade."

      Jean said, "We went to the principal's
      office."

      Tommy said, "We saw the nurse putting
      something on a kid's knee."

      Debbie said, "We come back to the room."
```

as he said it, unedited by the teacher. Correct spelling, however, is to be used. A finished story might look like the one in Figure 13.1.

This example is rather long for a first day, first grade story, but it is likely to appeal to children and motivate them because they dictated it themselves.

The procedure is much like the old "experience story" or "experience chart" used in many primary grades for a number of years. The difference is in the way the experience-dictated story is used for instruction and in the fact that it is unedited for grammar. Many teachers oppose the no-editing idea, saying that the children should see from the beginning a proper model of good grammar. The rationale for not editing is that the grammar used by the child in his conversation is the grammar he knows and can understand as he begins to move from spoken language to written symbols — as he begins to "read." He will read what he says. Likewise, some teachers would not write the story in the form of quotations, as in the example, because the children have not yet been introduced to the required punctuation. However, it helps the children to identify printed names and to remember what is in the story, because the names are recorded for each contribution. Also, the quotation marks are included in a natural way and are not commented on by the teacher unless some child raises a specific question about them. Even then the teacher keeps her response as brief and clear as possible (for example, "These marks show us exactly what Tommy said").

As the teacher records each line, she reads it for the children. The authors (speakers) are asked to reread their contributions. When the entire story is recorded, the teacher rereads it, asking each author to locate his sentence. The teacher now has the story reread for the group, with each child reading his own contribution. Since name tags are usually a big part of the beginning first grade, most of the children will soon recognize their own names as they are printed. The order of the story helps them remember, also, because they know their part came after some specific other child's. As each child "reads" (this process is not actually reading, or recognizing the printed word; it is more of a memorization), the teacher points to the words. She gives help when a child hesitates or falters.

As a follow-up activity, and to extend the ideas, the teacher may distribute drawing paper to the students. She prints at the top of each sheet the title the group chose for their story, such as, "Our Trip." She then directs the children to draw a picture that tells about their trip. As the pictures are finished, the teacher asks each child for a brief description of what he has drawn and writes it, again as dictated, on the picture. The child reads back the title and the caption for his picture. In this way, each child gets an opportunity to take part in oral discussion of an experience, to help dictate a story or an individual line, and to read his own and other contributions — and all on the first day of school!

The next day the story written by the group is again placed before the total group. It is reread by individual children with the teacher following the words with a pointer or her hand. Then she conducts some drill work, such as: "Mark, can you find what you said?" and "Where is Jean's part of the story?" She gives both the contributors and the rest of the class a chance to apply their knowledge. Prior to the class, the teacher has re-copied the story onto large poster paper and has cut the individual contributions into strips. The strips are now brought out and placed as they are read by the teacher or a student (depending on how quickly the students can read the chart) next to the story on the chart. If the lesson is progressing, the teacher can remove the strips and have the students take one at a time to place it next to the proper place in the story chart. (This step might need to be saved for a later session.) The teacher can now have each child present his picture and read (with help when needed) the caption (a description) to the class. The teacher can collect the pictures at this point and bind them into a book for the class library. The children now have a book they can at least partially read and that has meaning to them. If desired, the teacher could make several books using a few of the pictures in each. The picture interpretation might also be done in smaller groups, especially if attention spans are short.

If there is difficulty with the lesson, or if progress is not satisfactory, the teacher may choose either to start at the beginning (day one) again or to scrap the story and begin with a different experience and another story. The latter would be necessary if the story were based on an experience not motivating or one that had been replaced by something more relevant and interesting. With some groups it may take more than one start to gain the interest necessary for a sustained lesson.

The teacher makes duplicated copies of the group story for the next step of instruction. After the copies are passed out to the children, they follow along as the story is read again. The children can use markers at this stage to keep them on the right line as they read their stories. Later, the teacher divides the class into smaller groups to do more work with the words in the story. Each group "reads" from their own papers and is asked to draw a line under the words they can read on their own. Groups (or individuals) having difficulty can go back to the large chart and the sentence strips before doing the more independent readings.

At the next session the children again read their stories from the duplicated sheets and again underline the recognized words. The words recognized previously and at this session will therefore have two lines. The teacher makes a negation mark ─/─ on the line of words known previously but not recognized at this later session. For example, Sue's paper might look like Figure 13.2.

The students are now ready to claim the words they knew in both sessions as part of their sight reading vocabulary. The teacher acknowledges their mastery by having students create a word bank. The word bank consists of cards on which the child can record the words he recognizes. Each word he recognizes is printed on a separate card (2″ × 3″). For an example, see Figure 13.3.

Figure 13.2. A sample paper marked for word recognition.

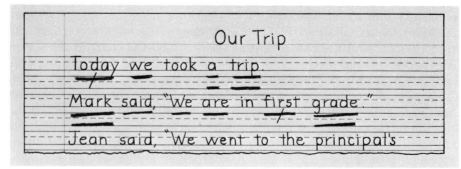

Figure 13.3.

Language Experience Approach

The card is placed in a box or envelope labeled with the child's name, and it is stored in a place to which the child has easy access. At a later session, the teacher can have each child read the words from his word bank. The word card may then be placed over (or next to, or under) the word as it appears in the story.

During this phase of the instruction the teacher may wish to make a "word window" or "window card." This is an index card with a rectangle cut out of the center. The cut-out portion can be placed over words in the printed story to isolate them and to test if the child recognizes the word. A lot of practice and positive encouragement is needed at this point in the instruction. When the children have enough words in their word banks, they can begin to create other stories and phrases independently by arranging the word cards. The more advanced children can then copy their stories onto beginning writing paper. Some first graders have made books for their classmates to read during the beginning month of school. However, do not expect this from very many children.

Other skills that can be learned during this step are those related to phonics and structural analysis. The words of the bank that are known to the students as sight words become excellent examples on which to build the lessons.

The teacher will need to keep track of the child's mastery of skills during instruction. A chart such as Table 13.1 might be useful. The skills taught on the chart can come from the school system's curriculum guide, from the scope and sequence of skills in the basal series being used, or from the teacher's personal knowledge of skill needs at that grade level or by that student. Such a record-keeping system helps the teacher to keep track of progress and to provide learning experiences meaningful to each child.

The instruction on a particular story is carried on as long as the teacher senses the children have an interest. It is not expected that all the children will be able to read every word at any time. If interest begins to wane, turn to another story or technique. Many teachers find that having several group stories going at once is a way to hold interest. Others find that after a few class group stories, it is better to divide the class into smaller groups based on ability and have each group compose stories. Many teachers start individualized instruction in reading at this point by having the children write individual stories and using them in the same way as the

Table 13.1. Skills Mastery Checksheet

	Long /a/	Short /a/	Etc.
Johnny	x	x	
Susie	x	/	
Mary	/		

/ = taught; x = mastered.

large-group stories. To a person who has never tried the technique, it may sound time consuming. But practicing teachers find the stories are usually short and the time is no longer than that traditionally used for small-group instruction in a preprimer.

Using Language Experience in the Total Reading Program

QUESTIONS TO GUIDE READING

Literal
What are some ways beginning reading skills can be taught through the use of the language experience approach?
What reasons does the author give that would indicate that the language experience approach is especially useful for linguistically different learners? for exceptional learners?

Inferential
Under what conditions can the language experience approach be useful beyond beginning reading?

Evaluative
How and when could a combination of language experience and basal reading approaches be effective?

The section on the methodology of the language experience approach presented its use in introducing beginning reading and sight vocabulary. This is one portion of the reading program in which the language experience approach has been found successful (Foerster 1974; Garcia 1974). There are other places in the reading program in which the language experience approach can be effectively used. These include: (1) in the development of beginning reading skills, (2) in conjunction with a basal reading program, (3) in working with the exceptional learner, (4) in middle grade reading instruction, and (5) with adult illiterates.

USE IN TEACHING BEGINNING READING SKILLS

The section on methodology gives some suggestions for the use of language experience stories in teaching beginning sight vocabulary. The language experience story is also useful to develop a variety of reading skills — such as left-to-right directionality, phonics, classification of words (i.e., like beginnings/endings, rhyming words, vowel sounds, etc.), structural analysis, word meaning, and beginning dictionary skills.

As the teacher writes the dictated story, she is introducing the left-to-right pattern. It is further reinforced when the teacher uses a pointer or her hand to follow the story during the rereading. Each reading of the story serves to practice the left-to-right pattern. The eye movement from the end of one line to the beginning of the next is another important pattern that can be introduced and practiced with the language experience story.

The teaching of phonics comes as the teacher begins asking such questions as:

"How are these words alike (*today, took*)?"
"Can you think of a word that starts like *today* and *took*?"
"Which word rhymes with *play*?"

At this point the teacher can focus on other beginning sounds such as: What words begin with /w/? What sound does ⟨w⟩ represent? The words need to be presented in as many ways as possible to build sight vocabulary. See Chapter 4 for other phonics skills. Many such experiences can lead the students to make generalizations about word families and to create lists of words to add to the word bank as they master them in sight vocabulary.

Long and short vowel sounds can also be introduced using the story words; for example, the teacher asks, "What sound does ⟨a⟩ represent in *grade*? How is the ⟨a⟩ in *saw* different? What other word in the story has an ⟨a⟩ that represents a sound like ⟨a⟩ in *grade*?"

One word attack skill very prominent in language experience is the use of context clues. The children can easily recognize words as they read the context and remember each particular contribution. The teacher can give practice by asking the children questions requiring reading the context, such as: "What did our class do?" and "Where did the nurse put something?" The children then find the word in the story that answers the question.

As the children build word banks, they can begin to arrange their words into groups, or classes, based on different criteria. This exercise will both strengthen the sight vocabulary and help children to clarify the multiple meanings of many words. The assignment may simply be to put all the words that belong together in a set and then to tell why the words belong to the set. Another classification scheme is to have the teacher ask that all words belonging to a particular set (such as words that tell names of people) be identified.

Other skills can be taught by such activities as asking the child to find words that are alike in some way. Words beginning or ending with the same letters can be matched. As the number of stories increase, there will be words to match for initial consonants and for rhyming. Children learn to identify compound and root words as they compare and classify words in the word banks.

Children are learning to analyze word meanings when they try to think of a synonym or antonym for certain words. Meaning and comprehension are also the basis for the drawings of the experience the children sometimes make.

As the children begin to acquire a sight vocabulary, they can use or construct a picture dictionary. This endeavor will lead them to realize they need to know the alphabet and alphabetical order. As the word bank becomes larger, children may feel a need to arrange the words in a more organized fashion; alphabetical order can be introduced here, too, as a useful way of organization. In addition children could arrange words by classification; i.e., animal words, people words, "doing" or action words, place words, etc. This will help them to see words in "go together" groups, which will increase story writing ability.

One of the advantages of the language experience approach is the opportunity to use more words than usually appear in basal readers. Children learn words from listening to others and are able to put into print words from their speaking vocabulary, which is by nature larger than the reading and writing vocabularies. One activity of great value in language experience is the word list created by the children apart from the story writing (or perhaps prior to the writing exercise). Children dictate words in categories for the list such as words for special days; words for seasons; words for experiences, etc.

Most advocates of the language experience approach believe that basic skills of reading can be meaningfully and successfully taught using this approach. The key is for the teacher to have a thorough knowledge of reading skills and to be able to carry through on careful planning and sequencing.

Use with a Basal Reader Program

Recent research in reading has led to the conclusion that no one method or program is best in successful beginning reading but that an eclectic approach (combining the best elements of several programs) appears to be the most desirable. The results of the twenty-seven First Grade Studies funded by the United States Office of Education give strong support to that conclusion (Bond and Dykstra 1967b). Since the basal reading program is the most widely used approach, it was compared to several other methods or programs. In this chapter we are concerned with the language experience program, so we will look at the results of the three studies that compared the language experience approach to the basal reader approach. The language experience groups were significantly higher in two of the studies in the area of word recognition. The other study reported no significant difference. In the three studies on paragraph comprehension, the language experience approach and the basal approach were each significant in one study, while the remaining study showed no significant difference. No differences in spelling ability were found in two of the studies, but language experience did produce higher spelling scores in the third. Even with such a small representation of studies, a pattern appears to emerge — neither appears to be significantly better as a way to teach beginning reading.

Many teachers feel a combination of the two is very useful. The approaches can be combined in instruction by: (1) using language experience to introduce the children to the form and philosophy of reading prior to experience with a basal reader, (2) providing concrete experiences to help build background for basal reader story comprehension and appreciation, and (3) supplementing the content and skills taught through the basal reader.

When the children have dictated or composed a story, there is very little, if any, need for external motivation to read the story. The story is based on experiences and interests of the children and therefore easily comprehended. As the children begin to write more and to write in smaller groups or individually, stories will become more diverse. The child will recognize that, in order to share a story, he will need a listener or a reader. He has now discovered that stories are written primarily for others to read. This learning can be used to introduce a basal reader by pointing out that other writers (like him) have written stories to be shared and that the basal reader contains many such stories. The stories are now shared experiences with the writer and not just words to be recognized. Likewise, the child understands the story form because he has used it in the dictation exercises, and his recognition is easily transferred to the basal.

Although new basal readers are much more realistic and aesthetically appealing than they used to be, they still contain some stories based on topics with which children are not familiar. For example, many children have not seen nor ridden an elevator or escalator. Providing a first-hand or vicarious experience and then having the children dictate stories would better prepare them to read a story about an event involving the elevator or escalator. The same is true for many experiences teachers take for granted, from animals to vacations. The teacher needs to be very alert to children's experiences, or lack of them, and to fill in the gaps as much as possible. Similarly, after reading a basal story the children might experiment with the ideas and write stories comparing their own experiences with those of the story characters.

As the different reading skills are introduced in the basal program, they can be reinforced, practiced, and strengthened when students apply the words of the word bank, which originated in the language experience stories. In programs that are individualized, the child's own language experience stories can be very effective and efficient ways to work on skill development, comprehension, and creative expression.

Use with the Exceptional Learner

Language experience can prove an invaluable tool in instruction of children with emotional disturbances. Often the disturbance is accompanied by a very low feeling of self-worth. The language experience approach can give the child a feeling of success: he can compose a story, and he can read the story. Working with words he has created may make him feel worthy and may develop a sense of pride. However, the teacher would need to proceed slowly and be sure each learning experience was a success experience.

Another area where the reading experience should be useful is in the instruction of the slow learner. Many of the printed materials are too difficult and too complicated for the slow learner. The language experience approach gives the child with a learning difficulty a chance to communicate his own ideas and then to see them written and be able to "read" them. Stories and sentences should be kept short and given much reinforcement. Slow learners can experience success in learning to read; they just take more instruction and a longer period of time to do so.

Some appropriate activities for slow learners include the following:

1. Show a short story film (such as a children's book or a fairytale). Then repeat the showing, but turn off the sound track. Have the students tell the story.
2. Read a short, interesting story to the students. Let them illustrate or dramatize the story.
3. Bring in an animal (e.g., a rabbit or gerbil) for observation. Have students describe the animal. Record the descriptive words on a chart or word card.
4. Present a story by film, record, or dramatization. Have students retell the story. Record their sentences on a chart or sentence strips.
5. Have students dramatize events in the school day such as going to lunch, getting ready for art, music, or physical education.
6. Draw or locate pictures that describe daily lives of students or special interests of students.

The teacher's imagination and the students' interest and enthusiasm will unearth many more ideas to develop and extend language. Slow learners need much practice in oral language prior to beginning the written forms.

Language experience could provide a special outlet for the gifted student. Many experiences lead naturally to expressing the outcomes, feelings, and creative thoughts of activities in a manner to be shared with others. Gifted students can use the approach to create their own books and activity reports for sharing and for future reference.

Although there are numerous activities for the gifted student, some suggestions are: have the students create their own myths in social studies and science about the origin of a thing or custom; have them identify a problem that they can work on and write a report of their progress toward solution; have them research a topic related to an area of study and write a report to be given to other students.

USE IN MIDDLE GRADES

A great concern of teachers in the middle grades is the child of apparently normal ability who falls below expectations in reading. One reason often stated for this lag is lack of interest in the reading material. The language experience approach could remedy this situation by giving the student material of interest that contains the vocabulary he can successfully handle. By writing his own material, based on his interests and experiences, the child is creating reading materials that he not only can understand but can enjoy. The teacher explores the children's interests through class activities and discussion, through survey techniques, and through individual conferences. He can use the interests expressed to provide an experience (or he can draw on a previous experience) to motivate the student to record his descriptions and feelings. The student may dictate to the teacher or he may write down the story himself. The teacher uses the content of the experience stories to work with the basic reading skills such as those described in the beginning reading program. Gradually, the student builds a positive attitude toward reading because it is about something that is a part of himself; at this point, the student should be able to transfer the skills to other printed materials.

The teacher must choose the first materials with great care, ensuring the child's success. She must also maintain close supervision during this experience to make it successful and rewarding. The teacher must approach the experience with a great deal of positive encouragement and follow through with such encouragement to the end of the experience. In this way she ensures that the child will be experiencing success and developing a more positive feeling about himself and his abililities. As time passes, the student has many more basic skills essential for using the approach.

Language experience activities should not be reserved in the middle grades for remedial or special students. All students can benefit from such experiences at every level. Stories and writings created by the students serve as great motivators in areas such as self-expression, creative writing, increasing vocabulary, sharing ideas and feelings with others, and expressing oneself clearly and in an interesting manner. Students can create cont →

writings in large groups, in small groups, and individually. They can prepare books and other materials to share or to keep for their own private reading. They can develop vocabulary banks — much like the primary word bank but at a more advanced level. (See Chapter 6, for more discussion of word banks.) The banks can be used for working with language skills such as syllabication, parts of speech, synonyms and antonyms, and any other areas of language in which practice is needed. Word banks are also excellent resources for analyzing and applying spelling concepts. The creative teacher will find many instructional opportunities in the language experience writings of her students.

Language experience is not reserved just for reading. It carries over into all the content areas of the middle grades. For example, in science the students can explore natural phenomena such as storms, floods, snow, stars, plants, etc. They can create word lists about the topics, and they can write about their experiences with the topics or about researched aspects of the topic. Some writing may be by students, using the word lists; other writing could be group-dictated to a writer. They can also share common experiences through experiments or demonstrations such as measuring how long a candle burns when placed under jars of varying sizes. Field trips in science and social studies furnish another motivation for writing. Activities involving drama and the study of realia in social studies are real story motivators as well as vocabulary builders. In mathematics students can share activities involving number processes and then put these into story form. The opportunities in art and music range from making puppets to producing the puppet show complete with appropriate music.

Students who have difficulty in reading various subject texts could create their own texts by writing or dictating about class reports, discussions, experiments, films, etc. The texts would be resources for information as well as practice in the communication skills.

The language experience approach has much promise for the teacher. It does require planning and carefully sequenced instruction. Merely having children dictate a story and then reading it back is not language experience instruction. We must always be sure the story is used in leading the child to reading, not as the end of reading in itself. Dictation must be used for instruction in reading skills in order to be true language experience.

USE WITH LINGUISTICALLY DIFFERENT CHILDREN

There has been much concern expressed about the oral language and reading skills of children who have a nonstandard language background. This group includes all children whose language patterns differ from that found in the traditional reading and trade books. Some materials — such as Bank Street Readers — purport to meet the particular needs of specific groups. However, these materials do not deal effectively with the variety of language patterns found in the minority cultures. How then can these needs be met? Recently the use of language experience instruction has been found successful in aiding Black and Chicano children to read (Foerster 1974; Garcia 1974; and Hall 1972).

The language experience approach is based partly on the assumption that the relationship of oral and written language can best be shown by using the language of the students and on the psychological factors of success, motivation, and attitude (Hall 1972, p. 5). The language experience approach also yields a better match between oral and written language of the child than any other major approaches to reading instruction can achieve. The linguistically different child of a minority culture speaks a language that is his primary or native language, and it is this language that should be the basis for his first reading experiences. Through language experience the child observes his spoken language being written and read. O'Brien (1973, p. 104) contends that ideas need to be spoken before they are written, especially in the beginning stages. This author believes that language is something you understand and say before you can successfully read and write it. Through language experience the student can be led from his home or community language patterns into the more standard patterns of the social, economic, and educational world. Thus he is in essence bilingual and does not learn that his home language is undesirable, a factor greatly contributing to his self-esteem.

When using the language experience approach with linguistically different students for the goals just described, it is important that the language patterns be recorded exactly as they are dictated by the student. If the child says, "Her going to the store," that is what is written (not "She is going to the store"). Some specialists still do not agree with this and believe the teacher should restate what the child says in a positive manner and record the restated language, "Yes, Mike, she is going to the store." But in this case, the recorded language then is not the thought pattern expressed and does not reproduce the child's "native" language.

One standard form that should be observed is spelling. Do not try to spell in dialect, but rather be sure of the word meant and record the standard spelling form. People usually hear themselves saying the word in the standard way, even if they don't. They react with shock to their voices on tape: "I didn't know I had an accent!"

On the basis of available theory and data (Foerster, Garcia, and Hall, whom we've just seen), the language experience approach appears to be a procedure that permits the linguistically different student to experience success in learning to read. It can serve as the transition from cultural language, or dialect, to standard language by first recording and accepting the child's cultural language, thus causing him to recognize that there are other ways of expressing the same ideas. He can record these ways side by side with the original. The approach is also appropriate as a basis for instruction for the bilingual child (Ching 1976, p. 34).

Again we must emphasize that the language experience approach is only one procedure to lead students into a reading program. It is not a panacea for all difficulties experienced by linguistically different students. Properly used, it can be a way for reading to be more successful for them.

Advantages and Disadvantages of the Language Experience Approach

QUESTIONS TO GUIDE READING

Inferential
What are some cautions a teacher should exercise in using the language experience approach?

Evaluative
Considering the advantages and disadvantages cited, under what conditions would you elect to use the language experience approach? How would you rate each of the advantages and disadvantages of the language experience approach (1 = very important; 2 = moderately important; 3 = not too important)?

The language experience approach has many advantages built into the method. Some of these follow:

1. The first reading experiences are successful because they use the every-day language patterns of the children. Children who speak a nonstandard language are not penalized or made to feel inferior because they do not measure up verbally to the standard. Likewise, children whose language patterns are beyond those expected are not frustrated by the task of having to learn simpler sight words.
2. The approach requires fewer and more inexpensive materials, which are readily available.
3. Children can utilize the sight vocabulary they bring to school (from signs, labels, and television.)
4. It is individualized in that each child is working at a level he can comprehend and with words he understands and can recognize.
5. Children learn that listening, writing, and spelling are a part of the reading process and, thus, that the language arts are interrelated.
6. Both phonics and sight words are used. Children see the relationship of sounds to the symbols used to represent them in writing.
7. Children learn to make choices and to function independently as they work with the skills.

8. Children feel their ideas are respected and accepted. This helps develop a positive self-image.
9. Motivation for and interest in reading are greatly increased, which may result in a positive attitude toward reading and creative expression.
10. Children are motivated to increase their spoken and written vocabulary.
11. When the approach is used with the basal program, the teacher may find that many of the words found in the preprimer may actually be learned before the books are presented; this situation generally permits a successful experience with the formal reading program.
12. Children have insight into what goes into a story and can critique and discuss the writer's ideas because they, too, are writers.

Even though the list of advantages looks impressive, there are certain limitations that need to be recognized:

1. The teacher is totally responsible for preparing all the materials for reading instruction. Each class must be allowed to dictate its own material. Materials dictated by other classes are not the work of the class present at the moment and cannot serve the purpose of the language experience materials. To ensure smooth progress, the teacher must provide interesting experiences from which to write.
2. In group dictation the vocabulary might not reflect the language level of all the children. Often it may be the level of the most able. The teacher needs to be sure all students are given a chance to contribute and that the material is understood by all the children.
3. The approach could foster memory reading. The child can memorize the story rather than know the words. This possibility is why the techniques for word isolation suggested earlier are important. Reviewing and using the words dictated in as many situations as possible will help eliminate this.
4. The instruction may become incidental, overlooking developmental aspects and the necessary basic skills. Each experience must be well planned and carefully followed up to ensure value.
5. The child may become too dependent on his own writing, failing to take the opportunity to share the ideas written by others. Encouragement to read other materials needs to be ongoing to offset this possibility. The teacher can point out materials she thinks the child can have success reading and will enjoy reading.
6. The success of the method depends on the teacher's ability to relate to the students, to motivate creative expression, and to be competent in teaching reading skills.

Putting Language Experience into Practice

QUESTIONS TO GUIDE READING

Literal
What are some activities teachers can provide for children as a basis for a "language experience" approach to reading?

Evaluative
Under what conditions would a teacher use each of the classifications of activities mentioned in this section?

Language experience is based on the idea that things familiar in the child's environment are used to direct him toward oral language expression, then to the recording of the language, then to reading what he has dictated. There is an endless source of material in the everyday environment of the child, and the teacher is usually perceptive enough to recognize the stimuli. However, often the teacher will want to set the stage, so to speak, by providing the stimuli so that the children share the *same experience*. This sharing is important so that the children will be interpreting from a common ground. It furnishes a focal point for their attention and gives each child a base from which to contribute ideas. Some suggestions for a common experience are: a field trip; a current happening in school or community; a story read to the class; a television program or movie the class has seen; classroom pets or projects; special visitors; and activities such as baking cookies, popping corn, and making butter. These are only starters meant to be springboards to many and varied creative stimuli.

The next few paragraphs contain some activities for use with a language experience approach in a classroom. They are broken down for the total class, for a small group, and for the individual. However, the classification is only for the purpose of clarity. Many teachers find it more manageable to start by having the total class dictate stories, as in the example given earlier in the chapter. From there they divide the class into smaller dictating groups, and finally they work with the individual children. The teacher does not need to feel this is the only way to implement the language experience approach into a classroom; it is offered as a suggestion to be adapted to specific situations.

CLASSROOM ACTIVITIES

1. Make name labels with the first and last names of the students. Make a chart of the names as they appear on the labels. Have students match the labels with the names on the chart.

2. Make helper charts, using the names as they appear on the name labels. Have each student find his job, matching his name label with the chart. At first, pictures may be used to name the jobs. Later, pictures with words may be used. Finally, just words may be used.

3. Read stories to the children and leave the books where the children can look at them independently. Also, records (with stories written on the cover or in a separate leaflet) can be used.

4. Use children's drawings and write sentences dictated by the children on them. Display the pictures or make books of them.

5. Have the children classify labeled objects into categories they define. The labels can be moved and placed in groups based on their classifications. Remember to return the labels to the proper place when finished.

6. Show a film without sound. Have children dictate a dialog to a writer or the tape recorder.

7. Take a walk to see fall colors, snow, or other seasonal conditions. On return students list all words they can for the subject. Students can write about their experience using their writing for reading and sharing.

8. Have an outside speaker for the class. The class prepares in advance a list of questions for the speaker. After the visit a thank-you letter is composed.

SMALL-GROUP ACTIVITIES

1. Have the children dictate a group story. Give each child a copy and have each read the story and underline the words he knows. At a later session, the process is repeated. The child again underlines the known words, so that there are double lines under the ones remembered. Copy these words onto word bank cards for the child.

2. Use the word bank to play word games such as: Match words that have the same beginning letters or beginning sounds; find words that are opposites.

3. Show a film or filmstrip without narration. Have the children compose the narration dictating it either on a tape recorder or to the teacher. Have them share their filmstrip with another group.

4. Have the children make pictures of a group story on newsprint, mural paper, or overhead transparencies; then they write a sentence or two for each picture under the picture. Make a box "movie" of the pictures, or

use the overhead projector to show them in sequence to the rest of the class.

5. Have the groups write letters to each other and to the other groups or classes. The letters will need to be dictated to the teacher at first, but when the children are capable they should copy their own.

6. Have students do a group activity such as making a mobile on weather, food, types of rocks, etc. Groups may compose a narrative about the mobile.

7. Have students plan a class election for social studies. Campaign speeches and slogans may be written by groups for their candidate.

8. Have each group choose a topic and prepare a radio-type skit. Time limits may be imposed.

INDIVIDUAL ACTIVITIES

1. Have the child dictate his own story; write it on large, primary paper, leaving room for pictures at the top. Have the child illustrate his story. Stories could also be tape recorded.

2. Have each child make his own book of the stories he has dictated. When he gets to dictating stories several pages long, each story can be a book by itself.

3. Have each child make his individual word bank of words he can recognize and read. Have him add to his bank from other sources, such as the preprimers and storybooks when he shows he can read the word. Use the word bank to create sentences.

4. Have each child classify the words in his word bank by making an alphabet book, using one page for each letter of the alphabet and copying the words from the cards onto the pages.

5. Let the child serve as teacher for another child. Do not have only the faster children as teachers, but let every child have a chance to play the role!

6. Have each student pick a person he admires and write a biography. These may be shared.

7. Have each student grow a plant under special conditions such as no light, upside down, turned on side, sitting on moving turntable, etc. A diary may be kept of the project.

8. Have each student pretend he is from another planet. He may write a news account of his arrival on Earth.

Summary

Language experience is the process by which the experiences of children are dictated by the children in their own language and are recorded for reading. The teacher makes use of the child's dictation as a tool in introducing the skills necessary for success in reading. There are many activities to use in developing the language experience approach.

The language experience approach is one method used successfully to create interest in and a positive attitude toward reading. It also serves to motivate children to write and to expand their vocabularies. It has been found useful in teaching reading to remedial readers, slow learners, children with learning disabilities, gifted students, and linguistically different children.

The language experience approach is by no means a panacea to teaching beginning reading. However, it is an approach that has been successful and it is worthy of consideration as a part of the total reading program.

Questions for Further Reading and Thinking

1. How would you employ the language experience approach using Initial Teaching Alphabet (ITA) or another changed alphabet?
2. How could the language experience approach be utilized with shy children?
3. What are some ways that the transition between experience stories and other reading materials may be accomplished?
4. How might language experience stories serve as an incentive to creative writing?
5. How might fantasy be used in the language experience approach?

Activities and Projects

1. Plan an activity for language experience that uses a science activity to stimulate the dictation.
2. Use a creative language experience, such as a puppet show or play, as the background experience for a classroom language experience lesson.
3. Write a critique of one of three widely used books on language experience (Hall 1981; Lee and Allen 1963; Stauffer 1970).
4. Check with some primary teachers who use language experience and have them evaluate their program.
5. Have a young child dictate a story to you. Try some of the suggestions for teaching reading skills using the story. Evaluate the results.

Leonard G. Breen

14

Additional Approaches, Materials, and Programs

Teachers-in-training are often confused by the bewildering variety of reading instructional approaches, materials, and programs available to teachers. However, as they gain experience in teaching, they begin to realize that there are broad classifications possible. (See the introduction to Part IV for broad definitions of approach and program).

Proponents of each approach, material, or program have definite feelings about what reading is. They often disagree on such issues as the role of language in reading, the nature of reading readiness, the most effective way to teach phonics skills, and on the questions of how best to control vocabulary loads in beginning readers or whether vocabulary should even be controlled at all. Each represents a point of view about the teaching/learning process. But the ultimate objective is the same regardless of the approach or material used — that the reader be able independently to decode and comprehend the printed page. Defining the best way to achieve that objective identifies the characteristics of the different programs used in reading instruction.

Chapters 12 and 13 discussed basal programs and the language experience approach. Though perhaps the most widely used, they by no means exhaust the range of ways devised to lead readers toward independence. This chapter will introduce several others such as individualized reading, linguistic approaches, changed alphabets, phonic approaches, programmed materials, and systems programs. You should study the characteristics of each and watch for commonalities and differences. You must carefully consider what approach or materials you would feel most comfortable in using as a supplement if basals or language experience were used in your school. Or conversely, you may find that one of the approaches or materials discussed in this chapter is the basis for instruction in your school; if so, how would you bring in basals or language experience as teaching supplements? Many teachers combine a variety of approaches and materials into effective programs.

Individualized Reading

Individualized reading is an approach that is widely used today both as a major approach and as a supplement. It is based on research by Olson (1956, pp. 36–37), and involves three principles in the planning for instruction: seeking, self-pacing, and self-selection. By *seeking*, Olson meant that each child carries within himself his own guide and timetable for development: external influences cannot force the development of the child. In other words, readiness is not imposed, but is an internal development. Olson believed that the child will *pace* himself through the developmental stages of learning and will tend to select materials to read that meet his level of readiness for new learning experiences. Consequently, in a program based on the individualized reading approach, children are given the opportunity to select and read widely in many books of all kinds and descriptions.

Individualized reading, however, is more than just wide reading. Hunt (1967) sees the approach as a highly organized way of providing reading instruction that treats reading as an interaction of three factors:

1. Skills development — from simple word recognition skills through application of skills to complex contextual material.
2. Response to ideas — from specific recall to deeper understandings and sensitive interpretations.
3. Attitudes and values — from lack of interest to developing lifetime values and positive patterns of tasteful reading.

Because individualized reading deals with several dimensions of the reading process, and involves a classroom of readers performing a variety of reading activities, the role of the teacher is vital to its success. Coordinating a program based on individualized reading requires much more organization and teaching than does managing a program that is preplanned and preorganized for you. The major variables fall under two major categories:

1. Organization procedures — selecting reading materials and classroom orientation.
2. Program mechanics — teacher-pupil conferences, skills development, follow-up activities, and record keeping.

ORGANIZATIONAL PROCEDURES

Advance organization by the teacher is most important for the success of a program based on the individualized reading approach. Before the program is initiated the teacher must have access to a variety of children's books, magazines, basal readers, and other types of reading materials. A sufficient number to begin with would be two — preferably three — times as many books as there are children in the class. Since a prime objective of this approach is to lead children to explore and appreciate the world of stories, language, and ideas, children need to read materials having a variety of literary patterns and an increasing complexity of language and story line. For these reasons teachers should use caution in including in their collections too many magazines and comic materials. Although this would seem to contradict previous arguments that students should be able to read whatever they want, some people feel that such materials lend themselves more to "picture looking" than to reading. The teacher will also want to collect a variety of exercises and games from cut-up workbooks, teacher-made ditto sheets, and other resources for use as group and individual skills activities.

Next the teacher must plan who will be involved in the program and how it will be introduced to the class and to the parents. Some teachers prefer to begin with only a few students from the class, such as the gifted or the slower learners, and add others as they feel comfortable. Other teachers may wish to use individualized reading for the entire class from the beginning. The decision will depend on the teacher's own ability to handle a wide variety of materials and children.

Because of its uniqueness, individualized reading should generally start with a short period of orientation to allow the children to get used to the idea of such a program and how it is run. Encourage browsing and free selection of books for a week or two. During this time help the students develop some criteria for the selection of books. If they are unsure, for example, whether a book they have chosen is at their level teach them to

Individualized Reading

[margin note: ☆ method child should use before going on.]

use the "five-finger method" for deciding. (Open the book and begin reading. If you come to a word you don't know and can't figure out hold out your thumb and continue reading. If you come to a second word you don't know put out another finger and continue reading. If you use up all the fingers on one hand while reading one page the book is probably too difficult for you to read with enjoyment. See if you can find another one that is easier.) This might also be a good time to share and discuss the results of interest inventories you have administered so that your readers have a clearer understanding of their individual and collective reading interests. (See Chapter 15 for a discussion of interest inventories.) By the end of the orientation period the children should know just what you as teacher will expect of them and fully understand how to proceed. What content knowledge of books read will you expect of them? Will they be responsible for vocabulary in the book? Will they be responsible for meaning or spelling or both? Will they be expected to do follow-up activities and/or keep reading records? How will they be evaluated and graded?

The Mechanics

[margin note: 1 to 1 basis]

The focal point of individualized reading is the individual conference during which the teacher meets with the student on a one-to-one basis to discuss the material the student is reading and to check his reading skills. During this time the teacher and child may discuss appealing aspects of the book, ideas developed by the author, and the child's reaction to his reading. Occasionally parts of the book will be chosen by either the child or the teacher for reading aloud, and sometimes plans will be made to share parts of the book with the entire class.

[margin note: question by the teacher.]

The key to the conference lies in the questions asked by the teacher. According to Hunt (1967), learning to discuss books through intelligent questioning is the most important instructional tool at the teacher's command. Teachers must practice to develop the art of discussing books with children whether or not they know the content of the book. Examples of questions that might be used for discussion follow.

In order to gain information concerning the child's knowledge of the content of the book, the teacher might ask:

1. Why did you choose this book?
2. What kind of story is this one?
3. What part did you like best? Why?
4. Was there a part that you did not like? Why?
5. What did the book teach you?
6. What characters did you like best? Why?
7. What do you think the writer wanted to tell in this book?
8. If you had the opportunity, what would you like to ask the author about this story?

In order to check the child's understanding of the meaning of specific passages or chapters, the teacher might ask:

1. What do you think the character (or writer) meant when he said this?
2. How else could this problem have been solved?
3. Has this ever happened to you?
4. If you could become one of the characters, which one would you choose?
5. Is there something in the book you would like to happen to you?

In order to encourage vocabulary growth, to develop deeper meanings, and to share interesting words, the teacher might ask:

1. What does this word, phrase, or part mean?
2. Read the part that shows conversation.
3. How did the writer show sadness?
4. Why did the author choose to use the word *bellowed* (or any good descriptive word)?
5. Can you find many unusual words that the author used?
6. Did anybody speak in a different way from what you or your parents do?
7. Robert Frost wrote:

   Let us pretend the dew drops from the eaves
   Are you and I eavesdropping on their unrest.[1]

   Langston Hughes wrote:

   Let the rain kiss you.
   Let the rain beat upon your head with silver liquid drops.
   Let the rain sing you a lullaby.[2]

   Did you find any writing like this in your book?

In order to check on the child's independent use of word attack skills the teacher may select certain words and ask:

1. What is the root word?
2. What is the prefix for this word? The suffix?
3. Can you think of another root word that rhymes with this?
4. What two words does this contraction stand for?
5. What words did you get stuck on?
6. Were there any words that you didn't know but were able to figure out? How did you do it?

These questions, or others appropriate to students' ages and abilities, might be listed on a bulletin board near your classroom library. They

1. From "A Cabin in the Clearing" from *The Poetry of Robert Frost* edited by Edward Connery Lathem. Copyright 1951, © 1962 by Robert Frost. Copyright © 1969 by Holt, Rinehart and Winston. Reprinted by permission of Holt, Rinehart and Winston, Publishers.
2. Langston Hughes, "April Rain Song," from *The Dream Keeper and Other Poems*, (New York: Alfred A. Knopf, Inc., 1932).

Individualized Reading   329

might also be mimeographed on cards or paper for students to take with them when they check a book out. This will allow readers to prepare ahead for the conference and not be forced to respond to all of the questions in an unrehearsed manner.

Organizing the conference also varies. Some teachers ask students to volunteer, others assign conference time, and many require students to make appointments for their conferences. Some teachers have found that having one child waiting close by while a conference is conducted will eliminate wasted time in getting to the next conference. This is sort of an "on deck" arrangement. Conferences need to be carefully timed, carefully planned, and usually are from five to twenty minutes in duration. Not all conferences need be teacher-pupil meetings. Children often like to work together in a common interest group and will frequently decide to read the same book independently and then meet to discuss common understandings, feelings, and what the book meant to them. Such student meetings should be encouraged.

During the conference, teachers note the skills that need practice and either provide some on-the-spot instruction or plan to form small groups for skills instruction. This group then exists only for the time necessary to master the needed skill. Group membership varies as children master, or are identified as needing, the particular skills being taught. Additionally, there are times planned for glossary activities, to work on word card files and games, to discuss a newly discovered language or literary technique, or perhaps simply to share a technique for attacking polysyllabic words. Skill development in individualized reading is different in that the child chooses, in part, the words and skills he needs to learn. Additionally, skill development goes beyond learning sounds and syllables and single words. It becomes the process of assisting the reader to use these skills to aid thinking and reasoning with printed language.

Teachers who use individualized reading find it necessary to use ways of keeping records of children's development in reading. Some of these records can be kept by the children, whereas others are the responsibility of the teacher. Each child can be asked to keep a list of the books that he has read on a form that might look like one of the two samples in Figure 14.1.

Teachers may also wish to refer to and use "My Reading Design" as discussed and illustrated in Chapter 15.

Teacher records can be as simple as a card or a notebook page made out for each child following a conference session or as complex as a formalized checklist on which the teacher periodically records her observations and reactions in such areas as word attack skills, comprehension skills, and oral reading skills. These can then be used as guides for planning future activities and materials selections or as a basis for reporting pupil progress to the child and his parents. Teachers do well to remember the importance of simplicity, however, when compiling such checklists. Gather as much information as you need for instructional record keeping

Figure 14.1.

PUPIL READING RECORD NAME				
Book Title	Author	Date(s)	Opinion of Book	Sharing Activity Chosen

<table>
<tr><td colspan="5" align="center">PUPIL READING RECORD</td></tr>
<tr><td colspan="5">Name_____</td></tr>
<tr><td>Book Title</td><td colspan="2">Student Comment*</td><td>Date Started</td><td>Date Finished</td></tr>
<tr><td>Tom Sawyer</td><td>B</td><td>1</td><td>9/4/81</td><td>9/18/81</td></tr>
<tr><td></td><td></td><td></td><td></td><td></td></tr>
</table>

*Select one number and one letter to express your reaction.

A—easy book	1—very enjoyable
B—average book	2—interesting but not great
C—hard book	3—didn't like it at all

and decision making, but keep your format uncluttered and easy to fill out and to read. Two sample teacher records are shown in Figure 14.2.

Individualized reading requires much from both teachers and children. The teacher must be open and flexible as well as knowledgeable in the area of reading skills. Children must be independent and to a great extent self-motivated and self-confident. One thing to remember is that individualized reading does not mean that every child is working on something unique at all times. Children can work individually in groups formed by interest or needs. True individualization implies that each child is working on something he needs at that point in time.

If you are interested in more information and some suggestions about individualized reading, you will find the following books helpful:

Barbe, Walter B. 1961. *Educator's guide to personalized reading.* Englewood Cliffs, N.J.: Prentice-Hall.

Brogan, Peggy; and Fox, Lorene. 1961. *Helping children read: A practical approach to individualized reading.* New York: Holt, Rinehart.

Figure 14.2.

TEACHER RECORD OF BOOKS READ					
John Doe					KEY
TITLE	AUTHOR	Flu.*	Voc.	Comp.	U—Unsatisfactory
Rabbit Hill	Robert Lawson	F	VG	E	F—Fair
Kidnapped	Robert L. Stevenson	F	E	E	VG—Very Good
					E—Excellent

*Flu. = Fluency
Voc. = Vocabulary
Comp. = Comprehension

TEACHER READING RECORD				
John Flynn				
Book & Date	Understanding of Plot	Attitude	Word Recognition*	Skills Needed
12/10 How the Grinch Stole Christmas	O.K. Got moral of story. Offered it.	Needs pushing. Some improvement.	But/by (self-correction) snows/snooze tripping/trapping	Punctuation Medial vowels Good attack on new words Careless on old words

*Word said/Word in story

Veatch, Jeanette. 1978. *Reading in the elementary school,* 2nd ed. New York: John Wiley.

Linguistic Approaches

QUESTIONS TO GUIDE READING

Literal
What are the major features of linguistic approaches to reading?
Can you name at least two major linguistic reading series?

Linguistics is the scientific study of language. Linguists have spent a great
deal of effort in describing the structure of English — its units and patterns of sounds, its meanings, and its grammatical structures. As they
studied the oral aspects of language, some linguists began to wonder if
they might apply the findings of their work to reading, the written aspect
of language. In the most basic sense, they hypothesized, a child can "read"
when he can recognize the correspondences between the oral-language
signals for meanings and the written-language symbols for the same
meanings (i.e., he can pronounce the words he sees written). Because
written language is a code representing the sounds of spoken language,
they suggested that when a learner can break the code (i.e., recognize in
printed form those sounds and words he knows in spoken language), he
has learned to read.

Leonard Bloomfield (Bloomfield and Barnhart 1961) and Charles Fries
(1963) were two of the first linguists to create reading materials based on
what they felt is the fairly regular phoneme-grapheme correspondence of
the language. They selected word forms for beginning reading based on
scientific principles of regularity, simplicity, and frequency of use. In
creating their linguistic reading materials they and others incorporated
the following principles into their programs:

1. Speech is the primary vehicle of communication. Any child who has
   mastered oral language is ready for beginning reading.
2. The first steps in learning to read are learning the names of the letters
   of the alphabet, acquiring a left-to-right orientation, and learning to
   discriminate likenesses and differences in letter and word shapes.
3. Words selected for beginning reading materials should have consistent
   phoneme-grapheme or spelling patterns. This consistency forces the
   reader to attend to sound-symbol relationships rather than using other
   recognition techniques. Practice materials should consist of word families and nonsense syllables.
4. Pictures and illustrations should be eliminated from beginning reading
   materials because they furnish artificial cues to the words and detract
   attention from the words themselves.

5. Comprehension and interpretations are secondary to sound-symbol recognition. It is quite possible that one can learn to read without being able to understand.

THE PHONOLOGICAL APPROACH

Bloomfield's materials, *Let's Read, A Linguistic Approach* (Detroit: Wayne State University Press), are based on linguistic information about the most frequently used vowel and consonant sound elements in our language. In his exercises Bloomfield starts with words and phonic elements that will be easy and useful for beginning readers to master. These elements are short vowel sounds in easy three-letter words; the first words contain the /a/ vowel and proceed to /e/, /i/, /o/, and /u/ words. Because of this system of phonological patterning, Bloomfield's reading exercises read like this: "Dan can fan a tan man." When the student has mastered this pattern with the short vowel sounds, he proceeds with the second pattern — the long sounds of vowels.

Another linguist, Charles Fries, used much the same approach but based the selection of words taught on consistent spelling patterns (see Chapter 4). Like Bloomfield, Fries (1963) insisted that readers master those words utilizing the simpler spelling patterns before being asked to identify irregular words. The two major spelling patterns encountered in the English language, and therefore forming the basis of the *Merrill Linguistic Readers* at the primary levels, are:

1. Consonant-vowel-consonant;   p-a-n, p-a-t, p-a-d.
2. Consonant-vowel-consonant-vowel;   m-a-t-e, m-a-d-e.

Further, words utilizing the second pattern should not be introduced until the child has mastered and can make high-speed recognition responses to words written in pattern 1.

The most popular linguistic reading series currently in use is the Lippincott *Basic Reading* series (McCracken and Walcutt 1981). The writers of this series have tried to incorporate the best features of typical basal readers with a linguistic approach to word recognition (see Figure 14.3). Their purpose is not to provide teachers with a full basal series but rather to help children learn to read through a controlled step-by-step procedure to phonics mastery. Instructional sequences for word recognition skills in the beginning materials are limited by the patterned linguistic features previously discussed. As in other linguistic materials this one also follows the policy of introducing only one new variable at a time. As with all linguistic series the *Basic Reading* series moves quickly through their phonics program hoping to attain skills mastery by the end of the second grade. Features that make this series unique and noteworthy include

Figure 14.3.

Peg is upset.
Peg's dress is a mess.
The pig is a mess.
Peg must get damp rags.
Peg and the pig miss the show.

From *Starting Out*, Book A of *Lippincott Basic Reading*. Copyright © 1981, 1975 by J. B. Lippincott Company. Reprinted by permission of the publisher.

attention to an extensive readiness program, a strong emphasis on an auditory approach to teaching/learning at the primary levels, well-developed teacher's manuals, and an abundance of good-quality literary selections using a variety of genres for reading purposes.

Fishbein (1967, pp. 46–48) summarized the phonological approach to linguistic readers by comparing it with other phonics approaches to reading; he identified the following contrasts:

1. Linguistic approaches present one regular pattern at a time, which is based on minimal contrasts within the words: for example, *man, ran, pan, fan, fat,* as opposed to *fair, farm, fat, father* presented in other materials.
2. Linguistic approaches avoid drill on rules and generalizations; they emphasize instead drill on recognition of word features.

3. Linguistic approaches use a single method of word attack. Coupled with controlled introduction of sound-spelling patterns, this limitation makes it possible to present reading skills in a much more organized fashion.

THE STRUCTURAL APPROACH

Not all linguists are in agreement with the patterned approach to sounds presented by the phonological method. Structural linguists insist that phrases and sentences are the meaning-bearing units of language and should therefore be used as the basis for reading instruction. Linguist Ronald Wardhaugh (1975) has suggested that reading selections for the beginner should reflect the natural language of speech and should not be artifically controlled, except perhaps in skills practice exercises.

One of the few sets of instructional materials to reflect this point of view is the delightful *Sounds of Language* readers (written by Bill Martin, Jr., in collaboration with Peggy Brogan, and published by Holt, Rinehart and Winston (1970–1974). These materials were constructed on the premise that reading should be a natural extension of the child's knowledge and use of oral language. Materials in each of the readers, therefore, are selected on the basis of what is known about the naturally developing language patterns of children and about the ways they use language to communicate meanings and feelings.

LINGUISTIC APPROACHES: A SUMMARY

The research and literature growing out of the use of linguistic materials have raised a number of questions about linguistics and the teaching of reading. What parallels exist between patterns of sounds and letters in spoken and written words? Although speaking, reading, and writing are all part of the process of language, are they learned or taught in the same ways? Does knowing about language help children learn to read it more effectively? The answers to these and other questions are by no means conclusive but there are indications that what is "good" linguistically is not necessarily good reading practice. Wardhaugh (1969), for example, reported that the use of phonological linguistic materials produces oral readers who are inferior in terms of rate and word accuracy. Further, his research indicated that emphasis on structural language knowledge yields no measurable improvement in reading comprehension. Sheldon and others (1967, 1969), Schneyer (1969), and Ruddell (1967) conducted a series of controlled studies comparing linguistic readers with typical basal readers; they either found little difference in the effectiveness of linguistic approaches over typical basal programs or found that what differences did exist in word-decoding ability or oral reading disappeared by the end of the second or third grade.

Proponents of linguistic reading materials have pointed out that linguistics can make a contribution, as other disciplines have, to the teaching of reading. It may turn out that the contribution of linguistics is to show us the best learning sequence and teaching methods for the presentation of basic sounds. Gunderson (1972) contends that linguistic science will make contributions to the understanding of relationships among dialect, context clues, and comprehension. It is the teacher, however, and not the linguist who can determine the best ways to use knowledge about language.

For a further evaluation of linguistic materials the reader may wish to study "Linguistic-Phonemics Approaches" in *Approaches to Beginning Reading* (Aukerman 1971, pp. 141–227), where various materials with linguistic orientation are described.

Intensive Phonics Approaches

QUESTIONS TO GUIDE READING

Literal
What are some characteristics of the intensive phonics approaches?

Evaluative
Should intensive phonics approaches be basically supplemental? Why or why not?

Another category of materials available to teachers is in many respects similar to linguistic materials. These materials, referred to as intensive phonics materials, also focus on decoding in the reading process. Proponents of the intensive phonics approaches generally believe that when the child has mastered decoding, he is on his way to handling independently all written materials.

Most intensive phonics materials are supplemental. Since they stress initial decoding skills, few are designed to be used beyond grade three, except for remedial purposes. Several of these materials emphasize the synthetic approach to teaching phonics (see Chapter 4). Children learn letter-sound associations in isolation and then are taught to blend these sounds to form words. Initially, children blend sounds to produce two- or three-letter words, then proceed to progressively longer ones. In a sense this is a spelling approach to reading, and some teachers have so used it.

Another characteristic of these materials is their tendency to stress memorization of rules and generalizations. Most teach children twenty to sixty phonic generalizations, which they then apply to the decoding of new words. (Refer to Chapter 4 on phonics teaching to find what is known about the utility of most phonic generalizations.) The drilling necessary for learning these rules creates an instructional problem for phonics-based materials in maintaining learner interest and motivation.

INTENSIVE PHONICS PROGRAMS AND MATERIALS

Several of the intensive phonics approaches purport to be similar to basal programs in that they are total programs. They provide the teacher with readers, teacher's manuals, teaching charts, workbooks, and supplementary materials. Among the most widely known are:

McCracken, Glenn; and Walcutt, Charles C. 1981. *Lippincott Basic Reading Series*. Philadelphia: J. B. Lippincott.

Trace, Jr., Arthur S.; and Carus, Marrianne, eds. 1979. *Open Court, Headway Program*. La Salle, Ill.: Open Court.

These readers differ from other basal programs in that there is an intensive emphasis on sound relationships or patterns. Vocabulary control is regulated by these patterns rather than by the frequency of word use or occurrence of words in children's language.

In addition, there are several programs that are designed to be supplementary: they contain supplementary charts, games, and exercises. Among the better known examples of this type of material is the *Phonovisual Method*, written by Lucille Schoolfield and Josephine Timberlake (1960) and published by Phonovisual Products Company of Rockville, Md.

DISTAR READING PROGRAM

The Distar Reading Program (Science Research Associates) was designed to teach reading and academic skills to culturally deprived children, slow learners, and children with below-average communication skills. According to its developers the program should enable children who have mental ages of four years or above to learn to read (Engleman and Bruner 1969).

The Distar Program uses a highly structured behavioral approach to teach the following skills:

1. Symbol-action activities. These activities are designed to teach left-right progression and the association of a sound with a symbol. The children are taught the sounds in fixed order in words and to spell by orally pronouncing the sounds: e.g., /c/-⟨at⟩ = /kuh/-⟨at⟩.

2. Blending tasks. The children are taught that sounds of words can be said slowly by carefully saying the sounds of each letter, /kuh-aaa-tuh/, and then blended by saying it fast (*cat*).
3. Rhyming tasks. These activities are used to teach children to recognize the relationship between sounds and words. After twenty sounds have been learned the children begin reading storybooks that contain from one to twenty-five words.

Children are taught in small groups of no more than five each. Each twenty- to thirty-minute lesson is preplanned with prepared materials and written dialog for the teacher, which specifies suggestions for what to say, what tone of voice to use, and what hand movements would be appropriate. Student materials include take home blending sheets, sound-symbol sheets, short stories, writing sheets, and workbook pages.

Because of the emphasis on auditory skills upon which the program is structured, some teachers report that Distar is not effective for children who have difficulty with auditory processing. Other teachers react negatively to the rigidity of the structure of the program. Some, however, have found the program to be effective with certain children and praise its organization, structure, and written format (Boyd 1975). According to Haring and Bateman (1977), Distar appears to be successful with children who have had extensive school failure in the past.

STRENGTHS AND WEAKNESSES OF INTENSIVE PHONICS APPROACHES

In his report on first grade reading programs, Kerfoot (1965) summarized the claims of strength and the charges of weakness made about phonics approaches to teaching beginning reading. Among the strengths claimed by proponents are these: (1) that phonics-based approaches aid the child with auditory perception and visual-auditory discrimination; (2) that phonics approaches build confidence in word recognition skills by teaching the child a systematic way to learn letter sounds and to unlock strange, new words; and (3) that phonics approaches aid the learner in spelling and composition skills.

strengths

Opponents, on the other hand, level several charges against the phonics approach: (1) that the phonics approach inhibits the learning of other reading skills, such as comprehension, by overemphasizing phonics in the beginning stages of learning to read; (2) that memorization of phonics rules is harmful because of their many exceptions and because the learning of these rules does not ensure the child's ability to use them anyway; (3) that intensive phonics materials place more emphasis on sounding out words than on the meaning of the words; (4) that they are ineffective for children with hearing problems; and (5) that they can seriously interfere with a child's motivation for reading by overemphasizing intensive drill on sounds.

opponents.

Changed Alphabets

QUESTIONS TO GUIDE READING

Literal
What is ITA? Unifon? DMS?

Inferential
Does a changed alphabet make decoding easier for the child?

Evaluative
Considering dialectal and ideolectical differences, is a one-sound/one-letter written language system possible?
Under what circumstances would a teacher elect to use ITA?

The English language uses twenty-six letters of the alphabet to represent what linguists have variously described as forty to fifty-two speech sounds. It is obvious that many letters have to be used in multiple combinations if all the sounds of the language are to be represented in writing. There are, therefore, occasions when the letter ⟨a⟩, for example, represents several different sounds, as in *cat, car, fair, father, hall,* or is silent in words such as *boat.* Critics of the English spelling system have seen this lack of a one-to-one correspondence between the phonemes and graphemes of our language as one of the major sources of difficulty for beginning readers. How can a child learn decoding, they ask, if he cannot rely on a given sound always being spelled the same way?

For centuries reformers have been attempting to change the alphabet to achieve a greater correspondence between the sounds and the spellings of our language. George Bernard Shaw left a portion of his estate to be used as a prize for the best developer of such an alphabet. Even Benjamin Franklin wrote about the inadequacies of the English spelling system. A recent effort in this direction gained prominence in England in 1961 under the development and direction of Sir James Pittman and was introduced to this country by John Downing of England in 1963. This new alphabet is called the Initial Teaching Alphabet, or ITA; as used in America it consists of forty-four symbols — one for each phoneme in our language.

The ITA is made up of twenty-four of the letters found in the traditional alphabet plus twenty new ones. (See Figure 14.4.)

Proponents of ITA recommend that it is not a program for teaching reading but rather a system of writing and spelling. As such, it should be used only in beginning reading instruction — to help young readers make the sight-sound associations necessary for decoding. From the beginning, students are also encouraged to write in ITA because it enables them to avoid the traditional hazards of spelling (Downing et al. 1967). Dallmann

Figure 14.4. The ITA.

b bed   c cat   d dog   f fish   g goat

h hat   j jug   k key   l lion   m man

n nest   p pet   r rabbit   s sun   t table

v voice   w window   y yellow   z zipper

a apple   e engine   i insect   o octopus   u umbrella

æ angel   ŒŒ eel   iͤe ice   œ oatmeal   uͤe uniform

wh wheel   ch chair   ſh shoe   th thumb   th that

au auto   oi oil   ou ow!   ŋ ring   ʒ dogs

ʒ garage   ɼ bird   a father   ω book   ᘯ moon

and others (1978, p. 162) identify the major advantages of the ITA system as claimed by its proponents:

1. It is much simpler for the child to learn to read by means of a symbol-sound code in which every character has but one sound and in which every sound is represented by only one symbol.
2. Children learn to read much more rapidly with ITA than with traditional orthography.

3. Making the transition from reading ITA to reading traditional orthography is relatively easy, so that soon after making the changeover the learner can read even in traditional orthography more effectively than one who started reading in that orthography.

4. Pupils taught with ITA have greater skill in written self-expression than boys and girls using traditional orthography.

5. Children with speech defects who are taught with ITA as a beginning method of reading instruction are likely to be helped more toward lessening or overcoming their speech difficulties than are other children with comparable defects who learn reading with traditional orthography.

There are also opponents of ITA. The problem they cite most frequently is that of making the transfer from reading in ITA to reading in the traditional alphabet once the child has gained proficiency in reading. Because a certain amount of unlearning must take place, they question whether any initial gains experienced are worth the confusion during the transition. Critics also point to the possibility that spelling problems may result from the transition. Harris and Smith (1976, p. 182), however, indicated that most studies do not bear out this criticism. The cost of purchasing a second set of instructional readers, library materials, or teaching charts is also seen as a negative factor in considering ITA materials. Opponents also point to the mobility of the American population as being a problem. The adjustment process for those children moving into or out of such a program, they say, is not worth the effort. Finally, critics of ITA claim that comparative research studies are inconclusive, and subject to the Hawthorne effect (i.e., the child knows he is part of an experimental program and he tends to perform better than might be anticipated in response to the attention he is getting, not necessarily because superior materials elicit a superior response); they feel that the problems of ITA are great, especially since research findings are not conclusive (Marsh 1968).

There are other modified alphabet programs sometimes found in use. Unifon is a forty-symbol alphabet developed by John R. Malone of Park Forest, Illinois. Malone developed Unifon (an acronym for uniformly phonetic) to help his son learn sound-letter relationships. Unlike ITA this program uses only capital letters and adds a few new symbols for vowel phonemes. A major disadvantage of Unifon is the lack of published materials for teaching and supplementary reading.

Another changed alphabet system is the Diacritical Marking System (DMS) developed by Edward Fry. Fry describes his system as follows (1972, pp. 393–394):

> The Diacritical Marking System (DMS) that I have developed has over 99 percent phoneme-grapheme regularity and aims at achieving essentially the same goals as the Initial Teaching Alphabet without distortion in word form or change in spelling.

The DMS is somewhat simpler than the diacritical marking systems found in most dictionaries, since the intention is to aid beginning readers rather than to give extreme accuracy. Regular consonants and short vowels have a bar over them. Regular two-letter combinations which make unique sounds such as the consonant digraphs and diphthongs have a bar under both letters. Silent letters have a slash mark through them. These marks plus a few others, such as those used for the broad a and other sounds of u, constitute the bulk of the marks used. Nearly every word used in first-grade reading books is marked; likewise, all work that a teacher duplicates or puts on the board contains the DMS marks. In writing, children have the option of using or not using the marks.

As with Unifon there is a lack of materials published for teaching or supplementary reading.

There are few school systems using modified alphabet programs today, and the popularity they enjoyed during the early 1960s seems to have disappeared. It is sometimes possible to find them being used for remedial purposes with children who have failed to see consistency in traditional spelling-pronunciation relationships. They are also able sometimes to motivate the reluctant reader who is having limited success in the regular program. The secret code aspect of the new alphabet enables this child to rekindle an excitement with reading that has been lost. As with all materials and programs they can be used to meet the needs of some of the children at some times.

Programmed Materials and Systems Programs

QUESTIONS TO GUIDE READING

Literal
What are the different formats in which programmed instruction appears in the classroom?

Inferential
What learner needs are met by programmed materials?

Evaluative
When would a teacher consider using programmed instruction as a part of the reading program?
Is the high expense of computer programs justified?

RATIONALE FOR PROGRAMMED MATERIALS

In the mid-1950s educational methods and materials began to be influenced in a significant way from a hitherto quiet quarter of the profession, the educational psychologist. Bolstered with fresh successes in the field of animal psychology, this group began to apply concepts of operant conditioning to the arena of classroom teaching and in so doing was influential in helping to produce several types of programmed learning materials.

The psychological premises underlying all programmed materials are the same, whether we are examining a simple programmed workbook or a sophisticated talking computer. They are as follows:

1. Objectives are stated as observable behaviors. This is an essential feature; if it is not immediately obvious in the materials themselves, it can certainly be documented in detail in teacher's manuals.
2. The learner makes a response at each step. It is through these responses that the learner's behavior is shaped.
3. The learner receives immediate feedback and support.
4. The learner works at his own pace.
5. Programs focus on specific skills.
6. All skills are carefully sequenced.

MATERIALS, METHODS, STRENGTHS, AND LIMITATIONS

Programmed instructional materials generally appear in classrooms in one of three formats: workbooks, or software; teaching machines, or hardware of various kinds; and management systems. Of these, programmed workbooks are perhaps best known and the most widely used. Programmed reading materials usually consist of books of very short problems boxed in linear frames. Each book or series of books is designed to lead the student toward proficiency in identifiable reading skills. Generally the materials have an answer column which the student covers with a marker. He then proceeds to work his way through the material frame by frame, reading the enclosed material and answering the questions asked. As he works he checks his responses and, if correct, moves on to the next frame. If incorrect, he has a chance to stop, look for his errors, make the necessary corrections, and move on. The best known of these materials, the *Sullivan Programmed Readers* (McGraw-Hill), uses a series of twenty-one books to lead the learner from alphabet knowledge through sound-symbol relationships (via a linguistic format) to reading for facts and main ideas on approximately a fifth or sixth grade reading level. (See Figure 14.5.)

There are several additional sources of programmed workbook materials, including:

Bondanze, William J.; and Bacci, William A. *Phonics for pupils.* New London, Conn.: Croft Educational.
Two programs covering the entire phonics curriculum.

Figure 14.5.

fits

Ann f___ts it in a pan.

pats

Sam ___ats Nip.

singing

Ann is $\Big<$ sitting.
singing.

pin

This is a $\Big<$ pin.
pan.

pa **n**

This is a pa___.

Reprinted from *Programmed Reading, Book I*, by C. B. Buchanan, copyright 1963, with permission of Webster/McGraw-Hill.

Lepehne, Renate. *Building words.* Cambridge, Mass.: Honor Products.
   A short program in structural analysis.
Loretan, Joseph O., ed. *Building reading power.* Columbus, Ohio: Charles
   E. Merrill Publishing Company.
   Several programmed booklets on contextual clues and structural
   analysis for upper grade students.
Mott reading programs. Galien, Mich.: Allied Education Council.
   Phonics workbooks written in a semiprogrammed format for each
   grade level.

Because of their methodical step-by-step presentation of information
and their reliance on repetition and reinforcement, programmed learning
materials and devices seem to be very effective with remedial readers and
with corrective-level readers (those reading slightly below grade level) in
need of catch-up skills reinforcement. These materials are particularly
well suited to the teaching of word recognition skills, vocabulary, and
lower level comprehension skills. In addition, they have value in that they
can be used to free teachers from drill-type instruction so that their
instructional time might be used more effectively elsewhere.

There are problems associated with the use of programmed teaching
materials, however. Foremost has been the lack of well-written, well-
structured programs. It is easier to produce programs than to produce
programs of high quality. Those programs mentioned in this text are
among the exceptions. Programmed materials cannot do an adequate job
of teaching higher level comprehension skills — such as interpretation,
analytic thinking, and critical reading. Nor can they contribute effectively
to the development of study skills and flexible reading rates. Their use
with above-average readers should be discouraged because the repetition
is often boring and of little use to these students.

TEACHING MACHINES AND COMPUTERS

The second type of programmed learning device used in reading programs
is teaching machines; these range in sophistication from the *Cyclo Teacher*
(Field Enterprises), which is a phonic wheel inserted in a special plastic
machine, to such devices as the *Systems 80* program (Borg-Warner), talking typewriters, and computer-assisted learning devices. With these materials the objective and basic format is the same as that utilized with the
software materials. However, the child interacts with some sort of audio-
visual device. He may sit before a TV screen or that of a small projector.
He often has a terminal similar to a typewriter or a multiple-choice set
of keys to activate when he wishes to indicate his responses, and is corrected or reinforced by the machine — either through an auditory comment or through a continuation of the materials being taught.
   The new generation of computer hardware goes far beyond these mod-

est initial efforts. The development of microtechnology has resulted in a new era of computer hardware and computer assisted reading programs. Suddenly we are being assaulted with Apples, TRS-80s, floppy-disks, softcards, and printers. This new generation of sophisticated computer technology is creating new opportunities and challenges for tomorrow's readers and reading teachers. It is now possible for readers to interact with "intelligent" machines that will listen with infinite patience to their reading lessons. Computer equipment can now diagnose a learner's abilities, select lessons appropriate to specific needs, and store an up-to-date record of progress made. The same equipment can supply teachers with hard copy printouts of a reader's diagnostic profiles and progress reports, run readabilities using a choice of formulas, or call up bibliographies of library materials grouped by interest area and reading level. Jinks (1981) envisions truly amazing possibilities for tomorrow's classrooms.

> Picture a junior high history class studying the Twentieth Century using ethnotronic systems capable of holographic simulations. Teddy Roosevelt could actually appear to visit the class. The vision, unlike film, would be interactive. In other words, the simulated Mr. Roosevelt would respond directly to the class much as an actor might.
>
> The difference would be that the hologram is backed by an information base which has in storage every piece of information known about the man. It can pull information about him and his time from storage at practically light speed while adjusting its responses to information it also contains about the class. Neither actors nor teachers have such capabilities. . . . A student would not be restricted to reading books, looking at still and moving pictures, and listening to lectures about Teddy Roosevelt — the student could interview him.

Tomorrow's reading teachers face the possibility of having to redefine literacy or at least accept responsibility for teaching a second type — a computer literacy. A time of excitement and challenge is ahead of us.

MANAGEMENT SYSTEMS

Another development in programmed instruction consists of those programs best described as management systems. Among the best known of these systems are the Croft Inservice Reading Program (Croft Educational Services), Fountain Valley Teacher Support System (Richard L. Zweig Associates), Prescriptive Reading Inventory (CTM/McGraw-Hill), and Wisconsin Design for Reading Skill Development (Interpretive Scoring Systems).

These new systems approaches integrate one of the major features of the programmed materials discussed previously, behaviorally stated program objectives, with a new feature, the criterion-referenced test. Instead of comparing a student to norms based on broad national groups, a criterion-referenced test evaluates a student's mastery of specific and explicit behavioral objectives. Every item on the test is associated with one of these objectives. The systems programs, then, are made up of the following elements:

1. a list of explicitly stated behavioral objectives (often a list of more than 300 objectives ranging from primary through upper level skills);
2. a battery of criterion-referenced tests designed to measure competency with the stated objectives;
3. student profile sheets that record and display a profile of student or class strengths and weaknesses on skills;
4. prescription guides keyed to widely used reading programs to provide teachers with the pages in the teacher's editions and workbooks that can be used to teach or reinforce specific skills; and
5. (in some programs) a prepared set of suggested classroom activities or worksheets keyed to the behavioral objectives listed and tested; these can be used for instruction or practice.

We can see that these programs are in reality classroom management systems, having the very real potential of redefining the role of the teacher to that of manager and record keeper for individual learners and groups of learners.

Combining Approaches and Materials: Is There a Best Way?

QUESTIONS TO GUIDE READING

Literal
How do the authors of this text feel that approaches and materials are best used?

Evaluative
Could an approach or program other than basals, language experience, or individualized reading be the core for a reading program? Why? On what bases would a teacher decide what the "core" should be?

You have probably sensed that the authors of this text have an eclectic attitude about the approaches and materials discussed in this part; we feel that differing approaches and materials are generally best used in combination, with special consideration being given to the unique conditions within the instructional setting — for instance, the needs of the learners, experience and competency of the teacher, physical restrictions of the classroom, and materials available for use. For many children the language experience approach — with its close relationship to the language patterns and concept load of the learner — may be a most effective approach with beginning readers, especially with the culturally and linguistically different. A basal program — with its structure and planned sequence of skills — may provide a basis for students who need to move methodically through a developmental sequence of skills. Individualized reading may be especially effective with gifted learners, who would be turned off by the structure of a basal program, or as a strategy for capitalizing on the interests and backgrounds of all students, regardless of their levels of reading ability.

Most experienced teachers select basals, language experience, or individualized reading as the core on which to center instruction, keeping the other two to reinforce, extend, or enrich the skills of the class members. The alternative approaches and materials presented in this chapter may also be used in programs for meeting specific specialized needs or interests.

Let us consider an illustration: In a second grade classroom, Mr. Farrell decides to use basal readers as the central component of his program. This program, using reading groups, provides Mr. Farrell with direction, along with well-planned lessons and resource materials. In addition, the framework and structure of the program assure him that he is presenting the needed reading skills in a systematic and developmental fashion. Children in the classroom who are experiencing reading difficulties or who are culturally or linguistically different pose a different challenge for the teacher; Mr. Farrell decides to have them work with language experience activities and he may continue with the approach for some time to help them see the relationship between spoken and written communication. The more able boys and girls in his class may occasionally utilize and extend their writing skills via the language experience approach — by writing and illustrating booklets about the units of work they are doing in other subjects. Mr. Farrell makes certain that many trade books are available so that the children can select and read materials that are interesting and useful to them. It may be especially important for his better readers to begin learning how to keep reading records, as well as to learn to collect and report back information. As need arises, Mr. Farrell has the option of selecting from various programmed instruction, phonic or linguistic workbooks, and audio-visual materials to meet specific skills deficiencies in his learners, or to enrich and extend the reading program.

Mr. Farrell, like most of today's professional educators, has found that there is no best material, approach, or program for reading instruction. What is most appropriate changes as the students change. Determining the best fit to students is accomplished only after looking carefully at student needs, characteristics of the school and community, and teacher abilities and instructional goals.

As children are at the center of the school program, selecting materials without considering their collective and individual needs would be foolish. What are the language needs and abilities of your learners? What kinds of out-of-school experiences and activities do they bring with them? Do they work better independently or in groups? Do they have good work habits and do they value reading as an activity?

Schools do not exist in isolation but are part of a larger community structure. Knowing about the community and school structure is helpful in deciding how best to accomplish your instructional goals. Do you have any choices in the selection of materials and approaches in your program or have these choices been made for you? If they have, can you deviate from them should you wish to? Does your school show evidence of valuing open, flexible teaching or is it highly structured? Is there an adequate variety of materials for instruction and library reading?

Of course teachers as classroom managers must look to their own teaching styles and abilities when selecting appropriate teaching vehicles. What are my instructional goals in reading? What do I expect my students to know and be able to do as a result of participation in my program? Am I a creative teacher who enjoys making materials? Do I prefer having the structured guidance of a manual? Am I comfortable with several group activities going on at once or do I need to feel more control over my classes? Do I enjoy teaching reading and am I an active reader myself?

Thoughtful answers to these questions are a necessary part of selecting appropriate approaches, materials, and programs for your school and class. There are many combinations appropriate for given populations at differing grade levels. The important point is that the best programs must be developed to meet the goals of the instructional situation and the needs of the learner.

Summary

A variety of approaches, materials, and programs for reading instruction have been reviewed and discussed in this chapter. Each of these reflects the philosophy of an individual or group of specialists about the teaching process as it relates to reading instruction. Each wants the same thing for children: independence in reading. Each differs, however, in its way of achieving that goal. It is imperative that you react to and reflect on each of these approaches, materials, and programs in light of your own philosophy of reading, what is known about child growth and development, and how you feel about your role and that of the learner in the teaching/learning process.

Questions for Further Reading and Thinking

1. Considering all the materials and the several approaches available for teachers to select from, what distinguishes a "good" program from a "bad" one?
2. What is your understanding of what constitutes high-interest controlled-vocabulary materials? What need do they fulfill in the teaching of reading?
3. Assuming that no single instructional approach or set of materials is adequate as a total reading program, what combination of approaches or materials would you select for use in your classroom? Why?
4. It has been said that the techniques and materials of reading are greatly influenced by the social patterns and educational philosophies of a society and by the teaching philosophy of its teachers. If this is true, how do you account for the continued popularity of, and heavy reliance on, the basal reading method and materials in light of the growing emphasis on individualized learning styles, open classrooms, etc.?
5. Compare ITA as a changed alphabet with UNIFON (Western Publishing Educational Services, 1220 Mound Avenue, Racine, Wisconsin, 53404). What are the similarities and differences between the two? What are the advantages and disadvantages of UNIFON?

Activities and Projects

1. Compare a basal reader for the first grade with a linguistic reader for the same level. How are they alike, and how do they differ? Do the same with readers for the third grade level.
2. Examine and read a book printed in ITA. Do you find it to be very easy or difficult to read? Why?
3. Use the form that follows to examine and evaluate at least six kinds of reading materials:
   Programmed readers
   Basal readers (from at least two different publishers)
   One set of linguistic readers
   Sounds of Language readers (Holt, Rinehart and Winston)
   ITA readers
   One set of phonic reading materials or series

TEXTBOOK EVALUATION FORM
(Suggestions of things to look for)

Subject:

Title:

Author:

Publisher:

Copyright date:

	Excellent	Good	Fair	Poor
1. Content	☐	☐	☐	☐
a. Appropriateness of content	☐	☐	☐	☐
b. Accuracy and correctness	☐	☐	☐	☐
c. Up-to-dateness	☐	☐	☐	☐
d. Objectivity and freedom from bias	☐	☐	☐	☐
e. Treatment of controversial issues	☐	☐	☐	☐
f. Adequacy of coverage and detail	☐	☐	☐	☐
2. Organization	☐	☐	☐	☐
a. Organization into units or themes	☐	☐	☐	☐
b. Continuity and sequence of presenting materials	☐	☐	☐	☐
c. Use of examples, illustration, and incidents	☐	☐	☐	☐
3. Style	☐	☐	☐	☐
a. Sentence structure and correctness of usage	☐	☐	☐	☐
b. Literary style	☐	☐	☐	☐
c. Simplicity, clarity, and directness of presentation	☐	☐	☐	☐
4. Supplementary	☐	☐	☐	☐
a. Workbooks	☐	☐	☐	☐
b. Exercises, reviews, and discussion guides	☐	☐	☐	☐
c. Annotated bibliography	☐	☐	☐	☐
d. Chapter and unit introductions and summaries	☐	☐	☐	☐
e. Audio-visual tapes (masters, filmstrips, etc.)	☐	☐	☐	☐
5. Format	☐	☐	☐	☐
a. Cover, binding, and size	☐	☐	☐	☐
b. Quality of paper	☐	☐	☐	☐
c. Legibility of type	☐	☐	☐	☐

	Excellent	Good	Fair	Poor
6. Cost per pupil	☐	☐	☐	☐
a. Expensive	☐	☐	☐	☐
b. Average	☐	☐	☐	☐
c. Inexpensive	☐	☐	☐	☐
7. Manual	☐	☐	☐	☐
a. Ease of use	☐	☐	☐	☐
b. Adaptability	☐	☐	☐	☐
c. Variety of suggestions	☐	☐	☐	☐
d. Usefulness of suggestions	☐	☐	☐	☐
e. Background information for teachers	☐	☐	☐	☐

Part Five

PROGRAM PLANNING

An effective reading program involves more than a foundation of readiness experiences, the development of cognitive skills, and the utilization of specific approaches for managing skills and experiences in some logical order. Other variables impinge on the act of processing print. Perhaps the most important of these is the teacher. It is the teacher, more than program, materials, skills sequence, or organizational pattern, that is crucial in an effective program. Ways that teachers can contribute to an effective program permeate this entire text.

In addition to the role of the teacher, there are other important considerations for program planning. Among these considerations — which are developed in this part — are *crucial* aspects of the affective domain, ways to help culturally and linguistically different children, ways to diagnose and evaluate reading proficiency, ways to organize the classroom, ways to utilize parents in the instructional program, and the fact that the "hows" and "whys" of reading instruction change over time.

J. Estill Alexander

15

Affective Dimensions

Today one hears much about the need for a "return to basics" in our schools. Most persons who make such statements are referring to the cognitive domain — knowledges and skills. The cognitive domain is indeed basic. Yet the affective domain is also important. In Chapter 1 it was stated that affect has an important function in reading. In the opinion of this writer the affective function is one of the basics that is badly in need of attention.

Certain affective behaviors or dispositions have been labeled with terms such as attitudes, interests, self-concept, values, and motivation. As noted in Chapter 1, Mathewson (1976, pp. 655–676) delineated an affective model of the reading process that focused on five components: attitude, motivation, attention, comprehension, and acceptance. In this model he posits attitude (evaluative responses to aspects of reading input such as form, content, and format) as the central construct. The second component, motivation, is said to represent the presence of a strong action orientation or interest.

This chapter focuses primarily on three aspects of affect — attitudes, self-concepts, and student interests as motivators. Discussion is provided on assessment and on techniques for promoting positive attitudes, positive self-concept, and lasting interests. The thesis of this chapter is that a reading program, to be successful, must foster learners who read, and who feel good about themselves and about their ability to use reading to satisfy some felt personal or informational need.

Attitudes and Reading

This section focuses on the research that seems relevant on attitudes, on ways to assess attitudes, and on strategies for developing and maintaining positive attitudes.[1] Attitudes are defined as how students feel about reading in general. Some theorists have proposed that attitudes consist of three components: cognitive, affective, and behavioral (both intended and actual). The cognitive component is defined differently here than is cognition in Chapter 1. Here, the cognitive component refers to beliefs, information, and perceptions about the reading act. The affective component is concerned with the student's evaluation of how he feels about reading; and the behavioral refers to the student's intention or action in relationship to his feelings. It may be difficult for teachers to distinguish among these components. Teachers often view attitudes only as positive or negative evaluations. Such evaluations can lead to effective assessment and instruction, however, inasmuch as they may involve significant

1. The material in this section is based on *Attitudes and Reading* by J. Estill Alexander and Ronald C. Filler (Newark, Del.: The International Reading Association, 1976).

knowledge about how students feel and may result in teacher behaviors that help students deal more effectively with the reading environment.

CORRELATES

Research on the factors that correlate with attitude development and maintenance is limited. An excellent synthesis of quality research done on attitudes as they relate to reading has been written by Patsy McLain Davis (1978). The discussion that follows will be based partially on her work and on a monograph coauthored by the present writer (Alexander and Filler 1976).

Defensible generalizations are difficult to make from the available data since the findings are based mostly on correlational data that do not denote cause-and-effect relationships. We should also note that factors do not necessarily operate independently of each other. The nature of these interrelationships has not been established.

Achievement. The findings of the studies dealing with the relationship between positive attitudes and reading achievement are somewhat contradictory. There is frequently a positive relationship between higher achievement and positive attitudes (Dotson 1977); but this is not always the case, and teachers should not expect such a relationship to exist necessarily (Alexander and Filler 1976). Teachers may gain some valuable insights into possible relationships from the studies that have been done. For example, Ransbury (1973) found that some children may attribute their own reading attitudes primarily to their ability to read. In such a situation, a reading improvement program would logically be a high-priority item for underachievers. Also, the selection of appropriate materials might be crucial because the reader's attitude toward the content of the material may affect his level of comprehension (Groff 1962).

On one hand, Healy (1965) found that it is possible to change attitudes toward reading, which resulted in increased achievement and more reading; the attitudes were maintained over time. Yet on the other hand, it is only fair to caution the teacher that positive attitudes are not necessarily self-maintaining. In Johnson's study (1965), students exhibited poorer attitudes toward reading at each successively higher grade level. Thus, while it may be possible to effect a permanent change in attitudes, it may also not happen. Attention to the affective domain must be given at all grade levels.

Self-concept. Self-concept, defined as an individual's perception of himself, is said to determine how the individual will behave (Moustakes 1956, p. 10). The research in this area has been largely related to achievement. According to Quandt (1972, p. 7), there is strong evidence that a positive relationship exists between levels of reading achievement and levels of self-concept. Attitudes toward reading also are related to levels of self-concept (Glick 1972).

Home environment and classroom atmosphere. The quality of the environment from which the student comes (parents and home environment) and in which the student learns (the teacher and classroom atmosphere) may also affect attitudes. This "quality" environment includes both the verbal and overt behaviors of teachers and parents and their nonverbal behaviors. Expectations for student performance and evaluations of their reading behaviors are often signaled through tone of voice, facial expressions, and posture movements. It is important to remember that students interpret these signals very well.

Findings from some studies that focused on the quality of the learner's environment have serious implications for teachers. For example, teachers may find in students what they expect to find. The results of one study (Palardy 1969) showed that in the classrooms of teachers who felt boys would be less successful than girls in learning to read, boys were truly less successful. The data also revealed that in classrooms of teachers who felt boys would be as successful as girls, the boys were as successful.

In addition to teacher expectations of success or failure, there are many other environmental factors that affect a student's attitude. A warm, friendly, and approving classroom atmosphere may alter a child's attitude and motivation for reading, according to Carver (1971). In a study of classroom atmosphere, Cleworth (1958) stated that pleasant surroundings, a cooperative spirit within the group, adequate and appropriate materials, and an organized study plan are important in attitude formation.

The role of parents is also crucial. For example, Hansen (1969) notes that parent involvement with the child's reading activities through "working with homework; encouraging, helping select, and discussing his reading; reading to him; assistance in looking things up in dictionaries and encyclopedias; and setting reading goals . . . may be related to positive attitude formation." What parents *do* with their children is important; and as Davis (1978) concluded is more important than the father's occupation or socioeconomic status, parental educational level, or the number of books available in the home.

Parents influence attitude in another way. Preston (1939) found that parents exhibit more negative attitudes toward children once they develop reading problems. Maladjustment may increase as the parents make derogatory remarks about the child, reproach him, or deny him privileges in an effort to get him to overcome his problem. How the parents *feel* about the child and his reading often makes a difference.

Instructional programs. There have been several studies to investigate the change in attitudes toward reading when special programs or practices are used. The results are not definitive. Perhaps the most valid

generalization that can be made is that the effects of instructional practices and special programs *can* but not necessarily *will* affect attitudes
(Squire 1969). There may be interactions occurring with other factors,
such as the teacher and the classroom atmosphere. The teacher and his
enthusiasm for a given practice or program may often be the key ingre-
dient in any attitude change that occurs. Class size does not appear to be
related to reading attitudes (Huser 1967).

Sex, intelligence, socioeconomic status, and race. There are a few beliefs,
held by some teachers, that are sometimes but not *always* supported by
research and may be harmful since teacher expectations may affect outcomes. These include the beliefs that girls have more positive attitudes
toward reading than boys (Hall 1977; Greenberg et al. 1965), that more
intelligent students have more positive attitudes than less intelligent students (Groff 1962), that students from higher socioeconomic classes have
more positive attitudes than do students from lower levels (Hansen 1969),
and that race may be related to positive or negative attitudes (Johnson
and Jacobson 1968). Teachers are cautioned not to make assumptions
about the effects that sex, intelligence, socioeconomic status, and race
may have on attitudes until they have assessed the specific attitudes of
the students in their classrooms. The findings may be different from what
was expected.

Interests. There is not much research on the specific nature of the relationship between interests and attitudes. Student interests are said to be
related to a number of factors within the learner and his environment.
These factors will be discussed in a later section of this chapter.

ASSESSING ATTITUDES

If teachers are to promote positive attitudes or change negative attitudes,
they must use some assessment tool or technique. Many good teachers
assess attitudes informally — at times intuitively and pretty much unconsciously. Yet many teachers, especially beginning teachers, may need
or wish to assess attitudes consciously and objectively. The purposes of
this section are to assist teachers in devising assessment instruments and
to make suggestions for the administration and interpretation of such
instruments.

In assessing attitudes both reactive and nonreactive measures should
be used (Reed 1979). These forms complement each other when teachers
are making determinations about attitudes. In the reactive situation students are aware they are being assessed and often participate in that
assessment. Interviewing and paper-and-pencil techniques often fit in this
category. In the nonreactive situation (such as observation) students are
not aware they are being assessed.

Accuracy of student responses in attitude assessments is often difficult to ensure. It is not enough to tell students that they should respond as they feel and that the teacher will not evaluate their responses punitively. More accurate responses may result if the student is told that the teacher is gathering information to help him choose more appropriate materials, decide what points to emphasize, and formulate new organizational patterns. An effective way to ensure honesty is to be calm and natural, treating the assessment situation as an ordinary routine classroom activity. In any event, interpretations should be based on assessment situation over a period of time. Specific suggestions to consider follow.

Observation. As a nonreactive tool, observation is a valuable way to assess attitudes. When possible, the teacher should determine in advance what behaviors she will observe, and develop a checklist to guide the observation process. The needs of the teacher will determine the specific behaviors she includes on the checklist. The best way to note significant behaviors is to observe students in informal, nonstructured situations such as play time, lunch, conversations with peers, library time, and independent reading or work/study periods in the classroom.

An observational guide (Table 15.1) has been developed by Heathington and Alexander (1978), with checklist items based on interviews with children in grades 1 through 6. The children were asked to talk about the behaviors they thought indicated positive or negative attitudes toward reading. It is recommended that the observation time consist of a period of two weeks or more.

Another observational guide is *A Scale of Reading Attitude Based on*

Table 15.1. Observation Checklist to Assess Reading Attitudes

In the two-week period, has the child:	Yes	No
1. Seemed happy when engaged in reading activities?		
2. Volunteered to read aloud in class?		
3. Read a book during free time?		
4. Mentioned reading a book at home?		
5. Chosen reading over other activities (playing games, coloring, talking, etc.)?		
6. Made requests to go to the library?		
7. Checked out books at the library?		
8. Talked about books he/she has read?		
9. Finished most of the books she/he has started?		
10. Mentioned books she/he has at home?		

Source: Betty S. Heathington and J. Estill Alexander, "A Child-Based Observation Checklist to Assess Attitudes Toward Reading," *The Reading Teacher,* April 1978, page 770. Reprinted with permission of the authors and the International Reading Association.

Behaviors developed by C. Glennon Rowell (1972). This scale gives the observer an opportunity to rate students on a five-point scale (always occurs, often occurs, occasionally occurs, seldom occurs, and never occurs). Some of the behaviors observed relate to the reading group activities, eagerness to respond and discuss, desire, efforts made, and free reading activities.

Some observers tend to see that which they wish to see; thus, every effort should be made to avoid preconceived ideas. The only behaviors that should be permanently recorded are those which occur repeatedly over time. Record keeping is essential with this technique since it is necessary to observe students over a period of weeks in order to ensure accuracy in assessment. An anecdotal record is a fruitful device for summarizing significant behavior patterns. Applegate (1968) states that the following information should be included: how children value reading, ways children use reading, evidence of application of reading skills taught, work/study behaviors, and tension signs in a reading situation.

Interviewing. Interviewing is more structured than observation but is less time consuming. For best results, the teacher should determine in advance the questions he will ask; he should also have them arranged in categories. To help make the interview situation more valid, it is important for him to ask questions in the beginning that are not related to reading. In this way the child may adjust to the interview and feel more at ease in responding. It is also important to ask questions in areas other than reading toward which the student is felt to have positive attitudes; the student will feel freer to make negative responses to reading related questions if he has been able to provide positive responses to some other questions. Asking questions that have little or no significant relationship to school in general may be helpful in masking the basic intent of the interview situation. Despite these cautions, some students may tell the teacher what they feel the teacher wants to hear.

Incomplete sentences. In the incomplete sentence technique, students usually respond to twenty to forty sentence starters. The age level of the student will determine, in part, the number of sentence starters to use. Typical sentence starters look like this:

> Reading is _____.
> I like to _____.
> I don't like to read _____.

The intent of this technique may be masked by including items related to areas other than reading. Since it is possible, and often probable, that the responses given indicate how a student feels on a given day, the information obtained should be verified through observation, in order to determine specific attitudinal patterns. The fact that students may respond as they feel the teacher wishes them to respond is a limitation of this technique.

An incomplete sentence instrument that is frequently used was developed by Boning and Boning and may be found in *The Reading Teacher* (April 1957), pages 196–199.

Questionnaire. One of the most direct methods of assessing attitudes toward reading is the questionnaire. Most questionnaires ask students to respond directly to specific questions, either orally or in writing. There are generally ten to twenty-five questions included. Examples are:

1. Why don't you read more in your spare time?
2. What are your favorite school activities?

This technique may be varied through the use of yes–no questions. For example:

1. Do you like to read?
2. Do you use the library frequently?
3. Do you read in your spare time?

Because there is no universal set of behaviors that must be sampled, teachers may choose a variety of behaviors to sample in a questionnaire. When teachers wish to sample specific reading situations, they should choose behaviors that seem to be most indicative of attitudes in those situations. Tinker and McCullough (1975, p. 367) suggest that six categories should be included when a comprehensive instrument is needed. These categories are: school in general, books and reading, the teacher, the reading environment, class activities, and work/study habits.

Obviously, the questionnaire is quicker and easier to use than are observation and interview techniques. Questionnaires are less time consuming since they may be administered to an entire group at one sitting. But the teacher should be aware that students may respond as they feel the teacher wishes them to respond.

A questionnaire frequently used is the *San Diego County Inventory of Reading Attitude*. It may be obtained from the Department of Education, San Diego County, San Diego, California, 92101.

Other techniques. Two other valuable devices, which are more difficult for teachers to construct, are pairing instruments and summated rating scales.

In a pairing assessment instrument, reading is compared in terms of preference with other activities in which the student is likely to engage. With each pair, the student selects the activity he prefers if he had only one option — reading or the other activity. Pairing may take the form of multiple comparisons or of simple forced-choice comparisons. Words and phrases, statements, or pictures may be used as stimulus situations. An available instrument (using pictures) is the *Primary Pupil Reading Attitude Inventory* by Eunice N. Askov (Kendall/Hunt Publishers, 2460 Kerper Blvd., Dubuque, Iowa, 52001).

The summated rating scale requires the student to respond on a four- or five-point scale to a series of statements about reading. A scale typically includes ten to twenty items. Response categories are generally: strongly agree, agree, undecided, disagree, and strongly disagree. This type of scale makes it possible to check "degrees" of feeling. Two such scales were recently developed by Betty S. Heathington (1975) — one for grades 1–3 and the other for grades 4–6. These scales, with directions for administering and scoring, follow (see also Alexander and Filler 1976).

HEATHINGTON PRIMARY ATTITUDE SCALE[2]

The Primary Scale consists of 20 questions which are to be read to the student. After listening to a question beginning with the words "How do you feel . . . ," the student is asked to mark one of five faces (ranging from very unhappy, to unhappy, to neutral, to happy, to very happy) which shows how he feels about the question. A score of 5 is given for each very happy face chosen, a 4 for a happy face, a 3 for a neutral face, a 2 for an unhappy face, and a 1 for a very unhappy face.

The directions for the primary scale are as follows:

Your answer booklet is made up of two pages. Page one goes from number 1 to number 10; page two goes from number 10 to number 20. Beside each number are five faces: a very unhappy face, an unhappy face, a face that's neither happy nor unhappy, a happy face, and a very happy face. I will ask you how you feel about certain things and you will put an X on the face that shows how you feel. Suppose I said, "How do you feel when you eat chocolate candy? Which face shows how you feel?" Someone may have chosen an unhappy face because he doesn't like chocolate candy; someone else may have chosen a happy face because he likes chocolate candy. Now I'll read some questions to you and you mark the face that shows how you feel about what I read. Remember to mark how *you* feel because everyone does not feel the same about certain things. I'll read each question two times. Mark only one face for each number. Are there any questions? Now listen carefully. Number 1 . . .

Certain groupings of questions indicate specific areas of a child's reading environment toward which he may feel positively or negatively. . . .

The following groupings are suggested:

1. Free reading in the classroom (items 3, 17)
2. Organized reading in the classroom (items 4, 7, 8, 13)

2. From J. Estill Alexander and Ronald C. Filler, *Attitudes and Reading* (Newark, Del.: The International Reading Association, 1976). Reprinted with permission of Betty S. Heathington and The International Reading Association.

3. Reading at the library (items 1, 18)
4. Reading at home (items 6, 12, 15, 19)
5. Other recreational reading (items 2, 5, 9, 16)
6. General reading (items 10, 11, 14, 20)

The scale items are:

How do you feel . . .
 (1) when you go to the library?
 (2) when you read instead of playing outside?
 (3) when you read a book in free time?
 (4) when you are in reading group?
 (5) when you read instead of watching TV?
 (6) when you read to someone at home?
 (7) about the stories in your reading book?
 (8) when you read out loud in class?
 (9) when you read with a friend after school?
(10) when you read stories in books?
(11) when you read in a quiet place?
(12) when you read a story at bedtime?
(13) when it's time for reading circle (group)?
(14) when you read on a trip?
(15) when you have lots of books at home?
(16) when you read outside when it's warm?
(17) when you read at your desk at school?
(18) when you find a book at the library?
(19) when you read in your room at home?
(20) when you read instead of coloring?
    Figure 15.1 is a sample from the answer sheet.

A score of 80 and above represents positive responses to items on the scale. Scores below 40 represent negative responses. Scores between 40 and 80 suggest neutral or possibly mixed feelings about the items on the scale.

Figure 15.1. Sample from the answer sheet, Heathington Primary Attitude Scale.

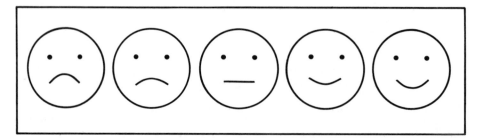

HEATHINGTON INTERMEDIATE SCALE[3]

The Intermediate Scale consists of 24 statements about reading. The student responds by marking whether he strongly disagrees, disagrees, is undecided, agrees, or strongly agrees with the statement read by the teacher. In scoring, a 5 is given for a very positive response, a 4 for a positive response, a 3 for a neutral or undecided response, a 2 for a negative response, and a 1 for a very negative response.

On nine of the items (numbers 2, 6, 10, 14, 15, 16, 20, 21, 23), a very positive response is indicated by marking "strongly agree" and receives a score of 5. On the remaining 15 items, a response of "strongly disagree" indicates a very positive attitude, receiving a score of 5.

The directions for the intermediate scale are as follows:

On your answer sheet, numbers on the right-hand column go from number 1 to number 14. Numbers on the left-hand column go from number 15 to number 24. Beside each number are five boxes. Over each box are one or two letters. *SD* stands for strongly disagree, *D* for disagree, *U* for undecided, *A* for agree, and *SA* for strongly agree. I will read certain statements to you and you are to mark an X in the box that shows how you feel. Suppose I said, "You enjoy eating chocolate candy." What box would you mark? Someone might love chocolate candy and would mark "agree." Remember that everyone may not feel the same about the statements, so make sure you mark how *you* feel. Mark only one box for each number. I'll read each statement two times. Are there any questions? Now listen carefully. Number 1. . . .

The Intermediate Scale also has groups of questions. . . .

The categories are:

1. Free reading in the classroom (items 5, 6, 15)
2. Organized reading in the classroom (items 1, 24)
3. Reading in the library (items 3, 4, 9, 17, 21)
4. Reading at home (items 7, 10, 11, 20)
5. Other recreational reading (items 12, 13, 23)
6. General reading (items 2, 8, 14, 16, 18, 19, 22)

The scale items are:

(1) You feel uncomfortable when you're asked to read in class.
(2) You feel happy when you're reading.
(3) Sometimes you forget about library books that you have in your desk.
(4) You don't check out many library books.
(5) You don't read much in the classroom.
(6) When you have free time at school, you usually read a book.
(7) You seldom have a book in your room at home.

3. From J. Estill Alexander and Ronald C. Filler, *Attitudes and Reading* (Newark, Del.: The International Reading Association, 1976). Reprinted with permission of Betty S. Heathington and The International Reading Association.

(8) You would rather look at the pictures in a book than read it.

(9) You check out books at the library but never have time to read them.

(10) You wish you had a library full of books at home.

(11) You seldom read in your room at home.

(12) You would rather watch TV than read.

(13) You would rather play after school than read.

(14) You talk to friends about books that you have read.

(15) You like for the room to be quiet so you can read in your free time.

(16) You read several books each week.

(17) Most of the books you choose are not interesting.

(18) You don't read very often.

(19) You think reading is work.

(20) You enjoy reading at home.

(21) You enjoy going to the library.

(22) Often you start a book, but never finish it.

(23) You think that adventures in a book are more exciting than TV.

(24) You wish you could answer the questions at the end of the chapter without reading it.

Figure 15.2 is a sample of the answer sheet.

Figure 15.2. Sample from the answer sheet, Heathington Intermediate Scale.

Scores of 96 and above represent positive responses to items on the scale. Scores below 48 represent negative responses. Scores between 48 and 96 suggest neutral or possibly mixed feelings about the items on the scale.

DEVELOPING AND MAINTAINING POSITIVE ATTITUDES

This section contains suggestions to help the teacher develop and maintain positive attitudes in students. Attention is given to teacher attitudes and behaviors, selected instructional practices and organizational patterns, and the importance of working with parents. Each area will be discussed in the following paragraphs.

Teacher attitudes and behaviors. There is little doubt that the teacher is often the most significant force in the development of positive attitudes.

Frequently, he is more important than the techniques, practices, and materials used.

Students perceive that the teacher's responses to the things they say and do are forms of evaluation. These responses include overt actions, oral communications, and indirect statements and actions — with some of the most influential communications being indirect. Rosenthal and Jacobson (1968) have stated that teachers communicate their expectations to students through "tone of voice, facial expression, touch and posture." It is important for teachers to be cognizant of these aspects of their behavior and to evaluate the effects that their nonverbal behaviors have on students. (For a further discussion of classroom environment, see Chapter 9.)

It is also important that the teacher be a good model for his students. The teacher who seldom enjoys reading will often have more difficulty in producing enthusiastic readers than will a teacher who clearly does enjoy it. The good "reading" teacher will read to his class, and he will read while his students are reading. He will become knowledgeable about books (old and new) on the age and grade level of his students in order to be able to make recommendations in terms of their interests and achievement levels. Students will see him reach for a book when he wants information, and they will often do the same.

Reading authorities consider certain teacher attitudes and behaviors conducive to positive attitudes in students. Teachers should analyze themselves in terms of these attitudes and behaviors. The following questions, which incorporate some of those behaviors Robinson (1952) and Zintz (1977) felt important, may assist in this self-analysis (Alexander and Filler 1976):

1. Do you value each student as a reader and respect his efforts in attempting to become a better reader?
2. Do you permit the student to express his fears and dislikes even if they are directed toward you?
3. Do you consider the feelings of your students and give immediate attention to their needs and interests?
4. Do you convince your students they need not be afraid to make mistakes?
5. Do you believe that each student can achieve some measure of success with reading?
6. Do you change methods and materials whenever student progress indicates that the methods and materials being used are not producing the desired results?
7. Are you aware of the ways, both verbally and nonverbally, that you communicate your feelings about reading to your students?

If a teacher answers no to any of these questions, she should make a conscious effort to change her behavior.

Instructional practices and organizational patterns. It is difficult if not impossible to suggest particular programs and strategies that work in most situations since attitudes tend to be highly specific to given individuals. The tasks of the teacher are to try out ideas and utilize those that are the most productive for given individuals or groups and to change strategies when those used are not effective. To effect an attitudinal change, teaching strategies and organizational patterns need not be sensational or spectacular. In most instances, the matching of tried-and-true strategies and patterns with the interests and needs of given students is all that is needed. Many such tried-and-true strategies and patterns are suggested elsewhere in this text.

Particularly notice strategies and patterns that:

1. attend to the development of a more positive self-concept.
2. consider the teacher's attitudes and nonverbal behaviors.
3. help students see a need for reading.
4. make sure a learner is ready to handle an instructional task before it is assigned.
5. teach relevant skills, thereby giving students tools with which to read.
6. utilize student interests in program planning.
7. involve selecting materials for use in school that are on the student's independent or instructional levels.
8. make interesting materials available and provide a time for reading.
9. involve reading or telling stories to students to show that reading is important.
10. provide time for the sharing of books or materials since enthusiasm is often caught from other students.
11. provide opportunities to read creatively, that is, to use reading in some unique way.
12. organize classrooms in such a way that learning to read is facilitated and the learner is not frustrated.

You should consider each strategy presented in this text for its potential for facilitating the development of positive attitudes. Recall from Chapter 1 that a significant role of teachers is the fostering of positive attitudes so children will want to read. Appropriate selection of strategies is crucial to this role.

Working with parents. Since parents and the home environment have an important impact on attitudes, it may be necessary for the school to work closely with some parents in order that positive attitudes be fostered in the children. There are several ways that may be effective: eliciting assistance from cooperative parents in working with problem readers; helping parents improve the reading environment in the home; apprising parents of the effects of their attitudes and behaviors on their children; and suggesting professional literature for parents to read. (See Chapter 19 for a fuller treatment of ways parents can help youngsters learn to read.)

Self-Concept

QUESTIONS TO GUIDE READING

Literal
What is self-concept?
What are two paper-and-pencil tests used to assess self-concept?
What types of behaviors should be observed when assessing self-concept?
What are some guidelines to follow when attempting to build self-concept?

Inferential
What is the relationship between self-concept and reading achievement?
How are the limitations of self-concept measures similar to, or different from, those used to measure attitudes?

Evaluative
Is observation superior to paper-and-pencil tests that purport to measure self-concept? Explain your position.
How would you decide whether a given strategy, material, method, or organizational pattern might enhance self-concept?

Self-concept has been defined as all the perceptions that individuals have of themselves, especially of their values and abilities (Quandt 1972, p. 5). Positive self-concept was defined in Chapter 1 as including self-confidence, liking oneself, and a feeling of appreciation by others. That self-concept is related to school achievement is not questioned. Purkey (1970, p. 14) has stated, "For generations, wise teachers have sensed the significance and positive relationship between a student's concept of himself and his performance in school." The purpose of this section is to help you see the importance of considering "reading" self-concept (a subcategory of global self-concept) in program planning. Attention is focused on research correlates, assessment, and strategies for promoting positive self-concepts.

THE CORRELATES

In general the relationship between levels of self-concept and levels of reading achievement is strong. As noted in Chapter 1, good readers' self-concepts tend to be more positive than those of poor readers.

Ivan Quandt (1972), who has synthesized research on self-concept in reading, states that when students feel that they are regarded as incompetent by others who are important to them, they tend to counteract this perception some way. For most children this counteraction involves disguising incompetency or withdrawing effort from those areas in which they are regarded as incompetent. Such withdrawal of effort may occur when the learner's efforts at reading are considered inadequate and may result in such behaviors as showing apparent disinterest in reading, showing apparent lack of effort in learning to read assignments, or showing apparent carelessness or professed hatred of reading. Quandt also states (pp. 8–9) that children who come to school thinking they may not succeed or those who develop this feeling as a result of their school experience may become victims of their own beliefs. Disabled readers may, because of lack of self-confidence, become discouraged and stop or reduce efforts to improve.

How children feel about themselves can be crucial to initial success in reading. In a study of how kindergarten children's self-concepts are related to beginning reading achievement, Wattenberg and Clifford (1964) found that children's attitudes about themselves were more closely related to reading success than was intelligence.

Relative to intelligence and self-concept, Anastasiow (1964, 1967) found that bright children who were reading below expectations had lower self-concept scores than those who were reading as expected. Girls with reading problems seemed to be more affected relative to self-concept than were boys with reading problems.

Maehr (1969) has suggested that learners' reactions to failure experiences are more a function of the views that persons important to them hold than to the failure experience itself. Teachers, parents, and peers have tremendous potential for affecting self-concept development either positively or negatively.

ASSESSING SELF-CONCEPT

Assessing self-concept, as with attitudes, presents some problems. Self-concept is most often assessed in schools through self-report (paper-and-pencil) techniques or through observations. A child may have difficulty in verbalizing feelings about himself in a self-report measure. The problem of accurate responses also exists when the child is able to verbalize feelings.

Observation is probably the most valid way for teachers to assess self-concept. However, there are limitations with this procedure also. Teachers may see what they expect to see or may not know which behaviors indicate the most useful information. Quandt (1972, pp. 12–13) suggests five types of behavior that may be observed in a school setting:

1. Positive or negative comments that children make about themselves or about reading.
2. Reactions to reading instruction and reading tasks (such as facial expressions, gestures, apparent lack of interest, or low motivation).
3. Interactions with peers (such as avoidance behaviors or attention-getting behaviors).
4. Voluntary answers to questions.
5. Apparent confidence level as tasks are performed.

Sanacore (1975) has suggested ten questions that can serve as a guide when observing levels of self-concept.[4] These are:

1. Does the student frequently make negative comments about himself?
2. Does the student frequently avoid working with peers?
3. Do the student's peers usually avoid working with him?
4. Do the student's peers often ridicule him?
5. Does the student constantly seek attention?
6. Does the student seldom volunteer?
7. Does the student compulsively seek information concerning his progress?
8. Does the student rarely seek information concerning his progress?
9. Does the student frequently manifest negative non-verbal behavior (for example, nail-biting, facial expressions)?
10. Does the student often set goals for himself that are not within his ability to attain?

Teachers are cautioned to make judgment on patterns of behaviors observed over time. A given single behavior may be attributable to a cause other than level of self-concept. For example, how a child is feeling physically or emotionally on a given day may affect behaviors significantly.

BUILDING SELF-CONCEPT

Teachers must strive to develop, enhance, or maintain a positive level of self-concept. Particular strategies will depend on individual learners. In working with students who have low self-concepts the teacher should keep in mind the following guidelines, based primarily on Quandt's work (1972):

1. Accept the student as a valued person. Find something in the student that you like and let him know about it.

4. Joseph Sanacore, "Reading Self-Concept: Assessment and Enhancement," *The Reading Teacher*, November 1975, page 165. Reprinted with permission of Joseph Sanacore and The International Reading Association.

2. Reduce negative comments. When a negative comment is necessary, precede it with some comment that is positive.
3. Make children's successes known to others. Find something about the student's reading that is deserving of praise. Give this praise in the presence of others who the student feels are significant or important.
4. Place failure in a given area of reading with success in other areas (possibly another area of school work). Find something that the student does adequately or well and show how this is important to learning or in the individual's life.
5. Minimize differences between reading groups. Structure some reading activities such as skills groups or interest groups that cross traditional group lines. A child's reading activities should not always be with the same individuals or materials.
6. Compare the student's progress against his previous level of proficiency, not with that of a group.
7. Utilize student interests when selecting materials for skill instruction or when recommending books for recreational reading. Students generally do better when they have an interest in a particular area or material.
8. Use materials for class assignments on the child's instructional or independent level. Frustration-level experiences may enhance or lead to a negative level of self-concept.
9. Select the skills for instruction that a child needs for success and show him how mastery of these skills will lead to higher levels of achievement.
10. Feel positive about yourself and be enthusiastic about your teaching. Enthusiasm is often caught rather than taught. Children generally feel better about themselves in a classroom in which the teacher feels good about himself.

Promoting Lasting Interests as Motivators for Reading

QUESTIONS TO GUIDE READING

Literal
What does motivation involve?
What are the four major steps in promoting lasting interests?
What are the personal and institutional factors involved in the formation of reading interest?
Can you describe three techniques for assessing interests?
What are some ways that a teacher can utilize student interests in program planning?

Inferential

How are interests related to motivation?

Why should a teacher not take for granted that a particular group of children (or an individual child) fits the typical patterns of interest?

What are the major strengths and weaknesses of the various techniques for assessing interests?

How do the suggestions given for promoting positive attitudes and positive self-concepts serve as motivators?

Evaluative

To promote a lasting interest in reading, does a teacher need to follow the steps discussed in this section in sequence? Why or why not?

What should a teacher do initially to extend interests?

How do teacher behaviors relate to student interests?

Motivation is a basic factor in developing reading proficiency and a prerequisite to actual reading (See Chapter 1). Progress is slow for those learners who are not concerned with progress and/or who do not enjoy trying to learn to read better. The effect of positive motivation is that of providing greater effort, encouraging concentration, and increasing cooperation with those involved in the instruction process.

The literature does not provide general agreement on precisely what motivation involves or how it can be generated or maintained. DeCecco and Crawford (1974) have stated, however, that motivation involves arousal, expectancy, incentive, and discipline. These are defined as follows:

Arousal — the initiation of an activity. Rupley and Blair (1979, p. 35) note that the level of activity can range from low (boredom) to high (emotional excitement) and suggest that the most conducive level to learning is somewhere between these extremes.

Expectancy — the establishment of goals, objectives, and purposes that enable the learner to function with understanding in the instructional setting.

Incentive — the rewarding of achievement in ways that encourage further learning and higher levels of achievement. These rewards may be intrinsic (satisfaction from within) or extrinsic (provided by someone else). When incentives are used, they must be powerful enough to unbalance any negativism that may have been associated with the stimulus situation (Robeck and Wilson, 1974, p. 197). Different learners need different incentives for the proper level of motivation to be aroused and sustained. Incentives should not be utilized beyond the point at which they are considered rewarding to the learner. Teachers should observe carefully the student's level of interest in the incentive.

Discipline — the management of behavior as the learner pursues tasks in the instructional setting. Student behavior must be appropriate for his learning and for the learning of others.

In the Mathewson affective model of reading processes cited in Chapter 1, motivation was posited as a crucial component. Among the motives discussed that impinge on reading were curiosity and exploration, desire for achievement, self-actualization, activity, and anxiety.

This section focuses on how teachers can develop or utilize the curiosity or exploration motive; that is, how they can develop and extend interests as a way of motivating readers. Of course, teachers can utilize motivational forces other than student interests, per se. The suggestions for promoting positive attitudes and self-concepts discussed earlier in this chapter are motivational for many students. The development of efficient reading skills, a major focus of this entire text, obviously relates to achievement motivation.

There is little disagreement about the importance of student interest in reading. It is unfortunate that many students learn the skills necessary to read but do not develop a permanent interest in reading. A major goal for reading programs should be to help students find lasting pleasure and satisfaction from reading.

To promote lasting interests, there are four major steps that it may be fruitful for teachers to take. First, the teacher may learn about the factors that correlate with interest formation. Second, he may familiarize himself with the interest patterns students typically have at the age or grade level he teaches. Third, he may study the individual interests of his students — since these individual interests may be unique and different from the normative interest patterns. And fourth, he may seek to develop and extend interests. We will focus on each of these steps, in the order given.

THE CORRELATES

A variety of different methods have been used to study the factors related to interest formation. It is difficult to synthesize and summarize the data available because of differences in the methodology of the studies, in the assessment techniques, in the populations sampled, and even in the definitions of what an interest is. In addition, not enough attention has been given to interrelationships among the factors to make definitive statements. Probably the best synthesis of the research to date has been done by Purves and Beach (1972, pp. 62–144). They discussed the factors in two categories — personal and institutional. The summary that follows is based, for the most part, on important highlights from their summary. Many of the implications of their summary are omitted; the reader is referred to the original work for an in-depth treatment.[5] It should be

5. In addition, a fuller treatment of this work is provided in Albert J. Harris and Edward R. Sipay, *How to Increase Reading Ability*, 7th ed. (New York: Longman, 1980), pp. 518–524.

noted that the generalizations presented here have limited value in predicting or understanding the specific interests of a particular child.

Personal. The factors briefly discussed in this category are age, sex, intelligence, reading ability, psychological needs, and attitudes.

There seems to be a definite developmental pattern in relationship to age at the elementary school level. Children tend to have an interest in stories that deal with their own age level. At the earlier levels, there is an interest in fantasy figures who represent childlike experiences. These fantasy figures are usually animals. At later elementary levels, there is a shift to more realistic stories that involve suspense and the unknown.

Sex has been found, in many studies, to be the most important determinant of reading interests. Cultural influences and sexual maturation, rather than intelligence, appear to be reflected in these differences, which may emerge as early as the first grade (Byers 1964).

The relationship between intelligence and interests is not clear from the available research. While the overall interests of bright students appear to be advanced beyond their age level, actual choices of book titles selected do not vary a great deal (Spache 1974, p. 5). While this statement appears contradictory, it is probably a combination of high IQ and high reading ability that is the primary determinant of the relationships found.

Reading ability does not appear to correlate directly with reading interests, however. The comprehension of superior elementary students does not appear to be affected by interests; on the other hand, comprehension is often affected by interests for students reading at or below grade level.

Psychological needs (self-concept, intellectual, emotional, social, and aesthetic) appear to be strongly related to interests. Children do not always utilize reading to satisfy needs, however. They frequently turn to other sources (such as persons they consider important), using reading as a recreational activity.

Very little is known about the relationship between attitudes and interests. The factors related to attitude development and maintenance were discussed earlier in this chapter.

Institutional. In this section, the following factors are identified and briefly discussed: availability of books; socioeconomic status and ethnic background; peer, parent, and teacher influences; and TV and movies.

Readers develop interests regardless of availability of books, yet accessibility and availability have a strong influence on children's book choices. In some studies, the amount and kind of reading materials in the home have been found to be related to the child's reading habits. Even when there are many options available, the children's choices are often affected by other factors — such as provision for sampling portions of a book, the title and content of the book, teachers' and friends' recommendations, illustrations, author's name, and introduction by mass media.

Socioeconomic factors do not significantly affect interests, according to the findings of most research studies. There does not appear to be much difference in the reading interests of rural, urban, and suburban children. There do appear to be differences in interests among ethnic groups, with the widest differences occurring at intermediate grade levels. Most of the research has focused on interest differences between Blacks and whites: the differences found seem to be more related to whites choosing material related to their cultural backgrounds than to Blacks choosing material related to their cultural backgrounds.

The influence of peers, friends, parents, and teachers is frequently direct: someone recommends a book. These persons may also influence interests because they are role models to the child. Teacher enthusiasm is often an important factor, although teachers sometimes misjudge student interests. Friends and peers are also potent forces for influencing interests.

The effect of media (such as TV and movies) on reading interests is complex. Only short-term effects have been studied. Students do devote more leisure time to TV than to reading. According to Harris and Sipay (1980, p. 523), the best research on the effects of TV on school achievement suggests a small negative effect (Hornik 1978). This effect is not established, however. Individual differences preclude any convincing generalizations relative to recreational reading (Purves and Beach 1972).

Other factors. In addition, Harris and Sipay (1980, pp. 525–527) consider illustrations and the difficulty level of the material to be important factors. Children seem to prefer realistic pictures in color. They also prefer a realistic black and white picture over a less realistic colored one (Rudisill 1952). Few children can really become interested in a book that is frustrating to them. A student can generally understand difficult material better if he has a strong interest in the material, however.

Interest Patterns of Elementary School Children

In addition to the difficulties involved in synthesizing interest studies, the teacher meets additional problems when he attempts to make definite statements about the interest patterns of elementary children. One problem of paramount importance is the categories used. Generally, these categories are determined in advance by an adult investigator and thus sample only those interests that the investigator feels important. Second, different definitions have been given to category designation. The same story may be classified as *humor* by one investigator and as *animal* by another. In addition, when a child is asked to choose among categories, it is possible that his top choices are not among the categories. Also, it should be noted that the choices of many students are not included at all in summaries of interest findings because they were not among those most frequently mentioned in the group studied. Group studies frequently suggest topics that only about half the students prefer (Robinson and Weintraub 1973). Hundreds of studies have attempted to assess student interest patterns; in summarizing the results, Robinson and Weintraub (1973)[6] state that at the preschool level:

> The limited research dealing with preschool pupils' reading interests is inconclusive and a fertile field for further study. Although kindergarten children seem to report more reliably than those who are younger, it is quite possible that interests are fleeting and do not stabilize until children can read by themselves. Moreover, it seems that illustrations have as much, or more, appeal than the content. Young children like repetition and ask to hear familiar stories again and again. Whether particular characteristics of stories, such as ease of understanding or the sounds of the words read, have appeal which leads to repeated requests for particular stories is not known.

Of interests at primary grade levels they state:

> Within the past decade, investigations continue to show a strong interest in animals, make-believe, and some interest in children's activities.... With regard to poetry, most . . . primary pupils appear to consider humorous poems as their first choice; poems about animals tended to be the next most popular; and then poems that carry a story line related to their own experience and with action are frequently liked.

Of interests at the intermediate grade levels they report that:

> The research dealing with reading interests at the middle-grade level shows that children have a greater variety of interests than at the primary-grade level. Pupils read books about a wide range of topics, read comics, and also read magazines and newspapers. Sex differences are generally quite pronounced. Boys tend to prefer adventure and action as well as historical and scientific topics. Girls often enjoy realistic and fanciful stories, mysteries, and humor. Both boys and girls begin to read children's magazines and many favor adult magazines by the sixth grade. The newspaper is read at times by nearly three-fourths of the middle-grade pupils. Poetry is not especially liked by most of these pupils.

For a more in-depth analysis of interest patterns of elementary school children, the reader is referred to the Robinson and Weintraub summary (1973).

One recent study conducted by Feeley (1982) illustrates the sex differ-

6. From Helen M. Robinson and Samuel Weintraub, "Research Related to Children's Interests and to Developmental Values of Reading," *Library Trends* 22:2 (October 1973): 81–108. Reprinted with permission of the Graduate School of Library and Information Science, University of Illinois at Urbana-Champaign.

ences that occur in intermediate grades in what they like to read and watch on TV. Her study indicated that middle graders have different interest patterns but that the difference may be less than the differences found in an earlier study (Feeley 1974). The combined preferences of viewing and reading were:

Boys	Girls
1. Sports	1. Media (recreational)
2. Media (recreational)	2. Animals
3. Historical adventure	3. Fun–fantasy
4–5. Informational	4. Social empathy
4–5. Fun–fantasy	5–6. Sports
6. Social empathy–Arts	5–6. Arts
	7. Historical information

Teachers often find that areas of student interest are similar for both TV viewing and reading. This affords teachers an excellent opportunity for using student TV preferences as a springboard for encouraging reading in a given area.

Assessing Student Interests

Since it is difficult to make judgments about what student interests will be at given age or grade levels and since interests are often unique to given students or groups, it is necessary for teachers to assess the specific interests of the students whom he teaches. Some of the techniques are the same basic types suggested for attitude assessment. These include observation, questionnaires and inventories, and interviews. In an inventory, Purves and Beach (1972, p. 68) state that some form of checklist is better than open-ended response-type questions because some students may have difficulty recalling appropriate information. They suggest that probably the best type of checklist is one that uses actual or fictitious titles, or descriptions. However, students are limited to responding to the items that the teacher has listed. Another limitation of the inventory or questionnaire is that there may be a tendency for some students to respond in a socially acceptable manner rather than as they really feel.

In deciding on content for interest inventories, the investigator should consider: free time activities; interactions with peers, siblings, and parents; play activities; TV and movie preferences; clubs; pets; trips; the library; wishes; and career preferences (if appropriate to age level). The following is an example of an interest inventory that includes all those items.

ALEXANDER INTEREST INVENTORY

Name _____ Room _____

1. In my free time, I like to _____.
2. My father and I like _____.
3. My mother and I like _____.
4. I have ___ brother(s) and ___ sister(s).
   My _____ and I like to _____.
5. My friends and I like _____.
   We play at _____.
6. I like to help at home by _____.
   But I do not like to _____.
7. I (like-do not like) to play with toys and games.
   My favorite toys and games are _____.
8. I (like-do not like) TV. My favorite programs are _____
   _____.
9. I (like-do not like) to go to the movies. My favorite movies are _____
   _____.
10. I (like-do not like) pets. My favorite pets are _____
    _____.
11. I go to scouts (yes-no); church (yes-no); clubs (yes-no). My favorite
    clubs are _____.
12. I (like-do not like) to take trips. I have visited _____
    _____.
    I would like to visit _____.
13. I (like-do not like) to collect things. My favorite collections are _____
    _____.
14. (I like-do not like) to make things. I have made _____
    _____.
15. I (like-do not like) to read. I read storybooks (yes-no); newspapers
    (yes-no); magazines (yes-no); comic books (yes-no). My favorites are
    _____.
16. I do not like to read about _____.
17. I (like-do not like) to go to the library.
18. I (like-do not like) to read at home. My parents like for me to read at
    home (yes-no).
19. If I could have any three things I could wish for, I would like _____
    _____, _____
    _____, and _____.
20. When I grow up, I think I would like to _____
    _____
    _____.

In addition there are other sources from which information about student interests may be obtained: library records, autobiographies, diaries, voluntary hobby club memberships, school records that have anecdotal notes, and incomplete sentence tests (see earlier section). It should be noted that the most important source of information is the student himself — listen to his conversations, note his creative writing topics, and observe his free reading choices.

Developing and Extending Interests

There are many ways a teacher may develop or extend the reading interests of his students. For one thing, the teacher can promote interests through "sales techniques," using the spectacular, but the results are generally only transitory (Robinson 1956, p. 24). It is generally more effective to use more subtle, creative ways in which reading becomes a natural part of the total school life. The ideas that follow are for the most part of this nature and are organized under teacher behaviors, classroom environmental influences, and special ways to extend interests.

Teacher behaviors. Because interests are acquired, they are amenable to training or teaching. The role of the teacher is crucial, for the teacher himself — his enthusiasm for and his love of books — is a strong motivating factor.

One good way to develop interests is to read to students (at any age level). Many reluctant readers will ask the teacher if they might finish reading a book after listening to an interesting portion read by the teacher. The teacher must be a good reader of books if this activity is to be effective. The story should be one that the teacher likes because enthusiasm for a story shows and is often contagious. In a longer story, it is often desirable to read only the more interesting parts. The more descriptive, less interesting parts may be summarized orally. At times, it is appropriate to read an interesting episode to students to whet their appetites for more reading.

Storytelling often has a similar motivating effect. Students often wish to read a story after listening to an interesting episode that is well told. To be effective, the teacher should like the story and should know it well. And, of course, the story should be of interest to the students.

Reading to children and telling stories to them are both forms of recommending books to children. They are especially effective ways to develop interests in children who come from cultural groups in which reading has not been a valued activity. The teacher may also find it useful to recommend specific books directly because children are frequently responsive to teacher suggestions.

The teacher should provide opportunities for the student to read creatively (see Chapter 8) because creative reading activities are frequently highly motivating. Reading can lead into creative writing and dramatics, which are activities that may be appealing enough to make a reluctant reader much more enthusiastic. Another activity with potential for sparking an interest in reading is to allow the student to devise unique ways of reporting on books.

The teacher can also work with parents to strengthen and broaden the students' interests. According to Tinker and McCullough (1975, p. 315), the teacher may: (a) discuss with parents the importance of positive attitudes on their part; (b) encourage them to provide suitable books and magazines; and (c) encourage them to talk about books, to read to their children, and to tell stories to them. These activities should be spontaneous — not staged — if they are to be effective.

It was noted earlier that many children do not like to read poetry. The encouragement of poetry reading is one of the teacher's most difficult tasks in extending interests. (See Chapter 11 for ways that may help.)

Classroom environmental influences. The type of classroom atmosphere and the physical environment the teacher establishes may also be conducive, or nonconducive, to the strengthening of reading interests.

Classroom collections of trade books and paperbacks may be motivational at any level. The important element is exposure. Such collections suggest to students that reading is an important and appropriate behavior. The collections should be within the reading level and interest ranges of the students, and they should be changed frequently. Also important are provisions for a *time* and a *place* for unassigned reading in the classroom.

It is important to house the classroom collection in an attractive setting with tables, chairs, bookshelves, and bulletin boards available. A "book nook" is one good way to feature a classroom collection. A book nook may be housed in a quiet corner of the room and furnished with comfortable chairs (perhaps even a rocker), carpeting for those who enjoy reading while sitting or lying on the floor, and a wide selection of books and magazines on appropriate reading levels. There should be adequate time for browsing and silent reading.

Reading interests are often promoted through voluntary participation in book club discussion groups: Two sources of books are libraries and inexpensive commercial book clubs.[7] Discussion groups give learners an opportunity to share books in ways that may spark an interest in another student who has not been curious about the topic previously. Peer recommendations are often powerful forces in developing interests.

Interest centers in the classroom may provide a source of variety for students.[8] Interest centers may include a wide range of materials such as

7. An example of a comprehensive commercial book club service is Scholastic Book Service (904 Sylvan Avenue, Englewood Cliffs, N.J. 07632). The following clubs are available at the elementary level: *See-Saw* for grades K–1; *Lucky* for grades 2–3; *Arrow* for grades 4–6; and *Tab* for junior high school.
8. For help with establishing interest centers, see *Individualizing Reading with Learning Stations and Centers* by Sue Don and others. (Evansville, Ind.: Riverside Learning Associates, 1973).

library books, content area materials, newspapers and magazines, comics, experience stories, creative book reports, and tape recordings of students' reactions to books. Centers are most effective when they relate to one specific interest area and contain only materials that relate to that area. (See Chapter 18 for further information on interest, or learning, centers.)

The use of media (print and nonprint) should not be overlooked. Such means often are effective in awakening interests. These media include — in addition to books and magazines — phonograph records, radio and TV programs, films and filmstrips, and slides and pictures. A dramatic recording, an exciting film, or an interesting and colorful picture may trigger a desire to learn more about the topic or happening being presented. Attractive bulletin boards focusing on books are also often effective.

Because children spend more hours watching TV than in any other leisure time activity, it may be profitable to utilize this medium as a motivational tool for recommending books. Becker (1973, pp. 17–25) suggests that teachers collect coloring books related to TV characters, books related to popular TV themes, and newspaper and magazine accounts of important current events. These print resources may be recommended to students (or portions may be read to them).

A special way to extend interests. A frequently used, structured plan to extend and broaden interests is G. O. Simpson's "My Reading Design" (1962). This circle graph (see Figure 15.3) enables the child to keep a record of the reading he has done in various curricular areas. In addition to filling in the chart, the child also keeps a separate listing of the titles of books read, by topics. A child should be permitted to color several circles (read several books) in one area as long as he samples each of the areas. The following forms of the design are available: Form E for grades 1–2; A for grades 3–4; B for grades 5–6; C for grades 7–9; and D for grades 10–12.

Utilizing interests in the instructional program. Children often make greater progress in reading when they read about things that interest them. Thus, the instructional program should make provision for the integration and utilization of student interests as often as possible. How can this be done? The following suggestions are illustrative:

Provide a choice among appropriate materials. Students should be given choices among reading materials when more than one piece of material will accomplish the teacher's or learners' objectives. For example, a comprehension skill may be taught from more than one skill development material. One student may prefer a programmed book while another may prefer narrative materials that reinforce or teach the same skill.

Give students choices in content area reading. Permitting a student to become a resource person in a specific content area is often helpful in extending interests. One way to accomplish this is to let the student share his knowledge in his special interest area by constructing a learning center

Figure 15.3. Simpson's "My Reading Design," Form B.

TO THE READER:—Here is an unfinished design. You may make it yours, if you complete it, as you read and enjoy the books which you like to read. First, find the book which you wish to read. Read it and write the title on the opposite page. Recall the things which you enjoyed in the book. Then, note the categories around the circle, and select those which tell what you enjoyed in the book. Check the subareas on the back page. They may help you to find the categories which do tell what you enjoyed in the book. Put the number of the book in the small circles nearest the center of the design, under the categories which tell what you enjoyed in the book. Then trace the small circles with your pencil. See Sample, opposite page. Very few books belong in more than three categories. Some books belong in one category only. If you read many books and record each book as you read, it will be fun to watch your pattern grow.

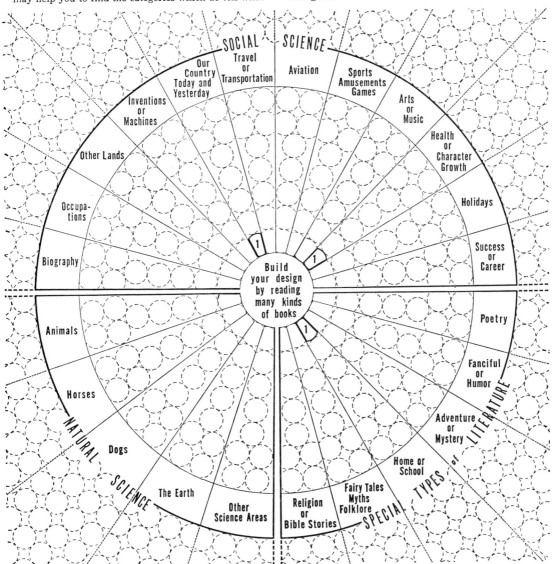

for other students to work through. A learner often feels motivated to read more and feels better about himself for having developed some degree of expertise in an area when he sees that his interests are valued and that he can work (partially at least) in his interest area.

Utilize interest groups. Interest groups are important because the teacher can tie education to hobbies and also because they promote content area reading. (See Chapter 18 for a discussion of interest groups.) Such groups offer a change of pace from the traditional ability groupings and may exist concurrently with these groups.

Utilize high interest–controlled vocabulary materials. Many materials, especially basals, do not provide for the interests of older children reading below grade level (Gillespie and Johnson 1974, p. 230). But there are several series available, frequently referred to as "high interest–controlled vocabulary" series; these attempt to use formats and story content that would appeal to a child at a given age level and at the same time use sentence patterns and vocabulary items at a lower level of difficulty. These series have met with much success in stimulating interest in reading for the low achiever. Two companies that provide a wide variety of types of such materials on many reading levels are Benefic Press (10300 W. Roosevelt Rd., Winchester, Ill. 60153) and Addison-Wesley (Sand Hill Rd., Menlo Park, Calif. 94025).

Utilize materials acceptable to students. In the Mathewson affective model, which we have referred to several times in this book, the acceptance component was stressed. This component involves the reader's integration of previously formed values, attitudes, and beliefs into his comprehension of the material he reads. Mathewson also suggested that the acceptance or rejection of materials read influenced attitudes toward further reading. Without a positive attitude, interest would be lacking. Thus, teachers should consider the use of materials congruent with the values, attitudes, and beliefs of children. A source for suggesting and evaluating books for use with children with minority cultural heritages, such as Blacks and Native Americans, is Maska Kabakow Rudman's *Children's Literature: An Issues Approach* (Lexington, Mass.: D. C. Heath, 1976).

Summary

It is essential that teachers consider how students feel about reading and what students like to read. An important outcome of reading instruction is to foster children who can and do read.

There are no guaranteed strategies that will promote positive attitudes. It is important to consider the effects of a student's positive self-concept, positive teacher attitudes toward reading and toward the learner, and instructional strategies that utilize students' interests and meet their instructional needs.

Student interests are motivating and determine largely the extent and nature of nonrequired reading. In promoting lasting interests, there are four steps that teachers should consider. First, they should understand the factors that correlate with interest formation. Second, they should understand typical interest patterns at the age and grade levels they teach. Third, they should study the individual interests of the students whom they teach. Fourth, they should make an effort to develop or extend interests.

It is important that teachers assess student attitudes, self-concept, and interests. One of the most valuable techniques is observation over time in nonstructured settings. Since this technique is time consuming and since teachers may wish information early in the instructional process, paper-and-pencil techniques such as questionnaires and summated rating scales may be helpful. It should be noted, however, that students may respond to these techniques as they feel the teacher wishes them to respond.

Questions for Further Reading and Thinking

1. What are the implications for teachers of research findings on attitudes? On self-concept? On interests?
2. How can you, as a teacher, determine the effects of your attitudes and behaviors on students' attitudes? On their interests?
3. Why is it desirable for developing attitudes and interests that a school have both a library and a classroom book collection?
4. Read Purves and Beach's account (1972) of the research relating to reading interests. Then read Chapter 1 in Spache's *Good Reading for Poor Readers* (1974) and pages 518–524 of Harris and Sipay's *How to Increase Reading Ability*, 7th ed. (1980). How has your reading refined your understanding of the research related to interests?

Activities and Projects

1. Prepare a card file of ideas that may be useful for developing and maintaining positive attitudes toward reading. Prepare another for developing and extending interests.
2. Construct an attitude assessment questionnaire. Give the questionnaire to a small group of students in your field experience program. Compare the results with the teacher's opinions. If possible, verify your findings through observation over time.
3. Devise a self-concept observational guide for a classroom with which you are familiar. State why you selected specific behaviors to observe.
4. Construct an interest inventory that would be applicable to the students with whom

you are working in your field experience program. Administer the inventory. Then compare the results with the contents of the basal reading series in use. Is the basal adequate? If not, what materials may be used to supplement the basal?

5. In your visits to elementary schools, note the techniques that teachers use to stimulate interest in reading, to improve reading attitudes, or to promote positive self-concepts. List other techniques they might use.

6. Study an individual child and recommend books you feel would help develop or extend his reading interests. List the techniques and activities you would use to help him become interested in reading the books you have recommended.

7. Prepare a list of high interest–controlled vocabulary materials that may be useful in working with low achievers.

8. Study one or more of the resources for teachers listed in the following section. How has your reading refined the learnings gained from this chapter?

Materials for Further Reading

Alexander, J. Estill; and Filler, Ronald Claude. 1976. *Attitudes and Reading*. Newark, Del.: International Reading Association.

Criscuolo, Nicholas P. 1979. Effective Approaches for Motivating Children to Read. *The Reading Teacher* 32 (February): 543–546.

Epstein, Ira. 1980. *Measuring Attitudes Toward Reading*. Princeton, N.J.: Report #73 of Eric Clearinghouse on Tests, Measurement and Evaluation, Educational Testing Service.

Graves, Michael F.; Boettcher, Judith A.; and Rydel, Randall A. 1979. *Easy Reading: Book Series and Periodicals for Less Able Readers*. Newark, Del.: International Reading Association.

Heathington, Betty S. 1979. What To Do About Reading Motivation in Middle Schools. *Journal of Reading* 22 (May): 709–713.

Henderson, Mary Ann. 1977. Reading While Becoming: Affective Approaches. *Journal of Reading* 20 (January): 317–326.

Huck, Charlotte S.; and Kuhn, Doris Young. 1976. *Children's Literature in the Elementary School*, 3rd ed. New York: Holt, Rinehart and Winston.

Johns, Jerry L.; and Hunt, Linda. 1975. Motivating Reading: Professional Ideas. *The Reading Teacher* 28 (April): 617–619.

Larrick, Nancy. 1960. *A Teacher's Guide to Children's Books*. Columbus, Ohio: Charles E. Merrill.

Mager, Robert F. 1968. *Developing Attitudes toward Learning*. Belmont, Calif.: Fearon.

Spache, George D. 1975. *Good reading for the disadvantaged reader*. Champaign, Ill.: Garrard.

Spache, George D. 1978. *Good reading for poor readers*, 9th ed. Champaign, Ill.: Garrard.

Lester N. Knight

16
Reading for the Linguistically and Culturally Different

Providing success for children in reading has for decades been a major goal of American schools. The mode for determining whether this goal has been met has typically been the use of a test. The results of such tests have been interpreted to indicate that the schools have not produced the desired *universal* success in reading. A substantial portion of those students who have not achieved success are referred to as the linguistically and culturally different (Harber and Bryen 1967; Shuy 1969). Although children in this group may be penalized somewhat by the tests themselves, it is nevertheless apparent to educators that many of these children do in fact perform below expected levels in reading tasks.

Prior to the 1960s the linguistically and culturally different child's failure in reading was frequently accepted as "to be expected." However, with the governmental War on Poverty and its associated programs, the schools began to recognize and accept some accountability for helping such children achieve reading success. The school's initial response was to view such children as essentially void of many of the prerequisites generally recognized as pertinent to reading success. As evidence has accumulated from research and experience, however, it has become increasingly clear that the language and experiential base (so important to reading success) of the linguistically and culturally different child is neither absent nor deficient. It *is* different, however, and this fact has many important implications for reading instruction.

Linguistically and culturally different children have at least one thing in common. They are often outside society's main stream of influence and social mobility. Poverty is a major factor in societal alienation because it places the child in a group whose language and culture tend to be viewed by the population at large as substandard. There are a number of subgroups in the linguistically and culturally different category, but many are economically poor. This factor tends to perpetuate the condition generation after generation.

Some linguistically and culturally different children speak a variation or dialect of English that is considered to be nonstandard. There are two major categories of nonstandard dialects spoken in this country. One of them includes various Black dialects and the other includes Appalachian dialects. Black dialects are used by children in both rural and urban areas, whereas Appalachian dialects are spoken mainly in mountainous rural areas of the Appalachian area. In either case the dialect is spoken across wide geographical areas, resulting in slight variations within the dialects.

Other children in our society considered to be linguistically and culturally different speak little English or no English at all. Among these groups are the Mexican-Americans of the Southwest, the Cajuns of portions of the Southeast, and the various Indian tribes, principally in the Southwest. And in more recent years some American educators have also worked with Cuban, Vietnamese, Cambodian, and other refugees. These groups represent a wide variety of language systems.

Each of the above groups, whether different in dialect or language, represents a unique and special culture. Consideration of the cultural differences is as important as the language differences in structuring reading programs. For each cultural system a potentially different value system, experiential base, and societal contribution are represented.

None of the groups considered above can be described as monolithic. Aside from the vast differences between such groups as Blacks and Navajo Indians, there are also important differences within groups (intragroup). This is particularly true among Indians and the Spanish speakers of the Southwest and the Spanish speakers from Cuba. In the paragraphs that follow these factors will be considered: (1) language differences and their role in reading; (2) cultural differences and their role in reading; (3) general suggestions for working with the linguistically and culturally different; and (4) teaching reading to the linguistically and culturally different.

Language Differences and Their Role in Reading

QUESTIONS TO GUIDE READING

Literal
What are some distinguishing characteristics of standard and nonstandard dialect?

Inferential
Which factor is the most crucial in determining potential success in reading — linguistic performance or linguistic competence?
What different language characteristics should be considered for non-English speakers when compared to nonstandard English speakers?

Evaluative

What degree of importance should teachers attach to language differences in reading?

A strong language base is widely viewed as essential to success in reading (Loban 1976; Ruddell 1966; Strickland 1962). Language is basically a human invention whereby members of the species are able arbitrarily to express and receive messages from each other. These messages are conveyed and received through a complex system of sounds that are combined into meaningful units (e.g., words). These units are then arranged in various ways to create longer utterances such as sentences. Sentences are then sequenced into longer discourse through discussion, written paragraphs, and even longer units. Additional meanings are conveyed through the language support systems of nonverbal cues and intonational variation.

If that constitutes language, what constitutes the *strong* or qualitative language base that is considered important to reading success? The answer to this question is not simple and will be explored further. However, it is clear that the first language of the linguistically and culturally different child has not been typically viewed as strong or qualitative. To reach this conclusion glibly is, as we shall see, entirely too simplistic.

DIALECT

Although the term dialect is sometimes erroneously used to denote a "bad" style of language, it actually is a nonqualitative term and refers to variation *within* a particular language that is unique to that language group. Everyone uses a dialect. Even American Sign Language includes dialectal variation (Dale 1976). One can expect to find different dialects across any language community, whether it be English, French, Spanish or some other language. Geography, socioeconomic status, educational level, age, and sex are some of the factors that may determine one's dialect. These variations are classified generally as either standard or nonstandard. Specific consideration here is given to standard English (SE) and nonstandard English (NSE).

Standard English (SE). Standard English is what some have believed to be synonymous with *strong* language, but who among us uses it? Is it those who speak like television news reporters or pronounce all their words as Webster suggests? I think not. However standard English is defined, the possibility of some variation must be taken into account. This means that more than one pronunciation may be "acceptable" and thus

Table 16.1. Standard Regional Variations

Pronunciations	Vocabulary
pen = pen or pin	sofa or couch
idea = idea or idear	blanket or comforter
Carter = Carter or Cahtah	let or leave
Mary = Mary or Merry	elevator or lift

create no problems of social acceptance for the user. It also means different labels may be applied to the same object. What *is* acceptable is determined regionally and by those with the most influence — the educated of the region. Hence a standard dialect might be described as that dialect used by the educated group of a particular region. In practical application this would imply that mere regional variations such as "car" versus "cah" or "faucet" versus "spigot" are not determiners of standard versus nonstandard English (see Table 16.1).

Nonstandard English (NSE). Since variation is "allowed" in standard English, what characterizes nonstandard variation? The above examples given are either of pronunciation or vocabulary label. Regional variations in these features of language are frequently considered standard, although some pronunciations, wherever they occur, are not considered standard (e.g., "keer" for "care"). Variations that are most frequently viewed as nonstandard occur at the level of grammatical construction. Therefore an utterance that substitutes *his'n* for *his* or omits the linking verb as in "She a pretty girl" is likely to be considered nonstandard. The influence of social standing determined by economic and educational opportunities is apparent since most nonstandard English speakers are not a part of the educated populace of a particular region. Nonstandard forms, when compared to standard, are fairly easily recognized (see Table 16.2). Nonstandard dialect has been viewed by some as weak language and consequently a major contributor to the disproportionate number of failures in reading among its users.

Nonstandard English and Reading

Written language or the printed page is not just talk written down. It follows the same basic grammatical structures as oral language but tends to be more polished and formal. Actually, *no one* talks like a book. Oral language is typically punctuated with false starts and with some rambling and fragmented sentences. It is also accompanied by variation in pitch, pause, stress, facial expressions, and gestures. However, few would dispute that most printed materials that confront school children are written

Table 16.2. Standard versus Nonstandard Features

	Standard	Nonstandard[a]
Pronunciations	this	dis
	rinse	rinch
	chair	cheer
	police'	po'lice
	window	winder
	told	toll
Grammar	Those aren't his.	Those ain't his'n.
	Joe climbed a tree.	Joe clumb a tree.
	Those are Jack's shoes.	Those Jack shoe.
	Mary heard it.	Mary heared it.
	The dog looked at me.	The dog look at me.

[a]Although these and other examples are *predominant* in some nonstandard dialects, they may also appear in some informal situations among some standard English speakers. SE speakers, however, are likely to use the standard form in most situations.

in standard English. Such nonstandard features as "Those Jack shoe" do not appear in children's reading or other texts. Given the fact of such divergence between the text and the nonstandard speaking child's dialect, can it be assumed that: (1) the child's language is weak? and (2) NSE interferes with success in reading?

Qualitative level of NSE. In the 1960s, when the War on Poverty programs were initiated, the prevailing view of NSE was that it was a weak rendition of SE and therefore deficient (Bereiter et al. 1966; Deutsch 1964; Deutsch 1967; Frost and Rowland 1968). This view was not new to the sixties but seemed to some people to be authenticated at that time. The major assumption, quite naturally, was that the reason for the widespread failure in reading among NSE speakers was their weak language. Later studies, of Black dialects in particular, have quite clearly shown that NSE is *not* merely a weak version of SE. It is rather a well-structured system with its own rules of grammar and vocabulary, which are followed by speakers of the dialect (Baratz 1969; Dillard 1977; Labov 1970; Wolfram 1970). As a complete linguistic system, the NSE used and understood by linguistically and culturally different children should not be viewed as weak SE but as a *well-developed* language in and of itself.

Interference of NSE with reading. As pointed out in the previous paragraph, earlier views held that NSE interfered with successful reading (Deutsch 1964; Goodman 1965*b*). Three factors probably contributed to this view. The first was that NSE was viewed as weak at the same time that a strong language base was being espoused as necessary to reading success. Second, there was little distinction between the *performance* (or use of) and *competence* (or understanding of) of SE by NSE speakers. Competence was not really considered and thus such speakers were viewed as being too deficient in language for success in reading. Finally, reading success was frequently measured in terms of oral reading performance rather than comprehension. Therefore every NSE rendition of the SE text was viewed as reading failure. All three of these factors have now been seriously questioned. Nonstandard English is clearly not an inherently weak language, and though spoken, does not preclude the existence of a high degree of competence in or understanding of SE. It is also clear that comprehension of the printed page should take precedence over any oral NSE renditions. The current view is that NSE *in and of itself* does not interfere with reading (Goodman and Buck 1973; Laffey and Shuy 1973; Rigg 1978; Wolfram 1979). It is extremely important to separate NSE oral language productions from reading comprehension. Oral productions that do not interfere with comprehension should not be regarded as a significant reading *miscue* (Cunningham 1977). The term miscue was coined by Goodman (1965*a*) to represent unexpected responses by the reader to the printed page. It may be concluded, therefore, that NSE does not directly interfere with reading success.

NON-ENGLISH SPEAKERS AND READING

A major difference between most NSE speakers and some non-English speakers (e.g., Mexican-Americans, Indians, Cuban refugees, etc.) is a lack of competence in English at all. Such children may be expected to have a well-developed language, but its linguistic composition may be substantially different in all aspects from English. (See Table 16.3.) Because of these basic differences, frustration can be expected if these children are required to begin to read from *English* materials immediately in first grade. For example, unless the reader knows Spanish, little meaning would be obtained from *¿Como está usted?* Imagine being confronted with pages of the same! This is not to suggest that all reading related experi-

Table 16.3. Some Interference Phenomena Samples Between English and Spanish

	English	Spanish
Vowels	Much variation in pronunciation (e.g., i — sĭt or sīte)	Little variation in pronunciation (e.g., i — bonita /bonēēta/)
Verb form change to indicate person	Not present	hablo = I speak. ellá habla = She speaks.

ences should be delayed. Certainly the child may begin reading with materials in her own language. And perhaps some reading instruction can occur along with development of an English language base, although some interference from the child's first language may still be expected (Gonzalez and Rafael 1981).

Cultural Differences: Their Role in Reading

QUESTIONS TO GUIDE READING

Literal
What kinds of cultural differences are important considerations in reading programs?

Inferential
How might a teacher inventory the cultural heritage of children?

Evaluative
Should any particular kind of cultural difference be considered more important than other cultural differences? Why or why not?

The cultural heritage of the reader has both direct and indirect influence on potential for reading success. Every culture tends to perpetuate a set of common experiences out of which concepts are developed. The conceptual framework of the reader has much to do with comprehension of printed materials. Even if the reader can decode all the words and understand the language structure, comprehension will falter if very many words represent unknown concepts. Each culture operates within a particular set of values, traditions, and customs. The members of one culture may place a high priority on preparation for the future, whereas another may be almost totally present oriented. There are cultures with traditions of literacy and others that may be basically action oriented. Such variations wield a powerful indirect influence on how reading can and should be taught. When the school program runs counter to the cultural mores of the child, problems may occur unless teachers are knowledgeable and sensitive to points of divergence.

Experiences and related concepts, values, traditions, and customs of the linguistically and culturally different may vary rather significantly from those of "mainstream society." There are also differences across the various groups designated as linguistically and culturally different. Some of those differences are discussed below.

EXPERIENTIAL VARIATION

Notice that the label for this section is "experiential *variation*" and not "experiential *deprivation*." The latter would apply only when the teacher did not take into account the possibility that the linguistically and culturally different child may not have experienced things represented in school materials. However, it is quite clear that every child does have a rich storehouse of experiences. Only a sampling of differing cultural experiences can be reviewed here, but let it remind the teacher that he must inventory what experiences and concepts the child has.

Compare the experiences of an Appalachian Mountain child with her middle-class, SE-speaking counterpart. Suppose the printed material refers to a *lavatory*. This probably would be an entirely foreign concept. However, the word *craklin'* would be recognized as pork rind and fat. Other terms that might be unrecognizable would include: *escalator, microwave, subway, atlas,* or even *orchestra*. On the other hand, if confronted with terms like *bee gum, sorghum, lye,* or *poke salad*, the child would likely have no conceptual problem. Since school materials and tests generally include the former rather than the latter terms, the teacher will need to make the necessary adjustment, to ensure that success is possible.

VARIATION IN VALUES, TRADITIONS, AND CUSTOMS

The values, traditions, and customs of each linguistically and culturally different group must be taken into account not only in the day-to-day lesson plans for reading, but in the teacher-child interaction associated with the actual execution of those plans. Rodrigues and White (1981, p. 3) suggest several examples:

> Does one point at a Navajo? Does one pat Vietnamese children on their heads when praising them? Does one point the soles of his or her shoes toward students of Arab descent? Does the lowering of one's eyes indicate the same thing in all cultures? How close does one stand to another when talking? Or, under what conditions may one person touch another? Knowing the answers to such questions can avoid unintended insults and facilitate cross-cultural communication.

It must be understood that the value system of some persons will mitigate against just what the school is working toward. For example, reward from hard work may not have been the experience of many children within the linguistically and culturally different group. Much value may be placed on the status quo or even the past because of lack of reward or even time to work for future goals. Some children, such as Appalachians, may be highly individualistic and find it difficult to work in groups. For many of these children the family is highly valued, although

Reading for the Linguistically and Culturally Different

the dominant parent may tend to be the father (as with Appalachians) or the mother (as with Blacks). The values, traditions, and customs should not be criticized or side-stepped, but should be accepted and used to the fullest extent possible. If this is not done, communication between the teacher and pupil is unlikely. If accepted, the child can thus develop a sense of acceptance and security, an absolute prerequisite for successful reading experiences in school.

General Suggestions for Working with the Linguistically and Culturally Different

QUESTIONS TO GUIDE READING

Literal
What are three major guidelines for teachers to consider when working with the linguistically and culturally different?

Inferential
What reasons can be identified that support the cruciality of positive teacher attitudes in working with children in reading?
What is the importance of standard English as a prerequisite to learning to read material written in standard English for nonstandard English speakers as compared with non-English speakers?

Evaluative
Should teachers approach the teaching of reading to linguistically and culturally different children any differently than to other children? If so, how?

Educational research has shown that the teacher is as important to the linguistically and culturally different as to any other population. There are no universally acceptable descriptions of the traits of a good teacher, but surely most educators would agree that among them would be sensitivity, flexibility, resourcefulness, and a respect for and rapport with students. Certainly these general traits will be beneficial to the teacher whose goal is to be successful with the linguistically and culturally different. Experience and research with this population have shown several important guidelines that such teachers should follow. Among these are: (1) know as much about the children as possible; (2) develop positive attitudes and expectations concerning them; and (3) avoid confusion between the oral language production and reading comprehension of children.

Role of Knowledge about the Children

Good teachers always begin their work with any child by learning as much as possible about him and then starting the instructional program "where he is." They also know that all children are different and they adjust the program accordingly. Good teachers of linguistically and culturally different children will need to make a special effort to *know* them because of their atypical characteristics.

As we have seen, specific differences can be expected not only in the oral language production of the child but in her cultural framework as well. The teacher must learn, with all possible specificity, just what these differences are.[1] Answers to such questions as the following should be sought:

1. In what ways does the first language or dialect spoken by the child differ from standard English (SE)?
2. If the first spoken language is a form of nonstandard English (NSE), what effect will it have on the child's initial experience in SE reading materials?
3. If the first spoken language is not English, what effect will it have on the child's initial experiences in SE reading materials?
4. What is the child's level of understanding (competence) in SE and how should this affect experience in reading SE materials?
5. Based on knowledge of the child's cultural heritage:
   a. What differences in conceptual framework can be expected and how does this affect the reading program (e.g., amusement park concepts versus "games at home" concepts)?
   b. What special cultural contributions can be utilized in the school (e.g., the crafts of Appalachia)?
   c. What effect should the represented value system, traditions, and customs have on the day-to-day interactions between the teacher and the child (e.g., present goal orientation versus future goal orientation)?

Attitudes and Expectations Concerning the Children

The attitudes and expectations of the teacher concerning linguistically and culturally different children may be the most crucial influences of all. The importance of teacher attitudes and expectations is not new (Frost and Rowland 1971; Johnson 1971). With increased evidence that NSE does not interfere directly with reading success, however, a sharper focus

1. Excellent materials are available from such professional groups as the Center of Applied Linguistics (CAL), Teachers of English for Speakers of Other Languages (TESOL), International Reading Association (IRA), and the National Council of the Teachers of English (NCTE). Also notice the suggested materials for teachers at the end of this chapter.

has been placed on teacher attitudes and expectations (Wheat et al. 1979). It is possible that failure results more from negative teacher attitudes and expectations (a phenomenon all too likely, as Blodgett and Cooper 1973; and Williams et al. 1972 show) than from any language or conceptual characteristics of the children.

A possible consequence of "getting to know" as much as possible about the linguistically and culturally different is a positive attitude toward them and realistic expectations from them. Consider attitudes about NSE for example. Wheat et al. (1979) have suggested that one might initially ask, "What do I know about language?" "Do I use different language styles?" and "What do I know about the child's language and how it is used?" A language attitudes inventory might also be used to check agreement or disagreement to such statements as: "Most Black children can easily understand the language of White teachers in school" or "Native Americans have great difficulty learning English because their own language and culture are so much less complicated."[2] If the teacher determines that her attitude is negative, she must strive to acquire the knowledge necessary about language in general (and the dialect or language of the child in particular) to develop a positive one.

It is absolutely essential that the teacher be able to accept the child's first dialect or language as a viable means of communication. The child should be encouraged to use that language in school without fear of rejection by constant correction or reminders of a "better" way to say things. Furthermore, it is equally crucial that the child's cultural heritage be accepted and appreciated. Beginning language and reading activities should make abundant use of the concepts, traditions, and customs of the child's representative culture.

The teacher's attitudes will bear directly on his expectations of the child. Positive ones will result in realistically high expectations, which will be transmitted throughout the day. These attitudes are conveyed not only verbally but through a myriad of nonverbal cues as well. Fortunate indeed is the linguistically and culturally different child who is able to work in an environment of acceptance and trust so conducive to learning. For that child, half (or more) of the battle is won.

CONFUSION BETWEEN ORAL LANGUAGE PRODUCTION AND READING COMPREHENSION

Some confusion has existed between oral language and reading for the linguistically and culturally different. Part of this confusion has resulted from the belief that a NSE oral rendition of reading of SE materials was a significant reading miscue or error and that proficiency in SE was a prerequisite for reading success. In addition, there was seldom a clear

2. Items from inventory by Susan H. Houston and published in *Attitudes, Language, and Change* by Gere Anne Ruggles and Eugene Smith. Urbana, Ill: NCTE, 1979.

focus between the goals of teaching reading and the goal of teaching standard English as a language alternative.

The reader should reread pages 394–96 to be reminded that NSE miscues probably do not interfere with reading comprehension and that speakers of other languages can begin reading in their own language. Hence divergent first language or dialect appears to be less consequential when the teacher is able to make necessary adjustments. These will be illustrated in a later section of this chapter (see pp. 409–10).

Everyone agrees that a primary responsibility of the school for the linguistically and culturally different child (NSE speaker or non-English speaker) is to teach her to *read* SE. What must be clear is that this responsibility is a totally different issue from teaching her to *speak* SE. If speaking SE is desirable and even essential for reasons other than reading, teachers should have a realistic goal. They should also consider some similarities and differences in learning the first and second language or dialect and should structure a language arts program to maximize the possibilities for achieving that goal.

Goal for teaching SE. The major reason for learning SE is sociological. This means that since it is difficult to achieve social mobility in our society without proficiency in oral SE, the schools should attempt to ensure that all children can use it in situations where it is desirable. Actually the ability to vary language style according to the situation is a desirable goal for all speakers. This goal is not necessarily in contradiction to the total acceptance of the child's first language or dialect. Such acceptance should always take precedence. However, dialects and languages can be compared in terms of *alternatives*. The SE alternative should always be viewed as another style or register, much as the SE speaker changes styles when speaking intimately to a close friend or about business with an employer. Great care must continually be taken to keep this goal separate from that of reading. Teachers should also realize that learning the SE alternative is closely tied to motivation in learning it. Since children may not see the need for it until the late elementary years or later, the goal must be viewed as long range.

Similarities and differences in first and second language or dialect learning. Children learn their language in much the same way (Slobin 1972) and most of them come to school having internalized most of the rules of their language (Dale 1976). Linguistically and culturally different children cannot, therefore, be viewed as linguistically impoverished in any sense at all. For the NSE speaker the task of learning to speak SE may be to some extent one of motivation since understanding of SE is already intact and since the dialectal differences are not as great as those between languages. The non-English speaker, faced with the task of learning a totally different language in an environment quite unlike that in which the first language was learned, meets a unique challenge. Some researchers suggest that learning a second language is a matter of adopting or extending existing skills and knowledge rather than relearning a completely new set of skills (Ervin-Tripp 1973; Ravem 1969). Other evidence suggests that in second language acquisition the learner may suffer from interference from the first language (Rodrigues and White 1981) and that morphemes (or meaningful units) are not learned according to semantic–syntactical difficulty as is the case in learning the first language (Mace-Matluck 1977). More research is needed to clarify differences and similarities in learning the first and second language.

Teaching Standard English. No best method can be recommended for providing the SE alternative. Approaches used may be generally classified as unstructured or structured. Unstructured procedures emanate from the notion that SE should be modeled consistently and in various ways so that the child receives maximum exposure to it. The language arts program includes many listening experiences to provide this exposure.[3] Gradually, nonqualitative comparisons may be made between the dialects or languages. In more structured approaches short periods of intensive practice periods are provided. The so-called audiolingual approach is such an approach. By this technique specific linguistic features (e.g., use of the possessive marker) are modeled and practiced immediately. Nonstandard English speakers may have the greatest prospect of learning SE from the more unstructured approaches. Non-English speakers may require a more structured approach unless the situation involves only one or two children who are in a classroom with SE speakers. Whatever the situation the principle of use of the child's first dialect or language in the school (especially during the early primary years) must be upheld.

Teaching Reading to the Linguistically and Culturally Different

QUESTIONS TO GUIDE READING

Literal
What are some characteristics of some nonstandard Black English dialects that may affect instruction in auditory discrimination and phonics?

Inferential
What should be the response of the teacher to nonstandard dialect translations in reading?

---

3. Note specific suggestions in *Language Arts for the Exceptional: The Gifted and the Linguistically Different* by Lester N. Knight. Itasca, Ill.: F. E. Peacock, 1974.

How can maximum potential for reading comprehension be realized for the linguistically and culturally different?

To what extent can typical programs and approaches to the teaching of reading be used with the linguistically and culturally different?

Evaluative

How could one describe the "ideal" program for teaching reading to the linguistically and culturally different?

Many Blacks, rural Appalachians, Native Americans, Mexican-Americans, and others labeled linguistically and culturally different do learn to read successfully. But far too many experience delayed success when compared to their SE-speaking peers, especially more affluent ones. Others simply do not succeed at all. Some possible reasons for this failure and some general suggestions for rectifying them have been reviewed in the preceding pages.

In the sections that follow, some of the aspects of reading, as defined in Chapter 1, are specifically considered with the unique characteristics of the linguistically and culturally different in mind. Although specific examples are given, you should recall the great diversity represented by the label "linguistically and culturally different" and attempt to avoid making faulty applications. The following aspects of reading are considered: (1) readiness, (2) word recognition, (3) comprehension, and (4) approaches and programs.

READINESS

Although readiness for reading is a concern at all reading levels, it has special significance for beginning reading. These concerns were highlighted and discussed in Chapter 2. The beginning reading readiness factors most likely to require special consideration by the teacher are discussed here. These include cognition, experiential background, linguistic background, and auditory discrimination.

No real evidence exists to indicate that linguistically and culturally different children are deficient cognitively. When the teacher relates to them on a basis similar with other children, there is no reason to expect any handicaps in abilities to think and solve various problems. Given a supportive situation to which they can relate, such children can demonstrate their cognitive skills. Carroll (1973) points out that they, in such a situation, are able to express thought equal to their peers.

The experiential framework and associated concepts of the linguistically different may be decidedly atypical: the fact that some "school type" concepts are absent does not in any way imply the *lack* of experiences and concepts. Where divergence exists between the child's experiences and concepts and those represented in beginning materials, adjustments must be made.

Initial adjustments most assuredly should include delay in using materials that are too diverse and development of procedures that capitalize on the child's own experiential base. For example, perhaps the story about the city factory can be delayed and another one developed about dyeing homespun yarn, our way of "getting rid of" a cold, or going fishing. Such story development involves the use of the language-experience approach discussed later in this chapter in more detail (as well as in Chapter 13).

As materials are developed utilizing his own experiential base, the linguistically and culturally different child should be provided with experiences whereby the concepts represented in the SE beginning reading materials are developed.[4] However, these concepts should never be viewed as in any way superior to their own. This can be done either directly or vicariously. The implication is that the educational program will be replete with well-planned field trips that involve much before and after discussion with the children. Carefully chosen resource persons should be invited to the classroom. Such persons could represent various vocations and professions represented in the SE materials. However, they would need help from the teacher to ensure that needed experiences are shared in a manner to which the children can relate. In addition the classroom activities should include much use of such media as carefully chosen filmstrips, cassette tapes, and records. No day should end without the teacher sharing an appropriate selection from children's literature.

The language power of the linguistically and culturally different child is well documented and has already been discussed. The school's task is to ensure that the child has success in initial reading experiences. Readiness experiences for the non-English speaking child should utilize materials and experiences in the child's native language. English as a second language may be introduced as a separate program from reading. The NSE speaking child is likely to have a relatively high level of understanding of SE as long as no unknown terms are used. However, the program should give continuous opportunities for hearing SE as a preparation for reading it. A major consideration for either the NSE speaker or non-English speaker is the probable interference of the first dialect or language with auditory discrimination of SE phonemes or sounds (see Table 16.4). Because of such interferences, standardized tests such as the Wepman Auditory Discrimination Test are of little value with this population. You are urged to reread the section on auditory discrimination in Chapter 2. It must be reemphasized that it is not necessary to master auditory discrimination of all SE phonemes in order to read SE materials. Recall that

4. Various Compensentory Education programs are now in existence. Programs such as Head Start and Title 1 may contain some features that may well be included in the total reading and language arts program. Care should be taken to ensure that such features are compatible with a total program whose philosophical foundation honors the funds of the child.

Table 16.4. Sample Characteristics of Some Nonstandard Black English

Phonological (sound) variations[a]

Omissions and reductions:	a*ks* (for *asks*)
	to*ll* (for to*ld*)
	be*ll* (for bel*t*)
	toe (for t*ore*)
	gho*ss* (for gho*st*)
	bre*fis* (for br*eakf*ast)
Substitutions:	*den* (for *then*)
	Ru*fie* (for Ru*thie*)
	S*kr*eet (for s*tr*eet)

Morphological (word form) variations

Omission of pluralizer:	I've got two *cent*. (for I've got two *cents*.)
Omission of past tense marker:	Mary *drop* it. (for Mary *dropped* it.)
	or Bill *lift* his bag. (for Bill *lifted* his bag.)
Omission of possessive marker:	Those *Jack* shoe. (for Those are *Jack's* shoes.)
Lack of subject-verb agreement:	Jill *like* it. (for Jill *likes* it.)

Syntax (sentence structure) variations

Use of *be* to indicate habituality:	He *be* workin'. (for He *has a job*.)
Omission of the copula:	Bill tired. (for Bill *is* tired.)
Multiple negation:	Jack *don't* have *no* shoes. (for Jack *doesn't* have *any* shoes.)
Question inversion of noun and auxiliary verb:	I axed Joe *could he* do it. (for I asked Joe *if he could* do it.)

Based on material from Burke (1973); DeStefano (1978); Labov (1970); and Zintz (1975).
[a]All variations can easily be recognized in the language production or speech of the child. The nonstandard form is provided but the standard form is often understood.

auditory discrimination may not be a very important readiness skill unless the program is heavily phonics oriented.

WORD RECOGNITION

The recognition of words is but one aspect of reading. Nevertheless, it is essential. Words are the language symbols used to represent meanings that refer to the reality of our world. A person faced with a passage whose sentences contain very many unknown words will generally fail to receive the writer's message.

For the beginning reader a word may be unknown because it cannot be decoded or pronounced correctly. Once this can be done the word can be recognized instantly and is hence referred to as a part of that child's sight vocabulary. Lack of word recognition is more likely to be due to a decoding problem rather than a meaning problem at this level. Because of this problem most beginning reading programs emphasize the acquisition of decoding skills more than other levels do. Such skills as phonics, structural analysis, and the use of contextual clues are discussed in Part Two. Since all of them are directly related to the language of the child, it is clear that teaching them may require some adjustments that take into account the first language or dialect of the linguistically and culturally different. See Table 16.4. The unique features of that language or dialect, as illustrated in the following paragraphs, must be considered as word recognition skills are taught.

Phonics. Phonics, as suggested in Chapter 4, refers to matching a particular sound of the language with a printed letter or letter combination. An important prerequisite to learning such a relationship is the auditory discrimination of the sound. Many children enter school with a rather high degree of mastery in auditory discrimination of SE sounds. However, as the various *sound–letter* relationships are considered, it will soon become apparent that such mastery cannot be assumed for the linguistically and culturally different. Therefore, what might otherwise be pedagogically routine becomes a special challenge for the teacher. Suppose the material being used instructs the teacher to say "Draw a line under every word that *begins* like the word I'm about to pronounce. The word is *this.*" The child's printed material looks like this:

they
moth
did
those
with

The child whose first language or dialect substitutes /d/ for /th/ is placed at a disadvantage and may select the word *did.* Since similar problems may occur when materials clash with any of the phonological variations, the teacher should be especially patient with such choices and should, as much as possible, either select or construct materials that do not place the child in the position of possible confusion. The same kind of consideration is due the non-English speaking student. Vowel sound–letter relationships may be particularly troublesome for the native Spanish speaker, for example, since only five vowel sounds exist in Spanish.

Structural analysis. Structural analysis refers to the utilization of the meaningful parts (morphemes) of words in decoding. These parts include the base or root of the word plus any addition to or alteration of it through prefixes, suffixes, plurals, past tense and comparative endings, or contractions. Since the use of structural analysis is based on knowledge of these parts as they are used in SE, any language or dialectal deviation

Table 16.5. Expected Nonstandard Translations of SE Forms

Printed materials	Nonstandard translation[a]
Will *has* two brothers.	Will have two brotha.
Josie park*ed* the car.	Josie park the car.
Tha*t's* Mary*'s* book.	That Mary book.

[a]Children who speak other dialects may make translations compatible with their first dialect. Appalachian speakers may translate "Those are his." to "Them are his'n." Similarly, the child's pronunciations may translate "window" into "winder" or "salad" into "salit."

from SE rules must be considered. The items under the "meaningful unit variations" category in Table 16.4 are examples. Therefore printed materials written in the SE forms in Table 16.5 might be expected to be translated by the child into his own language.

Nonstandard dialect translations in reading. Experience has shown that NSE English speakers will generally translate SE materials into their own dialect when reading orally. Therefore, the NSE Black child may read "Bill doesn't have any shoes" as "Bill don't have no shoe," and the NSE Appalachian child's rendition of "He may hurt himself if he isn't careful" could be "He may hurt hisself if he ain't keerful." We have seen previously that such dialectal NSE renditions do not interfere with comprehension of the materials. Such translations suggest that the child is finding meaning in her reading. The teacher, when confronted with such translations, should merely *accept* them in the oral reading setting. The only way this can be done is for the teacher to know the dialect. Only those deviations which change the meaning should be discussed at that time (Dillingofski 1979). At the same time plans can be made to assist these children in the development of the SE alternative as a part of the total language arts program. Ways to develop SE involve a number of processes too lengthy to describe here. However, teachers who make sure that SE is modeled not only by themselves but through children's literature will have made a meaningful start.

Contextual clues. The ability to use clues within the total context of the printed materials is of unquestioned value. Their importance is well documented in Chapter 5. The extent to which context can be used depends very much on the degree of compatibility existing between the material and the language and experience of the reader. Since important divergence may exist for the linguistically and culturally different child, care should be observed to choose materials of minimal divergence. The child's language, for example, might interfere with a correct choice in the first sentence, but be clarified in the second sentence.

1. Her (past, pass) made her famous.
2. His perfect (pass, past) to the man down the field made him famous.

Similarly, the Appalachian child is more likely to be able to be successful with contextual clues in a story about the game "Annie Over" than "Atari."

COMPREHENSION

Most reading authorities would agree that true reading does not occur with mere "word calling." Even if a child can correctly pronounce most words in the printed material, that material has not been *read* unless the message is understood. By rereading Chapters 1 and 8 you will be reminded of the complexity of defining just what is involved in comprehension. However, it is clear that once the words are recognized and decoded they must be understood in the total context of the material. This apparently involves a complex array of interrelating skills based on experiences and concepts, language, cognition, and attitudes. When anything in the reading experience interferes substantially with these factors, comprehension, and therefore reading itself, will suffer.

As we have seen, NSE speakers apparently possess a level of SE competence regardless of their performance. This competence ensures little interference from the features of NSE dialect itself. However, the non-English speaking child may not be expected to read successfully in SE materials until he gains some proficiency in English. Initial reading should be in materials printed in the child's first language.

The different cultural milieu of the linguistically and culturally different child may provide experiences that conflict with those represented in some SE materials. This may be expected for the NSE speaking child, though perhaps to a lesser degree, as well as for the non-English speaking child. The teacher must inventory the child's concepts and vocabulary through study of available materials and observation and determine to include them in reading materials, while avoiding materials heavy with unknown words. Table 16.6 contains examples of concepts that might be typically understood.

Table 16.6. Familiar Navajo and Appalachian Concepts

Navajo concepts[a]		Appalachian concepts	
creosote leaves	turquoise	pounding	poke salad
manzanita tea	loom	britches	smokehouse
maize	prickly pear	tow sack	kindling
griddle cake		light bread	

[a]The Navajo concepts must be printed in the Navajo language.

The cognitive skills necessary for reading comprehension (and reviewed in Chapter 1) are not as easily inventoried for the linguistically and culturally different as they are for other children. Typical standardized intelligence tests used to assess cognitive strengths and weaknesses are of even less value for them. However, there is little evidence that they are cognitively impoverished. The linguistically and culturally different child, it would appear, possesses the necessary cognitive skills. However, some of these children may have received sensory and intellectual stimulation that is somewhat different from the kind on which school learnings are based. For example there may have been very limited exposure to printed materials and problems may have tended to be solved physically more often than verbally. It is crucial that the teacher be aware of such differences and make allowances for them in his planning. In so doing, games and action-oriented activities could be selected rather than passive ones.

Finally, the teacher must not in any sense view the child negatively. This means that the child without the tradition of literacy, who seems to "butcher the King's English," who doesn't speak English at all, or who seems to "lack" *school* concepts and traditions must be accepted as she is. A nonaccepting attitude will ensure interference with reading, whereas acceptance of the total child plus a vigorous attempt to inventory her language, concepts, and attitudes will do much to ensure success.

PROGRAMS AND APPROACHES TO TEACHING READING

Based on what is now known about teaching reading to the linguistically and culturally different, it is clear that it is neither necessary nor wise to develop totally new approaches, programs, materials, or procedures. We have seen that much of what has to be done lies instead in adjustments in the classroom based on realistic, and yet positive, views of the total child. Certainly the development of materials written in all the various NSE dialects is not only virtually impossible, but is also unnecessary because such speakers automatically translate SE materials into their own dialect as they read (Hall and Turner 1974: Kachuck 1975). Yet the common programs and approaches used in teaching reading, and reviewed in detail in other chapters of this volume, can be successful only when adjusted to the population. Some possible adaptations are suggested below.

Basal programs. Since the evidence is clear that differences between NSE and SE do not interfere with reading comprehension, basals should not be abandoned on that basis. Furthermore there is some evidence that there may be a fair match between the speaking vocabulary of these children and the vocabulary of basals (Cohen and Kornfeld 1970). In using basals, however, the teacher should follow these guidelines:

1. Avoid the use of word examples that conflict with the child's dialect or language in teaching word recognition skills.
2. Accept NSE renditions of the basal materials that are compatible with the meaning of the text. Do not expect word-for-word accuracy.
3. Select basal material that does not conflict, to any great extent, with the concepts of the child.
4. Select basal material that is basically congruent with the child's cultural values, traditions, and customs.
5. Delay the initiation of the use of basals if necessary until the child can relate to them experientially and conceptually.
6. Supplement basals with other materials directly representative of the child's background.
7. Select basal materials, when possible, *written in the first language* of the non-English speaking child. Reading skills that are learned in the first language have been shown to transfer into faster acquisition of second-language reading (Cohen 1974; Gutiérrez 1975).

Language experience approach. The language experience approach (LEA) implies much opportunity to hear and use language prior to the development of materials for reading. This is one reason why LEA seems to hold considerable promise for teaching reading to the linguistically and culturally different. The child should be given much opportunity to *use his own language* through such activities as relating stories about past experiences, playing games, responding to classroom experiences in caring for pets or conducting experiments, or responding to stories and poems read aloud in class (Wheat et al. 1979). As a result of such talk based on the child's experiences, LEA stories (using the techniques suggested in Chapter 13) can be constructed and reading instruction initiated. The fact that such stories are written in the child's own language is another plus for the use of LEA. As the teacher writes the story, phonological variation should be represented by standard spelling, but the syntax should be written as the child speaks. By using the child's syntax the teacher is showing that the child's language is being accepted. It also allows the beginning reader to start with material close to her own oral language production. A story such as the following might result:

Fluffy

Our rabbit name Fluffy.
She have white hair.
She like two carrots every day.
And she jump and hop.

Such a procedure promotes taking of risks because it becomes clear that the teacher's acceptance of the child is not based on a standard that the child does not reach. The language experience approach can also be used with children whose first language is not English. In addition to the possibilities present in using the first language, it may serve as a useful tool in moving from learning to speak English to reading it.[5]

Individualized reading. To the extent that individualized reading refers to meeting the needs of each student, it is totally compatible with working with the linguistically and culturally different children. Adjusting methods in all aspects of teaching reading to the unique characteristics of these children is not only desirable but essential. To do anything less is to invite failure. Materials must be carefully selected and should include those from which the children can select to read with some assurance of identification and success. (See Chapter 14.)

Summary

Linguistically and culturally different children either speak a nonstandard variety of English or little or no English at all and come from a culture that also varies in important ways from the dominant culture. They have consistently achieved at a low level in reading. Reasons for lack of reading success have been the target of research and theory for a number of years.

Since a strong oral language base has been determined to be a key factor in reading success, much of that research has focused on the first language of the linguistically and culturally different. The research has shown that so-called nonstandard dialects are well-formed and predictable language systems and are not impoverished versions of standard English. The evidence suggests further that such dialects do not in and of themselves interfere with reading comprehension of standard English materials. Children whose first language is not English at all, however, cannot be expected to succeed in reading such materials until they have developed an oral English base.

The cultural variation of linguistically and culturally different children bears both direct and indirect influence on reading success. Experiences and related concepts, values, traditions, and customs vary rather significantly from those of mainstream society. Such variations must be taken into account as materials are chosen and as techniques are employed in teaching reading.

The teacher, as always, plays a key role in providing a reading program

5. See Katherine Davis Wilsendanger and Ellen Davis Birlem's suggestions in this regard in "Adapting Language Experience to Reading for Bilingual Pupils," *The Reading Teacher* 32 (March 1979): 671–673.

that can maximize the potential for reading success among these children. Attempts must be made to know as much as possible about them. Specific language and cultural differences and their implications for teaching should be well understood. In addition, the teacher must approach the linguistically and culturally different learner with positive attitudes about her language and culture and have realistically positive expectations concerning possible achievement. Finally, the teacher must avoid confusion between oral language production and reading comprehension by not viewing dialectal translations as reading errors and by clearly differentiating the goals of the reading program from those of the oral language program.

As the reading program is developed for linguistically and culturally different children, specific adjustments should be made in its every aspect. Atypical experiences and associated concepts will thus be considered in selection of materials and experiences will be provided when needed to develop concepts necessary for success with other materials. Particular differences in language should also be considered as such word recognition skills as phonics and structural analysis are taught. As adjustments are made, some of the common approaches and programs for teaching reading such as basals and the language experience approach can be used with success. Having done so, the teacher will have done what is the hallmark of most good teaching — *individualized for instruction.*

Questions for Further Reading and Thinking

1. Assume you are assigned to a first grade class in an Appalachian school. Your reading materials consist of only an outdated basal. What will be your first positive reaction to this situation?
2. Suggest how as a teacher you might utilize the parents of linguistically and culturally different children.
3. Respond to this position: "All reading instruction for non-English speakers should be delayed until some proficiency in English is attained."
4. What guidelines would you suggest be followed in situations where standardized IQ and readiness tests must be given to all students (including the linguistically and culturally different)?
5. Identify several programs commonly referred to as part of compensatory education. To what extent would you wish to utilize them and why?
6. You are teaming with a teacher who insists on "correcting" all nonstandard dialectal renditions of Standard English materials. What will be your response?
7. As a fifth grade teacher in a middle-class suburban school you are suddenly confronted with the enrollment in your class of an adopted Vietnamese child. What will be your response?

Activities and Projects

1. Develop a list of references that describe the language characteristics of Black dialects and Appalachian dialects.
2. Identify references that describe the cultural characteristics of the various linguistically and culturally different populations.
3. Structure a broad-based plan for ensuring that standard English is modeled extensively for the nonstandard English speaker and for the non-English speaker. Include pertinent recordings and children's literature in the plan.
4. Plan a talk that you might give to parents on "Back to School" night concerning your approaches to teaching reading to the linguistically and culturally different.
5. Identify sources that might be helpful in teaching English to non-English speakers.
6. Suggest some possible beginning reading materials for the Mexican-American; the Navajo.
7. Develop a set of guidelines of assessment in reading for linguistically and culturally different learners.

Materials for the Teacher

Cheyney, Arnold B. 1976. *Teaching children of different cultures to read: A language approach*, 2nd ed. Columbus, Ohio: Charles E. Merrill.

Ching, Doris C. 1976. *Reading and the bilingual child*. Newark, Del.: International Reading Association.

Cullinan, Bernice. 1974. *Black dialects and reading*. Urbana, Ill.: Council of Teachers of English.

Davis, A. L. 1972. *Culture, class, and language variety: A resource book for teachers*. Urbana, Ill.: National Council of Teachers of English.

Harber, Jean R.; and Beatty, Jane N. 1978. *Reading and the black English speaking child*. Newark, Del.: International Reading Association.

Knight, Lester N. 1974. *Language arts for the exceptional: The gifted and the linguistically different*. Itasca, Ill.: F. E. Peacock.

Rodrigues, Raymond J.; and White, Robert H. 1981. *Mainstreaming the non-English speaking student*. Urbana, Ill.: National Council of Teachers of English/ERIC.

Thonis, Eleanor W. 1976. *Literacy for America's Spanish speaking children*. Newark, Del.: International Reading Association.

Wolfram, Walter. 1979. *Reading and dialect differences*. Washington, D.C.: Center for Applied Linguistics.

Wolfram, Walter; and Christian, Donna. 1976. *Appalachian speech*. Washington, D.C.: Center for Applied Linguistics.

Brenda Kolker

17

Classroom Evaluation Procedures

The continuous evaluation of students' reading achievement has as its goal independent readers — those who can read words, understand concepts, react to print critically, and evaluate ideas for problem solving. Diagnostic instruction as part of continuous evaluation is a dynamic process. It is reacting to the needs of the individual learner in a continuous, positive way to ensure learning.

Diagnostic procedures involve the continuous assessment of the interplay between teacher-directed activities and student behaviors during those activities. This assessment assumes that the teacher knows: (1) what reading skills the school system has outlined as important (the curriculum guide), (2) what developmental reading skills are presented in the basal reading system (or other approach) the school uses, and (3) some specific teaching strategies to develop and maintain those skills. The use of diagnostic procedures also assumes that teachers understand — in addition to developmental reading and the act of reading — the tests and terminology associated with test interpretation so that they can make insightful decisions for program planning for a specific group of students. Diagnostic teaching is a form of evaluation or assessment and should be distinguished from evaluation to assign a grade. The former is a strategy in the teaching/learning process, whereas the latter is an assessment after the strategy has been carried out.

This chapter is organized into three main sections. In the first section, norm-referenced tests (and associated terminology) used in school systems will be the subject; we will look at some examples and make tentative interpretations. In the second section, we will take up specific strategies for classroom use, i.e., criterion-referenced methods of evaluation. The third section deals with teacher-made tests as well as the informal reading inventory.

Norm-referenced Measures

QUESTIONS TO GUIDE READING

Literal
What are several general testing conditions found in test manuals?
What are some different ways that test scores can be used?

Inferential
On what bases would a teacher select a norm-referenced test?

Evaluative
How can a teacher use test scores to improve the instructional program in reading?

School-wide norm-referenced evaluation usually occurs every few years in the elementary grades. Some school systems require teachers to administer tests in grades two, four, and six (or some combination) whereas others require tests every year. Teachers do not usually have much input into the question of whether students should be evaluated by these tests, although some school systems have a committee of teachers to make decisions regarding testing time and protocol. Because of the prevalence of norm-referenced tests, familiarity with certain concepts of testing can help the teacher to interpret scores: First, what is involved in test standardization? Second, what concepts are required to interpret test scores? Last, what does a teacher do with the scores after he has interpreted them?

TEST STANDARDIZATION AND CONCEPTS

In test standardization, those creating the test develop uniform procedures for administration and for scoring (DeCecco and Crawford 1974, p. 473). Items or questions within the test are assigned a difficulty level by the objective method of trying the test out with a large number of students (a sample). Test items solved correctly by the largest proportion of students are taken to be the easiest. Items passed by few students are said to be more difficult (Anastasi 1954, p. 25). It is not uncommon for a test to have a student sample of 10,000 or 20,000.

When a norm-referenced test is administered by school personnel, it must be done under uniform conditions. The beginning of each teacher's manual for a test always contains an example of test conditions. The example in Figure 17.1 is from the Scott, Foresman *Comprehensive Assessment Program*.

Figure 17.1.

Administrator's Preparations

The test administrator must handle several aspects of the administration in advance of testing.

Advance preparations. In advance of the week of testing, the test administrator should become thoroughly familiar with the test content and materials and should be sure adequate materials are available.

- Read through the test items to become familiar with the sample items and the pages on which subtests appear.
- Read and rehearse the test administration directions in this manual carefully, noting the method of: marking answers in the booklet, informing children of places in the booklet for starting and stopping, and monitoring testing time.
- Assemble all necessary test materials:
  1. One test booklet for each child and for the test administrator
  2. Extra booklets in case of extreme mismarking or damage
  3. Administration manual for the test administrator
  Inform the school principal or test coordinator if there is not an adequate supply of materials.
- You may want to assemble these optional materials:
  1. Two pencils with erasers (or crayons) for each child, or, if children have been instructed to bring their own, an extra supply of pencils (or crayons) to provide for those who forget and to replace pencils that break
  2. "Test in Session" sign
- Set aside a place for keeping test materials between test sessions.
- Fill in the back cover of each child's booklet. Print each child's last name, first name, and middle initial on the appropriate line. Complete the lines for school, teacher, and the child's grade and date of birth.

Organizing on the day of testing. *Before children arrive,* the test room should be organized so that testing takes place under the best possible conditions.

- Check that all materials are assembled and ready for distribution.
- Place "Test in Session" sign on the door, and attempt to avoid distracting noises and interruptions.

In addition to the organization of the room, also note the following:

- Plan to monitor the children's work closely, checking that they are: looking at the right test item for all items; marking answers acceptably; and marking only one answer for each item. Help children with their marking, but do *not* let them know the correct answer to an item.
- Carefully observe the signs to "go on" or to "stop," one of which appears at the bottom of each test page.
- In succeeding administration sessions, be sure that children have received their own test booklets.
- Be alert for genuine problems students may have (i.e., an obvious illness). Students who are ill may be excused from testing, and a make-up session may be planned. Bilingual children may need help in understanding directions.

Information for children. The following information has been incorporated in the administrator's script. It is presented here as general information.

- The test is intended to help children by discovering not only what they know but also what they need to learn.
- Children should try to answer each item; and all children should finish each subtest.

When the teacher reads test directions to the students, she must read them exactly as they are written. Figure 17.2 is a reproduction of a page in the examiner's manual for the *CTBS* (1974).

Along with the standardization of procedures for administration, the reliability and validity of the test are determined. *Reliability* refers to the consistency of scores obtained by the individual when he is given the same test after a specified period of time or after he is given an alternate form of the test. *Raw score* refers to the actual number of test items correct.

Table 17.1 shows that the consistency between Test 1 and the retest would be relatively high. There were only one or two point variations between the test and the retest for each child. The more alike the two scores for each student, the more accurately the test is measuring an achievement variable or trait (and not something due to chance) (Tyler 1963, p. 33).

The degree of relationship between the test and the retest is mathematically expressed in a correlation coefficient (r). A correlation coefficient is a numeral ranging from +1 to −1. The closer the correlation comes to +1, the greater the degree of positive relationship. For example, for a reading test, if the test-retest correlation were 0.2, the test would not be considered reliable. However, if the correlation were 0.95, the test would be considered highly reliable.

Validity refers to the concept of whether the test is measuring what it is designed to measure. For example, if a test for juvenile delinquency can distinguish between two groups, those who have not been judged by the courts to be juvenile delinquents and those who have, then the test would be a valid test for juvenile delinquency. If the test did not discriminate between the groups, then it would be invalid (DeCecco and Crawford 1974, p. 452). Similarly, reading comprehension tests should distinguish between those students who can comprehend ideas in print and those who cannot.

Along with reliability and validity coefficients, a standardized test also has norms. A *norm* is a score that indicates average performance (DeCecco and Crawford 1974, p. 454). For example, if the average second grader can identify twelve beginning blends in words after hearing the teacher pro-

Table 17.1. Raw Scores for Two Tests

	Test 1	Retest
Susie	12	11
Joe	15	17
Jimmy	8	6
Bruce	10	9
Laura	6	7
Ben	11	12

Figure 17.2. A page in the Examiner's Manual for the *CTBS*.

TEST 2

LETTER NAMES

Test 2 is given after a brief rest period following Test 1. The test books should still be on the students' desks. Proctors should check the test books to make sure that the markers are between Pages 4 and 5. Test 2 takes approximately 20 minutes.

SAY: Open your test book to the page that has the marker. Take out the marker. Fold your book back like this.

Demonstrate.

Put your book on your desk with this page showing.

Hold up a test book with Page 4 showing.

Proctors should check to see that the students have only Page 4, the Letter Names test, showing.

Place your marker under the first long row that starts with the picture of the airplane. Next to the airplane are four small boxes. Inside each box there are two letters, a capital and a small letter. There is also a little circle in each box . . . . I am going to tell you the name of a letter and I want you to find the letter that I name. Mark a circle to show your answer. Now listen carefully. We are going to do this one together.

Check to see that all students have their markers placed correctly.

Item D1
SAY: Look at the letters. Find the letter "S.". . . Under the letter "S" is a circle. Look at the mark covering the circle. This is the kind of mark that you should make.

Item D2
SAY: Now move your marker down to the picture of the flower. Look at the letters. Find the letter "X" and mark the circle. Show your answer to the helpers.

nounce them, the norm for second graders is twelve. When a test has national norms, a student's performance can be compared to that of his peers on a national basis; this requires that the sample contain representative groups of students for whom the test is designed. In the manual for the *Comprehensive Tests of Basic Skills*, Form S, Level C, Examiner's Manual (1973, 1974, p. 2), it is specified that the sample of students tested was the following:[1]

> *CTBS/S* was standardized on a large national sample of students from Kindergarten through Grade 12 in schools randomly selected from all regions and states of the United States. The sample included public and private school students proportionate in number to actual enrollments.

Norms are mathematically and conceptually based on the bell curve, or *normal curve*. When a large sample of students is tested, there is much individual variation. However, there is usually a pattern, or order, in the variation. The pattern is the bell-shaped curve. A large number of scores cluster in the middle, forming the average. The farther away from the middle, the smaller the total group proportion (Tyler 1963, p. 13).

Figure 17.3 shows that when a norm-referenced test is given, approximately 68 percent of the scores will cluster around the middle of the bell curve. Test makers usually use the curve to derive the standard scores, which are raw scores converted to a common standard or distribution (Champion 1970, p. 64). For example, out of a 180-item test, the average score might be 100. This average score (mean) is calculated by summing a group of scores and dividing by the number of scores (DeCecco and Crawford 1974, p. 481).

Another concept pertaining to scores is how much they vary. For example, on the 180-item test, do students in one class range from 30 to 150? Or are they clustered around the middle, say from 80 to 110? The *standard deviation* is a mathematical operation used to compute variability. Mathematically, it is based on all scores within the group (DeCecco and Crawford 1974, p. 483). Where all the scores cluster around the mean, as in the test results of 80 to 110, the standard deviation is much smaller than it is in the class that scores between 30 and 150.

The standard deviation is related to the normal curve. One standard deviation on either side of the mean contains 68.26 percent of the scores (σ is the mathematical notation for standard deviation). These concepts of norm, normal curves, and standard deviation can now be used to interpret test scores.

Look at Table 17.2. In terms of the bell curve, these scores for vocabulary would look like the representation in Figure 17.4.

Sixty-eight percent of the scores would fall between 27 and 53. If

1. From Comprehensive Tests of Basic Skills, Form S, Examiner's Manual. Reprinted by permission of the publisher, CTB/McGraw-Hill, Del Monte Research Park, Monterey, CA 93940. Copyright © 1973 by McGraw-Hill, Inc. All Rights Reserved. Printed in the U.S.A.

Figure 17.3. A bell curve.

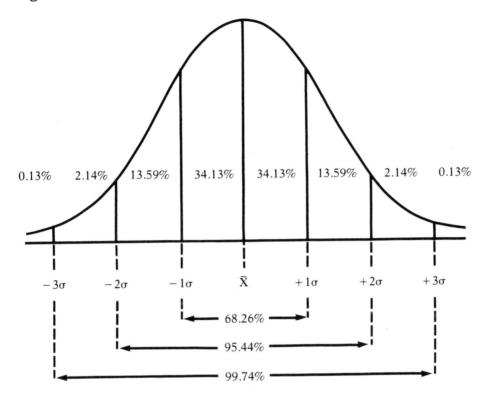

student X obtained a score of 32, it would be a bit below the mean, but within the 68 percent. So one can say that his score is between the mean and one standard deviation below the mean. What could one say of a student who received a raw score of 60 on the test?

Standard error of the mean is presented in test manuals in numerical form. It indicates how much error there is in the statistic rather than the people (Tyler 1963, p. 22). In other words, it tells what percentage of the time an individual's score will fall between certain points. Table 17.3 can be interpreted using this concept.

Again using the bell curve, we see that 68 percent of the students on the vocabulary test will fall between grade levels 2.4 and 4.0 (Figure 17.5).

The vocabulary test has a standard error of measurement of .4 grade level. If a student achieved a grade level score of 4.0 on the vocabulary subtest, his true score would fall somewhere between 3.6 and 4.4, 68 times out of 100.

In presenting the results of testing, publishers use derived scores. Assume that the student who took the test achieved a certain number of correct answers — perhaps 10 out of 15. Ten is referred to as the raw score. Through mathematical manipulation, the raw scores are converted

Figure 17.4. Bell curve for scores in Table 17.2.

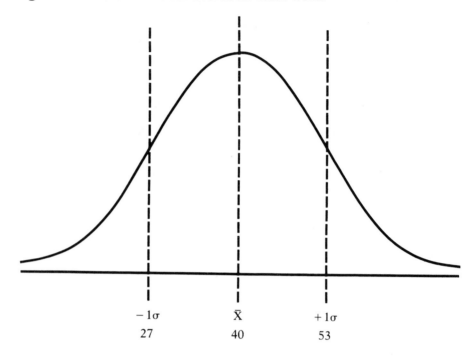

	-1σ	$\bar{X}$	$+1\sigma$
	27	40	53

Table 17.2. Raw Scores

	Mean	Standard deviation
Vocabulary	40	13
Comprehension	45	17

Table 17.3. Grade Placement

	Mean	Standard deviation	Standard error of measurement
Vocabulary	3.2	.8	.4
Comprehension	4.0	1.0	.6

to percentiles, stanines, or equivalent grade scores. These conversions facilitate interpretation.

Percentiles refer to scores in terms of the percentage of a group the student has scored above (DeCecco and Crawford 1974, p. 485). If a student scores in the thirteenth percentile, he has scored above 12 percent of the group. Percentiles range from 1 to 99.

Figure 17.5. Bell curve for vocabulary grade levels in Table 17.3.

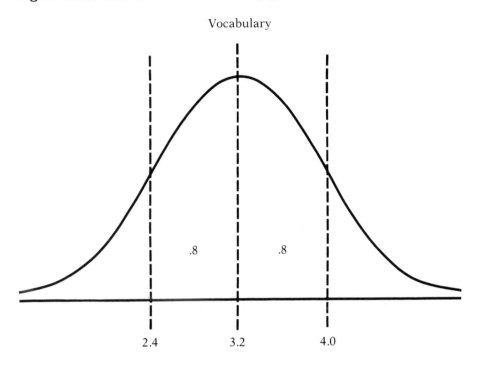

Figure 17.6 reproduces two pages from a test examiner's manual. It shows percentile (%-ile) rank, stanines, and standard scores. *Standard scores* are raw scores converted to a common standard that permits comparisons on different tests (Champion 1970, p. 64). For example, a student obtained a raw score of 52 on a math test and 42 on a spelling test. Table 17.4 shows the conversion to standard scores. From the standard scores we can see that he performs much better in math than in spelling. *Stanines* are very similar to standard scores, only they do not have as many discrete points.

Stanine refers to a nine-point scale (STAndard NINE-point scale). The numerical values are from one to nine with a mean score of five. One is

Table 17.4. Conversion to Standard Scores

	Spelling	Math
Raw score	42	52
Class average	60	38
Standard score	48	80
Stanine	4	8

Figure 17.6. A table from *California Achievement Tests Norms Tables,* Forms C & D, Level 15.

Table 6
RAW SCORE TO PERCENTILE RANK AND STANINE

Level 15   Middle of Grade 4: 4.3 to 4.5 (Dec, Jan, Feb)   Form C

Stanine	%ile Rank	Read Vocab	Read Comp	Total Read	Spell	Lang Mech	Lang Expr	Total Lang	Comput	Concepts & Applc	Total Math	Total Battery	Refer Skills	%ile Rank	Stanine
	99	29-30	37-40	65-70	19-20	23-25	36-38	57-63	32-40	40-45	68-85	205-238	25	99	
	98	28		64			35	56	30-31	38-39	66-67	199-204		98	
9	97		36	63	18	22		55	29	37	63-65	194-198	24	97	9
	96		35	62				54	28	36	61-62	190-193		96	
	95					21	34		27		60	186-189		95	
	94	27	34	61	17			53		35	58-59	183-185		94	
	93			60					26	34		180-182		93	
8	92		33	59		20	33	52	25	33	57	177-179	23	92	8
	91			58							56	175-176		91	
	90	26	32	57				51	24	32	55	172-174		90	
	89			56	16		32	50		31	54	169-171		89	
	88		31			19					53	167-168		88	
	87			55				49	23	30	52	165-166		87	
	86		30	54			31		22	29	51	163-164		86	
	85	25									50	161-162	22	85	
	84		29	53	15	18		48		28	49	159-160		84	
7	83			52					21		48	158		83	7
	82							47				156-157		82	
	81	24	28	51		17	30			27	47	153-155		81	
	80			50				46			46	151-152		80	
	79		27	49								150		79	
	78				14				20	26	45	148-149	21	78	
	77	23	26	48			29	45			44	147		77	
	76											145-146		76	
	75			47					19	25	43	144		75	
	74	22	25	46		16		44			42	142-143		74	
	73											140-141		73	
	72		24	45	13		28	43	18	24	41	139	20	72	
	71										40	137-138		71	
	70			44								136		70	
	69	21	23	43		15		42		23	39	135		69	
6	68											133-134		68	6
	67			42			27			22		131-132		67	
	66	20	22		12			41	17		38	130	19	66	
	65			41							37	129		65	
	64									21		128		64	
	63		21	40		14	26	40			36	125-127		63	
	62	19										124		62	
	61			39					16	20	35	123		61	
	60		20	38				39				122	18	60	
	59										34	121		59	
	58	18		37			25			19		118-120		58	
	57		19			13		38			33	117		57	
	56			36					15			116		56	
	55				11					18	32	115	17	55	
5	54	17	18	35			24	37				114		54	5
	53										31	111-113		53	
	52			34				36		17		110		52	
	51		17						14			109		51	
	50	16		33		12	23				30	108	16	50	

Level 15   Table 6 (continued)   Form C

Stanine	%ile Rank	Read Vocab	Read Comp	Total Read	Spell	Lang Mech	Lang Expr	Total Lang	Comput	Concepts & Applc	Total Math	Total Battery	Refer Skills	%ile Rank	Stanine
	49							35				107		49	
	48			32						16		105-106		48	
	47		16								29	104		47	
5	46	15		31	10			34	13			103	15	46	5
	45						22					102		45	
	44			30		11		33		15	28	101		44	
	43		15									99-100		43	
	42			29							27	98		42	
	41	14					21	32				97		41	
	40			28						14	26	96	14	40	
	39							31	12			94-95		39	
	38		14	27	9	10						93		38	
	37	13					20				25	91-92	13	37	
	36			26				30		13		90		36	
	35										24	89		35	
	34		13	25				29	11			88		34	
	33	12				9	19					87		33	
	32											86		32	
	31			24				28		12	23	85	12	31	
4	30		12		8				10			84		30	4
	29	11		23			18	27			22	83		29	
	28					8				11		82	11	28	
	27		11	22			17	26				81		27	
	26	10						25			21	79-80	10	26	
	25			21	7		16	24	9	10	20	77-78		25	
	24		10	20		7		23			19	74-75	9	24	
	23											73		23	
3	22			19	6		15	22*	8	9	18	72	8	22	3
	21	9		18		6		21				71		21	
	20		9					20			17	70	7	20	
	19	8		17	5	5	14	19	7	8	16	69		19	
	18		8	16			13					68	6	18	
	17	7					12	18		7	15	67		17	
2	16		7	15	4	4	11	17	6		14	66	5	16	2
	15			14			10	16		6		65		15	
	14	6	6	13				15	5	5	13	64-65	4	14	
1	13	4	5	11-12	3	3	9	14			11-12	52-53	3	13	1
	1	0-3	0-4	0-10	0-2	0-2	0-8	0-13	0-4	0-4	0-10	0-48	0-3	1	

considered low and nine is high. Stanine 1 contains 4 percent of the population whereas stanine 5 contains 20 percent of the population.

Stanine	1	2	3	4	5	6	7	8	9
Percentage	4%	7%	12%	17%	20%	17%	12%	7%	4%
Meaning	Poor	Below average		Average			Above average		Superior

Stanines have several advantages. The first is that they are broad units and therefore more dependable. The second is that they are easy to report to parents because they give a broader range than either a percentile or grade level score.

The International Reading Association (IRA) has recently passed a resolution cautioning teachers on the misuse of grade equivalents.[2] This prominent teacher organization states that use of grade equivalents promotes misunderstanding of a pupil's reading ability. The IRA advocates abandonment of grade equivalent use for reporting performance to individuals and groups. Teachers should consider reporting stanines.

Using Tests in Classrooms

The overriding question is "How can group test scores be used in a classroom setting?" When students are tested systemwide, usually the tests are sent to a center to be scored, and teachers do not see the actual tests again. However, the teacher receives some sort of profile on each student's test achievement. Using the information presented so far in this chapter, we can interpret the profile in Figure 17.7 for the *CTBS*.

Figure 17.7 profiles a second grade pupil. The reading portion of the test includes scores on vocabulary, sentences, passages, and total reading. The percentile rank for each subtest is charted. Below the chart itself are stanine scores, grade equivalent scores, and scaled scores. On the vocabulary subtest, the student achieved a raw score of 26, which was converted to a percentile rank of 68, and a stanine of 6. It can be tentatively said of the student's profile that she is somewhat above her grade placement of 2.2 in all areas measured by the test.

Several tests utilize grade scores to report the student achievement level to parents and teachers. The *CTBS* (see Figure 17.7) reports a grade placement level score for Total Reading, Total Language, Mathematics Computation, Concepts and Applications, and Total Mathematics, the Total Battery, as well as Science and Social Studies. The Total Reading grade score was 2.7, but it does not mean that the student should be placed in second grade, seventh month basal material because of at least two factors: first, the standard error of the test itself, which has been discussed; and second, the test norms have not been standardized against

2. Resolution of Delegates Assembly, International Reading Association, April 1981.

Figure 17.7. A student profile.

Student's Name _Martha Rogers_

Grade _2_

Teacher _Pat Rameriz_

Test Date _October 6, 1975_

School _Oceanside_

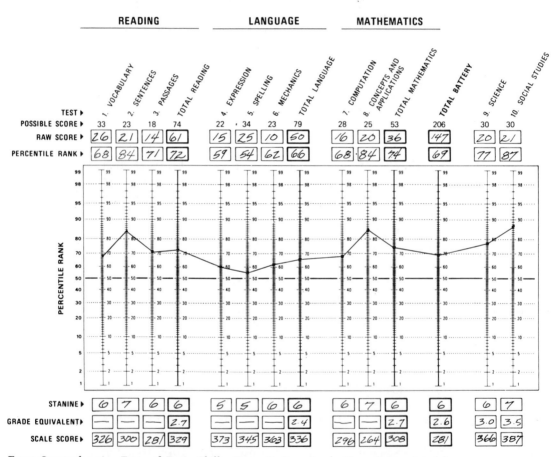

From Comprehensive Tests of Basic Skills, Form S, Examiner's Manual. Reprinted by permission of the publisher, CTB/McGraw-Hill, Del Monte Research Park, Monterey, CA 93940. Copyright © 1973 by McGraw-Hill, Inc. All Rights Reserved. Printed in the U.S.A.

the content of a specific material but within the test itself. If a student achieved a certain score, that score was related to other students' scores on the test, and not to a basal reader or library book. Therefore, the teacher will have to assess student achievement in other ways for placement in the appropriate instructional material.

Achievement tests show a student's progress from year to year. Is this progress continuous or erratic? Achievement test scores can also show strengths and weaknesses within a school or school system. Do all students perform poorly on vocabulary? If so, then vocabulary should receive greater instructional time within the school.

Points to Remember about Norm-referenced Testing

1. In the administration of standardized tests, the tester must follow the directions in the manual *precisely*.
2. Reliability refers to the consistency of test scores over a period of time.
3. The degree of relationship between, or among, test scores is expressed in a correlation coefficient.
4. Validity refers to the concept of whether the test is measuring what it is designed to measure.
5. Norms are based on the bell curve concept.
6. Standard deviation refers to the variability of test scores of pupils.
7. Standard error refers to the error within the test or statistic rather than to pupils.
8. Approximately 68 percent of the scores fall between -1 and $+1$ standard deviations on the normal curve.
9. Percentiles refer to scores in terms of the percentage of a group the student has scored above.
10. Stanines are similar to standard scores but they do not have as many discrete points.
11. A grade score obtained by a student on a standardized test does *not* mean the student can be placed in that grade level instructional material.

Criterion-referenced Tests

QUESTIONS TO GUIDE READING

Literal
What is meant by the term "criterion-referenced" in regard to reading tests?

Inferential
Could criterion-referenced tests also be norm-referenced?

Evaluative
How do criterion-referenced tests used in reading instruction differ from norm-referenced tests? Which would you use most?
How would the use of criterion-referenced tests affect classroom organization?

Tests in the previous section, such as the *Comprehensive Tests of Basic Skills*, are called norm-referenced tests. These tests have reliability and validity data, and students can be compared with others at the same age or grade level. Another category of tests is criterion-referenced. These tests do not have statistical reliability and validity; rather, they measure the specific achievement of one student against a criterion, or acceptable score. This type of testing is useful on a day-to-day or week-to-week basis. Criterion-referenced tests are not norm-referenced; that is, students are compared only to what they themselves can do and not to what other students do on the test. For example, if the teacher teaches five blends from Monday to Thursday (*bl, tr, fl, br, cr*), on Friday she might make an informal evaluation to ascertain whether or not the children have retained the blends. She will set her criteria of four out of five blends retained in order for the children to continue to learn new blends. If the children have not retained at least four out of five blends, reteaching of the blends will be necessary. Criterion-referenced testing is concerned with mastery learning. Skills are taught by the teacher, and students are evaluated for their mastery of the skills.

There are several criterion-referenced tests published, although many teachers develop their own. One of the published tests is the *Prescriptive Reading Inventory* (PRI) by CTB/McGraw-Hill (1972).

The first three items on the PRI deal with silent letters (see Figure 17.8). After the teacher scores the test she goes to the Individual Diagnostic Map to record the raw score and to check the mastery score necessary (see Figure 17.9). By comparing the scores, she can begin to plan an instructional program based on individual needs.

Teacher-Made Tests and the Informal Reading Inventory

QUESTIONS TO GUIDE READING

Literal
What types of assessment are included in the IRI?
What are two specific procedures to quickly "try on a book for size?"

Inferential
What is the relationship between an IRI and miscue analysis?

Evaluative
Would the time constraints necessary for administering informal teacher-made tests limit their use in your classroom?

Other criterion-referenced tests are the informal tests that teachers devise (instead of using a published test) for individuals within the classroom

Figure 17.8. Criterion-referenced test excerpt.

2 · PART A ────────────────

DIRECTIONS: In Items 1-3, read each word. Then read the small letters on the same line. Find the letter that is silent in the underlined word. Mark your answer.

1. <u>knife</u>

k	n	i	f
K	N	I	F

2. <u>fruit</u>

f	r	u	i
F	R	U	I

3. <u>hour</u>

h	o	u	r
H	O	U	R

DIRECTIONS: In Items 4-9, read the word with the underlined letters. What is the sound of these letters? Read the words across from the first word. Find the one that has the same sound as the underlined letters. Mark your answer.

4. v<u>oi</u>ce | E cool | F enjoy | G hole | H visit
5. str<u>aw</u> | A away | B caught | C crowd | D crow
6. p<u>oo</u>l | E broom | F hood | G floor | H shook
7. t<u>ur</u>n | A pear | B fearless | C early | D here
8. h<u>er</u> | E learn | F hear | G cherry | H mere
9. d<u>ea</u>r | A search | B heard | C dead | D appear

DIRECTIONS: In Items 10 and 11, read the four words. Find the one that is made out of two words. Mark your answer.

10. E mailman | F Saturday | G shouted | H winter

11. A feather | B sandbox | C boxing | D gladly

Figure 17.9. Individual Diagnostic Map.

For each objective on the Individual Diagnostic Map (first column), count the number of items answered correctly (check marks on the Scoring Key). The items testing a specific objective are listed by number in the ITEMS column. (Since this test is divided into two sections, Part A and Part B, each item number is preceded by the letter that designates in which part of the test the item is found. Note that for certain objectives, the item numbers are not consecutive.) Enter the number of correct responses for each objective in the RAW SCORE box. Then check the appropriate box, MASTERY, REVIEW, or NONMASTERY, that contains the same number as the RAW SCORE. For example, if the student answered two of the items testing Objective 9 correctly, the MASTERY box, containing the numerals 2/3, would be checked. If all items testing an objective have been omitted, mark the OMIT circle.

OBJECTIVE NUMBER	ITEMS	RAW SCORE	MASTERY	REVIEW	NON-MASTERY	OMIT	OBJECTIVE DESCRIPTION
PHONIC ANALYSIS							
9	A1, A2, A3	☐	2/3	1	0	◯	Silent Letters
13	A4, A5, A6	☐	2/3	1	0	◯	Variant Vowel Sounds: Digraph, Diphthong
14	A7, A8, A9	☐	2/3	1	0	◯	Phonetic Parts: Variant Sounds
15	A14, A15, A16	☐	2/3	1	0	◯	Phonetic Parts: Blending
STRUCTURAL ANALYSIS							
22	A60, A61, A62, A63	☐	3/4	2	0/1	◯	Pronouns: Referent
25	A10, A11, A12, A13	☐	3/4	2	0/1	◯	Compounds: Forming
30	A79, A80, A81, A82	☐	3/4	2	0/1	◯	Sentence Building: Phrase Selection
31	A83, A84, A85, A86	☐	3/4	2	0/1	◯	Phrase Information
32	A17, A18, A19	☐	2/3	1	0/1	◯	Affixes: Identifying Prefixes, Suffixes
33	A33, A34, A35, A39, A40, A41	☐	5/6	3/4	0/1/2	◯	Affixes: Building Words
34	A36, A37, A38	☐	2/3	1	0	◯	Defining Affixed Words

From Prescriptive Reading Inventory. Reprinted by permission of the publisher, CTB/McGraw-Hill, Del Monte Research Park, Monterey, CA 93940. Copyright © 1972 by McGraw-Hill, Inc. All Rights Reserved. Printed in the U.S.A.

— to measure the attainment of skills such as phonics or fact-recall comprehension, or sight vocabulary. The criterion for attainment or adequate performance is set by the teacher, either in number correct or percentage correct. For example, after teaching ten consonant sounds a teacher devises a test to measure whether or not the students have retained the sounds. A criterion score could be 80 percent; the students must get at least eight of the ten correct in order to move to new sounds. Less than eight sounds known would mean reteaching the sounds.

"Informal assessment" is a term that describes all the strategies a teacher uses to determine the baseline behaviors or skills (a needs assessment) to begin teaching or to determine achievement in order to develop a skill over a period of time. It is a specific skill behavior and skill processing assessment, as opposed to a global assessment by norm-referenced tests.

Underlying the scores on formal and informal tests of reading are the motivations, interests, and attitudes of students; these manifest themselves behaviorally while a student is actually performing reading tasks. Therefore, it is important not only to establish needs (and progress made) by means of test scores, but also to observe the student while he is reading because his actual reading behaviors could indicate achievement levels different from those indicated by the tests. Specific to reading are such behaviors as the following:

The student looks at a word he doesn't know and will not try the word. He might: (1) look to the teacher for help, (2) skip the word as though it weren't there, (3) say "I don't know," (4) make up a word that seems to fit the context, or (5) call the first letter of the word correctly and miscall the middle and ending.

When asked to read orally in a group, the student: (1) does not hesitate and reads fluently, (2) hesitates but begins reading and miscalls many words, causing other group members to make fun of him or poke each other or giggle, (3) reads word by word, (4) begins to read and squirms in his chair, kicks his feet against the chair, plays with his pencil, or begins to perspire, or (5) refuses to read.

The student is asked to read part of a story silently and: (1) reads willingly, (2) gazes out the window, (3) stares at the page but doesn't read, (4) keeps asking for help with words, or (5) finishes two pages in ten seconds or ten minutes while the other students take three or four minutes.

When the teacher asks questions orally about the material the student has read, the student: (1) knows every answer plus some, (2) keeps his eyes averted, (3) talks to the student next to him, (4) gives a wrong answer, (5) sits and doesn't respond at all, or (6) says "I don't know."

These types of behaviors can probably be observed in all children to a varying degree. It is the persistence and pattern of the behaviors that should be noted in conjunction with test scores themselves.

GROUP PROCEDURES

Dolch (1953) has suggested a group procedure using a basal reader as a quick assessment for locating poor readers. Using this technique, the teacher tells the group or class they are going to become acquainted with a new book. The new book can be a basal reader or a supplementary text of which there are enough copies for a group of students. Each child then individually reads a sentence in the book aloud, as fast as he can. The teacher supplies any unknown word to any child. If the teacher observes that a child stumbles over many words, then the book is probably too difficult for him. According to Dolch, there will be little embarrassment for a poor reader because each child reads only one sentence. This technique deals primarily with the mechanics of reading rather than comprehension.

A group comprehension test, suggested by Harris and Sipay (1980, p. 175), involves a short reading selection of four or five pages which students read silently. The teacher then asks short-answer questions orally, and students write the answers. The students are not permitted to look back at the selection to find the answers. If the students score below 60 percent on the questions, the book is probably too difficult for them. Beginning primary students might have difficulty writing the answers so other techniques would have to be used. This technique of a quick silent reading and oral questions survey can be used for library books in addition to basal readers and content area books. Chall (1953) refers to this approach as "trying a book on for size."

Another group procedure deals with phonics. Group phonics tests are available to teachers for use in the classroom. For example, the *Stanford Diagnostic Reading Test*, Level 1 (Karlsen et al. 1968) measures, among other skills, syllabication, beginning and ending sounds, blending, and sound discrimination. If group tests are not available, the teacher can construct her own informal tests assessing any skill. Several informal tests are presented in the next section. These examples are not meant to be all-inclusive.

INDIVIDUAL PROCEDURES

Phonics. Individual phonics tests are easy to construct. First, skim the basal reader teacher's manual (or sequence of skills chart published by the company that published the basal system) to ascertain the sequence of phonics skills taught; this preview is important because different basal systems often present these skills in different orders. Second, list the elements presented. Next, construct a test and administer it. The way the informal test is administered will depend on what type of information is wanted. Do the students know the isolated sound elements — such as vowels, consonants, and trigraphs — or can the students apply the isolated element knowledge in contextual settings?

For example, a second grade teacher studied the first grade basals and has decided that the students should have learned certain elements in isolation. She then made a ditto sheet of the elements, as shown here, with a place to mark what the child said as he responded to the items. The items were spaced so that there would be no confusion of the elements running together.

b ___	r ___	t ___	l ___	c ___	d ___
g ___	f ___	s ___	h ___	j ___	t ___
v ___	k ___	m ___	n ___	p ___	y ___
br ___	bl ___	st ___	wh ___	pr ___	sl ___
oi ___	ow ___	ail ___	ake ___	ell ___	
a ___	e ___	i ___	o ___	u ___	

She took the child aside when there were a few free moments and asked him to pronounce the sounds of the elements. This measure gave the teacher a baseline from which to begin the instructional program in phonics, and it also served as a record keeping device.

Structural analysis. Words change meaning when prefixes and suffixes are added to basic elements (see Chapter 6). Therefore, in the intermediate grades an assessment of this skill is warranted. To devise an informal test for prefixes (or suffixes), first identify several prefixes with high utility (such as *ab, con, ex, pre, dis*) and place them at the top of a page. Then, place root words in two or three columns on the same page. The task of the child is to insert the prefix in front of the root word to make a new word. The page would look like the following:

ab   *con*   *ex*   *pre*   *dis*

___tract   ___it   ___normal
___fix   ___enchant   ___determine

The student then could write what the word or the prefix means. Initially, it is usually better to test informally with a few elements rather than with all elements because unknown elements can be isolated more quickly. If the student does not perform well on the informal tests, follow the teaching procedure in Chapter 6.

This same skill area should be tested in the middle grades for content area understanding. Burmeister (1976, p. 484) recommends assessing prefixes and suffixes utilized in content areas. Some content area prefix and suffix families include the following:

Science:
- logy (geology)
- multi (multiangular)
- epi (epidermis)
- tele (telepathy)
- retro (retroactive)
- ultra (ultraviolet)

English:
- pre (predate)
- mono (monologue)
- para (paradox)

Social studies:
- auto (autocrat)
- bi (bipolar)
- gamy (misogamy)
- dem (demagogue)
- the (atheism)

Math:
- gon (pentagon)
- bi (biannual)
- circum (circumference)
- tri (triangle)

A multiple-choice pretest or assessment would include a word like *predate*, with a choice of: (1) date after, (2) omit date, (3) date before, and (4) date again. The student selects the response out of a choice of four items. The teacher then tallies which morphemes are causing difficulty and reteaches them.

Dictionary skills. As stated in Chapters 5 and 10, many subskills are involved in dictionary usage. In the primary grades, it is appropriate for the teacher to assess alphabetization. Worksheets for informal assessment would look like the following samples:

EXERCISE 1

Directions: Place the following words in alphabetical order.

cat, deer, apple, pizza, zebra, train, little, fox, rug, snake

This exercise deals with initial letters only. To progress to a more difficult exercise, utilize several letters, as in Exercise 2.

EXERCISE 2

Directions: Place the following words in alphabetical order.

turkey, play, park, dress, simple, trade, drop, shut, dip, told, tree, shout, time

Any subskill for dictionary usage can be assessed in the manner of these two exercises.

Informal Reading Inventory (IRI). One of the most widely used techniques for informal assessment is the informal reading inventory. While by no means the only way of assessing specific skill and processing print needs, it does provide an initial framework for a classroom teacher. The IRI provides a mechanism for observing a child process prose and consists of a series of short tests that help the teacher place the student at an appropriate instructional level. The IRI usually consists of a sight vocabulary test, silent and oral reading passages with comprehension questions, and a listening capacity test.

The IRI is usually constructed from material in graded readers. It contains word lists the teacher has constructed by making a random selection from the graded readers. The teacher also takes short passages of between 50 and 150 words from a set of readers and has the child read them silently or orally. Then she asks questions covering the material. A final section requires the teacher to read to the student, then ask him questions to test his comprehension.

There are several commercial IRIs available (Silvaroli 1982; Rinsky and deFossard 1980), and many basal reading systems include an IRI as part of their total program. An IRI takes from ten to twenty minutes to administer, not including interpretation time and time to plan instructional lessons. The process used in administering and interpreting the IRI is not an isolated strategy. It can be carried over to a reading group if students read orally several times a week within the group. Using this process, the teacher is diagnostically teaching — trying to plan specific lessons based on daily needs.

As the teacher listens to students read orally and watches them complete tasks, he should be informally evaluating their progress. Several students within a class will be reading above grade level and several will be reading below grade level. It is in finding the extremes in achievement that the informal measures will be initially useful.

The sight word list. Giving a word list is a first step in administering an IRI. The purpose of administering a word list is to ascertain the *specific* words in the student's sight vocabulary, to assess word analysis skills in isolation, and to place the student in passages for oral and silent reading. Oral reading passages should begin at the point at which the child makes a few sight word errors (0–4). Those words not known also provide a basis for instruction.

To administer a sight vocabulary test both the teacher and the child should have a copy of the words to be read. The student is asked to read the list of words as quickly as he can. Next to the words called correctly the teacher writes a "c." The teacher can write the words called incorrectly next to the printed word.

Sight vocabulary assumes that the student knows the words instantly, after a one-second exposure. Therefore, if the student hesitates for several seconds (count to yourself 1001, 1002), do not count that word as being in his sight vocabulary because the student is probably utilizing word attack techniques in order to pronounce the word. Also, if the student is moving his lips sounding out the word, it signifies that the word is not in his sight vocabulary.

Assessing oral reading. When a student reads orally, a teacher can assess and interpret types and numbers of errors. This assists him in determining the independent and instructional levels of the student. The *independent level* is the grade level materials on which the student makes few word recognition errors, with which he feels at ease, and on which he comprehends well. It is the level for pleasure reading. The *instructional level* is the level at which the student should be taught. At this level, the student makes more word recognition errors than at the independent level, and comprehension is not as high. These levels have been quantified by at least ten authors. Two of these will be discussed as an overview.

The Betts Criteria (1946) yielded the percentages shown in Table 17.5. Betts defined the independent level as the one at which the student misses 1 word out of 100 running words, and comprehension is 90 percent. At the independent level there are no symptoms of difficulty. (Symptoms of difficulty include such behaviors as lip movements while reading silently, pointing a finger at each word while reading, slow word-by-word reading, and any overt nervous habits [Betts 1946, p. 448].) At the instructional level, on the other hand, the student can miss 5 out of 100 running words, and comprehension should be 75 to 90 percent. There should be few (0–2) symptoms of difficulty. The frustration level is the level at which the student makes too many word recognition errors for adequate comprehension. Betts determined the above levels by having students read silently before reading orally. Thus, there were two readings of the same passage.

Powell (1969) also determined reading levels of students in grades one through six, but in his sample students read orally at sight. Basically he found that students at lower grade levels could make more word recognition errors for the instructional level and still maintain 70 percent comprehension. From Table 17.6, we can see that in grade one and the beginning of grade two, students could miss 16 words out of 100 running words and maintain 70 percent comprehension (Powell and Dunkeld 1971). In grade six, however, the 5–6 word recognition errors approximate the Betts criterion.

Table 17.7 simplifies and compares the results of Betts and Powell.

Table 17.5. Betts Criteria

	Word recognition		Comprehension	Symptoms of difficulty
Independent	99%	1/100	90%	None
Instructional	95%	5/100	75%	Some
Frustration	90%	10/100	50%	Many

Table 17.6. Powell Criteria — Instructional Level

Grade	Word recognition	Comprehension
1–2	1/6 (16–17/100)	70%
2²	1/8 (12–13/100)	70%
3²	1/11 (9/100)	70%
4	1/13 (7–8/100)	70%
5	1/12 (8/100)	70%
6	1/17 (5–6/100)	70%

Table 17.7. Betts and Powell Criteria — Instructional Level

	Betts	Powell
Word Recognition		
Grade 1–2	5/100	12–16/100
Grade 3–5	5/100	7–9/100
Grade 6	5/100	5–6/100
Comprehension		
Grade 1–6	75%	70%

To summarize the two sets of criteria, Betts required students to read silently and then orally, while Powell required students to read orally at sight. Betts based his criteria on fourth graders reading, and then generalized to the other grades. Powell obtained his scores by requiring students in grades one through six to read.

Betts was probably not incorrect in his criteria because of the practice effect (Powell 1973): When a student reads material twice, on the second reading his errors are reduced by 25 to 33 percent. Therefore, one reading versus two readings would have different error ratios. Which error ratio to use depends on the purpose of the teacher. Usually, in a reading group, students read silently first and then orally; hence, the Betts criteria would be appropriate. When students read orally only, the Powell criteria would be appropriate.

An additional criterion, based on research by Goodman (1965a), is referred to as *miscue analysis*. Instead of quantifying errors or miscues, the teacher evaluates the type of miscue. Miscue simply means that the student has said something different from what is on the printed page. Therefore, miscues are samples of overt behavior and intellectual processing, rather than something "bad."

There are nine questions to ask about each miscue (Goodman and Burke 1972), and interrelationships between and among miscues are usually involved. Table 17.8 presents the nine miscues, their definitions, and examples.

Table 17.8. Goodman-Burke Miscues, Definitions, and Examples

Miscue	Definition	Examples
1. Dialect	Is there dialect variation in the miscue?	wif — with goed — went John he went away — John went away
2. Intonation	Is there a shift in intonation?	project — project (*also shifts in phrases and sentences*)
3. Graphic similarity	How much similarity in looks was there between the miscue and the text?	walked — walk (*similar*) is — the (*not similar*)
4. Sound similarity	How much similarity in sound was there between the miscue and the text?	handle — handy (*similar*) bee — sweep (*not similar*)
5. Grammatical function	Is the grammatical function between the text and miscue similar? Is a noun replaced for a noun? Adjective for adjective?	She was a dog — she saw a cat. (*identical*)
6. Correction	Is the miscue corrected?	
7. Grammatical acceptability	Does the miscue alter the grammatical structure, or is it acceptable?	Patty was happy — Pete was happy (*acceptable*) Patty was happy — The was happy (*unacceptable*)
8. Semantic acceptability	Does the miscue alter semantics or is it acceptable?	Patty was happy — Patty was her (*unacceptable*) Patty was happy — Patty was glad (*acceptable*)
9. Meaning change	Does the miscue change the meaning?	Patty was happy — Patty was glad (*acceptable*) Patty was happy — Patty was angry (*unacceptable*)

Source: Adapted with permission of Macmillan Publishing Co. Inc. from *Reading Miscue Inventory Manual: Procedure for Diagnosis and Evaluation* by Yetta M. Goodman and Carolyn L. Burke. Copyright © 1972 by Yetta M. Goodman and Carolyn L. Burke.

One way (Tortelli 1976) to utilize the qualitative aspect of errors with the quantitative aspect is to try the following procedure:

1. Have students read aloud only.
2. Use the same marking system as the IRI and mark all miscues.

Figure 17.10. Oral reading passage.

FORM A, PART II—Level 1 (43 words)

Motivation: This story is about a type of spider that builds its web between flowers or plant stalks. Read this selection to find out more about this type of spider.

PLANT SPIDERS	Comprehension check
There are ~~all~~ *many* kinds of spiders.	(F) 1.___ Is there more than one kind of spider? (Yes—many more) *yes*
This ~~black~~ *blue* and green one is ~~called~~ *named* a plant spider.	(F) 2.___ What two things do plant spiders quickly learn? (<u>Hunt for food</u> and <u>build new nests</u>)
A plant spider has ~~small~~ *smelly* feet.	
All spiders have small feet.	(F) 3.___ What color was the spider in this story? (Black and green) *blue and green*
Plant spiders live in ~~nests~~ *nuts*.	(F) 4.___ What size feet does a plant spider have? (Small) (Little) *Small, I guess*
They soon learn to ~~hunt~~ *hurt* for food and build new nests.	(I) 5.___ At what time of year do we see more spiders? (Check answer in your area; usually more are seen during the warm weather—spring and summer.) *It didn't say that in the story*

Source: From Silvaroli, Nicholas J., *Classroom Reading Inventory*, 4th ed., © 1969, 1973, 1976, 1982 Wm. C. Brown Company Publishers, Dubuque, Iowa. Reprinted by permission.

3. After the student is finished reading, use another piece of paper marked off in four columns that carry these headings:
   Unexpected readings (different from text)
   Intended readings (words in text)
   Language (grammatically correct)
   Meaning (is meaning same or different)

Figure 17.10 reproduces an excerpt from a grade one passage in the *Classroom Reading Inventory* (Silvaroli 1973, p. 23). Student miscues are written above the word. Let us assume you have a child read it and afterward you make the four-column chart first described. Your chart might look like Table 17.9.

This particular child appears to be aware of language relationships but needs more instruction focused on meaning.

If a combination of the qualitative and quantitative assessments is to be used, error quantity as well as quality should be evaluated. The follow-

Table 17.9. Chart of Student Miscues

Unexpected readings	Intended readings	Language	Meaning
many	all	yes	same
blue	black	yes	different
named	called	yes	same
smelly	small	yes	different
nuts	nests	yes	different
hurt	hunt	yes	different

ing should be counted as errors to be tallied when a quantitative approach is used:

1. Omission — whole word or words (Gray and Robinson 1967).
2. Addition — whole word (Gray and Robinson 1967).
3. Substitution or mispronunciation — every mispronunciation is an error; adding a letter to a word is a mispronunciation; reversals are a form of mispronunciation (Gilmore and Gilmore 1968).
4. Aided words — after a five-second time lapse the child is told the word (Gray and Robinson 1967).

The following miscues or errors should not be counted:

1. Dialect (Spache 1972).
2. Self-corrections (Gray and Robinson 1967).
3. Repetitions. (Count for Betts Criteria but not Powell.)
4. Omission of punctuation.
5. Mispronunciation of proper names.
6. Hesitations.
7. Word-by-word reading.

Whether or not to count repetitions as errors is disagreed upon. Some authorities count partial words repeated, one word repeated, or more than one consecutive word repeated as errors (or some combination of the three). Others do not count repetitions at all. Ekwall (1974) used a polygraph to measure students' frustration level while reading and concluded that all repetitions should be counted as errors. Repetitions could also mean, however, that the student is unsure of a word following and repeats in order to derive additional meaning. Another interpretation is that what the child read did not make sense and he repeats to try to correct himself, thereby measuring a processing variable. It is the opinion of this author, after observing students process prose, that repetitions serve to provide insight into processing and should not be counted as errors. Rather, they should be recorded and inspected as a pattern, and not an error.

The passage in Figure 17.10 has 43 words so the student can make approximately half as many word errors as on the Powell criteria (see Table 17.6). The student read the selection orally only and made 6 word errors. Looking at Table 17.6 (the Powell criteria), we can see that for grade one, a student can make 16 or 17 word errors per 100 words and still maintain 70 percent comprehension. The student who read Plant Spiders made only 6 word errors, which is well within the criterion limit of about 7 errors per 43 consecutive words. The student missed only one comprehension question, number 5, so he correctly answered 80 percent of the questions.

Several of the miscalled words changed the meaning of the sentence somewhat: *blue, smelly, nuts,* and *hurt.* There was graphic similarity between blue–black, smelly–small, nuts–nests, and hurt–hunt.

In a classroom setting, the teacher would want to administer a higher grade level oral reading selection because of the adequacy of student response in word recognition and comprehension.

Marking systems. Several marking systems have been devised so that the teacher can inspect miscues. After the student has completed the oral reading and answered the questions, he can note patterns of errors. Does the child call the first part of the word correctly but miscall the middle and end? Do the word miscues affect the meaning? Questions such as these are difficult to answer while the child is reading.

Marking systems vary. The important thing is that the teacher establish his own system so that when he looks back over what he has marked he will be able to interpret it (Kennedy 1977, p. 127; Zintz 1977, p. 64). An example is shown in Figure 17.11.

The following illustrations (Figures 17.12 through 17.15) show partial IRI test results from a student in fifth grade. The administration procedures for the IRI were as follows:

Figure 17.11. A sample ranking system.

Error	Mark
Repetitions	∧∧∧∧∧ or ⟵—
Hesitations	(3 sec) ' or ✓
Mispronunciations	*sit* / *like* over ~~sat~~ ~~look~~ *(write word said)*
Added words	∧ *(insert word)*
Omission of words and punctuation	◯ *(circle word omitted)*
Teacher help	H
Self correction	sc
Word by word reading	is/going/to *(slash lines between words)*
Don't know	DK *(child comes to word and says "I don't know that one")*

Figure 17.12. Word lists.

Grade 2		Grade 3	
1. stood *stud*	11. corn	1. hour	11. crowd *cord*
2. climb	12. everyone	2. senseless *DK*	12. crawl *count*
3. isn't *DK*	13. strong	3. turkeys	13. unhappy *DK*
4. beautiful	14. I'm	4. anything	14. clothes *cloths*
5. waiting	15. room	5. chief	15. hose *horse*
6. head	16. blows ✓	6. foolish *DK*	16. pencil ✓
7. cowboy	17. gray ✓	7. enough	17. meat
8. high	18. that's	8. either	18. discover
9. people	19. throw *threw*	9. chased *chance*	19. picture
10. mice *miss*	20. own *one*	10. robe *rub*	20. nail

Source: From Silvaroli, Nicholas J., *Classroom Reading Inventory*, 4th ed., © 1969, 1973, 1976, 1982 William C. Brown Company Publishers, Dubuque, Iowa. Reprinted by permission.

Figure 17.13. Oral reading passage.

FORM A, PART II—Level 2 (49 words)

ORAL

Motivation: This story takes place at a rodeo. At a rodeo cowboys show their skill with horses, steers and ropes. Read to find out more about the horse and cowboy in this story.

THE RODEO	Comprehension check
The people ~~at~~ *that* the rodeo ~~stood~~ *stand* up. ←	(F) 1.___ What did the people do? (Stood up, were waiting, etc.) *sat & watched*
They were all waiting for the big ride. ←	(F) 2.___ What was the name of the horse? (Midnight) *C*
Everyone came to see Bob/Hill ride/ Midnight. ←	(F) 3.___ What did he (Midnight) look like? (Big, black, strong, etc.) *dark*
Bob ~~Hill~~ *held (H)* ~~is~~ *his (sc)* a top rider.	(F) 4.___ Why do you think that Bob Hill was a good rider? (Story said he was a top rider; he had practice) *Been in business a long time*
Midnight is the best horse in the show. He is big and fast. ←	
Can Bob ~~Hill~~ *Hell* ride this great horse?	(I) 5.___ Did the story say that Bob Hill rode Midnight? (No, he did later, only in the picture) *No, said he was gonna ride*

Source: From Silvaroli, Nicholas J., *Classroom Reading Inventory*, 4th ed., © 1969, 1973, 1976, 1982 William C. Brown Company Publishers, Dubuque, Iowa. Reprinted by permission.

Figure 17.14. Silent reading passage.

FORM B, PART II—Level 2 (43 words)

SILENT

Motivation: Can you imagine 25 mean bulls loose in a crowd of people? It would be a mess. Read this story to find out what some people do when bulls are loose.

PEOPLE AND BULLS	Comprehension check
Before a bull fight some people wait in the streets.	(F) 1.___ Why did the people run from the bulls? (Because the bulls might hurt them) *because they chased them*
Then angry bulls chase them down the streets.	(F) 2.___ What did the people do just before a big bull fight? (Waited in the streets) *Did I read that? sit & wait I guess*
Some people try to hide.	
Here come the bulls, they yell;	(I) 3.___ Why do some people like to wait for the bulls? (See if they can get away from the bulls, etc.) *They thinks it's fun*
Run for your lives.	
Some people get hurt.	(I) 4.___ What makes the bulls angry? (People tease them, they are frightened, etc.) *Tease them & wear red*
Others think it is great fun.	(V) 5.___ What does the word "chase" mean? (to run after, etc.) *running after somebody*

Source: From Silvaroli, Nicholas J., *Classroom Reading Inventory*, 4th ed., © 1969, 1973, 1976, 1982 William C. Brown Company Publishers, Dubuque, Iowa. Reprinted by permission.

1. Administer a word list(s) so that you can get an idea of basic sight words known and the reading level.
2. Have the student begin reading passages similar to the grade level word list on which he made few errors.
3. Administer a silent reading passage and an oral reading passage at the same grade level (one oral and one silent at grade two or whatever grade level passage is selected) because many students at lower reading levels appear to comprehend better while reading orally. Hence, silent reading with good comprehension would be at a lower level and would be the independent level.
4. Keep administering silent and oral passages until comprehension drops below 90 percent and 70 percent respectively.
5. Administer the listening capacity test (you read to her and ask her questions) when the child's reading comprehension drops below 70 percent. From this test you can find out to what level she could be reading if she had adequate reading skills; it is one indicator of potential level for primary grade students.

Figure 17.15. Oral reading passage — to test at a higher level.

FORM A, PART II—Level 3 (100 words)

ORAL

Motivation: Some people say birds are smart and some say they are silly. See if you will agree with the author when he says that most birds are smart.

SMART BIRDS	Comprehension check
Everyone knows that birds like to eat/seeds and ~~grain~~ [*grain / green (H)*]. Birds also like to eat little/stones called ~~gravel~~ [*gravnel*]. Birds have/to eat the gravel/ because they don't/have teeth/to/grind [*grin (H)*] their food. The gravel stays in the bird's ~~gizzard~~ [*gizzs*] which is some~~thing~~ [*time*] like a ~~stomach~~ [*storch*]. When the bird eat~~s~~ seed, the gravel and the seed grind together. All of the seed is mashed up. ~~Tame~~ [*Time (sc)*] birds must be given gravel. Wild birds find their own gravel on the road sides. Now you can see how ~~smart~~ [*storm (sc)*] birds are.	(F) 1.___ Name two things birds like to eat. (Seeds, grain, <u>gravel</u> stones, sand) (F) 2.___ Why do birds have to eat sand or gravel? (Grind their food) *Grind food cause don't have teeth* (V) 3.___ What does the word "grind" mean? (Crush, make smaller, etc.) *make into little bits* (I) 4.___ What do you think would happen to birds that can't get any gravel in their food? (Probably die, get sick) *I guess they would die* (I) 5.___ A bird's gizzard works somewhat like what part of your body? (Stomach) *Intestine - stomach*

Source: From Silvaroli, Nicholas J., *Classroom Reading Inventory*, 4th ed., © 1969, 1973, 1976, 1982 William C. Brown Company Publishers, Dubuque, Iowa. Reprinted by permission.

6. Administer any informal phonics tests that have been devised (see Figure 17.16). (Optional.)

The checklist of Table 17.10, in addition to the Tortelli (1976) checklist (see Table 17.9), will provide the teacher with needed information to use in planning an instructional program.

Comprehension. The Powell Criteria specifies that 70 percent comprehension should be maintained for an instructional level. Several questions about comprehension need to be asked when determining levels, however. First, would the children know the answer to the question without first reading the story? It has been found that on some tests, children can answer 30 percent of the questions without reading the story (Allington et al. 1977). Second, are the questions all fact-recall, inference, or critical types? Depending on your purposes, the questions should be perused before administering the test to children so that the teacher knows what type of comprehension is being measured. Third, how is comprehension measured? Is it by use of the cloze procedure? Does the child read the question silently/orally? Does the teacher ask the question without the

Figure 17.16. Informal phonics test.

(The child pronounces these elements; his responses are recorded in the blank.)

br	_br_	bl	_bl_	st	_st_	ake	_ike_	ell	_ill_
oi	_DK_	ow	_ō_	ail	_ail_	o	_ō_	u	_ū_
a	_ā_	e	_ē_	i	_ī_	wh	_wer_	pr	_per_
sl	_sl_	dw	_DK_	tion	_TON_	pl	_Pl_	sm	_sem_

Table 17.10. Checklist for Informal Reading Inventory

Word List 2 _____   Word List 3 _____

Total number of errors

	Total number of word recognition errors	Comprehension
People and Bulls		
The Rodeo		
Smart Birds		
(Listening comprehension was adequate at the Grade 5 level.)		

Patterns

	Errors that change meaning	Patterns of errors
People and Bulls		
The Rodeo		
Smart Birds		

Phonics elements known _____
Phonics elements unknown _____
Instructional level _____
Independent level _____

child reading it? These questions and concerns aid the teacher in interpreting the comprehension results of any test more adequately.

Content area tests. Up to this point the reading skills assessment discussed was done during the reading portion of the language arts block. It is also important to assess content area reading. After having determined: (1) the reading skills of the student and (2) the readability of the content area text, the next step is to match the text to the child. It is relatively easy to mismatch because of the "one-text" content area system. Bond,

Tinker, and Wasson (1979, p. 28) state that at the fifth grade level, the range of reading achievement could be six or seven years. With this wide range of achievement in mind, Smith, Guice, and Cheek (1972) have devised IRIs for science and math. Content areas offer a different challenge to the reader, and it is worth the effort to assess content area reading skill inasmuch as library facilities can be used to provide material more suited to the student's reading level in each content area.

Summary

Both norm-referenced and criterion-referenced assessment are integral parts of current school practices. Standardized tests are normed using the bell curve concept. In the administration manual, directions prescribe how to have effective testing sessions, and other directions tell the teacher precisely how to administer the test to a group of students. The administration manual also contains tables for converting raw scores to percentiles, stanines, standard scores, or grade placement scores. These tables help a teacher compare the achievement of students in his classroom to other students who took the test. Usually norm-referenced tests are more global than criterion-referenced tests in the evaluation of skills. Norm-referenced tests such as the *CTBS* measure reading vocabulary, reading skills, and reading comprehension. If the teacher gets the test booklet back, he can see what specific items were missed. If not, all he has is the student profile.

Criterion-referenced evaluation on a day-to-day basis is more helpful in planning instruction. Teacher-constructed tests give specific information on skills development and reading processing. The informal reading inventory is a useful tool for placing students at appropriate instructional and independent levels.

Diagnostic teaching is the heart of the classroom instructional program. The IRI (with the associated concepts of instructional and independent levels, patterns of errors, and errors that change meaning) is useless unless instruction is planned based on the findings. The diagram in Figure 17.17 depicts the cyclical nature of teaching and assessing.

Questions for Further Reading and Thinking

1. What are additional advantages and disadvantages of norm-referenced tests and testing procedures?

2. Why might the skills to be mastered at one grade level from two basal systems be different?

Figure 17.17. The teaching–assessing cycle.

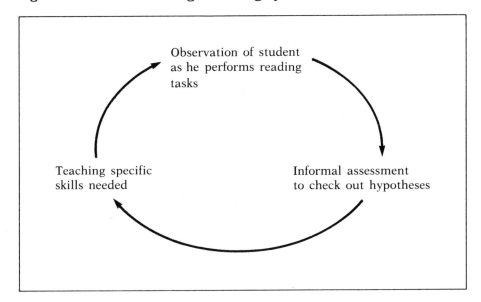

3. How does diagnostic teaching affect the organization of a classroom?
4. What do different authors of reading textbooks write about criteria for the instructional level?

Activities and Projects

---

1. Administer an informal reading inventory. Ascertain independent level and instructional level.
2. After you have administered formal or informal tests, list five *specific* ways to teach each of five *specific* skills.
3. Devise and administer two specific skill area tests to a student. Chart strengths and weaknesses in the specific skills.
4. Peruse a norm-referenced reading readiness test and a norm-referenced intelligence test. How are they the same, or different?
5. Administer an informal reading inventory to a first grader and a fourth grader. Are the oral reading miscue patterns the same?
6. Make an annotated bibliography of ten widely used norm-referenced achievement tests that include reading subtests. Include the name, publisher, reading skills tested, and how results are reported.
7. Construct five informal skills tests for a specific grade level.
8. Devise a checklist of skills for a particular grade level. The skills should be able to be measured informally, and the checklist should form a record keeping device.

Phyllis Huff

18

Classroom Organization

By this point in your study of reading, you have seen a lot written about several methods of instruction and you are well aware of the many skills and competences a reader needs to develop. The complexities of teaching reading may make you wonder how an effective reading program can possibly be realized within the short hours of a school day. It is the intent of this chapter to provide some background for the organization of a classroom that permits as much as possible to be accomplished within the given limits of time, teacher energy, and students' individual differences.

The organization of a classroom experience implies two things: organization of the physical environment (chairs and tables, for example) and organization of the ways in which the human components work and interact. The physical environment is often comparatively static and cannot be manipulated to a large degree (as, for example, by providing additional equipment or space). However, the vital element is the human organization that provides the best possible learning situation for each child, and this can be manipulated.

This chapter focuses on several major organizational patterns that attempt to meet the needs of learners — including intra- and interclass grouping, and individual and independent learning programs. Under intraclass grouping, we will discuss grouping for instruction by ability, interest, age, and total class; and we will also look at alternative within-class grouping, such as pupil learning, the nongraded approach, and team teaching. Interclass grouping refers to the grouping from more than one class for instruction. The individual and independent learning programs include use of learning stations in the reading programs and independent reading programs. Some of the topics mentioned are covered in detail in other chapters and will be presented here only as they relate to the organizational pattern of the classroom.

Intraclass and Interclass Grouping

QUESTIONS TO GUIDE READING

Literal
What are the various forms possible for intraclass grouping?

Inferential
What are the most important advantages and disadvantages of each form of intraclass grouping? of interclass grouping?

Evaluative
Which forms of intraclass grouping would you consider using (and under what conditions)?
Would different forms of intraclass grouping be more appropriate for content area classes?

A key word frequently used in planning for the organization of students in a reading program is "grouping." A group can consist of one child, several children, the total class, or a combination of several classes. Any organization (or group) is good only to the degree that it allows for meeting the needs of individual children.

Groups should be flexible. Otto and Sanders (1964, p. 67) believe that children should have an opportunity to work in a variety of groups: "The organization of instruction programs and grouping practices should be such that each pupil will have an opportunity to participate in groups of varying size and with pupils of different ages, abilities, interest, and backgrounds . . . some passive but mostly active experiences." Bush (1964) supports this position, summarizing the need for groups that will avoid creating, or allowing, passive learning situations; he considers the most beneficial groupings to be those that foster cooperative experiences between teachers and students.

I. · INTRACLASS GROUPING

This section will deal with the various organizational patterns of grouping for instruction in reading within a given class. The more traditional approaches to grouping, total class and ability level groups, are discussed along with some more innovative approaches — interest grouping, age level grouping, and team teaching (both teacher teams and student teams).

Total class grouping. The total class group is what the name indicates: the total class is taught as a single reading group with all the children reading from the same text and completing the same assignments. An argument for the total class grouping is the elimination of children's being placed into high-average-low groups and thus labeled. If all children are working at the same level on the same material, then all are, in theory, capable of working with equal ability. However, it has been said that the more varied the experiences of children are, the wider the range of reading ability among them. If this claim is valid, it implies that total group instruction is not meeting the needs of very many children within any group. The reason often given for the use of total group instruction in the intermediate grades is: "I don't have time for many reading groups." In such situations, the priorities for use of class time should probably be closely examined. After all, without the skills of reading, the students are very limited as they attempt to learn in the content areas.

Some other disadvantages for teaching the total class as a group relate to motivation and discipline. When all children are working on the same project, it cannot often be expected that they will maintain the same level of interest and attention. Thus, a few possess motivation, with the others only "doing what they have to to get by." This may result in the building of negative attitudes toward reading and toward school. Many of the children will be bored with the activity because it is not challenging, whereas others will be frustrated because it is too difficult. Either of these factions is likely to exhibit behaviors that will tend to disrupt and to frustrate the teacher. Many seemingly difficult discipline problems can be alleviated by providing experiences for all children which will interest them and in which they can have success.

Although the preceding arguments tend to discourage total class grouping for reading at any level, there are times when it is not only usable but advisable. One such time is when the students are working in a common interest or skill area — such as listening or discussion, or with unit topics in content areas (e.g., magnets or current events). The teacher then can provide the entire class with the same material (a film or other media aids) as a focus for discussion or informational reading. An example of such an activity is showing a film without sound and letting the students provide a dialog either individually or in a group as the film is shown again. Various dialogs could be tape-recorded and played with the film.

Other appropriate total class groupings include experiences in interpretive reading and choral reading. Also, students need to learn to listen and interpret in order to be able to read critically. Reading newspapers or current events articles and listening to news reports in a total class setting can form the basis for critical discussions that are much needed in the reading program. One such activity is comparing a leading news story from several sources — newspapers, television, and radio. Students can examine each to see how the information differs and how much is given the same treatment in all sources. The teacher must keep in mind that all newspapers are not printed at the same readability level and must provide those within the reading level of the children.

Caution is urged in the use of the total class as a unit for instruction. The teacher should be sure that there is both a common point of interest and a common need before planning such experiences: this condition will occur infrequently in most reading programs.

Ability grouping. Probably the most commonly used form of grouping is that based on the level of perceived ability of the child. This level is usually determined by testing the child either with formal, standardized reading tests or with informal, teacher-made tests to determine the relative level of reading performance (see Chapter 17), which is usually given in terms of grade level. After testing, the teacher places the children in groups that are considered homogeneous according to the scores of the tests used. The children in such groups are generally treated as a unit for the purpose of instruction.

There are several pros and cons to ability grouping. First, we will examine the strengths of the technique. As we have seen, the level of achievement within any given class is varied. The studies of Piaget also show that children develop at different rates (Flavell 1963). Thus, the grouping of children into smaller units makes it easier to provide the instruction necessary for their growth in reading. It is easier for the teacher to find materials that will meet their needs than when the group is larger and has a wider achievement range. Teachers also find that they can work more comfortably with a smaller part of the class at one time, that they can get closer to the child's learning needs, and that they are better able to provide tasks that are challenging (Otto and Sanders 1964, p. 124).

It appears that small-group instruction based on ability does have its strong points. What, then, are the weaknesses of this pattern? For one thing, ability grouping too often tends to reflect the social class of the students. Lower socioeconomic classes usually fall in low reading groups. As a result, many lower group students view themselves as inadequate. The students in the lower groups never have the feeling of being "someone special," and as a result most discipline problems tend to be centered in this group. Behavior problems make the independent learning tasks that are necessary for growth very difficult to assign and get completed. In reviewing psychological research on grouping, Alexander and Filler (1974) found that group cohesiveness, a feeling of liking and belonging, exists only in the reading groups at the upper ability levels.

The research comparing homogeneous to heterogeneous patterns is inconclusive; the number of studies indicating significant advantages to one form is approximately equal to the number finding differences in favor of the other form (Spache and Spache 1977, p. 465). The conclusions reported were that high-ability pupils are favored by homogeneous grouping. The lower ability students seemed to be hampered by the label of "slow" when grouped homogeneously. Perhaps more study should be done on the attitudes and self-perception that grouping practices foster.

Another problem is that ability grouping is too often static. Students are frequently placed in one group — never to leave for another level regardless of the rate of progress they display. When this happens, students label themselves as "smart," "just average," or "stupid or dumb." This leads them to the self-fulfilling prophecy that they can do no better or no worse than their reading group has designated for their performance level.

The current pattern of mainstreaming is another factor to be considered in ability grouping. Most mainstreamed children have learning difficulties, thus placing them in a group where they can function successfully is difficult. Teachers need to be very supportive of the mainstreamed children and to structure success experiences. In addition the physically handicapped will require special environmental conditions to function. This may mean a different technique for presenting lessons so that each need is met.

Even with the shortcomings, ability grouping does afford more provision for many individual needs than does total class instruction. However, when ability grouping is used, the teacher should also incorporate alternate grouping procedures that provide viable ways for meeting the individual needs of the students within all ability levels.

Interest grouping. Interest grouping is based not on achievement but on the common interests of the particular groups. Although the achievement levels of the students may be widely varied, motivation for the group comes from sharing a common interest in learning about something. There is evidence to suggest a dependent relationship between motivation and success (Olson 1956). The student is successful because he is motivated. The motivation leads him to attempt material more difficult than he otherwise would be inclined to tackle. He works hard, he experiences success, and he feels good about himself. The interest, together with past experiences that created the interest, gives the student a broader background than is found in the previously mentioned grouping patterns. Likewise, the more able student responds better to simple tasks without the usual boredom because he is interested.

One disadvantage to interest-based grouping lies in the various achievement levels of the students — despite the children's willingness to accommodate the group to some degree. The teacher must provide assignments that are on the success level of each child, and that involve much time and energy in preparation. The teacher must also provide books and reading material on a wide range of reading levels, while also covering the interest range of the group. Besides, the group is not static: as the interests wane or change, the group composition must also change. Interest in any given topic can be sustained only so long by most students.

Examples of topics for interest groups include horses, cars, prehistoric animals, mysteries, etc. Books can be available, and activities such as worksheets or art projects developed for each topic.

Most teachers like to use interest grouping to augment their ability level or other types of groups. The experiences in the interest group put together children with differing achievement levels, thus giving each a chance to be a part of a success group and to work with students whose achievement is not like his own. This diversity is needed in learning how to cope with everyday and adult life.

Age grouping. Another (and probably less used) type of grouping involves putting together children of like ages, or children of a range of ages, in one group. The children can come from the same classroom or from any number of classrooms in the school. The like-age grouping, sometimes equated with the ungraded plan, puts all six-year-olds together, all seven-year-olds, and so on. Many of the graded schools were started with this concept, but they grouped by the number of years the child had been in school, not by age. Age grouping has the advantage, in theory, that all children are roughly at the same developmental stage. However, research in child development doesn't support this theory (Flavell 1963; Olson 1956). At the same age, children can be at a variety of levels of development — from several months or years behind to years ahead of normal developmental patterns. In fact, in younger children a few months in age make a significant difference (Huff 1971; Riechard 1970). If there is an attempt to group by age in months, as opposed to age in years, there might be a closer developmental level, but there would still be a range of achievement for the teacher to cope with.

Multiage level groups have become popular in many schools, generally in "open" schools. In this approach, children of several ages are placed in common groups or, as they are called in some schools, communities. The basis for this type of grouping goes back to "Dewey days," when the effort was to provide a "family" type of experience in the schools, with older and younger children working together as they would in the typical home (Dewey 1916). The older children were to help the younger ones and were to serve as models for them. In reality, the teachers often regroup the multiage groups into ability groups, having each child work with the group most in line with his ability. The problems of such an arrangement are quite apparent. The older children often have difficulty working with younger children, and their self-image may be harmed. Younger children placed with older children often have identity problems. Careful preparation must be made for the groups to work well together, for understanding of the grouping pattern, and for acceptance by all people involved.

Alternate groupings. The previous discussion has dealt with some practices used in organizing a class for reading. Innovation in the area of grouping for reading instruction has led to several alternatives that will interest the beginning teacher. Teaming is one such approach. The process of teaming for learning and instruction involves more than one person taking an active role. Team teaching involves two or more teachers working together in some way so that the responsibility for instruction and for assisting the pupils is shared. Usually this means that some instructional technique is presented to a large group by one or more team members. Then the group is divided into subgroups for follow-up instruction and more individualized attention. The subgrouping may be made on the basis of ability, of interest, or by random assignment. For this technique to be successful the total large group instruction must be of value and of interest to all the students. For example, it might consist of a specific skill development such as using an index or card catalog. It could be a demonstration of a device or instrument such as a tape recorder or a microscope. Large group can be used to introduce a new unit of study. It can have a function for any topic relevant to instruction, providing it is applicable. The other important aspects of team teaching are how the subgroups are divided and how instruction is handled so as to enable each child to receive materials meaningful and useful to him.

Another teaming approach is pupil teaming, or buddy reading. This approach teams two students for a specific purpose. The team membership can vary according to the need. For example, a child having trouble with oral reading is teamed with a child who is accomplished in oral reading: the accomplished student helps the other by reading to him and by listening to him read. A unique approach that has been successful for some teachers is to team a slow reader, or to place a problem reader, with another reader with the same or a different problem. The two then can assist each other without either feeling inadequate in the presence of his teammate. I have found that this approach has worked very well with problem readers at the intermediate level. Likewise, more capable students may be teamed with their peers; thus, each benefits by having a teammate who can challenge him. Another approach to teaming that has worked with discipline-problem readers is teaming them with younger children who have similar difficulties. The older child is then given the responsibility for working with a younger child for a designated period of time each week. In my experience, the results have shown that both improve in their reading skills.

The teacher must carefully implement a pupil teaming plan by setting an atmosphere where neither child feels inferior or superior. This can be done to some extent by letting the children have some choice, such as "Alan, would you rather work with Sam or Joe?" Giving each child some choices helps toward a more positive feeling. The same attitude can be conveyed by asking the child if he would like to work on word skills with Jane today. Helpers should be flexible so that no permanent attitudes toward other children can be formed and so that children have a chance to work with a variety of others.

The nongraded approach was mentioned in the age grouping discussion. It merits some attention here since it is a recognized form of grouping in many open classrooms. This puts children in a group on the basis of ability, interest, or need as opposed to a specific grade assignment. It is just what the name implies: that no grade equivalent is attached and that each child is where he can most successfully operate.

INTERCLASS GROUPING

As an alternative to grouping within one classroom, it is possible to combine several classrooms at one level and to group from the total population for reading instruction. An example of such an approach would take all the third grades in a given school and divide them into reading groups according to the number of teachers at the third grade level. For instance, there are six third grade classes in the school. All these are combined, and the children are divided into six groups according to their reading level as measured by reading test scores. Each teacher agrees to work with one specific level of reading achievement. Each group consists of approximately one-sixth of the third graders, but they need not be equal in number. The children move to the room of the teacher assigned for the reading period.

Many teachers view this technique as homogeneous grouping and as an easier way to prepare and instruct. In reality, there is a wide difference within the groups. Also, this arrangement means that reading must be taught for exactly the same amount of time in each group every day. Unless there is much communication between teachers, this limits the teacher in what can be covered and in follow-up activities during the rest of the school day. It can cause the teacher to lose touch with the progress of the students with whom he works in the other curricular areas and, thus, to lose a great deal of control over instruction and material.

Interclass grouping also occurs in departmentalized instruction. In this organization one teacher teaches all the children of a given grade or set in one subject area, i.e., Teacher A teaches all English, Teacher B all math, and so on. Students are often grouped by ability in reading as presented above. Some teachers feel this is an advantage as there is less broad subject preparation and they can go in depth into one area. The same disadvantages are here as those listed above. Also it gives very little, if any, integration of subject matter, making units and other activities almost impossible.

Individual and Independent Learning Programs

QUESTIONS TO GUIDE READING

Literal
In what way can learning centers assist in the reading program?
What steps do you need to take in planning a learning center?

Evaluative
Since reading is an individual act, are individual approaches more desirable than group approaches?

We have seen conclusive evidence that children learn in different ways and at different rates. In order to meet all these individuals' specific needs, the teacher must provide more than a single type of organizational scheme and structure. Two means to meet differing needs are: (1) the use of learning centers and (2) independent reading.

LEARNING CENTERS

Recently there has been much emphasis on the use of the learning center, or learning station, in the classroom. Learning centers do provide both for individualization of instruction (through assignments geared to individual needs) and for the development of independent work habits. Learning centers give a focus to the child and help him attain goals by working independently of the teacher. The skill in working independently is one that is learned, and the learning center offers a good setting in which to learn it; children cannot learn if they do not receive instruction, direction, and — above all else — practice. Such centers can be developed around specific skills in reading.

Planning a learning center involves several steps: (1) define the purposes, (2) consider the characteristics of the students to be using the center, (3) define the concepts or skills to be developed, (4) outline the expected learning outcomes, (5) select the appropriate activities and materials, (6) evaluate the center, and (7) implement needed changes (Sherfey and Huff 1976).

In defining the purposes it is important to be specific so that it is clear to both teacher and student what is expected; e.g., "At this center you will develop the skill of using letters and sounds to attack unfamiliar words." A learning center must have a definite purpose. It will not be effective if it is merely the whim of the teacher, a reward for students who finish assignments, or an assignment prepared without a stated purpose.

The center must be appropriate in content and design for the students using it. The tasks should be graduated in difficulty to meet ability of both the slowest and the most advanced child. All children do not need to complete all tasks. For students with reading difficulty, a taped direction (rather than printed direction) or a pictorial direction may be used.

A clear statement of the skills and concepts the center is designed to develop is necessary. Also, the center must be planned to develop skills sequentially. Many centers fail on this point and thus evolve into busy-work stations.

The expected outcomes are the objectives that state exactly what the student should gain from the center. The specific goal is precisely what the directions to the student say; for example, "Create new words by joining two small words together."

The teacher should evaluate the students' learning, as well as the over-all learning effectiveness of the center. Any weakness in the center should be changed to ensure more efficient operation. See the annotated bibliography on learning centers at the end of the chapter.

 INDEPENDENT READING

The need for all children to reach a level of competence in reading that will enable them to read at a level of independence is one of the major goals of reading instruction. Once the child has command of enough sight words and has interest in some topic that is presented in story or book form, he can begin to read independently. There is no formal skills instruction during independent reading. The primary purpose is for children to learn to enjoy reading and to read materials for sheer pleasure. A time should be set aside for every child to have some experience in independent reading at some time during the course of the week's planning for the reading program. This could take the form of Sustained Silent Reading (SSR) discussed in Chapter 6.

Another way to provide for independent reading is for the child to read aloud to friends or to younger children. Any encouragement that will make the child feel that reading is enjoyable, not only for himself but for others, is desirable.

As a means of motivation and evaluation (as well as guiding students into a varied reading program), the teacher can make use of a contract. The contract is a written agreement between the teacher and the student that specifies what the student will do and the time limit for completion. Contracts can also be used in learning centers and individualized reading.

The preceding organizational approaches are those you can observe in many classrooms. There are creative teachers now trying other approaches as well. As a teacher gets to know his students and as he gains confidence and experience in his teaching, he will explore new and successful classroom organizations. However, it is important to mention again that there is no pattern that is "best."

Organizing a Classroom

QUESTIONS TO GUIDE READING

Literal
How can a beginning teacher plan and work with several groups of children at one time?

Evaluative
What is the most practical and efficient way to organize a classroom for successful reading?
Why is the independent reading assignment important in grouping?

With all the possible alternatives for grouping, the novice will probably be tempted to ask, "Which method is the best for teaching reading in the school setting?" Much research was done in the 1950s and 1960s on grouping for reading in the elementary school. But most of it compared one method of teaching with another, such as individualized versus basal approaches and homogeneous ability grouping versus heterogeneous grouping. Research appears to be conclusive in one aspect — there is no one organizational pattern that guarantees achievement. It is the teacher that makes the difference, not the pattern (Aaron 1960; Earle and Mosley 1974; Fay 1971; Spache 1965).

As the teacher begins planning the reading program several things need to be considered. The first and foremost is the providing of meaningful and appropriate instruction for each child. In order to accomplish this the teacher needs to give careful attention to the selection of the type of grouping to be used and how instruction will be planned for the groups. The teacher must also consider how the groups will be managed during the reading instruction time.

The ideal type of organization is one that provides each child with a meaningful experience and thus is individualized. In this sense individualized does not mean that each child needs to be working alone but that each child is receiving instruction that meets his needs. To provide the best instruction for each child most teachers find some combination of grouping more workable for them than a single approach. For example, some sort of achievement or ability grouping may be used for initial instruction, whereas for other purposes grouping in total class, interest groups, occasional age groups, and some individualization may be feasible. This imples that a lot of reading activity is going on in the classroom at one time and frightens many teachers in terms of their losing control over the situation. If each child is meaningfully occupied, that is less likely to happen. More will be discussed on this topic later in this section.

Before deciding on the grouping to be used the teacher must determine the readiness of the students for group and independent work. If the children have been working both in groups and independently, there will be very little preparation for the teacher to do other than to decide on the number of groups needed and to provide interesting and meaningful independent activities. If the children have not worked very often in groups or have had little or no exposure to independent work, the task will be much more difficult. In the latter case, most teachers prefer to work into the process very slowly, giving themselves and the children time to adjust and to learn to work without constant supervision.

A teacher might decide that the best working arrangement to begin the year is to have two groups based on reading level. This would allow one group to be working independently on a skill or other assignment while the teacher works with the second group on directed reading instruction. The groups would then be rotated. With only one group to supervise and one to work independently, the management of the reading period is less involved.

As the teacher and the students gain in skill to work independently, the number of groups can be expanded to three, four, or a fully individualized program depending on the teacher and the student needs. The teacher can also consider combining the various patterns discussed in this chapter. For example, children might be in a group for formal skills instruction but pursuing an individualized program during assignment time. Many such combinations are possible for a creative program.

Even though the ultimate goal is to have every child reading and working at his individual level, either in a group or alone, it is impractical for the beginning teacher to believe he can do this at the start of the school year. It must be done step by step, taking into account the size of the class, the range of abilities and the kinds of differences in the class, the teacher's experience and competence in the management of a class, the teacher's personality and philosophy of reading, and the background of the children in reading and in group and independent work. Taking all these factors into account, the program should still be striving to give each child a chance to succeed and to attain the highest level of which he is capable.

A concern of beginning teachers is the management of two or more groups of children during reading instruction. It entails providing for the group with which the teacher is working in the directed instruction and at the same time managing the group not under her direct supervision. In order for this to be a smooth process the students must be able to work independently. Teachers can develop independence in students by structuring the assignment so that it is within the ability of the students, is relevant to the students, and is perceived as a learning task. Examples of independent activities are: a follow-up assignment from the previous reading lesson; specific tasks such as handwriting and spelling; or a related language skill practice. The teacher can also make use of the time allotted for practice in other subject areas such as mathematics. Depending on the level and ability of the students there may be more than one task to complete during independent work time. An example of this is to have one assignment as the followup of the lesson by sequencing the happenings in the story and also having a practice exercise activity on the mathematics facts being studied.

In planning and presenting the assignment, the teacher must make the directions clear so that the students can follow them with ease. These may be written on the board to enhance understanding and remembering. The teacher must not get caught in the trap of giving repeated directions. Directions that are given well need only be given once with a review.

When the groups are increased to three or more the structure of the assignment is crucial to success. Following is an example of how three groups can function.

The teacher divides the class into three groups by using the reading ability levels of the students. These groups might be called Blue, Orange, Green. In addition she assigns each child a number: 1, 2, 3, 4, or 5. The teacher has prepared five centers for independent work: (1) a listening center for phonics, (2) a number center, (3) a creative play center using puppets, (4) a science center to find objects that sink or float, and (5) a watercolor painting center. She has two large disks on display. The disks have movable centers.

Each morning the disks are set for the beginning of the reading period (see Figure 18.1). Disk 1 tells each group where they should be for the first period (about twenty minutes for each period); disk 2 tells each child assigned to the centers which center he will work in for that day. Disk 1 is rotated for each period of the day's reading whereas disk 2 is only rotated once per day. This structure clearly tells the children what they are to do and keeps a minimum of children in each center. Any number of groups or centers may be used, adjusting the disks accordingly.

In summary, the vital elements in the management of multiple groups are having carefully planned structure; clear, easy-to-follow directions; and an expectation for children to follow these directions without direct teacher supervision. It requires specific and careful planning by the teacher. All materials needed must be available. It also requires that students learn to be responsible for their own behaviors. If the teacher begins slowly by having short independent work periods and gradually extends the time, she is more likely to have a well-managed class.

Figure 18.1. Sample disks.

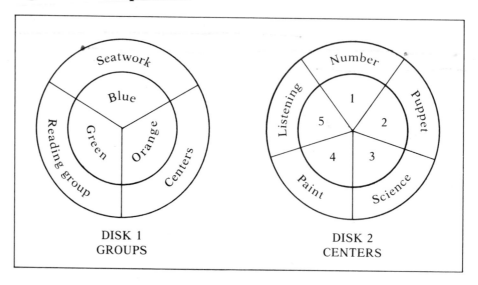

DISK 1
GROUPS

DISK 2
CENTERS

Summary

A major factor in the success of a reading program is the organization of the program. This chapter has presented three main organizational tactics: intraclass grouping, interclass grouping, and individual and independent learning programs. Several suggestions for organization for instruction were given for each major pattern.

The deciding factor in determining which organizational pattern to use in the classroom should be the teacher responsible for using it. Through study and experimentation the teacher can determine which pattern or combination of patterns is best suited to the particular class and instructional setting.

The provision of meaningful activities for children not actively working with the teacher is a vital part of any grouping or individualized pattern. Children must also be trained to work efficiently without constant teacher guidance. The novice teacher should perhaps begin with fewer groups and add more as both he and the children become proficient in group and independent work.

One way to develop independence in learning is the use of the learning center. The learning center provides for several levels of activities and offers the child some choices or alternate ways for learning basic and extended skills. The center must be carefully planned and designed so the child can work independently on the activities. Learning centers offer opportunities for creative expression as well as formal skill development.

The success of a reading program depends not only on the teacher's knowledge and the selection of content and skills but also on how the environment is organized for learning. The more the students are expected to be independent in their activities, the more the program must be organized. Students must know what is expected of them and how they can best accomplish the tasks assigned.

The final decision about the best arrangement for a particular class will depend on careful study and application of various procedures in several trial-and-error experiences by the teacher. Most teachers tend to favor those patterns and ideas which most nearly match the successful experiences they have had. The innovative teacher should try to avoid this tendency and give each pattern an equal chance to contribute to success in reading.

Questions for Further Reading and Thinking

1. What preparations should a teacher make for grouping a class of children in reading?
2. What are the first steps to take in classroom organization to ensure effective reading instruction?
3. What limitations are set on grouping by such factors as children's ages, materials available, students' ability levels, and class size?
4. If you could have the ultimate in a reading program, with no restrictions as to cost and materials, which type of organization would you choose? Why do you make this choice?
5. Describe your ideal of an elementary reading curriculum. Outline how this program would look in a school guide.
6. How may the procedures described in Chapter 17 be utilized in classroom grouping?

Activities and Projects

1. Using a teacher's manual or guide for a textbook series, plan at least three independent work activities that the student could be assigned relating to a specific story.
2. Games are often used in classrooms as independent activities. Find two such games that you think would be appropriate and tell how you would implement them in a classroom.
3. Draw an outline of an elementary classroom to scale. Arrange it to accommodate thirty students of varied reading abilities.
4. If possible, talk to some elementary teachers about their classroom organization. Record your observations and draw some conclusions about the type of teacher using the various types of organization.

Selected Activities for Learning Centers

Note: These need to be adapted to various levels of difficulty to meet varying student ability.

Activity: Sequencing (Figure 18.2)

Materials: Comic strips cut into frames.

Directions: Have the comic strip frames available, with table space enough to place them in the order they would occur in. A simple checking technique is to have a word clue spelled out on the strip, one letter to a frame, so that when the child has the strip in correct sequential order, the word is easily read. It is more interesting if the word in some way relates to the pictures.

Example: The comic is a four-frame sequence showing a romantic encounter between two birds on a balloon. The clue word: *love*.

Activity: Main ideas

Materials: Pictures and paragraphs from newspapers (without headings).

Directions: Have the child choose a picture or a paragraph and study it for a few minutes. Now he writes the main idea for his picture or paragraph. If you want this activity to be a self-checking activity, have some appropriate responses on the back of the picture or the paragraph or on a separate answer card numbered the same as the item chosen.

Activity: Writing a telegram (adapted from *Center Stuff*; see bibliography that follows)

Materials: Dittoed telegram forms.

Directions: Have the children choose a book they have read that they would like to tell a friend about. Give them these additional instructions: "Send a telegram to your friend that summarizes the book. Remember, telegrams cost by the number of words, so be brief, yet cover the main ideas."

Activity: Antonyms

Materials: Dittoed or printed lists of words.

Directions: Tell children to choose a list of words and write at least one opposite for each word. The same procedure works for writing synonyms or for writing describing words (adjectives).

Activity: Analyzing oral reading

Materials: Tape recorder and tape.

Directions: Give children these instructions: "Choose a story you especially like and read it into the tape recorder. Play the tape and

Figure 18.2. Sequencing.

listen without looking at the printed story. Can you understand the story? Can you understand the story better for listening? Was it interestingly read? Now follow the story in the book. Did you make any mistakes? What words or phrases gave you trouble?"

Example of using the newspaper in a learning center

Purpose. To introduce students to the newspaper and its importance in our culture.

Target students. Designed for use in second or third grade, but could be adapted to any level.

Concepts and skills. Identifying the parts of the newspaper; reinforcing alphabetizing; interpreting pictures; sequencing; identifying advertisements; compiling a newspaper.

Expected learning outcomes. All the skills; at conclusion, the student will be able to compile his own newspaper.

Activities and materials. Introduction: Before the children use the center, the teacher will show pictures from a newspaper and ask, "What are these pictures telling us about?" He will also show samples of other things that are found in the newspaper — e.g., ads, comic strips, headlines, stories, and sports. He will explain that the task cards at the center are designed to help the students work through the Newspaper Center on their own. Any task that needs extra information or material is color-coded to match a color-coded envelope containing the necessary supplies. To keep track of his work, each child will have a folder in which to store his material. The folder also contains a Task Card Check Sheet, on which the student will record the date he completed the task. Tasks do not need to be completed in order, but he does need to do all tasks. Continue creating tasks for all areas — create an advertisement; draw a comic strip; report a sports event, and so on. Have children put these together into a newspaper of their own.

Sample task cards:

TASK B
Find and cut out all the letters of the alphabet. Glue them to a piece of construction paper in alphabetical order.

TASK E
Open the envelope and put the cartoon frames in correct order to tell the story.

TASK C
Find pictures of things that begin with the alphabet letters. Paste them on the letter sheet beside the letter.

TASK F
Find an advertisement. Cut out any words that name colors. Paste these on paper.

TASK D
Find a picture in a newspaper. Cut the picture out and make up a story about it. Tape-record your story and place the tape with the picture.

TASK G
Take a newspaper. List the sections that are in the paper.

```
┌─────────────────────────────────────────┐
│ TASK H                                   │
│   Write a news story of something that   │
│   happened to you. Give your story a     │
│   headline.                              │
│                                          │
│                                          │
│                                          │
└─────────────────────────────────────────┘
```

Evaluate the center by checking each child's progress and interest.

Annotated Bibliography on Learning Centers

Allen, Roach Van; and Allen, Claryce. 1976. *Language experience activities*. Boston: Houghton Mifflin. (A guide for developing centers based upon language and vocabulary development. Includes creative activities.)

Davidson, Tom et al. 1976. *The learning center book*. Pacific Palisades, Calif.: Goodyear. (Suggestions for learning centers.)

Forte, Imogene et al. *Mini-center stuff*. 1976. Nashville, Tenn.: Incentive Publications. (A collection of model learning centers complete with diagrams and activity ideas.)

Forte, Imogene; and MacKenzie, Joy. 1976. *Nooks, crannies and corners*. Nashville, Tenn.: Incentive Publications. (Guide to learning centers.)

Forte, Imogene; Pangle, Mary Ann; and Pupa, Robbie. 1976. *Center stuff for nooks, crannies and corners*. Nashville, Tenn.: Incentive Publications. (The "how-to" for putting together and implementing a learning center.)

Horton, Lowell; and Horton, Phyllis. 1973. *The Learning Center: Heart of the school*. Minneapolis: Denison. (A book of learning center models and ideas for development.)

Johnston, Hiram. 1978. *The learning center ideabook*. Boston: Allyn and Bacon. (A book of plans and models for constructing a learning center.)

Kaplan, Sandra; Kaplan, Jo Ann; Madsen, Sheila; and Taylor, Bette. 1980. *Change for children*. Pacific Palisades, Calif.: Goodyear. (Excellent suggestions for learning centers, record keeping, and evaluation; includes worksheets.)

Lorton, Mary Baratta. 1972. *Workjobs*, pp. 17–125. Menlo Park, Calif.: Addison-Wesley. (Activities for readiness and perception for young children.)

Miles, Kate; and Stahl, Paula. 1974. *Use the news*. Englewood Cliffs, N.J.: Prentice-Hall. (Many unique suggestions for using the newspaper in the reading and language program.)

Nation, Jimmy E. (ed.). 1975. *Learning centers in the classroom*. Washington, D.C.: National Education Association. (Another book of ideas and plans for centers.)

Thomas, John I. 1975. *Learning centers: Opening up the classroom*. Boston: Holbrook Press. (Guides to developing and using learning centers at all levels.)

Sammye J. Wynn

19

Involving Parents in the Reading Program

Traditionally, educators have perceived the teaching of reading as the undisputed province of the school, generally ignoring their most effective and accessible source of help — parents. In recent years, however, educators are becoming increasingly aware of the many benefits that can accrue from parental involvement in the reading program. McDonald (1976) observed, after analyzing the correlation of pupil achievement scores with academic aptitude estimates, that no more than 36 percent of learning can be attributed to school efforts. He concluded that since about two-thirds of a child's knowledge is gained from the home and community, it seems essential for educators to capitalize on parents as resources in developing reading skills.

Children from every socioeconomic stratum benefit greatly from reading programs that involve parents; but for economically deprived children parental involvement is imperative if reading success is to be achieved. Historically children of low-income family groups have experienced pervasive reading failure in the nation's schools, with the attendant problem of high dropout rates. An overwhelming number of these children fail to master reading skills and merely stumble along in the first few years of school, after which they become confirmed nonlearners. This devastatingly low achievement rate can often be reversed for children of the poor (and all children can achieve greater reading success) through a preventive approach to the teaching of reading that focuses on parental involvement.

The preventive aspect should actually begin in the prenatal period. Prospective parents are given much information by their obstetricians, for example, on such things as malnutrition and the prevention of communicable diseases. But who gives information on how to prevent reading failure? The Parents and Reading Committee of the International Reading Association is now making an effort to provide this crucial information; a substantially stronger effort by educators is needed, however.

Prior to the advent of schools in early America, there were no parent surrogates involved in the education of children. Parents, though limited to primitive and haphazard methods, were the sole purveyors of knowledge to their children. The curriculum consisted primarily of survival content, with little time and effort allocated to teaching the major reading material available — the Bible. Considering the historical role of parents as the first teachers of their children, it is obvious that the modern-day school has long been remiss in assuming responsibility for institutionalizing the practice of involving parents in their children's reading programs and helping them assume this role by providing background information, guidance, and encouragement.

Although a few schools are beginning to recognize the importance of involving parents in the reading program, this is generally a neglected area in education. Schools must maximize the influential role parents could play in helping their children achieve reading success through creating a stimulating home environment and providing readiness for reading and support for continued progress. School-age children cannot, and certainly should not, be insulated from the influence of the home, as it is the learning arena for them during their first and most impressionable years; therefore, a portion of the school's total efforts must be directed toward involving parents in reading activities.

Parents as Cognitive Stimulators in the Preschool Years

QUESTIONS TO GUIDE READING

Literal
How may parents use everyday living to provide cognitive stimulation to their children?
What are some of the activities parents might plan to develop an enriched experiential background and oral language facility?

Evaluative
How may a teacher encourage parents to provide a more effective home reading environment?

Beginning at infancy, a stimulating home environment has positive effects on the educational development of children. Some homes provide this stimulation as a part of the daily routine, but many parents must be given assistance in creating a home environment where learning is fostered and everyday living develops readiness for reading. Parents must be helped to understand how specific activities contribute to reading success.

Listening to and Talking with Children

Generally parents do not recognize that sincerely listening to and talking with their children and encouraging further conversation provide the foundation for success in reading. It is important that parents understand that conversations with their children provide a backlog of information that is basic to reading progress. This activity also aids in developing the concept that printed symbols represent things that exist in life. Children learn many words through talking with their parents — names for objects and words for expressing ideas. As parents listen, they are also conveying the idea that the child has something worthwhile to say, which encourages him to speak often and freely; moreover, the child's self-concept is greatly improved.

It is not suggested that parents make special preparation or provide specific structured content as they talk with their children; rather they should just share some of their acquired information and understandings. For example, these topics may be discussed:

Time: Minutes make hours, hours make days, days make weeks, weeks make months, months make years.

Seasons: The four seasons and what they are like in terms of temperature and activities.

Holidays and special events: Origin, how observed.

Animals: Classification and natural habitat, how they interact with or help humans.

Food: Sources, nutritive qualities, classification.

Transportation: Different modes.

Weather: Winds, clouds, storms, rain cycle, snow, changes.

As parents talk with their child, they should model the speech patterns of speaking clearly and in complete sentences. They may further increase a child's speaking vocabulary by teaching him to make associations and relate new words to those already known.

Reading to Children — How It Helps

In addition to a shared enjoyable experience, many other valuable by-products accrue when parents read to children. Among these is facility in the use of oral language, which is a prime prerequisite for the development of effective reading skills; another is the joy and security of having the total attention and closeness of the parent. Moreover, the child's curiosity about books is heightened and his interest in learning to read quickly is aroused. As the youngster asks questions, describes pictures, repeats favorite parts, develops an awareness of rhyming words, and retells stories, he is acquiring an excellent foundation in essential reading skills. The child's listening and speaking vocabularies are increased as he learns the usage and meaning of words through pictures, context, and parent definition. Children are able to experience vicariously, storing valuable information to be drawn on later for interpretive purposes. (When we consider that the reader interprets all that is read in light of his experiences, we see that it is increasingly important that he develop an extended experiential background.)

As a result of being read to, children are able to see the link between speech and printed symbols; they begin to understand at an early age the relationship of oral language to print. This basic understanding enables them to move with greater ease into the realm of books. Additionally, proficiency in the use of context clues is developed as children begin to anticipate appropriate words which fit and "make sense" with preceding context. This skill will be most useful as children begin to read on their own. Reading to children not only lays the foundation for success in reading, it aids in developing a permanent interest in reading as well as an affinity for good books.

EXPLORING THE COMMUNITY FOR LEARNING SITUATIONS

The community is an excellent resource for learning and aids the child enormously in developing an enriched experiential background so essential for reading progress. Parents must be helped to develop an awareness of the numerous opportunities for acquiring background information from community explorations: a trip to the supermarket, dime store, drug store, bank, service station, airport, and nature walks are a few examples. Envision this parent-guided tour of the supermarket as the various departments are introduced and discussed.

> This is the meat department. Here we have all kinds of meat and sea foods. We get our meat from selected animals such as the cow, hog, chicken, lamb, and duck. Animals such as the fish, oyster, and shrimp give us seafood. They live in the water, which is sometimes called the sea. This is beef right here; the cow is the animal that gives us beef. When the cow's meat is cut, the different parts are given names such as steak (which you see here), hamburger, roast, and liver. The cow not only gives us beef, but milk as well, which is used to make butter, cheese, ice cream, and other dairy products.
>
> We call this the produce department. Fresh fruits and vegetables are found here. Vegetables and fruits come from plants, which grow in the ground. These green beans grow on a bush or vine. We call these greens "leafy vegetables" because we eat the leaves. With these potatoes it is different; only the roots of the potato are eaten. Look at these green peas; we eat only the seeds of the peas.

On subsequent trips to the supermarket, fruits can be discussed in a similar manner; other departments can also be explored, and much more information given regarding the sources and classification of foods. A most fascinating department for the young child is the area in which baby food and accessories are stocked. This is his domain — or was until recently; all discussion pivots around food and other items especially prepared for very young children. He will be delighted to learn how the fresh vegetables, meat, and fruits he saw earlier are cooked and prepared for babies. The role of the farmer and grocer as community helpers and the equipment used in supermarkets provide further opporunities for "talk starters."

Using the community as a backdrop, parents can be guided into planning countless activities that can provide an enriched experiential background and further stimulate learning. As parents share acquired information with their children, they will develop greater facility in communicating concepts and will serve increasingly as sources of information for their children. In addition, as parents and children share these experiences, much conversation between them will be stimulated, thus further promoting facility in oral language. It is reasonable that parents in the lower income stratum are often preoccupied with survival problems; they will need special encouragement to provide these educational experiences for their children. Although most of their energies may be expended on immediate goals, every effort should be exerted to inform them of the wealth of learning situations available in the community.

MAKING MAXIMUM USE OF THE PUBLIC LIBRARY

Some parents, along with their children, are regular patrons of the library; reading in the home is a way of life for the family. There are many parents, however, who do not perceive the library as an avenue to success in reading for their children. These parents must be given special assistance in discovering the library as a marvelous source for stimulating their children and getting them ready for reading — a source that is readily available at no extra cost. Since it is so important that parents make maximum use of the public library, specific information should be discussed with them. Ideas such as the following are suggested:

1. Introduce the child to the public library at an early age. Help him develop the concept that the library is a supermarket of knowledge, information, and fun-type reading.
2. See that the youngster has his own library card, and take him to the library often to look at books and check out books in line with his interests and stage of development. Teach him the organization of the library.
3. Acquaint the child with the various departments and services of the

library: children's department, reference, audio-visual, story hour, film showings, and book clubs.

4. Give more than lip service to the notion that reading is important. Use the library with enthusiasm as a source of pleasure and information. Read for information and enjoyment in the presence of the children.

Although using the public library is extremely beneficial, attention should be given to helping children develop their personal libraries of books received on birthdays, Christmas, and other special days and on trips to the supermarket, drugstore, and variety store. Diplomatic suggestions may be made to relatives so that they, too, may acquire the habit of giving books as presents. The child's personal collection of books will add much to his interest in reading and will play a dominant role in creating a reading environment in the home. Another very valuable service which may be rendered parents is helping them develop book lists appropriate for various stages of development and interests. By all means introduce parents to Nancy Larrick's *A Parent's Guide to Children's Reading* (New York, Bantam Books, 1975).

FURTHER SUGGESTIONS FOR PARENTS

We have been considering many activities that lay the foundation for proficiency in reading. These are activities for parents to implement — with the guidance and encouragement of teachers. To these, we add the following, which also provide cognitive stimulation to children in their preschool years, their "wonder" years.

1. Help the youngster acquire good work habits. Give him reasonable tasks to perform and encourage him to complete whatever is started without too many interludes. In conjunction with the establishment of effective work habits, teach the child that there is a place for everything and that he is to put things in their proper places after finishing with them.

2. Develop the child's ability to observe closely and to notice details; help him refine his ability to see likenesses and differences in pictures, objects, people, animals, and growing things. Also lead him to make comparisons in size (such as big, middle-sized, little, tall, and short) and in shape (such as round, square, and triangular).

3. Begin at an early age stressing to the youngster the importance of listening carefully. Praise him for growth in facility to note likenesses and differences in environmental sounds and gradually call attention to likenesses and differences in words:

"Do these begin with the same sound: *man, milk, money?*"
"Do these rhyme: *two-shoe, four-door?*"

Listening is a most vital skill since so much of the child's learning is facilitated through this avenue.

4. Provide practice for the little ones in following directions. Initiate the activity by giving very simple directions, gradually increasing in difficulty as beginning instructions are mastered. For example:

"Go to the kitchen and bring me a spoon."

"Look in the closet and get my bedroom slippers."

"Hop to the kitchen like a rabbit and walk back to me."

"Run to the front door, touch it three times, turn around two times, and run back to me."

Parent-Teacher Partnership

QUESTIONS TO GUIDE READING

Literal
What course of action might teachers take in establishing a working relationship with parents?
What are some ways of establishing better home-school relationships?
How can a teacher prepare for a parent conference?

Evaluative
How is the teacher's attitude toward home-school relations reflected in his effectiveness in establishing a parent-teacher partnership?
Why are parent-teacher conferences so important?

There are reports in the literature of strong parent-teacher relationships, but these are few in comparison to the ideal. There is an urgent need for this partnership if children are to experience success in reading initially and to continue to make gains in this important skill. Such a partnership can facilitate prevention of reading failure, rather than remediating it.

ESTABLISHMENT OF RELATIONSHIP

As a first step in establishing a working relationship with parents, the teacher must examine his own attitude toward parental involvement. The superintendent, supervisor, or principal can issue a decree that teachers develop close home-school ties, but this will become a reality only if the teacher's attitude is positive. Assuming that the teacher is receptive to the idea, the second step, of actually involving parents, can be taken. This may well require initiative on the part of the school because parents often have not felt welcome in the schools, especially the parents in the low socioeconomic stratum. There have been far too much alienation and estrangement between parents and teachers in the past; both have mutual concern for the child's academic progress, yet they have spent little time together mapping strategies and exchanging information.

An effective public relations program must be launched with a view toward gaining the confidence of parents and welcoming them as partners in education. There are many ways singly or in combination that this goal can be reached:

1. Prearranged home visits.
2. Parent-teacher conferences at school.
3. Parent visits to classrooms during reading periods.
4. Organization of parent study groups or clubs.

The inventive teacher, of course, will think of many other ways to bring parents and teachers together to promote the student's proficiency in reading.

PROVIDING BACKGROUND INFORMATION TO PARENTS

The school must accept the assistance currently available from some parents and actively seek avenues through which less prepared parents may be helped to develop background information, competencies, and confidence in their abilities to help. Parents need general background information, as well as specific "how-to-do-it" instructions related to their supporting roles in their children's reading success. The following topics are recommended as starters in enlisting the informed assistance of parents:

1. What we know about how children learn.
2. The importance of the self-concept in learning.
3. Making selective use of mass media (developing TV logs).
4. Continuing the library habit (preparing book lists).
5. The use of learning games to reinforce reading skills.
6. Supervision of home study and reading (providing a special place and special atmosphere).
7. Development of personal library.
8. Parents as pace setters in reading.

This information could be disseminated through such means as educational television, parent-teacher conferences, organized parent programs, or informal coffee hours. Armed with information and confidence, parents can be productive partners in combatting the reading problems now facing the nation's children.

Keeping Parents Informed

It is extremely important to keep parents informed about the school's reading program and to familiarize them with procedures and materials currently used in the teaching of reading. An excellent way to achieve this goal is to invite parents to participate in classroom reading programs by trying an activity such as:

Assisting with book club activities.
Supervising small groups engaged in reading games.
Providing needed practice for children on an individual basis using materials prepared by the teacher.
Reading to children.
Listening to beginning readers who insist that someone witness their newly developed skill.
Constructing reading games under teacher supervision.
Assisting with library and reading skills centers.

The teacher, of course, will think of many other ways to involve parents in the classroom setting; the preceding list is just recommended as a starter.

Conferencing with Parents

The parent-teacher conference is a vital component in the parent-teacher partnership and must be carefully planned so that success can be ensured. The following guidelines from Wynn's *Making the Most of Parent-Teacher Conferences* (1972) are suggested.

1. Establish a friendly atmosphere free from interruptions.
2. Be positive; begin and end the conference by discussing favorable points.
3. Be a good listener.
4. Be truthful and objective but avoid labeling. Give a realistic picture of a child's performance in terms of his ability and suggest specific ways parents may help if assistance is needed.
5. Communicate with parents in terms they can understand.
6. Respect parents' and children's information as confidential.
7. Help parents find more than one solution to a problem if possible.
8. Base judgments on all available facts and actual situations.
9. Refer parents to resources such as school counselors and community agencies when needed.
10. Invite parents to visit and participate in school functions.

11. If possible have helpful information in print available for parents; it can be very brief.
12. If notes are made during the conference, share them with parents.

PARENT POWER IN ACTION

In preceding sections we have discussed the parents' involvement in getting their children ready for success in reading. The child's entry into formal reading instruction in the school setting in no way diminishes the need for parental involvement; rather, the role of parents shifts to one of supporting the teacher in keeping alive the child's interest in reading and assisting as needed in reinforcing reading skills and providing practice in reading. Home activities should be directed and supervised by the teacher. The parents must understand that they are not being asked to usurp the teacher's role; they are only to provide a much needed support system by extending reading activities into the home. When parents see themselves as partners with teachers and possess some background information, it is only logical that this ready source of parent power be utilized.

An example of parent power follows. It is included here to show the strength of informed parental influence:

William must go directly to a class for the severely mentally retarded; that was the verdict for six-year-old William, as pronounced in a psychological evaluation predicting cognitive failure in a school situation. The principal, however, had other ideas; William was to have a chance in a regular classroom for at least the first six weeks of school. Through the usual procedure of placing students, William was assigned to my classroom. That indeed was a challenge. But with the support and assistance of his parents, William was able to develop oral language facility as well as skill and interest in reading during his first school year.

My first visit of the school year was to William's home to solicit the support and cooperation of his parents. Reading readiness (with emphasis on background experiences, oral language, and the urgency of helping William feel good about himself--) was discussed in great detail. Specific reading readiness activities were developed for implementation by the parents. Instructions to the parents were of this sort:

1. Talk with William often and listen carefully when he speaks to you.
2. When you go to the grocery store, drug store, post office, or other appropriate places, take William with you and tell him something about these places; encourage and answer questions.
3. Take William to the library for story hour and film showing. Let him check out books and read to him every evening. Discuss illustrations and encourage William to retell stories. Make reading a very special time.

4. Look at selected television programs and follow them up with discussions.
5. Take him to the zoo, airport, and other places of interest.
6. Give simple directions to William and help him learn to respond appropriately.

Fortunately William's parents were cooperative and interested in encouraging him and in providing background information. They were very much involved in providing a variety of experiences and helping with materials sent home to reinforce reading skills being taught in the classroom. William is now a senior in college and still an avid reader. His reading success must be attributed largely to the support and assistance given by his parents.

This is just one example of parent power. There are many more in schools throughout the nation.

Reading Games and Activities for Developing Skills and Interests (for Home Use)

QUESTIONS TO GUIDE READING

Literal
What are some activities through which parents may extend the reading program into the home?

Inferential
How may specific reading skills be reinforced through parent-teacher cooperation?

Evaluative
What evaluative procedures can a teacher use to assess the effectiveness of reading games and activities provided for home use?

FOR PRIMARY GRADE CHILDREN

In addition to reading to the child, reading along with him, and listening to him read on a regular prearranged schedule in a special place, there are many activities and reading games in which parents may participate with their primary grade children at the direction and under the supervision of the teacher.

Most teachers have a collection of commercial and teacher-made games for teaching vocabulary and word recognition skills. The teacher can invite parents to come to school and check out games to take home in order to reinforce specific skills after they have been introduced in class. Each game should include clear, thorough directions. A few possibilities follow.

Activities and Reading Games for Home Use

1. Arrange reading parties, complete with "goodies," and invite friends to come and bring their favorite books to read and share.
2. Make a big production of letting the child see tangible evidence of books he has read; help him display on a wall chart, mobile, or poster the books or stories he has read. This is a great incentive builder.
3. As a joint project with the youngster, make a special bulletin board for daily messages and information instead of telling him everything orally.
4. Emphasize (by demonstrating) the need for reading for practical purposes: to assemble a toy, to care for a pet, to prepare simple foods (popcorn, popcorn balls, cookies, candy, instant pudding), to read pattern directions to make simple garments, to read about a city or country to be visited, etc.
5. Use a small clothes line, snap clothes pins, and 5 × 8 file cards or colorful construction paper to make a "conversation line." Write a question to the youngster and pin it up on the line; let him answer in writing and replace the card on the line. Engage in this activity with regularity, ingenuity, and enthusiasm. You could write nursery rhymes with large blanks for missing words. Or try

riddles on the cards, with ample space for the child to write his answer.
6. Instead of directly giving the youngster a surprise you have purchased, use the format of a scavenger hunt to let him "read his way" to the gift; leave notes in various places in the house to lead him to the gift.
7. After looking at a children's classic on television with the child, encourage him to check the book out of the library so that the family can enjoy reading the book together.
8. Encourage the youngster to compose stories based on his experiences, interests, or imagination. Write down these stories in booklet form and help him to read them. Share the stories with family and friends, emphasizing the author. Generally the child will read his stories to others without too much prompting — again getting valuable practice.
9. Solicit the support of relatives; have them write letters to the child and encourage him to answer. There is something magical about receiving mail; besides, it seems so grown-up to get a letter. Children generally respond quite well. This activity affords an additional opportunity to practice reading skills.

Vocabulary games. These are examples of teacher-made games:

Word Dominoes
Word Bingo
Sorting and Classifying Words (using pockets of a shoe holder)
Antonym, Synonym, and Homonym Games
Yours or Mine (Words are placed face down in a stack in front of the child. He pronounces words as he selects them from the stack. Known words become his words and are placed in the "mine" stack. Unknown words become the parent's words and are placed in the "yours" stack as they are identified by parent. When all words in the

stack are used, the youngster then has another opportunity to identify words held by parent.)

Uncle Wiggly Variation Board Game (with objective of moving from a beginning point to a goal by identifying words)

Developing Word Bank (of known words for use in game situations)

Picture Match (matching pictures with words — a favorite with younger children)

Fishing Pond with Magnet (an old familiar game)

These are examples of commercial games:

Group Word Teaching Game with Popper Words, I & II (Garrard)

Dolch Basic Sight Words, Picture Words, and Phrase Cards (Garrard)

Rolling Readers (Scott, Foresman)[1]

Word recognition skills games. These are some teacher-made games:

Picture and Sound Match

Sound Bingo

I Am Thinking (select word card, supply a clue to the word, and have the child produce the initial sound of word)

Consonant Dominoes (depicting consonants, consonant digraphs, and consonant blends)

Spell-eeze (child practices using common word parts — consonants, consonant digraphs and blends — to form words according to instructions such as, "Show me how you would form the word *start*.")

Growing Words (adding variant endings to root words)

Break-Apart Words (compound words)

Wacky Animals (Three sets of cards depict animal heads, bodies, and tail — along with prefixes, root words, suffixes.)

These are examples of commercial games:

Affixo, Vowel Dominoes, and Go Fish (Remedial Education Press)

Doghouse Game and Phonic Rummy (Kenworthy)

Group Sounding Game and Phonic Lotto (Garrard)

Scrabble (Selchow and Righter)

Syllable Game and Take (Garrard)

The preceding are some of the games that parents might borrow from the teacher's materials center to reinforce specific reading skills. Not only must parents understand the purpose of the game, but the children must understand as well. Additionally, the overall purpose of all games must be clearly understood — that of helping children gain independence in

1. These can also be used in a variety of games.

reading. The child should be reminded, too, of the relationship of reading games to successful reading in home practice. An occasional "This is what we learned from our game," as the child unlocks a previously unknown word, would be a helpful reminder. Parents must take care that games are meaningful and of short duration. They should be terminated while interest and enthusiasm are still high. Also, make sure that the mechanics of the game do not overshadow the skill being reinforced.

Learning games and other reading activities extended into the home can aid the child tremendously but must not take precedence over the reading sessions. The library card as the passport to greatness must be kept in the foreground and used with regularity. Also the personal library collection deserves special attention. Most children take pride in having their very own books and often demonstrate greater skill in reading books from their own libraries.

FOR MIDDLE GRADE CHILDREN

The notion is often advanced that students develop basic reading skills in the primary grades and have diminished needs for concentrated reading instruction and parental assistance as they move into the intermediate grades. Teachers should dispel this misconception emphatically. They should emphasize to parents that, in fact, the need for their support and active involvement in the child's reading program increases as he pursues more extensive independent and peer-related interests. At this grade level it becomes increasingly difficult for parents to get children to cooperate willingly, although it is an attainable goal. The critical precondition for success, of course, is a close working relationship between parents and teachers.

Students in the middle grades might not be excited about fishing for prefixes, roots, and suffixes to form words, but there are many meaningful exercises and games that they would find interesting and appealing. The following are illustrative of reading activities that teachers can prepare and make available to parents for developing and reinforcing reading skills with their older children; instructions and self-checking devices (if needed) would accompany the activities. It must be remembered that it is not enough merely to ask parents to help. They need specific instructions, which is the rationale for suggesting that teachers prepare activities complete with instructions.

Selecting specific words. The objectives of this exercise are to provide reading practice and vocabulary development. The teacher writes several sentences with choices of words for completion. The child reads the sentences and chooses the appropriate words. Sentences such as these could be formed:

A beautiful sunset is _____.
      resident magnificent miserable

The _____ of the house was not at home.
    occupant innocent establish

Vocabulary review. Selecting from a list of basal words sent home, parents may place words in piles on seasonal motifs (Christmas presents, autumn leaves, Easter eggs, turkeys, witches, etc.) located on a table. The student pronounces words as he picks them up. He keeps all known words while the parent gets the unknown words. The parent puts the unknown words in context on small sentence strips; then the child and parent take turns reading the sentence strips. Following this activity, the problem words are again placed in a pile — with the expectation that this time the youngster will recognize all the words and, thus, they will belong to him.

Nightly read-in. With the advice and assistance of the librarian, the child selects books of special appeal and interest. Each night the parent and child take turns reading for about thirty minutes or until interest begins to wane. The parent supplies missed words without any effort to teach word recognition skills. She notes any missed words, then places them on word cards and sentence cards for review. When parents display interest and enthusiasm, this could be a most fruitful experience.

Working with word parts. Parents should not be expected to teach word recognition skills, although there is much they can do via key words or pictures for consonants, consonant blends, consonant digraphs, and common syllables. The teacher can develop key charts with separate cards. Parents could use them in a variety of ways to ensure familiarity — flashing, matching, sorting, and classifying. Examples follow:

Consonant Chart			
b boy	*c* cat	*d* dog	*f* fish

Consonant Digraph Chart			
ch chair	*wh* who	*th* thumb	*sh* shoe

Consonant Blend Chart			
bl blue	*cl* clown	*fl* flag	*gl* globe

| b | c | d | f |

| ch | wh | th | sh |

| bl | cl | fl | gl |

Common Syllable Chart			
ar	*ir*	*ill*	*ay*
car	bird	hill	play

ar	ir	ill	ay

When the parent feels his child is sufficiently familiar with the key charts, he can move on to word formation. The task he sets for the child utilizes the new knowledge of consonants, consonant digraphs, consonant blends, and common syllables in this manner:

Phonogram card with slots:

Consonant, consonant digraph, and blend cards:

c	m	ch	th	bl

We know this common word part *ar* as in *car*. Let's form the word *charm* by selecting the right cards to fit into the slots. Yes, we need these cards:

ch	and	m

Let's fit them into the slots:

Next, parent uses the common "ar" to form many words, and the child is constantly reminded that utilizing his knowledge of word parts is an effective way to attack unknown words. These are some possibilities for "ar": ch*ar*t, sh*ar*k, m*ar*ch, *ar*m, sm*ar*t, st*ar*t, sp*ar*k, y*ar*d, and sc*ar*f. As the exercise continues, the parent keeps a record of words learned in this manner. Sentences incorporating these words can be used in a variety of situations, ensuring instant recognition and meaning.

Making a word center. Using a corrugated box covered with contact paper, the teacher can develop an interesting word center for home use. The instructional areas suggested for the four sides of the box are: Compound words, Synonyms, Antonyms, and Multiple meanings.

Place the appropriate caption on each side, also pasting on a large heavy-duty envelope for each, to hold materials for activities, including answer sheets. Suggestions for an activity for compound words are given below.

Compound words

Materials needed: Root words on cards, sentences with compound words missing (enclosing in acetate folder), and answer sheets.

Instructions: Form compound words using root words. Read incomplete sentences and write in appropriate compound words. Check your work jointly with parent using answer sheet.

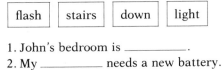

| flash | stairs | down | light |

1. John's bedroom is _____.
2. My _____ needs a new battery.

Activities for synonyms, antonyms, and multiple meanings can be developed in a similar manner. Use these words as starters:

Synonyms:	huge — enormous	annoyed — bothered
	delighted — happy	invent — discover
	certainly — surely	difficult — hard
	awful — terrible	frightened — scared
Antonyms:	ugly — beautiful	trash — treasure
	gentle — rough	shorten — prolong
	destroy — preserve	impoverish — enrich
	agree — protest	dangerous — safe
Multiple meanings:	bank, spring, light, stamp, model, bridge, mask, switch, brand, crook, draw, strip	

The youngster may file, in his word bank, words mastered in this center.

Getting it all together. The objective of this game is to use and understand the meaning of prefixes and suffixes in order to develop proficiency in reading in the content areas.

Instructions: Beginning with the first chapter of a specific content book, identify problem words and list them in any one of ten groups. Look them up in a dictionary. Make three cards for each problem word, using 3 × 5 cards: a puzzle card, marking the word into prefix, root, and suffix (for example dis–content–ment); a definition card; and a sentence card (containing the sentence in which the word was first discovered in the content area reading).

Shuffle all the cards and give each player (parents and child) three cards. Place five cards face up on the table. The first player checks to see if he can make a book consisting of a puzzle card, definition card, and sentence card. When a player can match all three cards he can make a book.

Players continue in this manner until the "books" have been completed. Parent and child then take turns reading their game words and the portion of the chapter from which the words were taken. They work their way through the chapters, learning the vocabulary of the text by adding new words and reviewing those learned previously.

Materials: puzzle cards, definition cards, sentence cards, and textbook.

Synonym search. The objective of this game is to increase vocabulary through an understanding of synonyms and synonymous terms.

Instructions: All players make a careful check of the newspapers for accounts of sports events: baseball, swimming, basketball, rowing, hockey, golf, tennis, track, and others. Find synonyms and synonymous terms for *victory* and *defeat* as well as for *won* and *lost*. Compile and compare the lists. Consult the dictionary for clarification. The player with the longest list is the winner. Use these lists as a beginning for studying synonyms and synonymous terms on TV commercials, in printed materials, and in conversation. Players can jointly develop a book of synonyms.

Materials: newspaper, dictionary, paper and cards, pens, and a small notebook for the synonym book.

The preceding activities are some in which parents may engage with their intermediate grade children to improve reading capability and foster interest in reading. In addition to these suggestions, the traditional activities are also recommended: the matching games, sentence cards, use of the encyclopedia, reading to children, and listening to them talk.

Reading takes on a new dimension for children when parents and teachers truly become partners in this crucial learning area. Although it sometimes requires extra work and infinite patience on the part of both parents and teachers to extend reading activities into the home, the benefits that accrue far surpass the effort exerted.

A Parent Involvement Program That Worked

QUESTIONS TO GUIDE READING

Evaluative

Would the parent involvement program described in this section work in a situation with which you are familiar? Why or why not?

That parents can help their children achieve success in reading was demonstrated by a volunteer program this author conducted over an eight-year period. Although the program was designed for parents in the low socioeconomic stratum, it has implications for parents of all economic strata. The program was conducted in a severely depressed area of Knoxville, Tennessee, for parents of first graders. These families were not library users even though there was a library within easy walking distance. As could be expected, reading materials in these homes were extremely limited, and there were few toys available.

The program was initiated because of the appalling number of reading failures noted throughout the elementary school. The groundwork for the program was laid by home visits during the first three weeks of school, followed by the organization of a First Grade Parents' Study Group. A program of parent education and involvement was designed; the program was explained in detail to parents, who were told that the school needed their help in order to improve the reading achievement of their children. As each component of the program was explained, the parents were helped to understand how it related to reading readiness or reading skills.

The parents' group had evening meetings in the format of a social hour. Information was presented in an informal manner. Each year a mother was chairman and catalyst for the group; she sent out notices regarding the meetings and kept other parents interested and involved. During the course of the school year the following topics were discussed:

1. How parents can help their children make better progress in school.
2. Child growth and development (with emphasis on individual differences).
3. The importance of the self-concept.
4. Book lists, television logs, and lists of inexpensive learning materials.
5. Organization and use of the public library.
6. Supervised home study.

At one meeting each year the librarian from the public library brought a collection of books, including offerings for the entire family; she encouraged the parents to use all services of the library. The librarian also cooperated very closely with parents in their summer reading program for the children.

Although money was a source of difficulty, parents seemed able to rearrange their priorities to help provide experiences for the children. (This was before the poor were "discovered" — before the War on Poverty). The parents pooled their meager resources to provide buses to take children to places of interest — such as the zoo, a dairy farm, a bakery, a fire station, a bottling company, and TVA dams. Many of the mothers accompanied the children on trips and seemed to derive as much pleasure and stimulation from these experiences as did the children. These shared experiences provided many opportunities for conversation between parents and children.

Through the years, the name of the organization changed but the objective remained constant. As time progressed, a positive change in child rearing practices became evident:

1. Parents spent more time reading to their children.
2. Parents and children used the library on a regular basis.
3. Inexpensive picture dictionaries, paperbacks, records, and learning games were bought with a portion of the family's limited income.
4. The children showed marked improvement in both reading skills and interest in reading.

This change did more than alter the home environment and affect the lives of the children enrolled in the first grade class; the benefits clearly reached the preschoolers and other school-age children in these families as well. There were fewer reading problems as the preschoolers reached first grade, and the other school-age children generally showed improvement in reading achievement and interest as well.

Summary

Throughout the nation, children are failing in reading (disproportionately large numbers from low-income family groups) despite the many programs designed to combat this problem. One deficiency in our educational systems is the tendency of schools to overlook, or reject, the significant roles parents could play in helping children learn to read. This deficiency may be overcome through a partnership with parents, one that stresses strong background information and a confidence-building component. Well-informed parents are able to create a learning environment in the home and provide cognitive stimulation for their children in the early years. This advantage enables a child to develop a strong experiential and oral language base along with general readiness for success in reading.

This coalition between parents and teachers could continue to function over all the years the children are in public school. Parents could extend reading activities into the home to maintain interest in reading and provide a support system to reinforce skills as needed. Working with parents and involving them in their children's reading programs can be very demanding for a teacher; that it is well worth the effort, however, is substantiated by descriptions of successful programs that involved parents in the education of their children.

Questions for Further Reading and Thinking

1. How do schools in England involve parents in their children's reading programs and extend related activities into the home?
2. What would you consider the ideal age for beginning reading readiness activities with children? Support your answer.
3. Since American education is committed to teaching all children to read, how may the importance of involving parents in the reading program be communicated and implemented on a national basis?
4. Other than the mention made in this chapter, how else may television be used to stimulate parents to develop a higher degree of awareness of their roles as the first and most long-term teachers of their children?
5. Do you think that very young children should be taught to read by their parents? What is your reaction to Glenn Doman's *How to Teach Your Baby to Read* (Random House)? Do you approve or disapprove? Explain fully.
6. How may community agencies be used to involve parents in the reading program?

Activities and Projects

1. Design a lobbying project to get your senators and representatives sensitized to the need for legislation to incorporate parent involvement and education into the educational system through an organized staff, just as other special services are provided.
2. You are a teacher at Happyvale Elementary School and your principal asks you to make suggestions for initiating a program to bring parents and teachers together in the interest of raising the reading achievement level of the children. List a minimum of six suggestions.
3. Develop content for three vignettes dealing with the topic, "How Parents May Contribute to the Reading Success of Their Children." Exclude content discussed in this chapter.
4. Prepare a short presentation for parents, explaining to them the rationale for becoming active partners of their children's teachers.
5. Prepare six home-based activities for developing oral language facility. Exclude activities described in this chapter.
6. Construct six games for extending reading activities into the home in these specific skill areas:
   a. Sight vocabulary
   b. Use of initial substitution
   c. Synonyms and antonyms
   d. Use of compound words
   e. Use of common syllables
   f. Use of the final *e*

Resources for Teachers and Parents

Arbuthnot, May Hill. 1969. *Children's reading in the home*. Glenview, Ill.: Scott, Foresman.

Baghban, Marcia. 1972. "How can I help my child learn to read English?" Micromonograph. Newark, Del.: International Reading Association.

Blumenfeld, Samuel L. 1973. *The new illiterates and how to keep your child from becoming one.* New Rochelle, N.Y.: Arlington House.

Buskin, Martin. 1975. *Parent power: How to deal with your child's school.* New York: Walker.

Chan, Julie M. T. 1974. "Why read aloud to children?" Micromonograph. Newark, Del.: International Reading Association.

Chess, Stella. 1974. *How to help your child get the most out of school.* Garden City, N.Y.: Doubleday.

Criscuolo, Nicholas. 1982. *You can help your child in reading by using the newspaper.* Parent brochure. Newark, Del.: International Reading Association.

———. 1981. *You can use television to stimulate your child's reading habits.* Parent brochure. Newark, Del.: International Reading Association.

Ervin, Jane. 1979. *Your child can read and you can help: A book for parents.* Garden City, N.Y.: Doubleday.

Glazer, Susan Mandell. 1980. "How can I help my child build positive attitudes toward reading?" Micromonograph. Newark, Del.: International Reading Association.

Granowsky, A. et al. 1977. *For parents and children: A guide for better reading.* Asheville, N.C.: Tarmac.

Larrick, Nancy. 1975. *A parent's guide to children's reading.* New York, N.Y.: Bantam Books.

Pickering, C. Thomas. 1977. *Helping children learn to read: A primer for adults.* New York, N.Y.: Chesford.

Ransbury, Molly Kayes. 1972. "How can I encourage my primary-grade child to read?" Micromonograph. Newark, Del.: International Reading Association.

Rogers, Norma. 1972. "How can I help my child get ready to read?" Micromonograph. Newark, Del.: International Reading Association.

———. 1972. "What books and records should I get for my pre-schooler?" Micromonograph. Newark, Del.: International Reading Association.

Sartain, Harry W. 1981. *Mobilizing family forces for worldwide reading success.* Newark, Del.: International Reading Association.

Wynn, Sammye J. 1972. The ancillary role of parents in the correction and prevention of reading difficulties. In *Remedial reading: Classroom and clinic,* eds. Leo Schell and Paul C. Burns, pp. 556–566. Boston: Allyn and Bacon.

Arnold R. Davis

20

A Historical Perspective

Languages are man-invented. Some are spoken by a relatively small number of people, others by millions. No one knows for sure just how language began. One theory suggests that humans heard the sounds of nature or of animals and from the effort to imitate those sounds, words were gradually developed. New words were added as labels were needed for new things and ideas.

Actually, the basic sounds of any given language are not numerous. The same few sounds are put together in various combinations to produce all the words of a given language. There are more than 3000 different languages spoken throughout the world, and the majority of these are spoken with fewer than 50 phonemes, or sounds. These phonemes may be put together to produce as many as 100,000 different words in any single language.

Man's first attempt to record his language was through the use of drawings. People who could recognize the drawings and their relationships to each other were actually reading. At first, the pictures represented single objects and were adequate for communicating simple, concrete ideas. But picture writing had many limitations; for example, it was inexact and it could not express abstract ideas.

During the course of history, more accurate ways of recording things and ideas developed. One of the systems that evolved was alphabetic writing. This system was based on the concept that spoken language consists of sounds that are put together in fixed combinations to produce words. The letters are recorded in the same sequence as the sounds of the spoken words to produce recorded speech. Learning to read alphabetic writing involves (among other considerations such as syntactic and semantic cues) making the correct associations between the letter symbols and sounds they represent.

More than 2000 years ago the Greeks and Romans achieved alphabetic writing. The Greeks borrowed letter forms from the Phoenicians and developed a complete set of symbols or letters in which they could represent every sound in their language. The Romans borrowed from the

Greek alphabet in order to develop their system of alphabetic writing. Greek and Roman children learned to read by first mastering the names and forms of letters and then by learning the syllables that combined consonants and vowels in two- and three-letter combinations. The teaching of reading to early Greek and Roman children apparently did not require any particular skill and knowledge. According to Mathews (1966, p. 9),

> those who taught children to read were regarded with great disdain and contempt. Whenever possible, slaves were assigned to this monotonous, unimaginative task. In old Athens there was a saying of one who was missing that he was either dead or had become a school-master and was accordingly ashamed to appear in polite society. It was thought that kings and others of high rank who had lived evil lives would, in the next world, be forced to maintain themselves by teaching reading and writing.

The Romans took with them their Latin language and literature when they invaded England in the first century. It is thought that probably in the seventh century English was written for the first time by Christian missionaries who knew both English and Latin. As soon as English was written, there was reading instruction. The responsibility for the teaching of reading to early English children fell by edict of the Pope to the secular priests and monastic institutions. The children were taught the alphabet, the syllables, and if they progressed, the Primer, or prayerbook (W. J. Davis 1973).

Since sounds have changed more rapidly than the symbols used to represent them there is not a consistent one-to-one relationship between sound and symbol in *Modern American English*. Twenty-six different letters represent approximately 45 phonemes of the spoken language, and these 45 phonemes can be spelled about 350 ways (Pollack and Pickarz 1963, pp. 4–9). This makes learning to read a difficult process.

When a child comes to school he has been immersed in a world of spoken language. Now he must learn to associate the written language that represents particular sounds. He must learn, for example, that the sound of long *a* /ey/ can be spelled many different ways: *a, aye, eh,* m*ai*d, th*ey,* n*eig*h, pl*ay.* In addition, he learns that the letter *a* also represents other sounds, as in h*a*t, *a*long, and *a*re. Further confusion may arise when a reader must switch from upper to lower case letters and from manuscript to cursive writing.

The purposes of this chapter are to describe some of the ways that have been used to teach reading in America and to focus on some of the changes that have occurred in reading instruction since 1607. You will note that some changes are cyclic. An understanding of these changes will help us view "new" methods and approaches in proper historical perpective.

QUESTIONS TO GUIDE READING

Literal
Why was education first considered important for the common man?
What procedure was followed in the alphabet method?
What were some of the most common textbooks used in early America?

Inferential
When and for what reason did the stress on phonics begin?
What controversies persisted over the entire period?

Evaluative
How do you think the purpose of teaching reading changed in America between the time of the Puritans and the Civil War?
Based on your reading throughout this book, what would you identify as some shortcomings of the reading instruction materials prior to the Civil War?
What controversies about teaching reading in the late 1800s still exist today?
Why do these controversies persist?
Why do some of today's parents want to go back to the *McGuffey Reading Series*?

Early instruction in America was based directly on influences from England. As the Church of England gradually shed the doctrines of Catholicism, one of the important new doctrines to emerge was that each individual is directly responsible to God for his own salvation. About this time (1524) Martin Luther initiated education for the common man so that he could read the Bible for himself in order to achieve that salvation. Thus, the Bible was established as the chief material used for reading instruction, as well as the chief objective. In early protestant America, reading was stressed for the same religious reasons that had motivated Martin Luther. To be responsible to God, one must be able to read and interpret God's word; for, if a person couldn't read, he could not be his own "priest."

The alphabet method was the first method used to teach children how to read in America. The typical procedure was for the child to first memorize the names of the letters and to learn to identify both the capital and lower case forms. Next, the child learned to spell and pronounce combinations of two letters, then three-letter combinations, and finally monosyllabic words. Multisyllabic words, phrases, sentences, and stories were gradually introduced. The child was required to memorize prayers, the

Ten Commandments, and other Biblical material. Oral reading was stressed because literate members of Puritan families read Scripture aloud to family and friends.

The first reading textbook printed in America was the *New England Primer*, published about 1685 (Smith 1965, pp. 18–19). This was a very small book, 2½ by 4½ inches. The print and illustrations were very small, and the book contained about 100 pages. Throughout the many editions of the *Primer*, the selections varied slightly but the content remained basically the same. First, it introduced the alphabet, then the vowels, consonants, double letters, and capitals. After these, it taught word lists with two-letter syllables. It increased the length of the words to six-syllable words. Famous rhyming couplets illustrating letters of the alphabet were included, as was the Lord's Prayer. Much of the material came directly from the Bible, but some of it was paraphrased by the *Primer*'s author, Benjamin Harris. The *New England Primer* was by far the most popular textbook of that period. (See Figure 20.1.)

The Hornbook was used as a supplement to the *New England Primer* during the years in colonial America before 1776. The Hornbook was not actually a book. Rather, it was a short-handled paddle made of wood or cardboard, about 2½ by 5 inches. A leaf of vellum or paper was pasted on the paddle. On it was inscribed the alphabet in both small and capital letters, the vowels and vowel-consonant combinations, and the exhortation: "In the name of the Father and of the Sonne and of the Holy Ghost." Also on the Hornbook were the Lord's Prayer and the Roman numerals. A transparent sheet of horn covered the papered side. A string through the handle enabled the child to carry it around his neck or attach it to his clothing (Smith 1965, pp. 15–17). (See Figure 20.2.)

After the child in colonial America had learned the alphabet, could spell syllables and simple words, had memorized many selections, and could read orally from the *Primer* and Hornbook, he graduated to the Bible, which was the only book found in most homes.

In 1782, a New England school teacher, Noah Webster, published a reading textbook, *Grammatical Institute*. The book had sections on beginning reading, grammar, and advanced reading instruction. He developed a scheme of phonics, not as a means for teaching reading, but to establish a standardized American speech and destroy the differences in dialect that existed just after the Revolutionary War (Emans 1968, p. 603). In 1790, Webster's work was offered as three separate texts. One of these, the *American Spelling Book*, referred to as the "Blue-back Speller" because of its blue cover, became one of the most influential books America has known. This book, which would eventually sell about 24 million copies, was about 4 by 6½ inches in size. It had about 158 pages encased in wooden covers. The print was small and the lines were crowded close together. The book contained many lists of words and syllables, with few repetitions. In fact there often were as many as 100 new words on a page. There were many pages of rules for correct reading, speaking, and pro-

Figure 20.1. Two pages from the *New England Primer*, edition of 1727.

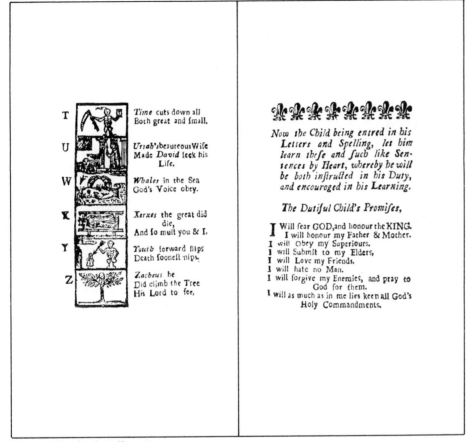

Courtesy Teacher's College Press.

nunciation. Selections were patriotic, historical, and informative in nature. The Blue-back Speller was widely used for both reading and spelling instruction. It required the child to laboriously spell out each word he would need to use in reading sentences and stories in the book (Witty 1949, Chap. 1).

Lyman Cobb was one of the first educators to compile a graded set (one book per grade level) of reading textbooks. Other educators who prepared sets of readers in the early 1800s included Caleb Bingham, George Hillard, Lindley Murray, John Pierpont, and Samuel Worcester.

There was nothing unusual about the content of Worcester's books, first published in 1828, but his approach was unique. He appears to have been the first American author to suggest the adoption of the word method for teaching reading. Although it is not known just when the word method began, educators in Europe had been using this method long before this

Figure 20.2. Replica of a Hornbook.

Used with permission of The Horn Book, Inc.

time. Reading was taught in Europe by presenting an object or a picture together with a word that represented it. Basically, the word method involves concentrating on the word as the instructional unit. The student is taught to recognize words without sounding them out. The new word is repeated over and over until the child learns it. During the 1840s, American educators, including Horace Mann, visited schools in Prussia and Switzerland and observed the word method being used to teach reading. Upon their return to America, these educators advocated, through speeches and articles, the adoption of this method.

It is not, perhaps, very important that a child should know the letters before he begins to read. The child may learn first to read words by seeing them, hearing them pronounced, and having their meanings illustrated, and afterwards he may learn to analyze them or name the letters of which they are composed. (Smith 1965, p. 86)

It was not until 1850 that the whole word method was popularized through the widespread use of Josiah Bumstead's *My Little Primer*, and later John Webb's primer, *The New Word Method*.

A study by Cattell in 1885 supported the teaching of whole words. He showed that in a given unit of time only a few unrelated letter sounds could be recognized, but in the same amount of time it was possible to recognize entire words. According to Smith, "This was the only period in American history in which the word method was advocated by editors and authors as a general method of teaching reading" (1965, p. 86).

Despite the general acceptance of the word method by educators, protests were numerous. Parents became disturbed when they discovered that their children did not know the names of the letters in words they could pronounce. More protests arose when it was found that children taught to read with the word method were unprepared to attack new words in unfamiliar settings (Witty 1949, Chap. 1). To remedy this problem, some critics suggested phonics as a method for teaching children to attack new words. But this method of reading instruction also had its critics.

Some of the complaints leveled against the use of phonics were these:

1. Some letters have more than one sound (for example, ⟨c⟩ with its two sounds as in *cat* and *city*); and some sounds are represented by more than one letter (for example, the sound /s/, which is represented by the letter ⟨s⟩ as in *so* but also by the letter ⟨c⟩ as in *cell*.
2. Phonics instruction tends to produce word-by-word readers.
3. Using phonics requires so much effort in unlocking a word letter by letter that the reader may achieve less understanding of the meanings of words than other readers using other reading methods.
4. Phonics places emphasis on the mechanics of reading rather than on understanding the ideas that are being communicated.
5. Phonics is likely to make learning an uninteresting experience (Tinker and McCullough 1962, pp. 14–15).

The most popular of the graded series of readers was the *McGuffey Readers*, prepared by William Holmes McGuffey in 1840. It is estimated that more than 122 million copies were sold between 1840 and 1920, when the last printing occurred. The *McGuffey Readers Series* was a clearly defined and graded set of books with one reader for each grade level. The cardboard books were about 5 by 7½ inches in size. The material in these readers emphasized commendable traits of human character: truth, honesty, fair dealing, initiative, and self-reliance. These readers played a significant role in determining the attitudes and moral values of young people and were instrumental in shaping literary taste. Mark Sullivan (1927, p. 15) stated: "to millions, probably nine out of ten average Americans, what taste of literature they got from McGuffey's was all they ever had; what literature the children brought into the home in McGuffey's Readers was all that ever came."

The selections in *McGuffey's Readers* were from the areas of science, history, art, philosophy, economics, and, of course, the Bible. The lessons were probably easier in this series than in the *New England Primer* or the Blue-back Speller. McGuffey was the first author to limit the number of new words on each page. He also recognized the need for the repetition of new words. Although some of the earlier readers might have had as many as 100 new words per page, the new words in McGuffey's books were limited to 10 to 12 per page, and the review lessons had no new words at all (Figure 20.3).

We have seen that the desire to maintain religious practices was the driving force behind the emphasis on literacy. This country's first edu-

Figure 20.3. Page from *McGuffey's First Reader*.

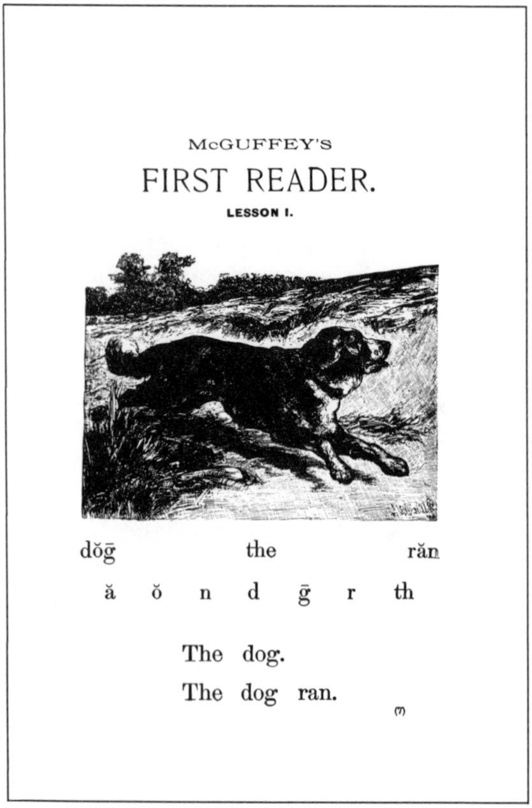
McGUFFEY'S

FIRST READER.

LESSON I.

dŏḡ the răn

ă ŏ n d ḡ r th

The dog.

The dog ran.

(7)

Courtesy of the Trustees of the Boston Public Library.

cation law was the Massachusetts Education Act of 1647, sometimes called the "Old Deluder Satan Act," which ordered the establishment of schools for reading instruction. In the 1600s, teachers "listened to children's lessons." Children were expected to learn on their own and the teacher's primary function was to see that they did. When the children couldn't recite their lessons, they were sent back to their seats for more self-help. Many of the children who experienced difficulty with reading simply dropped out of school. In 1852 the first compulsory education law was passed; this was in Massachusetts. Compulsory attendance meant that children were required to remain in school whether they were successful students or not. Now teachers had to do more than listen to lessons; they had to teach those students who could not teach themselves. Various methods of teaching evolved and controversies arose concerning the best way to teach reading to all children.

The Twentieth Century

QUESTIONS TO GUIDE READING

Literal
When did research into remedial reading begin?
What were some of the approaches advocated for reading instruction in the 1960s?
What are important research areas in reading instruction today?

Inferential
Why do some persons describe the development of reading instruction in the twentieth century as "cyclical"?
What was the motivation for the "Right to Read" program?

Evaluative
Are new teaching materials and methods necessarily better? Why or why not?
What impact may current developments have on reading instruction for you as a teacher?
What would you consider to be the five most important twentieth-century developments in reading?
Of what importance have standardized tests been in twentieth-century reading instruction?

There has been a strong interest in reading instruction in the twentieth century. This interest has reflected the tenor of the times and has continued to show the influences of educational, religious, economic, and political institutions. Of special importance has been the standardized testing movement, research with better controls, and attempts at individualizing instruction.

At the beginning of the twentieth century, the word method was expanded to include sentence and story methods (Schreiner and Tanner 1976, p. 470). Thought getting, which emphasized meaning and thinking, was stressed rather than word mastery. In the sentence method, the teacher read an entire sentence to a child while he looked on. Then the teacher focused on particular words in the sentence. Also popular at this time was the story method, which was similar in that a short story was read to the pupil and his attention was focused on selected words and sentences in the story (Minshall 1914, pp. 568–571).

The sentence and the story methods caused parents to complain that children were memorizing some words and developing dependence on the teacher to tell them the other words. As a result phonics came back with renewed emphasis (Betts 1956, p. 357). (Incidentally, the content of the basic textbooks during the early 1900s was primarily fables, folk tales, rhymes, and selections from classical literature.) By 1910, children were spending large amounts of time and drill on the mastery of phonics. They memorized lists of phonic families and studied phonic charts and cards.

THE START OF READING RESEARCH

In 1915, the *Gray Oral Reading Test* was published. Through the use of this test, teachers discovered that many children could not pronounce words; and of those who could pronounce the words, many did not know their meanings. This situation was blamed on the emphasis on phonics: children seemed too concerned with decoding or unlocking words, without regard to their meaning. Critics stated that teachers spent too much time developing the skills of phonetic elements at the expense of teaching children to get meaning from their reading. By the end of this decade, phonics was considered old-fashioned and outmoded, and was practically abandoned (Emans 1968, p. 604).

The 1920s have often been referred to as the "Golden Era of Reading" in America. During this time many research studies on reading were conducted in classrooms as well as in controlled laboratory situations. Not only did the number of studies increase, but the scope of problems investigated widened. The three areas to be most investigated were silent reading, individual differences, and remedial reading. The concept of reading readiness began to receive attention in the professional literature.

As a result of the strong reaction to the phonics method of teaching reading in the previous decade, the story method became the predominant instructional technique in the 1920s. The story method of reading instruction was an expansion of the sentence method. First, the entire reading selection was read to the children by the teacher. Later the children would read the story. The prereading by the teacher was done to allow children to get meaning from a complete unit or story, while following the sequence of development with anticipation of upcoming events. Consequently, this method emphasized meaning while teaching children to anticipate and follow the sequential ideas of the story. Although a chief drawback of this method was the great number of new words presented in the books for young readers, the concept of vocabulary control was introduced in an effort to keep word count low while attempting to maintain interesting content.

Also about this time, standardized instruments for measuring reading achievement began to be devised. The study of reading problems on a more scientific basis was now possible. Research studies during the 1920s related mostly to test development and resulted in tests that were widely administered later.

After World War I, silent reading was advocated as the primary objective of reading instruction. Some proponents even advocated the abandonment of instruction in oral reading. This change in practice was largely accounted for by two factors: (1) the development of tests that revealed that silent reading was superior to oral reading in comprehension and speed; and (2) the publication of the yearbooks of the *National Society for the Study of Education*, especially the *Twentieth Yearbook*, which pertained almost exclusively to silent reading (Spache 1963, Chap. 11).

During the 1930s, reading programs reflected the application of knowledge learned from the reading research of the 1920s. Now, a new approach to teaching reading was introduced — that of teaching as a part of the "activity program." In this approach, children worked freely, actively, and spontaneously in following their own interests. The teachers tried to incorporate all subject matter in a "unit of work." Rather than using one basic reading textbook, many classrooms had charts and booklets, as well as materials the students prepared themselves (Smith 1965, p. 7).

Research studies on reading continued during the 1930s and were generally superior to those conducted in the previous decade. They were better in isolating problems, in design, and in controls. Research studies on reading readiness and the application of the readiness theory reached a peak during the 1930s. Remedial reading studies had begun in laboratories in the 1920s; during the next ten years, many studies were conducted in classrooms in public schools. The studies during this decade focused on the causes of difficulties, diagnosis, and corrective procedures.

THE BASALS TAKE HOLD

The concept of the controlled vocabulary which was introduced in the 1920s resulted in the development of several series of basic reading textbooks. The series were designed to take the child in a systematic and sequential manner from the preprimer level of instruction through the sixth or eighth grade. Use of these series of basic reading textbooks became known as the basal reading program. In these books, careful attention was given to the number of new words the student would encounter in each lesson.

During the 1940s there was a concentrated effort by many educators to encourage classroom teachers to divide their heterogeneously grouped classes into subgroups to accommodate varying levels of ability in reading. Ability or homogeneous grouping was seen as a solution for the perplexing problem of meeting the educational needs of the wide variety of children found in the typical classroom of the graded elementary school.

Most teachers found that three groups was a number they could manage efficiently. Once the high, average, and low groups were established, they "worked through" the textbook, reading each story, studying the related vocabulary, and doing the workbook pages (West 1964). By the end of the decade, almost every school system in the nation had adopted the idea of the basal reading program with ability grouping within individual classrooms.

Also during the 1940s educators came to realize that reading was not an isolated skill, but was instead one aspect of the language arts program which included spelling, handwriting, vocabulary development, listening and composition. Educators began to see that reading does not develop in a vacuum but is affected by all other aspects of child development. For example, a child's oral language is the raw material for reading and contributes to the development of skills in reading, listening, speaking, writing, and spelling. Reading in the content areas also began to receive more attention in the 1940s, and there was increased attention given to teaching reading at the high school level.

THE PUBLIC GETS INVOLVED

About 1950, many articles in educational journals and popular magazines were critical of the reading instruction in America. Many educators felt there were too many poor readers in the public schools. Surveys showed that few students did reading on their own and that most students had failed to develop any permanent interest in reading as a leisure-time activity (Barbe 1961, p. 9).

Interest by the lay public in reading instruction became widespread during this period — partly as a result of popular magazine articles about reading written for laymen. In 1955, Rudolf Flesch's *Why Johnny Can't Read* (Harper & Row) was published. This book stayed on the bestseller list for over thirty weeks and was serialized in many newspapers. While the general press reacted favorably to it, reviewers in educational periodicals almost unanimously rejected it. Flesch challenged the prevailing views on beginning reading instruction which emphasized the sight or word method. He advocated a return to a phonic approach for beginning instruction.

Dissatisfaction in the United States continued to spread. The public was becoming more and more concerned about how their children were being taught to read. Educators reacted by proposing and developing a wide variety of solutions. The criticisms caused public school personnel to examine their methods of teaching carefully. It also gave them a chance to explain the research, psychology, and philosophy on which their teaching methods were based. The furor of the 1950s created more interest on the part of parents and laymen than at any other time in the history of reading.

There were several results from this newly created interest in reading instruction. More reading courses were taught in teacher training institutions. Standards were raised in regard to qualifications of teachers. The number of research studies in reading increased, including investigations in the areas of perception, comprehension, critical reading, the effect of the classroom climate on reading success, parental influence, and listening.

A big innovation in reading instruction was the movement toward individualized reading approaches. Many of these approaches were based on the theory that a student would be more interested in reading if he could select the books that interested him and if he were allowed to proceed at his own rate according to his individual needs and abilities. In order to implement a reading program that provided for self-selection and self-pacing, it became necessary for the classroom environment to contain reading materials of various types. This need for many kinds of learning materials was responsible for an increase in the use of trade books in the basic curriculum. Trade books (sometimes called "library books") are those books which are not a part of a graded or developmental series. These are books of adventure, animals, family life, humor, mystery, or travel. Many educators recommended a minimum of four to six different books for each child in the classroom for individualized reading instruction, changed on a regular basis. During this period of time, silent reading was still being advocated, along with opportunities to read orally to the teacher. Both of these factors of reading instruction are components of an individualized reading program.

FEDERAL INVOLVEMENT IN EDUCATION

Until the 1960s Congress had resisted many demands for federal financial assistance for elementary and secondary education, arguing that federal aid to education meant federal control of what was to be taught. Many educators and lay school boards had the fear that federal financial assistance or control would lead to socialism or even communism.

However, Russia's Sputnik changed the picture. A bill was drawn —

the National Defense Education Act (NDEA) — which was a blend of efforts to increase the nation's scientific and technical competence. The 1958 bill provided financial support for guidance counseling and testing; aid for improving the teaching of science and mathematics; vocational training; and research in the use of television. Later amendments to the National Defense Education Act of 1958 broadened the scope of subsidy considerably to include aid for the improvement of reading instruction.

Although there were several important research studies conducted during the 1960s, perhaps the most significant investigations during that period dealt with instruction in beginning reading. Many approaches, both old and new, were advocated for beginning reading instruction. Some of these included: phonic approaches, basal reading texts, language experience approaches, changed alphabets such as ITA, Words-in-Color, the Montessori method, programmed learning, and linguistic approaches. Each of these claimed to be the logical way to begin reading instruction (Chall 1967, p. 13). And there were approaches which combined methods such as the phonic-linguistic or the phonic-word (Smith 1965, pp. 71–82).

A concerted effort to find out if there really were superior methods or approaches for teaching beginning reading was sponsored by the U.S. Office of Education, with its "First Grade Reading Studies." The coordinators of this project concluded that combinations of approaches and methods seemed better than single approaches or methods and that pupil and teacher characteristics affected reading progress, regardless of the approach or method used in instruction (Bond and Dykstra 1967*b*). In addition to the many different methods and approaches being advocated for reading instruction, there were several patterns of classroom organization being tried — including individualized reading, multilevel reading instruction, ungraded reading programs, departmentalized reading, ability grouping, grouping within the classroom, and team teaching plans.

Although President John F. Kennedy was able to get Congress to pass the Higher Education Facilities Act of 1963 and the Vocational Education Act of 1963, he was unable to achieve what he had especially wanted — a general aid law for elementary and secondary schools. It was not until 1965, under President Lyndon B. Johnson, that the Elementary and Secondary Education Act (ESEA) was passed. This act authorized appropriation of 1.3 billion dollars for the following: aiding "educationally deprived" children from low-income families; centers for counseling, remedial instruction, new teaching methods, and vocational guidance; support for educational television; aid for school library resources and textbooks; and educational research. Johnson's expectations of expanding the federal aid to elementary and secondary education were not fulfilled because of military commitments for the Vietnam War.

The Head Start and Follow-Through programs under the federal sponsorship of the Office of Economic Opportunity emerged during the mid-1960s. These were special programs for children from low-income families designed to improve instruction, achievement levels, self-image, health, nutrition, and other academic or social goals. Active participation of parents was also stressed. Head Start provided a wide range of curriculum experiences for preschool children. Programs included experiences to foster language development, social development, cognitive development, physical skill development, and many other activities. Follow-Through programs were designed to sustain and augment in later years the gains that children from low-income families made in Head Start and other special programs.

Head Start and Follow-Through were programs mainly developed at the local level with no national direction. The success of these programs has been varied: commendable in some places and lacking value in others (King-Stoops 1977, p. 12).

In 1966, the United States Office of Education established the Educational Resources Information Center (ERIC). The ERIC Center for Reading and Communication Skills (ERIC/RCS), one of the sixteen clearinghouses for educational research and materials, is located at the headquarters of the National Council of Teachers of English in Urbana, Illinois. This center continues to be a useful source of information for anyone interested in the teaching of reading.

In the early 1970s decoding was still a popular and controversial issue. Present-day programs focus the beginning reader's attention on both the development of a sight vocabulary and the study of sound-symbol relationships. Changes in reading instruction are occurring, however. For example, research in the fields of psycholinguistics and sociolinguistics is contributing new information for program planners of reading curricula. Evidence from the research in these two emerging fields indicates that initial reading practices should consider aspects of oral language development, how children think, and how language is acquired. The search for meaning should also be a concern of any initial reading program (Lamb and Arnold 1976, pp. 108–114).

Interest in education has continued to exist in the federal government. In 1970, the U.S. Office of Education announced a campaign aimed at eliminating illiteracy. The "Right to Read" program was designed to coordinate all efforts, public or private, to ensure that all children learned to read before they left school. Dr. James E. Allen, then Commissioner of Education, stated that one out of every four students in the United States had reading deficiencies and that there were more than three million illiterates in the adult population (Allen 1969, p. 2). His goal was that by the end of the 1970s, no one should leave school without being able to read.

SCHOOL ACCOUNTABILITY

As the decade moved along, an emphasis on school accountability and proof of achievement developed. The decline of average student performance on the verbal portion of the Scholastic Aptitude Test (SAT) was widely reported by the media and was interpreted as evidence that children's reading abilities and skills had declined. Competency testing and legislation were two efforts directed toward increasing the accountability of the public school system for developing effective reading programs.

Increasing academic standards by mandating that competency tests must be passed before a child can be graduated from high school or a child can be promoted to the next grade was the most common reaction to SAT score declines and has been adopted in some form in nearly all fifty states (Farr and Olshavsky 1980, p. 528). Many educators hoped that the competency tests would enable school systems to have quality control and ensure a congruence between what a teacher teaches, what a teacher should teach, and what students learn. In many states competency tests were administered at the elementary school level for the purpose of locating reading deficiencies before students enter high school. It was thought that the content of the tests would establish what constitutes basic skills and teachers would help children learn at least enough to pass the tests before leaving school. The ultimate goal was that children would leave school with sufficient skills to function independently in our society.

Legislation was also enacted to increase the accountability of the public school system to teach children to read and reduce the number of nonreaders in the United States. Public Law 94-142 was passed to ensure the right of children to quality education and to obligate the school system to operate on the assumption that every child can indeed learn. The intent of the law was to involve parents in the planning of their child's program of study. This law in effect placed legal responsibility for helping children learn to read on the public school system and on the instructors themselves (Harper and Kilarr 1978, p. 23.).

The National Assessment of Educational Progress (NAEP) was initiated during the 1970s. The purpose of this project was "to make available baseline, census-like data on the educational attainment of young Americans relative to certain evidence and periodically to obtain evidence concerning progress in meeting these objectives" (Foreman 1972, p. 293). The National Assessment of Educational Progress test was administered to several thousand children in 1970–71, 1974–75, and 1979–80 in order to obtain information about the levels of achievement of nine-, thirteen-, and seventeen-year-old students in several reading skill areas. NAEP was also concerned with the growth or decline in reading skills over that period of time. Test results indicated significant improvement between 1971 and 1980 for nine-year-old students. There was no significant change in the overall reading skills of thirteen- and seventeen-year-olds, although seventeen-year-olds did decline slightly in inferential comprehension. Scores on this test indicate that minimal literacy is at a very high level among children in the United States (National Assessment of Educational Progress 1981).

The Present Scene

In 1981 President Ronald Reagan signed the Omnibus Budget Reconciliation Act (HR 3982), which changed all federal education spending. This law created three new chapters under the Education Consolidation and Improvement Act of 1981, which affected elementary and secondary education. Chapters I and II of the Education Consolidation and Improvement Act replaced the Elementary and Secondary Education Act of 1965 as amended, except for Bilingual Education. This act changed the old Title I to Chapter I, "Financial Assistance to Meet Special Educational Needs of Disadvantaged Children." Chapter II, with its subchapters, is the block grant. This part of the legislation deals with improving basic skills, teacher centers, gifted and talented programs, as well as "Reading is Fundamental." In all, the amount of money and the federal regulations have been cut. Now the states will be responsible for the regulations and for decisions to increase funding.

Reading research continues to bring about changes in reading instruction. Comprehension is currently receiving considerable attention. Decoding is still an important research area. Increased attention is also being given to reading in the content areas, attitudes of both teachers and students, and the quality of the learning environment (Davis, Davis, and Alexander 1976, pp. 40–41).

Provision for a great variety of learners must be made in today's reading programs. The gifted, the retarded, the bilingual, and the child with specific learning disabilities all have a place in today's reading programs. Existing reading programs for the culturally different child vary widely in rationale, scope, and teaching strategies. (Teaching suggestions for working with the culturally different child are found in previous chapters in this text, especially in Chapter 16).

Summary

This chapter traced the teaching of reading in the United States from the 1600s to the present time. Throughout the history of America, educators have adhered to the philosophy that written or printed words are used to recall an idea. The methods and materials for teaching reading have changed over the years. There has been a progression from one method and one book to our current situation, in which there are several prominent approaches and many combinations of these approaches. The changes discussed in this chapter were often the subject of controversy. Some of the religious, educational, economic, and political forces involved in these controversies were noted.

Schools in twentieth-century America have been greatly influenced by research. The number of research studies dealing with the various aspects of learning to read and the teaching of reading during this century runs well into five figures. It is evident that there has been and *is* a tremendous interest in and concern about the techniques of teaching children to read.

Questions for Further Reading and Thinking

1. How has reading instruction been influenced by research on how children learn?
2. How have research studies on the teaching of reading affected classroom instruction?
3. How could current methods of teaching reading utilize the best of the old and the best of the new?
4. How are government-funded programs affecting American reading programs?
5. Will history record any changes in the teaching of reading with the invention of television?
6. Since the 1600s, people have been coming to America from other countries. The languages these people speak and read are numerous. How have these immigrants influenced reading programs?
7. Various linguistic communities have existed on the North American continent for centuries. How have/will/should these communities and their language patterns influence(d) reading instruction?

Bibliography

Aaron, Ira E. 1960. Patterns of classroom organization. *Education* 80 (May): 530–532.

Abrams, Jules C. 1969. Further considerations on the ego functioning of the dyslexic child — A psychiatric viewpoint. In *Reading disability and perception*, ed. G. D. Spache. Proceedings of the 13th Annual Convention, International Reading Association, Newark, Del.: 13(3): 16–21.

Alexander, J. Estill; and Burns, Paul C. 1974. Words and their changing ways. *Elementary English* 51 (April): 477–481.

Alexander, J. Estill; and Filler, Ronald C. 1976. *Attitudes and reading*. Newark, Del.: International Reading Association.

———. 1975. Measures of reading attitudes. *Elementary English* 52 (March): 376–378.

———. 1974. Group cohesiveness and reading instruction. *The Reading Teacher* 27 (February): 446–450.

———. 1973. Questioning strategies and reading comprehension. *Tennessee Education* 3 (Spring): 5–10.

Allen, James E., Jr. 1969. The right to read — Target for the 70's. Washington, D.C.: U.S. Department of Health, Education, and Welfare, Office of Education.

Allen, Roach Van. 1965. *Attitudes and art of teaching reading*. Washington, D.C.: National Education Association.

Allington, Richard L.; Chodos, Laura; Domaracki, Jane; and Truex, Sharon. 1977. Passage dependency: Four diagnostic oral reading tests. *The Reading Teacher* 30 (January): 369–375.

Ames, Wilbur S. 1966. The development of a classification scheme of contextual aids. *Reading Research Quarterly* 2 (Fall): 57–82.

———. 1964. The understanding vocabulary of first grade pupils. *Elementary English* 41 (January): 64–68.

Anastasi, Anne. 1954. *Psychological testing*. New York: Macmillan.

Anastasiow, Nicholas J. 1967. Sex differences in self-concept scores of high and low ability elementary students. *The Gifted Child Quarterly* 11 (Summer): 112–116.

———. 1964. A report of self-concept of the very gifted. *The Gifted Child Quarterly* 8 (Winter): 177–178, 189.

Anderson, Richard C.; Reynolds, Ralph E.; Schallert, Diane L.; and Goetz, Earnest T. 1977. Frameworks for comprehending discourse. *American Educational Research Journal* 14 (Fall): 367–381.

Applegate, Don J. 1968. Individualizing reading as its philosophy, research and implementation. ERIC ED 019 182.

Ashton-Warner, Sylvia. 1963. *Teacher*. New York: Simon and Schuster.

Athey, Irene. 1976. Reading research in the affective domain. In *Theoretical models and processes of reading*, eds. Harry Singer and Robert B. Ruddell, pp. 352–380. Newark, Del.: International Reading Association.

———. 1966. Personality factors and the development of successful readers. In *New frontiers of college-adult reading*, eds. George B. Schick and Merrill M. May, pp. 133–139. Milwaukee: Yearbooks of National Reading Conference.

Aukerman, Robert C. 1981. *The basal reader approach to reading*. New York: John Wiley and Sons.

———. 1972. *Reading in the secondary school classroom*, pp. 132–206. New York: McGraw-Hill.

———. 1971. *Approaches to beginning reading*. New York: John Wiley and Sons.

Ausubel, David P. 1968. *Educational psychology, a cognitive view*. New York: Holt, Rinehart and Winston.

———. 1965. A cognitive structure view of word and concept meaning. In *Readings in the psychology of cognition*, eds. Robert C. Anderson and David P. Ausubel, pp. 58–75. New York: Holt, Rinehart and Winston.

Bader, Lois. 1980. *Reading diagnosis and remediation in classroom and clinic*. New York: Macmillan.

Bailey, Mildred. 1967. The utility of phonic generalizations in grades one through six. *The Reading Teacher* 20 (February): 413–418.

Baker, Linda; and Stein, Nancy L. 1981. The development of prose comprehension skills. In *Children's prose comprehension: Research and practice*, eds. Carol Hayes Santa and Bernard L. Hayes, pp. 7–43. Newark, Del.: International Reading Association.

Bamman, Henry A.; Hogan, Ursula; and Greene, Charles E. 1961. *Reading instruction in the secondary school*, pp. 174–185. New York: David McKay.

Baratz, Joan C. 1969. Linguistic and cultural factors in teaching reading to ghetto children. *Elementary English* 46 (February): 199–203.

Barbe, Walter B. 1965. *Teaching reading: Selected materials*. New York: Oxford University Press.

———. 1961. *Educator's guide to personalized reading instruction*. Englewood Cliffs, N.J.: Prentice-Hall.

Barrett, Thomas C. 1974. Taxonomy of reading comprehension. In *Teaching reading in the middle grades*, eds. Richard F. Smith and Thomas C. Barrett. Reading, Mass.: Addison-Wesley.

Becker, George J. 1973. *Television and the classroom reading program*. Newark, Del.: International Reading Association.

Bereiter, Carl; Engelman, Siegfried; Osborn, Jean; and Reidford, Philip A. 1966. An academically oriented pre-school for culturally deprived children. In *Pre-school education today*, ed. Fred M. Hechinger, pp. 105–135. New York: Doubleday.

Betts, Emmett A. 1956. Phonics: Practical considerations based on research. *Elementary English* 33 (October): 357–371.

———. 1946. *Foundations of reading instruction*. New York: American Book Company.

Bleismer, Emery P.; and Yarborough, Betty H. 1965. A comparison of ten different reading programs in first grade. *Phi Delta Kappan* 46 (June): 500–504.

Blodgett, Elizabeth G.; and Cooper, Eugene B. 1973. Attitudes of elementary teachers toward black dialect. *Journal of Communication Disorders* 6 (June): 121–133.

Bloom, Benjamin S., ed. 1956. *Taxonomy of education objectives*. New York: Longmans, Green.

Bloomfield, Leonard; and Barnhart, C. L. 1961. *Let's read: A linguistic approach*. Detroit: Wayne State University Press.

Bond, Guy; and Dykstra, Robert. 1967a. The cooperative research program in first-grade reading instruction. *Reading Research Quarterly* 2 (Summer): 5–142.

———. 1967b. *Final report, project no. X–001*. Washington, D.C.: Bureau of Research, Office of Education, U.S. Department of Health, Education, and Welfare.

Bond, Guy L.; Tinker, Miles A.; and Wasson, Barbara B. 1979. *Reading difficulties: Their diagnosis and correction*. 4th ed. Englewood Cliffs, N.J.: Prentice-Hall.

Bormuth, John R. 1969. Development of readability analysis. Final Report, Project No. 7-0052, Contract No. OEC-3-7-070052-0326. Bureau of Research, Office of Education, U.S. Department of Health, Education, and Welfare (March).

Bouise, Louise M. 1955. Emotional and personality problems of a group of retarded readers. *Elementary English* 32: 544–548.

Boyd, John E. 1975. Teaching children with reading problems. In *Teaching children with learning and behavior problems*, eds. Donald D. Hammill and Nettie R. Bartel, pp. 15–60. Boston: Allyn and Bacon.

Bradley, John M.; and Ames, Wilbur S. 1978. You can't judge a basal by the number on the cover. *Reading World* 17 (March): 175–183.

Brazemore, Judith S.; and Gwalthney, Wayne K. 1973. Personality and reading achievement: The use of certain personality factors as discriminatory. *California Journal of Educational Research* 24 (May): 114–119.

Brown, Ann L. 1980. Metacognitive development and reading. In *Theoretical issues in reading comprehension*, eds. Rand J. Spiro, Bertram C. Bruce, and William F. Brewer, pp. 453–482. Hillsdale, N.J.: Lawrence Erlbaum.

Brown, James I. 1966. Reading improvement through vocabulary development, the CPD formula. In *New frontiers in college-adult reading*, eds. George Schick and Merrill May, pp. 197–202. Milwaukee: Yearbooks of National Reading Conference.

Brown, Roger; and Bellugi, Ursula. 1964. The processes in the child's acquisition of syntax. *Harvard Educational Review* 34: 133–151.

Bruner, Jerome, 1960. *The process of education*. New York: Vintage Books.

Bruton, Ann. 1977. A review of reading comprehension research reports in journals from 1900–1975.

Unpublished doctoral dissertation, The University of Tennessee.

Burmeister, Lou E. 1976. Vocabulary development in content areas through the use of morphemes. *Journal of Reading* 16 (March): 481–487.

———. 1971. Final vowel-consonant -e. *The Reading Teacher* 24 (February): 439–441.

———. 1968. Usefulness of phonic generalizations. *The Reading Teacher* 21 (January): 349–356.

Burns, Paul C.; and Broman, Betty L. 1979. *The language arts in childhood education*. 4th ed. Chicago: Rand McNally.

Burron, Arnold; and Claybough, Amos L. 1974. *Using reading to teach subject matter*. Columbus, Ohio: Charles E. Merrill.

Bush, Clifford L. 1964. Three kinds of grouping in the same classroom. In *Improvement of reading through classroom practice*. Newark, Del.: International Reading Association Conference Proceedings 9: 5–51.

Bush, Clifford L.; and Huebner, Mildred. 1979. *Strategies for reading in the elementary school*. 2nd ed. New York: Macmillan.

Byers, Loretta. 1964. Pupils' interests and the content of primary reading text. *The Reading Teacher* 17 (January): 227–233.

Camden, Hazel. 1954. Materials and procedures to develop reading efficiency in the sciences. In *Supplementary educational monograph, No. 81*, p. 105. Chicago: University of Chicago Press.

Cardinell, C. F. 1976. Rewriting social studies materials to lower reading levels. *The Reading Teacher* 30 (November): 168–172.

Carillo, Lawrence W. 1957. The relations of certain environmental and developmental factors to reading ability in children. Unpublished doctoral dissertation, Syracuse University.

Carroll, John B. 1973. Language and cognition: Current perspectives from linguistics and psychology. In *Language differences. Do they interfere?*, eds. James L. Laffey and Roger W. Shuy, pp. 173–185. Newark, Del.: International Reading Association.

Carver, Clifford. 1971. Motivation versus cognitive methods in remedial reading. ERIC ED 050 921.

Cattell, Janet. 1947. On the time required of recognizing and naming letters and words, pictures, and colors. *James McKeen Cattell — Man of Science*, pp. 13–23. Lancaster, Pa.: Science Press.

Cazden, Courtney B. 1968. The acquisition of noun and verb inflections. *Child Development* 32 (1968): 433–448.

Chall, Jeanne. 1967. *Learning to read: The great debate*. New York: McGraw-Hill.

———. 1953. Ask him to try the book for fit. *The Reading Teacher* 7 (December): 83–88.

Champion, Dean J. 1970. *Basic statistics social research*. Scranton, Pa.: Chandler Publishing Company.

Chan, Julie M. T. 1974. *Why read to children*. Newark, Del.: International Reading Association.

Ching, Doris C. 1976. *Reading and the bilingual child*. Newark, Del.: International Reading Association.

Chomsky, Carol. 1974. When you still can't read in third grade. Unpublished manuscript. Cited on p. 18 of *The Recognition of Words*, 1978, eds., Linnear Ehri, Roderick W. Barron, and Jeffrey M. Feldman. Newark, Del.: International Reading Association.

———. 1969. *The acquisition of syntax in children from 5 to 10*. Cambridge, Mass.: M.I.T. Press.

Church, Marilyn. 1974. Does visual perception training help beginning readers? *The Reading Teacher* 27 (January): 361–364.

Cleland, Donald L.; and Miller, Harry B. 1965. Instruction in phonics and success in beginning reading. *Elementary School Journal* 65 (February): 278–282.

Cleworth, Maud C. 1958. *Evaluation of reading*. Chicago: University of Chicago Press.

Clymer, Theodore. 1963. The utility of phonic generalizations in the primary grades. *The Reading Teacher* 16 (January): 252–258.

Cohen, Andrew D. 1974. The Culver City Spanish immersion program: The first two years. *The Modern Language Journal* 58 (March): 95–103.

Cohen, Dorothy. 1966. Effects of a special program in literature on the vocabulary and reading achievement of second grade children in special service schools. Unpublished doctoral dissertation, New York University.

Cohen, S. Alan; and Kornfeld, Gita S. 1970. Oral vocabulary and beginning reading in disadvantaged Black children. *The Reading Teacher* 24 (October): 33–38.

Comprehensive Tests of Basic Skills Examiner's Manual, Form S, Level A. 1973, 1974. Del Monte Research Park, Monterey, Calif.: CTB/McGraw-Hill.

Corle, Clyde G. 1972. Reading in mathematics: A review of recent research. In *Reading in the content areas*, ed. James L. Laffey, pp. 75–94. Newark, Del.: International Reading Association.

Coulter, Myron L. 1972. Reading in mathematics: Classroom implications. In *Reading in the content areas*, ed. James L. Laffey, pp. 95–126. Newark, Del.: International Reading Association.

Cullinan, Bernice E.; Jagger, Angela; and Strickland, Dorothy. 1974. Language expansion of Black children in the primary grades: A research report. *Young Children* 29 (January): 98–112.

Cunningham, Patricia M. 1977. Teachers' correction responses to Black dialect miscues which are non-meaning-changing. *Reading Research Quarterly* 12: 637–653.

Dale, Edgar; and Chall, Jeanne S. 1948. A formula for predicting readability. *Educational Research Bulletin* 27 (January 21 and February 17): 11–20; 37–54.

Dale, Philip S. 1976. *Language development: Structure and function.* 2nd ed. New York: Holt, Rinehart and Winston.

Dallmann, Martha; Rough, Roger L.; Chang, Lynette Y. C.; and Deboer, John J. 1978. *The teaching of reading.* 5th ed. New York: Holt, Rinehart and Winston.

Davies, W. J. Frank. 1973. *Teaching reading in early England.* London: Pitman.

Davis, Arnold R. 1973. An annotated bibliography for organizing information. *The Clearing House* 47 (February): 382–384.

Davis, Arnold R.; and Miller, Donald C. 1974. *Science games.* Belmont, Calif.: Lear Siegler/Fearon.

Davis, Frederick B. 1968. Research in comprehension in reading. *Reading Research Quarterly* 3 (Summer): 449–545.

Davis, Patsy McLain. 1978. An evaluation of journal published research on attitudes in reading, 1900–1977. Unpublished doctoral dissertation, University of Tennessee, Knoxville.

Davis, Patsy M.; Davis, Arnold R.; and Alexander, J. Estill. 1976. Reading instruction: Past and future. *Tennessee Education* 6 (Spring): 38–42.

DeCecco, John P.; and Crawford, William R. 1974. *The psychology of learning and instruction.* 2nd ed. Englewood Cliffs, N.J.: Prentice-Hall.

Dechant, Emerald V. 1970. *Improving the teaching of reading.* 3rd ed. Englewood Cliffs, N.J.: Prentice-Hall.

Dechant, Emerald V.; and Smith, Henry P. 1977. *Psychology in teaching reading.* 2nd ed. Englewood Cliffs, N.J.: Prentice-Hall.

Delawter, Jane Ann; and Eash, Maurice J. 1966. Focus on oral communication. *Elementary English* 43 (December): 880–883.

DeStefano, Johanna S. 1981. Research update: Linguistic consciousness-raising in children — Carol Chomsky. *Language Arts* 58 (May): 607–612.

———. 1978. *Language: The learner and the school.* New York: John Wiley and Sons.

Deutsch, Cynthia P. 1964. Auditory discrimination and learning: Social factors. *Merrill-Palmer Quarterly* 10 (July): 277–296.

Deutsch, Martin. 1967. The role of social class in language development and cognition. In *The disadvantaged child: Studies of the social environment and the learning process,* ed. Martin Deutsch. New York: Basic Books.

Dewey, John, 1916. *Democracy and education.* New York: Macmillan.

Dillard, J. L. 1977. *Lexicon of Black English.* New York: Seabury Press.

Dillingofski, Mary Sue. 1979. Sociolinguistics and reading: A review of the literature. *The Reading Teacher* 33 (December): 307–312.

Dolch, Edward W. 1960. *Teaching primary reading.* Champaign, Ill.: Garrard Press.

———. 1953. How to diagnose children's reading difficulties by informal classroom techniques. *The Reading Teacher* 6 (January): 10–14.

Donald, S. M. 1968. The SQ3R method in grade seven. *Journal of Reading* 11 (October): 33–35, 43.

Donnelly, Mona M. 1973. Science or fiction: The elementary teacher's dilemma. *Tennessee Education* 3 (Winter): 10–15.

Dotson, Mary Margaret Seldidge. 1977. The relationship between fifth grade children's attitudes toward reading and factors such as success or failure in reading, intelligence, sex, grade retention, level of grade retention, and socioeconomic status. Unpublished doctoral dissertation, The University of Tennessee, Knoxville.

Douzat, Jo Ann; and Douzat, Sam V. 1981. *Reading: The teacher and the learner.* New York: John Wiley and Sons.

Downing, John A.; Cartwright, Daphne; Jones, Barbara; and Lotham, William. 1967. Methodological problems in the British ITA research. *Reading Research Quarterly* 3 (Fall): 85–100.

Downing, J.; Ollila, L.; and Oliver, P. 1975. Cultural differences in children's concepts of reading and writing. *British Journal of Educational Psychology* 45 (November): 312–316.

Drum, Priscilla A.; Calfee, Robert C.; and Cook, Linda K. 1981. The effects of surface structure variables on performance in reading comprehension tests. *Reading Research Quarterly* 16: 486–513.

Durkin, Delores. 1981. Reading comprehension instruction in five basal reader series. *Reading Research Quarterly* 16: 515–544.

———. 1978–1979. What classroom observations reveal about reading comprehension instruction. *Reading Research Quarterly* 15: 481–533.

———. 1978. *Teaching them to read.* 3rd ed. Boston: Allyn and Bacon.

———. 1977. Facts about pre-first grade reading. In *The kindergarten child and reading,* ed. Lloyd O. Ollila. Newark, Del: International Reading Association.

———. 1966. *Children who read early: Two longitudinal studies.* New York: Teachers College Press.

Durrell, Donald. 1968. Phonics in beginning reading. In *Forging ahead in reading,* ed. J. Allen Figurel, pp. 19–25. International Reading Association Proceedings, 12 Part 1.

Earle, Richard A. 1976. *Teaching reading and mathematics,* p. 64. Newark, Del.: International Reading Association.

———. 1969. Reading and mathematics: Research in the classroom. In *Fusing reading skills and content,* eds. H. Alan Robinson and Ellen Lamar Thomas, pp. 162–170. Newark, Del.: International Reading Association.

Earle, Richard A.; and Morley, Richard. 1974. The half-open classroom: Controlled options in reading. *Journal of Reading* 18 (November): 131–135.

Eberwein, Lowell D. 1979. The variability of readability of basal reader textbooks and how much teachers know about it. *Reading World* 18 (March): 259–272.

Ekwall, Eldon E. 1974. Should repetitions be counted as errors? *The Reading Teacher* 29 (January): 365–367.

Ellis, Henry C. 1965. *The transfer of learning.* New York: Macmillan.

Emans, Robert. 1968. History of phonics. *Elementary English* 45 (May): 602–608.

———. 1967. The usefulness of phonic generalizations above the primary grades. *The Reading Teacher* 20 (February): 419–425.

Emans, Robert; and Fisher, Gladys Mary. 1967. Teaching the use of context clues. *Elementary English* 44 (March): 243–246.

Engleman, Siegfried; and Bruner, Elaine C. 1969. *Distar reading: An instructional system.* Chicago: Science Research Associates.

Ervin, Susan M.; and Miller, W. R. 1963. Language development. Sixty-Second Yearbook of the National Society for the Study of Education, Pt. 1, pp. 108–143. Chicago: University of Chicago Press.

Ervin-Tripp, Susan M. 1973. Some strategies for the first two years. In *Language acquisition and communicative choice: Essays by Susan M. Ervin-Tripp,* ed. Anwar S. Dil. Stanford, Calif.: Stanford University Press.

Farr, Roger. 1969. *Reading: What can be measured?* Newark, Del.: International Reading Association.

Farr, Roger; and Olshavsky, Jill Edwards. 1980. Is minimum competency testing the appropriate solution to the SAT decline? *Phi Delta Kappan* 61 (April): 528–530.

Fay, Leo. 1971. *Organization and administration of school reading programs,* p. 64. Bloomington, Ind.: ERIC/CRIER.

———. 1965. Reading study skills: Math and science. In *Reading and inquiry,* ed. J. Allen Figurel, pp. 92–94. Newark, Del.: International Reading Association.

———. 1954. What research has to say about reading in the content areas. *The Reading Teacher* 8 (October): 68–72.

Feeley, Joan T. 1982. Content interests and media preferences of middle grades: Differences in a decade. *Reading World* 22 (October): 11–16.

———. Interests patterns and media preferences of middlegrade children. 1974. *Reading World* 13 (March): 224–237.

Fernald, Grace M. 1943. *Remedial techniques in basic school subjects.* New York: McGraw-Hill.

Fishbein, Justin M. 1967. Reading and linguistics. *The Instructor* 77 (November): 25, 46–48.

Flavell, John H. 1963. *The developmental psychology of Jean Piaget.* New York: Van Nostrand Reinhold.

Fodor, Janet Dean. 1980. *Semantics: Theories of meaning in generative grammar.* Cambridge, Mass.: Harvard University Press.

Foerster, Leona M. 1974. Language experience for dialectically different Black learners. *Elementary English* 51 (February): 193–197.

Foreman, Dale J. 1972. National assessment of elementary reading. *The Reading Teacher* 26 (December): 293–298.

Forgan, Harry W.; and Mangrum, Charles T. II. 1981. *Teaching content area reading skills.* 2nd ed. Columbus, Ohio: Charles E. Merrill.

Frase, Lawrence T. 1967. Learning from prose material: Length of passage, knowledge of results and position of questions. *Journal of Educational Psychology* 58 (October): 266–272.

Frederiksen, C. H. 1977. Inference and the structure of children's discourse. Paper for the Symposium on the Development of Processing Skills, Society for Research in Child Development meeting, New Orleans. Summarized in *Teaching reading to every child* (1978) by Diane Lapp and James Flood, pp. 302–304. New York: Macmillan.

Freedman, Glenn; and Reynolds, Elizabeth G. 1980. Enriching basal reader lessons with semantic webbing. *The Reading Teacher* 33 (March): 677–684.

Freeman, Evelyn B.; and Wolfgang, Charles H. 1978. A Piagetian view of reading readiness. *Reading World* 18 (October): 72–80.

Freeman, Joseph F. 1973. Differential clues employed in word recognition for known and unknown words. Unpublished doctoral dissertation, University of Arizona.

Fries, Charles C. 1963. *Linguistics and reading.* New York: Holt, Rinehart and Winston.

Frost, Joe L.; and Rowland, G. Thomas. 1971. *Compensatory programming: The acid test of American education.* Dubuque, Iowa: William C. Brown.

———. 1968. Cognitive development and literacy in disadvantaged children: A structure process approach. Mimeographed. Austin, Tex.: The University of Texas.

Fry, Edward. 1980. The new instant word list. *The Reading Teacher* 34 (December): 284–289.

———. 1977. Fry's readability graph: Clarifications, validity, and extension to level 17. *Journal of Reading* 21 (December): 242–252.

———. 1972. *Reading instruction for classroom and clinic,* pp. 49–60. New York: McGraw-Hill.

———. 1968. A readability formula that saves time. *Journal of Reading* 11 (April): 513–516, 575–578.

Furth, Hans J. 1970. *Piaget for teachers.* Englewood Cliffs, N.J.: Prentice-Hall.

Gambrell, Linda B. 1978. Getting started with sustained silent reading and keeping it going. *The Reading Teacher* 32 (December): 328–331.

Garcia, Ricarde L. 1974. Mexican Americans learn through language experience. *The Reading Teacher* 28 (December): 301–305.

Gates, Arthur I. 1937. The necessary mental age for beginning reading. *Elementary School Journal,* 37 (March): 508.

———. 1930. *Interest and ability in reading.* New York: Macmillan.

Gatheral, Maryann. 1979. Super research: What to do if "They" use it against you. *Learning* (August, September): 71, 76, 78.

Gendler, Everett. 1975. . . . that well I re-tell old tales . . . *Elementary English* 52 (April): 555–559.

Gibson, Eleanor J.; and Levin, Harry. 1975. *The psychology of reading.* Cambridge, Mass.: M.I.T. Press.

Gillespie, Patricia H.; and Johnson, Lowell. 1974. *Teaching reading to the mildly retarded child.* Columbus, Ohio: Charles E. Merrill.

Gilmore, John V.; and Gilmore, Eunice C. 1968. *Gilmore oral reading test.* New York: Harcourt Brace Jovanovich.

Gipe, Joan P. 1980. Use of a relevant context helps kids learn new word meanings. *The Reading Teacher* 33 (January): 398–402.

Glennon, Vincent J.; and Callahan, Leroy G. 1968. *Elementary school mathematics: A guide to current research.* Washington, D.C.: Association for Supervision and Curriculum Development.

Glick, Oren. 1972. Some social-emotional consequences of early inadequate acquisition of reading skills. *Journal of Educational Psychology* 63 (June): 253–257.

Golub, Lester S. 1971. Stimulating and receiving children's writing: Implications for an elementary writing curriculum. *Elementary English* 48 (January): 33–49.

Gonzalez, Andrew; and Rafael, Teresita C. 1981. Transitional reading problems in English in a Philippine bilingual setting. *The Reading Teacher* 35 (December): 281–286.

Good, Carter V., ed. 1973. *Dictionary of education.* New York: McGraw-Hill.

Goodman, Kenneth S. 1976a. Behind the eye: What happens in reading. In *Theoretical models and processes of reading.* 2nd ed., eds. Harry Singer and Robert B. Ruddell, pp. 470–496. Newark, Del.: International Reading Association.

———. 1976b. Reading: A psycholinguistic guessing game. In *Theoretical models and processes of reading.* 2nd ed., eds. Harry Singer and Robert B. Ruddell, pp. 497–508. Newark, Del.: International Reading Association.

———. 1968. *The psycholinguistic nature of the reading process.* Detroit: Wayne State University Press.

———. 1965a. A linguistic study of cues and miscues in reading. *Elementary English* 42 (October): 639–643.

———. 1965b. Dialect barriers to reading comprehension. *Elementary English* 42 (December): 853–860.

Goodman, Kenneth S.; and Buck, Catherine. 1973. Dialect barriers to reading comprehension revisited. *The Reading Teacher* 27 (October): 6–12.

Goodman, Yetta M.; and Burke, Carolyn L. 1972. *Reading miscue inventory manual procedure for diagnosis and evaluation.* New York: Macmillan.

Gould, Rosalind. 1972. *Child studies through fantasy.* New York: Quadrangle Books.

Gray, William S.; and Holmes, Eleanor. 1938. *The development of meaning vocabularies in reading.* Chicago: University of Chicago Press.

Gray, William S.; and Robinson, Helen M., eds. 1967. *Gray oral reading tests.* Indianapolis: Bobbs-Merrill.

Greenberg, Judith W.; Gerver, Joan M.; Chall, Jeanne; and Davidson, Helen H. 1965. Attitudes of children from a deprived environment toward achievement-related concepts. *Journal of Educational Research* 59 (October): 57–62.

Greif, Ivo P. 1980. A study of the pronunciation of words ending in vowel-consonant-final E pattern. *The Reading Teacher* 34 (December): 290–292.

Groff, Patrick. 1975. Reading ability and auditory discrimination: Are they related? *The Reading Teacher* 28 (May): 742–747.

———. 1962. Children's attitudes toward reading and their critical-type materials. *Journal of Educational Research* 55 (April): 313–314.

Gumperz, J. 1968. The speech community. *International encyclopedia of the social sciences*, pp. 381–386. New York: Macmillan.

Gunderson, Doris. 1972. Are linguistic programs different? In *Some persistent questions on beginning reading*, ed. Robert C. Aukerman. Newark, Del.: International Reading Association.

Gunning, Robert. 1968. *The technique of clear writing.* Rev. ed. New York: McGraw-Hill.

Gurren, Louise; and Hughes, Ann. 1965. Intensive phonics vs. gradual phonics in beginning reading: A review. *Journal of Educational Research* 58 (April): 339–347.

Guszak, Frank J. 1969. Questioning strategies of elementary teachers in relation to comprehension. In *Reading and realism*, ed. J. Allen Figurel, pp. 110–116. International Reading Association Conference Proceedings.

Guthrie, John T.; Seifert, Mary; Burnham, Nancy R.; and Caplan, Ronald I. 1974. The maze technique to assess monitor reading comprehension. *The Reading Teacher* 28 (November): 161–168.

Gutierrez, Arturo L. 1975. Bilingual education: Reading through two languages. In *Reading and the Spanish-speaking child*, ed. Don E. Critchlow. Laredo, Tex.: Texas Council, International Reading Association.

Hafner, Lawrence E. 1965. A one-month experiment in teaching context aids in fifth grade. *Journal of Educational Research* 58 (July-August): 472–474.

Hall, Diane Sprawls. 1977. Teaching the relationship of reading attitudes to achievement, sex, and social class among fifth grade pupils. Unpublished doctoral dissertation, The University of Tennessee, Knoxville.

Hall, MaryAnne. 1981. *Teaching reading as a language experience.* 3rd ed. Columbus, Ohio: Charles E. Merrill.

———. 1972. *The language experience approach for the culturally disadvantaged.* Newark, Del.: International Reading Association.

Hall, Vernon C.; and Turner, Ralph R. 1974. The validity of the "different language explanation" for poor scholastic performance by black students. *Review of Educational Research* 44 (Winter): 69–81.

Hammill, Donald; Goodman, Libby; and Wiederholt, J. Lee. 1974. Visual-motor processes: Can we train them? *The Reading Teacher* 27 (February): 469–478.

Hansen, Harlan S. 1969. The impact of the home literacy environment on reading attitudes. *Elementary English* 46 (January): 17–23.

Harber, Jean R.; and Bryen, Diane N. 1976. Black English and the task of reading. *Review of Educational Research* 46 (Summer): 387–405.

Hargis, Charles; and Knight, Lester N. 1975. The language of children and the language of their reading instructional materials. *Tennessee Education* 5 (Fall): 13–17.

Haring, Norris Grover; and Bateman, Barbara. 1977. *Teaching the learning disabled child.* Englewood Cliffs, N.J.: Prentice-Hall.

Harms, Jeanne McLain. 1975. Children's responses to fantasy in literature. *Language Arts* 52 (October): 942–946.

Harper, Robert J. II; and Kilarr, Gary, eds. 1978. *Reading and the law.* Newark, Del.: International Reading Association.

Harris, Albert J. 1968. Research on some aspects of comprehension: Rate, flexibility, and study skill. *Journal of Reading* 12 (December): 205–210, 258–260.

Harris, Albert J.; and Sipay, Edward R. 1980. *How to increase reading ability.* 7th ed. New York: Longmans.

Harris, Larry A.; and Smith, Carl B. 1976. *Reading instruction.* 2nd ed. New York: Holt, Rinehart and Winston.

———. 1972. *Reading instruction through diagnostic teaching*, pp. 25–28. New York: Holt, Rinehart, and Winston.

Harris, Theodore L.; and Hodges, Richard E., eds. 1981. *A dictionary of reading and related terms.* Newark, Del.: International Reading Association.

Haskinson, Kenneth. 1973. "False" questions and "right" answers. *The Reading Teacher* 27 (November): 159–162.

Hasselriis, Peter. 1972. Reading in literature: Student involvement is just the beginning. In *Reading in the content areas*, ed. James L. Laffey, pp. 31–74. Newark, Del.: International Reading Association.

Hay, Julie; and Wingo, Charles E. 1967. *Reading with phonics, teacher's manual.* Philadelphia: J. B. Lippincott Company.

Healy, Ann Kirtland. 1965. Effects of changing children's attitudes toward reading. *Elementary English* 42 (March): 269–272.

Heathington, Betty S. 1975. The development of scales to measure attitudes toward reading. Unpublished doctoral dissertation, The University of Tennessee, Knoxville.

Heathington, Betty S.; and Alexander, J. Estill. 1978. A child-based observation checklist to assess attitudes toward reading. *The Reading Teacher* 31 (April): 769–771.

Heffernan, Helen. 1960. Significance of kindergarten education. *Childhood Education* 36 (March): 313–319.

Heilman, Arthur W.; Blair, Timothy R.; and Rupley, William H. 1981. *Principles and practices of teaching reading.* 5th ed. Columbus, Ohio: Charles E. Merrill.

Herber, Harold L. 1978. *Teaching reading in content areas.* 2nd ed. Englewood Cliffs, N.J.: Prentice-Hall.

———. 1972. Reading in the social studies: Implications for teaching and research. In *Reading in the content areas*, ed. James L. Laffey. Newark, Del.: International Reading Association.

———. 1970. *Teaching reading in content areas.* Englewood Cliffs, N.J.: Prentice-Hall.

Herber, Harold L.; and Sanders, Peter L., eds. 1969. *Research in reading in the content areas: First year report.* Syracuse University: Reading and Language Arts Center.

Hittleman, Daniel R. 1978. Readability, readability formulas, and cloze: Selecting instructional materials. *Journal of Reading* 22 (November): 117–122.

Hoisington, Arthur R. 1968. An experimental investigation of a linguistic approach to vocabulary development which emphasizes structural analysis: Prefixes, suffixes, and root words. Unpublished doctoral dissertation, Washington State University.

Holden, Marjorie H.; and MacGinitie, Walter H. 1972. Children's conceptions of word boundaries in speech and print. *Journal of Educational Psychology* 63 (December): 551–557.

Hong, Laraine K. 1981. Modifying SSR for beginning readers. *The Reading Teacher* 34 (May): 888–891.

Hornik, Robert C. 1978. Television access and the slowing of cognitive growth. *American Educational Research Journal* 15 (Winter): 1–15.

Horvath, Barbara M. 1977. Sociolinguistics and reading. In *Linguistic theory: What can it say about reading?*, ed. Roger W. Shuy, pp. 95–107. Newark, Del.: International Reading Association.

Howell, Wallace J. 1953. Work-study skills of adolescents in grades VII–XIV. *School Review* 61 (May): 277–282.

———. 1950. Work-study skills of adolescents in grades IV–VII. *Elementary School Journal* 50 (March): 384–389.

Huck, Charlotte S. 1976. *Children's literature in the elementary school.* 3rd ed. New York: Holt, Rinehart and Winston.

Huff, Phyllis E. 1971. The effects of the use of activities of science — A process approach on the oral communication skills of disadvantaged kindergarten children. Unpublished doctoral thesis, Ohio State University.

Hunt, Lyman C. Jr. 1967. *The individualized reading program: A guide for classroom teaching.* Newark, Del.: International Reading Association.

Huser, Mary K. 1967. Reading and more reading. *Elementary English* 44 (April): 378–382, 385.

Ignoffo, Matthew F. 1980. A thread of thought: Analogies as a vocabulary building method. *Journal of Reading* 23 (March): 519–521.

Informal reading inventory. 1976. Boston: Houghton-Mifflin.

Informal reading inventory levels 1–12 13–24. 1973. New York: Scott Foresman Company.

Jackson, Philip Wesley. 1968. *Life in classrooms.* New York: Holt, Rinehart and Winston.

Jacobson, Paul B. 1932. The effects of work-type reading instruction given in the ninth grade. *School Review* 40 (April): 273–281.

Jeffrey, W. E.; and Samuels, S. J. 1969. Effect of method of reading training on initial reading and transfer. *Journal of Verbal Learning and Verbal Behavior* 6: 354–358.

Jenkins, Joseph R.; and Pany, Darlene. 1981. Instructional variables in reading comprehension. In *Comprehension and teaching: Research reviews*, ed. John Guthrie, pp. 163–202. Newark, Del.: International Reading Association.

———. 1980. Teaching reading comprehension in the middle grades. In *Theoretical issues in reading comprehension*, eds. Rand J. Spiro, Bertram C. Bruce, and William F. Brewer, pp. 555–574. Hillsdale, N.J.: Lawrence Erlbaum.

Jinks, Jerry. 1981. Computing the future: Smart machines will change our schools. Billings, Mont.: *Eastern Montana Update* (June): 6–8.

Johnson, Dale D. 1971. The Dolch list reexamined. *The Reading Teacher* 24 (February): 449–457.

Johnson II, Dale D.; and Pearson, P. David. 1978.

Teaching reading vocabulary. New York: Holt, Rinehart and Winston.

Johnson, Joseph C.; and Jacobson, Milton D. 1968. Some attitudinal and comprehension factors operating in the middle grades. *Educational and Psychological Measurement* 28 (Winter): 825–832.

Johnson, Kenneth R. 1971. Teachers' attitudes toward the non-standard Negro dialect — let's change it. *Elementary English* 48 (February): 176–184.

Johnson, Lorenzo Gail. 1965. A description of organization, methods of instruction, achievement, and attitudes toward reading in selected elementary schools. *Dissertation abstracts*, volume 25, no. 7A.

Johnson, Roger E. 1977. The reading level of elementary social studies textbooks is going down. *The Reading Teacher* 30 (May): 901–906.

Kachuck, Beatrice Levy. 1975. Dialect in the language of inner-city children. *Elementary School Journal* 76 (November): 105–112.

Karlin, Robert. 1980. *Teaching elementary reading: Principles and strategies*, 3rd ed. New York: Harcourt Brace Jovanovich.

———. 1975. *Teaching elementary reading: Principles and strategies*. 2nd ed. New York: Harcourt Brace Jovanovich.

Karlsen, Bjorn; Madden, Richard; and Gardner, Eric F. 1968. *Stanford diagnostic reading test*. New York: Harcourt Brace Jovanovich.

Kemper, Richard. 1969. Developing attitudes toward reading. *Conference on reading: University of Pittsburgh report* 25:101.

Kennedy, Eddie C. 1977. *Classroom approaches to remedial reading*. 2nd ed. Itasca, Ill.: F. E. Peacock.

———. 1974. *Methods in teaching developmental reading*. Itasca, Ill.: F. E. Peacock.

Kerfoot, James F., ed. 1965. *First grade reading programs, perspectives in reading no. 5*. Newark, Del.: International Reading Association.

King-Stoops, Joyce. 1977. *The child wants to learn*. Boston: Little, Brown.

Klare, George R. 1974–75. Assessing readability. *Reading Research Quarterly* 10: 62–103.

Knight, Lester N. 1972. Oral-aural language instruction and reading achievement of selected Spanish-speaking children. *California Journal of Educational Research* 23 (September): 188–197.

Krause, Kenneth C. 1976. Do's and dont's in evaluating textbooks. *Journal of Reading* 20 (December): 213.

Kulhavy, R. W.; and Swenson, Ingrid. 1975. Image

instructions and the comprehension of text. *British Journal of Educational Psychology* 45: 47–51.

LaBerge, David; and Samuels, S. Jay. 1974. Toward a theory of automatic information processing in reading. *Cognitive Psychology* 6 (April): 293–323.

Labov, William. 1970. Language characteristics of special groups: Blacks. In *Reading for the disadvantaged: Problems of linguistically different learners*, ed. Thomas D. Horn, pp. 139–157. New York: Harcourt, Brace and World.

———. 1970. *The study of nonstandard English*. Champaign, Ill: National Council of Teachers of English.

Laffey, James; and Shuy, Roger, eds. 1973. *Language differences: Do they interfere?* Newark, Del.: International Reading Association.

Lamb, Pose; and Arnold, Richard. 1976. *Reading: Foundations and instructional strategies*. Belmont, Calif.: Wadsworth.

Lasswell, A. 1967. Reading group placement: Its influence on enjoyment of reading and perception of self as a reader. Paper presented at the American Educational Research Conference, New York.

Lee, Doris; and Allen, Roach Van. 1963. *Learning to read through experience*. New York: Appleton-Century-Crofts.

Lefevre, Carl A. 1964. *Linguistics and the teaching of reading*. New York: McGraw-Hill.

Legenza, Alice; and Knafle, June D. 1979. The effective components of children's pictures. *Reading Improvement* 16 (Winter): 281–283.

———. 1978. How effective are pictures in basal readers? *The Reading Teacher* 32 (November): 170–173.

Lesiak, Jude. 1978. Reading in kindergarten: What the research doesn't tell us. *The Reading Teacher* 32 (November): 135–138.

Loban, Walter. 1976. *Language development: Kindergarten through grade twelve*. Urbana, Ill.: National Council of Teachers of English.

———. 1963. *The language of elementary school children*. NCTE Research Report No. 1. Urbana; Ill.: National Council of Teachers of English.

Lundsteen, Sara. 1971. *Listening, its impact on reading and the other language arts*. Urbana, Ill.: National Council of Teachers of English.

Lundstrum, John P. 1976. Reading in the social studies: A preliminary analysis of research. *Social Education* 40 (January): 10–18.

Mace-Matluck, Betty J. 1977. The order of acquisition of English structures by Spanish speaking children: Some possible determinants. Paper presented at the annual meeting of the Teachers of English to Speakers of Other Languages (April), Mexico City.

MacGinitie, Walter H. 1976. Difficulty with logical operations. *The Reading Teacher* 29 (January): 371–375.

Maehr, Martin L. 1969. Self-concept, challenge, and achievement. *Lutheran Education* 105 (October): 52–57.

Mager, Kenneth. 1972. Computer assisted instruction and reading. In *Reading process and pedagogy*, eds. William E. Blanton and J. Jaap Tuinman, pp. 77–98. Bloomington, Ind.: Bulletin of the School of Education, Indiana University, volume 48 (September).

Manzo, Anthony V. 1979. The ReQuest procedure. In *Reading comprehension at four linguistic levels*, ed. Clifford Pennoch, pp. 57–61. Newark, Del.: International Reading Association.

Manzo, A. V.; and Sherk, J. K. 1971–72. Some generalizations and strategies for guiding vocabulary learning. *Journal of Reading Behavior* 4 (Winter): 78–89.

Marchbanks, Gabrielle; and Levin, Harry. 1965. Cues by which children recognize words. *Journal of Educational Psychology* 56 (April): 57–61.

Marsh, R. W. 1968. The London I.T.A. experiment: A rejoinder. *Reading Research Quarterly* 4 (Fall): 120–123.

Martin, Bill; in collaboration with Peggy Brogan. 1972. *Sounds of language readers*. New York: Holt, Rinehart and Winston.

Mathews, Mitford. 1966. *Teaching to read: Historically considered*. Chicago: University of Chicago Press.

Mathewson, Grover. 1976. The function of attitudes in the reading process. In *Theoretical models and processes of reading*, 2nd ed., eds. Harry Singer and Robert B. Ruddell, pp. 655–676. Newark, Del.: International Reading Association.

McCarthy, Dorothea. 1954. Language development in children. In *A manual of child psychology*, ed. L. Carmichael, pp. 492–630. New York: John Wiley and Sons.

McCracken, Robert A. 1971. Initiating sustained silent reading. *Journal of Reading* 14 (May): 521–524, 582–583.

McCracken, Glenn; and Walcutt, Charles C. 1981. *Lippincott basic reading*. Philadelphia: J. B. Lippincott.

McCullough, Constance M. 1958. Context aids in reading. *The Reading Teacher* 11 (April): 225–229.

———. 1957. Responses of elementary school children to common types of reading comprehension questions. *Journal of Educational Research* 51 (September): 65–70.

———. 1945. Recognition of context clues in reading. *The Elementary English Review* 22: 1–5.

McCutcheon, Gail; Kyle, Diane; and Skovira, Robert. 1979. Characters in basal readers: Does "equal" now mean "same"? *The Reading Teacher* 32 (January): 438–441.

McDermott, Roy P. 1976. Achieving school failure: An anthropological approach to illiteracy and social stratification. In *Theoretical models and processes of reading*. 2nd ed., eds. Harry Singer and Robert B. Ruddell, pp. 389–428. Newark, Del.: International Reading Association.

McDonald, Frederick J. 1976. Report on phase II of the beginning teacher evaluation study. *Journal of Teacher Education* 27 (Spring): 39–42.

McLaughlin, G. Harry. 1969. SMOG-grading — a new readability formula. *Journal of Reading* 12 (May): 639–646.

McNeill, David. 1970. The development of language. In *Carmichael's manual of child psychology*, 3rd ed., ed. P. H. Mussen, pp. 1061–1161. New York: John Wiley and Sons.

———. 1966. Developmental psycholinguistics. In *The genesis of language: A psycholinguistic approach*, eds. F. Smith and G. A. Miller, pp. 15–84. Cambridge, Mass.: M.I.T. Press.

McWilliams, Lana; and Rakes, Thomas A. 1979. *Content inventories: English, social studies, science*. Dubuque, Iowa: Kendall/Hunt.

Melmed, Paul J. 1971. Black English phonology: The question of reading interference. *Monographs of the Language-Behavior Research Laboratory*, no. 1. Berkeley, Calif.: University of California.

Meltzer, Nancy S.; and Herse, Robert. 1969. The boundaries of written words as seen by first graders. *Journal of Reading Behavior* 1 (Summer): 3–14.

Mentfessel, N. S. 1966. In *The disadvantaged child*, eds. J. L. Frost and G. R. Hawkes. Boston: Houghton Mifflin.

Menyuk, Paula. 1963. Syntactic structures in the language of children. *Child Development* 32 (June): 407–422.

Milner, Esther. 1951. A study of the relationships between reading readiness in grade one school children and patterns of parent-child interaction. *Child Development* 22 (June): 95–112.

Minshall, Martha J. 1914. Vanquishing the reading bogey. *Education* 34 (May): 568–571.

Mitchell-Kernan, D. 1969. Language behavior in a Black urban community. Unpublished doctoral dissertation, University of California, Berkeley.

Moustakes, Clark E. 1956. *The self*. New York: Harper and Brothers.

Napell, Sondra M. 1978. Using questions to enhance classroom learning. *Education* 99 (Winter): 188–197.

National Assessment of Educational Progress (Washington, D.C.). 1981. *Newsletter* 14 (Spring): 1–3.

Neuman, Susan B. 1981. Effect of teaching auditory perceptual skills in reading achievement in first grade. *The Reading Teacher* 34 (January): 422–426.

Nobel, Clyde E. 1952. An analysis of meaning. *Psychological Review* 59: 421–430.

Noel, Doris I. 1953. A comparative study of the relationship between the quality of the child's language usage and the quality and types of language used in the home. *Journal of Educational Research* 47 (November): 161–167.

O'Brien, Carmen A. 1973. *Teaching the language different child to read*. Columbus, Ohio: Charles E. Merrill.

O'Donnell, Roy C.; Griffin, William J.; and Norris, Raymond C. 1967. *Syntax of kindergarten and elementary school children: A transformational analysis*. Urbana, Ill.: National Council of Teachers of English.

Olson, Willard D. 1956. *Psychological foundations of the curriculum*. UNESCO Educational Studies and Documents, no. 26.

Osgood, Charles E.; and Sebeok, Thomas A. 1965. *Psycholinguistics: A survey of theory and research problems*. Bloomington, Ind.: Indiana University Press.

Otto, Henry J.; and Sanders, David C. 1964. *Elementary school organization and administration*. New York: Appleton-Century-Crofts.

Otto, Wayne, 1977. Design for developing comprehension skills. In *Cognition, curriculum, and comprehension*, ed. John T. Guthrie, pp. 193–232. Newark, Del.: International Reading Association.

Paivio, Allan. 1969. Mental imagery in associative learning and memory. *Psychological Review* 76 (May): 241–263.

———. 1965. Abstractness, imagery and meaningfulness in paired-associate learning. *Journal of Verbal Learning and Verbal Behavior* 4: 32–38.

Palardy, Michael J. 1969. What teachers believe — What children achieve. *Elementary School Journal* 69 (April): 370–374.

Pearson, P. David; and Camperell, Kaybeth. 1981. Comprehension of text structure. In *Comprehension and teaching: Research reviews*, ed. John Guthrie, pp. 27–55. Newark, Del.: International Reading Association.

Pearson, P. David; and Johnson, Dale D. 1978. *Teaching reading comprehension*. New York: Holt, Rinehart and Winston.

Piaget, Jean. 1970. Piaget's theory. In *Carmichael's manual of child psychology*, Part I, ed. P. H. Mussen, pp. 703–732. New York: John Wiley and Sons.

Pick, Ann D. 1972. Some basic perceptual processes in reading. In *The Young Child*, ed. Willard W. Hartup, pp. 132–157. Review in Research, Washington, D.C.: National Association for the Education of Young Children.

Pieronek, Florence Terese. 1979. Using basal guidebooks — the ideal integrated reading lesson plan. *The Reading Teacher* 33 (November): 167–172.

Pollack, Myron F. W., and Pickarz, Josephine A. 1963. *Reading programs and problem readers*. New York: David McKay.

Powell, William R. 1976a. *Project to improve education in the basic skills*, technical report #2 (August). Department of Education, Tallahassee, Florida.

———. 1976b. Teachable concepts from reading research. Paper presented at the National Reading Conference, Atlanta, Georgia, December 5–7.

———. 1973. Acquisition of a reading repertoire. *Library Trends* 22 (October): 177–196.

———. 1969. Reappraising the criteria for interpreting informal inventories. In *Reading diagnosis and evaluation*, ed. Dorothy DeBoer, pp. 100–109. Newark, Del.: International Reading Association.

Powell, William R.; and Dunkeld, Colin G. 1971. Validity of the IRI reading levels. *Elementary English* 48 (October): 637–642.

Prescriptive Reading Inventory. 1972. Del Monte Research Park, Monterey, Calif.: CTB/McGraw-Hill.

Preston, Mary I. 1939. The reaction of parents to reading failure. *Child Development* 10 (September): 173–179.

Purkey, William Watson. 1970. *Self-concepts and school achievement*. Englewood Cliffs, N.J.: Prentice-Hall.

Purves, Alan C.; and Beach, Richard. 1972. *Literature and the reader: Research in response to literature, reading interests, and the teaching of literature*. Champaign, Ill.: National Council of Teachers of English.

Quandt, Ivan. 1972. *Self-concept and reading*. Newark, Del.: International Reading Association.

Ransbury, Molly Kayes, 1973. An assessment of reading attitudes. *Journal of Reading* 17 (October): 25–28.

Ravem, Roar. 1969. Language acquisition in a second language environment. *International Review of Applied Linguistics* 6 (February): 175–185.

Raygor, Alton L. 1977. The Raygor readability estimate: A quick and easy way to determine difficulty. In *Reading: Theory, research, and practice*, ed. P. David Pearson, pp. 259–263. Twenty-sixth Yearbook of the National Reading Conference.

Readance, John E.; Bean, Thomas W.; and Baldwin, R. Scott. 1981. *Content area reading: An integrated approach*. Dubuque, Iowa: Kendall/Hunt.

Reed, Kathleen. 1979. Assessing affective responses to reading: A multi-measurement model. *Reading World* 19 (December): 149–156.

Reid, J. F. 1966. Learning to think about reading. *Educational Research* 9: (November): 56.

Riechard, Donald E. 1970. The acquisition of selected life science concepts by beginning kindergarten children from three different community settings. Unpublished doctoral thesis, Ohio State University.

Rigg, Pat. 1978. Dialect and/in/for reading. *Language Arts* 55 (March): 285–290.

Rinsky, Lee Ann; and deFossard, Esta. 1980. *The contemporary classroom reading inventory*. Dubuque, Iowa: Gorsuch Scarisbrick.

Robeck, Mildred; and Wilson, John A. R. 1974. *Psychology of reading: Foundations of instruction*. New York: John Wiley and Sons.

Roberts, Leslie. 1981. First graders understanding of reading and reading instructional terminology. Unpublished doctoral dissertation. The University of Tennessee at Knoxville.

Robinson, Francis P. 1961. Study skills for superior students in the secondary school. *The Reading Teacher* 14 (September): 29–33.

Robinson, H. Alan. 1978. *Teaching reading and study strategies: The content areas*. 2nd ed. Boston: Allyn and Bacon.

Robinson, Helen M. 1972. Perceptual training — Does it result in reading improvement? In *Some persistent questions on beginning reading*, ed. Robert C. Aukerman, p. 145. Newark, Del.: International Reading Association.

———. 1966. The major aspects of reading. In *Reading: Seventy-five years of progress: Supplementary educational monograph no. 96*. Chicago: University of Chicago Press.

———, ed. 1956. *Developing permanent interests in reading*. Chicago: University of Chicago Press.

———. 1952. Fundamental principles of helping retarded readers. *Education* 72 (May): 596–599.

Robinson, Helen M.; and Weintraub, Samuel. 1973. Research related to children's interests and to developmental values of reading. *Library Trends* 22 (October): 81–108.

Rodenborn, Leo V.; and Washburn, Earlene. 1974. Some implications of the new basal readers. *Elementary English* 5 (September): 885–888.

Rodrigues, Raymond J.; and White, Robert H. 1981. *Mainstreaming the Non-English speaking student*. Urbana, Ill.: National Council of Teachers of English.

Roehler, Laura R. 1974. Techniques for improving comprehension in social studies. In *Reading in the middle school*, ed. Gerald G. Duffy, pp. 140–152. Newark, Del.: International Reading Association.

Rosen, Carl. 1966. An experimental study of visual perceptual training and reading achievement in first grade. *Perceptual and Motor Skills* 22: 979–986.

Rosenthal, Robert; and Jacobson, Lenore F. 1968. Teacher expectations for the disadvantaged. *Scientific American* 218 (April): 19–23.

Rothkopf, Ernst Z. 1966. Learning from written instructive materials: An exploration of the control of inspection behavior by test-like events. *American Educational Research Journal* 3: 241–249.

Rowell, C. Glennon. 1972. An attitude scale for reading. *The Reading Teacher* 25 (February): 442–447.

Ruddell, Robert B. 1967. Reading instruction in first grade with varying emphasis on the regularity of grapheme-phoneme correspondences and the relations of language structure to meaning — Extended into second grade. *The Reading Teacher* 19 (May): 730–739.

———. 1966. Oral language and the development of other language skills. *Elementary English* 43 (May): 489–498.

———. 1965. Effect of the similarity of oral and written patterns of language structure on reading comprehension. *Elementary English* 42 (April): 403–410.

———. 1963. An investigation of the effects of the similarity of oral and written patterns of language structure in reading comprehension. Unpublished doctoral dissertation, Indiana University.

Rude, Robert T. 1973. Readiness tests: Implications for early childhood education. *The Reading Teacher* 26 (March): 572–580.

Rudisill, Mabel. 1952. Children's preferences for color versus other qualities in illustrations. *Elementary School Journal* 52: 444–451.

Rudman, Masha Kabakow. 1976. *Children's literature: An issues approach*. Lexington, Mass.: D.C. Heath.

Rumelhart, David E. 1981. Schemata: The building

blocks of cognition. In *Comprehension and teaching: Research reviews*, ed. John T. Guthrie, pp. 3–26. Newark, Del.: International Reading Association.

———. 1980. Schemata: The building blocks of cognition. In *Theoretical issues in reading comprehension*, eds. Rand J. Spiro, Bertram C. Bruce, and William F. Brewer, pp. 33–58. Hillsdale, N.J.: Lawrence Erlbaum.

Rumelhart, David E.; and Ortony, Andrew. 1977. The representation of knowledge in memory. In *Schooling and the acquisition of knowledge*, eds. Richard C. Anderson, Rand J. Spiro, and William E. Montague, pp. 99–135. Hillsdale, N.J.: Lawrence Erlbaum.

Rupley, William H.; and Blair, Timothy R. 1979. *Reading diagnosis and remediation*. Chicago: Rand McNally.

Ryan, Frank L. 1973. Differentiated effects of levels of questioning on student achievement. *Journal of Experimental Education* 41 (Spring): 63–67.

Samuels, S. Jay. 1976. Modes of word recognition. In *Theoretical models and processes of reading*, eds. Harry Singer and Robert B. Ruddell, pp. 270–282. Newark, Del.: International Reading Association.

———. 1967. Attentional process in reading: The effect of pictures on the acquisition of reading responses. *Journal of Educational Psychology* 58 (December): 337–342.

Sanacore, Joseph. 1975. Reading self-concept: Assessment and enhancement. *The Reading Teacher* 29 (November): 164–168.

———. 1973. A checklist for the evaluation of reading readiness. *Elementary English* 50 (September): 858–860; 870.

Sanders, Norris M. 1966. *Classroom questions: What kinds?* New York: Harper and Row.

Sartain, Harry W. 1960. The Roseville experiment with individualized reading. *The Reading Teacher* 13 (April): 272–281.

Schneyer, J. Wesley. 1969. Reading achievement of first grade children taught by a linguistic approach and a basal approach — Extended into third grade. *The Reading Teacher* 22 (January): 315–319.

Schoolfield, Lucille; and Timberlake, Josephine. 1960. *Phonovisual method*. Washington, D.C.: Phonovisual Products.

Schreiner, Robert; and Tanner, Linda R. 1976. What history says about teaching reading. *The Reading Teacher* 29 (February): 468–473.

Shapiro, Bernard J.; and Willford, Robert E. 1969. ITA — Kindergarten or first grade? *The Reading Teacher* 22 (January): 307–311.

Sheldon, William D. 1969. Basal reading programs: How do they stand today? In *Current issues in reading*, ed. Nila Banton Smith, pp. 295–299. Newark, Del.: International Reading Association.

Sheldon, William D.; Stinson, Frange; and Peebleo, James. 1969. Comparison of three methods of reading: A continuation study in the third grade. *The Reading Teacher* 22 (March): 539–546.

Sheldon, William D.; Nichols, Nancy J.; and Lashinger, Donald K. 1967. Effects of first grade instruction using basal readers, modified linguistic materials and linguistic readers — Extended into second grade. *The Reading Teacher* 20 (May): 720–725.

Shepherd, David L. 1978. *Comprehensive high school reading methods*. 2nd ed. Columbus, Ohio: Charles E. Merrill.

———. 1973. *Comprehensive high school reading methods*. Columbus, Ohio: Charles E. Merrill.

Sherfey, Geraldine; and Huff, Phyllis. 1976. Designing the science learning center. *Science and Children* 14 (November–December): 11–12.

Shuy, Roger W. 1977. Sociolinguistics. In *Linguistic theory: What can it say about reading*, ed. Roger W. Shuy, pp. 80–94. Newark, Del.: International Reading Association.

———. 1969. A linguistic background for developing beginning materials for Black children. In *Teaching Black children to read*, eds. Joan C. Baratz and Roger W. Shuy, pp. 117–137. Washington, D.C.: Center for Applied Linguistics.

Silvaroli, Nicholas. 1982. *Classroom reading inventory*. 4th ed. Dubuque, Iowa: William C. Brown.

Simons, Herbert D. 1974. Black dialect and learning to read. In *Literacy for diverse learners*, ed. Jerry L. Johns, pp. 3–13. Newark, Del.: International Reading Association.

Simpson, G. O. 1962. My reading design. Defiance, Ohio: Hubbard Company.

Slobin, Dan I. 1972. They learn the same way all around the world. *Psychology Today* 6 (July): 71–74; 82.

Slobin, Daniel I. 1966. Grammatical transformations and sentence comprehension in childhood and adulthood. *Journal of Verbal Learning and Verbal Behavior* 5: 219–227.

Smith, E. Brooks; Goodman, Kenneth S.; and Meredith, Robert. 1970. *Language and thinking in the elementary school*. New York: Holt, Rinehart and Winston.

Smith, Edwin; Guice, Billy; and Cheek, Martha. 1972. Informal reading inventories for the content areas: Science and mathematics. *Elementary English* 49 (May): 659–666.

Smith, Frank. 1975*a*. *Comprehension and learning: A conceptual framework for teachers.* New York: Holt, Rinehart and Winston.

———. 1975*b*. The role of prediction in reading. *Elementary English* 52 (March): 305–311.

———. 1971. *Understanding reading: A psycholinguistic analysis of reading and learning to read.* New York: Holt, Rinehart and Winston.

Smith, Helen K. 1967. The responses of good and poor readers when asked to read for different purposes. *Reading Research Quarterly* 2 (Spring): 33–45.

Smith, James A. 1973. *The creative teaching of the language arts.* 2nd ed. Boston: Allyn and Bacon.

———. 1967. *Creative teaching of reading and literature in the elementary school.* Boston: Allyn and Bacon.

Smith, Nila Banton. 1965. *American reading instruction.* Newark, Del.: International Reading Association.

Smith, Richard J. 1969. Questions for teachers — Creative reading. *The Reading Teacher* 22 (February): 430–434.

Smith, Richard J.; and Johnson, Dale D. 1980. *Teaching children to read.* Reading, Mass.: Addison-Wesley.

Soar, R. S. 1966. Pupil needs and teacher-pupil relationships: Experience needed for comprehending reading. (Mimeographed.) Philadelphia: Temple University.

Spache, George D. 1974. *Good reading for poor readers.* 9th ed. Champaign, Ill.: Garrard Press.

———. 1972. *Diagnostic reading scales.* Monterey, Calif.: California Test Bureau.

———. 1965. *Classroom organization for reading instruction — An annotated bibliography.* Newark, Del.: International Reading Association.

———. 1963. *Toward better reading.* Champaign, Ill.: Garrard Press.

———. 1953. A new readability for primary grade reading materials. *Elementary School Journal* 53 (March): 410–413.

Spache, George D.; and Spache, Evelyn B. 1977. *Reading in the elementary school.* 4th ed. Boston: Allyn and Bacon.

———. 1973. *Reading in the elementary school.* 3rd ed. Boston: Allyn and Bacon.

Spearritt, Donald. 1972. Identification of subskills of reading comprehension by maximum likelihood factor analysis. *Reading Research Quarterly* 8 (Fall): 92–111.

Spencer, Doris U. 1967. Individualized vs. a basal reader program in rural communities, grades one

and two. *The Reading Teacher* 21 (October): 11–17.

Spiegel, Dixie Lee. 1981. Six alternatives to the directed reading activity. *The Reading Teacher* 33 (May): 914–920.

Squire, James R. 1969. What does research in reading reveal about attitudes toward reading? *English Journal* 58 (April): 523–533.

Stauffer, Russell G. 1975. *Directing the reading-thinking process.* New York: Harper and Row.

———. 1970. *The language-experience approach to the teaching of reading.* New York: Harper and Row.

———. 1942. A study of prefixes in the Thorndike list to establish a list of prefixes that should be taught in the elementary school. *Journal of Education Research* 35:453–458.

Stauffer, Russell G.; and Harrell, Max M. 1975. Individualizing reading-thinking activities. *The Reading Teacher* 28 (May): 765–769.

Strickland, Ruth. 1962. The language of elementary school children. *Indiana University School of Education Bulletin* 38: 1–131.

Suchman, J. Richard. 1966. *Developing inquiry.* Chicago: Science Research Association.

Sullivan, Mark. 1927. *Our times: The United States 1900–1925; America finding herself,* vol. II. New York: Charles Scribner's Sons.

Sutton, Marjorie J. 1969. Children who learned to read in kindergarten: A longitudinal study. *The Reading Teacher* 22 (April): 565–602.

Taba, Hilda. 1965. The teaching of thinking. *Elementary English* 42 (May): 534–542.

Templin, Mildred C. 1957. Certain language skills in children: Their development and interrelationships. *Child Welfare Monograph* 26. Minneapolis: University of Minnesota Press.

Terwilliger, Paul N.; and Kolker, Brenda. 1981. Sight vocabulary learning of first and second graders. *Reading World* 20 (May): 251–258.

Thelen, Judith. 1976. *Improving reading in science,* p. 45. Newark, Del.: International Reading Association.

Thorndike, Robert L. 1973. *Reading comprehension education in fifteen countries.* New York: Halsted Press.

Tierney, Robert J.; Readance, John E.; and Dishner, Ernest K. 1980. *Reading strategies and practices: Guide for improving instruction.* Boston: Allyn and Bacon.

Tinker, Miles A.; and McCullough, Constance M. 1975. *Teaching elementary English.* 4th ed. Englewood Cliffs, N.J.: Prentice-Hall.

———. 1962. *Teaching elementary reading.* New York: Appleton-Century-Crofts.

Torrance, E. Paul. 1970. Influence of dyadic interaction in creative functioning. *Psychological Reports* 26 (April): 391–394.

Tortelli, James P. 1976. Simplified psycholinguistic diagnosis. *The Reading Teacher* 29 (April): 637–639.

Trabasso, Thomas. 1981. On the making of inferences during reading and their assessment. In *Comprehension and teaching: Research reviews*, ed. John T. Guthrie, pp. 56–76. Newark, Del.: International Reading Association.

Turner, Thomas N. 1981. Question games for social studies. *Social Education* 45 (March): 194–196.

———. 1980. Making the social studies textbook a more effective tool for less able readers. In *Improving the use of social studies textbooks*, ed. William E. Patton, pp. 21–26. Washington, D.C.: National Council for the Social Studies.

———. 1977. Critical reading as a values clarification process. *Language Arts* 54 (November–December): 909–912.

———. 1976a. Figurative language: Deceitful mirage or sparkling oasis. *Language Arts* 53 (October): 758–761.

———. 1976b. Making the social studies textbook a more effective tool for testable readers. *Social Education* 40 (January): 38–41.

———. 1973. Creative writing with the news. *Tennessee Education* 3 (Spring): 29–36.

Turner, Thomas N.; and Alexander, J. Estill. 1975. Fostering early creative reading. Language Arts 52 (September): 786–789.

Turner, Thomas N.; and Marino, Sheila B. 1975. Creative reading: Keeping the magic while casting the spell. *Tennessee Education* 5 (Fall): 27–31.

Tyler, Leona E. 1963. *Tests and measurements.* Englewood Cliffs, N.J.: Prentice-Hall.

Vacca, Richard T. 1981. *Content area reading.* Boston: Little, Brown.

Veatch, Jeannette; Sawicki, Florence; Elliott, Geraldine; Flake, Eleanor; and Blakey, Janis. 1979. *Key words to reading: The language experience approach begins.* Columbus, Ohio: Charles E. Merrill.

Viox, Ruth G. 1968. *Evaluating reading and study skills in the secondary classroom.* Newark, Del.: International Reading Association.

Wanat, Stanley F. 1977. Introduction: Attention and individual differences in comprehension. In *Linguistics and reading series* 2 (papers in applied linguistics), ed. Stanley F. Wanat, pp. v–xii. Arlington, Va: Center for Applied Linguistics.

Wardhaugh, Ronald. 1975. Linguistics and reading. In *Teacher's resource book — Series R*, eds. Carl B. Smith and Ronald Wardhaugh, pp. 32–44. New York: Macmillan.

———. 1971. Theories of language acquisition in relation to beginning reading instruction. *Reading Research Quarterly* 7: 168–194.

———. 1969. Is the linguistic approach an improvement in reading instruction? In *Current issues in reading*, ed. Nila Banton Smith, pp. 254–267. Newark, Del.: Proceedings International Reading Association, 13, Part 2.

Warren, James E., Jr. 1960. The heart of language. *Education* 20 (January): 259–263.

Wattenberg, William W.; and Clifford, Clare. 1964. *Child Development* 35, Part 1 (June): 461–467.

Webber, Bonnie Lynn. 1980. Syntax beyond the sentence: Anaphora. In *Theoretical issues in reading comprehension*, eds. Rand J. Spiro, Bertram C. Bruce, and William F. Brewer, pp. 141–161. Hillsdale, N.J.: Lawrence Erlbaum.

Wertsch, J. V. 1972. Adult-child interaction and the roots of metacognition. *Quarterly Newsletter of the Institute for Comparative Human Development* 2: 15–18.

West, Gail B. 1974. *Teaching reading skills in content areas: A practical guide to the construction of student exercises.* Orlando, Fla.: Sandpiper Press.

West, Roland. 1964. *Individualized reading instruction.* Port Washington, N.Y.: Kennikat Press.

Wheat, Thomas E.; Galen, Nancy D.; and Norwood, Molly. 1979. Initial reading experiences for linguistically different learners. *The Reading Teacher* 33 (October): 28–31.

Wick, John W.; and Smith, Jeffrey K. 1980. *Achievement series beginning education assessment 4.* Glenview, Ill.: Scott Foresman.

Williams, Frederick; Whitehead, Jack L.; and Miller, Leslie. 1972. Relations between language attitudes and teacher expectancy. *American Educational Research Journal* 9 (Spring): 263–277.

Winkley, Carol K. 1966. Which accent generalizations are worth teaching? *The Reading Teacher* 20 (December): 219–224.

Witkin, Belle Ruth. 1973. *Reading improvement through auditory perceptual training.* Final project report. Hayward, Calif.: Alameda County Superintendant of Schools.

Witty, Paul A. 1974. A rationale for fostering creative reading in the gifted and the creative. In *Creative reading for gifted learners: A design for excellence*, ed. Michael Labuda, pp. 8–24. Newark, Del.: International Reading Association.

————. 1949. *Reading in modern education*. Boston: D.C. Heath.

Wolf, Willavene; with Cansneder, Bernice, and Cansneder, Bruce M. 1967. *Critical reading ability of elementary school children*. U.S. Office of Education. Contract No. OF-4-10-187, OE Project No. 2612. (June 1967.) Columbus, Ohio: Ohio State University Research Foundation.

Wolfram, Walter A. 1979. *Reading and dialect differences*. Arlington, Va.: Center for Applied Linguistics.

————. 1970. The nature of non-standard dialect divergence. *Elementary English* 47 (May): 739–748.

Wylie, Richard E.; and Durrell, Donald D. 1970. Teaching vowels through phonograms. *Elementary English* 47 (October): 787–791.

Wynn, Sammye J. 1972. *Making the most of parent-teacher conferences*. Knoxville, Tenn.: University of Tennessee.

Zimit, Sara G.; Rose, Cynthia; and Camp, Bonnie W. 1973. Relationship between reading achievement and Rosenzweig picture-frustration study in early grades. *Psychology in the Schools* 10 (October): 433–436.

Zintz, Miles V. 1977. *Corrective reading*. 3rd ed. Dubuque, Iowa: William C. Brown.

————. 1975. *The reading process: The teacher and the learner*. 2nd ed. Dubuque, Iowa: William C. Brown.

Index

Guided reading, in basal reading
  program, 286–87
Gumperz, J., 19
Gunderson, Doris, 337
Gunning, Robert, 249
Gurren, Louise, 83
Guthrie, John T., 133
Guszak, Frank J., 210
Gutiérrez, Arturo, 411
Gwalthney, Wayne K., 5

"Habit retorts," 216
Hafner, Lawrence E., 132
Hall, Diane Sprawls, 361
Hall, MaryAnne, 303, 317
Hall, Vernon, 410
Hammill, Donald, 29
Hansen, Harlan S., 360, 361
Harber, Jean R., 391
Hargis, Charles, 29, 31
Haring, Norris Grover, 339
Harms, Jeanne McLain, 178
Harper, Robert J., 510
Harrell, Max M., 270
Harris, Albert J., 107, 239, 376, 378,
  434
Harris, Benjamin, 498, 499
Harris, Larry A., 288, 342
Harris, Theodore L., 49, 248
*Harrison-Stroud Reading Readiness
  Profiles*, 34
Hasselriis, Peter, 264
Hawthorne effect, 342
Hay, Julia, 93
Head Start programs, 405, 508, 509
Healy, Ann Kirtland, 359
Heathington, Betty S., 280–301, 362,
  365
Heathington Attitude Scales
  intermediate, 367–68
  primary, 365–66
Heffernan, Helen, 25
Heilman, Arthur W., 49, 238
Herber, Harold L., 247, 255, 259, 260,
  268
Herringbone technique, 241–42
Herse, Robert, 42
Higher Education Facilities Act (1963),
  508
Hillard, George, 499
Hints, in reading comprehension, 170
History
  of compulsory education, 502–3
  of federal involvement in education,
    507–9
  of language recording, 495–96
  of reading instruction, 497–503
    in colonial America, 498
    in eighteenth century, 498–99
    grouping in, 506
    during nineteenth century, 499–
      503
    public involvement in, 506–7
    school accountability in, 509–10
    in the twentieth century, 503–11
  of reading research, 504–5
Hittlemen, Daniel R., 249, 251

Hodges, Richard E., 49, 248
Hoisington, Arthur R., 107
Holden, Marjorie H., 31
Home environment. *See also* Parent
  involvement
  and attitude toward reading, 360
  and developing positive attitude, 370
  reading games and activities for
    for middle grade children, 484–88
    for primary grade children, 481–84
Homographs, 170
Homonyms, in vocabulary
  development, 136
Homophones, 170
Hong, Laraine K., 127
Hornbook, 498, 500
Hornik, Robert C., 378
Horvath, Barbara M., 20
Houston, Susan H., 401
Howell, William J., 221
Huck, Charlotte S., 264
Huebner, Mildred H., 50, 303
Huff, Phyllis, 302–23, 450–68
Hughes, Ann, 83
Hughes, Langston, 329
Hunt, Lyman C. Jr., 127, 326, 328
Huser, Mary K., 361
Hyperbole, definition for, 174

Ignoffo, Matthew F., 132
Illustrations, and reading interests, 378
Imagery, in reading behavior, 13
Incentive, in motivation, 375
Incomplete sentence technique, in
  attitude assessment, 363–64
Indexes, for locating information, 227–
  29
Independent reading, providing for,
  460
Individual Diagnostic Map, 430, 432
Individualized reading
  components of program, 507
  for culturally different learner, 412
  definition for, 326
  evaluation of, 349
  for linguistically different learner,
    412
  mechanics of, 328–32
  organizational procedures for, 327–
    28
Inductive method
  of phonics instruction, 83
  in propaganda assessment, 181, 182
Inferential comprehension, 151
  ambiguity in, 170
  anaphora in, 170–71
  causality in, 172
  context signals in, 171
  definition for, 167
  figurative language in, 172–76
  function of, 169
  types of, 170–76
Inflectional endings, identifying, 111
Informal assessment
  behaviors underlying scores in, 433
  defined, 433

of dictionary skills, 436
group procedures for, 434
of phonics skills, 434–35
of structural analysis skills, 435–36
Informal Reading Inventory (IRI), 436,
  443–46
  assessing oral reading in, 438–43
  checklist for, 447
  comprehension in, 446–47
  sight word list in, 437–38
  for vocabulary assessment, 123
Information
  locating, 223
    dictionary use, 224–25, 226
    encyclopedias for, 225–26
    indexes for, 227–29
    reference books for, 225
  organizing, 231–34
  selecting, 231
Initial Teaching Alphabet (ITA), 340–
  42
Innuendoes, 170
Inquiry strategies, 211. *See also*
  Questions
Instant words, Fry's, 50, 65–67
International Reading Association,
  Parents and Reading Committee
  of, 471
Interpretation, and question
  classification, 202
Instructional programs
  and attitudes toward reading, 360–
    61
  mass, 43
  phonics, 82–93
  utilizing interests in, 384, 386
Intellectual development
  and formal reading instruction, 10,
    11
  of kindergarten children, 41–42
  Piaget's view of, 9–12
Intelligence. *See also* Cognition
  and attitudes toward reading, 361
  and reading interests, 377
Interest centers, 383. *See also* Learning
  centers
Interest groups, 386
Interest in reading
  and formal reading, 29
  and reading readiness, 38
  teacher observation of, 32
Interests, 374. *See also* Motivation
  assessing student, 380–82
  and attitudes toward reading, 361
  correlated with reading
    achievement, 376–78
  developing and extending, 382–86
  of elementary school children, 378–
    80
  grouping by, 455–56
  promoting lasting, 374–86
  utilized in instructional program,
    384, 386
International Reading Association
  (IRA), 427
Interviewing, for attitude assessment,
  363
Irony, definition for, 174
ITA. *See* Initial Teaching Alphabet

interpreting graphic and pictorial representations, 263
interpreting symbols and signs, 262
skills, 260–62
solving word problems, 262
Mathews, Mitford, 496
Mathewson, Grover, 6, 22, 158, 357
Mathewson model, of effective behavior, 376, 386
Maturity, and reading readiness, 25
May, Merrill, 134
Maze exercises, in vocabulary development, 133
Maze test, for vocabulary assessment, 123
Mean, calculation of, 422
Meaning. *See also* Semantics; Vocabulary development
acquisition of, 16
multiple, 136–37
reading for, 143. *See* Comprehension
Meaning banks, for word study projects, 138
Media, and reading interests, 378
Melmed, Paul J., 19
Meltzer, Nancy S., 42
Memory
comprehension and, 147, 152–53
and question classification, 202
in reading behavior, 13
Mental Measurements Yearbook (Buros), 34
Meynuk, Paula, 17, 18
Metacognition, 168
questions in, 200
in reading comprehension, 158
Metaphor, definition for, 174
Metropolitan Readiness Tests, 34
Middle grades, language experience approach in, 315–16
Miller, Harry B., 82
Miller, W. R., 17
Milner, Esther, 19
Minorities, and language experience approach, 317. *See also* Culturally different learner; Linguistically different learners
Minshall, Martha J., 504
Miscue analysis
defined, 439
example, 440, 442
Mitchell-Kernan, D., 19
Modification, as context clue, 100
Mood, as context clue, 100
Morpheme
definition for, 71
free vs. bound, 105
Mosley, Richard, 461
Motivation. *See also* Interests
and content area reading, 247
and language experience approach, 315–16
promoting, 375
questioning and, 206–7
and total class grouping, 453
Mott reading programs, 346
Moustakes, Clark E., 359
Murphy-Durrell Reading Readiness Analysis, 34

Murray, Lindley, 499
My Little Primer (Bumstead), 501
"My Reading Design" (Simpson), 384, 395

Napell, Sondra M., 200
National Assessment of Educational Progress (NAEP), 510
National Defense Education Act (NDEA) (1958), 508
Navajo, familiar concepts of, 409
Neuman, Susan B., 29
New England Primer (Harris), 498, 499, 502
Newspapers, 230
creative reading of, 190–91
index use, 227, 229
reading in class, 453
New Word Method, The (Webb), 501
New York Times Index, 230
Nobel, Clyde E., 16
Noel, Doris I., 19
Non-English speakers, and reading, 396–97
Nonstandard English (NSE), 393
example of, 409
qualitative level of, 395
and reading, 394–96
sample characteristics of, 406
Norm, definition for, 420
Normal curve, 422
Norm-referenced measures
of general word knowledge, 123
standardization and concepts, 418–27
using, 427–29
Notebooks, for word study projects, 138
Noun-adjective relationship, 101–2
Nouns
and articles, 101
and verbs, 102

O'Brien, Carmen A., 317
Observation, teacher
for assessing attitudes, 362–63
informal assessment, 433
for matching content area texts and children, 253
for oral language, 19–20
for reading readiness, 30–31
O'Donnell, Roy C., 42
Office of Economic Opportunity (OEO), 508
"Old Deluder Satan Act," 503
Olshavsky, Jill Edwards, 510
Olson, Willard D., 326, 455, 456
Omnibus Budget Reconciliation Act (HR 3982), 511
Onomatopoeia, definition for, 174
Opinion, distinguishing fact from, 179–80
Oral language
development of, 19
figures of speech in, 173–74
and reading acquisition, 18

Oral reading
assessing, 438
IRI test results for, 444, 446
Orientation skills
in formal reading, 29–30
and reading readiness, 39–40
teacher observation of, 32
Ortony, Andrew, 8
Osgood, Charles E., 14
Otto, Henry J., 452, 454
Overview, structures, 275–76

Pairing instruments, for attitude assessment, 364
Paivio, Allan, 13
Palardy, Michael J., 360
Pany, Darlene, 157
Paragraphs
meaning of, 161–63
types of, 162
Parent involvement, 43–44, 370–71, 471
example of, 488–90
games and activities (for home use)
for middle grade children, 484–88
for primary grade children, 481–84
parent-teacher partnership
background information for parents, 478
conferencing with parents, 479–80
establishing relationship, 477–78
keeping parents informed, 479
parent power, 480–81
in preschool years, 472
community resources for, 474–75
library use, 475–76
listening to and talking with children, 473
reading to children, 473–74
suggestions for, 476–77
Pearson, P. David, 106, 119, 120, 129, 130, 131, 149, 157, 172
Percentiles, definition for, 424
Periodicals, 230
Personification, definition for, 174
Phonemes
acquisition of, 15
/c/ and /g/, 72–73
definition for, 71
teaching of, 84
Phonetics, definition for, 71
Phonics
consonants in, 72–73
content of, 70–71
definition for, 69
in history of reading instruction, 501
individual tests in, 434
informal testing of, 447
instruction in
language experience approach for, 311
methods, 84–93
principles of, 82–84
synthetic vs. analytic approach, 93
self-test on, 78–80
teaching
activities and projects in, 337–39
analytic vs. sythetic approach, 93

Phonics (*cont.*)
  auditory-visual association in, 86,
    88, 89
  application in, 85, 86, 88–89, 90–
    91
  decoding in, 93
  inductive vs. deductive method,
    82–83
  reinforcement in, 85
  sequence of, 84–85, 86, 88–89, 90–
    91
  terminology in, 71
  vowels in, 73–76
Phonics program, 80
  important concepts in, 81
  sequence of teaching in, 81–82
Phonograms
  definition for, 71
  teaching, 92
  usefulness of, 84
Phonological approaches, 21, 334–36
  Distar reading program, 338–39
  linguistics, 337–38
  programs and materials, 338
  strengths and weaknesses of, 339
Phonology, in language acquisition, 15
Piaget, Jean, 8, 9
Pick, Ann D., 42
Pickarz, Josephine A., 496
Picture dictionary bulletin board, 57–
  59
Picture Potency Formula, for basal
  series, 291
Pieronek, Florence Terese, 294
Pierpoint, John, 499
Pittman, Sir James, 340
Poetry reading, 191, 265
Pollack, Myron F. W., 496
Possessives, teaching, 155
Powell, William R., 12, 438, 439
Powell Criteria, for oral reading, 438–
  39, 443, 446
PQRST (preview, question, read,
  summarize, test) technique for
  science, 241
Prefixes
  home exercises on, 487–88
  informal tests for, 435
  in vocabulary development, 134–35
  and word recognition, 107
Preoperational period, of intellectual
  development, 9
Preschool children
  community resources for, 474–75
  library use for, 475–76
  listening to and talking with, 473
  reading to, 473–74
  suggestions for, 476–77
Prescriptive Reading Inventory (PRI),
  347, 430–32
Preston, Mary I., 360
Primary grade children, home
  activities for, 481–84
*Primary Pupil Reading Attitude
  Inventory* (Askov), 356
Processing Print, concepts in, 22
Program, definition for, 279
Programmed approaches
  management system in, 347–48

materials for, 343–44, 345
methods, 344, 346
teaching machines, 346–47
Pronunciation
  of consonants, 72
  dictionary aids in, 108–13
  prefixes and suffixes as aids for, 108
  standard, 395
Propaganda, 181–84
Property relations, in vocabulary
  development, 120
Psycholinguistics
  defined, 14
  and reading, 20–21
Public Law 94-142, 510
Public relations program, 478
Puns, 170
Pupil teaming, 457
Purkey, William Watson, 371
Purves, Alan C., 376, 378, 380

Quandt, Ivan, 359, 371, 372, 373
Question clusters, 210
Questioning
  building environment for, 213–15
  importance of, 199
  reciprocal, 212
  skills
    dealing with unexpected or
      unfamiliar, 203–4
    developing child's own, 215–17
    use with content areas, 205
    using generic questions, 204
Questionnaire, for attitude assessment,
  364
Questions
  categories of, 200–201
  cognitive-level, 210–11
  definition for, 199
  following up, 209–13
  generic, 204
  interest-arousing, 206–7
  motivational, 206–7
  for preparation for reading, 206–8
    aids to comprehension, 208
    providing reasons for reading,
      207–8
  Sander's system of classifying, 201–2
  teaching, 199–202

Race. *See also* Culturally different
  learners; Linguistically different
  learners
  and attitudes toward reading, 361
  and reading interests, 378
Rafael, Teresita C., 397
Rakes, Thomas N., 253
Ranking system, for informal reading
  inventory, 443
Ransbury, Molly Kayes, 359
Ravem, Roar, 403
Raw Score
  definition for, 420
  example of, 424
Raygor, Alton L., 249
Raygor Readability Estimate, 249

Readability
  cloze procedure for, 250–52
  definition for, 248
  matching text and pupils, 253
  teacher analysis of, 252–53
Readance, John E., 241, 242, 253, 254
Reader's Guide to Periodical Literature,
  229, 230
Read-in, 485
Readiness
  assessing, 26–28
    informal, 30–33
    standardized tests, 34–35
  auditory discrimination and, 28, 29
    teaching, 39
    tests, 33
  of culturally different learner, 404–6
  divergent views regarding, 25–26
  kindergarten reading, 40–44
  of linguistically different learner,
    404–6
  teaching, 36–37, 39–40
    general guidelines for, 36–37
    language arts skills in, 37–38
    strategies for, 39–40
  visual discrimination and, 28, 29
    teaching, 39
    tests, 33
Reading
  providing reasons for, 207–8
  wide
    in sight vocabulary development,
      54–55
    in vocabulary development, 126–
      27
Reading acquisition, 18
Reading behaviors, types of, 12–14
Reading rate
  activities for working with, 238–39
  basal reading program grouping
    and, 293–94
  flexibility of, 236
Reality, distinguishing fantasy from,
  178
Reading skills, 40. *See also* Skills
Reagan, Ronald, 511
Record keeping, in individualized
  reading programs, 330–31
Reed, Kathleen, 361
Reference books, for locating
  information, 225. *See also*
  Information; *specific references*
References, as context clue, 100
Reid, J. F., 31
Reinforcement
  in phonics instruction, 85, 86–87,
    88–91
  in vocabulary development, 130
Relationship signals, 171
Relevancy, determining, 180–81
Reliability, of norm-referenced
  measures, 420
Religion, and reading, 497–98, 502
Repetition, in learning of sight words,
  51
Respellings, dictionary, 110–11
Reynolds, Elizabeth G., 295
Rigg, Pat, 396
Rinsky, Lee Ann, 437

and phonic clues, 69
sounding out in, 92
structural analysis for, 104
   compound words, 105–7
   prefixes and suffixes, 107–8
teaching
   to culturally different learner,
     406–9
   to linguistically different learner,
     406–9
Words. *See also* Sight words

compound, 105–7, 487
Fry instant, 50, 65–67
multisyllabic, 112
signal, 155
Word study projects, individualizing,
   137
Word train, for sight vocabulary
   development, 57
Writing, creative, for sight vocabulary
   development, 55–56. *See also*
   Literature

Wylie, Richard E., 84
Wynn, Sammye J., 48–64, 470–92

Yarborough, Betty H., 83
Yoakam, Gerald A., 239

Zecchini, Sandra, 275
Zimit, Sara G., 5
Zintz, Miles V., 109, 369, 406